THE EARLY CHRISTIAN CHURCH

VOLUME II

THE SECOND CHRISTIAN CENTURY

CONTENTS

v

CONTENTS

LIST OF ILLUSTRATIONS

LIST OF MAPS AND TABLES

THE SOURCES

SELECTED LIST OF ANCIENT CHRISTIAN AUTHORITIES FREQUENTLY QUOTED

(1) HISTORICAL WRITERS OF THE FOURTH CENTURY

(*a*) The *Ecclesiastical History* of EUSEBIUS, written A.D. 305–24, quoted as *E.H.* Eusebius had access to good libraries which contained important second-century documents from which he gives numerous quotations. His work is the basis of research into second-century church history. See chapter 26.

(*b*) The *Panarion* of EPIPHANIUS, written 374–7, and also his treatises *Concerning Weights and Measures*. Epiphanius also had access to good second-century documents, but he reproduces them without identifying the source from which he takes them; yet his transcriptions and adaptations are very valuable. One writer on whom he drew was HEGESIPPUS. See vol. I, chapter 23.

(2) THE CONTEMPORARY SOURCES

(*a*) The New Testament and associated literature, which includes

The Epistle of Clement, or I Clement, 96–7: see vol. I, chapter 20.
The Shepherd of Hermas, or *Pastor*: various dates from about 100 to 140: see vol. I, chapters 20 and 21, also vol. II, chapters 5 and 6.
The Epistles of Ignatius and Polycarp, 110–17: see vol. I, chapter 24.

To which may be added the so-called *Epistle of Barnabas* (about 125?) and the *Didache* or *Teaching of the Twelve Apostles* (120–50?) (see vol. I, chapter 26). And probably in the same period the pseudonymous writings described in vol. II, chapter 1.

(*b*) PAPIAS, bishop of Hierapolis, one of the Johannine School, collected oral traditions of the disciples, and used them to illustrate his *Interpretations of the Oracles of the Lord*. The book is lost, but quotations from it are given by IRENAEUS and EUSEBIUS; other quotations, some of them dubiously authentic, are found in other authors. Its date may be about 125 or 135: see vol. I, chapter 16 and vol. II, chapter 2.

(*c*) JUSTIN MARTYR, a Samaritan philosopher who was converted about 125.

The *Dialogue with Trypho* took place in Ephesus *c.* 135, but was written down perhaps as much as twenty years later.

The *Syntagma of Heresies*, written before 150, is lost, but was used by IRENAEUS and HIPPOLYTUS.

The *First Apology* in Rome about 150–52; the *Second Apology* in Rome before 161.

See vol. II, chapters 4, 7, and 9.

(*d*) The APOLOGISTS and other writers on the relations between Christian and Greek thought: Aristides of Athens (see vol. II, chapter 6); Tatian, a pupil of JUSTIN (see vol. II, chapters 9 and 12); the anti-Christian philosopher Celsus, known only through the refutation written by Origen (see vol. II, chapters 11 and 24); Athenagoras of Athens (see vol. II, chapters 11 and 14); Theophilus of Antioch (see vol. II, chapters 12 and 16).

(*e*) HEGESIPPUS, a Palestinian scholar who settled in Rome between 155 and 185, wrote the *Hupomnemata* or *Note-books*, containing traditions of the Jewish church, and information on episcopal successions and heretical schools. The book has not survived, but is known from quotations in later authors.

Identified and unidentified quotations in EUSEBIUS.

Unidentified quotations in IRENAEUS and EPIPHANIUS, some of which are recognizable without serious doubt, others more problematical.

Extracts in a document attributed to Philip of Side. See vol. I, chapters 5, 10, 12, 13, 22, 23, vol. II, chapters 2, 4, 8 and 15.

(*f*) IRENAEUS, a disciple of Polycarp of Smyrna and a pupil of JUSTIN. His principal work was the refutation of Gnosis in five volumes, usually cited as *Adversus Haereses*, or *Against Heresies*, or *Ad. Haer.*, or *A.H.* Called for short the *Refutation* (or *Elenchos*). Written about 185. It is often possible to recognize where he is making use of earlier works, e.g. the *Interpretations* of PAPIAS, the *Syntagma* and *Against Marcion* of JUSTIN, the *Note-books* of HEGESIPPUS, gnostic myth, ritual and theology, catholic creeds and other traditions.

(*g*) HIPPOLYTUS, a disciple of IRENAEUS, a devotee of the theology of JUSTIN, was a bishop in Rome about 217 to 235.

His *Syntagma of Heresies*, written about 205, in which he made use of the *Syntagma* of JUSTIN, and lectures given by IRENAEUS or possibly books of his. This book has not survived in Greek; but a Latin adaptation of it exists which was called the *Libellus against All Heresies*, and wrongly attributed to Tertullian.

His larger *Refutation of All Heresies*, or *Philosophoumena*, was written later.

He wrote a few separate monographs on contemporary heretics, among which most scholars would include the *Little Labyrinth* from which EUSEBIUS quotes.

Also the *Apostolic Tradition*, a liturgical work; and the *Chronicle*, which does not survive, but is incorporated in the Liberian (Philocalian) Catalogue, A.D. 354.

(*h*) CLEMENT OF ALEXANDRIA and TERTULLIAN wrote voluminously from about 190 or 195 to 220. Clement was head of the catechetical school at Alexandria from about 190 to 200, and quotes oral traditions, apocryphal literature, gnostic theologians, and Jewish, Christian, and pagan authors of the second century. Tertullian wrote his *Apology* about 197. He became a Montanist about 205–7. His anti-heretical writings shed light on second-century history; and his other books on liturgy, church controversy and relations with society and the state.

ORIGEN succeeded Clement in Alexandria, and afterwards migrated to Caesarea; he wrote many books on scripture and general theology; his book *Against Celsus* is our only source of information for that second-century author.

(*i*) The Apocryphal Gospels, Acts, Epistles, etc. of the period.

(*j*) The Mishnah and other rabbinic material.

CHAPTER 1

ANONYMOUS CHRISTIAN LITERATURE

ON PSEUDONYMOUS LITERATURE

About a hundred years after the crucifixion, a new kind of literature begins to appear in the church, probably in the eastern lands. It comes down to us without the names of its authors, and is sometimes written in dramatic form in the name of an apostolic personage. These books are described by modern writers as pseudonymous, that is written under a false name; but this word is apt to give the impression that there was an intention to deceive, which does not appear to have been the case. They were, on the whole, as innocent in intention as any work of fiction in modern times which brings historical characters on the stage.

We know what pseudonymity was for the period about which we are writing. It was a literary convention of the Jewish synagogue, comparable to the novel or the drama or the motion picture and enabled the writer to present his message in the style of a bygone age and so give it prestige. They were literary imitations of the great religious classics. The prophet or sage of olden days was put on the screen and made to speak again, and give his message to a later age, in reference to its problems. The two dramatic planes can be readily distinguished; the ostensible historical setting in which the revelator is placed, and the actual historical setting for which the book was written. To create the effect, it was necessary for the author to reconstruct the earlier period by an exercise of the imagination and to carry through the fiction consistently, or else, of course, the illusion would be destroyed.

This kind of literature was still being produced in the synagogue. From the synagogue it passed into the church, and the church was beginning to imitate it. An interesting example is the Apocalypse of

Ezra (or Esdras) which had been written for the Jews in the first century, and enlarged early in the second by the addition of three rather elaborate visions at the end. This 'pseudepigraph' was taken over by a Christian author, who added two introductory chapters at the beginning; and in this form we find it appended to the Latin Apocrypha as II Esdras. It has passed into the Apocrypha of the English Authorized Version.

But the most interesting example of these christianized Jewish romances is the *Ascension of Isaiah*.

THE *ASCENSION OF ISAIAH*

There was apparently a Jewish romance which described the persecution of the prophet Isaiah by the wicked king Manasseh, and his martyrdom by being sawed in two by a wooden saw: a rather widespread legend which was known apparently to the author of Hebrews. This Jewish romance, which was originally of an anti-Samaritan character, was used as an historical platform on which to stage a picture of the Christian gospel. Isaiah himself is the ostensible author of some parts of it. He ascends stage by stage through the seven heavens, and in the seventh he joins in the worship of the primal Father, with the Beloved and the Holy Spirit. Here he looks into the future, and sees the descent of the Beloved through the seven heavens, unknown to the angels who guard their portals; the virgin birth at Bethlehem with legendary detail; the crucifixion; the descent into the underworld; the resurrection; the instruction of the twelve apostles for eighteen months; their sending out into the world; and the ascension of the Beloved to his former condition of glory.

It is a notable text, for it contains some Christian material of the first century which partakes of an apocalyptic and gnostic character; but its present form is later, since it seems to make use of the Matthaean Gospel, and its view of the virgin birth shows a certain amount of development in a docetic direction.

The attitude of the four Gospels to the Virgin Mary might be described as reverent and discreet. In Luke we have a charming portrait encircled in a halo of devotion and associated with songs and prophetic utterance. In the others she is silent and withdrawn. In John, it is true, she stands by her son twice, once at the beginning of his ministry

2

in Galilee, and once during his Passion in Jerusalem. But there is no sign of special honour or veneration. By the end of the century she had her place in the gospel and the creeds, as we see them in the letters of Ignatius. Ignatius says that her virginity and her child-bearing were mysteries of silence to be ranked with the death of the Lord; they were performed in the silence of God and deceived the ruler of the aeon. This same thought is found in the *Ascension*, but the author goes further. It was no ordinary birth.

> And Joseph did not approach Mary, but kept her as a holy virgin, though with child; and he did not live with her for two months; and after two months of days, while Joseph was in the house, and Mary his wife, but both of them alone, it came to pass that when they were alone, Mary straightway looked with her eyes and saw a small babe, and was amazed; and after she had been amazed, her womb was found as formerly before she had conceived.
>
> (*Ascension of Isaiah*, IV, 11, 5–9.)

It is a sheer miracle. The virginity of Mary is not impaired by the birth of her divine son; it is not a real birth; a certain element of docetism has been infused into the catholic tradition. This idea developed still further in the border-land between gnosticism and catholicism. Various writers elaborated the narrative, and the stories of the infancy of Jesus may have grown up in these circles too. We do not know who or what they were, but they were not Jews; they were Gentile circles where the pious imagination loved to muse upon the Jewish-Christian mysteries.

Many scholars regard this paragraph as a later addition to the text, and some assign the whole book to a later date; but Justin seems to know it in one form or another.

THE IDEALIZATION OF PETER

If we turn now to the Second Epistle of Peter in the New Testament, we shall find another example of the same kind of literature, though the pious imagination is more restrained in its operation. This author has built up a complete and self-consistent fictitious situation which is based on the apostolic documents of an older generation. This fictitious situation can be clearly distinguished from the actual situation to which the author is really addressing himself.

We can make a number of deductions about this actual situation. The author makes mention of a collection of the Epistles of St Paul which he describes as scripture; he refers to I Peter as the former Epistle; he incorporates the Epistle of Jude into his work bodily. He is an early witness to the existence of a collection of apostolic writings which had by now become sacred. The figures of the apostles have receded far enough into the past for their writings to be regarded as classics, and so soon as this happens the literary imitations begin to appear; for 'pseudonymity' is the tribute paid by a later generation to a classical and creative period with which it has lost touch.

A more radical school of criticism would like to add to the list of 'pseudepigraphs' the Epistles of James and Jude, the Pastorals, and even I Peter and Ephesians; but these documents belong to a different class of literature. They are not imitative. Mediate authorship may be allowed for, no doubt, in some cases, but they bear the marks of being sent out as messages from the men whose names they bear, even if some literary assistant or executor has prepared them for the public. Their background is provided by the Judaeo-Christian church life of the first century; their references to persons and events come in naturally and in a casual manner; they build up no fictitious picture; they create no illusion; they do not even make the identity of their author clear in every case, and that is what a 'pseudepigraph' must do at all costs. Their effect depends upon their being genuine messages from the men whose names they bear, even if the actual composition be the work of a disciple or colleague, as is stated in the case of I Peter.

The effect of II Peter, on the other hand, depends upon literary art. It is a work of the creative imagination. When it was first read in the ecclesia the feeling would have been similar to that of reading a historical novel or watching a historical play or film. A past situation was being conjured up and contrasted with the life of the present day.

As men looked back into the past, it was the figure of Peter that caught the imagination; or Peter with the twelve apostles. The grandeur of Peter which is revealed in the first chapter of the Acts, and supported by the Gospel of Matthew, is enhanced further in these tributes from the third generation. A number of romantic works appeared, in which he was the main figure and also the narrator and revelator. The high standing of some of these books in the later second century makes it necessary for us to regard them as products of the earlier part of it.

Furthermore, the idea of Peter in the mind of the second-century church was not based solely on New Testament evidence; he was a

4

historical figure and the founder of a tradition, who continued to be remembered and discussed among the elders in his churches; the Jewish Christians had a similar memory of James, which was magnified and idealized in the same way. Doubtless the predecessors of Marcion cherished a similar idealized picture of Paul. So the old people in my diocese continued to talk of Bishop Mountain and Bishop Stewart, a century after their great pioneer work.

THE SECOND EPISTLE OF PETER

The Second Epistle of Peter is written in the form of a testament, and purports to give the last message of the great apostle just prior to his death. The suggestion is, therefore, that it was written from Rome. The Lord has revealed to him that he is shortly to die, and he is writing in order to stir up the pure minds of his hearers by way of remembrance. A fictitious situation is thus created for which many precedents existed; there are many such pieces which profess to give the last words of a saint or sage, the greatest example being the last words of Moses in Deuteronomy. No intermediary appears, since that would lessen the dramatic effect. Peter writes this Epistle for himself.

The central part of the Epistle is occupied with a diatribe (entirely borrowed from Jude) against the false teachers with lax morals, who reject the Hebrew revelation and the old-fashioned eschatology. 'The fathers have fallen asleep', they complain, 'and none of the things which were expected have come to pass.' There is a similar passage in I Clement, and for the matter of that in II Clement, thus linking these three books together. Peter is made to say that the Lord is not slack about his promise; the delay is designed so as to allow time for every one to repent. A day with the Lord is like a thousand years, an idea found in Barnabas and Justin and other writers of the period; it will come suddenly like a thief in the night; the heaven and earth will pass away with a great noise, and the elements will melt with a fervent heat.

The authentic 'First' Epistle was written too early to have to deal with such doubts; they had not arisen. Nor had it anything to say about the false teachers. But it did say that these were the last times, and that judgement had begun; it spoke, too, of a fiery ordeal. But these were indefinite terms. Its realistic and sober message failed to

5

satisfy an age which wanted to hear about the fires of judgement and the dreadful things which were to come upon the earth. In all this early second-century literature we see the more concrete and materialistic imagination of the Gentile mind crystallizing the visionary and spiritual language of the apostolic age into a system of literal eschatological predictions. The apocalyptic tradition loses touch with current history.

In I Peter the apostle is simply a fellow-elder and a witness of the sufferings of Christ; he assures his readers or hearers that suffering will be succeeded by glory; but he does not indicate how this will come to be. In II Peter he is presented as an eyewitness of the glory. The author builds up his picture from the authentic Gospels; he is not guilty of inventing anything. He presents the mountain of transfiguration as the point when the illumination of Peter began; and a revelation of a holy mountain had behind it the excellent literary precedent of Moses on Mount Sinai or Mount Abarim. It became a favourite scene in the imaginative literature of the second century. Its use here establishes the authority of Peter to speak about the glory that is coming in the revelation of Jesus Christ. He has another authority, however, in the 'prophetic word' which is like a light shining in a dark place. This seems to be the Hebrew scripture or Old Testament, which he adds, is 'not for private interpretation'.

Fortified in this way, he is able to make strong statements about the future. The idea of a destruction of the world by fire is not to be found in any other New Testament book; but it appears in Hermas and the *Didache*, and became the common belief of Christians early in the second century. The fires of judgement were often in their thoughts, and were conceived in a very literal fashion. II Peter provided the doctrine with apostolic authority.

THE *REVELATION* OF PETER

The 'Second Epistle' is not mentioned by any second-century writer, though traces of it may perhaps be found here and there; the *Revelation*, on the other hand, was valued by Clement of Alexandria, and read in the Roman Church, in the hundred-and-nineties. It is a work of sheer imagination. A case might be made out for some degree of contact between II Peter and the apostolic age. About 120, if II Peter is as old as that, there would have been old men who could affirm without fear of successful contradiction what the teaching of Peter had been on certain points. The question of the day of judgement could have been one of them; and II Peter might conceivably be in touch with such traditions. In any case it gives us a valuable picture of the apostle as he now appeared in the tradition of the church, a visionary, a Hebraist, a moralist, and an eschatologist; just what Marcion and the docetics disliked. It is interesting to have such a picture. No such nucleus of respectable tradition could possibly be imagined for the *Revelation*.

The Second Epistle made an advance in the doctrine of Christian eschatology by its assertion that this heaven and earth would be destroyed by fire, and new ones created; an idea which was not without its precedent in the Jewish apocalypses. In the *Revelation*, the expectation of a kingdom of God on earth is abandoned in favour of a Paradise in another world.

A small fragment of the text was discovered at Akhmim in Egypt, and in its opening words the Lord is concluding an address about false teachers which is reminiscent of the Second Epistle. Once again Peter is the narrator. 'We, the twelve disciples,' go with Jesus to a mountain which is probably the mountain of the resurrection mentioned at the end of Matthew. There they are shown Moses and Elijah as examples of the glorified saints. The vision does not satisfy them, and they ask where are all the righteous, or what sort of 'aeon' it was in which they dwelt. In other words the old Transfiguration vision to which II Peter had appealed was felt to be inadequate; more powerful revelations were given on the mountain of resurrection.

They were shown a vast space outside the world, brighter than any light. 'The air was incandescent there with the rays of the sun, and the earth was flowering with unfading flowers... Angels ran about them there, and the glory of those who dwelt there was equal, and with one voice they praised the Lord God, rejoicing in that place.' After this they were shown hell and the torments of the ungodly, who had blasphemed the 'way of righteousness'. They saw the punishment of the various classes of sinners enumerated in such books as the *Two Ways* or the *Pastor* of Hermas. They were plunged in streams of blood or pools of boiling filth; they hung suspended by their tongues; they said, 'We never thought we would come into this place.'

The unfading incorruptible Paradise is faintly suggested in I Peter; and there are several points of contact with II Peter, with its denuncia-

7

tion of false prophets, and its holy mountain, and its strong passage about the torments of hell. The word used in both is Tartarus, which is the name of hell in Greek mythology; and the Paradise certainly suggests the Elysium of the Greek poets or the Orphic mysteries. At one time we think of the *Book of Enoch*, and at another of the *Sixth Aeneid* of Virgil. *The Revelation of Peter* is an important book to keep in mind in the study of second-century history. It struck deep roots in the popular tradition. It gave the martyr an immediate paradise on which he could meditate, like the good thief in Luke's Gospel; it provided him with an inferno for the apostates and the persecutors. Yet the torments of these souls might be shortened, it was suggested, by the prayers of the martyrs. This idea is clearly enunciated in the Christian *Sibyllines*, which may be indebted to lost passages from the *Revelation of Peter*.

The Greek imagination was now turning the old oriental symbols into a lively and exciting popular poetry. There was a great change in Christian piety and aspiration when the poetry of the church began to emphasize a blessedness in heaven rather than a kingdom which was to be established upon the earth. For the present a variety of ideas coexisted without being co-ordinated; and it was possible to combine the two principal ideas, as Jewish apocalypse had already done.

THE *PREACHING OF PETER*

At the end of the century Clement of Alexandria quotes from *Barnabas*, Clement, the *Pastor* of Hermas, the *Revelation of Peter*, and the *Preaching of Peter*, almost in the same way as he quotes from the New Testament books. Undoubtedly they had come down to him in company with them. If the *Revelation* appealed to the poet in him, the *Preaching* must have appealed to the philosopher. This book seems also to have been known to the Athenian philosopher Aristides (before 148) and was quoted by Heracleon the gnostic, in Rome, a generation later. Its influence in the second century seems to have been widespread; but all we know of it is a few quotations in Clement of Alexandria and one in Heracleon.

The Peter who appears in this book is neither a visionary nor a prophet; he is a teacher, and even a philosopher. He lays down, in the name of the Twelve (for he does not appear or act alone in this sort of literature), some of the elementary and fundamental propositions of the Hellenized Judaeo-Christian monotheism. God is

The invisible who seeth all things, the uncontainable who containeth all things; he has need of nothing and all things have need of him; it is for his sake they exist; the incomprehensible, the eternal, the incorruptible, the uncreated, who made all things by the Word of his power...that is to say the Son. (*Preaching of Peter*, in Clement Al., *Strom.* VI, 5.)

Having established an acceptable view of God, he passes to the consideration of the three ways of worshipping him, that of the Greeks, that of the Jews, and that of the Christians, to whom he alludes as the 'third race'. This is a way of thought which Aristides picked up, and, through him or through other channels, it spread widely and was widely adopted.

These races were all monotheists; they all believed in one God; the difference was to be found in their manner of worship. The Greeks worship idols; the Jews worship angels; but Christians adore God in a new way through Christ. We have here the beginning of the Christian philosophy of the apologists, the first of whom were Quadratus, Aristides, and Justin.

These words seem to be part of an address given by Peter and the Twelve to their hearers. There was another dramatic scene in the book, in which Christ sent them out to preach, after his resurrection. They were to evangelize all men throughout the world to know that God was one. First they were to offer repentance to Israel; but after twelve years they were to go out into all the world, lest any one should say, 'We have not heard.' This tradition is a very interesting one. It appears in other writers, such as the anti-Montanist Apollonius, who wrote about A.D. 200.

There is a third important quotation in which the apostles say, or Peter says in their name, that they have examined the books of the prophets and have found that they all name Jesus as the Christ, either in parables, or in riddles, or else absolutely in so many words; and that was why they made no statements apart from the scriptures. This is the theology of the 'Books of Testimonies', of course, and we know that the *Preaching* made use of testimonies. It maintained, for instance, that Christ was the Law and the Word; and it used Jeremiah's prophecy of the new Covenant. It will be remembered that Peter laid claim, in the Second Epistle, to the possession of an official interpretation of the 'prophetic word' of the Old Testament; it looks as if there were quarters in which the testimony material was regarded as having the authority of Peter and the Twelve.

The three 'pseudepigrapha' which we have now studied are rich in material for the background of second-century Christian history, short as they are; but the *Gospel* seems to stand rather apart. It was in all probability a later work.

THE *GOSPEL OF PETER*

We may be passing beyond the reign of Hadrian in considering the *Gospel of Peter;* it may be dated before 150, but not all scholars would agree. It makes use of all our four Gospels, though it shows no fidelity to the sources which it is using. The portions of it which we possess deal with the Passion and the Resurrection, and it has been suggested that it was never anything more than a Passion Gospel. It has also been suggested that the *Gospel* and the *Revelation* were originally parts of a single book; for both were included in the Akhmim fragments. We know, however, that the *Revelation* did circulate separately, since it was still being read in the fifth century in the churches of Palestine on Good Friday. If the *Gospel* was simply a Passion narrative, it would probably have been read on the same day. It has notes of time which suggest a quite peculiar view of the Paschal fast; the day of the Crucifixion was the Passover as it is in John; the disciples fasted and mourned and wept, night and day, from the Crucifixion 'till the sabbath'; but this appears to mean the sabbath a week later, so that they fasted through all the 'days of unleavened bread'.

The gospel is strongly anti-Jewish, and therefore favourable to Pilate. Pilate and the centurion on guard at the tomb, whose name is given as Petronius, are made into witnesses of the Resurrection. The whitewashing of Pilate, and the use of Pilate as a witness to the truth of the gospel, is carried a good deal further in some later writers. In time there was a book called the *Acts of Pilate* in which Pilate himself was the narrator; but the existing versions of it are much later than this period. Yet we are left with the impression that something of the sort must have existed in the mid-second century; we hear of *Acts* of Pilate, of epistles of Pilate to Tiberius, and even a portrait of Jesus made by order of Pilate.

There is a docetic touch in this Gospel. Jesus is silent on the cross as if feeling no pain; and, at the end, he says, 'My power, my power, why hast thou forsaken me?' The mistranslation shows a certain knowledge of Hebrew, since *Eli* (my God) is not unlike *Heli* (my power); and it suggests that the spirit which had entered Jesus at his baptism had now left him; but the reference to feeling no pain does not necessarily imply a divine impassibility. In the Acts of the Martyrs, it is often said that they behaved as if they felt no pain; they were in a state of ecstasy, or absorbed in communion with the Lord. The *Ascension of Isaiah* says that when Isaiah was being sawn in two, he neither cried aloud nor wept, but his lips spake with the Holy Spirit until he was sawn in two. Basilides says that the martyr should seem not to feel pain.

The Resurrection story is taken from Matthew, but is much elaborated. There is a great voice from heaven; two men descend, and the stone rolls away of its own accord. The two men enter the tomb and bring out Jesus; the heads of the two men reached to the heavens, but the head of Jesus overpassed the heavens. The *Ascension of Isaiah* has a very similar picture; but in *Peter* the cross comes out of the tomb, following him, and the voice from heaven says, 'Hast thou preached unto them that sleep?' and an answer is heard from the cross, which says 'Yes'.

The women see a vision of an angel at the empty tomb, but there is no appearance of Jesus for a whole week. When the days of unleavened bread are over, the twelve disciples, still mourning and grieving, return to their own homes; Simon and Peter take their nets and go to the sea; Levi the son of Alpheus is with them.... Here the Akhmim manuscript breaks off. There is something very peculiar and dramatic in the absence of any Resurrection appearances on Easter Sunday, and the adherence to the idea suggested in Mark, of appearances in Galilee only. The supplementary ending to the Marcan Gospel was clearly unknown to the author.

It does not seem that this Gospel was ever very widely known or highly thought of. It has been suggested that it was known to Justin Martyr; but this is not certain. A Gospel of this name was in use among the Docetae of Antioch by the end of the century. It survives in an Egyptian manuscript. It clearly enjoyed a certain amount of favour in more than one quarter. Perhaps it was a counterblast to the *Hebrew*

Gospel, in which the first Resurrection appearance was given in Jerusalem to James the Just, the patron saint of the Jewish Christians.

We have dealt with three non-canonical Gospels now, two of which were current in the church by the year 130, or at any rate by about 140; they are the *Hebrew Gospel*, the Marcionite revision of Luke and the *Gospel of Peter*; we have the feeling that the *Gospel of Peter* may have been rather later than the others. They were all composed for actual use in the services of the church; the first two, of course, to the exclusion of all other Gospels; the latter, perhaps, as a supplement; we do not really know. It is hard to say to what extent we are witnessing here an extension of the original process of Gospel-writing, or an imitation of it.

THE PAPYRUS FRAGMENTS

The discovery of two fragments of Gospel manuscripts dating from the period which we are now discussing has shed unexpected light on these studies. In the first place they are the oldest remains of books produced in codex form, that is to say, with leaves folded and sewn together in the fashion we are accustomed to today. In the second place they are assigned by the experts to the first half of the second century, and earlier rather than later; the same range of dates that we have assigned to the *Revelation* and *Preaching of Peter*.

The fragment of St John may be seen at the John Rylands Library at Manchester. It is only about three and a half inches by two and a quarter. Fortunately it is a piece of the top outside corner of a page; that is, it has part of the top margin and the outside margin. This enables the expert to calculate the length of the lines in the complete page; the writing on the back makes it possible to check this; a comparison of the results obtained makes it possible to calculate the number of lines to the page. Further calculation shows that St John's Gospel would have taken up a hundred and thirty-three pages of this size (about eight inches by eight and a quarter). The experts do not think that it contained more than the one Gospel, since the four Gospels in this format would be rather bulky; but of course it might have been a little larger without difficulty. It could have contained the Johannine Epistles or other material.

From this study we may proceed to study the 'Egerton papyrus', which had a smaller page in a similar style of handwriting. Two pieces remain, with writing both on back and front; but there is no way of calculating the number of pages in the complete book. The narrative, so far as it can be reconstructed, is a free rendering of material from John and Mark (or Matthew); there is a line which suggests that the author knew Luke. It consists mainly of passages in which Jesus is in conflict with the Jewish authorities, so that its interest may be apologetic; it may have been prepared for use in connexion with argument against the Jews. The sentences chosen from John are not in their original context or order, and are very freely paraphrased. The story of the leper from Mark or Matthew comes in quite abruptly without any kind of transition.

And behold a leper comes to him and says, Jesus, Master, I was travelling with lepers and eating with them in the inn, and I too became a leper; if, therefore, thou wilt, I am made clean. Then the Lord said to him, I will: be thou made clean; and immediately the leprosy departed from him. But the Lord said to him, Go and show thyself to the priests....

The story is more respectful than its Marcan original; Jesus is called the Lord; the leper makes a courteous address and explanation, instead of bursting in with his request; Jesus does not touch him. Such differences would seem to have arisen in oral delivery or preaching. It is how somebody told the story in the course of preaching. We visualize a community like that of Papias, in which the 'living word' was still powerful.

There is a fragment from a story which is not preserved in any of our four Gospels, but there is too little of it for successful reconstruction. Jesus is standing on the banks of the river Jordan; he stretches out his hand and takes water; he sows the water on the...he takes of the water that has been sown...but that is all that remains. It may be compared with Exodus iv. 9.

The book seems to be some Alexandrian teacher's own handbook of selected passages from the written and oral tradition. Other free associations of written and oral matter appear in the so-called *Second Epistle of Clement*, which it is convenient to consider here, though it is not in any sense a piece of fictitious literature; neither, of course, is the Egerton papyrus.

THE SECOND EPISTLE OF CLEMENT

We have already mentioned II Clement in connexion with II Peter. It is not a pseudonymous work. It received its name from the fact that it happened to follow I Clement on certain rolls or codices. It is a later work than I Clement, but it has a real connexion with it in a quotation from some unknown scripture, which it gives in a more extended form. This passage also forms a point of contact with II Peter, referring as it does to a generation which has been disappointed in its eschatological hope. Like II Peter it uses the expression 'prophetic word'.

Hear also what the prophetic word saith: Wretched are the double-minded, who doubt in their hearts, and say, We heard of these things long ago, even from our fathers, but we who are expecting them from day to day have seen none of them.

O men without understanding, compare yourselves to the tree; take the vine; first it puts out its leaves, then the bud comes, after that the unripe grape, then the cluster standing ready. So also my people had confusions and afflictions; then shall it receive good things.

(II Clem. XI, 2–4 and I Clem. XXIII, 3–4.)

This passage, with its harvest symbolism and its echo of the Marcan Gospel, is the sort of thing which we also find in Papias and the elders.

II Clement was an 'entreaty', which was designed to be read after the scripture lessons in the ecclesia. It was composed by someone with pastoral authority, possibly a bishop. Its purpose was to persuade Christians to repent before it was too late. It has all the conventional ideas of the third generation and the literature which it produced; but it has no room for chiliasm. It is not to be placed in that circle of thinking. It is in the New Testament tradition, and we are conscious of echoes of I Peter and I John, without ever being able to say that they are being quoted. There is an apparent quotation from Ignatius of Antioch in IX, 3 (see Ignatius, *Philadelphians* VI, 4). I Corinthians is very plainly referred to, and there are a number of explicit quotations from the words of Jesus. These are the most striking features of the book; for while most of them appear to come from Matthew, and some from Luke, there are others which come from an unknown source. In one of these the Lord is asked when the kingdom will come, and he gives a riddling reply:

> When the two shall be one,
>> And the outward as the inward,
> And the male with the female,
>> Neither male nor female. (II Clement XII, 12, 2.)

A similar saying is attributed to the *Egyptian Gospel* by Clement of Alexandria; but the likeness is not close enough to make it probable that II Clement borrowed from this pseudepigraph, which should probably be dated rather later in the century.

In another instance, II Clement quotes the saying in which the Lord sends out his disciples like lambs among wolves, and Peter asks, 'What if the wolves tear the lambs to pieces?' Jesus says, 'Let not the lambs fear the wolves after they die', and goes on to give the canonical saying about not fearing those who can only kill the body. The little dialogue has rather inexpertly welded together two sayings from Matthew. On another occasion, a saying from Matthew is introduced by a clause which has a Johannine ring:

If you were gathered together with me in my bosom, and do not my commandments, I will cast you off, and will say to you, Depart from me: I know not whence ye are, ye workers of lawlessness. (II Clement IV, 5.)

If II Clement belongs to the same period as 'Barnabas' and Papias, there were still many sayings of Jesus afloat in the oral tradition, and the combination of old and new material into new books had not ceased; homiletic variations were still possible. These, and similar causes, are sufficient to account for the Gospel sayings in II Clement; the use of a non-canonical gospel is quite possible, but it is not a necessary assumption. The character and teaching of Jesus was not yet confined in men's minds to an impression produced by reading the Four Gospels. He was a person who had lived on earth not very long ago; his immediate disciples had passed away within living memory; and his splendid sayings were being repeated by men who had studied under those disciples.

THE BACKGROUND OF II CLEMENT

We are associating II Clement with 'Barnabas' in the period after Ignatius, between 120 and 131. Its place of origin is quite unknown; but it was accepted with I Clement into the New Testament in eastern churches known to Eusebius and Epiphanius in the fourth century. They are both included in the great fifth-century Bible known as Codex Alexandrinus (A); they are counted as New Testament books in the *Apostolic Constitutions*; they were included in the canon of the Syrian church. They are found in the Bryennios manuscript, which formed a supplement to the New Testament and included 'Barnabas' and the *Didache*. This massive evidence all points to one conclusion; I Clement and II Clement were held in the highest estimation in Syria. II Clement seems to have left no imprint in Egypt or the west.

It is a mirror of its times. The Christians to whom it is written were conscious of their superiority to Jew and Gentile alike. They were proud of their emancipation from the worship of idols and did not hesitate to tackle their pagan friends on the subject. They told them about the marvellous 'oracles of God', a phrase which may have meant the sayings of Jesus; but their conduct fell so far below the standard of the Gospel teaching that the pagans laughed at them and said that the whole thing was a fraud and a deception. There was need of true repentance, therefore, from the heart; and such repentance, it would seem, was offered without restriction until the Day of Judgement came. Then indeed it would be too late. It would be a fiery judgement, such as we find in Hermas, II Peter, the *Didache*, 'Barnabas' and the *Revelation* of Peter.

Things are said about keeping the flesh holy and the seal of baptism unspotted; but these warnings had to do with the inroads of the teachers of evil, who doubted the doctrine of the coming judgement. They did not believe that Christ had been manifested in the flesh, or that man would rise again to be judged in the flesh. Our author is a strong anti-docetic of the school of John and Ignatius, though he cannot be called a theologian. He says that we must think of Christ 'as God'; he was formerly Spirit, and became flesh in order to call us.

He was not a writer of any originality, and he has not been highly thought of by the moderns. He was a competent pastor, possibly a bishop, and he gives us a picture of the average Gentile believers who are proud of their emancipation from idolatry, devoted to their Saviour and his marvellous words, instructed out of the 'Bible' (*biblia*) and the 'apostles', forgetful of the words of the 'elders' which they hear in church, apt to be impressed by strange teachers, not always free from sins of the flesh, not offering the world a spectacle of unalloyed love,

I. THE JOHN RYLANDS PAPYRUS

2. HADRIAN

but ready apparently to give their lives for their faith, without too much fear of the evil 'aeon' in which they live. Life in this world is brief and unpleasant; but the promise of Christ is great and wonderful; and so too is the refreshment of the coming kingdom and of eternal life.

CONCLUSION

Different as the tone of this document is from II Peter, we note that it has in common the idea of the supreme authority of the prophets or of the 'prophetic word', which has to be defended in the face of growing doubts about the *parousia* which are spread by docetic teachers. Perhaps we have an indication here of a date previous to the second Jewish war of 131–5. After that date the argument from prophecy received new strength, since the Christians saw many of the old prophecies fulfilled in the final defeat of the Jews and the devastation of their country. It became a strong conviction and a favourite line of argument. The complaints of II Peter and II Clement seem to suit the period of the hundred-and-twenties, when a former generation had passed away without seeing the outward and visible fulfilment of the apocalyptic hopes in which they had been persuaded to believe. On the other hand, both authors had a good collection of apostolic literature, including quite likely I Clement; and this does not allow of a much earlier date.

The books which we have been considering form a group with curious and complex interrelations. They form a catholic and sub-apostolic group, which can all be thought of, in a sense, as belonging to the school of Peter and the Twelve; for Clement, in the imagination of the east, was guaranteed by Peter; and Hermas, of course, was guaranteed by Clement. II Peter is a supplement to I Peter; II Clement appears as an appendix to I Clement. The *Didache* appears in the name of the Twelve, and as a supplement to Matthew. They bear witness to a busy interchange between east and west. I Peter, I Clement, and Hermas came from Rome to the east; the others may have originated in the east, and travelled Rome-wards. 'Barnabas' and a version of the *Two Ways* reached Rome, as we judge by the fact that Latin translations were made.[1] The *Preaching of Peter* reached Alexandria, Athens, and

[1] Nor should we forget the association of Barnabas with Clement in Rome and Alexandria, which appears in the *Recognitions* and *Homilies* of Clement.

Rome. The *Revelation of Peter*, wherever it originated, was accepted at Rome along with the Revelation of John. Clement of Alexandria used them all except II Clement and II Peter. These books are all, in varying degrees, on the fringe of the New Testament, except for the *Preaching*. The *Gospel of Peter*, too, seems rather to stand apart from the rest of the group.

They show a considerable intellectual and spiritual decline from the authentic literature of the apostles and their associates.

CHAPTER 2

THE CHURCH IN ASIA

THE TIMES OF HADRIAN

The Emperor Publius Aelius Hadrianus was a Spaniard by descent, a Roman by birth and breeding, and a Greek by temperament and culture. He had a restless and inquiring mind which was always interested in some new thing. He had succeeded his uncle Trajan, not without difficulty, in 117. He had withdrawn from oriental adventures, leaving kings of his own choosing in the principalities east of the Euphrates; a course of action which had settled the frontier for the time being, but allowed the Parthian king to build up his power once more. He abandoned the province of Dacia, north of the Danube. He secured the frontier in Britain. He created what seemed to be a workable Roman empire on the lines which Augustus had laid down for the benefit of his successors; the ocean on the west, the deserts on the south, the Rhine, the Danube and the Euphrates on the north and east, would seem to be its natural frontiers.

The middle years of this century were the last serene years of the Hellenistic world; the fusion of Roman power and Greek wisdom was complete; the foundations of the European culture had been laid. All that was now required was the influx of oriental religion, and this was coming fast.

Hadrian's reign marks the end of the old classical Latin literature. Pliny had died under Trajan. Tacitus and Suetonius and Juvenal were still writing when he came to the throne; but the Greek tongue would soon predominate as the language of culture and business in Rome, though the senate, the magistrates and the army would continue to use Latin. Greek had always been the language of the Roman church, though we cannot rule out the possibility of a derivative Latin Christianity in Rome from very early times.

The writings of Tacitus show that neither Judaism nor Christianity was understood by the governing classes. The Jew was well known for his total intolerance of all the gods and goddesses. His was the spirit that denied; he was commonly called an atheist. He was known, of course, to have peculiar superstitions of his own, including the rite of circumcision which was regarded as revolting, the institution of the sabbath which was inconvenient, various daily washings, and distinctions of clean and unclean meats. The gnostic type of Jew had produced a host of discreditable teachers who performed magical rites and knew the names of angels and devils. The sublimity of their ideas about God, in their legitimate tradition, was not widely understood. Tacitus, for instance, shows himself culpably ignorant about them, and seems to have swallowed whole the libels of controversial writers like Apion, who stated that they were lepers and criminals of Egyptian origin who had been expelled from Egypt by the Pharaohs and worshipped a god with an ass's head. Celsus, the critic of Christianity, repeats this information, which must, therefore, have been widely accepted in literary and official circles. The Jews had recently attempted to wage a desperate war against the empire, and were working up for a new one. Their record of rebellion was a bad one.

The Christians, as a branch from the root of Judaism, inherited this bad reputation; and more was added. Celsus says that they originated as a rebellious faction among the Jews, just as the Jews themselves had originated as a rebellious faction among the Egyptians. Tacitus knew that their founder had been executed as a criminal under Pontius Pilate, a statement which produced the worst impression. They were classified with bandits and outlaws. The Jewish view of the Christians is preserved by Justin and Celsus; it was that they had abandoned the worship of the one God to set their hope upon a man, and that man a convicted criminal. Nor did they hesitate to compare their faith in Christ crucified with the myths of Greek and oriental religion.

It was widely believed that they met together to murder a new-born infant and feast upon its flesh and blood; after that the lights went out, and the so-called brothers and sisters indulged in promiscuous sexual intercourse with one another. Every effort had been made, by torture and by executions, to get them to give up their allegiance to their crucified founder, and to worship the lawful gods, especially the divine emperor; but it was known now that no real Christian could be persuaded to do it. So great was their obstinacy that they would rather die; and they had convinced themselves that if they did die in this way, they would go straight to God and enjoy a blessed life in his kingdom for evermore. The miserable creatures, Lucian remarked, had convinced themselves that they were immortal. It would appear that the magistrate or philosopher often wished heartily that they would all die and go to heaven and trouble him no more.

We should assume that the gospel had now spread in some shape or form to every part of the empire, and even beyond its borders. About 150 Justin offered his *Apology* to the emperor on behalf of Christians 'from every race of men'. Allowing for some exaggeration in that statement, we may yet think that Christianity had spread to all the main centres, and was everywhere well known.

HADRIAN IN ATHENS: A.D. 124–5

On his accession in 117 Hadrian had the difficult task of withdrawing from military adventures, fixing the boundaries of the empire, and restoring peace. In the course of his work, he personally visited all the provinces. He built a great palisade from the Rhine to the Danube as a means of defence against the German tribes, and a 'wall' across northern Britain from the mouth of the Tyne to the Solway Firth, as a means of defence against the Picts and Scots. The latter defence marks the furthest extension of the Roman power in Britain, which was due to the energy and ability of the great general, Julius Severus. Caerleon, Chester and York were the three principal centres of military administration. No doubt Christianity had reached these points, along with Mithraism and other oriental cults.

On his return from Britain, Hadrian paid a visit to Athens. This was in 124 or 125. Athens was participating in the Hellenic revival and basked in academic and literary glory. A millionaire named Herodes Atticus was providing it with new buildings and endowments. Naturally, too, it benefited from the liberality of a monarch who everywhere interested himself in the monuments and traditions of the past. He rebuilt a great part of the city, a part which came to be known as Hadrian's City. He submitted to the mysteries and was initiated at

Eleusis; for there was probably no experience that he would not try once. This must have occurred either in 124 or in his later visit in 129.

It would be perfectly in accord with his broad-minded disposition to receive an 'apology' or defence of the Christian tradition; and Eusebius tells us that two such 'apologies' were presented to him in Athens, one by Quadratus, and one by Aristides. It has been proved now that Eusebius was wrong about the Apology of Aristides, which was written some fifteen years later, and presented to Antoninus Pius; and this has sometimes been taken to imply a later date for Quadratus too; but surely the probabilities are in favour of an opposite conclusion. Eusebius possessed a copy of Quadratus and followed whatever indications he found in the text; he did not possess a copy of Aristides, and simply adds a notice about Aristides to his account of Quadratus. The modern scholar differs from Eusebius in having Aristides but not Quadratus.

THE *APOLOGY* OF QUADRATUS

It is hardly possible, in any case, to place the *Apology* of Quadratus much later than 124 or 129, because, in the short extract which Eusebius quotes from it, he makes the statement that some of the persons healed by Jesus had survived 'even into our times'. How late could such a claim be plausibly made? The phrase is an elastic one, but a date after the hundred-and-twenties is rather difficult to accept.

The passage which is quoted by Eusebius runs as follows:

But the works of our Saviour remained permanent, for they were genuine; that is to say, those who were healed, and those who rose from the dead. They were not only seen when they were being healed or raised; they remained permanently—and not only while the Saviour was dwelling [on earth] but also after his departure—they lived on for a considerable time, and some of them survived even into our own times.

(Quadratus, *Apology*, in Eusebius, *E.H.* IV, 3, 2.)

The use of the expression '*our* Saviour' rather suggests that Quadratus was presenting the figure of Christ as a saviour or healer, in contrast to the pagan healers or saviours, such as Apollo and Asclepius, whose cures he may have said were not permanent. Eusebius calls his book an apology on behalf of our *theosebeia* or way of worshipping the deity, which looks as if it were a refutation of the charge of atheism and a defence of Christianity as a pure monotheistic worship, through Christ, on the lines of the old Jewish Hellenism. Something of this sort had appeared already in the *Preaching of Peter*, a book which must have been known in Athens, since it appears to have been used by Aristides.

The production by Quadratus of the first Christian book to be written in the Greek manner was occasioned by a persecution. Certain wicked men had molested our people. About thirty-five years later, Dionysius of Corinth mentions a persecution in Athens in which Publius, the bishop at that time, died as a martyr, and his successor Quadratus had great difficulties in reorganizing the church. The words of Dionysius give no help in dating this persecution, which may not have been the one to which Quadratus alluded in his *Apology*; but doubtless it was the same Quadratus.

On the other hand, the Quadratus who is mentioned by the Phrygian Montanists is probably another man.

PERSECUTION IN ASIA

The years 122–3 certainly saw a severe persecution in Asia Minor. It was due to popular demonstrations against the Christians. So formidable were they that the Roman legate in Asia, Silvanus Granianus, wrote to Hadrian asking him whether he ought to yield to such campaigns of violence. We shall see what they were like when we come to study the martyrdoms of St Polycarp and of the martyrs of Gaul. There were times when it was customary to satisfy the religious and patriotic sentiments of the populace with scenes of violence and bloodshed in the arena, and on these occasions an excited crowd was apt to make demands to which it was politic to yield. Pontius Pilate had found himself in just such a predicament.

HADRIAN'S RESCRIPT: A.D. 124–5

Granianus finished his term of office without receiving any reply from the emperor who may have been in the east in 123; but his successor, Minicius Fundanus, whose years of office were 124–5, received an official reply or 'rescript'. This was the year when Hadrian paid his visit to Athens. It is a remarkable document.

I have received the letter which was written to me by your predecessor, Serenius[1] Granianus, a most distinguished man, and it did not seem to me

---

[1] An error for Silvanus.

that I could pass over the question in silence, lest innocent persons might be interfered with and informers be given an opportunity of doing harm. Therefore if the inhabitants of your province are willing to support their petition against the *Christians* openly and to plead their case in a court of law, I am not forbidding them to do it, but not to rely on petitions and outcries only. The right procedure is for you to inquire into the allegations, should anyone consent to bring a charge. So, if anybody accuses them of doing something contrary to the law and proves their case, it is for you to decide the punishment in proportion to the offence. But, by Hercules, you must be very careful to see that, if anybody accuses one of them falsely, you assign *him* severe penalties in proportion to his malice.

(Rescript of Hadrian in Eusebius, *E.H.* IV, 9.)

The law was not in any way changed, but this directive with regard to procedure must have operated in favour of the Christians. Trajan had ruled out anonymous letters; Hadrian ruled out malicious accusations and popular clamour. It would appear that he was no persecutor.

The rescript is quoted, in a Greek translation, in Justin's *Apology*.

THE CONVERSION OF JUSTIN

Many of those who watched the Christians marvelled at their faith and courage, and were attracted towards their religion. Among these was Justin of Samaria, who ultimately became a martyr himself and is known by that title. When he wrote his own *Apology*, twenty-five years later, he appended to it the text of Hadrian's rescript, which must have become known to him at this time. He was, by then, the successor of Quadratus and Aristides as champion and defender of the much-maligned Christian philosophy.

He gives us an amusing account of his search for the truth. He had received the usual education, and had read about the loves and wars of the gods and goddesses in the Greek poets. After this he went to the philosophers to find out the truth about God and the soul. His first master was a Stoic; but he said that he knew nothing at all about God, and that such studies were of no importance. Justin left him for a 'Peripatetic', an exponent of the philosophy of Aristotle, who insisted on fixing his fee, so that both of them might have pleasure and profit withal. Disgusted with this commercial attitude, Justin passed on to a Pythagorean, who asked him if he had been grounded in music and geometry. As he lacked these academic prerequisites, he passed on to a

Platonist 'of our town', and fell in love with his doctrine of an eternal reality which was infinitely superior to this world and could be known only by the pure intellect. The words 'in our town' were spoken in Ephesus, but the inference that they referred to Ephesus is a little uncertain. It might equally well be Athens or any other centre of learning where philosophers abounded.

While he was walking by the sea (and this shows that he was no longer in Samaria), he fell in with a venerable old man who was no mean hand at a philosophic argument; and it was this unnamed Christian teacher, whom he met by chance and never saw again, who directed his attention to the highest philosophy of all, which had been set forth by the divine prophets, as Justin describes the Hebrew scriptures. He read these books, and imbibed their sublime doctrine of God. He was deeply impressed by their predictions, which he found fulfilled in the Christian Gospels and in contemporary history. He studied the words of the Saviour, which he found short, precise, terrible, and yet full of refreshment. And he became a Christian in the manner which he describes in one of his books. He was baptized in the laver of regeneration in the name of the Father of all things, even the Lord God, and of our Saviour Jesus Christ, and of the Holy Spirit. He did not cease, however, to be a philosopher. He went about wearing the gown which all philosophers wore, but he preached the new 'barbarian' philosophy, which was the oldest of them all.

THE CHRISTIAN PHILOSOPHY

It is clear that the presentation of Christianity as a form of philosophy was no new thing. He had run into a Christian school in which the apostolic tradition had undergone a certain amount of formal definition. We find in his *Apology* a certain number of general propositions with regard to the faith, which he introduces by the formula, 'We have been taught and instructed'; and he regards them as expressions of the common Christian faith which would be valid everywhere. In the philosophic schools they would be called 'dogmas', that is to say, authoritative formulations of the received opinions. The Christian teachers from whom he had received them seem to have been following in the trails of certain Jewish scholars of the Hellenistic tradition who had for a long time been trying to commend Jewish monotheism as the best form of 'philosophy'.

25

These authoritative doctrines included such propositions as these: There is but one God, eternal, invisible and immaterial. He stands in no need of such sacrifices as were offered in the pagan temples, or for that matter in the old Jerusalem Temple either. He had created the whole universe by his 'Word'; the creative Word of the Lord having been equated with the divine Mind or Reason of the Stoics which ordered and governed the world. Justin had a developed theology of his own about the Word, but in one form or another it was among the doctrines which he had received.

Here is the same equation of the Hebrew and Greek monotheisms which Jewish Hellenists had already attempted and Christian apologists would continue to preach. It would be the stock-in-trade of the Christian philosopher as he made his approach to the intellectuals. Actually Justin does not stray far from the teaching and instruction of this kind which he had received in the church; he goes to the Hebrew scriptures to 'prove' his doctrine of the divine Word, however much he may universalize it in the Stoic manner or find it in some germinal form in every human heart; and his access to the Father of all things was through Christian worship and revelation.

His dependence upon the Judaeo-Christian tradition is proved most effectively by his uncritical faith in the apocalyptic of the school of Papias, which he thought was taught in the Revelation of John. The same rather over-realistic form of imaginative thinking is manifested in his doctrine of the dominion of daemons in the cosmos, which was in harmony with the usual Platonic theory as well as with the mythology of *Enoch;* and in his conventional belief in the dissolution of the cosmos by fire, which was in harmony with the Stoic philosophy as well as with II Peter and the Sibyllines; and in the final judgement, for which he could find analogies in the Greek poets. In all these matters he was a man of his own age. He accepted the current Christian philosophy as he found it, though his individual genius rises superior to it at many points.

HADRIAN IN ASIA MINOR: A.D. 129

In the year 129 affairs in the east demanded the personal attention of the emperor, who had not been there for twelve years. He passed through Athens for the second time, crossed the Aegean Sea and arrived in Asia.

Among the young men who attended upon him were two whose names appear in later Christian records, Antinous and Florinus. Florinus was either a Christian already or else deeply interested; and while the royal party was in Smyrna he visited the local bishop, Polycarp, and listened eagerly to his anecdotes about St John and others who had seen the Lord. We are still within hearing of the apostolic period.

There was a boy named Irenaeus who was present on these occasions, and fifty years later he recalled the scene in a letter to Florinus, in which he describes him as 'faring sumptuously at the royal court'. The visit of Hadrian to Smyrna is the obvious occasion to which to assign this encounter, since there is no other record of an imperial visit to Smyrna during the lifetime of Polycarp. Irenaeus was still a boy at the time, he says; and if he was fifteen years old in 129, he would be in his sixties or early seventies when he wrote his great book *Against Heresies*, and about five years older when he took part in the Paschal controversy. (There are some scholars, however, who think that this chronology makes Irenaeus too old at the time when he appears as a bishop and an author; and they suggest that there may have been some later unrecorded imperial visit, when this encounter with Florinus, in the presence of Polycarp, took place.)

IRENAEUS AND FLORINUS

Fifty years later Florinus had taken up with gnostic heresy, and this is what Irenaeus wrote to him by way of reminder.

I have a better remembrance of the things which happened then; for the things we learn in childhood grow together with the soul and become united with it. I can tell you the very place where the blessed Polycarp used to sit and talk; I can tell his goings forth and his comings in, and the way of life he had, and his bodily appearance, and the speeches which he made to the multitude, and how he told us about his intercourse with John and the others who had seen the Lord, repeating their words from memory; and certain things about the Lord which he had heard from them, about his miracles and his teaching; as Polycarp received them from eyewitnesses of the life of the Word, so he reported everything in harmony with the scriptures.

And I, by the mercy of God which was given me, was listening eagerly to all these things and committing them to memory; not on paper but in my heart; and by the grace of God I ponder on them continually; and I can testify before God that if that blessed and apostolic elder had heard these things, he would have cried out aloud and stopped his ears, as his manner was, saying, 'O good God, what times hast thou preserved me unto, that I must bear with this?' And he would have fled from the spot where he was sitting or standing when he heard such words.

(Irenaeus, *Epistle to Florinus*, in Eusebius, *E.H.* v, 20, 4–8.)

We would give much to have a few more vivid eyewitness pictures like this from the second century, and less contentious theology. The lapse of years is reduced to nothing when elderly men recall the memory of their school-days. Irenaeus and Florinus had a common memory to which confident appeal could be made.

The critics who deny the reality of the ministry of John the apostle at Ephesus have to take into account this honest straightforward evidence; and are obliged to argue that Irenaeus and Florinus made a mistake about the identity of the John of whom Polycarp was speaking; and of course that everyone else in their circle was mistaken, too; Justin for instance, who was teaching in Ephesus a year or two later, and received the Revelation as the work of the Apostle. In fact the whole Ephesian church must have fallen into the same error. Quite frankly, it does not seem possible that so gross a misconception of the truth can have become current when Polycarp himself and other pupils of John were in a position to correct it. It was hardly thirty years since his death. All the older people would remember him.

THE JOHANNINE SCHOOL

It was the period when the great masters of the school of John were presiding in their own schools and passing on the teaching which they had received from him and from others who had seen the Lord; they were the men to whom Irenaeus alludes as the elders. Polycarp was now sixty years of age, and had twenty-five years more to go; he had been baptized about the year 69 or 70 in the height of the apostolic age; he became the grand old man of the Christian church. Only less venerable was Papias, who is described by Irenaeus as a pupil of John and a companion of Polycarp; but the critics who reject his evidence about John, are obliged to regard this as another of his mistakes. Irenaeus himself was an example of the younger men who were being trained in their schools, and would spread their teaching and influence far and wide during the remainder of the century.

We do not know who was the bishop or leading teacher in Ephesus at this time; but we have information about a curious phenomenon, a family succession of bishops; for Polycrates, who was born at this time, says that seven members of his family had been bishops before him, and it would not be unreasonable to suppose that this remarkable family was already prominent in the church life of the time. He was bishop of Ephesus himself about 190–5. He left on record interesting statements about Philip and John and Polycarp.

PAPIAS THE PHRYGIAN

Papias of Hierapolis was a familiar ecclesiastical type, the crusted conservative who does not change his opinions from youth to old age; a most valuable authority for the historian, and a protection to the church in an age of transition. Hierapolis, where he was bishop, had been the headquarters of the apostle Philip,[1] with whose daughters he was personally acquainted; it was about one hundred miles east of Smyrna and Ephesus, and had become the leading church in eastern Phrygia. No doubt it had its own rather different tradition. Papias was a native Phrygian, judging by his name, and we can already detect a certain individuality about Phrygian Christianity. We see signs of the preoccupation with apocalypse, which gave birth to Montanism in a few years; we may even see the forerunners of the feminist movement in the two daughters of Philip who lived there 'in the Spirit' as virgins, to a great age. The third lived in Ephesus, and may have been married.[2] The near-by city of Philadelphia had its prophetess, whose name was Ammia. An otherwise unknown Quadratus also exercised a prophetic ministry in these parts; he should be carefully distinguished from the Athenian Quadratus.

Papias was deeply interested in the Judaeo-Christian apocalypses and studied the Revelation of St John, which had been written in his lifetime and contained special messages for the Phrygian churches. He was a famous promoter of the doctrine of the 'chiliad' or millennium, the thousand-year period after the resurrection during which Christ

---

[1] A Roman theologian named Proclus, about A.D. 200, thought that he was the Philip of Caesarea mentioned in the Acts; many critics think he was right, but if so Papias, Irenaeus and Polycrates have made another mistake.
[2] The Philip who lived at Caesarea had four virgin daughters who prophesied, so that Proclus can be excused for confusing the one with the other.

would reign with the saints on this earth, which would then become miraculously fertile. Justin received a form of 'chiliasm', which located the centre of this earthly kingdom in Jerusalem, but we do not know whether Papias held this form of the belief. He may simply have thought of an earth redeemed from sin and death, and free from war and hunger and toil. He took very simply the hope of the kingdom coming on earth as it is in heaven, and elaborated it with detail from the Hebrew prophets and other sources.

It is most unfortunate that the five volumes of his *Expositions of the Oracles of the Lord* have been lost; but even so we are grateful for the quotations which have come down to us in the works of other writers.

PAPIAS AND THE GOSPEL TRADITION

We see Papias mainly through the eyes of Eusebius, who had a low view of his intelligence. He may be perfectly right, of course, but he was unsympathetic with eschatological fancies and impatient with him on that account. He blames Papias for the dogmatic chiliasm of Justin and Irenaeus and other second-century fathers, who, he thought, were too deeply impressed with the 'antiquity of the man'. This is a just criticism, but it admits that he was a person of influence in his time.

Modern writers represent him as a devotee of the oral tradition, who had an antipathy to books; but this opinion seems to go beyond the evidence; for he was one of the first Christians to write a book after the secular or Gentile manner. Let us look at what he said.

> I supposed that things out of books did not profit me as much as the utterances of a living and abiding voice.
>
> (Papias, *Expositions*, *Preface*, in Eusebius, *E.H.* III, 39, 4.)

It is a single sentence, and too much may be built upon it. He has been calling to mind a period in his youth when the voice of Jesus was still echoing in the oral tradition of the apostolic church. He had heard the words of Jesus repeated by disciples of Andrew, Peter, Philip, Thomas, James, John, and Matthew. It must have been a memorable experience. Their words must have come with an authentic intonation which was no longer to be heard in his old age when the church had to depend on written Gospels. The memory of that experience naturally meant more to him than anything he now heard read in church.

The 'Oracles of the Lord' on which he commented in his book were taken from written Gospels, and his oral traditions were brought in as supplementary material. This is made perfectly clear in another sentence from his preface.

I will not hesitate *also* to set down for your benefit, *along with* my 'Expositions', everything that I carefully remembered from the elders, guaranteeing its truth.   (*Ibid.* III, 39, 3.)

Eusebius did not think highly of these oral traditions of Papias. He remarks that he frequently referred to John and Aristion by name, and set forth their traditions. Other traditions were received from the two daughters of Philip. Others were quoted as from an unwritten tradition; and these included certain strange parables and teachings of the Saviour and other matters of a rather mythical character, among which Eusebius includes the doctrine of the millennium. He explains these as misunderstandings of the apostolic narratives, since Papias did not realize that they were expressed in figurative or mystical language; which may be a very just criticism.

One example of this kind of material was given in an earlier chapter and other examples are found in Irenaeus. The following extract is given by him on the authority of the elders generally, but no doubt he takes it from the *Expositions*.

As the elders say: Then also shall they which have been deemed worthy of heaven go thither; while others shall enjoy the delight of Paradise; and others shall possess the brightness of the city; for in every place the Saviour shall be seen according as they who see him shall be worthy.

They say moreover that this is the distinction between the dwelling-places of those who bring forth a hundredfold, and those that bring forth sixtyfold, and those that bring forth thirtyfold. . . .

The elders, the disciples of the apostles, say that this is the arrangement and disposition of those that are saved.   (Irenaeus, *A.H.* v, 36, 1–2.)

Here is a piece of eschatological fancy which has been fitted to an 'Oracle of the Lord' taken from a written Gospel; for the parable of the sower in Matthew and Mark is the source of the thirtyfold, sixty-fold and hundredfold, and it is linked by Mark with teaching on spiritual vision. The second-century fathers uniformly explain this parable as a symbol of the Resurrection, as the Asian elders do here.

THE TRADITIONS OF PAPIAS

The book has vanished; but it made a deep impression. We can see the old bishop among his people, like the wise scribe in the gospel, bringing out of his treasury things new and old; what the elder used to say about Mark's Gospel; how the Lord answered Judas when he found the apocalyptic imagery rather thick; or how old the Lord was when he began teaching. He dealt out mystical explanations of the parables and commandments in answer to teachers who brought in strange commandments; he supported them by references to the Revelation of St John, which had arrived from Patmos in his time; he quoted John; he quoted the unknown Aristion, whom he called the disciple of the Lord; he recalled what had been said by the pupils of this or that disciple; he drew on the tales that used to be told by the daughters of Philip. It was from them that he heard how Justus Barsabbas drank a draught of deadly poison, and by the grace of the Lord took no harm from it; and also of the resurrection of a corpse in their time, the 'mother of Manaim' according to the unreliable Philip of Side.

He had a revolting tale from some source or another about the death of Judas Iscariot, and a story about a woman who was falsely accused of many sins before the Lord; a tale which was also to be found in the Gospel of the Hebrews, Eusebius says; possibly the story of the 'woman taken in adultery', which has found its way into the texts of the Bible.

Our picture of Papias is a very important one, since it gives us a glimpse of the gospel tradition as it was when the apostolic age was not quite out of hearing, and sayings and stories of Jesus were still passing from lip to lip in the preaching and teaching of the church. It shows us the kind of source from which additions and emendations crept into the Gospel manuscripts, and how material could be found for new Gospels like the Hebrew Gospel or the Egerton fragment. Papias was not the only venerable elder who could hand on personal memories in this way. He happens to be so well remembered because he wrote a book. The date of writing cannot be determined; it is usually assigned to the latter part of the reign of Hadrian.

3. JEWISH COINS

4. ANTINOUS

CERINTHUS AND THE EBIONITES

Asia Minor was not destined to produce an abstract other-worldly theology of the superior gnostic type. Asian Christianity had a firm hold on the old-fashioned gospel in its literature and in its manifestation as religious fellowship. It gloried in the apocalyptic and liturgical language of the Judaeo-Christian tradition, and it gained its understanding of the new spiritual life through the prophetic and sacramental media of the fellowship. Such a temperament was not likely to run into the refined form of gnosis which proclaimed a remote nameless deity and an immaterial Christ. We know from the evidence of John, Ignatius and Polycarp that docetism did exist among the Asian Christians as a separate sect; but when gnosticism clearly appears at Ephesus, it is the gnosis of magic and ritual and sex; not the gnosis of absorption into the infinite.

The only heretical name which comes down to us from this early period is that of Cerinthus, the traditional opponent of St John. His views are far from clear. According to Irenaeus, who ought to know, he reposed his faith in a higher deity than the God of the Jews. Some higher sovereignty sent down the 'Christus' in the form of a dove, to enter the man Jesus after his baptism; he then proclaimed the hitherto unknown Father, and worked miracles; he flew back to the Father before the Passion. This is mythological thinking, though it expresses a theological theory. It is found again in the Basilidian sect and in Carpocrates, a later gnostic of Alexandria, the centre where Cerinthus had received his training. It was, no doubt, an Alexandrian idea.

Cerinthus rejected the virgin birth and called Jesus the son of Joseph and Mary; Carpocrates did this too. He must have rejected the Jewish Law with the Jewish God, as Carpocrates did. Carpocrates saw no harm in participation in idol-sacrifices and sexual pleasures; and Cerinthus may have taken the same line. St John denounces teachers of this sort in the Revelation. They are veiled under the names of Jezebel and Balaam; anti-Jewish characters both.

We arrive at a paradox at this point. Cerinthus, who rejected the Jewish God, is coupled by Irenaeus with the narrow sect of Jewish-Christians which he calls the Ebionites, since both deny the virgin birth. Both explained the divine element in Jesus as the indwelling of a Holy Spirit, though with considerable differences theologically. It seems that Cerinthians and Ebionites existed side by side in Asia and were bracketed together in the church catalogues.

Gaius of Rome, the opponent of Proclus, who wrote about the year 200, attributed to Cerinthus an eschatology not unlike that of Papias and Justin, though it is more sensually defined. There will be a resurrection of the flesh; the kingdom of Christ will be established on earth for a thousand years in Jerusalem; the flesh will once again serve the lusts and pleasures in nuptial festivities. A similar statement is found about fifty years later in Dionysius of Alexandria, but without reference to Jerusalem; he emphasizes the nuptial character of life in the kingdom and speaks of feasts and sacrifices and slaying of victims.

If this is correct, we may conclude that while Cerinthus rejected the God of the Jews, and also no doubt the Law which he gave to Israel, he recognized an element of inspiration in the prophets, as the Ophites did, for instance, and that he used the parables of Jesus and the poetry of Jewish apocalypse very much as Papias and the Elders did. The Ebionites very probably did the same. They interpret the prophecies in a curious way, Irenaeus says, and they adore Jerusalem as the house of God. It looks as if the apostolic-minded Papias, and the antinomian Cerinthus, and the Judaizing Ebionites, may all have been working in the same kind of apocalyptic material. The *Expositions* of Papias might thus be aiming at the establishment of a correct (traditional) understanding of this material in the face of divergent views.

On the other hand, Irenaeus and Hippolytus say nothing at all about the apocalyptic teachings which Gaius attributes to Cerinthus; and Irenaeus is our earliest and best authority on him. We cannot feel confident that Gaius at the end of the second century had any very reliable information to go on, especially as he makes the extraordinary statement that Cerinthus was the true author of the Revelation of John. Neither Gaius nor Proclus seems to have been very well informed.

CHAPTER 3

THE SECOND JEWISH WAR

HADRIAN IN ANTIOCH: A.D. 129–30

Hadrian passed through Asia and Phrygia and spent the winter of 129–30 in Antioch. It is very doubtful how much we can say about the church in Antioch at this period; it passes into relative obscurity for forty or fifty years. It is unlikely that its history was peaceful.

The heretical schools associated with the name of Satornil were directing the minds of their devotees to a purely spiritual deity outside of time and space, and a purely spiritual Christ. It is unfair, perhaps, to use words like 'unsubstantial' or 'nebulous' of this type of Christianity; no doubt its adherents felt that spirit was far more real and powerful than flesh or material substance. Their own spirituality was so intense as to lead to a denial of the bodily life, which they thought of as evil; they abstained from wine and flesh-meat; they practised celibacy. They could quote texts from Paul which seemed to support their idea of a current of spiritual power in the body so strong as to crucify the flesh and its lusts; he had said such things in Antioch (Galatians v. 24).

The same sense of the gospel as spirit and power is found, of course, in Ignatius, but it is a spirit-power which becomes flesh in Jesus Christ, and in the heart of the believer, and in the sacramental fellowship of the church; it has an affinity and affection for flesh. It is thus compatible for him with a very full participation in the catholic tradition which comes so clearly into sight in his writings; in fact it is in and through the catholic order that he has contact with spirit. Round these two conceptions the evolution of the future Syrian catholicism seems to take place; the idea of spirit and the idea of church order. The spirit-theology of Paul and John is balanced by the ecclesiastical Gospel of Matthew, in which Peter is the leading apostle, and Jewish tradition is made available to the Gentile churches.

CHRONOLOGICAL TABLE

(from Nerva to Commodus, A.D. 96–192)

A.D.

96	NERVA appointed by the Senate, 96. Epistle of Clement. *Visions* of Hermas.	
98	TRAJAN, adopted by Nerva, 98. Prophet Elkhasai in Transjordania, *c.* 100.	
100	Death of John at Ephesus and Clement at Rome, and Herod Agrippa II in Galilee.	EUARESTUS, 97/101: fourth bishop of Rome.
102		
104	Martyrdom of Simeon in Palestine, *c.* 104–7	
106		ALEXANDER, 105/110.
108		
110	Persecution in Bithynia under Pliny; Trajan's Rescript.	
112	*Parthian War* of Trajan, 113–17.	
114	Ignatius the Martyr, 108–17. Letters of Ignatius and Polycarp.	
116	Jewish Revolts in Mesopotamia, Egypt, Cyprus.	
118	HADRIAN (adopted by Trajan) succeeds in 117. End of the war.	XYSTUS (Sixtus I), 115/120: concordat with Asians.
120	Concordat of Xystus with Asians in Rome on Paschal question.	
122	Persecution in Asia Minor; Hadrian's Rescript, 124/5.	
124	*Apology* of Quadratus offered to Hadrian in Athens; or 129.	
126	Conversion of Justin Martyr? Date of *Barnabas? Didache?*	TELESPHORUS, 125/129: died as a martyr.
128	Hadrian visits Smyrna in 129; Irenaeus and Florinus with Polycarp?	
130	Hadrian in Palestine and Egypt.	
132	*Jewish War* begins (132). Justin's *Dialogue with Trypho*, 132–6.	
134	*Romans defeat Jews* (135); city of Aelia built on site of Jerusalem.	
136	Martyrdom of Telesphorus in Rome.	HYGINUS, 136/139: arrival of
138	ANTONINUS PIUS (adopted by Hadrian) succeeds, 138;	heresiarchs.
140	arrival in Rome of Cerdo, Marcion and Valentinus.	PIUS, 140/143; brother of
142	Completed works of Hermas according to the *Muratorian Fragment.*	Hermas.
144	Latest likely date for the *Interpretations* of Papias?	
146	Latest likely date for *Apology* of Aristides of Athens; Justin's *Syntagma?*	
148	MARCUS AURELIUS co-emperor, 147 (adopted by Antoninus).	
150	*First Apology* of Justin; in Rome; probably 150–2.	

A.D.

152	The prophesyings of Montanus in Phrygia?	
154	Visit of Polycarp to Rome; meeting with Anicetus.	ANICETUS, 155/158: with
156	Martyrdom of Polycarp and others at Smyrna; 155 or 156	Eleutherus as his deacon.
158	Martyrdom of Ptolemaeus and Lucius at Rome; before 161.	
160	Hegesippus comes to Rome in the time of Anicetus.	
162	MARCUS AURELIUS and LUCIUS VERUS, 161. *Parthian War*, 162–6.	
164	Martyrdoms in Asia, 160–6. Synods condemn Montanism.	
166	Martyrdom of Justin and others in Rome, 162–7.	SOTER, 166/169; epistle to
168	Correspondence of Dionysius of Corinth.	Corinth.
170	MARCUS AURELIUS sole emperor, 169. The Thundering Legion, 171 or 174.	
172	Tatian leaves Rome for Syria, before 173.	
174	*Rebellion in Syria*, 175. *Apologies* of Melito and Apolinarius, 176.	ELEUTHERUS, 174/178: had been deacon of Anicetus.
176	Gallican martyrdoms, 177; Irenaeus in Rome.	
178	COMMODUS made co-emperor, 177. *Apology* of Athenagoras of Athens.	
180	COMMODUS succeeds his father, 180; the African Martyrdoms.	
182	The *Autolycus* of Theophilus of Antioch; Hegesippus writes the *Note-books* under Eleutherus.	
184	Martyrdom of Apollonius at Rome, 183–5.	
186	The *Refutation* of Irenaeus; written under Eleutherus.	
188	Early history of Callistus, his imprisonment in Sardinia.	VICTOR, 189/193.
190	Paschal controversy and councils.	
192	SEPTIMUS SEVERUS succeeds Commodus (assassinated 31 December 192); accession 193.	

Notes

(1) The accessions of Roman Emperors and some other imperial dates are to be found on the left-hand side of this Table. The even numbers of years in the margin supply a chronological scale.

(2) In the centre the reader will find the events of Christian history which may be dated exactly, approximately, or relatively. Where no date is given, the position of the event is approximately correct; where a question mark is added, the date is less certain.

(3) The names of the bishops of Rome are given on the right-hand side. The figures given with the names are the dates of accession according to (a) the Chronicle of Hippolytus, which is the authority followed by the Liberian Catalogue, and (b) Eusebius, who is probably working from the chronographies of Africanus. The former are calculated from 64, and the latter from 68, as the date of the martyrdom of Peter and Paul. These dates are only approximate, and in the earlier entries are dubious. The Eusebian dates are not possible in the case of Anicetus and Victor.

This background material is our best guide to the nature of Antiochene Christianity at this time; and we may append to Matthew, in our consideration of it, the *Didache* or *Teaching of the Twelve Apostles to the Gentiles*, which is the first of the Syrian church orders, and yet tells us of wandering prophets and teachers so filled with Holy Spirit that it was impiety to question their words or acts. It gives us sacramental benedictions which retain a pronounced Jewish tinge, though the colour of the book as a whole is decidedly anti-Jewish. When we come to Theophilus, who was bishop of Antioch in the hundred-and-seventies, we find a theology which is quite definitely on the Jewish and biblical side, and yet it has a quiet spirituality of its own which defies definition. We get the impression, however, that the stronger, more dynamic, spirituality of Ignatius has rather given way to a liberal Law-and-Prophets Christianity based on Matthew and the Old Testament.

Can we go farther than this? Can we place in Syria, and at this period, the production of some of the 'pseudonymous' books which were issued under apostolic names? the second Epistle of Peter? his *Revelation*? his *Preaching*? his *Gospel*? the last of which is first reported from the neighbourhood of Antioch. They affirm the authority of Peter and the Twelve; they work from the Law and the prophets; they proclaim a fiery judgement which is to come. They belong to a different school from the millennial apocalyptic of the Phrygian and Asian tradition, so that we are justified in looking for their origin elsewhere; but Alexandria is not excluded, nor Rome.

Or may we suggest II Clement, which uses a verse from Ignatius, and passed into the Syrian New Testament along with I Clement?

Eusebius preserves a list of Antiochene bishops; but only one out of the first five is anything more than a name to us. They are Euodius, Ignatius, Heron, Cornelius and Eros; then Theophilus, who was still living in 180.

HADRIAN IN PALESTINE

From Antioch Hadrian passed on into Palestine and visited Jerusalem in 130. Work had already begun on the rebuilding of this city, and there was a population of some sort. It is a reasonably secure assumption that a Christian church had been established there. Hegesippus tells of a return of disciples from the church-in-exile at Pella; and another authority, quoted by Eusebius, gives the names of a number of Jewish-

Christian bishops, who claimed succession from James the brother of the Lord though it is not said that they were of the family of Jesus. The Jerusalem elders and bishops of this period would be the official custodians of the traditions about James the Just and the other members of the family which were written down some forty or fifty years later by Hegesippus. Hegesippus was another of the younger men who were destined to play a part in the history of the Roman church. All roads led to Rome for this generation.

It was about this time, or a little earlier, that the *Epistle of Barnabas* must have been written, as appears from one of its scripture elucidations:

Behold they who destroyed the Temple, the same shall build it. [Isaiah xlix. 17.] It is happening [Barnabas says], for through their going to war it was destroyed by their enemies, and now they and the servants of their enemies are building it up.   (*Epistle of Barnabas*, XVI, 3.)

This sentence suggests a policy of co-existence and collaboration in Jerusalem which would not have been possible in the years 130–2, at the end of which a serious war broke out. It appears to belong to an earlier time when Romans and Jews were co-operating, a time which is also reflected in the legend about Aquila which we gave in full in an earlier chapter. If Hadrian had not given orders earlier for the rebuilding, either in 117 at his accession or at some later time, at any rate he did so now; but not in the spirit of co-operation suggested by the verse in Barnabas, for his decision aroused the Jews to fury. The new city was not to be a Jewish sanctuary or ethnic centre; it was to be a Roman outpost on the eastern frontier. This was a natural policy, and may be compared with the rebuilding of Carthage and Corinth by Julius Caesar. It was in line with the Romanization of many other oriental cities which were growing wealthy on the caravan trade with the far east.

The late and fragmentary character of the sources does not enable us to decide precisely what steps Hadrian took before the war, but it is clear that there was enough friction now to create a very ugly situation. The war, which broke out after the departure of Hadrian, cannot have been engineered without considerable preparation, and we read in the Talmud of numerous journeys of Rabbi Akiba into Mesopotamia, to Nisibis and Nehardaea, where there were influential groups of Jews, and also into Cilicia and Cappadocia; it is possible that the Jewish communities in these border-line countries provided some assistance and support.

According to the Talmud, Hadrian had already taken severe measures. He is said to have forbidden the practice of circumcision and even the keeping of the Sabbath and the reading of the Law; but this sounds like an exaggeration.

SIMEON BAR COCHBA

The Jews seem to have restored their national organization and rural economy under the rabbinic sanhedrin, and its 'prince' or 'patriarch', Gamaliel III, whose death must have occurred about this time. Their temper was fiercely nationalistic and Zionist. They had set their hopes, with all the intense fervour of which their race is capable, on the restoration of the Jewish state, and the rebuilding of the Temple in Jerusalem, and they were ready to fight one more desperate war to attain this purpose. They had in readiness a military leader, whose name was Simeon the son of Cosebah. The great Rabbi Akiba, now a man of very great age, proclaimed him to the nation as the promised Messiah, under the title of 'Bar Cochba', the Son of the Star, which was taken from the prophecy of Balaam, which Christians also made use of for their Messiah.

> There shall come forth a star out of Jacob,
> And a sceptre shall rise out of Israel...
> And Edom shall be a possession;
> Seir also shall be a possession for his enemies,
> And Israel shall do great acts of war.
>
> (Numbers xxiv. 17–18.)

—the name of Edom, which was the country of origin of the Herod family, being often used in Jewish writings as a symbol for Rome.

We recognize in these religio-nationalistic activities the Jewish counterpart of the millennial fancies of Papias and Justin and others. The two interpretations of prophecy grew up, no doubt, side by side and in opposition to one another. The nationalist Jews dreamed of a renewed and restored Jerusalem under a military Messiah who would exercise empire over the earth. The Christians of Phrygia dreamed of a renewed and restored Jerusalem under their crucified Messiah Jesus, when he came again in glory. Both expressed their aspirations in imaginative apocalyptic language; for it was asserted, according to the

Talmud, that Bar Cochba blew flames of fire out of his mouth; and he seems to have set the pattern for the Antichrist of the later Christian poets and prophets; for apocalypse in the second century did not so completely lose touch with history as we would suppose if we only had the *Revelation of Peter*.

We have no information about the apocalyptic theology of the Jewish-Christian bishops, prophets and teachers in Israel. We only know that they refused to recognize Bar Cochba and would not take part in the war. The conflict with the national authorities passed into an acute phase and they were proscribed as heretics and very soon, no doubt, as traitors. The name of Jesus was cursed in the synagogues, and the 'Nazareans' themselves were forced to 'blaspheme Christ', as Justin tells us in his *Dialogue*. It is to this unhappy time that we must allot the virtual extinction of the oldest Christian churches, those that were formed among the Jews themselves.

HADRIAN IN ALEXANDRIA, A.D. 130–1

We do not know whether Hadrian realized how serious the situation was in Palestine. It is unlikely that he did. At any rate he went on to Alexandria, where he passed parts of 130 and 131, giving himself up to sight-seeing and pleasure.

It was in Egypt that an event occurred which demonstrated the incompatibility which existed between the 'ethical monotheism' of Jews or Christians and even the most enlightened paganism of the day. We have mentioned a young man named Antinous who attended upon the emperor. He was drowned in the Nile, and the emperor, who had a personal attachment to him, consoled himself as best he could by building a temple in his honour where he could be worshipped as a god; a town was founded on the site and ceremonial games were held every year in his honour. Now an infatuation of an older man for a boy would cause no remark among the Greeks. Zeus, the father of Gods and men, had his Ganymede. Achilles had his Patroclus. The *Symposium* of Plato finds a place for it in the life of an educated man. But the deification of an emperor's personal homosexuality seems to carry a romantic view of masculine love rather far. It shocked the Christian conscience, as we see in Justin and Hegesippus and other writers of the period. Eusebius has pointed out that Hegesippus dates himself by his statement that this event took place in his own time. He remarks that the pagan world was still erecting cenotaphs and temples to men,

one of whom was Antinous, the slave of Hadrianus Caesar, for whom the 'Antinoëan Games' are celebrated; who lived in our own time [or, which games were instituted in our own time]; indeed the emperor founded a city and named it after Antinous, and appointed prophets.

(Hegesippus, *Note-Books*, in Eusebius, *E.H.* IV, 8, 2.)

The childhood, or possibly the youth of Hegesippus thus falls into this period, along with Irenaeus, Florinus, Polycrates and Narcissus, who were all to play their part in church history for fifty years. Hegesippus was an oriental, probably a Jewish Christian, who had close con-nexions with the old Jewish church in Palestine, and preserved many of its historical traditions.

In Egypt anything could happen. The old and the new kept house together. The native cults of cats and crocodiles continued to flourish and furnished the Jewish and Christian apologists with material for their more satirical passages. It was the home of Isis, the queen of heaven, the most attractive of all the mother-goddesses. It was the home of magic and mystery; and Hadrian, like many sceptics, had a weakness for the wonderful. In the midst of these mystic raptures and primitive superstitions the most modern learning had its com-fortable home. It was here that Euclid had laid the foundations of the geometrical science. Eratosthenes had calculated the distance of the moon. Ptolemy was mapping out the heavens; unfortunately on a geocentric basis, though there were still those who held that the earth went round the sun. The first steam-engine had been made, or at any rate projected. The great Museum, or Institute of the Muses, was said to contain a copy of every book in the world, including the original manuscript of the Septuagint; or so at least Tertullian believed (though perhaps he had forgotten about the destruction of the old library by Julius Caesar). It has been calculated that it must have contained at least a million volumes. The principal Jewish synagogue, with thrones for its seventy or seventy-two elders, resembled a vast temple; so big it was, the Mishnah said, that an attendant had to wave a flag as a sign when the people were to say 'Amen'. In the Serapeum, the great compound god Serapis, who had been invented or imported by the first Ptolemy, was worshipped by all. In the Koreum a form of the

Eleusinian mysteries was celebrated, and on January 6, after a night of chant and vigil, the worshippers of Kore, 'the maiden', were shown her holy child, who was identified with 'aeon', the 'age': the new year itself, which was the offspring of endless time.

A third- or fourth-century writer in the *Historia Augusta* preserves a letter which Hadrian wrote during this visit to his brother-in-law Servianus, which is an excellent example of his light vein in literature. Everyone in Alexandria, he remarked, worshipped the same god:

The Egypt which you used to commend to me, my dear Servianus, I have discovered to be but lightly balanced, wavering with every motion of rumour.

The worshippers of Serapis are the *Christians*. Indeed those who call themselves 'bishops of Christ' are devotees of Serapis. There is no synagogue-ruler of the Jews, no Samaritan, no elder of the Christians, who is not an astrologer, an inspector of entrails, or a watcher of the flight of birds. The patriarch himself, when he visits Egypt, is forced by some to adore Serapis, and by others to adore Christ. . . .

They all have one sole deity, which is money. This is what all the Christians and all the Jews worship: and the Gentiles too.

(*Scriptores Historiae Augustae*, Loeb ed., vol. III, p. 398.)

ALEXANDRIAN CHRISTIANITY

It would be improper, of course, to use this lightly written document to establish the detail of church organization in Alexandria; nor should we take its picture of a financial syncretism too seriously; but the name of Christ is certainly much more prominent than we would have expected, even though it is not in the best company. It is plain that Hadrian had seen or heard gossip about the Christian bishops and elders, and had taken note of the official visits of the Jewish patriarch, Gamaliel III or some ill-fated successor—possibly even Bar Cochba himself.

We have already tried to give a sketch of the early organization of the church in Alexandria as it was seen in later legend. If these legends have any truth in them, the bishop had a position which resembled that of the patriarch; his sanhedrin of elders or bishops formed a close corporation; no deacon could aspire to the episcopate, as at Rome; the congregation or congregations can have had little power. But actually we must confess that we lack the materials to construct a reliable picture.

We have a list of bishops, however, with the number of years they held office, which is preserved in the pages of Eusebius. If we start in the year 62, a number obtained by working backwards from 190, the approximate date of the accession of Demetrius, we find that it works out like this: Annianus (or Hananiah) 62, Avilius 84, Cerdon 98, Primus 109, Justus 119, Eumenes 130, Marcus 143, Celadion 153, Agrippinus 167, Julian 178, and Demetrius 190. Demetrius is the first bishop about whom we have any real information. Annianus occurs in legend. The rest are mere names.

We shall return in our next chapter to the subject of the Alexandrian church. No doubt all the varieties, both Jewish and Gentile, were to be found there, and all the books were assiduously studied. Old Gospels were copied and new Gospels were written. Scholars and mystics wrote commentaries and evolved new theologies. Florinus, who had listened to Polycarp talking about John in Smyrna, may have bought a copy of Matthew or John at a bookstall. He may have met Valentinus, who studied the Johannine Gospel, and combined the wisdom of Jesus and the intellectualism of Paul in a wonderland of spiritualized mythology; a form of thinking to which Florinus himself ultimately succumbed. Basilides, the Alexandrian counterpart of the Antiochene Satornil, was fashioning a new philosophy out of the old gospel material with the help of Iranian gnosis. The Platonist Carpocrates was making strange use of Matthew. The reign of Hadrian was the flowering time of the heresies, it has been said.

The fact is that the figure of Jesus as saviour in the Pauline epistles, and the stories of his wonderful life and wise teachings as given in the Gospel according to Matthew, had come to the notice of the intellectuals. Among the courtiers of Hadrian was a certain Phlegon, a royal slave like Antinous (and very probably Florinus too), to whom he subsequently gave his freedom. Phlegon was an intellectual who wrote a number of books on history and antiquities and the wonders of the world. In one of these books he gave some account of the darkening of the sun and of the earthquake which are said to have occurred at the crucifixion. The Matthaean Gospel had come to his notice as a document which deserved serious consideration. It cannot, or course, be stated that he was with Hadrian in Palestine and Egypt at this time; but the fact shows that the interest in Christianity at the court of Hadrian was not confined to Florinus.

THE SECOND JEWISH WAR, A.D. 132–5

In the year 132 war broke out in Palestine, and the Jews made their last desperate attempt to regain their independence. It is pathetic to reflect how seldom, and for what brief periods, the Jews have succeeded in establishing an independent state in Jerusalem. It is a tragic history, and no episode in it is more tragic than the misguided effort in 132–5 to save the site of the holy city from desecration by the infidel and to realize the messianic dream. It was a heroic, fanatical, and hopeless effort. They had no allies, so far as we can see, and they were not supported by risings of Jews elsewhere. Yet the war dragged on for three or four years, and it cost the Romans much blood and treasure to bring it to a successful issue. No great historian, like Josephus, arose to chronicle its turns of fortune. It is a confused tale, illuminated by a few references in the historians of later times, and dimly recorded in the traditions preserved in the Talmud. The meagreness of our information blinds us to its importance.

It began, we may suppose, with fanatical guerilla fighting; and the Jews met with dramatic successes in its first phases. Bar Cochba took Jerusalem and seems to have reigned there for something like two years; for coins turn up which are marked with the names of 'Symeon the Prince' and 'Eleazar the Priest', and such inscriptions as 'The First Year of Freedom' and 'The Second Year of Freedom'. Two of Bar Cochba's letters have been discovered among the 'Dead Sea Scrolls', which confirm the name Simon or Symeon son of Cosebah. The coins confirm the title of nasi or prince. No doubt he was waiting for God to grant complete victory before he took the title of king.

Hadrian had returned to Rome in 132, and he entrusted the conduct of the war to his prefect Tineius Rufus. The Mishnah confounds this man with Terentius Rufus, who was the Roman commander at the end of the first war under Titus; it calls him Tyrannus Rufus or Turnus Rufus the Wicked. Despite all the Roman efforts the Jews maintained their hold on the holy city and other strong points in the country, and Hadrian had to bring his best general, Julius Severus, from Britain, with strong reinforcements. In the summer of 134 he visited the country himself. Had the empire been engaged in civil strife, or in serious external war, Akiba and Bar Cochba might have been successful for a time in establishing their free Jewish state; for this has only ever been done when the weakness or dissensions of the greater powers could be turned to advantage. It was not so to happen in this case.

The country was reconquered by the Romans at very great cost. The number of the Jewish casualties, as given in the Talmud, seems fantastic,[1] but should be treated with respect; and it is clear from the Roman evidence that their armies suffered heavy losses too. They recaptured Jerusalem, however, and the Jewish leaders, with the remainder of their army, were shut up and besieged in the strong city of Bitther, the modern Khirbet-el-Yehoud, which fell in 135 after a protracted resistance in which great numbers of Jews were killed or taken prisoner, only to be subjected to the most revolting tortures or sold as slaves. Among the prisoners was Akiba himself, now a very old man; for he was said to have reached the conventional complement of a hundred and twenty years. His flesh was slowly scraped from his bones with iron combs or 'shells', a regular procedure in the Roman legal system, as we shall see in the Acts of the Christian martyrs. At the end it was evening, and the time came when the pious Jew recited the *Shema*, which is recognized by Jews and Christians alike as the first commandment of the Law. Akiba made a heroic effort and performed this duty. 'Hear, O Israel,' he said, 'the Lord our God, the Lord is One'; and on that last word, the tradition tells us, he expired. His crazy dream of a military theocracy, centred in Jerusalem, brought ruin to his people in his time; but his example gave them lasting inspiration, and his labours on the interpretation of the scripture and the codification of the oral law provided the Judaism of the future with a sure foundation.

Not every Rabbi shared his apocalyptic hope. 'Akiba,' said one of them, 'the grass will spring from thy jawbone, and yet the Son of David will not have come.'

THE CITY OF AELIA

It was on the ninth of the month of Ab that Nebuchadnezzar had entered Jerusalem in 586 B.C., and it was on the tenth day of the same Jewish month (which fluctuates between July and August), that Titus watched the temple burn in A.D. 70. It was a fatal date in the Jewish calendar. The tractate *Taanit* of the Mishnah, which deals with fasting,

[1] 985 villages taken, 50 fortresses destroyed, 580,000 men killed.

and was composed not very long after this period, speaks of it as follows:

On the ninth of Ab it was decreed that our ancestors should not enter the Holy Land. On the same day the first and second Temples were destroyed, the city of Bitther was taken, and the site of the city was ploughed.

(Mishnah: Taanit, iv. 6.)

The ploughing of the site was an old Roman ceremony which was used in laying out a new city. The old Jerusalem was to be forgotten, and the day of destiny seems to have been chosen to inaugurate a new city with a new name and a new religion. Such was the policy now put into effect. It was called Aelia Capitolina; Aelia from the family name of Hadrian himself (Publius Aelius Hadrianus), and Capitolina from the great temple of the chief deity of Rome, Jupiter Capitolinus. A temple in honour of this god was erected on the site of King Solomon's Temple, and a statue of Hadrian was put up in it, so that, at long last, the emperor had succeeded in establishing himself in the place of the God of heaven. The Abomination of Desolation spoken of by Daniel the prophet stood where it ought not.

Hadrian was determined to avoid all possibility of disaffection in his new frontier city. No Jew was allowed to settle there, or even come in sight of it, though a curious privilege was allowed them as time went on. We have evidence from the fourth century that once a year, on the ninth of Ab, they were allowed to stand by the piece of the Temple wall which still remained and lament for the glory which had passed away. Even so they had to endure the mockery of the Roman soldiers and to pay bribes for the privilege.

The sanhedrin of rabbis had been dispersed, but in process of time it was reconstituted under Symeon III, the son of Gamaliel III. His court shifted from place to place, but was finally settled at Tiberias on the Sea of Galilee. The war must have weakened the hold of Judaism on the coast towns and in Palestine generally, and time was again required to recover. Thousands of Jews had been killed in battle, massacred, driven into exile, or sold as slaves. Few of the rabbinic band remained; but once again, the Mishnah says, there were five selected disciples associated with the patriarch. Among these were Simon ben Jochai, Judah ben Ilai and Rabbi Meir. Symeon III had a son named Judah, the seventh in descent from Hillel, who is known in history as Judah the Holy. Rabbi Judah the Holy is said to have been born on the day that Rabbi Akiba died; he died himself about 220; and it was under his direction that the Mishnah was reduced to writing. Rabbi Meir took a leading part in the work.

Their headquarters after the war were in Tiberias in Galilee; and some old rabbinic documents may have taken form as early as this: the midrashic commentaries like *Mekilta* on Exodus and *Siphra* on Leviticus, and the early Mishnah tractates like *Taanit* on the fast days, and *Megilloth* on the books to be read in the synagogues; and *Pirke Aboth*, which gives the pedigree of the rabbinic fathers, with characteristic sayings of each.

THE CHURCH IN AELIA

It follows of necessity that the Jewish church in Jerusalem came to an end, but there may have been a thin element of continuity; for there must have been some Gentile Christians in Jerusalem before the war, and Jewish Christians may now have taken refuge in the Gentile church.

The church which existed in Aelia after the war was entirely Gentile, and therefore its episcopate was Gentile. The document used by Eusebius gave the names of fifteen bishops of the Gentile succession whose accessions have to be fitted into the fifty-five years previous to about 190. Their names are Mark, Cassian, Publius, Maximus I, Julian I, Gaius I, Symmachus, Gaius II, Julian II, Capito, Maximus II, Antoninus, Valens, Dolichianus, and finally Narcissus. We have discussed this list before and have pointed out that it must have been preserved as the title-deeds of Narcissus. Various theories have been propounded to explain why there are so many names. We suggested that the first thirteen names might be those of a newly constituted bishop with twelve elders from whom successors might be chosen. Or did Maximus and Julian and Gaius enjoy two terms of office, like Narcissus himself? Or did episcopates sometimes overlap, like those of Alexander and Narcissus? Or is the number itself insecure? Eusebius gives fifteen names in his *Chronicle*, but only thirteen in his *History;* he omits the second Maximus and Antoninus, probably by error.

Narcissus was still living in 217 or thereabouts, and claimed at that time to be a hundred and sixteen years old, not far from the conventional hundred and twenty. We may doubt whether he remembered his age correctly; but we cannot doubt that he was a very old man, older than other old men who were living at that time. He can hardly have been born later than the hundred and twenties, and his memory would easily run back into the war and post-war period. He was a Christian counterpart of Rabbi Judah the Holy.

According to the testimony of Jerome, who lived at Bethlehem in the fourth century, a temple of Aphrodite, or Venus as she was called by the Romans, was built by Hadrian's order on the site of the Crucifixion; no doubt she was equated with Ishtar or some other equivalent Syrian goddess. This temple was demolished two hundred years later by the order of the Emperor Constantine and replaced by a Christian church, which was dedicated in 335; the present church of the Holy Sepulchre stands on this site. The traditional sites of the Crucifixion and Resurrection were so close together as to be included within one range of buildings. This local tradition agrees with the statement in the Johannine Gospel which says, 'There, because it was near at hand, they laid the body of Jesus.' It was inside the walls of Aelia, and therefore of course of the modern Jerusalem: but it should be outside the walls of the old city of the time of Herod. This may quite possibly be the case; but the line of the old wall is not known.

Jerome also states that the cave in which Christ was said to have been born had been surmounted by a shrine of Adonis, which was a title of the Syrian god Tammuz. It is not said in the Gospels that Christ was born in a cave, but the idea was established in the tradition before the war; for Justin speaks of the cave of the nativity at Bethlehem, which was thirty-five furlongs from Jerusalem, an exact measurement which suggests local knowledge. The cave is mentioned as a place of historic interest by Origen.

Another monument was the upright stone by the site of the Temple which marked the site of the martyrdom of James the Just, and is mentioned by Hegesippus in the story of his passion. The time came when the chair of James was also shown. No doubt it was simply the episcopal throne of the Jerusalem bishops, and may have been as old as the time of Narcissus. Eusebius himself had seen it. It is noteworthy that the Gentile succession at Aelia regarded itself as the heir of the old Jewish succession, and kept alive the historic traditions.

THE JEWISH-CHRISTIAN CHURCH

We have included this half-legendary material for what it may be worth. It seems to represent the historical tradition of the church at Aelia at the close of the century. There are hard critics, of course, who dismiss it all as imagination or fabrication; but this seems too strong a procedure. It is of equal value with the information preserved in the Mishnah, and if it were a fabrication, it is not unreasonable to suppose that it would have been made rather more impressive. It does not, of course, amount to direct evidence; but the lack of direct evidence, either Jewish or Christian, must not blind us to the importance of the events of this period, and the continued importance of Jewish Christianity as a factor in eastern church history. Its work was not yet done, though its pride and its glory had disappeared and its congregations were few and scattered.

The story of Jewish Christianity since the death of Symeon in 104–7 had been a story of disintegration under the pressure of persecution and heresy; and this process must have been accelerated by the events of 131–5. It was entering into its last phase, though it still had a contribution to make.

We can make out, to a certain degree, the geographical distribution of Jewish Christianity subsequent to 135. Jewish Christians were carried east and west in the drift of displaced persons which followed the Bar Cochba war. We find an interesting group of Jewish refugees in Ephesus who discuss the problem with Justin Martyr. The legends of Edessa suggest that others reached the Syrian principalities of the far east; the Christian missions to the far east cannot be placed any later than this. Nearer Palestine, on the River Orontes, which flows down to the sea below Antioch, there was a community of Elkhasaite Christians at Apamea, which sent a mission to Rome in the early third century; and there was a community of Nazareans at Beroea, the modern Aleppo, which was still flourishing in the fourth century. In Cappadocia, a Roman border-province, there were Greek-speaking Jewish Christians of the Ebionite type, who actually produced their own translation of the Old Testament towards the end of the century. There was a sophisticated Hellenistic Ebionism in the cities of the Phoenician seacoast, which produced the legends about Clement and Peter and their conflicts with Simon of Samaria. There must have been a considerable

Jewish-Christian expansion to produce all this evangelistic and literary activity.

Apart from these developments or offshoots of the original Jewish-Christian church, there were still the old communities round the Sea of Galilee, at Nazareth, Pella, Cochabha and other villages. Here was to be found the older Jewish Christianity, with its episcopal successions in the family of Jesus, its Hebrew or Aramaic gospel, its tolerance of Paul, and its not unfriendly relations with the Gentiles. Hegesippus, who arrived in Rome in the hundred-and-fifties or sixties, seems to have represented this kind of Palestinian Christianity.

The civilization of the west was making progress in this country, and the Greek language was more necessary than ever for purposes of business and administration, as well as for learning and literature. It would appear that the Jewish-Christian patriarchate at Pella was bilingual, and that its theological schools made use of the Septuagint, and published their learned works in Greek. By this means at any rate they could maintain relations with oecumenical Christianity.

ARISTO OF PELLA

In the period immediately after the war the church at Pella had a distinguished scholar named Aristo, who wrote a book called the *Dialogue of Jason and Papiscus*, the first Christian book in dialogue form. It was well known in the Greek-speaking churches, since it was singled out for attack by the philosopher Celsus about thirty years later, and was defended early in the third century by the Christian scholar Origen. Neither of them mention the name of the author, but this is vouched for by another Celsus, who translated it into Latin in the seventh century, so that it had a long life of usefulness in the church. Origen tells us that it was in the form of a debate between a Jewish Christian and a Jew of Alexandria on the subject of the Old Testament prophecies and their fulfilment in Christianity. He praises the author because he allows the Jewish debater to acquit himself nobly and worthily. The seventh-century Celsus says that he was convinced of the truth of Christianity and accepted baptism.

Eusebius made use of the writings of Aristo for information about the Jewish war; and the following paragraph is taken in whole or in part from one of his books and therefore gives us the evidence of a contemporary Jewish Christian.

The war came to a climax in the eighteenth year of the rule of Hadrian [A.D. 135] at Bith-thēra, a city of great strength, which was not a very great distance from Jerusalem. The siege went on for a very long time. The rebels were brought to utter destruction by hunger and thirst; and the man who was guilty of the folly paid the just penalty. After this the whole nation was forbidden ever to set foot in the country round Jerusalem, by a legal decree, and by commands of Hadrian, and not even to gaze from a distance on the soil of their fatherland. So Aristo of Pella relates.

(Eusebius, *E.H.* IV, 6, 3.)

Eusebius does not name the book of Aristo from which he quotes; but it is quite probably the *Dialogue*; for the defeat of Bar Cochba was hailed by the Christian schools as a new fulfilment of prophecy which confirmed all the rest. 'Your land is desolate', they quoted from Isaiah; 'As for your country, strangers devour it before your eyes'; and even more aptly, 'Your eyes shall see the land from far away.' These texts appear henceforth in the Christian 'testimony' books, and it is thought probable that *Jason and Papiscus* inspired this whole series of anti-Jewish compositions, many of which were composed in dialogue form.

Very few quotations from Aristo have come down to us, but, such as they are, they show that his theology was not out of line with that which prevailed in the Gentile churches. Christ was the pre-existent Son, by whom God created the heaven and the earth; he was the 'Beginning' which is spoken of in the first verse of Genesis (see Col. i. 18, etc.). It is an important historical fact that the old Jewish church at Pella had a scholar who could write in Greek in a manner which was acceptable to the church at large. The Jewish Christians were not all Ebionites in the narrower sense of the word; even the oldest Jewish Christianity prior to 70 A.D. was probably bilingual and had its Hellenistic wing. It is no more extraordinary for a Jew like Aristo to write in Greek, than for a Roman like Hermas, or a Phrygian like Papias or Epictetus.

It is a great loss to the historian that he does not possess the *Apology* of Quadratus, the *Interpretations* of Papias, or the *Dialogue* of Aristo; for they are the first Christian books composed in the Greek style by men who appeared as authors and used their own names. They belong to three different lines of thought. Athens gives the first approach to the Hellenistic world; Phrygia gives the first mystical interpretations of the prophets and evangelists within the fellowship; Palestine gives the first approach to the Jews. We have some notion of each, as it happens; and Papias is not badly represented in allusions and quotations; but we would like to be able to read them for ourselves and form our own impressions. They are the forerunners of a catholic theology.

CHAPTER 4

THE HERESIARCHS

TRYPHO THE JEW

Not all the Jews were pleased with the warlike policy of Akiba and his Messiah, and there were some who fled the country. Among these was a young Jew named Trypho, whose character is a revelation of the varieties which still existed in Judaism. He had a good acquaintance with the Scriptures, but not in Hebrew. He spoke an excellent Greek, and his education had left him with an open mind. He had received instruction from the rabbis, but they had warned him not to be enticed into arguments with Christians, whose folly and simplicity he smiled at. He had read the book called 'the Gospel', however, and had admired its teaching, though he thought it impossible to carry out in practice. He is the first person we hear of who has read a Gospel as literature; and this is an indication that they were now in the hands of the public.

On arriving in Greece he did not neglect the opportunity of finding out something about philosophy, and he attached himself to a teacher at Argos of the name of Corinthus. He learned that the philosopher was a man with a mission; he could be recognized by the gown or pallium which he wore; and he should be prepared to give an account of himself to all inquirers.

Passing over the Aegean Sea to Ephesus, he was walking with some friends along the Xystus, which was a long stone walk or colonnade intended for the public use, when he saw a man of middle age, wearing the philosopher's gown. He acccosted him with a friendly greeting, and the philosopher replied with a tag out of Homer. He was easily prevailed upon to give an account of himself, and Trypho was amazed to discover that he was a Christian and professed to expound the philosophy of the divine prophets. No philosopher could honourably decline a public disputation, and a debate was carried on for a couple of days, after which the Christian was obliged to leave, for his ship was sailing for some other port. He composed a report of the discussion, and enlarged it from time to time, with a view to making it a complete handbook on the subject. It was the famous *Dialogue with Trypho* of Justin Martyr; for Justin was the strange teacher in the philosopher's gown. The *Dialogue* survives almost entire, and is the most ambitious piece of early Christian literature known to us after the *Pastor* of Hermas; and before Justin's own *Apology*.

The dialogue was one of the accepted forms in Greek philosophy, the classical instances being the dialogues of Plato. We have come across another example of it in the *Dialogue of Jason and Papiscus*, which may have suggested to Justin the idea of writing up his own dialogue. There was another dialogue on the same subject, but of a more imaginative type, in which a Jewish debater was introduced disputing with Christ himself; this anti-Christian dialogue was incorporated by the philosopher Celsus into his book against the Christians which he called *The True Word*. (The assumption has always been that Celsus wrote these chapters himself; but they require a Jewish author, and suit this early period.) The Jew in the *Celsus Dialogue*, as we may call it, had read a Gospel which was obviously Matthew, but became confused later on when he discovered there were more.

THE *DIALOGUE WITH TRYPHO*, A.D. 135

The debate at Ephesus was remarkable for the good humour and broad-mindedness of the disputants. It is obvious that a personal friendship was established between them. Once or twice they become a trifle heated, and these exchanges help us to realize that we are reading the story of an actual debate, not a literary fiction; though Justin has supplemented the story with a massive weight of additional material drawn from the 'testimony' tradition.

Our authority for saying that it took place at Ephesus is the bare statement of Eusebius, but this has been accepted by scholars without demur. The works of Justin have come down to us in two manuscripts only, one of which is a copy of the other, and the text of the *Dialogue* which they give is not complete. Some pages are missing in the middle, and these contained the winding up of the first day's debate and the opening of the second; in another case Justin's treatment of a Psalm has dropped out; it has also lost a dedication at the beginning which was addressed to a friend named Marcus Pompeius, whose name occurs twice in the text. 'My dear Pompey', Justin says. No doubt he was a patron or friend who encouraged Justin to proceed with his work. This dedication probably stood in the copy which Eusebius used and provided him with his information.

The date of the discussion was either during the Jewish war of 131–5, or just after it. The characters speak as if it were going on, but Justin refers once or twice to the expulsion of the Jews from the neighbourhood of Jerusalem, which took place after it. These references could have been added later from the *Dialogue of Jason and Papiscus* or elsewhere.

There is a statement in Irenaeus that it was not customary in Asia Minor for a man to become a teacher before the age of forty. If Justin was forty in the period 132–5, he must have been born in the years 92–5, and was seventy or seventy-five when he became a martyr. It does not seem very likely that he was older than forty, therefore, and if we are prepared to discount the statement of Irenaeus we can make him younger and advance the date of his birth as far as 100. Justin was already a very proficient scholar and debater, as Trypho recognized. He had thoroughly mastered the intricacies of the 'testimony' theology, which justifies us in placing his conversion a few years previous to the date of the *Dialogue*. No doubt the events of the war and the messianic pretensions of Bar Cochba had stimulated the interest in these studies; they may be responsible, too, for his developed doctrine of a Christian kingdom to be established in Jerusalem.

THE PROBLEM OF THE JEWISH CHRISTIANS

The group of Jewish refugees who were with Trypho were not all interested in Christianity or in biblical discussions. Some laughed loudly and wandered away; some stayed and listened, or sat discussing the war-news; some jeered and had to be silenced. On the second day there were newcomers, however, including a certain Mnaseas. Those who stayed were favourably impressed by what Justin had to say. Questions were asked about the status of the Jewish Christians, for they were anxious to know what kind of reception their brethren of the Christian faith would receive from their Gentile co-religionists. Justin assured them that most Christians would receive them into their houses, provided they did not attempt to force their customs upon their hosts; but there were Gentile Christians who did not believe that Jewish Christians could be saved, and carried it so far that they would not talk to them or admit them into their homes.

Other historical conditions are brightly illuminated too; the Jewish rabbis, with their meticulous scholarship and their anti-Christian arguments, which were the counterpart of the anti-rabbinic arguments of Justin; the new translations of the Old Testament which were an embarrassment to Justin since they did not agree with the Septuagint texts in which he had been trained; the comparison of the Christian gospel with the pagan mystery cults, which is also made in the *Celsus Dialogue*; and the daemonic parodies of the true gospel which were being produced by heretics like Satornil and Basilides.

The principal complaint of Trypho is that the Christians do not observe circumcision or the sabbaths or the appointed festivals, or the other requirements of the Jewish Law; and that they have abandoned God to set their hope upon a man, as the *Celsus Dialogue* also points out. Justin affirms that the man Jesus was the eternal Word of the Father.

It appears, however, that there were Christians who accepted Jesus as the Messiah, but not as the eternal Word. There were some who thought of him as a 'man from men' who was made Messiah by anointing and election, at his baptism very probably. Trypho, who had been deeply impressed by Justin's arguments from the scriptures, much preferred this christology, and Justin did not discourage him from accepting Jesus on these terms as the Jewish Messiah, if that was as far as he could go.

The controversy was of grave concern to both sides precisely because a broad-minded Jew like Trypho, and a Christian of the old tradition like Justin, had so much in common. Both believed in the One God who had created the heaven and the earth, and conversed with the patriarchs, and brought the Jews out of Egypt, and spoken through the prophets. They agreed that the scriptures contained the words of divinely inspired men. They were trying to understand one another.

The situation was aggravated by the effects of the war. A long and desperate war sets masses of men in motion, prisoners, refugees, displaced persons generally and, in the ancient world, slaves for sale. The *Dialogue* enables us to see something of this state of affairs in Ephesus, and it must have been very much the same in Rome.

MARCION OF PONTUS

The controversy was not always carried on with the friendliness and candour of the *Dialogue*. There were extreme men on both sides, as Justin had said. No outstanding name comes to light on the Jewish side, though the name of Ebion was invented before the century came to an end. On the anti-Jewish side we have the great heresiarch, Marcion of Pontus, a contemporary of Justin, who regarded him as the greatest enemy of the church.

A great deal has been written about Marcion in recent theology, and it has become difficult in consequence to reduce him and his movement to their correct historical proportions. He was, perhaps, the strongest and most forceful Christian leader of his time; but he was not everything that his modern admirers have claimed for him. He is big enough however without that. He was born at Sinope, a seaport on the Black Sea in the province of Pontus. His father was the bishop there, according to the Latin *Libellus against Heresies* which epitomizes a short treatise which Hippolytus wrote in Rome about the year 200; it goes on to say that he was excluded from the church by his father for the seduction of a virgin. This tale is not to be found in the writings of Tertullian or in the longer treatise of Hippolytus on heresies, and it has not been taken very seriously by modern scholars, though it is supported by the fourth-century Epiphanius, who appears in this instance to have some earlier source before him as he writes. It sounds a little like a misunderstanding of some picturesque statement, such as Hegesippus made, about the church being a pure virgin until it was corrupted by heresy.

We have no information about the immediate predecessors of Marcion or the period of his life before he came to Rome; but it is highly probable that he was also in Asia Minor about the time of Justin's *Dialogue*. Irenaeus tells us that he once confronted Polycarp and asked for recognition. 'Recognize you,' said the old stalwart grimly,

'Recognize you? I recognize you as the first-born of Satan.' This encounter may have taken place much later, when Polycarp visited Rome
in the hundred-and-fifties; but if so, it seems to imply that he had been
acquainted with Marcion at some earlier time; so that an appearance
of Marcion in Smyrna in the thirties seems to be indicated.

Marcion had not parted from the catholic church when he came to
Rome about 137, but when he arrived there his theology must already
have been of a peculiar type. What seems to have been most deeply
rooted in him was his antipathy to Judaism and the Jewish God; and
just as Justin studied the scriptures and arranged his texts to prove the
perfect harmony of the Old Testament with the New, so Marcion
studied the scriptures with the object of proving their absolutely
irreconcilable character.

Marcion was given the nickname of *naukleros*, a ship-owner or
skipper, and as his birthplace, Sinope, was an important seaport, it has
been thought that he was in the shipping business before he became a
religious leader; but the nickname might have arisen from numerous
voyages taken in the interests of evangelization. He seems to have been
an evangelist or church-builder, like his favourite apostle, St Paul,
rather than a theologian like Basilides or Valentinus; and like St Paul
he may have had many journeys by land and sea to his credit. Certainly his church was very widely spread and was especially powerful
in the east. It is not unreasonable to suppose that he was travelling and
evangelizing in the east in the early thirties.

MARCION'S MYTHOLOGY

Marcion's bitter antagonism to the Hebrew faith was balanced by his
ardent enthusiasm for the figure of the Saviour, whom he regarded as a
'saving spirit' and a messenger of mercy and love unmixed with anger
or even with justice. No doubt we see here the secret of his appeal.
Much of the evidence from out-of-the-way sources suggests that what
impressed the Gentile mind in the Christian message was the personality of Jesus himself, whose appearance on earth was still so recent.
There were numbers who responded to this appeal which was broad-
casted now through written Gospels, and had no interest in, or even
detested, the Hebrew monotheism, moralism and apocalyptic which
came as its historical setting. Marcion felt no need for an historical

setting; he regarded Jesus as the son of a new or strange deity whose abode was far above the heavens. He inherited or adopted the theology of Syrian gnosis, which was docetic and ascetic and repudiated this creation altogether.

In this oriental gnosis the Christ-spirit descends from the high God into the material cosmos to do battle with the god of this world as Marcion calls the Creator, stealing a phrase from St Paul to serve his turn. The form of the myth which Marcion adopted included the descent into Hades and the liberation of the righteous souls from the dominion of death; for, according to Irenaeus, his Christus rejected the righteous men of the Old Testament, such as Abel and Enoch and Noah and Abraham, and set free Cain and the Sodomites and the Egyptians and the Gentiles generally; and this feature of the myth connects Marcion with those Ophites who regarded Cain as the forefather of the elect. These sayings should not be taken too literally, however. It looks as if the language of myth was still being freely used in this tradition as a form of expression for religious thought and controversy. A myth was refuted by an anti-myth, a poem by an anti-poem. There is no evidence which suggests that Marcion was concerned with formal theological consistency; he preached the descent of a saving Spirit who came to free mankind from the god of this world and his law and his jealousy and his Hades; this purely spiritual Saviour, who had no mortal body, nevertheless suffered and died upon the cross, which is a paradox indeed. In some strange way he allowed for the real passion and the real death which is the heart of the Christian gospel.

The docetic myth, which regarded Jesus as an angel or spirit, had appeared before this in Asia Minor and had been condemned in the Epistles of Ignatius and Polycarp. The theory which divides the Epistle of Polycarp assigns the major part of it to the present period and suggests that it was composed with Marcion in view, though indeed it does not touch upon Marcion's characteristic doctrines.

MARCION AND THE APOSTLES

Marcion was opposed to the efforts which were being made, especially in the east, to promote an historical and apostolic form of Christianity, under the authority of Peter and the Twelve. Peter and the Twelve had never properly understood their master. He followed the Epistle to the

Galatians very closely in this awkward part of his theology, and perhaps he was travelling in the footsteps of older Paulinists of the docetic type. Peter and the Twelve had never cleared themselves from Judaism and the Law. The Son of God had been obliged to reveal himself a second time, choosing for his purposes the persecutor Paul. Paul had resisted Peter face to face at Antioch.

Marcion was compelled to reject the Syrian Gospel according to Matthew which was being accepted very generally now as the premier Gospel. He was in all respects the opposite of the Ebionite Christian who built on Matthew and rejected Paul. But he was bound to have documents if he was to establish his theology. The documents on which he staked the truth of his gospel were the shortened version of Luke and a collection of the Pauline Epistles which had also been edited to some extent; the Epistle to the Romans in particular had been considerably cut down. These documents, on which everything depended, were the weakest point, morally and intellectually, in his theological system. His catholic opponents accused him of fabricating them himself, and his modern champions draw a strange picture of him as a higher critic before his times, removing what he took to be Judaistic interpolations. It is considered that he did this after his arrival in Rome, but there is evidence that this literature existed in the Syrian gnostic school before he arrived there.

The fact is that any reconstruction of the origins of the heresy of Marcion is bound to have conjectural features in it, especially in this period before he came to Rome; but it seems preferable to allow for a period of evangelization, and the influence of predecessors, before that date. The success of his church organization in the east suggests that his theological views were not completely unfamiliar, and he himself not entirely unknown in those parts.

THE BATTLE OF THE GOSPELS

As the oral delivery of gospel material by disciples of Jesus, and disciples of those disciples, was superseded by the use of written Gospels, there was probably a period when each church was equipped with a single Gospel for its liturgical purposes, as Antioch was in the time of Ignatius. Indeed, the Marcionites and the Ebionites continued in this condition, and had an old-fashioned look in consequence. The dissemination of more Gospels would throw this simple condition of affairs into confusion. There were four, five, or six to choose from. The Jew who is quoted by Celsus refers to this condition of transition.

When we read Justin's arguments with the Jews in his *Dialogue*, and his explanation of the faith for the Gentiles in his *Apology*, we find that he refers exclusively to written Gospels, which he calls the *Records* or *Memoranda of the Apostles*. He names no apostolic names; he makes few very exact quotations; he is quoting in a general way from the living evangelical tradition, and referring to written records as his authority.

He calls these records by the name of Gospels, and says that they were read in the liturgy, with the prophets; but this is not the same thing as setting up the fourfold Gospel as a sacred unity, though doubtless the position of the four was unassailable. They were not regarded as a fixed unalterable scripture, however, or at any rate not in all quarters, since his pupil Tatian felt free to combine them into a single narrative. Nevertheless, his fidelity to the text shows that it was not subject to substitutions; he confines himself to the actual words of the four, and called his book the *Diatessaron*, the fourfold harmony.

It follows that the adoption of the four Gospels for liturgical and didactic purposes was not exactly an act of canonization. It did not set up new scriptures in the church as yet. They approximated to the position of scripture, but the word does not seem to have been used before Irenaeus. It is claimed that Marcion made a new departure in this respect. It is possible that the heresiarchs in Alexandria took a similar step. Alexandria pioneered in literary studies.

BASILIDES

If Marcion can be thought of as the strongest figure of his day in Christian evangelism (as some maintain), it is equally possible to suggest that Basilides was the greatest figure among the Christian intellectuals; but it is not possible, in either case, to fill in the detail of the picture. He is said by Epiphanius to have been a disciple with Satornil of Menander of Antioch; but there is nothing in common between their two systems except the sexless character of their thought about the high God; a feature which they shared with Marcion and the catholic tradition. The affiliation is a mistake which arose from the attempt to form relations between the gnostic schools and to trace their origins.

The testimony of Clement of Alexandria places him in the reign of Hadrian, and this agrees with the other evidence. In Clement's time, at the end of the century, his school was still in existence in Alexandria and its writings were in circulation. It was not influential in the west, from which most of our documentary evidence comes; but it is thought that it had considerable influence in Syria. The theological systems which are ascribed to Basilides are hopelessly divergent, and modern scholars are not agreed upon what authority to follow; but it may be that he never worked out a system; he may have been a discursive writer and thinker like Clement of Alexandria himself.

A writer of his own day named Agrippa Castor wrote a *Refutation* of his heresy, which has not survived; but Eusebius had seen it, and drew some valuable information from it. Jerome also refers to it. It seems to provide the best starting point.

AGRIPPA CASTOR

Agrippa said that Basilides wrote a twenty-four volume commentary on the Gospel. It is not said what Gospel, but we know that it contained a comment on a passage in Luke. It may have commented on all the Gospels, or on the Lucan Gospel only. Origen, in his first homily on Luke, says that he wrote a Gospel called the Gospel of the Truth; but this seems to be a misunderstanding, or perhaps a confusion with Marcion. Irenaeus says that the Valentinians used a Gospel of this name (see *A.H.* III, 11, 13) and part of a Valentinian homily called the *Gospel of the Truth* has recently turned up in papyrus form.[1]

Agrippa also mentions two prophets called Barcabbas and Barcoph, with certain other non-existent persons, who were given barbarous appellations so as to amaze the impressionable. Isidore, the son of Basilides, wrote a commentary on the prophet Parchor, which is another form apparently of the name Barcoph. Isidore took his cue from the old Jewish Hellenists and claimed that Aristotle and the Greek philosophers borrowed their ideas from these barbarian writers. He makes them out to be descendants of the Jewish patriarch Ham, who is regarded in the Books of Clement as the forefather of the Iranian

[1] See *The Jung Codex*, ed. F. L. Cross (Mowbrays, Oxford, 1955).

religious founder Zoroaster. These Persian scriptures were thus introduced into the canon of the Basilidian church in close association with a Christian Gospel or Gospels.

Agrippa also says that the high God of Basilides was named 'Abraxas', a magical name which is found engraved on 'gnostic' gems. Its correct form appears to have been 'Abrasax', and it was corrupted in the course of time into the mystic word Abracadabra. The Greek letters in this name, when given their numerical value, add up to three hundred and sixty-five, like the letters in the name of 'Meithras', the Iranian deity who symbolized radiant light. The Basilidian school believed in a system of three hundred and sixty-five heavens, and it would appear therefore that their philosophy was based on an Iranian Hellenism and on the symbolism of the sun revolving round the heavens in the course of the three hundred and sixty-five days of the Alexandrian calendar.

Agrippa accuses Basilides of teaching that it was a matter of no moral significance to taste food offered to idols, in which indeed he might have argued, and probably did argue, that he was only following the teaching of Paul; and also that it was allowable to deny the faith in times of persecution, which is our first reference to persecution in Alexandria. But perhaps he did no more than allow those who had denied to return to the fold, which is what Hermas did in Rome. He imitated Pythagoras in imposing a five-year period of silence on those who came to him for instruction; and Isidore regarded Pherecydes the tutor of Pythagoras as a Zoroastrian; Pythagoras could therefore be aligned with the Iranian prophets. The discipline of silence was also accepted by the Pythagorean philosopher Apollonius of Tyana in the *Life of Apollonius*, which was composed by Philostratus in the third century out of second-century sources. A rather romantic oriental mysticism was becoming fashionable.

QUOTATIONS FROM BASILIDES

We are fortunate in having two fairly long extracts from the writings of Basilides himself, both from the *Exegetica* or Gospel commentary. In the thirteenth volume he dealt with the Lucan parable of the rich man and Lazarus, and then, after about five hundred verses, he proceeded to consider the views of certain barbarians on the subject of good and evil; and as they speak of an uncreated Light and an uncreated Darkness, they seem to be of Iranian origin.

Some of them say that there are two principles of all things, with which they associate good and evil; these principles are without beginning, and unbegotten. That is, in the beginning there were Light and Darkness, which existed separately and were not made.

(*Acts of Archelaus*, 67, in R. M. Grant, *Second-century Christianity*, pp. 18–19.)

The universe in which we live consists in the main of Darkness, but the Darkness is irradiated (or fertilized?) by some glimmer of Light. It is a form of the Iranian dualism which coloured much of the later Syrian gnosis.

The second extract is taken from the twenty-third volume, which was the last but one and must therefore have dealt with the story of the Crucifixion. The rigid logic of Basilides seems to have found satisfaction in the doctrine of the transmigration of souls, which is common to all gnostic theologies. The pain that men suffer in this world is explained by the theory that they are working out the just penalties for the sins which they committed in some former existence; for Basilides would do anything rather than call providence evil. He finds himself in difficulties, however, over the case of children who have not sinned, and ascribes the suffering which they undergo to their inherited sinfulness. He also finds himself in difficulties over the case of Jesus of Nazareth.

And if, as we pass from these observations you were to proceed to confound me by saying concerning someone, 'This man then has sinned, for this man has suffered', I would reply with your permission, 'He has not sinned, but is like a child suffering.' If you were to press me more closely, I would say, 'Whatever man you name is a man, but God is righteous; for no one is pure, it is said, from pollution.' (Clement Al., *Stromata*, IV, 12, 7.)

He appears to be speaking here of the man Jesus, in accordance with the Cerinthian christology, and not the divine Christus which dwelt in him for a time and returned to its heavenly home before the Crucifixion; and if so, we can understand the terms of his statement, and also the fact that gnostics of his school told their disciples not to put their faith in the crucified, or to join in the glorification of the martyrs, who were working out the penalty for their sins of ignorance, or at least for their inborn sinfulness. Nevertheless, it was an encouragement for them to think that they were not 'suffering as evil-doers', but 'as Christians', Basilides said, echoing the words of the First Epistle of Peter.

Clement, from whom we have taken these extracts, discusses the views of Basilides rather closely, and quotes also from the treatise of his son Isidore on ethical problems. Isidore distinguishes sharply between the passions which disturb the soul or 'adhere' to it, and the inner self which must resist them. Basilides meditated deeply on the problem of the soul; intellectualist though he was, he recognized a higher faculty in man than the intellect; it was the gift of faith by which a man had intuitive knowledge of God; but it was not the possession of every man.

THE SCHOOL OF BASILIDES

The account of the 'system' of Basilides in Irenaeus, which he probably obtained from the *Syntagma* of Justin, seems to be a conventional summary of the outstanding features of the popular teaching and practice in the organized school or church of the heresiarch. There is no trace of the Iranian mysticism, which may have been imparted only to the higher classes of initiates; but the abstract character of his thought appears in his sexless cosmogony. Unbegotten God gives birth to Intelligence; Intelligence to Word or rational thought; Word to Understanding; Understanding to Wisdom and Power. Below these come the first angels and the powers which made the universe; and below these are the three hundred and sixty-five heavens, the lowest of which is the one we see. The lowest heaven belongs to the God of the Jews, whose quarrels with the guardian angels or deities of the other nations were the cause of the Jewish wars. It was the first-begotten of the high God, Intelligence or Mind, who descended to earth, and appeared among the nations (a bold phrase indeed) in human form to deliver mankind from the tyranny of the creator; but the one who was crucified was not he; it was Simon of Cyrene—another bold statement, but it is a possible way of understanding the rather loosely articulated text of Mark.

What follows this in Irenaeus is a rather conventional tirade against gnosticism in general. The body is of no importance since it cannot be saved. Eating food which has been offered to idols is of no importance.

All sexual pleasures are lawful. The initiated gnostics use magical invocations and know the names of the angels, and the secret name of the Saviour, which is 'caulacau', a Hebrew word which means 'line upon line' (Isaiah xxviii. 10 and 13). They are unknown to the world, even as he was himself. 'Know every man,' they say, 'but let no man know thee.' They are few in numbers, one in a thousand and two in ten thousand. They tell their mysteries to none and keep their secrets in silence.

We seem to have a scrappy impression of the mysteries as they filtered down from the teachers at the top level to the rank and file. The immorality of which they are accused does not seem to be in line with the teaching of the master. On the other hand Hippolytus preserves a long piece of abstruse speculation which may represent the teaching of the movement at its higher levels, as it was systematized by the successors. This lower universe originated from a species of world-egg, in which everything existed in seed-form; an idea which is found in the Orphic poems. Three successive heavens rose up, each with its father-god, each of whom had a son who was wiser than himself. In this lowest world of all the elements of existence have not all been sorted out, and portions of the 'sonship' are still imprisoned in its material composition. Everywhere the natural motion of the sonship is upward; all that comes down from above is a voice or a current of power or a mere wave of energy, which liberates the imprisoned sonship and enables it to soar upward on the wing of the Holy Spirit. Some scholars regard this as the true theology of Basilides himself; others think it is not Basilidian at all.

While the school of Basilides was primarily an academic foundation which produced a number of intellectual expositions of the spiritual mysteries, it also had a church-like form, and a popular mythological aspect which was expressed in ritual and magic. Its churchly form seems to be proved by its institution of an astrological New Year festival on January 6 or 10, a date which depends upon the three-hundred-and-sixty-five day calendar which provided a mystical number for the Basilidian heavens and the mystery-word 'Abrasax'. The importance and influence of the organization is proved by the fact that it was still a force to be reckoned with in Alexandria at the end of the century.

VALENTINUS AND CARPOCRATES

It will be more appropriate to deal with the second great Alexandrian teacher, Valentinus, in the next chapter. Basilides built up the fabric of his thought and church organization in Alexandria itself. Valentine was a traveller. He left a strong organization behind him in Egypt which endured the test of time; but he taught in Cyprus and Rome as well. No doubt he continued to travel even after he had made Rome his headquarters.

We must deal briefly with the extraordinary case of Carpocrates, however. He accepted Jesus as a philosopher and wonder-worker of the same sort as Apollonius of Tyana, the wandering magus of the first century who is said to have acquired control over the body and over the material world by cultivating the powers of the mind. Somewhat in the same way, Jesus, who was the natural son of Joseph, possessed a powerful and pure soul, and was more righteous than other men. He could remember what he had seen in his heavenly pre-existence, and for this reason a heavenly 'power' came down upon him at his baptism, and enabled him to avoid the powers that had made the world. He disciplined his soul in the Jewish Law and thus learned to despise it, an advance in spirituality which gave him the power to work miracles and perform acts of healing. The power to work such miracles was available to all who would despise the daemonic rulers of this world, as Jesus had despised them; and the Carpocratians are credited with the belief that they were the equals in this respect of such apostles as Peter and Paul, or even of Jesus himself.

This mixture of magic and philosophy is based on the notion that this material world is inferior or useless, and that the potentialities of the mind are unlimited. The body is a prison, a favourite maxim of the mystery religions. The soul is an imprisoned angel, and must exercise its powers in order to obtain the victory over the body, and the world, and the daemonic rulers, and so return to the upper realms, where it belongs. To effect this, it must not hesitate to pass through all possible experiences in this bodily life; for unless it does, it will never free itself. It must take no account of the ideas of good and evil, which are only human opinions. Salvation comes by faith and love.

It seems likely that the moral life of the Carpocratians was just as free from moral restraint as these words imply. Carporactes had a son whose name was Epiphanes. He died at the age of seventeen, after writing a treatise *On Justice*, which advocated a Platonic communism in the matter of wives. Quotations from this treatise given by Clement show that he used the Gospel according to St Matthew, and interpreted it so as to support the duty of promiscuous sexual love; 'Give to everyone that asketh thee', Jesus had said. The beautiful text in which he promised his presence where two or three were assembled in his name was taken to support the old mystical idea that there are three who take part in sexual intercourse, the man, the woman and the god. It was in short a sacramental rite involving a divine presence. This idea was widespread in the ancient world, and the rite was duly performed in the temples. Undoubtedly it was taken into the non-ascetic types of Christian gnosis.

Clement tells us that in his day Epiphanes was adored as a god at Sama in Cephallenia. A temple had been built there of massive stone blocks, with altars, shrines and a museum. On the new moon the people of Cephallenia celebrated 'his birthday, when he was taken up among the gods', with sacrifices, libations, banquets and hymns. This sect was clearly blessed with wealth and culture, but it was hardly Christian. The figure of the Saviour was absorbed into an eclectic 'Platonic' system, which cultivated a romantic non-moral magical spirituality.

THE FEAST OF THE EPIPHANY

Clement also tells us that the Basilidians observed January 6 or 10 as the birthday of Christ, which meant in their theology his baptism in the River Jordan, when the heavenly Christus came down into the world and took possession of the body of the man Jesus. The Cerinthian preoccupation with the baptism, at the expense of the Passion, was a feature of all these Alexandrian sects. In some non-canonical gospel narratives, including one which is given by Justin, the voice which comes from heaven at the baptism says, 'Thou art my Son: this day I have begotten thee'; a quotation from the second psalm which refers to the enthronement of the Davidic king. A king's accession-day is his regnal birthday. The baptism could thus be regarded as the birthday or accession-day of the divine Christus.

This form of the words is also found in some manuscripts of the Lucan Gospel, and there are scholars who think it is the correct Lucan reading.

Now January 6 was a New Year festival in Alexandria at the Koreum, the temple of the Maiden. While the Basilidians were spending the evening of the 5th in vigil and readings, the devotees of Kore were keeping her festival with chants and devotions to the images of the gods; at dawn an image of a baby was brought up from the crypt and carried in procession, and it was said that the maiden had given birth to the aeon or age: another year was given to the world; it was the birthday of the new year.

January 6 has become the Christian festival of the 'Theophany' or 'Epiphany', the glorious appearance of the God. It was accepted in due course throughout the east as the festival of Christ's nativity, until the Roman date of December 25 took its place; and even now this has not happened everywhere; the Armenian church knows no other nativity festival but January 6. Even in Rome it took a long time to change January 6 over and dedicate it to the visit of the Magi; and traces of the baptism commemoration are still to be found in the ritual. It looks as if the Basilidian festival was so popular among Christians generally in Alexandria, that the church was bound to adopt it in self-defence, and mask its heretical character by assigning it to the nativity; but the association with the baptism was not forgotten.

It has been maintained that it had a nativity connexion from the beginning.[1]

[1] See *The Evolution of the Christian Year*, by A. A. McArthur, 1953.

CHAPTER 5

THE SCHOOLS IN ROME

TABLE OF ROMAN BISHOPS TO A.D. 235

(taken from the Chronicle of Hippolytus, A.D. 234–5 by the compiler of the Liberian Catalogue A.D. 354)

		A.D.	
(1)	Linus	64	(II Timothy iv. 21.)
(2)	Anencletus	76	(Also called Cletus.)
(3)	Clement	88	(Wrote an Epistle to the Corinthians.)
(4)	Euarestus	97	
(5)	Alexander	105	
(6)	Xystus	115	(Also called Sixtus; concordat with Asians.)
(7)	Telesphorus	125	(Died as a martyr.)
(8)	Hyginus	136	(Arrival of Cerdo, Valentinus, Marcion.)
(9)	Pius	140	(Brother of Hermas; arrival of Justin.)
(10)	Anicetus	155	(Visit of Polycarp; arrival of Hegesippus.)
(11)	Soter	166	(Correspondence with Dionysius of Corinth.)
(12)	Eleutherus	174	(Writings of Hegesippus and Irenaeus.)
(13)	Victor	189	(Paschal controversy.)
(14)	Zephyrinus	199	(With Callistus as deacon.)
(15)	Callistus	217	(Hippolytus as rival bishop.)
(16)	Urbanus	222	(Schism continues.)
(17)	Pontianus	230	(Schism continues.)
		235	(Martyrdom of Hippolytus and Pontianus.)

Notes. The number of years allotted to the first three bishops, twelve years, is obviously a conventional figure, and so possibly is the date 64, with which the list begins. It is the date of the fire of Rome and the Neronian persecution, which is taken to be the date of the martyrdom of Peter and Paul.

71

Clement's death is often allotted to 100 or 101, where Eusebius places it. With the accession of Hyginus and Pius the dates may be taken as approximately correct.

THE ROMAN CHURCH

The Rome of Hadrian differed considerably from the Rome of Nero. Numbers of magnificent buildings and monuments had been erected, and Hadrian had employed the Syrian architect, Apollodorus, to assist in this work; perhaps his influence may be seen in the domed temple called the Pantheon, which was rebuilt at this time; its appearance, as Spengler pointed out, resembles that of a mosque; it has the oriental touch, and was dedicated to the twelve gods of the heavens. Rome was becoming a cosmopolitan city. The old Roman families no longer controlled the senate. Hadrian himself was a Spaniard; his successor Antoninus belonged to a family from Gaul.

We learn from the Epistle of Ignatius to the Romans that the church in Rome was an influential body, and from Hermas that it had its wealthy households. Dionysius of Corinth, who wrote about thirty years later, looks back on the history of the previous generation and speaks of its wealth and generosity; it was their custom, handed down to them from their fathers, to extend help to other churches by sending funds to those who were in need, and especially those who had been condemned to work as convicts in the mines. It communicated with other churches, therefore, and helped them in their difficulties.

SIXTUS, TELESPHORUS, HYGINUS

The traditional dates for the Roman bishops of the second century can only be approximate, but are useful as guides nevertheless. Xystus (or Sixtus) became bishop about 115–18 not long after the martyrdom of Ignatius and the accession of Hadrian. He had consolidated his position by making a concordat with a community of Asian Christians in the city, who maintained a liturgical tradition of their own. They were doubtless in touch with Polycarp of Smyrna and must have possessed the Johannine books. Xystus imparted to them the eucharist from his own service, a symbol of unity which we find continued in later centuries between the popes and the principal parish churches. This alliance between Asia and Rome remained the most powerful factor in church history up to the end of the century, when it was dramatically broken. It contributed greatly to the leadership exercised by the Roman church.

The name Xystus appears as Sixtus in the Latin translation of Irenaeus, which was made not long after his book was written. He uses the Greek name Xystus in the Greek original, but notes the coincidence that Xystus was the sixth bishop from the apostles. Sixtus or Sextus, meaning sixth, was a common Roman name, and this bishop may have been of Latin origin.

The Jewish War of 132–5 broke out in the episcopate of the seventh bishop, Telesphorus. No doubt the Christians shared in the unpopularity of the Jews at this time, and we have some evidence of persecution in the fact that Telesphorus himself died as a martyr, probably in 137 or 138. The evidence for the martyrdom is quite clear; in the list of bishops given by Irenaeus, we find the statement that Telesphorus 'witnessed gloriously', which is the same phrase which he uses to describe the martyrdom of Polycarp a few paragraphs lower. No doubt there were other martyrs. The later Roman tradition, for what it is worth, supplies the names of martyrs who were believed to have died under Hadrian; St Symphorosa and her seven sons; and St Achilleus and St Nereus, who are buried in the cemetery of Domitilla.

In this troubled post-war period Hyginus became bishop, and held the position for only three years; but these three years, approximately 137–40, were years of momentous importance for the Roman church. Alexandrian and Syrian schools were established, or, if they were established already, received illustrious teachers from the east. These new teachers were welcomed at first without demur.

VALENTINUS OF EGYPT, c. A.D. 137

The new master of the Alexandrian school in Rome was Valentinus. He had established schools in Egypt and Cyprus, which were still flourishing in the fourth century. Epiphanius, who knew them well, says that he died in Cyprus. We also hear of Valentinian schools in Ephesus and Antioch.

It has often been said that it is difficult to obtain a fair view of the great heresiarchs through the controversial writings of their catholic opponents; still, the task can be attempted. Valentine appears as a man of intellectual genius, whose philosophic ideas were expressed in imaginative or poetic form; not at all in the analytic manner of Basilides. Myth, ritual, gospel, magic, astrology, mysticism and philosophy were all blended in his fantastic theology. He could explain everything and fit everything in.

He was definitely an exponent of the gospel, however; and we have a few words of his which make this clear.

There is one God, whose presence is manifested in the Son. By him alone the heart can become pure; by the expulsion of every evil from the heart. . . . As long as no thought is taken for it, the heart remains unclean, and the abode of many daemons; but when the Father who alone is good, visits it, it is made holy, and shines with light; and he who possesses such a heart is so blessed that he shall see God.

(Valentinus: in Clement of Alexandria, *Strom.* II, 20.)

The writer of these sentences has meditated deeply on the Gospels, and links three passages together by a penetrating devotional analysis; the story of the rich young ruler, the expulsion of the legion of devils and the beatitudes of the Sermon on the Mount. It illustrates the central thought of Valentinus, which tends to be lost altogether in the mazes of his theological 'system'; it is the visit to the soul of the believer of a divine power, an idea Hermas and Barnabas expressed in their mysticism about the Spirit. In Valentine's myth it was the descent of the Saviour into this dark world to be united with his spiritual bride.

Clement of Alexandria and Hippolytus of Rome preserve a few more sayings by which we can judge the personality of the master.

Many of the truths written in the ordinary books are found written in the church of God; for these are common words from the heart—the law written in the heart. This is the people of the beloved which is loved by him and loves him.   (*Ibid.* VI, 6.)

This passage recalls the saying of 'Barnabas' about the covenant of the beloved Jesus which is sealed in our heart;[1] and the author of 'Barnabas' is thought to have been an Alexandrian like Valentine.

[1] See also Barnabas XVI, 7: 'Before we believed in God the dwelling-place of our heart was corrupt and weak as being in truth a temple made with hands; for it was full of idolatry and was a house of daemons.' Had Valentine read Barnabas or been instructed in his school? Barnabas thanks God for a supernatural gift of knowledge (*gnosis*) and wisdom (*sophia*).

There is something in common between the 'gnosis' of the two writers.

Valentine says that he saw a new-born child, and questioning it he asked who it might be. It answered and said that it was the Word; and thence he frames some tragic myth and wants his heresy to consist of this.

(Hippolytus, *Refutation*, VI, 35.)

As Clement himself maintained, words are the children of the mind. The mind is fertile and brings them to birth; thought is genealogical; the relation of the sexes is the mirror of the eternal realities; the seed must be sown in the heart; the lover must visit the soul.

THE OGDOAD

Basilides is reported to have said that the deity was best defined in negative words, since it was misleading to make any statement about him. Even the statement that he exists is misleading. Valentine had no such inhibitions. He was a master of words.

His philosophy of the ultimate reality was expressed in a genealogical myth, some of the names in it being borrowed from St John's Gospel. We follow the guidance of his pupil Ptolemeus, though he seems to have sacrificed something of the poetry of his master. He begins with Bythos: the unmeasured abyss of eternal being; abyss or eternity conceives grace or thought or silence to be his consort. Their first-born son is mind who is united with truth; their offspring is word married to life; then man married to church; making up the supreme 'Ogdoad' of *eight* primal 'aeons'. Next to these come five more pairs of divine attributes called the 'Dekad ' or *ten;* and next to these the 'Dodekad' or *twelve*, which was the equivalent, at this infinitely higher level, of the zodiac circle or months of the solar year. The whole *pleroma*, or 'fullness' of the deity adds up to *thirty* aeons, the 'Triakontad', which corresponds to the days of the month or moon. The *pleroma* was the abode of perfect love and joy and harmony and praise.

The highest group, known as the Ogdoad or Eight, reflects the genealogy of the high gods of Egypt, and the number-mysticism of Pythagoras; but it is not possible to elaborate these points here. The system branches out in many directions before we come to the descent of the Saviour. It is brilliant and ingenious, but choked with too much detail.

THE VALENTINIAN MYTH

Valentine's drama of creation and redemption was derived from the old Ophite myth, though he discarded the symbolism of the serpent. The mysterious Semitic name Ialdabaoth (child of chaos) was retained for the creator of the universe; and the female spirit from the higher realm, who inspires him in his work and counteracts his blunders, carries the name 'Achamoth', which is a perversion of the Hebrew word *hokmah*, which means wisdom. Her name in Greek was Sophia, and was to be found in the Septuagint as a personification of the intellectual or imaginative power which flows from the deity. Holy Wisdom had shared in the creation of the world, and guarded the chosen people and inspired the prophets. She was an Alexandrian importation, and was known to Roman Christians through the *Wisdom of Solomon* which was read in the church alongside of the New Testament.

Sophia was the last and lowest of the thirty aeons, and had conceived an incestuous desire to know the Father of all, who was the ultimate source of her own being. She had fallen from her high estate before the world began, and had become submerged in the void and darkness outside the Pleroma. She received visits from certain male aeons but was not able to return to her heavenly home. A new being called Horus, the boundary line, barred the way; he was the 'firmament' of the old religion and the cross of the new religion; the factor in the universe which divided it and yet united it, and held everything firmly in place. She became the mother of Ialdabaoth and his six associate angels. She was the mother of all living.

Before creation took shape, however, she was overwhelmed by the waters of chaos. Her tears and sorrows and anxieties were the substance out of which creation was made; for in some sense she was the original formless matter of the Greek physicists. But she had a divine origin, and something of her divine nature, some 'seed' or light, was implanted in the gnostic man; for her passion represents the sense of crisis and frustration in the souls of the elect, who resent their imprisonment in the flesh and cry to the high God for deliverance from this inferior cosmos. They are the seed of the mother, and share her rather hysterical nature. Jesus, the divine Saviour, comes down from the heavenly realms to deliver her and them. Meanwhile Ialdabaoth, the God of the Jews, had prepared his human Christus or Messiah, who was to be born of a virgin; the 'aeon' Jesus, who is the perfect offspring of all the thirty aeons, descends into her womb and so enters into the body of the earthly Christus; he passes through Mary like water passing through a tube. Jesus Christ is two persons, the 'psychic' Christ of the creator who is believed on in the catholic church, and the indwelling invisible Jesus who is known only to the gnostic.

We must pause to explain the word 'psychic'. A 'pneumatic' is a person possessed by the '*pneuma*' or Spirit; the divine inward gift of Hermas; the heavenly spark of Satornil; the seed of the mother according to Valentinus. The 'psychic' has no *pneuma*, no seed of light, no spark of the divine; he has nothing but his soul or 'psyche', the ordinary life which animates the body. The ordinary catholic Christians are 'psychics'; they lack the 'pneumatic' endowment; they cannot see the pneumatic Saviour within the psychic Christ. The gnostics are 'pneumatic', they have perfect knowledge and a higher destiny.

The divine Saviour unites himself with his fallen consort, the erring Sophia, and restores her to the bridal-chamber in the pleroma above this visible universe. The souls of the gnostics (who are sons of this mother) will be delivered from the burden of the flesh and exalted to the same place whither their Saviour has gone before, where each will be united with an angel; for souls are feminine and angels are masculine. As for the common 'psychic' Christians, who live by faith and good works, they will rise from the dead and ascend to their 'psychic' Christ, who is sitting at the right hand of the creator, who has been converted too, and promoted from the seventh heaven to the eighth heaven at the top of the visible universe, which used to be the abode of his mother, Sophia. The abandoned earth, along with such men and women as are not even 'psychic', but only 'choic' or earthly, will be destroyed by fire.

The catholic type of Christian appears to get all he ever expected.

Disregarding the endless ramifications of the myth, we may remark that its central theme is a penetrating study of the neurotic intellectual type and anticipates the Freudian theory. The hysterical Sophia represents the unlawful incestuous desire which has to be repressed and kept under in the region of the unconscious. Horus is the 'censor' who bars its return into the realms of intellectual light. The word gnosis, or knowledge, has a sexual significance. The myth is sexual from start to finish; and the solution consists in the reunion of the separated sexual characters. The male saviour or angel represents the 'higher' intellectual factor, and the female spirit, or portion of the spirit, represents the more emotional factor, which suffers from frustration and is unable to express itself satisfactorily. Valentine invites the neurotic intellectual idealistic type to achieve sublimation by contemplating the passion of the mother, identifying his soul with her and sharing in the nuptial redemption, which she achieves through the visit of the bridegroom who is her saviour.

It is furthermore very remarkable how this high fantastic myth is based on traditional concepts which could be found, for instance, in Hermas; the spirit who is a bride; the glorious male angel; the touch of spirit in the soul of the believer; the unhappy divided state of the non-integrated soul, which leads to melancholia and madness; the hints of nuptial solutions in his visions, which however, never terminate in anything. What Valentine did with his material was to dramatize it.

VALENTINE AND THE ROMAN CHURCH

We may well wonder how the Roman Christians could have accepted Valentine as a legitimate teacher; but he did not oppose or contradict the traditional faith or practice. He allowed room for everything in his system; but perhaps he did not begin by promulging his system; perhaps he never promulged a system. If he spoke at first in psalms and hymns and spiritual songs, or visions and revelations, it might be long before the true character of his thought became apparent. Roman Christians were accustomed to the visions of Hermas, and must have listened to oracles and allegories of many kinds. It was indeed this kind of thing that had gone to seed in the gnostic schools.

How soon Valentine parted from the church we do not know. Tertullian says that he was disappointed at not becoming bishop; someone who had been a confessor was preferred before him. This might have occurred in the vacancy after the death of Hyginus; or possibly not in Rome at all. He remained in Rome right through the episcopate of Pius, Hegesippus says. Then perhaps he retired to Cyprus and died there as Epiphanius says. He left no books. His pupils carried on his school.

According to the evidence of the Muratorian Catalogue, Hermas was living at this time, and it is possible that the conflict with the great heresiarch has left some traces in his latest work. It may have been now that he produced the long and complicated rewriting of his tower vision, which is included in the *Pastor* as the ninth parable. In this he explains rather clumsily that the old woman of his first vision, who had originally been the Sibyl and was then transformed into the church, was also the Holy Spirit and a Son of God. His instruction by a spirit in female form belonged to an elementary stage in prophetic vision; but he had now advanced so far as to be instructed by a male angel whom he called the shepherd; and the principal actor in his later parables (or *Similitudes*) was the glorious angel or Son of God or Michael, who was the lord of the tower. The old vision with its feminine spirit could not be withdrawn from circulation, but it could be branded as elementary and inferior; the nuptial symbolism could be submerged, though it is only just below the surface.

In the new vision of the tower the apostles and teachers are definitely in the past. False teachers are a danger. They are described as the hypocrites who bring in strange teachings and pervert the servants of God, especially those who have sinned; not allowing them to repent but persuading them with foolish teachings. Much depends upon the bishops and deacons. The bishops are highly commended. They are the great spreading trees under which the sheep of the flock find shelter. The plural word constitutes a difficulty, since there is really no doubt that the single episcopate was established now in Rome; and Pius, the brother of Hermas, would succeed Hyginus in the chair of the church of the city of Rome, as the *Muratorian Fragment* says. But there must have been bishops in the adjacent communities, as there were in the case of Antioch in the time of Ignatius, who came in to councils in the city; and the writings of Hermas have the whole Christian world in view, and were sent out to many bishops.

There is also the picture of the false prophet which appears as the eleventh commandment. Close scrutiny of this chapter convinces one that it was written with a definite situation in view and a definite person. This person seats himself in a chair, as a teacher, or even as a bishop perhaps; he is filled with the spirit of the devil; he prophesies after the Gentile manner; he takes money. He leads astray the double-minded and the empty-headed. He is a schism-leader of some sort.

It is immediately after this, in the twelfth commandment, that Hermas is confirmed in his own ministry, and solemnly charged to adhere to the great and beautiful and glorious commandments, by means of which the heart is gladdened and men will live unto God.

CERDO AND THE SYRIAN SCHOOL, c. A.D. 137

We know very little about Cerdo, who was the head of the Syrian school. He represented the gnosis of Satornil of Antioch, and introduced his doctrine of the 'two gods', one of whom could be described as just, whereas the other was good, that it so say kind and benevolent. The former was the Hebrew God, of course, the other was the nameless deity who existed in the higher realms. His Christ was an immaterial spirit who never took human flesh. Hippolytus, as reported in the Latin *Libellus*, says that Cerdo used shortened editions of Luke's Gospel and Paul's Epistles, the same books that were used by his successor Marcion and this explains Marcion's own claim that his shortened Gospel had been used by Paul himself. If he believed what he said, it must have been in use for some considerable time before he received it. He must have received it from someone he trusted.

Nevertheless, most scholars hold that he produced this literature himself, and that is what Irenaeus and Tertullian unhesitatingly assert. If this is so, Hippolytus was mistaken in saying that Cerdo used it before him.

Irenaeus had a short account of Cerdo, which he drew without serious doubt from the pages of Hegesippus, to the effect that he arrived in Rome in the time of Hyginus and was received into the church after making a confession of faith; which is an interesting reference to the use of a creed-form to test the legitimacy of a teacher. He engaged in teaching privately or secretly, and made a second confession. He was then convicted or refuted by the majority, and withdrew from the convention of the brethren. The narrative is not perfectly clear, but it suggests a memorable secession from the whole church by a considerable group, who were led by a teacher from the east who had not been trusted by everybody in the first place. He now operated his own 'school'.

MARCION IN ROME, c. A.D. 137

The same excellent source states that Marcion arrived in Rome under Hyginus, continued under Pius and reached his greatest strength under Anicetus.

It is not at all certain to what extent the theology of Marcion was formed before he came to Rome. The best that can be said is that he had

5. THE TEMPLE OF ANTONINUS AND FAUSTINA

6. THE FABRICIAN BRIDGE

not yet parted from the catholic church. According to Tertullian, he attached himself to the church on his arrival and presented it with the magnificent sum of two hundred thousand sesterces; so he was a man who had control of considerable funds, whether as a successful ship-owner, or as a church organizer, or both. In due course the unusual character of his views brought him into conflict with the Roman elders. It occurred, according to Epiphanius, when the episcopal see was vacant. The trouble arose from the fact that his father, the bishop of Sinope, had not absolved him from the sin of incontinence; a story which is not taken seriously by modern scholars.

If we leave this on one side, we find next in Epiphanius a reference to a controversy about the *proedria* or first seat, which looks like the position of a teacher or bishop in the church. Following this there comes a very credible story of a debate in which Marcion asked the elders what was meant by the parable of Jesus about the patch of new cloth on the old garment and the new wine poured into old skins. The old skins, in his opinion, meant the outworn tradition of the Jewish religion, to which the catholic church in part adhered; the new wine was the intoxicating gospel which he was preaching himself. Some argument followed, and Marcion left the church, swearing that he would inflict upon it an enduring 'schism'; he would tear the old garment once and for all.

There is little doubt that Epiphanius is reproducing his excellent second-century source here (Hegesippus perhaps), and scholars are inclined to consider his evidence seriously. In any case Marcion parted from the church and joined the school of Cerdo, taking, no doubt, a number of like-minded followers with him. His two hundred thousand sesterces were returned to him, Tertullian says. Before long he succeeded Cerdo as master of the school. He seems at some time to have issued an Epistle, which was known to Tertullian, in which he reviewed his quondam connexion with the catholic church; but no trace of this Epistle remains. Ten years after this, Justin remarks that he was teaching his perverse doctrines to every race under heaven. Marcion or his emissaries must have travelled widely. We know, for instance that his disciple Apelles visited Alexandria. He picked up the docetics and the ascetics and the anti-Jewish fanatics, and became a formidable rival to the catholic church.

MARCION'S CHURCH, c. A.D. 140

Searching for the heart of the Marcionite theology, we find it in the sense of utter contrast between the God of the Jewish Law and the Saviour of the Christian gospel. It is possible that Marcion's modern admirers have failed to do him absolute justice by insisting too exclusively on his dependence on Paul. It looks as if the central idea of his preaching came straight from Jesus himself as he saw him in the pages of his *Gospel of the Truth*; a God so good that it was wrong to call him just.

As we read the Sermon on the Mount in Luke we find the good God and the doctrine of unlimited mercy and forgiveness which formed the core of Marcion's faith. These words are followed immediately by his favourite parable of the tree and the fruit, which he applied to the deity himself; a good tree produces good fruit; a good God could not have made a bad world; he could not be warlike or revengeful or severe.

On the other hand, this gospel of pure goodness was fortified by a heroic asceticism. The simple believer in the 'school' of Marcion had to renounce his wife, if he had one, and embrace perpetual celibacy. He must never partake of wine or flesh, though fish was permitted. The body must be mortified and starved; it belonged to the creator, and when it died it would be discarded for ever.

There is a point about Marcion which is worthy of some attention. Marcion's church did not depart from the pattern which was now everywhere adopted in the catholic tradition. It had bishops, presbyters and deacons. It had sacraments, though it used water for the eucharist instead of wine, the drinking of wine being altogether banned. In baptism the candidates were anointed with oil and given milk and honey to drink. These ceremonies were all in traditional use in the catholic church before the end of the century, as we learn from Hippolytus and Tertullian; and some of them appear in the Valentinian rituals. It would seem probable therefore that they were in general use before these three distinct traditions separated from one another. Of course they may have borrowed from one another, but in view of the feelings that existed between them it does not seem likely.

Barnabas uses the symbolism of milk and honey in connexion with baptism, and Theophilus of Antioch invites an inquirer to be anointed. These may refer to actual rituals, but could well be taken as figurative expressions.

MARCION'S NEW TESTAMENT

It has been strongly argued that Marcion was the first to 'organize' a 'catholic' church order. There is no evidence that anybody ever 'organized' a catholic church order, but there are two points in the theory which are deserving of some attention. The first is that he imposed on all his churches his own theology; the other is that he seems to have laid down a canon of apostolic scripture for reading in the churches. The catholic church of his time, meaning by this term what Celsus called the great church, the mass of Christian churches of apostolic foundation, had a large inheritance of apostolic and sub-apostolic literature; but it was not yet a canon of scripture like the books of the Old Testament. It is maintained that Marcion did something new when he brought his book of Pauline Epistles into close association with his *Gospel of the Truth*, and so substituted a canon of Epistles and Gospel for the old canon of the Law and the Prophets; though actually there seems to be no evidence that he called them scripture.

Undoubtedly this was an important development which must have led the catholic churches to re-examine the situation; but we do not know that it was without antecedents of any kind. It should not be forgotten that the old Gospel of Luke, from which his *Gospel of the Truth* was formed, had possessed an apostolic sequel in the Acts of the Apostles; Marcion or some predecessor substituted the Pauline Epistles for it, Galatians taking the place of Acts as a source-book of Apostolic history and doctrine. The same pattern may have appeared in other quarters, too. The so-called First Epistle of John seems to have been the sequel to John's Gospel. I Peter may have been regarded as the sequel of Mark. The *Didache* was certainly composed as an apostolic sequel to Matthew.

Another point is that it is not perfectly accurate to say that the Old Testament was not read in the Marcionite churches. There was a third 'canonical' book, if we may use the term, which Marcion composed himself, called the *Antitheses* or *Contradictions*. The catholic churches read extracts from the Law and the Prophets along with their extracts from the Gospels, thus proving their perfect harmony; and words of Jesus quoted in Clement, Justin and Theophilus are sometimes prefaced by such Old Testament quotations. Marcion copied this procedure in his *Antitheses*, but with the object of proving their absolute incompatibility; and this was regarded as his most important literary labour. Unfortunately we are not able to reconstruct this monument of his scholarship and controversial ability, though some information about it survives.

This does not detract from the originality and genius of Marcion, but it does suggest that his policies may have been determined to some extent by contemporary developments, which may not always be documented. Every point in the theology and church order of Marcion was related somehow to points which were established in the catholic church order of his time; but the position which he gave to his apostolic documents was necessarily a stronger one than they were given in the old tradition, which had no need to prove its theology or supply its credentials in quite the same way. For Marcion everything depended upon his combination of Galatians with the *Gospel of the Truth*.

THE ACCESSION OF PIUS, *c.* A.D. 140

The Syrian Chronicle dates the Marcionite schism in 138, and this date cannot be far out. It must have taken place by about 140 or 141, which is the approximate date for the accession of Pius as bishop of Rome in succession to Hyginus. If we take seriously the tales told by Tertullian and Epiphanius, this would be the episcopal election in which both heresiarchs were disappointed. Pius would be the 'confessor' who proved the more powerful candidate than Valentine.

Pius was the brother of Hermas, the *Muratorian Fragment* says, and Hermas 'compiled' his book called the *Pastor* while his brother Pius occupied the episcopal chair; that is to say, the definite edition of his various revelations. The book emphasizes the moral life, the coming judgement and the glory of martyrdom. The old Roman coalition of the bishop, the prophet and the martyr was firmly established. Senior men who could well remember the days of Clement were in the saddle, and nothing could have been more objectionable to Valentine and Marcion.

It looks as if Pius and his elders dealt firmly with certain novel tendencies and modernizing personalities in the ecclesia with which Hyginus had been more lenient or less fortunate. Hyginus had taken over the reins after a persecution in which his predecessor had been killed; and the parallel instance of the loss of Bishop Publius at Athens indicates that the task of reorganization in such circumstances was no easy one. But perhaps Hyginus' own views were on the modernistic side? Perhaps he was even the patron of Cerdo or Valentine?

Pius is a Latin name like Clement and Sixtus, but it is not possible to build much on that. He must have been a slave like his brother Hermas who had a Greek name and wrote in Greek though his prose style is marked by a number of Latinisms. Their acceptance after so many years as leaders in the Roman church is a tribute to their character and ability and sustained Christian faith. But could Hermas really have been alive at this period? He was a married man with an insubordinate family when Clement was at the end of his episcopate about 97 to 100; but marriage and families came early in those days. If he married at twenty (and he could have married even younger), and his oldest child was fifteen (which is old enough for unruly conduct), he would have been about thirty-five when he wrote the *Visions*. If this was in the year 100, he would be about seventy-five when Pius became bishop, only five years older than Polycarp, who was in good form fifteen years later, and not too old to supervise the preparation of a standard edition of his prophetic works.

SCHISMS AND SCHOOLS

We know next to nothing about the appointment of bishops at this time. It is quite possible that the old bishop was expected to consecrate his successor or at any rate to designate him, no doubt with the concurrence of the whole ecclesia; but even if this custom prevailed in Rome, for which there is no evidence at all, it might not be possible when the bishop died as a martyr as Telesphorus did, or died unexpectedly as Hyginus may have done, since his episcopate was so short. In such cases the new bishop would have to be chosen in some other way, the presbyters taking the lead no doubt, and neighbouring bishops co-operating perhaps, and the whole ecclesia concurring. All these features are to be found in one case or another; but according to Hippolytus at the end of the century, the Roman bishop was chosen by all the people and consecrated by neighbouring bishops, the elders standing by.

In any case these two elections, if they were elections, were held in a period of confusion due to various causes, the aftermath of war, the effects of persecution and the conflict with heresy.

It would appear that episcopal elections had a divisive effect upon the church. The state of affairs would appear to be this: after the accession of Pius the Roman church was seen to have broken into two or more parts, each of which was fully organized, and had oecumenical connexions. The more conservative part, which had Pius as its bishop, favoured the old concord of Jewish antecedents with apostolic tradition, and found a witness to it in the writings of Hermas, which were linked with the name of Clement, which now had a lustre of antiquity and apostolicity about it. The part of the church which accepted the doctrines of Marcion took a different line, by reducing the quantity of apostolic literature which was accepted as legitimate and adding to it the writings of Marcion himself. Whether Marcion was the bishop of Rome in the estimate of his church, or whether he had a bishop, we do not know. He certainly equipped his church with bishops; but he may have stood higher in the estimate of his followers than any bishop. They thought he was the only one who knew the truth, Justin sarcastically says.

Were there any other rival churches in Rome with rival bishops? We do not know. It seems rather unlikely that Valentine founded a church. He operated a school of more advanced studies for the intellectuals, and initiated them into a higher degree of illumination in the mysteries.

A word must now be said about the Christian schools. There were apostolic teachers in the church from the first, but we have so signs of schools being carried on separately from the church. But there were teachers now who gathered groups of pupils or inquirers round them, apparently in their own houses or lodgings, like St Paul, or in the houses of wealthy patrons who took them into their homes. We learn from the *Two Ways* and from the *Didache* that classes were held daily, and in the time of Hippolytus the proper time for this was the early morning. We may also begin to distinguish a class of inquirers who had not made up their minds to be baptized (the rolling stones of Hermas) from a class of hearers (the *neoi* or younger) who had been accepted, but were going through the long period of preparation which was now demanded before baptism; by the time of Hippolytus it was normally three years. It would include fasting and prayers and exorcisms, and Hippolytus says that it was competent for the teacher to bestow a laying on of hands, either in blessing or exorcism or both.

The Christian ecclesia consisted in theory of a circle of baptized saints, who possessed the Holy Spirit and were pledged to a life of perfect chastity, either as married persons or as bachelors or spinsters; to a complete renunciation of pagan life; and possibly to martyrdom. If they lapsed from this high standard, the way of reconciliation was hard or, in the opinion of some, impossible. By now there must have been many who remained for years in the class of hearers or catechumens, rather than adopt the heroic and saintly life which was incumbent on the baptized; and if so, the school must have been the centre of their Christian life. It seems that they were not admitted to the prayers of the brethren or to the eucharist. Had the bishop or elders any effective control over these schools?

If this was the situation, it becomes fairly easy to understand the influence of the great teachers and the success with which they organized their following. Cerdo and Valentine were the heads of important schools, which were fully recognized by Hyginus and the elders; they had an organization already. But there is a further point. When a schism occurred, it was natural for each episcopal group to regard the rival episcopal group as nothing more than a 'school'. It could not be called a church, since there could not be two churches of God sojourning in one city. Thus the organization of which Cerdo was the head is called a school by Irenaeus; but we can hardly doubt that Cerdo called it a church. It would be *the* church for him; and either he was its bishop, bishop of Rome in the estimation of his flock, or else he had a bishop, with elders to support him. Marcion took over the 'school' of Cerdo, Irenaeus says, and therefore he may have been bishop of Rome in that succession; he certainly regarded his organization as the one true church.

The loose organization attributed to the heretical churches by Tertullian may have had something to do with the fact that they developed out of schools. It would explain perhaps why they did not exclude the catechumens from the prayers of the brethren. He also says that women were allowed to baptize and that episcopal appointments were not permanent; but perhaps these were oriental features.

Furthermore, since celibacy was a requirement for baptism in the Marcionite churches, few of the hearers would hasten to baptism; his churches would always consist very largely of a mass of catechumens.

There was also another class of Christian adherent to whom an appeal could be made. In his picture of the 'false prophet', Hermas remarks that those who associated with him were the 'double-minded' who frequently repented; which suggests that he offered easier terms of repentance than Hermas did to those who had fallen from grace. The reference is easier to understand if the false prophet was a rival bishop; and the same charge was brought by Hippolytus against his rival bishop Callistus. It suggests that the penitents formed another class for whose allegiance rival groups could compete.

THE ROMAN TRADITION

The Roman church was thus forced to consolidate its organization and its theology, and by doing so it gained stability and gave leadership to the church as a whole. The divisions and controversies in Rome were felt to the very bounds of the catholic church. No doubt the views of Marcion and Valentine were discussed before long by the Britons on the banks of the Thames; they certainly reached the Syrians on the banks of the Euphrates. The true philosophy of Valentine lingered longer in Antioch than elsewhere, Tertullian said. Marcionite churches were numerous in the east.

Was the third Roman tradition, the tradition of Bishop Pius, equally influential? The evidence leaves no doubt at all that it was; but it appears in the east as the tradition of Clement. The veneration which was extended in Syria and Palestine to the name of Clement as the successor of Peter in Rome, shows how high the reputation of the old Roman tradition stood. The tradition of Peter and Clement was regarded as the strong champion against Marcion and all heretics of the anti-Jewish type. The conviction was expressed in the oriental manner in the 'Clementine' romances of the Hellenistic Ebionite school, in which an imaginary Peter, seen through the eyes of an imaginary Clement, triumphantly refutes an imaginary Simon Magus, who is Paul, Marcion, Valentine and Basilides rolled into one; and in the so-called *Acts of Peter* the defeat of Simon Magus is transferred to Rome itself.

The exaltation of Clement in these works of fiction is the reflexion in Syria, of the position of leadership which the Roman church occupied in the west, and in the catholic church generally, until the end of the century. In the Ebionite imagination the conflict was seen in simpler terms than it was in Rome; it was a conflict between Peter and Paul, which is how Marcion saw it too. In Rome, however, the tradition of Clement is traced back to Peter and Paul jointly; and Clement is not the first successor; he has predecessors.

CHAPTER 6

ARISTIDES AND JUSTIN

Antoninus Pius, A.D. 138–61, *p.* 90. The Legacy of Hermas, *p.* 91. Spirit theology, *p.* 92. Persecution and *apologia*, *p.* 94 The *Apology* of Aristides, before A.D. 147, *p.* 96. The third race, *p.* 96. Justin comes to Rome, about A.D. 150, *p.* 98. The *Syntagma* of heresies, *p.* 99. Semo Sancus, *p.* 100. The school of Justin, *p.* 101. The Western Text of the Gospels, *p.* 103. Textual variations, *p.* 105.

THE ANTONINE EMPERORS

Nerva, 96–98

Trajan, 98–117

Hadrian (Publius Aelius Hadrianus), 117–38

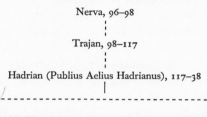

Lucius Ceionius Commodus Verus (renamed Lucius Aelius Verus and given title of Caesar). Died 1 Jan. 138. Known as 'the older Verus'

Lucius Ceionius Commodus Verus. Known as 'the younger Verus'. Aged about 7 in 138. Augustus, with Marcus Aurelius, from 161 to his death in 169.

Titus Aurelius Fulvius Boionius Antoninus. Adopted on death of the older Verus. Renamed Titus Aelius Hadrianus Antoninus, and known as **Antoninus Pius**. Married to Faustina. Adopted, by order of Hadrian, the younger Verus and his nephew and son-in-law (married to the younger Faustina)

Marcus Annius Verus, aged about 17 in 138. Renamed Marcus Aelius Aurelius Verus, known as **Marcus Aurelius**, 161–80. Co-emperor in 147.

- - - - - - represents adoption.
Bold type represents emperors of the Antonine family.

Lucius Aelius Aurelius **Commodus**, 180–92. Co-emperor with his father in 177, murdered in 192.

Note. The dynastic principle was introduced into the adoptive system inaugurated by Nerva by the action of Hadrian, who directed Antoninus Pius to adopt the son of the dead 'Caesar' Verus, and also his own nephew. Hadrian thought highly of young Marcus, whom he called Verissimus. Trajan, Hadrian, and Marcus Aurelius, all came of Spanish stock.

Furthermore, it was by Hadrian's direction that Marcus was married to his first cousin Faustina (the younger), whose mother (the Empress Faustina) was his aunt.

On adoption into the imperial family, a new name was conferred. The adopted son took a name or names from his adoptive father. It is this practice that made it so difficult for the fourth-century fathers to identify correctly the names which they found in their sources. Eusebius, for instance, states that Aristides addressed his *Apology* to Hadrian, but the Syriac text reads 'Caesar Hadrianus Antoninus Augustus Pius'.

Justin Martyr addressed his to the emperor 'Titus Aelius Hadrianus Antoninus Pius Augustus Caesar and to Verissimus his son a philosopher, and to Lucius a philosopher, natural son of a Caesar and adopted son of Pius'.

ANTONINUS PIUS, A.D. 138–61

On the slope of a hill overlooking the Roman forum, the visitor to Rome may still see the temple which the Emperor Antoninus Pius erected in memory of his wife Faustina, and Marcus his successor dedicated in memory of both. Antoninus succeeded Hadrian in the summer of 138 and reigned for twenty-three years. He was an excellent administrator, quite tireless in the duties of government, and his twenty-three years were years of comparative peace and prosperity, perhaps the best years the Roman empire ever saw. He was of Gallic descent, but his family was Italianized, and he owned rich estates in many parts of Italy. So far as we know, he never left the country after his accession. He was no philosopher, but he encouraged the philosophers. Literary men of the Latin and Greek traditions flocked to his court and were well rewarded. His two adopted sons, Lucius and Marcus, received the best training in both traditions that could possibly be given to them. His name 'Pius' implies not only devotion to the gods, but also an affectionate respect for the old traditions of domestic and civil life. The strong family feeling of the Antonine family was an integral part of the imperial system, and therefore had its place in the divine order. It became a religious cult.

Antoninus himself was a broad-minded and liberal man within these limits. He is said to have disliked shedding blood. There is good evidence that he discouraged the persecution of the Christians, or at least the savage popular outbursts which his predecessor Hadrian had also disapproved.

Antoninus was the central figure in a succession of able rulers who gave good government to the empire for the best part of a century. They carried on the imperial administration under the old Roman forms; but their conception of government was also influenced by Stoic monotheism, and its belief in a divine reason or intelligence directing the universe. All races and all religions might have their place in the world, if only they would get along with one another and obey the emperor. The reign of these philosopher-kings was certainly a remarkable period in human history and did much to form the mind

of Europe. Their dynasty was a proud one, but it did not last so long
as that of the other Pius, the one who became the bishop of the Christian ecclesia about 140, and counted his succession from the apostles
Peter and Paul.

THE LEGACY OF HERMAS

Hermas was an old man now, pottering about among his elms and vines
if indeed he was still living. In any case he lived on in his books, which
were highly influential not only in Rome but in Egypt and the east too.
It falls to few authors to bring out corrected editions of their books
forty-five or fifty years after their first appearance; but it does occur.
Its occurrence in the case of Hermas is the only hypothesis which does
justice to all the evidence. His successive revisions have left their mark
on his text. He had a way of adding to his *Commandments* and *Parables*
subsidiary morals and precepts which were never intended to be drawn
from them in the first place; and when this is done, we can sometimes
infer that he is dealing with changed conditions; and this draws our
attention to new problems in the church life of his time.

One of these is the question of marriage and divorce, which is dealt
with in an appendix to his fourth commandment, the subject of which is
chastity. This commandment condemns adultery not only in act but
even in desire. 'The very thought of it, for a servant of God, is a great
sin; and if anyone were to work this evil work, he would be working
his own death.' A question is then asked of a very curious nature. A
man has a wife who is faithful in the Lord, and he finds her 'in adultery'
does he sin if he continues to live with her? The answer is that he does
sin; he must separate from her; and he may not marry another woman.
The decision was in line with Jewish jurisprudence, which made divorce
compulsory under certain circumstances; but the prohibition of re-
marriage was based on words of Jesus (or Paul); and the reason which
Hermas gives for this prohibition is that the erring partner may repent
and ought to be received if she does.

The discussion calls to mind an uncanonical story of Jesus which was
current at this time and found its way eventually into the text of the
official Bibles. It is the story of the woman who was taken 'in adultery',
and was brought before Jesus by the scribes and Pharisees. 'He that is
without sin among you,' said Jesus, 'let him cast the first stone'; and
when her accusers disappear from the scene in confusion, he says to the

woman, 'Neither do I condemn thee; go, and sin no more.' This story, the origin of which is unknown, draws attention to two conflicting elements in the church tradition which were to cause increasing difficulties to the authorities. One was the doctrine of absolute morals, or even of utter sinlessness in thought and word and deed; the other was the doctrine of unlimited forgiveness.

This dilemma is brought forward by Hermas in a new question. There were teachers in the Roman ecclesia who had laid it down that there was no repentance for Christians after their baptism, when they went down into the water and took forgiveness of their former sins. This doctrine had powerful support, and something very like it is to be found in the Epistle to the Hebrews and the First Epistle of St John. It would appear that it was now hardening into a principle of church order; and Hermas defers to it. He is determined, however, to find a place for repentance in spite of it. He had done so once before by producing a document which had heavenly authority; but this special indulgence had been tied to a given date and was no longer operative. It was not intended for those who were now making their profession of faith; it was intended for those who were called before these days. Nevertheless, at that time the Lord did provide a place for repentance, and had given authority over it to the shepherd-angel who was the spiritual control of Hermas himself; and by that authority given unto him he was prepared to assert that Christians who had fallen into sin after severe temptation from the devil might be allowed one repentance; but if they sinned off hand and then repented, it would be unfortunate for them; they would with difficulty live.

This decision, equivocal as it seems to be, was of great importance in the church. It was widely adopted, and its repercussions continued into the early third century. The dilemma was not removed; but a way was found by which the two principles could both be respected. It may be added that we have no idea how this 'repentance' was administered: Hermas may be claiming that he administered it himself as the bearer of the spiritual revelation.

SPIRIT THEOLOGY

The moral perfectionism of the tradition to which Hermas belonged was not based on legalism. It was based on an intense faith in the Holy Spirit as a living power in the heart. The baptized Christian had the

Spirit in him, and therefore ought to sin no more. He ought not even to desire to sin. It was unfortunate for him if he did, for the Holy Spirit cannot dwell in the heart along with the evil desire; it will abandon that man and intercede against him.

Hermas summarizes his views on the Christian life in the time-honoured form of commandments; but he is really dealing with 'spirits' or inward dispositions. There is a spirit of holiness which animates the Christian personality and becomes manifest in such graces as faith or innocence or purity, which are therefore thought of as 'spirits'. Every Christian is possessed by a divine spirit. Hermas sometimes speaks of the indwelling spirit as though it were his own spirit or an extension of his own spirit; at other times it is a loan from God, a spirit which is 'made to dwell' in his 'flesh'. This ambiguity is ineradicable. It does not yield to analysis. The mysterious power within the Christian heart is me-and-not-me; it is all my own and yet it is all of God; God-in-me and I-in-God.

If the Spirit worked so powerfully and effectually in the case of the believer, what would be the case with regard to the Saviour ? Hermas approaches this subject in one of several extensions which he builds on to his parable of the servant in the vineyard, the proper subject of which was fasting. The servant in the vineyard is called the Son of God, and that is a simple thought; the Holy Spirit which dwells in him is also called the Son of God, and that is a simple thought too; but when we find Hermas speaking of the servant in the parable as the 'flesh' in which the Holy Spirit dwelt, his thinking is far from simple. The identity or personality is not fixed in the servant or in the Holy Spirit. It fluctuates between them.

Hermas was probably quite aware of that. It is probably just how he visualized the inward life of the spirit-possessed Christian. His inward and spiritual life had become identified with the Holy Spirit; and yet there was a distinction; he could talk in terms of one or the other.

He goes on to complicate matters even more by adding still another excursus to his parable. Just as the servant in the parable, who at one point represents the 'flesh' in which the Spirit dwelt, was made a fellow-heir with the Spirit, so the 'flesh' of the Christian believer will receive its reward if it is found undefiled and spotless. In simpler words, there will be a resurrection of the body.

One thing is clear about this confused pneumatic theology. It is based on a religion of inward experience in which a divine power or spirit moves the human heart; it may be oriental in origin; it has affinities both with Judaism and with Stoicism; it reminds us of docetism; but it is fundamentally anti-docetic. It is the same answer to docetism that Ignatius gave; spirit in flesh. On the other hand, it has none of the bold clear definition that we find in Ignatius. Many scholars think that Hermas shared the christology of Cerinthus in which the man Jesus receives a heavenly power or spirit at his baptism; Hermas does not say this, but his spirit christology is not altogether incompatible with it. It is an informal imaginative Christology which defies analysis.

PERSECUTION AND *APOLOGIA*

During the hundred-and-forties, at the end of the third Christian generation of forty years each, the old type of intuitive, or imaginative, or catechetical writing begins to give way to an analytic, objective, and philosophical literature on the Greek model, written by a new class of convert who had received training in Greek thought. The Christian church appears to have enjoyed comparative peace under the mild rule of Antoninus Pius, at least in his earlier years. The times were tranquil and prosperous; and just as Greek philosophers gravitated to Rome to enjoy the sunshine of imperial favour in a cultivated and literary court, so the Christian teachers flocked to the capital, where they enjoyed patronage or founded schools or carved out schismatic churches. The erroneous idea that the 'bad emperors' were the persecutors, and the 'good emperors' restrained persecution, seems to be based on the experience of the church under Hadrian and Antoninus, and is first found in the *Apology* of Melito or Sardis about A.D. 165.

Among these Christian teachers were men who thought the time had come to present the case in favour of Christianity to the emperors and to the educated world of which they were the patrons. They penned what were called *apologies*.

The word *apologia* is not to be taken in the English sense, but in the Greek. There was nothing apologetic about these documents. The word meant the case for the defence; especially a defence made by an accused person in a law-court. It is the name given by Plato to his report of the speech which Socrates made at his trial before the people of Athens; and there is nothing apologetic about that magnificent account of his life and mission. It is perfectly possible that the first Christian 'apologists' chose the title because of its Socratic connexions; for very soon they were claiming Socrates as one of themselves in his capacity as a martyr and a witness to the truth. The idea of the Christian apology first appears in Athens among men who had absorbed a reverence for Socrates in the course of their literary education. The apologies were addressed to the Antonine Emperors, who claimed to be philosophers.

Since the *Apology* of Quadratus has not survived, it remains that the *Apology* of Aristides is our earliest document of this kind. It was addressed to Antoninus Pius without the mention of any colleague, and was therefore composed before the year 147 in which Marcus Aurelius became joint-emperor. It is sometimes questioned whether the apologies were actually presented to the emperors; but there hardly seems to be room for literary fiction in such a matter. The emperor's name could hardly be affixed to them for decorative purposes. They look like genuine appeals to the highest legal authority, who was known to cultivate a humane and liberal policy and to extend his favour to philosophers in general. It is probable that Aristides found his way, with other gowned and bearded intellectuals, into the imperial halls on the Palatine Hill; for there is no recorded visit of this emperor to Greece, and the fact that the apologist calls himself Marcianus Aristides, a philosopher of Athens, suggests that he was not in Athens when he presented it. The opening paragraph sounds an objective and dispassionate, but rhetorical note.

By the providence of God, O King, I came into this world; and when I gazed upon the heaven and the earth and the sea, with the sun and the moon and everything else, I wondered at its beautiful order; and when I saw how the universe and everything that is in it, moved in accordance with a determined law, I realized that its mover and controller was God.

I maintain that this is the God who framed the universe. He is without beginning, invisible, immortal, in need of nothing, and above all passions and defects, such as anger and forgetfulness and ignorance and so forth. He needs no sacrifices or libations or anything else from this visible world. He stands in need of nothing, and everything stands in need of him.

(Apology of Aristides, I.)

THE *APOLOGY* OF ARISTIDES, BEFORE A.D. 147

There was nothing new in this. It sounded like Greek philosophy, but there was nothing that the Jewish Hellenists had not already said. He was following in the same lines as the *Preaching of Peter*. He also followed this pseudo-Petrine work in dividing mankind into three races, or four if we follow the Syriac and Armenian versions. The first of these were the barbarians, and particularly the Chaldeans who worshipped created things instead of the creator and made images to put in temples. He exposes the folly of worshipping the physical elements, which are subject to defilement and dissolution; or the dead idols, which have to be guarded so carefully for fear they may be stolen.

The Greeks were wiser than the Chaldeans, but their wisdom had betrayed them into greater follies. He runs through a number of the myths, and points out that they are full of violent and comic scenes in which the gods commit adultery and murder, and suffer injury or death. He adds an appendix on the Egyptian worship of animals. This material was not new either, for Jewish and Greek philosophers had both pointed out these absurdities. He goes on to condemn the worship in the temples, and asserts, as other apologists do, that human sacrifices still went on in them. He is amazed that the Greeks, who had advanced so far in many respects, should not have advanced beyond an obscene, cruel, and superstitious polytheism. Their laws are just, he says, but their gods are unjust.

His second race (or third according to the Syriac and Armenian versions) was the Jews, but he does not devote much space to them. He commends them for worshipping the one true God, and praises their compassionate and philanthropic social life; but he follows the *Preaching of Peter* in asserting that their liturgical tradition was really a worship of angels, and not of God, since they observed sabbaths and new moons and the passover and the great fast and circumcision, and rules of purity with regard to food. His third (or fourth) race was the Christians.

THE THIRD RACE

The confusion in the textual authorities about the number of races and the arrangement of the material about the Christian faith might be explained very simply if we assume that Aristides was making use of

7. SOCRATES

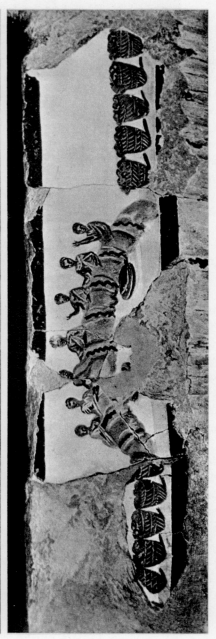

8. CATACOMB PAINTINGS: THE EUCHARIST

a Christianized version of a Jewish tractate against idolatry which spoke of three races of mankind, the barbarians, the Greeks and the Jews. There might have been two ways of accommodating the old document to the new material, and the new material to the old document.

The *Apology* is fundamentally a defence of a Jewish proselyte piety as the best monotheism and the best moralism. It has been Christianized to a certain extent by the introduction of a paragraph based on the creed, which comes quite at the beginning of the document in the Syriac and Armenian versions and serves to introduce the Christians as the fourth race. In the Greek version it comes later, after the Gentile and Jewish forms of worship have been criticized and thus leads on to the account of the wonderful moral and social life of the Christians at this later point as the Third Race. This account of the Christian life and manners is little more than a Judaeo-Christian catechism put into the third person. In addition to this the author refers the emperor to a written Gospel, probably Matthew.

The text of Aristides is not free from uncertainty, but comparison shows that his creed or kerugma included in it the declarations that Jesus Christ was the Son of the most high God, that he descended from heaven and was born of a Hebrew virgin, that he had twelve disciples in order to fulfill a certain dispensation, that he was pierced by the Jews, that he died and was buried, that he rose again after three days and ascended into heaven, and that his disciples went out into all parts of the world; a credal outline which is closely related to the 'testimony' theology.

The account of the unworldly life of the Christians has a certain charm, though its catechetical origin makes it distressingly conventional. 'They do not commit adultery or fornication; they do not bear false witness'; and so forth. It emphasizes the social virtues within the brotherhood. They fast two or three days so as to provide the needy with food. They provide for those who are imprisoned on account of the name of their Messiah. They pray every morning and at all hours; they give thanks to God over their food and drink. They take special care over the burial of the dead. The Syriac and Armenian versions rather extend these references to the self-denying other-worldly piety of the third race.

In conclusion Aristides affirms that he is a believer; he urges the emperor to read the Christian writings; he emphasizes their innocence and the injustice of the persecutions which they suffer; and he invites all who do not know God to approach the gateway of light and to receive the incorruptible words. And let them anticipate the dread judgement which is to come by Jesus Christ upon the whole race of men.

The *Apology* may have made some impression, since it seems to have been known to the philosopher Celsus, who wrote his attack on Christianity some twenty years afterwards. It was valued in the Christian church and was still current in the fourth century. After that it was lost until fairly recently, when the Armenian and Syriac translations of it were discovered. It was then recognized that the Greek text still existed in a strange form, the popular medieval romance called *Barlaam and Joasaph* (or Josaphat), which is a Christianized version of the life of Buddha. A long speech put into the mouth of one of the characters is nothing but the *Apology* of Aristides in a slightly edited form; or of course a slightly different form of the tractate which Aristides composed or used. This tractate in turn bore some relation to the *Preaching* of Peter.

JUSTIN COMES TO ROME, ABOUT A.D. 150

The *First Apology* (so-called) of Justin Martyr is addressed to Antoninus Pius 'and his son Verissimus a philosopher, and Lucius a philosopher, natural son of a Caesar and adopted son of Pius'. Verissimus is Marcus Aurelius, who was given the title of Augustus in 147; and it is strange that it does not appear here, since the book was almost certainly written after that date. It mentions a certain Munatius Felix, who was prefect of Egypt, whose term of office came to an end between 151 and 154. It states that it was written about a hundred and fifty years after the birth of Christ. Altogether the years 150–2 may be taken as a likely date for this book.

How long before this date Justin came to Rome we do not know. When we last saw him, some fifteen years earlier, he was debating with Trypho at Ephesus, and his boat was leaving for some other place, perhaps another Greek city on the shores of the Aegean Sea. We should not think of the great Christian teachers of this period as fixing their residence permanently in any one city. Justin states in his so-called *Second Apology* that he had resided at Rome twice. We should not assume, for instance, that Marcion or Valentine remained in Rome all the time; Marcion's nickname, the 'sea-captain', rather suggests a number of sea-voyages; and Valentine had connexions with Cyprus as well as with Rome and Egypt. Greek philosophers like Lucian of Samosata tried their luck in province after province. Rome and Athens were among the most tempting fields of contest; and Justin modelled his way of life on that of the philosopher. In his philosopher's gown, he must have been a familiar figure in more than one city. We can hardly doubt that he visited Athens, where the tradition of Socrates was maintained in several schools; for he remained to the end a pupil and admirer of the old rebel who had been put to death for bringing in new gods and saying that the gods of the city were not gods at all.

THE *SYNTAGMA* OF HERESIES

When Justin came to Rome he had two books to his credit. One was the *Dialogue with Trypho* in its original form, with many notes, no doubt, of additional anti-Jewish arguments drawn from the prophets. The other was his *Syntagma* or collection of heresies, a work to which he alludes in his *Apology*. The word *Syntagma* means an orderly arrangement or collection; and this *Syntagma* was a catalogue of the principal heresiarchs of the day, with a short sketch of the origin and errors of each; an indispensable handbook, one would think, for the bishops and elders of the period. It was very widely used, as is shown by its incorporation into the more extended heresiological works of Irenaeus and Hippolytus. The original has not come down to us; we only know it in these secondary forms; but it is not hard to identify some of the passages which have been taken from it, even though no acknowledgement has been made. We have drawn on it in our accounts of Simon Magus, Menander, Saturninus (as Justin spelt the name), Cerinthus, Basilides, Carpocrates, Valentine, and Marcion.

In his *Apology*, Justin speaks of Marcion as 'even now teaching those who have yielded to his persuasions', and says that 'he has persuaded a great number in every race, by the aid of the daemons, to deny God who is the Lord of the universe'. He regarded Marcion as the most formidable of the heretics and wrote a separate treatise on him, which has not come down to us, though no doubt its substance is incorporated into later works; for the authors of this period seldom took the trouble to write a thing for themselves if someone else had already done it satisfactorily. He did not pay much attention to Valentine. It is probable that he underestimated the extent of his errors and the danger that he presented to the church. It would seem that he did not sufficiently fortify the Roman church against Valentinianism (see Irenaeus, *Ad Haer.*, Preface).

SEMO SANCUS

We may trace to Justin the widespread conviction that Simon Magus was the father of all heresy. Simon had first appeared in Samaria, where he was excommunicated by Simon Peter, as we read in the Acts of the Apostles; but Justin does not refer to this record; he was born in Samaria, and had personal knowledge about the Simonian cult as it existed there in his own day. He was sensitive on the subject, and was concerned to distinguish himself from it.

As he was walking about Rome and examining its sacred places, he crossed the Fabrician bridge which leads from a point near the Theatre of Marcellus, to the Island. On the Island he says, he found a statue erected in honour of Simon Magus, with the inscription,

SIMONI DEO SANCTO
(To Simon the holy god)

He surmised, or was informed, that it had been erected in honour of the father of heresy about a hundred years before, when he had visited the city in the reign of Claudius and had so impressed the senate by his wonderful acts that they allowed the statue to be erected. He is so sure of this in the address to the emperor and senate in his *Second Apology*, that it is hard to believe that it was only a conjecture of his own, as many scholars would have us believe.

In 1574 an altar was discovered on the Island which bore an inscription beginning with these words.

SEMONI SANCO DEO FIDIO
(To Semo Sancus the god of good faith)

Semo Sancus was an old Sabine fertility god, who was a guarantor in the case of oaths; and more than one inscription of this sort, with his name in it, has been found. Now Justin may have seen this inscription, which may have had a statue over it; and he may have rashly identified it with Simon Magus and then permitted himself the conjecture that

16227

Simon had visited Rome in the days of Claudius and received this honour at that time. But it is hard to see how the sight of the statue would provide him with the name of the emperor in whose time Simon had paid this visit; and it is at least as likely that this conjecture, if it was a conjecture, was corroborated or even suggested by the evidence of others, perhaps of the Samaritan community at Rome, with which Justin would have contacts.

Justin includes the cult of Simon Magus, along with the sects of Valentine and Marcion, as one of the heresies with which Christians had to contend in his time. It is natural to suppose that the Samaritan community in Rome included a group which perpetuated the cult or teaching of Simon. They may even have combined it with the cult of the local fertility god, Semo Sancus, as the Jews of Apameia combined the cult of Jehovah with that of the local fertility god Sabazius. Such identifications were common in Hellenistic circles where various religions met. Justin had no motive for inventing the legend about the statue, if it was a legend; the local Simonians had such a motive, and the legend may have had some basis of truth. Perhaps the senate had permitted their cult; Origen says that the Simonians had no martyrs, which implies that they were a *religio licita* or legally recognized religion.

The Roman legend about the death of Simon is preserved by Hippolytus, and differs from the Syrian one which is told in the *Acts of Peter*. What it says is that Simon informed his followers that if they buried him alive he would rise again on the third day, which he failed to do. This could be a perversion of a legend, similar to that of John in the gnostic Acts, that the earth was observed to move above his grave, as if he were still breathing; or even of a fertility myth borrowed from the cult of Semo Sancus. None of the Syrian legends about Simon Magus and Peter appear in any early Roman source. The remarks of Justin about Simon have nothing to do with these legends; he obtained all his information in Samaria and in Rome.

THE SCHOOL OF JUSTIN

Justin established a school at Rome exactly as Cerdo and Marcion and Valentine had done. He propagated a philosophy or particular interpretation of Christianity, trained up personal disciples and produced a mass of literature. Unlike his rivals, he won the admiration and affection of the church at large.

One of his pupils was Tatian, an oriental with a brilliant mind and the rudiments of Greek culture, who came from the neighbourhood of Nisibis beyond the Euphrates. He called himself an Assyrian. Another was Irenaeus from Smyrna, a pupil of Polycarp. They serve to illustrate the cosmopolitan nature of Justin's school. It appears from the account of his martyrdom that it was a rallying-point for Asians and Phrygians. It was, in short a college of a non-Roman character, and may have been affiliated with the local community of Asian Christians, of whose existence we already know. The relations between Asia and Rome were still cordial, and the Roman church was strengthened in its contest with heresy by the establishment of an Asian theological school which it could trust.

A word may be said about the literature of Justin's school, of which we can infer something from his writings. He had, of course, the Old Testament in the Septuagint version; or, if he had not the full text of all the books which might be included in it, he had collections of extracts, some of which were made for liturgical or devotional purposes and some for controversy. Next to these he had the '*Apomnemoneumata*', the 'Relations' or 'Records' of the apostles, to which he also gave the name of *Euangelia*, Gospels. These certainly included the three synoptic Gospels, and possibly the fourth Gospel too, which he quotes on at least one occasion without mentioning however the source which he was using. This gospel must also have been one of the sources of his 'Logos' theology. He alludes to the Revelation as the work of the Apostle John. He makes use of the Epistles of St Paul occasionally, though he does not mention his name. The traces of the Acts are faint. An allusion is made to the Sibyl; and also to the *Acts of Pilate* which may be some extra-canonical book like the Gospel of Peter; or, as some scholars think, the reports of Pilate to the emperor, which Justin assumes the existence of. It would also appear that he knew the *Ascension of Isaiah*.

This is a peculiar and meagre list, but it must be remembered that a collection of his recognizable references and quotations gives only a meagre view of the books from which an author works. We are bound to assume that Justin's library of sacred books was considerably larger than this. There is also the difficulty that his quotations are never very exact; he has numerous slight variations from the canonical text, which are due to his habit of loose quotation or the influence of the oral tradition. In his classroom work, it would appear that sayings of Jesus from various Gospels were collected together and amalgamated with one another, and sometimes influenced by the catechisms. It is possible, too, that new Gospel texts were still being formed by combining the existing ones with one another and with sayings which were current orally.

The school of Justin may also have been a workshop where manuscripts were prepared. It may have provided the literary material out of which Tatian composed his harmony of the four Gospels.

THE WESTERN TEXT OF THE GOSPELS

It is unfortunate that no copy of the Gospels or of any other Christian book made at this date actually survives; but the dry science of textual criticism is able to make some inferences of value. The lines of research can be roughly summarized in this way. Whenever manuscripts are copied by hand, minor variations will be introduced into the text; and these minor variations will be transmitted to subsequent copies, and so on. A study of these variations enables one to group the manuscripts (or other authorities) into 'families' the members of which all exhibit the same characteristic variations, which must have had a common ancestor. We thus establish a type of text which was produced in some one channel of transmission, or in related channels; and we think in terms of common ancestors.

One such type of text is the so-called Western Text. It was used by Tatian and Irenaeus, who were both pupils of Justin; and, as far as we can see, something very like it was used by Justin himself. His methods of quotation do not enable us to fix this as precisely as we could wish; but it looks as if it was the kind of text which was used, or even produced in his workshop. Something very like it was produced in the workshop of Marcion, too, since it formed the basis of the text of his mutilated Luke. More interesting still, it was the type of text which was used for the Latin translation, which was made within a very few years, probably while Justin was still in Rome. It is easy to see why it has been called the Western Text. It seems to have been the type of text which was in general use in Rome in the hundred-and-fifties.

It does not follow, however, that it originated in Rome. The men who used it came from Asia Minor. We have to take into account, too, the fact that the Syriac gospels were translated about the end of the century from a rather similar type of text. It can be distinguished from the Western Texts; but it is, so to speak, a cousin. The textual critics think that this is true even when one has allowed for the influence of Tatian, who took back with him to the east a form of the Western Text as it was known in Rome. It is considered probable, therefore, that the Western Texts used in Rome, and the oriental text used for the Syriac translation, were derived from a common ancestor of still earlier date.

What is the character of the Western Text as compared with the texts of other families? It has a greater amount of free variation. It is not merely that the accidental variations are numerous; it is a question of alterations, assimilation of one Gospel to another, improvements in style or matter, and additions; especially additions, and particularly in Luke and Acts, which underwent a thorough rewriting at some early period. It would seem that scribes or teachers annotated their Gospels; they wrote in the margin, or between the lines, additional material, which might be incorporated into the text by the next copyist. Sometimes this additional material came from another Gospel, and sometimes from uncanonical sources or oral tradition; sometimes we can detect theological motives. Sometimes it was an improvement in the style, or at any rate a change. Sometimes it was an ingenious conjecture. In many western authorities we find the new ending to Mark; in practically all we find the woman taken in adultery.

A few interesting examples may be given. In the baptism of Jesus in Matthew a great light shines on the waters of the Jordan, and in Luke the voice from heaven says, 'This day have I begotten thee', not 'In thee I am well pleased.' When the Ethiopian is baptized in Acts, he is given a creed to say, 'I believe that Jesus Christ is the Son of God.' In the decree of the Jerusalem Council, the Gentiles are told to abstain from idol-offerings, from fornication and from blood, 'and what you do not wish to be done to yourselves, do not do to others...being carried by the Holy Spirit'. In the Last Supper in Luke, the account of the institution of the eucharist is much abbreviated; in the Garden of Gethsemane the sweat of the Lord is like great drops of blood falling to the earth, a reading which is found in Justin, though he omits the words 'of blood'.

Of course each case is carefully examined by the scholars on its merits, and it can be argued in certain cases that the Western Text has preserved the right reading. It may be intrinsically more probable, or it may be supported by other evidence. Its basic text, once the free variations are eliminated, has as much right to consideration as any other. It is argued, for instance, that the omissions of the Western Text are entitled to respect, since its tendency is to add; but any given omission may be due to accident or to theological prepossessions. The omission of the institution of the chalice in Luke, for instance, may be due to the influence of some heretical group which did not use wine in the sacrament. The Marcionites did not, for instance.

TEXTUAL VARIATIONS

In conclusion a few observations may be made. The first is that, numerous as the variations are, they do not make any significant alteration in the substance of the text; the great majority of them are merely superficial. Secondly, it looks as if nearly all the textual variants of any interest must have come into existence by about the year 150; for naturally the amount of free variation was greatest at the beginning, before the books were regarded as scripture. What occurred later was learned amendment. Thirdly, the process had taken a long time, and its analysis is a very complicated business. First came the stage of free variation, when most of the changes were due to the errors of copyists or well-intentioned correction from one motive or another; then came the revision of Luke and Acts, of which something was said in an earlier chapter, thus leaving in existence two texts of these books; then there was the production of the short version of Luke in the school of Marcion or his predecessors; and the short version of Romans, which was widely used; and lastly the dissemination of the text and its further development in its different traditions. The textual evidence provides data for the history of these books subsequent to the date of their first dissemination.

It is also an additional illustration of the fact that there was no central organization in the Christian church such as could have imposed a uniform text or a uniform New Testament on the catholic church. The production and distribution of the apostolic literature went on freely in more than one centre. The textual agreement which it possesses is an inheritance from its apostolic origins in the first century. Its diversity is due to its expansion. We do not yet know where the Western type of text originated, or how it reached Rome. We know about its dissemination there, simply because enough evidence comes in from the second half of the second century to prove it. At the end of the second century and the beginning of the third, enough evidence comes in from Alexandria to prove the existence of other independent types of text. This special, rather technical study, has its own very considerable historical value.

CHAPTER 7

THE *APOLOGY* OF JUSTIN

THE *APOLOGY* OF JUSTIN, *c.* A.D. 150

A great deal of interest attaches to what is called the *First Apology* of
Justin Martyr; for here we have at last an objective picture of what is
called primitive Christianity, with arguments in its favour, composed
by a leading intellectual with excellent knowledge. It comes at the end
of the third generation after the Crucifixion, allowing an average of
forty years to a generation; but two long lives easily cover such a period
of time; and Polycarp and Pius were both still living. The youth of one
was passed under the influence of John in Asia Minor, the youth of the
other under Clement in Rome. Justin belonged to the generation of
new men; but the old had not yet passed away.

The *Apology* of Aristides was not a long book. It could have been
read through at a single session, and may have been intended for this
purpose. The *Apology* of Justin was a longer and more ambitious enterprise. It was designed for careful reading and study. It gave a much
more complete picture of Christian faith and life; it met criticism on
various points; it argued that the policy of persecution was wrong; it
aimed at dispelling ignorance and prejudice; it produced logical and
philosophical proofs of the truth of the new religion. It cannot really
be said that Justin is a skilful writer; but he wins all hearts by his
simplicity and candour, which is touched with moral fervour and
accentuated by his indignation over the injustice of the persecutions
and his admiration for the fortitude of the martyrs. It was indeed the
faith of the martyrs that had predisposed him personally to accept the
new religion, though he attributed his conversion in the main to the
effect produced upon his mind by the books of the prophets and the
words of the Saviour. While he does not hesitate to reinforce his
arguments by references to a divine judgement both in this world and

that which is to come, his appeal is essentially a rational one. Christianity is put forward as the true philosophy, and he asks that it be understood. He does not argue the case like a lawyer, though he deals with the legal aspect of the matter briefly in his opening paragraphs; he argues like a philosopher, and his appeal is to the universal faculty of reason which the emperors honoured by their claim to piety and philosophy. His opening sentences emphasize this point of view.

It is reason itself which directs that those who are in very truth pious men and philosophers should honour and love the truth, and refuse to follow the doctrines of the ancients if they are worthless; for a sound reason is not content with forbidding us to follow those who acted or taught unjustly, but directs the lover of truth, even if he is threatened with death, that he must make up his mind to say and do what is just.

Now you are described as pious men and philosophers, and guardians of justice and lovers of education. Listen, therefore, and let it be proved whether you really are so. (Justin, *Apology*, II, 1.)

THE PRIMACY OF REASON

We are now in the same logical and terminological quandary that we found ourselves in when we studied the experiential theology of Hermas; for the word translated 'reason' is the word *logos* which can also be translated as 'word'. It has a long ancestry of usage in Jewish speculation, Stoic philosophy and Christian evangelism; and Justin heroically equates all three usages without really unifying his thinking. We must begin with the simple evangelical experience, which itself defies definition.

Justin accepts of course the Spirit theology of the old tradition which is represented by Hermas. He does not tell the emperors much about it; but the prophets and the virgins are there in the background. He speaks of the work of God in his soul by the name of the Word or Reason. Conviction of truth, especially of moral truth, is for him the voice of God, the primary inward revelation, for which he is prepared to die. This reason or word, that speaks in every human heart, is God in him, not merely he in converse with God: it is he, and it is not-he. The conception was familiar to the philosopher of the Stoic school; the element of reason in the being of man was a portion of the divine reason, a spark of the deity itself. The philosopher was a man set apart, a man devoted to the truth, a man who must be prepared to die for the truth that was in him. There had been examples in recent history, from the time of Nero downward; and Justin is prepared to accept them as authentic witnesses to God's truth. He quotes Socrates,[1] but he also quotes the quite recent Musonius, who had suffered under Domitian. The true philosopher, who suffered for the word of truth that was in him, was to some extent a Christian.

The breadth of this conception is astonishing. We need hardly say that it was not acceptable to everybody in the church. It looked as if Justin was taking into Christianity a quantity of Platonic and Stoic philosophy, just as Valentine and the gnostics were taking in a quantity of Hellenistic mythology and mystery lore. It raises the question to what extent the Christian church, in Justin and his successors, did affiliate itself to Greek learning and philosophy; and secondly to what extent this was a bad thing, or changed the character of the faith. We shall not attempt to answer these questions, which are beyond our scope or ability. What we must point out is the fundamental fact that in the Greek tradition everything had to justify itself at the bar of an impartial and universal reason, and Justin was sure that Christianity could do this. He had fallen in love with Christianity for two reasons; it was good, and it was rational. Aristides and his predecessors had insisted that it was good; it was Justin who first insisted that it was rational. From his time onward, Christians saw with increasing clarity that they must be able to make intelligent, logical and consistent statements about their religion.

THE THEOLOGY OF REASON

There was an opinion current in the second century that Jewish monotheism and Greek monotheism could be identified, as they are in the words of the pagan philosopher Numenius: 'What is Plato but Moses talking in Greek.' When one looks into this equation, it seems to amount to this, that both believed in a sole deity who governed the world by his providence or reason. There were grave differences, of course, in their ideas about the deity; but the experiential fact remained that both confessed faith in a universal God to whom they owed a moral allegiance.

[1] Socrates had used the word 'daemon' for the inward voice or power in which he recognized the guidance of the deity.

In accordance with the spirit of the age, both tended to conceive of God as remote or distinct from this world. Stoicism, indeed, approximated to pantheism and thought of God as the spirit of this world, animating it in the same way that the soul animates the body; but Platonists preferred to think of some divine medium or agency through which God worked on this world and in the heart of men. Justin interpreted the divine reason of the Stoics in this way; he rather Platonized the Stoic theology.

He has great difficulty in expressing this point of view. He had, it is true, the precedents of Philo, and even of St John; for in St John the logos or reason or word is the power by which God made the world, and also the light that illuminates every man who comes into the world, if that is the correct translation; but Justin attempted to define the matter more precisely. The divine reason is a second God. He is 'a second God in number, but not in mind'; that is to say, he is a second God and he is not a second God. Justin is not afraid to talk in paradoxes; but by doing so he falls into the same trap as Hermas. He commits himself to formulas that fall short of the standards of orthodoxy which were adopted at a later date. He imperils the fundamental doctrine of the 'monarchy' or sole sovereignty of God; a word which has a somewhat Aristotelian sound. But he wrote before the days of exact theology; he was a pioneer in the field of Christian philosophy, and uses many unguarded expressions; and he does not endear himself to us any the less by these signs of his primitive date.

Furthermore he had his other equations or identifications to consider. There was a Word of God in the Old Testament that came to the prophets. It came to Abraham; it came to Elijah; it came to Ananias, Azarias, and Misael in the burning fiery furnace. It was the authentic divine power which took hold upon the human heart in what is called evangelical or prophetic religion. And it was the same divine power which had come to Socrates and Heracleitus and Musonius Rufus. It had spoken with Moses out of the flame of fire, where Justin dares to speak of a fiery form. It had led the chosen people out of the land of Egypt. The Old Testament provided him with a personalized view of this mysterious divine power; but whereas in the older Hebrew tradition the Word was God himself in creation or revelation, mysteriously the same and mysteriously separate, in Justin he rather tends to become an agent; an angel or apostle, who speaks and acts on behalf of the High God, though indeed he is God. He is another and not another.

Then there is the most audacious equation of all, which identifies the Logos or Word with the divine being who became man by being born of the Virgin Mary, and taught his disciples personally, as a man, the truths of which the prophets and philosophers had only received a partial revelation.

This series of identifications establishes a system of a sort, though it does not resolve the intellectual difficulties which it creates. The fact is that it simply enables Justin to make use of his different categories by passing imperceptibly from one to the other. At one point he is speaking of the divine power by which the Hebrew God made the heaven and the earth; at another it is the divine agent in Hebrew history and revelation; at another it is the universal reason of the Stoic and Platonic philosophy; at another it is Jesus of Nazareth; and at another it is the truth which reveals itself in the heart of every man as absolute reality. The same divine power manifests itself in these different ways. It is a sketch for a philosophy; but not a philosophy.

THE DAEMONS AND THE PASSIONS

Justin is thus enabled to speak in the name of the true and virtuous reason which is common to all men, and call for an impartial investigation into the persecution of men of every race who are suffering under unmerited hatred and slander. The only charge against them is that they are called *Christians;* and they are put to death simply on account of this name. If they were found guilty of some actual crime there would be no cause for complaint; but no serious investigation has ever been made. They confess the Name, and they are put to death; they deny the Name and they are acquitted. Some of them, no doubt, are evil-doers, but why should all suffer because of that? A wise discrimination is shown in the case of the philosophers, and why not in the case of the Christians too?

The persecution of Christians is not an act of reason, therefore; it is an act of passion. In Stoic ethics a passion or emotion is regarded as a minor form of madness. It is an irrational element in the soul, which wise men learn to control by means of reason. The persecution of Christians, not being an act of reason, must be an act of passion or temporary madness.

What, then, is the cause of the insane passions which inspire persecution? Justin has no doubt about this. They are due to the influence of 'daemons'. In the Platonic schools, the 'daemons' were disembodied spirits, lower in degree than the gods. They were not regarded as evil; on the contrary they were, for the most part, good. Justin had believed in them before his conversion, and he continued to believe in them after his conversion; but he now thought of them as evil. He does not precisely identify them with the pagan deities. Aristides had said that the gods were either deified men, or personifications of the physical elements, or myths which originated in ritual; eminently rational conclusions. There was another view, however. They were the false fronts behind which the evil 'daemons' hid themselves in order to delude mankind and establish their tyranny over them. Christians who had been pagans only a year or two previously were only too well aware of the evil power and spirituality which existed in the cults which they had left, and were prepared to accept the theory of daemons as an adequate explanation of it. There was something, they felt, that haunted the temples, inspired the devotees, expressed itself in the myth and ritual, maddened the enthusiasts, sent the dreams, and worked the magic. It could well be personified and so given substantial existence under the name of daemons.

There was a myth at hand which gave a more dramatic expression to the belief. It was the old Hebrew myth of the fallen angels, which was cognate with the Greek myth of the Titans. It is excluded from the canonical books of the Old Testament, though it appears to have left a trace here and there; but it is fully told in the apocryphal *Book of Enoch*, which was very well known at that time in the Christian church, though it was not in any sense canonical. Hermas probably knew it; it is quoted in Jude and Barnabas; and it is discussed by Tertullian, who champions its claims. It tells the tale of the angels who fell from heaven, how they lusted after the daughters of men, how they begot giants, how they taught mankind charms and enchantments, how they fell to unnatural sin of all kinds, and how last of all they palmed themselves off as gods, or deluded mankind with temples and images, so that they might enjoy the rich offerings and sacrifices. It was these daemons who drove on their devotees to attack and persecute the Christians.

A nexus is thus established between the daemons and the passions which is similar to the nexus between the Word of God and the Logos conceived as the reasoning power in man. The divine reason leads the

Christian philosopher to attack polytheism; the unholy daemons excite the passions of pagan society to attack the Christians. Passion fights reason; reason fights passion. The mythological dramatization of the facts of history corresponds exactly to the psychological dramatization of the conflict in the soul.

PAGAN PARALLELS TO THE GOSPEL

In the *Dialogue* at Ephesus, Trypho had asked Justin about the parallels which existed between the Christian gospel and the pagan myths; the 'virgin births', the violent deaths, the resurrections and the ascensions. Justin brings this question up for further consideration in his *Apology*. He refers to the stories of Hermes, Asclepius, Dionysus, Heracles, the Dioscuri, Perseus and Bellerophon. He has an interesting and original answer to the question. Everything in the life of Jesus had been predicted by the Hebrew prophets. As he turns the pages of his Septuagint or book of Testimonies, and reads the words of the Hebrew prophets he sees the incarnation, crucifixion, resurrection, and ascension, with other Christian verities, prefigured by men who wrote long before; as much as five thousand years before, Justin thought, in some cases. It is his great 'argument from Prophecy', his favourite and probably his most effective argument. He favours the emperors with a great deal of it.

Now if the whole course of history and all the main points of the Christian gospel had been prefigured or predicted in the Hebrew prophets, it was perfectly possible for the daemons to obtain a preview of the plan of salvation and incorporate some of its features in the myths. Thus the god of the mysteries, Dionysus, riding on his ass, was an imitation of the expected ruler from Judah with his ass and his vine and his robes stained with blood. Similar Hebrew sources were found for Bellerophon riding his horse in heaven; Perseus, born of a virgin, and also ascending into heaven; Heracles like a giant running his course; and Asclepius healing the sick. But none of the sons of Zeus had been crucified. The daemons had missed this mighty symbol of strength and government, since the prophets had veiled it in baffling figures of speech. And yet it was everywhere visible in human affairs; in the mast of a ship, in the structure of a plough, and even in the upright figure of a man; even in the standards of the imperial army. The latter remark explains, perhaps, how Christian soldiers in the Roman Army reconciled themselves to the adoration which they were obliged to give to the *vexillum*. They saw the cross in it.

Justin, therefore, looked upon the pagan myths and mysteries as daemonic imitations of the Gospel; and not content with these, the daemons had put out others since the coming of Christ. He is referring to the heresies. He mentions specifically Simon and Menander, and the image of Simon which had been set up in the days of Claudius. He refers also to Marcion of Pontus and his numerous followers, who regard him as the only one to understand the truth and laugh at us though they have no proof for what they say. Justin is thinking of his own system of theology, which was so securely guaranteed by the proof from prophecy.

CHRISTIAN MONOTHEISM

Such is the system of theology which Justin worked out, with the help of the best science and learning of the day; in particular, the theory of the Logos, the theory of daemons, and the allegorical interpretation of holy texts. What interests us is that he thought it right to apply current philosophic concepts to his thinking about Christianity, and current methods of literary criticism to its holy books. If the results are sometimes rather fantastic, we may be sure that they did not seem fantastic at the time. Our own attempts at literary criticism may seem equally fantastic when they are reviewed a few centuries from now; if anyone troubles to do so.

He does not confine himself to argumentation, however. He gives an objective account of Christian faith and life which is of a totally different character from his argumentative passages, though it is interwoven with them. He has to meet the charge that Christians are 'atheists', that is to say, they fail to reverence the accepted deities by going through the customary rites and ceremonies. We refuse, says Justin, to honour with many sacrifices or with garlands of flowers the gods who are formed by men and set up in temples; they are lifeless and dead.

We *are* atheists [he says], so far as such supposed gods are concerned; but not in respect of the most true God, the Father of righteousness and chastity and similar virtues, unmixed with evil; he is the God we reverence and adore, and also the Son who came from him and taught us these things, and the army of good angels who follow him and are being made like unto him; and the prophetic Spirit too; honouring them in Word and in truth, and handing on ungrudgingly the tradition as we were taught it to all who wish to learn.

(Justin, *Apology*, 1, 6.)

Once again Justin has committed a theological blunder; he has combined an old apocalyptic formula about Jesus and the angels with an old Trinitarian formula, thereby putting the angels on a level with the Father and the Holy Spirit; but in any case the passage is liturgical, not dogmatic. It sets the tone for other passages which follow; for what he has to show is that Christians do have a rich tradition of worship, and are not 'atheists' who ignore the deity.

What sustains them in their devotion to truth is their longing for the eternal and pure life with that God who is the father and maker of the universe. He created all things in the beginning out of formless matter, for the sake of mankind; and all who prove themselves worthy by their works will have a part in his passionless and incorruptible 'kingdom'; a word which he has to explain, since it has been misunderstood. He refers it to the day of judgement when some will go to eternal punishment and some to salvation, in accordance with their deeds, which are not hid from God. He points out that this faith in God is a great assistance to the government, since it predisposes Christians to act virtuously. He discreetly says nothing about a millennial kingdom to be established on this earth, which was not accepted by all Christians.

The climax of his account of Christian monotheism is another passage on the worship of the Creator, who needs no blood-offerings or libations or clouds of incense; or so Christians were taught.

We speak to him with a word of prayer and thanksgiving (*eucharistia*) over everything that we offer; we praise him with all our power; for this is the only honour we can bring him that is worthy of him.

We do not waste in the fire the good things which he has given us for our food, but bring them for ourselves and those who are in need.

In thankfulness to him, therefore, we send up with a word our solemnities and chants, [praying] that we may have whatever is needful for our health, and various good things, and the changes of the seasons, and our return in incorruption through faith in him. (Justin, *Apology*, 1, 13.)

The picture is that of the eucharistic sacrifice. The meaning of the reference to the word is not perfectly clear. He means probably in the first place that the offering of praise and thanksgiving was directed to God in spoken prayers, and not in sacrificial victims, libations, and garlands; but it can hardly be understood apart from his doctrine of the Logos. It is the service offered in words as an act of the divine reason.

THE TEACHINGS OF THE WORD

Justin is not content, as Aristides was, merely to repeat clauses of the catechisms when he comes to describe the altruistic and other-worldly life of the Christians; he attempts it, but soon passes to the actual words of Jesus in whom the divine reason was incarnate. They are taken out of his own class-room practice, or possibly from the forms of teaching given in divine service. They are arranged in topics and have been selected from more than one Gospel, though the Sermon on the Mount of St Matthew predominates. Sayings from different Gospels have been combined, and even expanded under the influence of the catechisms. The topics are,

(1) Concerning chastity.
(2) Concerning loving one another.
(3) On communicating to the needy and not doing it for glory.
(4) Concerning unrevengefulness, and being of service to all, and not wrathful.
(5) Concerning not swearing at all, and always speaking truth.
(6) How one must worship one God only.
(7) Not only those who talk but those who do works will be saved.

The section on chastity is an important one because serious charges of sexual misconduct had been brought against Christians. No doubt the teaching about loving one another and the custom of the holy kiss were misunderstood. Justin explains that the standards are so high that only one marriage is permitted, and the desire for adultery is equally culpable with the act, the very thought which had so dismayed Hermas. Many Christians lived a chaste unmarried life; he knew of men and women of sixty or seventy years of age who had been made disciples in childhood and had never lost their chastity. The statement gives us a glimpse of a group of veteran Christians who had been baptized as children in the days of John and Clement, and had never declined from the lofty standards which had been impressed upon them then; but Justin does not deny that there were some who had.

He concludes this section with an eighth topic on the payment of taxes to the imperial government. The emperors would hear for the first time the famous saying, 'Render unto Caesar the things that are Caesar's and unto God the things that are God's.' They would learn that worship belonged to God alone, but that the Christians were prepared to serve their kings and rulers and to offer prayers on their behalf. They had nothing to fear from the Christians, therefore, but he reminds them that all kings had died the common death, and were liable like everyone else to the punishment of eternal fire.

He supports the doctrine of eternal fire from pagan sources. He quotes the Sibyl and an unknown Persian writer named Hystaspes. He also refers to the Stoic doctrine that the universe was periodically dissolved by fire.

THE SACRAMENTAL ORDER

We may omit from our survey the long series of extracts from the Old Testament and the inferences which Justin draws from them. It is interesting that they follow his extracts from the Gospels, just as he says they do in the liturgy itself. After these comes a plain straightforward account of the liturgy which is one of the most important of early Christian documents.

It is preceded by an almost incomprehensible piece of Christian gnosis, in which he links Plato with Moses, and then with the help of both imparts a mystic vision of creation which tells of the Word of God that called the primal light into existence, and of the Spirit that moved upon the face of the waters; it finds room for the sign of the cross, which was prefigured in the brazen serpent; and the hidden Name, which was communicated to Moses out of the flame of fire; for the mysteries of Genesis and Exodus formed the background of the baptismal ritual from the beginning. The Spirit moves again upon the waters, the threefold Name is solemnly uttered, and the new man is created. 'Egypt' is left behind and the land of promise entered.

He then describes objectively the actual rite and explains how we dedicate ourselves and are new-made in Christ. Those who are convinced, and believe in the truth of the Christian teachings, and undertake to live in accordance with them, go through a period of prayer and fasting in companionship with those who are already Christians, asking God for the forgiveness of their former sins. Then they are brought to some place where there is water and are born again by the new birth, in the name of the God who is Father and lord of the universe, and of our Saviour Jesus Christ, and of the Holy Spirit; for Christ said, 'Unless you are born again, you shall not enter the kingdom of heaven'—a loose quotation of John iii. 3. An explanation follows, in which he gives texts from the prophets and refers to what he regards as daemonic imitations of baptisms in the ceremonies of the pagan temples.

He now returns to the baptismal rite. The candidate who has received the 'illumination' is brought before the 'brothers', as they are called, who offer 'common prayers' for themselves, for him and for all men everywhere, praying earnestly that we, who are disciples of the Truth, may be found good members of the community in our works, and keepers of the commandments which we have received, so that we may be saved with an eternal salvation.[1] When the prayers are over we salute one another with a kiss. Then a loaf of bread with a cup of wine and water is brought forward to the president of the brethren, who takes it and sends up praise and glory to the Father of all things, through the name of his Son, and through the holy Spirit, and gives thanks (*eucharistian*) at great length for our being counted worthy to receive such things from him. At the conclusion of the prayers and eucharist the whole people that is present gives its assent by saying 'Amen', which is a Hebrew word which can be translated 'So be it'.

After the eucharistic prayer of the president and the assent of the people the deacons distribute to all who are present a portion of the eucharistic bread and of the wine and water. And they carry it away to those who are absent.

The general outline of procedure is much the same as what we found in the *Didache*, though different points are emphasized in the two documents. The *Didache* did not describe the introduction of the newly baptized into the prayer-life of the brethren and their first participation in the kiss and in the prayers. It is the moment which afterwards received the name of confirmation, but neither the *Didache* nor Justin says anything about the gift of the Holy Spirit; they are silent, too, about any laying on of hands or anointing, such as we find a generation later in the rites known to Tertullian and Hippolytus; but this does not prove that they were not in use. We have to remember that Justin was

[1] For 'disciples' and 'commandments' see Matthew xxviii. 19 f. and Ignatius to the Romans, III, 1, where making disciples is equivalent to baptizing. Cf. Vol. I, p. 454.

not giving instructions for carrying out the rites, but composing a short account of them for the emperors with the object of showing that there was nothing unseemly about them, and that they constituted a real form of worship of the universal deity through Jesus Christ. He adds a short explanation, as he did in the case of baptism, explaining that the bread and wine which have been made into 'eucharist' by a word of prayer which comes from God (or Christ) are not received as if they were ordinary food, but are the flesh and blood of the incarnate Jesus Christ. He quotes from the 'Records of the Apostles', which are called Gospels, the command of Jesus himself to make this act of memorial, and he does not fail to indicate that daemonic parodies of the rite are in existence, mentioning specifically the mysteries of Mithras.

THE SUNDAY ASSEMBLY

Justin follows the same general plan as the author of the *Didache* by making a second reference to the eucharist in his account of the Sunday-morning assembly. After our baptism and first communion, he says, we continued to remind each other of them; we are constantly together; we bless the Father of all through his Son Jesus Christ and the Holy Spirit, over everything we offer; and on the day called Sunday we assemble in the same place; we read the 'Records of the Apostles' or the writings of the prophets so long as time permits; and when the reading is over the president utters an admonition or invitation to imitate these excellent persons. Then everybody stands up together and offers prayers; after which the eucharist and communion follow as before. Those who are well off, and wish to do so, make a contribution which is entrusted to the president, who has the care of the widows and orphans, the sick and the needy, the prisoners and the strangers, and all who are in distress. He is their trustee or caretaker.

This general assembly was held on a Sunday because it was the 'first day', when God transformed the darkness and the matter and made an orderly world; and Jesus Christ rose from the dead on this same day. On the day previous to Saturn's day they crucified him, and on the sun's day, as it is called, he appeared to his disciples and taught them those things which we now submit for your perusal. Justin thinks that if his exposition of the Christian religion is in line with reason and truth, the emperors should honour it. If it seems to be the ravings of lunacy, or 'mania', they are at liberty to despise it; but on no account should they treat it with hostility. They may be sure that they will not escape from the impending judgement of God if they continue in their course of injustice. He appends a copy of the epistle of the great and glorious Caesar, 'Hadrian your father', in which he forbade the hunting down of Christians; and this rather suggests that the similar directive of Antoninus himself to the cities of Greece had not yet been issued. Hadrian's rescript had been issued twenty-five years earlier, about the time of Justin's conversion.

And so the *First Apology* ends.

THE LITURGY IN JUSTIN

Four points may briefly be mentioned in connexion with this notable liturgical text. The first is that it is not necessarily Roman. For all we know Justin may have composed the greater part of his *Apology* before he came to Rome. When he got there, he may have attended the liturgy of the Asian community. Possibly the local variations in the liturgy were not of great importance; or his lack of detail on many points may be due to a desire to present a picture of the service as it was offered everywhere.

The second is that the expression 'President of the brethren' is a non-technical description of the local bishop, just as 'Records of the Apostles' is a non-technical description of the Gospels. It has been suggested that this president was a chairman who was chosen for the occasion; but it must be a permanent official who takes responsibility for the administration of the church funds and looks after widows, orphans, sick people, prisoners and strangers, and is in short the trustee or caretaker of all who are in need. The word 'caretaker' would be a good synonym for the word *episcopos*, which has a very similar meaning in its secular use. We have here a clear picture of the Christian bishop, who is the chief actor in the liturgy, the principal teacher in the church and the steward of the household of God. It helps us to visualize the position of such venerable and apostolic men as Pius of Rome or Polycarp of Smyrna, with their staff of deacons. It is the council of elders that fails to appear.

The third point is the reading of lections from the New Testament and the Old, which he refers to as apostles and prophets, putting them in that order; but the only apostolic books which he actually mentions are the Gospels. He does not refer to other apostolic literature, but this would not be necessary in addressing the emperors.

The fourth point is that he makes no reference to psalms or hymns. We have various references to singing, and even (by way of symbolism or metaphor) to instrumental music, in Paul, John, Pliny and Ignatius; but it is a pity that none of our authorities give us clearer information on the use of the Psalms and other hymns or chants in the primitive church. Justin shows a great deal of interest in the Psalms as liturgical and devotional texts; and is said to have written a book called the *Psaltes*, or 'Performer on the Harp'.[1] It would seem that they had their place, but that is the most that can be said.

[1] But this might be a commentary on the Psalms of David; he comments on a number of Psalms in the *Dialogue*.

CHAPTER 8

THE MARTYRDOM OF POLYCARP

POLYCARP'S VISIT TO ROME

Pius, the bishop of Rome, died about 154, and was succeeded by
Anicetus. The figures which are given in connexion with the old
episcopal lists work out at 155–6–7; but we are obliged to place it a
little earlier so as to allow room for the visit of St Polycarp to Rome,
which must have taken place before his martyrdom in February of 155
or 156; for the object of his visit was to see the new bishop.

It is clear from the fact of the synchronism that Polycarp visited
Rome in honour of his accession, if not to be present at his election and
consecration. It was now about forty years since he had planned to
visit Antioch for the council which was held there when the see was
vacant by the martyrdom of St Ignatius; and, knowing the determination of his character, we may feel sure that he actually attended, unless
circumstances made it completely impossible. The present occasion was
a rather similar one. A veteran bishop, one of the elders of the whole
catholic church, had passed to his rest; a successor was being installed
in his place or had been installed.

The position of Anicetus was not easy. There were bodies of
Christians, or so-called Christians, who refused to accept him as their
bishop. We learn, for instance, that Valentine continued into his time
and that Marcion waxed strong. The differences and divisions which
occur at episcopal elections must have accentuated the gravity of the
situation. In such circumstances recognition by bishops of other
countries must have been looked for, and Anicetus would greatly value
the support of the pupil of St John and the tutor of St Irenaeus, who
must by now have been the most influential figure in the Christian
world. His visit made a deep impression on the Roman church and
Irenaeus records that many Christians who had joined the heretical

schools returned to its communion. We depend on Irenaeus for the story of this visit, and it is possible that he was in Rome at the time. He appends to it the tale of the attempt of Marcion to secure recognition from the aged disciple of St John, and the spirited reply, 'I recognize you as the first-born of Satan.' If we assume that this encounter took place during Polycarp's visit to Rome, as seems natural, we note that age had not robbed him of his characteristic vigour; for he was now eighty-four or eighty-five.

Many matters were discussed between the two bishops, and it has been suggested that a synod or council of visiting bishops took place. The points of difference were easily composed, Irenaeus says. They did not choose to be too contentious about the exact day of the Paschal fast. Polycarp was not prepared to abandon the tradition which he had received from St John, and Anicetus would not surrender the tradition of the Roman elders, a word of great honour in the Roman tradition which is used here to include the succession of bishops. The controversy was not allowed to disturb the harmony of the occasion. Anicetus conceded to Polycarp his own position as celebrant at the eucharist, and the concordat sanctioned by Bishop Xystus was allowed to continue. The alliance between Asia and Rome was firmly cemented.

The episode supplies a good background for a statement which Irenaeus made at a later date about the catholic tradition. We have seen that the witness was a dispersed witness, its authority being distributed among the various churches of apostolic foundation. Among these he very naturally singles out the churches of Asia and the church of Rome, which he calls the churches in 'the central parts of the world'. To Rome however, he allots a position of stronger leadership; *potentiorem principalitatem* are the words, as we find them in the Latin translation (*Ad. Haer.* III, 3, 1), for the Greek original has not survived. It was necessary, he adds, for every church to meet at Rome, since the faith was preserved there by the faithful who visited it from every quarter. This position as an international centre, where bishops, teachers and prophets from all parts of the empire and even beyond its borders, could meet together and so contribute to the preservation of the faith, was maintained until the end of the century. This picture agrees with the other evidence. During this whole period, from about 150 to about 200, we do not know for certain of a single eminent Roman-born teacher; they are all foreigners. The bishops may have been Roman-born, but from Linus to Pius only two (or three) out of nine have Latin names; between Pius and Victor all the names are Greek, and Greek is still the language of the church.

If we ask where the strong witness in the church is to be found after the death of Polycarp, we are bound to say that it passes to Rome. It passes to the church itself and its succession of bishops, rather than to any individual; the individual who stands highest after the death of Polycarp would probably be Justin, who is now accepted as a Roman teacher, and becomes a Roman martyr.

THE EPISTLE OF THE SMYRNEANS

Shortly after his return to Smyrna, either in 155 to 156, Polycarp met his death by way of martyrdom. We have not been so fortunate as to have a record of a martyrdom other than the Passion of Jesus himself and those of Stephen, James the Just and Symeon ben Clopas: all Palestinian.[1] These are the first 'Acts of the martyrs', designed perhaps for liturgical use at their anniversaries, and so related as to recall the Passion narrative itself and to assimilate the martyr to his Lord. Our account of the martyrdom of Polycarp belongs to this class of literature, which appears to have been well established by this time. It was composed by a certain Marcianus, on behalf of the 'church of God sojourning at Smyrna', and addressed to the 'church of God sojourning at Philomelium' and 'to all sojournings in every place of the holy and catholic church'. The technical terms here used are very interesting. The verb *paroikein* means to reside as a stranger or alien in a foreign city and is translated in the English Bible as 'sojourn'. Its use in the Christian church goes back to I Peter, an Epistle written in view of martyrdom and specially valued by Polycarp; it emphasizes the fact that all Christians are strangers and pilgrims in this world. Clement uses it in addressing the church of Corinth, and Polycarp in addressing the church of Philippi. It has now provided a new technical term in the word *paroikia*, a 'sojourning', which comes down to us almost unchanged in the word 'parish'. The *paroikia*, or sojourning, was the local Christian community under its bishop (what we would call his diocese) in contrast to the world-wide or 'catholic' church of which it is a part. The word 'catholic', which we first noticed in Ignatius, is also a tech-

[1] For Jewish examples see IV Maccabees and the Ascension of Isaiah.

nical term by now, and is used of the world-wide confederation of legitimate *paroikiai*.

The use of the word is particularly suitable here, because Polycarp of Smyrna had become a 'catholic' or universal figure, like Ignatius of Antioch or Clement of Rome before him. He had grown in strength and glory and occupied a unique position as a link with the apostolic age. Locally he was 'the blessed Polycarp', the 'most marvellous Polycarp, who had been in our times an apostolic and prophetic teacher, and bishop of the holy church in Smyrna'. The heathen called him 'the teacher of Asia, the father of the Christians, the destroyer of our gods, teaching men not to sacrifice or worship'. Allowing something for the literary style of Marcianus, we are still left with a picture of a powerful personality in a strong position. It is a mistake to read the records of primitive Christianity in terms of unpractical other-worldly idealists without any flesh-and-blood organization or interests. In actual fact we have a picture of a vigorous and turbulent democratic life balanced by an apostolic and prophetic leadership which was given increasing constitutional authority. Celsus does not picture the Christian bishops as lean ascetics; he says they were the kind of men you would choose to captain a band of brigands. The bishop was a man of authority and prestige, who had an adequate staff and resources. He was regarded with reverence and awe. The respect in which Polycarp was held may be measured by the simple fact that he had not been in the habit of taking off his own shoes; this was a duty which any of the faithful were ready and willing to perform as a tribute to his character and great age. It is the service which John the Baptist said that he was unworthy to perform for his strong successor; it was the work of a personal slave or servant. A man of any position did not dress or undress or bathe himself.

THE PERSECUTION AT SMYRNA, A.D. 155 OR 156

It was in the month of January of 155 or 156. Philip of Tralles, the Asiarch and high priest of the imperial cultus, was in Smyrna, to be present at the annual games as one of the duties of his office. Statius Quadratus, the proconsul, was also present to take official part in them. It was a festival occasion. Twelve Christians were to be given to the fire or to the wild beasts. Some of them were Phrygians from Philadelphia. One of these Phrygians, named Quintus, had voluntarily surrendered himself as a martyr and had persuaded a number of others to do the same. It accorded with the highly emotional Phrygian temperament and with the theology of enthusiasm which was cultivated in those parts, but it was not approved by the church, Marcianus says, 'because it is not what the gospel teaches'. There were Phrygian enthusiasts who did not agree with Marcianus on this point.

The more cautious attitude towards martyrdom is exemplified in Polycarp and defended by Marcianus. Acting on advice rather than inclination, Polycarp withdrew to a property in the country with a number of his clergy, including Marcianus himself, we would judge. Cyprian of Carthage and other leading men did the same in similar circumstances. It was a matter of policy rather than flight, though flight is counselled in the Gospels. 'When they persecute you in one city', we read, 'flee unto another.' It was a question of preserving the sacred order and administration intact. A persecution was an act of war upon the church; it required direction and organization on the Christian side; there were prisoners to be ministered to; the faithful had to be organized in prayer, the waverers encouraged, the families of prisoners supported, and so forth.

We have very few particulars about the opening days of the festival, of which, it would appear, Marcianus was not an eyewitness. He tells us how the victims were scourged with the Roman *flagellum*, a whip with leather lashes reinforced with lead; it tore the skin and flesh so as to expose the veins and inner organs. Many of the martyrs bore this without a groan; it seemed that they were with Christ in the spirit, or that the Lord was conversing with them. The exaltation of the martyr in the Spirit closely resembled the ecstasy of the prophet, in which he saw visions and heard voices. 'Attending to the grace of Christ, they despised worldly torments, and worked out their eternal punishment in a single hour.' This is, no doubt, the conventional language of martyrology, but it is of great historical, theological and psychological importance; it expresses in ultimate existential language the sheer dynamic faith which was at the core of the gospel; a faith which persecution served to intensify.

The fire seemed cold to these martyrs when compared with that which is eternal and unquenchable. They could endure it, because they saw before their mind's eye those good things which ear heard not, and eye saw not, nor did it ascend into the heart of man; but the Lord revealed it to to them because they were no longer men but angels.

And so it came to pass [Marcianus says] in the case of those who were condemned to the wild beasts, or suffered terrible tortures, or whose flesh was scraped off with shells, with the object of turning them, if it were possible, to denial... for there were many devices which the devil brought against us.

Marcianus brings his theology of persecution to an end with this mention of the devil; for how could Christians doubt that the men who operated these 'devices' and the crowds who took a delirious pleasure in watching them were impelled by a non-human frenzy? If it required a more than human fortitude to withstand these tortures, it also required a more than human ferocity and hatred to inflict them. The half-mythological language of Justin about the daemons, and the half-mythological language of the Revelation of Peter about eternal fire giving to spiritual realities a poetic form and substance, are explained now as being in origin the language of a martyr church, which had to assert in words which completely satisfied it the existential reality of the spiritual situation.

Marcianus mentions two men by name, one for eternal shame and one for eternal glory. One was Quintus the Phrygian, whose courage failed him when he saw the wild beasts, so that he was persuaded by the proconsul to 'swear and sacrifice'. The other was the noble Germanicus who lept upon the wild beasts, as Ignatius had resolved to do, wishing to pass quickly from this unjust and lawless life. The crowd marvelled at the nobility of the god-loving and god-fearing race of Christians, shouting 'Away with the atheists!' and 'Search out Polycarp!' The whole scene in the stadium has thus been brought before our eyes and for the first time we see what was meant by the popular clamour which Hadrian had deprecated.

THE ARREST OF POLYCARP

Polycarp, meanwhile, spent his time, night and day, in prayer for all his people in their hour of ordeal, 'and for all the churches throughout the world', as was his custom. The universal church was in his mind. If he were to fail when he saw the wild beasts it would be a day of defeat not only for Smyrna, but also for the catholic church and for the gospel of Christ. He stood now where Ignatius had stood forty years before, but with an even clearer consciousness of what it meant. His character and bearing were, of course, very different; for he was stolid, unemotional, and short of speech. Yet he had his visions. Three days before his martyrdom he dreamed that his pillow was on fire, and said to his company, 'I must be burned alive.' It would appear, therefore, that his heart was set on martyrdom, not on escape.

The 'pursuers' were now coming near, and Marcianus tells how Polycarp and his company moved to another farm; and a third flight could have been arranged if he had consented. On arriving at his first place of refuge, the officers found two of his slaves and tortured them until one of them confessed where he had gone. Justin had spoken of torture being applied to slaves in order to make them give evidence against their masters, and so does Athenagoras, rashly adding that they never did so. It follows that Christians were often men with estates and properties, and not, as some romantics think, mainly of the slave class themselves.

The narrative now begins to draw out the likeness between the martyrdom of Polycarp and the Passion of our Lord, which was fundamentally a strong and realistic sentiment, though it was compatible with some artificialities and led to an unbalanced reverence for the martyr. It was no doubt a very real thing, however, for those who lived through it, or died through it. The name of the 'officer of the peace', who was in charge of the pursuers, was Herod, and he was accompanied by his father Nicetes, whose sister Alke had received a special message of affection from Ignatius forty years previously. They had with them the wretched young slave who had played the part of Judas, the betrayer. It was a Friday at supper-time, and they found Polycarp in the upper room. They were amazed at his age and erect bearing. He invited them to eat and drink as his guests and asked for an hour in which to pray. He stood in prayer for about two hours, Marcianus says, remembering by name all those who had accompanied him and all the catholic church throughout the world; and when the hour was come to go forth, they mounted him on an ass, and brought him into the city, it being the Great Sabbath, a day which has now been identified with the Jewish feast of Purim, not with the Passover as older scholars thought.

On the way to the stadium, Herod and Nicetes did their best to

9. GLADIATORIAL COMBAT

10. THE SHRINE OF ST PETER

persuade him to deny; for the glory of breaking down the champion would be greater for them than the glory of making him a martyr, and far more damaging to the church. 'What harm can there be', they asked him, 'in saying Caesar is Lord, and making the offering, and so forth, and saving yourself?'

He kept them waiting for an answer for a considerable time, and all he said was, 'I do not propose to do what you advise.'

It was the first of a number of matter-of-fact answers, which were very different in character from the heroics of the more emotional brethren.

THE WITNESS OF THE MARTYR

The scene now changes to the crowded stadium, with its bedlam of angry voices. It was the afternoon of 23 February 155, or 22 February 156. The wild-beast show, the so-called dog-hunt, was over. We think naturally of the counsels which Ignatius had given to him; 'time for continual prayer...stand firm like an anvil under the blows...it is the part of a great athlete to be beaten and to conquer'. There were not wanting among the Christians present those who heard voices from heaven. 'Be strong, Polycarp,' a voice was heard to say, 'be strong and play the man.'

And now he stands before the proconsul, whose duty it was to certify the guilt of the accused, and the usual persuasions begin, 'Show some respect for your old age', they said. 'Swear by the genius of Caesar. Repent, and say, Away with the atheists!'

Polycarp groaned and looked up to heaven. 'Away with the atheists!' he said, indicating by a motion of his hand the crowd of howling heathen who filled the stadium.

'Swear, and I will release you. Revile Christ.'

'Eighty and six years have I been his servant, and he has done me no wrong. How can I blaspheme my King who saved me?'

It is the great saying of the century. It brings before us the lapse of time since the days when the apostles were preaching the gospel, and Roman armies encircled Jerusalem. Eighty and six years take us back to the year 69 or 70, when Polycarp began his life in Christ. He knew the answers to all the questions which the historian would like to ask; he knew Philip and Aristion and John; he had seen the development of the episcopate into a universal apostolic order; he had welcomed the

Gospels of Matthew and John when they were new; he had heard the Revelation when it was first unrolled in his own church of Smyrna, and a special message given to that church, 'Be thou faithful unto death, and I will give thee a crown of life.' It is fortunate for the historian that the Asian teachers laid great stress on seniority and therefore had a way of referring to their ages. Polycrates, for instance, who was bishop of Ephesus about 190, gave his age at that time as sixty-five; he was therefore about thirty years old when Polycarp died. He speaks of seven members of his own family who had been bishops, and some of these must have been in office at this time. He mentions the martyrdom of Polycarp at Smyrna, and of Thraseas of Eumeneia at the same place. A whole series of lives and events are thus seen to interlock, and fall into place along a hundred years of continuous history.

The interrogation went on. 'Swear by the genius of Caesar', the proconsul said again. The one question which was fatal to the Christian was purposely being delayed. Polycarp was being given the opportunity to evade it; but he went straight to the point himself.

'If you foolishly imagine that I am going to swear by the genius of Caesar, as you call it, and are pretending not to know who I am, hear it openly. *I am a Christian*; and if you want to learn the doctrine of Christianity, appoint a day, and you shall hear it.'

The incriminating words must have aroused a fearful uproar, for the proconsul again refers to the crowd. 'Persuade the people', he said: the *demos* which was the foe of constituted authority in every Greek city.

'I considered that you were entitled to an explanation', replied Polycarp, 'because we are taught to render a fitting honour, provided it is not hurtful to ourselves, to the powers and authorities which are ordained by God; but I see no reason why I should make any defence or explanation to *them*.'

It was a proud strong speech, and the proconsul turned from persuasions to the usual threats of wild beasts and fire; but Polycarp was unmoved and even spoke of the coming judgement and the everlasting fire which was reserved for the godless. The proconsul's part was now over, for his criminal had confessed his guilt. He had conducted the legal enquiry which was required by Hadrian's rescript. A herald was sent into the stadium, to proclaim three times, 'Polycarp has confessed that *he is a Christian*'; and once again an angry roar went up. Philip the Asiarch was urged to bring back the lion; for, contrary to the popular impression today, few municipalities possessed more than one lion. The lion, however, was in no mood for Christians after the 'dog-hunt', and the cry went up that Polycarp should be burned alive; and so, says Marcianus, his words were shown to be prophetic, when he said, 'I must be burned alive.'

THE PASSION OF POLYCARP

Marcianus now tells of the gathering of the faggots for the fire, in which the Jews were very much to the fore, 'as is their custom'. It was their feast of Purim, the leading idea of which was the fearful punishment executed upon the enemies of God and of their race. The story read at this feast was the story of *Esther*, and it is significant that Christian writers steer clear of this book,[1] which was only received with difficulty into the Jewish canon; it describes the hanging on a cross[2] of Haman, the enemy of the Jewish race. There is no reason to doubt that the more fanatical members of the synagogue played their part in the persecution of Christians. We have noted that Herod, the 'officer of the peace', had a Jewish name himself.

Polycarp put off his cloak, and loosened the girdle of his tunic, and unlaced his shoes—a service which others had always done for him. He was tied to the wooden upright, being spared the nails of crucifixion at his own request; for, said he, 'The God who will give me power to endure the fire, will also give me power to remain unmoved in the flame without the security of your nails.' He stood there, Marcianus says, like a notable ram out of a great flock, chosen for a whole burnt-offering, well-pleasing to God. He looked up to heaven, and uttered a prayer of blessing and thanksgiving, on the lines of the great eucharistic prayer. The flame was kindled, and bellied out like a great sail, as if it were unwilling to touch him.[3] He was in the midst like silver or gold being fired in the furnace,[4] or bread being baked in the oven; and there was a fragrance like incense or one of the costly spices. This is the customary phraseology of the Acts of the Martyrs, and suggests that

[1] It is quoted by Clement of Rome, but excluded from the canon by Melito and Athanasius.

[2] *Stauros* in the Septuagint.

[3] Compare the story of the Three Children in the Septuagint version of Daniel.

[4] Compare Ecclesiasticus ii. 5, I Peter i. 7, etc.

the Acts of Polycarp were not the first composition of their kind. The bread and the incense are, of course, liturgical symbols, and so, of course, is the cup in the prayer of Polycarp.

When it was seen that the body was not being consumed, a gladiator was sent in to despatch him. He stabbed him to the heart with a dagger, and there came out round the hilt so much blood as to put out the fire; and the crowd marvelled to see so much difference between the un-believers and the elect. There is a curious textual point connected with this passage. The manuscripts read 'there came out a dove and'. The words 'a dove and' appear in Greek letters as ΠΕΡΙΣΤΕΡΑΚΑΙ; the reading ΠΕΡΙΣΤΥΡΑΚΑ, 'round the handle', is a modern conjecture and a very good one. Nevertheless, the word 'dove' could be an ideo-gram or symbol for the soul leaving the body: it is a catacomb emblem of the Christian soul.

And now a strange contest takes place. The Christians in some way made known to the authorities their desire to have the dear body of their dead bishop; but the Jews joined battle with them as they were about to take it. Here is an interesting comment on all those theological dialogues and debates on the subject of Judaism; the antagonism under-lying them suddenly appears in its historical setting. The Jews were a powerful body, apparently, and harboured a great animosity against the Christians. At last Nicetes, the father of the sinister Herod and brother of the Christian Alke, persuaded the proconsul to refuse the request, 'lest they should abandon the crucified, and begin to worship this one';[1] at which Marcianus is highly incensed: 'for we worship Christ as Son of God', he says, 'but we love the martyrs as disciples and imitators of the Lord, on account of our never-to-be-exaggerated happiness in our king and teacher.' We are obviously dealing here with a tradition which has grown up on both sides with regard to martyrs and martyrdoms. The request for the body should be compared with the request for the body of Jesus at the end of the Passion narrative. The Romans nor-mally allowed the bodies of executed criminals to be given back for burial.

So the centurion burned the body, but later on, Marcianus says, we took up the bones, more precious than precious stones and more proved than gold (an echo of I Peter), and laid them up where it was

[1] Compare Trypho's statement that Christians had 'abandoned God' to set their hope on a crucified man.

fitting. 'And there, as it may be possible, we shall assemble in joy and gladness, and the Lord will grant us to celebrate the birthday of his martyrdom, and to commemorate also those who underwent the contest before him, and train and prepare those who are to do so.' And so we see clearly that the cult of the martyrs was well established, including the observation of their anniversaries or 'birthdays'.

THE WRITING OF THE EPISTLE

It was some little time, it would seem, before a request arrived from the church at Philomelium for a full record of the martyrdom. Our reconstruction of the events would be that the Philomelians were represented at the election or consecration of a successor to Polycarp; that different versions of the story were going round; and that some of these stories needed to be supplemented. The more fanatical Phrygian Christians may have been critical of the withdrawal of Polycarp. A summary account was drawn up by order of the church of Smyrna, 'through our brother Marcianus' for the information of that church and of the brethren in those parts. It was in the same manner that the Roman church had written to the Corinthian church 'through Clement', as Dionysius of Corinth says, and of course Peter to Pontus and Bithynia 'through Silvanus'. Marcianus was the actual author. The name of the scribe who wrote it was Euarestus, as he tells us himself, following the example of Tertius, the scribe who wrote St Paul's Epistle to the Romans.

Philomelium was in eastern Phrygia, north of Little Antioch; but the letter was not addressed to that region alone; it was for 'all the *paroikiai* of the holy catholic church'. It was a catholic Epistle in short, intended for circulation throughout the universal church. It went far and wide, for it influenced the writer of the Acts of the Gallican martyrs in 177. These churches in southern France were in close touch with the churches of Asia Minor, through their Phrygian and Asian members, one of whom was their presbyter Irenaeus, who dedicated one of his books to a certain Marcianus.

The liturgical use of this Epistle is fairly clear from its character, and from its reference to the birthdays of the martyrs. Possibly these anniversary celebrations were modelled on the annual commemoration of the Passion of Jesus, with its readings from the Passion narratives of the Gospels. The Acts of the Martyrdom of James the Just, which had occurred at the Passover, were written up in the Gospel style, in the version which Hegesippus brought to Rome about this time. The martyr was assimilated to Jesus himself; he was the imitator and perfect disciple, as Marcianus says. This is obvious throughout the Epistles of Ignatius and the Acts of Polycarp, and not least in the prayer which he utters at the stake. This prayer must, of course, owe something to the art of the composer of the Acts; but it must also contain many phrases which Polycarp uttered; they are expressed in the language of eucharistic prayer, which was full of stereotyped phrases.

O Lord God, the Almighty,
The father of thy beloved and blessed child, Jesus Christ, through whom we
    have received the Knowledge concerning thee.[1]
O God of angels and powers and all creation, and of all of the race of the
    righteous who live before thee:

I bless thee for that thou hast deemed me worthy of this day and this hour,
To receive my portion in the number of the Martyrs, in the cup of thy
    Christ, unto resurrection of life eternal, of soul and body, in incorruption
    of Holy Spirit,
Among whom may I be received before thee this day as a rich and accep-
    table sacrifice, even as thou hast prepared and revealed it beforehand,
    and fulfilled it, O real and true God:

Wherefore, for this cause, and on account of all things, I praise thee, I bless
    thee, I glorify thee, through the eternal and heavenly high priest, Jesus
    Christ, thy beloved child, through whom, to thee, with him and the Holy
    Spirit, be glory now and ever and into the ages to come. Amen.

This is perhaps our best example of the second-century eucharistic prayer. It divides into three parts. The first part is an address to God in the familiar style of the Jewish benedictions, through Jesus Christ the beloved 'child'; and the third part is another act of thanksgiving or eucharist of the same sort, terminating in a trinitarian ascription of glory; they are the familiar substance of eucharistic prayer. Between the two comes the thanksgiving for his martyrdom, which gives the

[1] Compare the benedictions over the bread in the baptismal eucharist of the *Didache*.

whole prayer its specific meaning. Marcianus would have no difficulty in reconstructing the prayer substantially along the lines of what Polycarp said. He had often heard Polycarp at prayer. He had prayed aloud for two hours, the night before.

THE COLOPHONS

The Epistle of Marcianus has been preserved in two ways. Eusebius gives a shortened version of it in his *Ecclesiastical History*, and Pionius appends it to his life of Polycarp. At the end of the manuscript, as he gives it, we find some colophons, or notes by scribes, which are of interest. The first is

This copy was made by Gaius from the papers of Irenaeus, a disciple of Polycarp: this Gaius also lived with Irenaeus.

and under this

And I, Socrates [or Isocrates] wrote it in Corinth from the copy of Gaius. Grace be with all.

and under this

And I again, Pionius, wrote it out from the above-mentioned copy, after I had searched it out...gathering it together when it was wellnigh worn out by age, that the Lord Jesus Christ may also gather me into his eternal kingdom....

The manuscripts do not agree in their wording, but both say that Pionius found the manuscript through a revelation given him by the blessed Polycarp himself. Pionius, who lived in the third century, had a great devotion to the memory of Polycarp, but he was a man of vivid imagination, and unfortunately it showed itself in the composition of a biography of the saint which must be regretfully dismissed as a pious fiction, even though here and there he may be preserving a small fragment of old tradition.

These colophons look as if they were genuine, but in one manuscript, the Moscow manuscript, they are considerably enlarged. We find additional stories which it says are taken from the writings of Irenaeus. The first is that of the encounter of Polycarp with Marcion, which we know to be genuine; the second has no outside support. They run as follows,

This Irenaeus, being in Rome at the time of the martyrdom of Bishop Poly-carp, instructed many; and many excellent and orthodox writings of his are in circulation. In these he mentions Polycarp and says that he was his pupil. He powerfully refuted every heresy, and handed down the ecclesiastical and catholic rule as he had received it from the saint. He mentions this fact too, that when Marcion, after whom the Marcionists are called, once met the holy Polycarp, and asked Polycarp to recognize him, he said to Marcion, 'I recog-nize you? I recognize you as the first-born of Satan.' And this is also current in the writings of Irenaeus, that on the day and hour that Polycarp witnessed in Smyrna, Irenaeus, who was in the city of the Romans, heard a voice like a trumpet saying, 'Polycarp has witnessed.'

This very shadowy testimony is the only ancient evidence which states in so many words that Irenaeus actually taught at Rome; but there is much circumstantial evidence which leaves us without any doubt that he did.

THE CATHOLIC CHURCH

We have seen in the tradition of Ignatius and Polycarp, that is to say of Syria and Asia Minor, a clear and consistent picture of the catholic church as the totality of all the local churches in Christ. It was closely related by Ignatius to the holy order of the episcopate, which he re-garded as established in his time to the ends of the earth. In Polycarp it is related to the liturgical order. It was his custom in prayer to remember all the churches throughout the world. These churches, therefore, formed a spiritual unity, and we have noticed how they were knit together by visits of bishops or their envoys, exchange of Epistles and other documents, and migrations of teachers and prophets. One of the responsibilities of the bishop was the provision of hospitality for visiting Christians, probably in the house or houses which were placed under his management for church purposes. In consequence the church was fully conscious of itself as a world-church; and in cases of persecu-tion, schism, or any other difficulty, one local church had no hesitation in addressing another and offering a word of comfort or advice or material assistance.

We are not aware of any constitution or system of canons which regulated this corporate unity. The idea of a catholic church was not an imposed idea; it was simply a recognition of the historical realities. The church felt itself to be the continuation in apostolic form of the old Israel or people of God, which was already dispersed throughout the world. It was conscious, of course, of a transformation in the body, but not of a break in the succession. This continuity was nowhere more clearly expressed than in the liturgy. Prayers for the gathering into unity of the Israelites dispersed throughout the world had been an important feature of the Jewish ritual; it was a prophetic and apocalyptic hope, and therefore a high point in the liturgy too. The idea passed quite easily into Christian apocalyptic and Christian liturgy. The Lord, when he came, would 'send out his angels to gather his elect from the four winds', and Christians prayed for the realization of this messianic hope both now and in the future. The chiliasm of Papias was only a specific too-concrete form of this hope; Montanism would soon provide another. In the liturgy, however, it remained on its primitive level of symbolism and spirituality; and there are a couple of prayers in the *Didache* which express this thought.

As this broken bread was scattered upon the mountains and was gathered together and became one, so may thy church be gathered together from the ends of the world into thy kingdom. (*Didache*, IX, 4.)

[And again after the communion has taken place.] Remember, O Lord, thy church, to deliver her from every evil, and to make her perfect in thy love; and gather her together from the four winds, when she has been made holy, into thy kingdom, which thou hast prepared for her. (*Didache*, X, 5.)

The *Didache* in its present form is probably no later than the martyrdom of Polycarp, and the substance of these prayers is doubtless much older; they may be used with confidence in connexion with the prayers of Polycarp, to illustrate the catholicity of the period, and particularly its devotional style. Their position in such intimate connexion with the breaking of the bread and the act of communion distinguishes them altogether from the ordinary 'prayers of the brethren'. They would appear to have been a part of the eucharistic action, and to have brought the whole universal church into the scope of the offering, in the spirit of St Paul's saying that 'we, being many, are one bread, one body'.

The unity of Christians was not centred in Jerusalem, then, or in any earthly city. It was centred in the exalted Christ, and realized locally in the breaking of the bread, in the full meeting of the whole *paroikia*, under the presidency of the bishop; 'for this is what is spoken by the Lord,

In every place and time to offer me a pure sacrifice; for I am a great King, saith the Lord, and my Name is wonderful among the Gentiles.'

(*Didache*, XIV, 3.)

Such is the form of the quotation in the *Didache*; but it is worth giving it in full, according to the Septuagint text, since it is the great eucharistic text of the second-century fathers, and exactly expresses their consciousness of themselves as a catholic church,

I have no pleasure in you, saith the Lord Almighty, and I will not receive sacrifice from your hands [he is speaking to the Jerusalem priesthood]; because from the rising of the sun even unto the setting, my name is glorified among the Gentiles, and in every place incense is offered to my name, and pure sacrifice; for my name is great among the Gentiles saith the Lord the Almighty. (Malachi i. 10b–11.)

For I am a great king, saith the Lord the Almighty, and my name is glorious among the Gentiles. (Malachi i. 14.)

The 'name' of the Lord was a symbol for the revelation of himself in his glory in response to the Temple worship at Jerusalem, which was the place which he had chosen to put his 'name' there. But now the sacrifices offered at Jerusalem were rejected; the divine presence was parted and distributed among the Gentiles. Worship was offered to him in every place. And yet it is one act. Such is the vision of the one catholic church which Christians of this generation were given in their eucharistic worship, when they still expressed themselves naturally in the forms and symbols drawn from the old Judaeo-Christian spirituality.

Note. Since the claims of the *Life of Polycarp* by Pionius to serious historical consideration have recently been revived (C. K. Barrett, *Commentary on St John*, S.P.C.K., 1955), it is worth pointing out that his story of the foundation of the church in Smyrna by St Paul is contrary to the express statement of Polycarp himself in his *Epistle*, 'we were not yet in Christ'.

CHAPTER 9

EASTERN PROPHETS AND TEACHERS

In studying the account of the martyrdom of Polycarp we noticed a certain apologetic tendency, as if the discreet non-provocative policy of Polycarp had to be defended against a different attitude which rushed upon martyrdom with enthusiasm. There were these two different types of martyrs in the church, and they corresponded to two different types of faith or theology. The exponent of the second type in the martyrdom of Polycarp is the Phrygian would-be martyr Quintus, whose courage failed him at the last moment; and Marcianus observes that his conduct in giving himself up was not in accordance with the gospel. The letter which tells the story was directed to the church of Philomelium in eastern Phrygia; and Phrygia was the home of Christian enthusiasm, using the word in the sense of utter surrender to a divine indwelling spirit. The man is 'en-theos'; a god is in him.

THE NEW PROPHECY; MONTANUS, A.D. 150–5

We are now in a position to approach the subject of the outbreak of prophetic enthusiasm in western Phrygia, which is known as Montanism. In the highlands of Mysia, which lay north of Laodicea and Hierapolis, it would seem that whole villages had embraced the Christian faith in its prophetic form. The Phrygians were an emotional people, who had been accustomed to worship Cybele, the mother of the gods, with wild music and the shedding of blood and unmentionable rites. Their priests were emasculated in honour of the jealous goddess, who must be served by 'half-men'. The horrible sacrament of the *taurobolium*, or immersion in hot bull's blood, is said to have originated in this cult. Their hero-god was the shepherd Attis, who cut himself

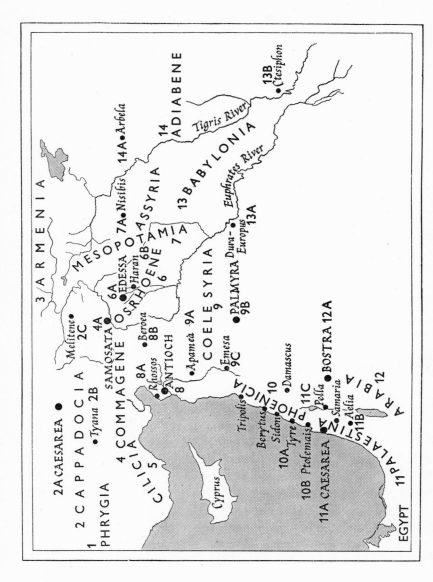

Map I. The oriental expansion of Christianity.

(1) *Phrygia*, the home of Montanism, was divided among several Roman provinces.

(2) *Cappadocia*, a border province of increasing importance, where Christianity was strong. Its capital was Caesarea (2A). Tyana (2B) was the home of Apollonius, the philosopher-mystic, who was converted into a rival of Christ. Melitene (2C) was the place where the Twelfth Legion was stationed, and took in Christian recruits.

(3) *Armenia* was an important semi-independent buffer-state, under Roman influence. The country became Christian by about 300.

(4) *Commagene* was a Syrian state. Its capital city, Samosata (4A), was the birth-place of the satirist Lucian, and of the third-century bishop of Antioch, Paul.

(5) *Cilicia*, an old Roman province, whose capital was Tarsus, the birthplace of St Paul.

(6) *Osrhoene*, an independent Syrian kingdom under Roman influence, ruled by the Abgar dynasty. Its capital, Edessa (6A), the modern Urfa or Urhai, was evangelized by the legendary Addai, who is said to have built a church there. Christianity was favoured by some members of the royal family, and well established before 200. Haran (6B), the Roman Carrhae, was associated with the story of Abraham.

(7) *Mesopotamia and Assyria* are names for areas of land between the two rivers. Their application does not seem to have been exactly defined. Nisibis (7A) was an important 'Assyrian' city, which came under Roman influence.

(8) *Antioch* was the second largest city in the empire, and the capital of the empire in the east. It was the chief city of Syria, and an apostolic see which claimed Peter as its founder. Not far off was Rhossos (8A), where Bishop Serapion found the church reading the Gospel of Peter; and Beroea (8B), a Jewish-Christian centre where the Hebrew Gospel was still in use in the fourth century.

(9) *Coele Syria* (Hollow Syria) was a name which was often given to the Syrian inland region between Antioch and Palestine. Apamea on the Orontes (9A) was a centre of the Jewish-Christian sect of Elkhasai. Palmyra (9B) was an important city, dominating the trade-routes, and in the mid-third century was the capital of an eastern empire. Emesa (9C) was an old Syrian city, devoted to the sun-god, El-Gabal; a dynasty descended from the priest-kings of Emesa ruled the Roman empire in the early third century.

(10) *Phoenicia* included various coast-towns which were the scenes of the legends about Peter, which form the substance of the Jewish-Christian Clementine books. The bishops of Tyre (10A) and Ptolemais (10B) were early connected with the Palestinian and Alexandrian churches.

(11) *Palestine* included the old apostolic centre of Caesarea (11A), which was a leading bishopric, and Aelia (11B), which was the new name for Jerusalem; they were in close touch with Alexandria. Pella (11C) was the town by the Lake of Galilee, to which the original Jerusalem church had migrated. Jewish-Christian communities were found east of Jordan and in northern Arabia, many of them heretical.

(12) *Arabia*, the Roman province east of the Jordan, ran as far south as the Gulf of Akaba, where there was communication by sea with India. Bostra (12A) was its capital.

(13) *Babylonia* is a name which may be assigned to the southern part of the land between the two rivers. Dura-Europus (13A) is a very advanced Roman outpost of the early third century, which was taken by the Persians in 268. Interesting synagogue and church remains have been excavated there. Ctesiphon (13B), with its companion city of Seleuceia, is near the site of the ancient Babylon. Ctesiphon and Seleuceia were, from time to time, the joint-capital of the Parthian empire.

(14) *Adiabene* was a Syrian kingdom east of the Tigris which early received a Christian mission. Its capital was Arbela (14A).

for love of the mother and died under the pine-tree. In the wild excitement of her mysteries, the mourners for Attis passed into a state of frenzy which resembled madness.

In the village of Ardabau, which has not been precisely located, there lived a Christian prophet named Montanus, who had once been a priest of Cybele, Jerome says. He set going a religious revival in the church, the effect of which would be felt far and wide. It was known as the New Prophecy by its friends and the Phrygian Heresy by its enemies; it was called Montanism by the theologians of a later time. Its strong features were fasting and asceticism, the seeing of visions, the hearing of voices, and possession by the Spirit. The condition of the prophet, during his seizure by the Spirit, was described as 'ecstasy'; he was 'beside himself', and had no control over what he was saying. Another mind was in command; another person was speaking through him; it was the Word of God, or the Spirit, or the Almighty Father who spoke. It was a non-rational influx of sheer supernatural energy, which was its own final authority. There was a word out of St John's Gospel which Montanus liked to use: the Paraclete, the Spirit of Truth who would come and lead the disciples into all truth, and convict the world of sin and of righteousness and of judgement. This hour had now struck.

Montanus could not be content with the older conception of the Spirit working organically in the whole body of the church through all its members and functions; nor with the Hermadic view of the interior life as a fusion of the divine with the human; he believed that when he was in ecstasy, the entire deity was speaking through him at that moment. All that was human was in abeyance. 'I am God Almighty', he is reported to have said, 'dwelling in a man'; 'I am neither angel nor envoy; I am the Lord God and Father, and have come myself.' Hermas had said that the inspiration of the prophet was due to an 'angel' from the divine Spirit, an impulse as we might say; Montanus made a more exalted claim for the power that spoke in him.

Behold the man is as it were a lyre, and I flutter as it were the key; the man sleeps but I awake. Behold it is the Lord that moves the hearts of men in ecstasy: and I that give them hearts.   (Epiphanius, *Panarion*, 48.)

The simile of the musical instrument was not peculiar to Montanism. It was used by such grave and learned writers as Athenagoras of Athens and Theophilus of Antioch in reference to the Old Testament prophets.

Why should it not be applied in stark realism to the prophets of the church?

The prophetic ministry was no new idea. It was indeed an essential element in the Jewish inheritance of the church, and therefore in its catholic order; but none except the Lord himself had enjoyed the whole fountain of the Holy Spirit, Justin said; a thought which appears to have been embodied in the story of the baptism of Jesus in the Hebrew gospel. He had given the Holy Spirit to his church. He had gone up on high; he had led captivity captive; he had 'given gifts to men'; but these gifts were parcelled out; one gift to one and one to another. Montanus introduced a new thing. The total prophetic authority was concentrated in one place. The voice of the Lord God himself was being heard in the valleys of Phrygia; and this new fact constituted it the centre of the universal church, a doctrine which soon assumed authoritative form.

PRISCILLA AND PEPUZA

There were a number of women who were associated with Montanus in his work. Among these were Maximilla and Priscilla. They too had the gift of prophecy.

Written records were made of the oracles which were uttered by Montanus and the women, and Epiphanius quotes some of them in his account of the sect. He tells us that Priscilla received an important revelation as she slept; 'for Christ came to her and slept with her, as the deluded woman herself says,

In the form of a woman Christ came to me in a shining robe, and infused wisdom into me, and revealed it to me that this place is holy, and here it is that Jerusalem cometh down from heaven.' (Epiphanius, *Panarion*, 49.)

The word 'here' in this oracle refers to the small village of Pepuza, and its neighbour, Tymion. Pepuza was the holy city of the New Prophecy, and Montanus gave it the name of Jerusalem, we are informed by the Ephesian writer Apollonius at the end of the century, because it was the scene of his religious assemblies; 'For everybody to assemble there', is what he says.

The language of Priscilla's oracle is taken from the Revelation of St John. The holy city, or New Jerusalem, is the vision of blessedness and peace on which the book closes; a spiritual vision, many Christians have thought, among them the hymn-writers who have interpreted it for the common people; 'Saviour, since of Zion's city, I through faith a member am.' Such may have been the meaning of this oracle for Priscilla herself. Where the saints were congregated and the Spirit fell from God and the prophets prophesied, there Jerusalem 'cometh down'. The verb is in the present tense.

This is not how the church historians and theologians have understood it, however. They think that the adherents of the New Prophecy expected to see a golden city appear visibly in the sky and descend to earth at Pepuza. The difficulty about this literal interpretation is that there is no trace of it in the evidence. Western Montanism certainly had never heard of it. Tertullian, the devoted adherent of Montanus, did indeed take the descent of the holy city literally, but he believed that it would come down on the site of the old Jerusalem in Palestine. His ignorance of what has been regarded as the official Montanist eschatology is exceedingly hard to explain.

Perhaps some light may be shed on the problem by going back to the original source of the vision. The Revelation of St John contains a special message for the Phrygian church of Philadelphia, not very far from Pepuza. This church was in serious conflict with Jews or Judaizing Christians, and John says,

To him that overcometh...I will inscribe upon him the name of my God, and the name of the city of my God, the new Jerusalem, which cometh down from heaven. (John, Revelation iii. 12.)

In other words, the name of Jerusalem now belonged, not to the actual Jews in Philadelphia, who were a synagogue of Satan, but to the despised and persecuted Christians. They were the true city of God; the new Jerusalem, which God had chosen 'to put his name there'.

Since that time, Philadelphia had boasted of a prophetess named Ammia, who was regarded as the predecessor of Maximilla and Priscilla. A connexion or pedigree of a sort appears here which may help to explain Priscilla's dream. When the prophetic witness was in Philadelphia, Philadelphia was given the name of Jerusalem; when the prophetic witness was in Pepuza, Pepuza was given the name of Jerusalem. There is no evidence that the Phrygian prophets were concerned with millennial forecasts like Papias and Justin. It would seem that they were con-

11. ST PETER'S FROM THE AIR

12. MARCUS AURELIUS

cerned with the fulfilment of Gospel prophecy in their own movement. They may have had prophecies of a golden future after the wars and disturbances predicted by Maximilla; but there is no record of them.

The two great promises of the Johannine books were both realized in their midst; the one was the presence of the Paraclete or Comforter in the persons of Montanus and the women; the other was the gathering of the saints with these prophets, in Pepuza and Tymion, which constituted the New Jerusalem, which cometh down from heaven.

What was the date when the New Prophecy began to lift up its voice? Eusebius gives 177 to 178 as the date when it was attracting world-wide attention, but this is much too late for its origin. The date which is given by Epiphanius is the nineteenth year of Antoninus, which works out at 157. Apollonius says that it was forty years before he wrote, which works out with a high degree of probability as about 152 or 153. We will not go far wrong in assuming that Montanus was beginning to prophesy when Polycarp died as a martyr; and this would help to explain the critical note in the story of his martyrdom; but one would suppose that there were prophesyings in Phrygia before Montanus. His movement cannot have come out of nothing, and it claimed to possess predecessors in Quadratus and Ammia.

A GLANCE AT ANTIOCH

Antioch on the Orontes was the centre of the imperial administration in the east and the gateway to Roman Syria. It grew wealthy on the trade in luxury products with the far-eastern countries, such as China and India, as Alexandria did in Egypt. The church in Antioch must have been numerous and powerful, and much divided by controversy; but we hear next to nothing of it, and are forced to fall back upon conjecture. We may reasonably consider, however, the docetic schools, the prophets of the *Didache*, and the case of Peregrinus.

At the end of the century, Bishop Serapion of Antioch found the so-called *Gospel of Peter* being used in the church at Rhossos in Cilicia. He made inquiries, and found that it was the gospel of a sect of Docetae, whose leader or founder had been a certain Marcianus, who, he said, had been in the habit of contradicting himself. Marcianus and his Docetae may have been flourishing at this time. A strongly docetic theology had existed in Antioch ever since the days of Menander and Satornil;

and their emphasis on an unsubstantial and 'spiritual' Christ may partially account for the emphasis on the historic and Judaistic side of the gospel in the official theology of the church, which sometimes seemed to err in the direction of humanism or adoptionism. The *Gospel of Peter* was not necessarily an Antiochene production, however. It may have been introduced there; from Alexandria for instance, where another sect of Docetae also existed, under the leadership of Julius Cassianus; but Julius quoted from the *Gospel of the Egyptians*, Clement of Alexandria says. Our information is so meagre, however, that for all we know, the Egyptian gospel may have had much in common with the so-called Peter, fragments of which were discovered in Egypt.

As for the *Didache*, we have taken the view that its origin is Syrian, and that it is not likely to be much later than 150 in its present form. Those who wish to assign it to an earlier date would not object, however, to the supposition that it was still exercising its influence in the neighbourhood of Antioch, where we may locate its ambitious and refractory prophets who aspired to step into the positions of the apostles of Jesus and the high priests of Judaism. We may visualize them going their rounds of the rural churches in the harvest seasons, receiving the first-fruits, and 'ordering tables' and demanding money in the Spirit, and celebrating their 'cosmic mystery of the church'; a mystery on which no light has yet been shed, though we may conjecture much. To question their oracles was to sin against the Holy Ghost.

Sacred teachers and sacred prophets seem to have been the glory and the shame of the church. Celsus, the philosophic critic of Christianity, tells us that they were specially active in Palestine and Phoenicia, where he had seen them at work.

There are many [he says] who, though they are people of no importance, yet affect the manner of inspired persons, both inside and outside of temples ...'I am God', they say, or 'I am the divine Spirit; I have come because the world is perishing through your iniquities; but I desire to save you, and you shall see me returning again in heavenly power. Blessed is he who now does me homage: on all the rest I will send down eternal fire.'

(Celsus, *The True Word*, in Origen, *Against Celsus*, VII, 9.)

Celsus has preserved some authentic Christian notes in this parody of the prophetic preacher. He represents the prophet as speaking in the person of Christ; but the example of the Phrygian prophets shows that this was not at all an impossible idea; and the prophet of the *Didache* also claims that the divine Spirit is speaking through him.

LUCIAN OF SAMOSATA

There was one Syrian kingdom which had been incorporated into the empire, since it lay west of the Euphrates. Its name was Commagene, and it bordered on the province of Cappadocia. Its capital city was Samosata; and Samosata was the birthplace of Lucian, the most graceful and witty of the Greek authors of the period. His satire was a finer and keener weapon than that of Celsus. He had wandered from country to country in his younger days, giving lectures in Greece and Italy and Gaul; but he settled in Antioch about the year 160, moving after a while to Athens. In both cities he fell in with the notorious Peregrinus, also called Proteus, or made enquiries about him; and after Proteus' famous act of self-destruction at Olympia in 165, he wrote the unkind sketch of his life, which sheds some light on Christianity. But the wit of Lucian spared neither gods nor men.

PEREGRINUS THE CHRISTIAN

In his skit which he calls *Concerning the Death of Peregrinus*, Lucian tells us that the subject of his satire was born at Parium on the Hellespont, where he committed many crimes, not even drawing the line at parricide. He was permitted to leave the city, however, after the confiscation of his property, which makes the extreme charges of Lucian sound rather improbable. He travelled as far as Palestine, where he became a Christian. He wandered from church to church as a 'synagogeus or prophet or thiasarchus'. These titles are not very serious appellations. The first has a Jewish look, and the last is decidedly Bacchic; they might be translated 'a master of assemblies, a prophet, a leader of divine revels'. He carried with him sacred books, some of which he had composed himself. He was imprisoned in Antioch and became a martyr of great fame. His fellow-Christians attempted to secure his release, and when this was found impossible they looked after his wants with unremitting care and zeal. In the day-time widows and orphans waited about the doors of the prison; the clergy bribed the guards to let them keep company with him at night; delicacies to eat were smuggled in; and envoys arrived from the far-off cities of Asia Minor to advise and console him. In the eyes of Lucian all this was very funny. The Christians were a simple people, easily imposed upon, and Peregrinus was doing remarkably well at their expense. To use the words of the *Didache*, he was a Christ-monger not a Christian.

The historian, however, must make some allowances for the mocking spirit of Lucian and give Peregrinus some credit for sincerity, and the Christians some credit for common sense. Peregrinus was not without his admirers at Athens a few years later, and he demonstrated his sincerity, at least, by his theatrical death at Olympia; for the martyrdom at Antioch was never consummated. Had the proconsul condemned Peregrinus, he might have shone in the pages of church history as another Justin Martyr. Like Justin, he was an author; like Justin, he was in love with philosophy; and the Christians called him the new Socrates. But the proconsul decided that he would not benefit the Christians by granting them another martyr. Peregrinus was released, and escorted on his way by jubilant Christians. Finally he fell from grace. He parted from the church after some controversy on the matter of forbidden foods, Lucian thought. We shall continue the story of Peregrinus in the next chapter, in which he will appear as a Cynic philosopher.

EAST OF ANTIOCH

In the desert cities between Antioch and the Euphrates, a wealthy and cultured society was coming into existence, which would have an increasing influence on the fortunes of the empire. The old Iranian and Babylonian religious traditions were going through a period of intellectual ferment under the stimulus of Greek thought. We cannot expect to find Syrian Christianity exactly like the Christianity of the west.

The Euphrates River was still the boundary of the Roman empire; and on the eastern side of its western bulge was the Syrian kingdom which the Greeks called Osrhoene. This name was a corruption of the native name of its principal city, Urhai, the modern Urfa; but the Greeks had called this city Edessa, and this is the name it was generally known by. The whole territory between the two rivers, in these latitudes, was vaguely known as Assyria.

Farther east still, across the Tigris, was the Syrian kingdom of

Adiabene, whose capital was Arbela. Its royal family had accepted Judaism in the first century, but this was now an affair of past history. Nevertheless the Jewish religion, in various forms, was spread far and wide in the lands between the two rivers, and beyond. It is natural to suppose that Christianity in its various Jewish forms had spread there too; but it is only now that we begin to find evidence of it.

The kingdom of Osrhoene, or Edessa, had a line of sovereigns of Arab origin, whose names were usually Abgar or Manu: they were connected in some way with the sovereigns of Arbela. Under the patronage of these sovereigns, or some of them, a form of Christianity took possession of the city of Edessa and was in a flourishing condition by the end of the century. The language spoken there was Syriac, and the local church expressed itself in that language. It became the medium of a widespread and illustrious Christian culture, which spread in due course as far as China. It is still the language of the Syrian liturgy, though modern Syrians speak Arabic. It was not identical with the Aramaic which was spoken by the Jews and the Palmyrenes, though it resembled it closely. The Syriac Christianity of Edessa was not continuous, on a language basis, with the Aramaic Christianity of Jesus and his disciples, of which no literary trace remains today; translation was necessary.

THE CHURCH IN EDESSA

The legendary founder of Christianity in Edessa (for Syrian Christianity abounds in splendid legends) was a certain Addai, who is said to have been one of the seventy-two disciples of Jesus. Eusebius had received from the Edessenes a long romantic story in which the legendary Addai had been transformed into the apostle Thaddaeus, or 'Thaddai'; but this is not apparently the oldest form of the legend. The native account of it, the *Doctrine of Addai*, which took its present form in the fourth century, does not make this claim, though it agrees in its main outline with Eusebius. It tells how King Abgar Ukkama (the Black) sent a messenger to Jesus, asking him to come to Edessa and cure him of his leprosy. Jesus could not accept this invitation, but he sent Abgar a portrait of himself, with an Epistle, in which he promised that an evangelist would come in due course. After the Ascension the apostle 'Judas Thomas' sent Addai, who cured the king and built a church at Edessa.

Now the Addai legends may not be entirely devoid of historical value; for a hard historical fact is found at the core of most legends, or, at any rate, they must attach themselves to history at some point. The *Acts of Paul*, for instance, may be classed as an historical novel, but their hero is the historical Paul, who actually existed and planted churches in the locations where the legend places him. The name of Addai may be received as historical. The legend tells how he was befriended by a Jew named Tobiah the son of Tobiah, who received him into his house, and helped him in various ways; and this suggests that the oldest form of Christianity in Edessa was Jewish.

The *Doctrine of Addai* goes on to say that he died in peace after consecrating his pupil Aggai to be his successor as bishop.[1] Aggai displeased the next king, whose name was Manu, and was put to death before he was able to consecrate as his successor a third bishop, Palut, who had also been a disciple of Addai; so Palut was consecrated by Serapion of Antioch, who had been consecrated himself by Zephyrinus of Rome. We have suddenly moved on more than a hundred years, for Zephyrinus did not become bishop before about 200, and cannot have consecrated Serapion, who became bishop of Antioch about 190. It is plain what has happened. A tradition about Palut has been awkwardly spliced on to a tradition about Addai. It is an important tradition. Palut appears to be an historical character, since the orthodox Christians of Edessa were nicknamed 'Palutians' by their heretical opponents, who may have represented the older tradition.

In the old Syrian chronicles there are various entries which add to the confusion. The great Syrian intellectual, Bar Daisan, or Bardesanes, who was born in 154, was converted to the faith in 179 by hearing the bishop Hystasp preaching in the church which had been built by Addai. This entry confirms the tradition about Addai and his church, but it adds more names to the episcopal succession; for Hystasp is given a predecessor called Yaznai (or Izani), and a successor named 'Aqai, who excommunicated Bar Daisan for heresy. We are quite unable to piece together an episcopal succession-list; but we are pleased to note that the Syrian chroniclers did not make the attempt to do so; nor did they invent names to fill the void. The names we have may well be genuine. They point to confusion and conflict, and the existence of more than

[1] Our first reference to an episcopal consecration, if the fact is accepted: in any case, a venerable tradition.

one succession of bishops. Palut seems to have been the first of a new succession, which was in touch with the Christian tradition of the west.

The existence of the church is put beyond all reasonable doubt by an entry in one of the chronicles, which says that it was destroyed in the year 202, when the River Daisan flooded. It looks as if it had been built on low ground as a convenient site for baptisms. It is our first reference to a church building, though there is evidence by the end of the second century that such buildings existed. The shadowy figure of Addai and his Jewish-Christian mission may be placed, perhaps, after the wars of Trajan (114–17) in which Edessa was destroyed by Lusius Quietus; or even after the Jewish wars of 132–5, when great numbers of Jews must have sought refuge in the east. The *Chronicle of Arbela*, the capital of Adiabene, suggests that Christianity reached the east of the Tigris about the same time.

APOSTOLIC MEMORIALS

We have reached a point now when the apostolic age, in the most generous interpretation of the phrase, was receding beyond the reach of man's memory. We have seen an instance in which two long lives have bridged the interval. John had stood by the cross of Jesus, and Polycarp his pupil had crowned his own career with martyrdom one hundred and twenty-five years later; three average generations of about forty years each had been covered by two long lives. We enter the fourth generation, and look now to men like Irenaeus and Hegesippus and Eleutherus to carry on the tradition to the end of the century.

Many changes occur at such a period of transition. It is the point at which, in every human community, an historical interest comes into existence, which is marked in modern times by jubilees and centenaries. The newer generation begins to ask questions about the historical origins of the community and the personalities of its pioneers and founders. In the church of the second century this becomes apparent in the construction of written lists of the bishops who linked it with the apostolic founders. It showed itself, too, in an interest in historic sites, and especially in the burial-places of the great men of the first generation. It played its part in ecclesiastical controversy.

Recent excavation has shown that it was marked in Rome by a certain amount of new construction in the cemetery on the right-hand side of the Via Cornelia as one goes up the Vatican Hill, a site which was revered as the burial-place of St Peter. A shrine was erected with a little altar or table which was supported by two graceful columns about four feet six inches in height the remains of which have recently been discovered. Behind it is a curved niche beneath which was discovered a rectangular cavity, which was empty. There are many burials around it. There are no inscriptions mentioning the name of Peter. The best that can be safely said is that this is the shrine mentioned by the Roman writer Gaius about the year 200; he calls it a *tropaion* or monument of victory, and adds that there was a similar monument of St Paul on the Ostian Way, but this site has not been excavated. On the other hand, the numerous second-century catacombs show how piously the Roman Christians took care of their dead. The Martyrdom of Polycarp shows that there was a religious service at the tomb on the anniversary of a martyr's death.

A Montanist champion named Proclus, in the course of an argument with Gaius, referred to the tomb of St Philip at Hierapolis in the Montanist country; and so did Polycrates, the bishop of Ephesus, who also mentioned the burial of St John at Ephesus. We have no second-century evidence about the sacred sites in Jerusalem, except for the *stele* or upright stone by the Temple, where James the brother of the Lord was martyred, which is mentioned by Hegesippus.

HEGESIPPUS AND HIS RESEARCHES

The figure of Hegesippus is an elusive one. His once famous *Note-books* have disappeared in the course of time, and we have nothing from his hand but a few extracts. There are several in Eusebius, and one or two in the Oxford manuscript which de Boor regarded as an epitome of Philip of Side.[1] These can be supplemented by a study of certain passages in which Irenaeus or Epiphanius, or both, have used the *Note-books* without acknowledgement. After careful comparison of these authorities, a useful picture emerges. We have made use of it, from time to time, in discussing the history of the old Jewish church and it helps us to work out the chronology of the second century.

Hegesippus came from Palestine, where he had learned the old traditions. He brought with him the traditional narratives about James

[1] See note appended to vol. I, chapter 19.

the brother of Jesus, who had suffered martyrdom in Nero's reign, and the less illustrious members of the family of the Lord, who had survived 'into the times of Trajan', that is to say into living memory. He was bilingual or even trilingual. He quoted his Hebrew Gospel in Hebrew and in Syriac; he quoted apparently from other sources in Hebrew, and from unwritten Hebrew traditions. The word Hebrew probably means Aramaic in all cases. It was the language of the Hebrews, and is referred to in the Gospels as Hebrew. Eusebius deduces from the use Hegesippus made of it that he was a Hebrew Christian himself.

This famous Palestinian teacher was probably younger than Justin and older than Irenaeus. Like Justin, he had devoted himself to the controversy with heresy, and arrived in Rome with a good deal of research on the subject to his credit; but this research had been done on Palestinian soil, and dealt with Jewish heresies which are mere names to us now. His mind worked in the oriental manner, and he constructed a sort of pedigree of heresy. First came the old Jewish sects which had opposed the Lord and his brother James; their offspring were the Jewish-Christian sects which opposed his cousin Simeon ben Clopas; and these were the progenitors of the third-generation heresies of the Gentile type, which had been catalogued by Justin in his *Syntagma*; the Menandrianists, and 'Marcianists', and Carpocratians, and Valentinians, and Basilidians, and Satornilians. (There may have been a sect called the Marcianists, but the word is an obvious clerical error for Marcionites in this catalogue.)

Among their Jewish predecessors in the episcopate of Simeon, he mentions Simon and Cleobius and Dositheus, whose names were not unknown in the Gentile Christianity of the east.

HEGESIPPUS AND THE EPISCOPATE

Hegesippus made much of the fact that the apostolic tradition was maintained in each city through its succession of bishops. His interest in this field of historical research had been awakened in Palestine where the episcopate seems to have been held in high esteem as an apostolic institution; and it was not unnatural that he should visit Rome to compare what he was accustomed to in Palestine with the tradition of Clement, of which he must have heard a great deal. The episcopal successions were everywhere established in his time, but he felt that he would like to verify their orthodoxy by actual research. He was not disappointed. He visited many cities and conversed with many bishops. He was most gratified with the results. In every city, and in every succession, he found the same teaching; and it was all in accordance with the Law, the Prophets, and the Lord—meaning by this the Gospel.

We could wish that we had the story of his journeys. It is likely that he passed through Asia Minor, like Ignatius, for it seems that he assigned John's imprisonment on the Island of Patmos to the reign of Domitian; and he too 'survived into the times of Trajan'. This reference is preserved in the 'de Boor' manuscript, and in Eusebius too, though he does not name Hegesippus as the author from whom he takes the information.[1]

He made the journey to Corinth by sea, where Primus was the bishop apparently. He gave some account, which has not survived, of the disorders of the church in the time of Clement but says that the right teaching was preserved down to the time of Primus. He mentioned Clement's Epistle. This is how Eusebius quotes him:

[After some remarks on the Epistle of Clement to the Corinthians, he goes on to say:] And the church of the Corinthians continued in the right teaching until Primus was bishop at Corinth:

And I associated with them on my voyage to Rome, and I abode with the Corinthians many days, during which we were refreshed together in the right teaching.

But when I came to Rome I made for myself a succession-list as far as Anicetus, whose deacon was Eleutherus.

And from Anicetus, Soter received the succession; after whom came Eleutherus. And in every succession, and in every city, that which the Law and the prophets and the Lord do proclaim, is faithfully followed.

(Hegesippus, *Note-books*, in Eusebius *E.H.* LV, 22, 2–3.)

HEGESIPPUS IN ROME, c. A.D. 160

When Hegesippus says that Eleutherus was the deacon of Anicetus, he does not mean that there was only one deacon in the Roman church. Eleutherus was the bishop's deacon or principal assistant. He was what came to be called the archdeacon. He had a long and honourable

---

[1] See Lawlor and Oulton, *Church History of Eusebius*, vol. II; note on *E.H.* III, 21.

career, and must have exercised a continuous influence on the policy of the Roman church, until he became bishop himself, dying about 190. At this period he was the head of the business administration. Among other matters, he may have looked after such cemeteries as were not in private hands, as his successor Callistus did. We may, perhaps, credit his administration with the work which was done on the Vatican cemetery and the monument of St Peter.

The list of Roman bishops which Hegesippus compiled was incorporated by Irenaeus in his Refutation, and helps us to map out the Christian chronology of the period. It did not give the years of the episcopates.

It appears, from a comparison of our evidence,[1] that Hegesippus then went on to speak of a lady named Marcellina, who arrived in Rome about the same time that he did. She was a teacher of the school of Carpocrates, an Alexandrian heresiarch, who combined breadth of mind with laxity of morals. He had created a philosophic cult out of a mixture of Plato and Jesus. Marcellina came from Alexandria; she had a chapel in her house which contained images of Pythagoras and Plato and Aristotle and other sages, among whom she placed an image of Christ which had been made by order of Pontius Pilate. The vision which we get of this intellectual lady, crowning her statues with garlands, and preaching the only true gnosis, is an astonishing one. We may be sure that she would not have put Christ in this elect company, if there had been no willingness on the part of the intelligentsia to welcome him. It is a notable sign that the spirit of the age might be willing to enrol him among the immortals if only the inheritance of Hebrew monotheism could be thrown overboard. Marcellina was in advance of her times. Fifty years later, this union of religions was the fashion in imperial circles.

As for Pontius Pilate, the legend of his portrait of Jesus is still going the rounds. It belongs to a cycle of legends which were incorporated into such works of fiction as the *Acts of Pilate* or the *Gospel of Nicodemus*, which we possess in rather late recensions. It should be compared with the legend of the portrait of Jesus in the Syrian *Doctrine of Addai*. Perhaps Addai's church in Edessa contained such a portrait,

---

[1] The text of Irenaeus is supported by the text of Epiphanius, which gives further particulars. They are using the same source without acknowledgement. See B. H. Streeter, *The Primitive Church*.

like Marcellina's chapel in Rome. As for legends, Hegesippus says that the fabrication of an apocryphal literature was well under way in his time, and there is no doubt that this was the case. He may have had in mind books like the so-called *Gospel of Peter* which had a friendly interest in Pilate. We have considered it already, but it is not likely that it was written before the hundred-and-fifties.

There is an important little group of chronological notes in Irenaeus, which also seem to come from Hegesippus. Cerdo arrived in Rome in the time of Hyginus, it says; Valentine arrived under Hyginus, flourished under Pius, and persisted under Anicetus; Marcion succeeded Cerdo in his school and grew in strength under Anicetus. It is the picture as Hegesippus saw it when he arrived in Rome, and as he placed it in relation to his episcopal chronology. Did he invent this method of dating ecclesiastical events by the episcopates in which they occurred? or did he bring this custom to Rome from Palestine? And did he relate his episcopal chronology to general chronology? to the regnal years of the emperors, for instance? The unknown second-century source used by Epiphanius did so, and this source may be Hegesippus; it dealt with Aquila in Jerusalem, Marcion in Rome, the Phrygian prophesying, and the return of Tatian to the east.

Rome now had at least three oriental teachers, Justin of Samaria, Tatian of Assyria, and Hegesippus of Palestine; but Justin represented the tradition of Asia Minor.

CHAPTER 10

PHILOSOPHY AND MARTYRDOM

The rescript of Antoninus, after A.D. 150, *p.* 158. Ptolemaeus and Lucius, *p.* 159. The *Second Apology* of Justin Martyr, *p.* 160. Tatian the Assyrian, *p.* 162. The *Address to the Greeks*, *p.* 163. Marcus Aurelius, *p.* 164. The Meditations, p. 166. Marcus and the Christians, p. 167. The martyrs of Asia, *p.* 168. The Parthian war, A.D. 162–6, *p.* 169. The martyrdom of Justin, A.D. 165? *p.* 171.

CHRONOLOGICAL TABLE

showing relations of events between 154 and 167

A.D.	Fixed dates	In Rome	Greece and Asia
154		*Anicetus bishop.*	Prophesying of Montanus.
155		Polycarp in Rome.	? Persecution in Greece: Athens.
156	Martyrdom of Polycarp.		? Martyrdom of Publius: Athens.
157		(Hegesippus arrives ?)	? Rescript of Antoninus: after 150.
158		? Ptolemaeus and Lucius.	
159		? Crescens the Cynic.	
160		? Justin: *Apology II.*	
161	*Accession of M. Aurelius.*	? Tatian: *Address to Greeks.*	
162		*Rusticus Prefect: to 167.*	(Possible date for Sergius Paulus.)
163	Parthian war.	(Hegesippus arrives ?)	
164			? Thraseas martyr: Montanist synods.
165		? Martyrdom of Justin.	Immolation of Peregrinus.
166	Sergius Paulus in Asia.	*Soter bishop.*	? Sagaris martyr: paschal controversy.
167	Sergius Paulus in Asia.	*Rusticus finishes term.*	? or Sagaris martyr.

Hegesippus arrived in Rome in the episcopate of Anicetus, 154–66: we placed him early in this episcopate so as to include him in a chapter dealing with oriental Christianity; the double entry in the above table symbolizes the fact that his arrival may have been later.

The martyrdoms of Ptolemaeus and Lucius must be placed before the prefecture of Junius Rusticus. They could be previous to the martyrdom of Polycarp, but this does not seem likely. Tatian's *Address to the Greeks* refers to Crescens, but some scholars place it later.

Justin was martyred under Rusticus, and Sagaris under Sergius Paulus; Thraseas in all probability before Sagaris.

The persecution at Athens in which Publius died is not necessarily to be identified with the persecution in Athens and other Greek cities, which elicited the rescript of Antoninus; but the identification seems natural.

THE RESCRIPT OF ANTONINUS, AFTER A.D. 150

It is quite a question whether the philosophic activities of leading Christian intellectuals served to moderate the imperial policy. Melito of Sardis, writing probably in 176, mentions a 'rescript' of the Emperor Antoninus, in which he checked certain onslaughts which had been made by the populace upon the Christians in Greece, mentioning particularly the cities of Larissa, Thessalonica and Athens; and since Justin quotes the rescript of Hadrian in his *First Apology*, and fails to mention the rescript of Antoninus, to whom the *Apology* was addressed, we are justified in allotting it to a date after the *Apology* was written, that is to say after 150 or 152. The anti-Christian outbreaks in Greece which it attempted to curb may have had some connexion with the wave of persecution in Asia which led to the martyrdom of Polycarp in 155 or 156. The indications, such as they are, make this a likely date.

If this is accepted, the next step would be to identify the persecution in Athens which was referred to in this rescript with the one mentioned by Dionysius of Corinth ten or fifteen years later. It brought about a crisis in the history of that church, Dionysius says. There were a number of apostasies; the Athenian bishop Publius died as a martyr; and the new bishop Quadratus had the greatest difficulty in reorganizing the church; nevertheless, by his zeal he brought the people together again and rekindled their faith. No doubt this was the Quadratus who presented an *Apology* to Hadrian in Athens some thirty years before, according to the date given by Eusebius; but one could wish that there was enough material to make a more substantial reconstruction of these events.

As the reign of Antoninus comes to its end in 161, we notice a deterioration in the position of the Christians. Under his mild rule, at least in its earlier years, it was possible, apparently, for the champions of Christianity to come forward publicly, and present the new religion for consideration as a philosophic cult which was entitled to the same immunities as the other philosophers enjoyed, though some of them were admittedly 'atheistic'. Such was the line which was taken by the *First Apology* of Justin, which we dated about 150, and it was hoped that the case for Christianity would be impartially examined. Some restraints were placed by Antoninus on lawless persecution, but apparently no such impartial examination took place. The *Second Apology*, which was written before 161, shows that the appeal had been disregarded by the authorities. What is more, it had aroused the resentment of the professional philosophers, and especially of Cynics like Crescens, and even of Platonists like Celsus. Fronto, the tutor of Marcus Aurelius, was bitterly adverse and Marcus himself was unsympathetic.

PTOLEMAEUS AND LUCIUS

In Rome the prefect of the city was Lollius Urbicus, an old soldier of Hadrian, who had made his reputation in Britain and had held this high judicial position in Rome from 144 to 161. He was no friend of the new faith, as can be seen by his conduct of a case which came before him.

There was a Christian teacher named Ptolemaeus, who numbered among his pupils a lady of rank and fortune, whose name is not preserved. Her husband was a notorious rake, and she had been guilty of marital irregularities herself before she became a Christian and adopted the life of virtue and self-discipline. Her position now became a difficult one, and while her husband was on a voyage to Alexandria, she divorced him. Such an action illustrates the disruptive effect of the Christian standards of chastity on the old pagan social life. The situation was open to misrepresentation, and her husband, on his return, determined to have his revenge. He informed the authorities that she was a Christian, a charge which she managed to evade by placing herself under the protection of the emperor, who was ready, it would seem, to shield a Christian from persecution, at all events if she was of high social standing. We hear no more of her. According to the principles of Hermas and Justin, she must have enrolled with the widows and virgins.

Foiled, in this attempt, the husband turned upon her teacher Ptolemaeus. The text is not perfectly clear at this point; but what is clear is that the husband bribed a centurion, who was a friend of his, to put to him the fatal question, 'Are you a *Christian*?' Ptolemaeus had no alternative but to confess and soon found himself in prison. It would seem that he might have gone on teaching the principles of Christianity, without disturbance, had he not provoked the enmity of the aggrieved husband.

He was kept in prison for a long time before his case was heard; and when he appeared in court before Lollius Urbicus, the same procedure was adopted. There was no enquiry or examination; he was simply asked, 'Are you a *Christian*?' and when he admitted it, he was summarily condemned to death. The whole story was probably very well known to everyone, and one of the spectators in the court, a man named Lucius, rose and protested.

'What is the crime?' he asked. 'This man is no adulterer or fornicator; no murderer or thief or robber; he has not been convicted of any crime. All that you have punished him for is his admission that he is called by the name of *Christian*. You are judging in a manner which is not worthy of the pious emperor, or his son the philosophic Caesar, or the sacred senate.'

Lucius was a Christian himself, and Urbicus knew this at once.

'I think you are another of the same sort', he said.

'I certainly am', replied Lucius, and was ordered off to execution; and according to the Christian custom he offered a thanksgiving.

A third Christian protested and was also condemned.

Justin did not let the matter rest there. He penned a document in which he brought the whole case to the attention of the highest authorities. This document is the so-called *Second Apology* and is found in the manuscripts appended to the *First Apology*; it certainly carries on some of the arguments contained in that document. It must have been written before 7 March 161, when Antoninus died; for Antoninus is the pious emperor, and Marcus Aurelius the philosophic Caesar. It was in this year, too, that Urbicus ceased to be prefect of the city; Marcus appointed Junius Rusticus in his place. Rusticus was even less sympathetic with the Christians.

THE *SECOND APOLOGY* OF JUSTIN MARTYR

The so-called *Second Apology* of Justin is the source from which we have drawn this very instructive narrative. He goes on to expatiate on the injustice and futility of a legal process which refused to make any effective inquiry into the nature of a crime, or actually a mere name, for which it condemns a just and innocent man to death. He also answers a few criticisms and objections which have been levelled, either at his *First Apology*, or at his public teaching. In particular he fastens upon a Cynic philosopher named Crescens, who had attacked the faith without even knowing what it was, a fact which Justin had demonstrated, he said, by coming forward and engaging in public argument with him. The debate had been reduced to writing, like the discussion which he had held with Trypho, and he hopes that the emperor has read it. It looks as if the Christian philosophy had made a stir.

Meanwhile he is fully expecting to be plotted against by 'Crescens the Philopsopher', and nailed to a cross. The comic title means a lover of sound (*psophos*), rather than a lover of sense (*sophia*). The philopsophic Crescens may also have had a friend who was a centurion, and his plans included the liquidation of Tatian as well as Justin; or so Tatian says.

Crescens [he says] who made his nest in the great city, and surpassed all men in his passion for boys, and was a great lover of money, and a despiser of death, was actually so afraid of death, that he made it his business to bring Justin (and me too) to death as if it were an evil thing, because he announced the truth, and convicted the philosophers of being gluttons and cheats: but which of the philosophers except you alone did he ever attack?

(Tatian, *To the Greeks*, XIX.)

The Greek text is a little corrupt in the last sentence, but this seems to be its sense. It is written in the spirit of Tatian, not the spirit of Justin, but it suggests that Justin had not hesitated to use strong language.

As if to compensate for his attack on Crescens, Justin opens up to its widest extent his generous recognition of the old philosophers like Socrates and Heracleitus, and even the more recent Musonius, the tutor of Epictetus. They were inspired men. In every human soul, Justin said, the word of God exists as a seed or germ. Socrates listened to the word of God as much as Abraham or Elijah.

I pray and contend with all my might that I may be found to be a *Christian*, and yet I profess that the teachings of Plato are not foreign to those of Christ. But I do say that they are not in all respects alike. And so it is too in the case of the others, whether it be the Stoics or the other writers; for each one saw what was akin, and spoke well...according to his portion of the divine germinative Word, so whatever was said well by any of them belongs to us as Christians.   (Justin, *Second Apology*, XIII, 2 and 4.)

It may be that Justin left Rome for a while after this incident, in connexion with which he seems to have attracted an undue amount of hostile attention. He states during the trial which preceded his martyrdom that he had resided in Rome for two separate periods. The most obvious point at which to place his departure from Rome is after the Crescens incident, and therefore prior to 161. It is convenient to take the *Address to the Greeks* of Tatian at the same time, since it alludes to the same incident; but some scholars place it at a later date.

TATIAN THE ASSYRIAN

Tatian, the pupil and devout admirer of Justin, had come, like him, from an eastern land. He was a pagan from the country which the Romans called Assyria, east of the Euphrates and west of the Tigris. He came to acquire the western culture. In Athens he had attended the schools and been admitted into the mysteries. No doubt he felt some glow of appreciation at the time, but that was turned into contempt and anger. He went on his way to Rome, and inspected the array of statues which had been brought there from every quarter of the world, and marvelled at their beautiful futility. He saw human blood being poured out in honour of Saturn and Latiarian Jupiter; or heard about it. We are surprised to hear of human sacrifice at this stage of the world's civilization; but Justin mentions it too, and so do the other apologists. The slaying of the king-priest of Diana at Aricia by his successor in office was still going on. The civilization which accepted torture as a normal part of legal procedure and delighted to watch men torn to pieces by wild beasts in the arena, would not have denied an ancient deity his offering of human blood.

Like other intellectuals, Tatian was drawn to Christianity by the study of the Hebrew prophets, which were so much older than any other literature he knew and so far in advance of it spiritually. It introduced him to the one sovereign deity, and delivered him from an infinite array of rulers and tyrants. He allowed himself to be initiated and put off evil and become like an infant. He attached himself to the school of Justin, 'the marvellous Justin', as he calls him, and developed into a teacher and writer of no small merit. We find him back in Athens, where he writes his treatise *Concerning Animals*, which has not been preserved, and his brilliant *Address to the Greeks*, from which we have drawn these particulars. The indications are not as firm as we would like, but the *Address* reads best as an appeal to the Greeks in Athens, and its reference to the hostility of Crescens seems to place it not long after the *Second Apology*. He seems to speak as if Justin were still living, and if so the date of writing must be before 165. In any case the hostility of Crescens is still fresh in his mind; he turns upon him fiercely as if he were present: 'which of the philosophers did he ever attack but *you?*'

THE *ADDRESS TO THE GREEKS*

Tatian is harsh, critical, emotional, inflated, unfair, and one-sided; but there is no denying his ability, sincerity and genius. He was a masterly and influential man; an oriental Tertullian.

He had an excess of temperament. He is all superlatives and extremes. He has no good to say about Greek culture; he finds it superficial, immoral, and lacking in originality. He ridicules the academic culture of Athens, its emphasis on verbal subtlety and felicity, and even its affected accent. If ever there was a case of an inferiority feeling, it is Tatian. He is the hapless outsider who has broken into the charmed circle of an academic tradition. Conscious of his genius, he has asserted himself too loudly, and has been laughed down. His return from Rome as a Christian will be hailed as the latest joke. 'Tatian', they will say, 'has turned aside from the Greeks with their vast multitude of philosophers, and has carved out something new for himself, the doctrines of the barbarians.' This reads as if it were written shortly after his conversion.

He glories in this word 'barbarian', which only meant a person who had no knowledge of the Greek language and letters. 'I said good-bye to the arrogant boasting of the Romans and the chilly verbosity of the Athenians, with their inconsistent doctrines, and embraced our own *barbarian* philosophy.' It was a piece of abuse, no doubt, which had been thrown at the Christian intellectuals, but they had picked it up with pride. Tatian introduces it with dramatic effect in the first sentence of his treatise. 'Gentlemen of Hellas,' he says, 'do not show yourselves too antagonistic to the *barbarians*, or look with ill-will upon their doctrines, for which of your pursuits has not been derived from the *barbarians?*' A rhetorical question which he immediately backs up with a host of examples. Tatian has ransacked libraries and made numerous journeys and personal researches, on which he prides himself. He empties the contents of treatises and note-books into the current of his satire. He grudgingly concedes some merit to Socrates among the philosophers, and Heracles among the demigods; but he has nothing but savage scorn for most of the great figures of Greek philosophy, literature, and religion. There is an emotional intensity about his writing which compares ill with the calm appeal to reason of his master. We can see the trends of thought which led him later on into heresy. He is formally orthodox in his doctrine, but he has a low view of man and of material existence; and his inability to see anything good in the Hellenic culture is in harmony with this attitude. He had a queer view of the heavenly world; he had a queer psychology. He followed Hermas and the Jewish moralists in looking on the spirit which was in man as a gift or loan from God. If he retains it, it enables him to live a life of heroic sanctity and renunciation; if he loses it, he is simply an animal. To repudiate matter is his summary of the good life. He combines an intense and unsteady spirituality with a strong and literal eschatology.

His book is not an apology. It is not a plea to the emperor on behalf of persecuted Christians; it is an onslaught upon the Hellenic culture which he patronized and endowed. It blames the Greeks, by which he means the intellectuals, for the policy of persecution, and derides their philosophy and literature and pretensions to wisdom. He is totally at variance with his master Justin, who reveres the great names of Plato and Socrates and accepts them as forerunners of the gospel. The fact is that he is not speaking altogether as a Christian. He is speaking as an oriental who has plunged into a western imperialistic culture and then turned from it again in disgust, and found truth and happiness in a new oriental philosophy, which was nevertheless older and truer than all the others.

Tatian reminds us of one point that Justin had forgotten; Christianity was an oriental religion, not a European one. He was destined to become the theologian of a Christian Syrianism, not of a Christian Hellenism. He reminds us that Syrian Christianity existed, and that it comprised a large proportion of all living Christians, who may not all have been loyal and devoted subjects of the Roman king.

MARCUS AURELIUS

Antoninus Pius died on 7 March 161, and was succeeded by Marcus Aurelius, in whose reign it would appear that persecution grew more intense. He had been co-emperor with Antoninus since 147, and he proceeded to give the same position to Lucius Verus, his brother by adoption, with the title of Augustus. It was an act of generosity and piety, but it was not wise. The older adoptive principle, which had permitted the choice of mature men with administrative experience, was thus brought to an end. The new method of educating promising young members of the imperial family and investing them with the purple step by step had, of course, been initiated by Hadrian himself when he chose Marcus and Lucius for this purpose; but the rigorous moral and intellectual training which they had received from the greatest rhetoricians and philosophers of the day produced strangely different effects in the two young men. Marcus had grown up serious and thoughtful, but without much trace of humour or social feeling, so far as we can see; he lived a life of monastic or puritan severity. Lucius indulged his natural desires and enjoyed the social pleasures which Marcus despised.

Marcus Aurelius describes his adopted father Antoninus as a man of splendid physical health and equable temperament. He found no difficulty in long hours of administrative labour. He was uniformly affable. Marcus lacked these natural advantages. We gather from his own words that he was physically unequal to the work which he imposed upon himself. He had to drive himself to face the daily routine and to endure discourtesy or bad manners. He had fits of giddiness and haemorrhages; he suffered from laboured breathing; and in view of these facts there is a pathetic interest in his repeated exhortations to himself to act like a man and a Roman, which covered such small but significant points as getting up in the morning. These exhortations were based ultimately on the example of Socrates, who was a miracle of physical vigour and endurance. There was no room for sentiment or tender feeling in Marcus, either as a Greek philosopher or as a Roman gentleman; he shows no sign of it in his writings, either for himself or for others; but in his relations with his family it certainly came to the surface.

He has been described by his detractors as a prig, a judgement which has been further elaborated in the phrase 'a great and good man, and he knew it'. These judgements are hard; but it must be confessed that he was too serious-minded. He was keyed up constantly to a high sense of duty and self-discipline, and had no sympathy with the weaknesses of the average man. He was no judge of character. When all this has been said, it remains that he was a great emperor, perhaps the greatest of

Roman emperors. If he had never written the book of confessions which reveal his inner life and thought, he might be remembered simply as a ruler and general of indomitable spirit, who met one military reverse after another with great ability and unfailing courage.

THE MEDITATIONS

Marcus Aurelius is of value to us in our historical researches as a favourable example of the Stoic idealism which transformed the old Roman culture in its last phase and prepared the way for the Syrian and Iranian religious ideas. It was not literary; for he warned himself against too much book-reading, which he regarded as a dangerous form of self-indulgence. He disliked the flowery and artificial style of the popular writers, and had no interest in metaphysical speculation. Philosophy was for him the art of living in accordance with nature and with reason. He attempted to face facts and to speak plainly. He took seriously the great masters of the moral life.

He was conscious of the existence of much evil in the world; but he strove to impress upon himself the dogma that the universe is governed in accordance with reason, and therefore everything that happens must be good when it is looked at from the point of view of the whole. This rather inhuman reason, which pervaded and directed all things, made itself known in the breast of man. It was the real man; his body and his passions were extraneous things and not parts of his true self. Nothing that happened to the body could be described as evil, since it was external; man should be superior to all external things. He should remain unmoved by good or evil fortune—death itself is only a fact of nature, and therefore must be good; the actor's part was ended and he walked off the stage. He must depart without emotion, and without concern. He must do it as a deliberate act of judgement, and not out of mere obstinacy like the Christians; there should be nothing loud or theatrical; it must be done with gravity and decorum.

The title which he gave to his book of meditations was *To Himself*. It is a spiritual diary which he wrote during his military campaigns. The analysis of the inner life is a form of literature which begins to appear about this time. St Paul was an example of it to a certain degree; the supreme examples are Marcus Aurelius and St Augustine. Marcus owes much to Epictetus, who had set the moral tone to which the best minds in the pagan world responded at this time. Their books were not lost. They were taken over in the Christian church and became manuals of piety in the cloisters of the middle ages. Once again we notice how the culture of an age which is often regarded as decadent did much to fix the modes of thought which helped to form the European civilization.

MARCUS AND THE CHRISTIANS

There is only one reference to the Christians in the writings of Marcus, and we have already quoted it. It proves that he had watched the martyrdoms, and had been repelled by the bravado of the more fanatical of the martyrs and by the 'obstinacy' of the more reasonable. He detected a note of what we would call exhibitionism. It is possible that he did not like persecuting; but he had trained himself to do many things that he did not like. As an emperor, he was bound to suppress disorderly and disloyal organizations which might prove dangerous to the government. He was bound to defend the recognized gods and goddesses who were so violently denounced in the Christian propaganda. He was a firm believer in the gods, whose existence, he thought, could be proved. He performed the unromantic rituals of the old Roman religion as a serious and sacred duty. It was the existence of these gods and the continuance of their rituals which was now the main issue in the battle between the church and the empire. The religion of the empire was a very real one. It was genuinely believed that the ancestral deities and virtues had made Rome great. Christianity threatened them.

Among the tutors who had left a deep impression upon his docile mind had been a certain Junius Rusticus, whom he appointed prefect of the city at the beginning of his reign, in succession to Lollius Urbicus. It was Rusticus who put Justin Martyr to death, and it is plain that he looked down on Christianity as a debased and extravagant superstition, as Pliny had done in his time. Another of his tutors was Aemilianus Fronto, a Latin grammarian and stylist of African origin, who had studied the subject of Christianity, and had come to the conclusion that the charges of cannibalism and incest were perfectly true.[1] We are not at all surprised therefore to find an increase of persecution during the reign of Marcus; and it will appear in the records of the Gallican persecution of 177 that he was personally responsible for the policy.

[1] See R. M. Grant, *The Sword and the Cross* (New York, 1955), pp. 75–6.

THE MARTYRS OF ASIA

Two more bishops were put to death in Asia Minor, both of whom were Phrygians; Thraseas, the bishop of Eumenea, was brought to Smyrna to suffer there, which suggests another high festival like that in which Polycarp had been done to death; Sagaris of Laodicea witnessed in his own city apparently. We have no Acts of these martyrdoms, but they were well remembered even at the end of the century, since other events were dated by referring to them. A conflict between the Phrygian bishops and the Montanist prophets is said to have occurred about the time that Thraseas witnessed; a controversy about the *Pascha* broke out in Laodicea about the time that Sagaris witnessed, which is further defined as 'when Servilius Paulus was proconsul of Asia'; a mistake for Sergius Paulus, whose years as proconsul would be 166–7, or else 162, which is not considered so likely. Thraseas is mentioned before Sagaris in the catalogue of names quoted by Polycrates of Ephesus about 190. The synchronisms are a little shadowy, but the relative dates are fairly probable.

There are also some Acts of Martyrs from Pergamum which may be assigned to the same period, since they make mention of emperors in the plural. They seem to be genuine and contemporary, but are written up in a rather inflated style, very different from those of Polycarp and Justin.

The first martyr was asked his name, and replied, 'My first and choicest name is *Christian*; but if you seek my worldly name, it is Carpus.'

He refused to sacrifice, and made a long discourse on the worship of the gods which we cannot help thinking may have been elaborated by the writer of the Acts. It is a declaration in favour of monotheism and an onslaught on the idols and the daemons. Carpus was tortured with the 'shell' or iron comb, but continued to repeat the words '*I am a Christian*' until he could speak no more.

The second martyr was an old man named Papylus, who came from Thyatira. He was a teacher, and in all probability an ascetic.

'Have you any children?' asked the proconsul.

'Many, by God's mercy', he answered; upon which one of the spectators broke in.

'That is the Christian way of speaking', he said. 'He means that he has children according to the faith.'

'Why did you tell a lie?' asked the proconsul.

'I have children according to God in every province and city.'

'Will you sacrifice, or will you not?'

'From my youth up, I have served God, and have never sacrificed to idols. *I am a Christian*, and you will get no other answer from me; for there is nothing greater or nobler that I can say.'

He was tortured like Carpus and bore it without uttering a sound. They were both nailed to stakes and burned to death. Papylus died more quickly than Carpus. Carpus smiled as he was nailed; 'he saw the glory of the Lord, and was glad'. He died with a prayer of thanksgiving on his lips and this so moved a Christian woman standing by that she offered herself for martyrdom and rushed eagerly into the flames. Her name was Agathonice.

Their bones were carefully guarded to the glory of Christ and the praise of his martyrs.

THE PARTHIAN WAR, A.D. 162–6

Another reason can be suggested for the increase of persecution between 160 and 165. Marcus Aurelius was unfortunate from the beginning of his reign, and had need of all his philosophy to sustain him. The peaceful administration of Antoninus may not have been sufficiently energetic, and a general policy of tightening up may have been necessary. This may have become apparent when a Teutonic tribe called the Hatti crossed the Danube and invaded the Roman provinces of Germany and Rhaetia. Simultaneously Vologases II, the Parthian monarch, invaded the empire in the east. He made himself master of Armenia and Cappadocia without difficulty, and raided into other parts of Asia Minor. Lucius Verus, the second emperor, was despatched to take command in the east.

Verus made his home at Antioch for five years (162–6), and lived a life of pleasure, while his generals conducted the war, pushing far into Media and Babylonia. In 165 his commander-in-chief, the energetic Avidius Cassius, who was a Syrian by birth, reached the twin cities of Seleucia and Ctesiphon, which were near the site of the ancient Babylon; he destroyed the cities and demolished the royal palace of Vologases. No attempt was made to hold this distant territory; he had reached the end of his tether, and his armies were beginning to suffer from the plague; but the more northerly country remained under his control. The province of Mesopotamia, which had been set up for two years by Trajan, was restored to the Empire. In 166 the Emperor Verus returned to Rome from Antioch with great reluctance, for he had come to look upon the east as his kingdom. It is the beginning of a Romano-Syrian connexion which will be of greater historical importance as we proceed. Romanized Syria grew in wealth and military power.

The war years of 162–6 were also the period of the Asian martyrdoms, and possibly of martyrdoms elsewhere. It is the background against which we must place the anti-Roman and anti-Greek diatribes of the oriental Tatian in his *Address to the Greeks*. It also provides an explanation for the appeals of Celsus to the Christians to fight in the army and not allow the empire to fall into the hands of barbarians; and we shall see that they did fight in the armies against the barbarians. Feeling runs high in times of war and calamity, however, and the public likes to find a scapegoat. This attitude is well summed up in a sentence from the *Apology* of Tertullian, written some thirty years later:

If the Tiber floods its banks, if the Nile fails to flood the fields, if heaven holds back the rain, if the earth shakes or famine comes, or pestilence; at once the cry goes up; 'The Christians to the lion!' (Tertullian, *Apology*, XL.)

It is a famous sentence; but it may be that Tertullian took the idea from an earlier apologist, Melito of Sardis, who wrote in the reign of Marcus. In the first year of the reign of Marcus, the Tiber did overflow its banks, and brought disaster to many; there was pestilence and famine; and in the year of victory, 166, when Marcus and Lucius celebrated their 'triumph' in Rome, the oriental plague which had decimated the armies of Avidius Cassius near the site of the ancient Babylon, struck the imperial city itself.

It is likely, therefore, that the pagan population blamed the Christians for these calamities, that Melito protested against this attitude in his *Apology*, and that Tertullian transferred the protest of Melito to his own pages, expressing it in his own epigrammatic style. It is possible, too, that oriental Christians may have taken the Parthian side in the war.

THE MARTYRDOM OF JUSTIN, A.D. 165?

During the years 162–7, Junius Rusticus, the tutor of Marcus Aurelius, was prefect of the city, and during his term of office Justin was in Rome for his second period of residence there. He had a well-organized school, and no doubt he was working on some of his books. Rusticus decided to suppress this centre of Christian propaganda.

It was not, after all, the enmity of Crescens the Cynic that brought Justin to trial, so far as we can see, though Eusebius comes to this conclusion. He and his companions were arrested by police action, and brought before the prefect for examination. In answer to the first question, he gave a simple account of the Christian faith in God and in Christ; but the prefect was not interested in his theology. He wanted to track down more Christians.

'Where do you assemble?' he asked; but Justin evaded the point of this question by giving a theological answer.

'Where each one chooses or can', he said. 'Do you suppose that we all meet in the same place? Not so. The God of the Christians is not limited by spatial conditions. He is invisible, and fills heaven and earth, and is worshipped everywhere, and glorified by the faithful.'

We recognize here the doctrine of a universal world-wide worship which has appeared in so many different forms in apologetic and liturgical texts. Rusticus changed the question.

'Tell me where *you* assemble,' he said, 'or in what place you collect *your* followers.'

Justin had nothing to conceal on this point, since the arrest had been made.

'I live above a man named Martin at the Thimotinian baths', he said; 'and during the whole time—for I am now residing in Rome for the second time—I have known no other place of meeting; and if anyone wished to see me, I communicated to them the teaching of the truth.'

He had answered strictly according to the letter of the question, which referred only to his own school. It is easy for us to see from his reply how his hearers and pupils could mix with the crowds that came to the baths, and find their way unnoticed to his upper room.

'Are you a *Christian*?' asked Rusticus.

'*I am a Christian*', answered Justin. It was the fatal question which the code of the martyr forbade him to evade by the use of theological subtleties or baffling answers. The same question was put to the other prisoners in turn.

'*I am a Christian* by the grace of God', answered Charito and Chariton. They were brother and sister, no doubt; and they were playing on the meaning of their own names, which were derived from the word *charis*, which means grace.

Euelpistus was a Cappadocian and a servant of Caesar; a member of the civil service, as we would say. He followed suit. '*I am a Christian*, too, set free by Christ; and by the grace of God I share the same hope.' He was a pupil of Justin, he admitted, but had learned to be a Christian from his parents in his own country. His answer contained a reference to his name, which means 'hopeful'.

'*I am a Christian*', said Hierax, who was a difficult and obstinate case; he refused to say whether Justin had converted him to Christianity. 'I *am* a Christian,' he repeated, 'I *was* a Christian, and I will *go on* being a Christian.' With regard to his parents he condescended to give a little information; 'Christ is our true father,' he said, 'and faith is our true mother; my earthly parents died, and when I was driven away from Iconium in Phrygia, I came here.' We note that it is the Phrygian who makes use of baffling answers. He reminds us of Carpus and Papylus.

Paeon and Liberianus also admitted that they were Christians. Paeon had received the good confession from his parents, like Euelpistus. None would incriminate Justin by saying that *he* had converted them.

The prefect now attempted to break them down by threats.

'Listen', he said to Justin. 'You call yourself learned, and think that you know true teachings; if you are scourged and beheaded, do you believe that you will ascend into heaven?'

'If I endure these things', said Justin, 'my hope is that I will receive his gifts.'

'Suppose we get down to business. Offer sacrifice to the gods.'

'No right-thinking person falls away from piety to impiety.'

'Unless you obey, you will be mercilessly punished.'

'Even if we are punished we can be saved through prayer, through our Lord Jesus Christ; for this will become our salvation and our confidence at the more fearful and universal judgement-seat of our Lord and Saviour.'

All the martyrs assented to this, saying, 'Do whatever you like; for *we are Christians*, and do not sacrifice to idols.'

It was the Christian martyr now, and not the enlightened pagan philosopher, who was standing for the sanctity of his convictions and the freedom of the human spirit, before the organized and educated tyranny of a deified world-power using naked force. The prefect proceeded to pronounce the sentence.

'Let those who have refused to sacrifice to the gods, and will not yield to the command of the emperor, be scourged and led away to suffer the punishment of decapitation according to the laws.' The holy martyrs glorified God, the narrative says, and went forth to the accustomed place, and were beheaded, and so made perfect their witness by the confession of the Saviour; and some of the faithful removed the bones secretly and laid them in a fitting place, the grace of our Lord having wrought with them: to whom be glory for ever and ever: Amen.　　　　　(*The Martyrdom of Justin.*)

The narrative seems to be taken from the records of the court, or else it was written down at once when the dialogue was still fresh in the memory; but its liturgical close and response prove that it was composed to be read in church, perhaps on the birthday of the martyrs, though nothing is said about this. In the cemetery of Priscilla there is a stone which bears the inscription 'MXOUSTINOS' in Greek letters; it looks almost like the name of Justin preceded by the letter 'M' for the word 'martyr'; and possibly it marks the resting-place of the body of the founder of Christian philosophy, awaiting the visitation from heaven. His day in early Roman martyrologies is 14 April; in the east it is 1 June. The Syrian Chronicle gives the year of his death as 165.

The catacomb legends tell tales of other martyrs under Marcus Aurelius.

CHAPTER 11

PHRYGIAN CHRISTIANITY

THE SEVEN CHURCHES OF ASIA MINOR

What appears before us now in Asia Minor is the circle of seven churches which St John addressed in his Revelation. It is only about seventy years later, and some of them have become increasingly conscious of their inheritance in it. It would appear to have been a book of local interest, which only spread slowly to the churches of the Christian world. It was known to Theophilus of Antioch and to Clement of Alexandria, but the east as a whole did not accept it. It played an important part, however, in forming the Christianity of the Phrygian churches, which had not been evangelized by Paul himself. The story of Montanism shows that western Phrygia was essentially Johannine country.

There were two cities on the inland territory which gave leadership at this time to the whole of Asia Minor. One was Sardis, and the other was Hierapolis. Sardis had been the capital city of the mythical Croesus, who was king of Lydia; it had received a message of its own in the Revelation, but its early Christian history is not known. Its bishop was Melito. The other was Hierapolis, the principal city of Phrygia. It had been mentioned by Paul in his Epistle to the Colossians, but had received no message from John. This may have been because it was the headquarters of the apostle Philip. The connecting link between the apostolic age and the mid-second century was Papias, who, judging by his name, was a native Phrygian. Its bishop now was Claudius Apollinarius, whose position resembled that of a metropolitan.

MELITO OF SARDIS

Melito was an ascetic of holy life. Polycrates called him the blessed eunuch and says that he lived continually in the Holy Spirit: but the words of Polycrates should not perhaps be taken too literally. We learn from Tertullian that he was regarded as a prophet, though not in Montanist circles. In addition to being a mystic he was a learned scholar, and in particular a student of the Old Testament. He was not satisfied, however, with the state of Old Testament studies as he found it. A certain Onesimus had frequently requested him to provide him with a book of extracts from the Law and the prophets referring to the Saviour and the faith as a whole. He even desired to be reassured about the exact number and order of the ancient books. The fact is that the old 'Books of Testimonies' such as Justin had used were now quite inadequate: the text and the canonicity of the verses quoted by him were freely disputed by the Jews. The text of the Old Testament had become a subject for learned discussion, and new translations were being produced. Leaders of Christian thought had to keep up with these movements.

In order to obtain some reliable information, Melito made a pilgrimage to Palestine, as Peregrinus had done before him, and visited 'the place where these things were announced and effected'; that is to say the city of Aelia, as Jerusalem was now called. We do not know at what period of his life he did this; we are narrating it here in order to build up the portrait of the man. At Aelia he would meet the great Narcissus, who was even more famous than Melito himself as a holy man and ascetic, and became in due course bishop of Aelia. Melito brought back to Sardis a list of Old Testament books which is almost identical with the list which was sanctioned by the Jewish Rabbis at Jamnia in the nineties, and accepted in due course throughout the Christian church; but the book of Esther is missing, as it is in the canon of Athanasius. He agreed with Hegesippus, a Palestinian scholar, in giving Proverbs the title of the 'All-Virtuous Wisdom'. From these books he composed six volumes of extracts for Onesimus. It is interesting to learn that there was an authority in the Palestinian church to which the western churches deferred on this matter.

He also agreed with Hegesippus in making quotations from the Aramaic and the Syriac. It is interesting that Rome and Asia should

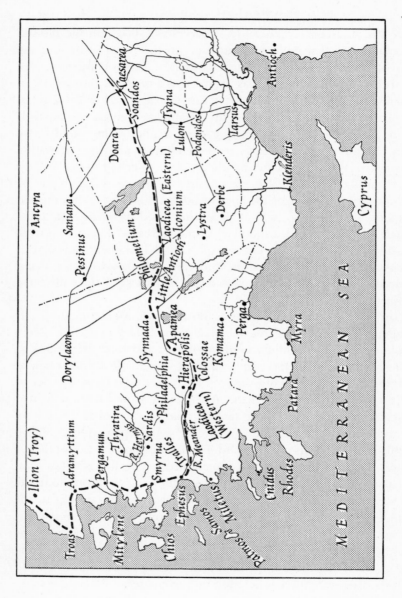

Map 2. The churches of Asia Minor.

(1) *The Churches of the Revelation*

The map shows the Island of Patmos, where the Revelation was written; and the seven churches to which it was sent. A broken line shows the division between the Roman provinces of Asia and Galatia (and, in the south, Pamphylia).

(1) From *Ephesus* there is a road north along the coast through Troas to Pontus and Bithynia, and another east through Phrygia and on as far as Mesopotamia. Melito and Avircius would follow this high-road on their eastern journeys. There would be Roman military establishments, inns, and facilities for travelling, all the way; but they would be entertained and sent on their way by the churches. This work was an episcopal responsibility.

(2) *Smyrna* had assumed the leadership of the coastal part of Asia, owing to the character and prestige of Polycarp. It was the scene of his martyrdom and of the subsequent martyrdom of Thraseas of Eumenea (on the Glaucus River),

(3) *Pergamus* (or Pergamum), was the scene of the martyrdom of Carpus, Papylus and Agathonice.

(4) *Thyatira* was the home of Papylus. The anti-Montanist 'Alogi', who were hostile to the Johannine writings, strangely insisted that there was no church there.

(5) *Sardis* was the capital of the ancient realm of Lydia, bordering on ancient Phrygia. Its bishop at this time was Melito. He was the most important Christian leader in Asia Minor.

(6) *Philadelphia* had a special prophetic tradition through a certain Ammia, who flourished in the period between the Revelation and the Montanist movement, and (apparently) formed a link between the two.

(7) *Laodicea* received an epistle from St Paul, of which no trace remains. It must be distinguished from the east-Phrygian Laodicea.

(2) *The Lycus River.*

The Phrygian cities are related to the river system. These rivers flow down from a mountainous country through wooded glens. The important cities of *Hierapolis*, *Laodicea* and *Colossae* are situated on the Lycus River, a little above its confluence with the Meander. All three are mentioned in St Paul's Epistle to the Colossians, and they are close enough together to have a common history.

Hierapolis had become the leading church, owing to the important work of the apostle Philip in the first century and his successor Papias in the second.

Further east, along the high-road, is the important city of *Apamea*, where there was a Jewish community which had combined the worship of Jehovah with that of a local deity named Sabazius. The city recognized this cult. There were many ancient Jewish settlements all through this region. The pressure of Judaism is felt in Philadelphia and elsewhere.

(3) *The Glaucus River*

The Glaucus River and its tributaries flow down into the Meander out of the high mountain country. In these deep valleys, a prophetic form of the gospel seems to have outstripped the church organization and created the Phrygian form of Christianity known as Montanism.

The principal Montanist centres were *Ardabau*, the home of Montanus, whose site is unknown; *Pepuza*, the 'New Jerusalem' of the sect; and *Tymion*, near Pepuza. These villages were the holy land of 'Montanus and his women'.

Higher up the Glaucus River was the Phrygian 'Pentapolis', or 'Five Towns'. In one of these the 'Anonymous' author of a work against Montanism wrote his book about 192; he was probably a bishop. He wrote at the request of Bishop Avircius of *Hierapolis* and of a synod which had met at Ancyra, which he attended with his friend Zoticus of *Otrous*. This Zoticus is, very likely, different from the Zoticus of Cumana who assisted Julian of Apamea to examine the prophetess Maximilla.

The site of this *Cumana* is unknown, but it is suggested that it was in the neighbourhood of Apamea, where the name Zoticus was common. There is a Komama in southern Galatia, and a Comana in northern.

(4) *The Southern Galatian Cities*

Farther to the east, the high-road veers north to avoid the Sultan Dagh Mountains, which run south of it, separating it from the Galatian part of Phrygia. *Little Antioch, Iconium, Derbe, and Lystra,* were the cities which Paul visited on his 'first missionary journey', before A.D. 50. His Epistle to the Galatians is addressed to them.

They do not seem to have been subject to the Johannine influence. They were 'Encratite' in character, rather than 'Montanist'. They cherished the memory of Paul, and are the scene of the exploits of Thecla in the 'Acts of Paul'.

(5) *Northern Galatia*

The map marks the two principal cities of northern Galatia, *Pessinus* and *Ancyra*; this is the true Galatia, which had received its name from invading Gauls about three centuries before Christ. Pessinus was the holy city of the goddess Cybele; it was from this town that her black fetish-stone had been taken to Rome two hundred years before Christ. Ancyra is the modern Ankara. It was the scene of an anti-Montanist synod about the year 192.

We do not know when Christianity reached these cities.

both have enjoyed the services of oriental scholars, which made possible some degree of contact with Jews and Jewish Christians on a bilingual basis. Some of the few scraps of Melito's writings which remain are in the Syriac language, and the suggestion has been made that he wrote them in that language. He may have been a Syrian. He was an exponent of the high monarchian theology like Ignatius, and rejoiced in the paradox of the incarnation.

He was begotten before the light, the creator of all things with the Father, fashioner of mankind...incarnate in the virgin, born at Bethlehem, wrapped in swaddling-clothes...pierced with the spear in the flesh, hanged upon the tree, buried in the earth, risen from the dead...the repose of the departed, the finder of the lost, the charioteer of the cherubim, the chief of the army of angels, God of God, Son of the Father, Jesus Christ king for ever. Amen.

(Melito, Fragment, from R. M. Grant, *Second-century Christianity*, p. 77.)

His passionate, hurried, efflorescent style, with its poetic manner and its eye for the dramatic, is not Greek; nor is it always Christian. Pagan myth provides its splendid images for this new mode of Christian rhetoric. The figure of Christ is arrayed in the glory of the unconquered sun.

As when a copper globe full of fire within, flashing much light, is washed in cold water with a great noise, but the fire within is not quenched but again flashes fierily; so the sun, burning like lightning, is washed wholly but not extinguished...washed in a mystic baptism, he rejoices exceedingly.... He rises as a new sun to men; driving out the darkness of night, he begets the light of day. On this course also the motion of the stars and the moon by nature moves; they are washed at the baptistery of the sun like good disciples. ... Now if the sun with the stars and the moon, is washed in the ocean, why not Christ too in the waters of Jordan? King of kings and governor of creation, the sun of the east who also appeared to the dead in hell and to mortals in the world, shone forth from heaven as the only sun. (*Ibid.* p. 74.)

CLAUDIUS APOLLINARIUS AND THE PASCHA

Melito wrote a book *Concerning the Pascha* whose opening words are quoted in Eusebius.

In the time of Servilius Paulus proconsul of Asia, at which season Sagaris witnessed as a martyr, there came a great controversy in Laodicea concerning the *Pascha*, which fell according to the season at that time: and these things were written. (Melito, *Concerning the Pascha*, in Eusebius, *E.H.* IV, 26, 3.)

We have made use of these words in fixing our chronology. The text is not in good shape. Servilius Paulus should be Sergius Paulus, whose proconsular years were 166–7 (or possibly 162); and the statement that the Pascha fell according to the season at that time has no meaning as it now stands.

Claudius Apollinarius, the bishop of Hierapolis, also wrote a book on this subject, a short extract from which is included in an Alexandrian document called the *Paschal Chronicle*. His manner is a little heavy and superior.

There are, to be sure, some who are contentious about these questions, owing to their ignorance; and we must forgive them for this; since ignorance does not merit accusation; what it needs is instruction.

Now what they assert is that the Lord ate the lamb on the fourteenth day [of the month Nisan], and that he suffered on the great day of the unleavened bread [which was the fifteenth]: and they interpret Matthew as saying what they imagine to be the case, so that their understanding of it is not in harmony with the Law; and according to them the Gospels appear to be at variance.   (Claudius Apollinarius, *Concerning the Pascha*, in the *Paschal Chronicle*, Preface.)

Apollinarius himself must have believed that the Lord suffered on the fourteenth, and so he must have somehow interpreted Matthew as saying what *he* imagined to be the case. He was attempting to harmonize it with John; but unfortunately the Gospels *are* at variance, and modern scholars are unable to reconcile them.

There were two customs then, but unfortunately it is not certain what they were. One's first impression is that the Matthaeans kept their Pascha on the fifteenth of Nisan, and the Johannines on the fourteenth; but there is another possibility which is more likely to be correct. Perhaps both observed the fourteenth, but in different ways; the Matthaeans keeping it as a Passover in imitation of the Jews,[1] the Johannines ignoring its connexion with the Passover, and keeping it as the annual commemoration of the Crucifixion.[2] Jesus was the true Paschal Lamb, and his sacrifice of himself upon the cross had fulfilled the type.

This is the first reference in the surviving literature to the Gospel of Matthew by name; and for Apollinarius, at any rate, there were a

---

[1] Their fast would begin after the Passover meal, as in the Hebrew Gospel (and the Gospel of Peter?).

[2] Presumably they kept the whole Passover day as a fast.

number of Gospels, which formed a harmonious group. It was inconceivable that they should disagree with one another. His opponents, of course, may have been Ebionites, who used Matthew only.

THE EXAMINATION OF MAXIMILLA

We now may return to our earlier synchronism, the martyrdom of Thraseas, which we assigned to the years 160–5. It was at the time of this martyrdom, Eusebius says, that a certain Zoticus confronted Maximilla at Pepuza, when she was making a pretence at prophesying, and attempted to refute the false spirit that was speaking through her; he gives as his authority for this statement a writer named Apollonius, who wrote an account of the New Prophecy at the end of the century: see Eusebius, *E.H.* v, 18, 13 and 14.

Eusebius depended for his information about the New Prophecy on two authors who wrote about 190 and 200. One of these was Apollonius; the other is referred to by scholars as 'The Anonymous', an unfortunate title, since it suggests that he put out his book anonymously, whereas he was actually a well-known ecclesiastic in his day whose name unfortunately has not been preserved. Eusebius gives the actual words in which he refers to the incident.

Approved men and bishops, Zoticus from the village of Cumana, and Julian from Apamea, were present to test and refute the spirit which was speaking; but Themiso and his followers stopped their mouths, and would not permit the false spirit which was deceiving the people to be refuted by them.

('The Anonymous', in Eusebius, *E.H.* v, 16, 17.)

The encounter was also referred to in a Montanist publication which was known as *According to Asterius Urbanus*. This work is thought to have been a collection of the inspired oracles of the Montanist leaders; for it contained the words in which Maximilla protested against such treatment.

I am driven away from the sheep as if I were a wolf; I am not a wolf; I am Word and Spirit and Power. (Asterius Urbanus, *ibid.*)

The scene is a dramatic one. The two bishops are clearly in a minority, and have come from a distance. The location of Cumana is not known, but Apamea was a large city situated on the highway. It was not denied that Maximilla was inspired. That was regarded as obvious. It was a spirit of some sort that spoke through the frenzied woman when she was in 'ecstasy'; and it had to be either the Spirit of God or the spirit of an unclean daemon. There was no other possibility. Paul and John had both said that the spirits should be examined or tested; and it was the duty of the church through its approved men and bishops to make the examination and to decide; but the venture came to nothing. Themiso was too strong for them. We hear of Themiso elsewhere; he was a high-ranking man in the hierarchy of the New Prophecy; a confessor, it was claimed, and the author of a 'catholic epistle'. It would seem that he was second in command to Montanus himself; perhaps his successor.

What we are watching here is a turning point in a conflict which had now become acute. The leaders of the church recognized that the New Prophecy was a strange phenomenon. They disliked the speaking 'in ecstasy', with its entire loss of mental control by the prophet. They tried to prove that the biblical prophets had not spoken 'in ecstasy'. At some time or another the prophets were ruled out of order.

This schism was bound to come. It was not possible for responsible constitutional leaders to accept the dictatorship of an irresponsible irrational spirituality. It might seem to be departing from the great freedom of prophesying which had existed in the former generations; but these were not prophets of the older Christian type; they were prophets of the pagan type; the frenzy that shook them was like the frenzy that shook the devotees of Attis. They were Christian corybantes. In the teachers of the type of Justin we see the primitive Christian teacher Hellenized; he appears in the guise of the Greek philosopher. In the prophets of the type of Montanus we see the primitive Christian prophet Phrygianized; he appears in the guise of the dervish.

APOLLINARIUS AND THE NEW PROPHECY

As the head of the most important of the Phrygian churches, Apollinarius was naturally bound to take a leading part in the controversy with Montanus and his women; and Eusebius states that he wrote on the subject when Montanus and his false prophetesses were still at the beginning of their deviation from the true path. His writings were strongly commended by Serapion, who became bishop of Antioch about 192. Serapion wrote an Epistle on the subject himself, with which he sent out some papers or documents of Apollinarius. Eusebius adds that he found in this Epistle of Serapion the signatures of certain bishops, two of which he quotes.

Aurelius Quirinius martyr [or witness]: I wish you well.

Aelius Publius Julius from Develtum, a colony, of Thrace, bishop: as God in heaven liveth, I swear that the blessed Sotas of Achialus wished to cast out Priscilla's daemon, but the hypocrites would not allow it.

(Eusebius, *E.H.* v, 19, 3.)

He says that he found these signatures 'in the Epistle'; but it is more probable that they belonged to the documents of Apollinarius which were sent with it. The bishop of Develtum in Thrace is more likely to have turned up at Hierapolis than at Antioch, and the fact to which he bears witness must have taken place long before the episcopate of Serapion.

Signatures of this sort are placed on official documents, and it looks as if the document in this case was a conciliar Epistle. We infer that Apollinarius presided over a synod which commissioned him to write an Epistle which would be signed by all the members of the synod. It is stated by the Anonymous that synods of the faithful were held at this time to deal with the Montanist crisis; and judging by these signatures they may have included martyrs, and possibly others, with the bishops.

In the ninth century, some unknown scholar or librarian compiled a list of church synods or councils from ancient sources. It is known as the *Liber Synodicus* or *Synodicon*; and the oldest entry on its list is a synod at Hierapolis under Apollinarius, which was attended by twenty-six other bishops. The evidence of this late document, taken by itself, might not be considered very high; but it is an interesting confirmation of an impression which we had already received from the evidence which Eusebius gleaned from the pages of Serapion. Its evidence is completely independent of Eusebius. It has no reference to Priscilla. It states that the synod condemned the errors of Montanus and Maximilla and Theodotus; but it confuses Theodotus the high steward of the Montanist oblations with a later Theodotus, a Byzantine theologian who was nicknamed the 'leather-worker'. The *Synodicon* appears to be making use of old material, and we shall return to the consideration of it later.

Thrace was a barbarous region like Phrygia, though it had its outposts of civilization, like the 'colony' of Develtum, whose bishop subscribes his name in the formal Roman style. It had its own orgiastic mystery cult, since it was the original home of Dionysus, the god of wine. We are not told whether the blessed Sotas came all the way from Anchialus to Pepuza to exorcize Priscilla, or whether Priscilla was on a visit to Thrace. The latter theory sounds the more probable. The form of oath used by Julius suggests that he was making a deposition on behalf of Sotas about something which had happened elsewhere. The *Synodicon* comes to our help again with a statement that a local synod was held at Anchialus in Thrace under Sotas, which was attended by twelve bishops, and that it condemned the same three persons.

The conflict was not only more widely extended; it was more acute. Zoticus had only attempted to 'prove' the spirit which spoke through Maximilla. Sotas attempted to exorcize Priscilla's daemon. He treated her as a person who was possessed by an evil spirit.

THE MONTANIST FASTS

Montanism was now an expanding movement, and it was acquiring a definite policy and organization under its highly authoritative leadership. It was making many decisions on spiritual problems. Apollonius begins his account of Montanus by saying that he laid down the law about fasting, and dissolved marriages. The latter statement has been taken to imply that Priscilla and Maximilla had abandoned their husbands before joining the Montanist movement as 'virgins'. The word 'virgin' was used rather loosely at the time for a holy person now living in a chaste and unwedded state. The virgins were grouped with the 'widows'. Ignatius had spoken of the widows who are styled virgins. Tertullian ranks a widow higher than a virgin. He is a first-hand authority on Montanism, and tells us that the Paraclete had definitely forbidden second marriages, which were therefore no longer lawful in the church. It was true that the apostles had permitted widows to marry again; but this was a concession to the weakness of the flesh, and the concession had been withdrawn by the Paraclete. Indeed Tertullian, though a married man, did not altogether approve the married state. The prophet himself cannot have been sympathetic to marriage either.

In those areas where the *Didache* was accepted, Wednesday and Friday were already set aside as fast-days. Elsewhere, it would seem, days of fasting were appointed by the bishop or by private devotion.

Hermas appears to have chosen his own. Sometimes the food which Christians denied themselves, or its monetary equivalent, was given to the poor, in accordance with a favourite passage from Isaiah (lviii. 6 f.) We find at the end of the century that it was customary to break the fast at 'the ninth hour', about three in the afternoon. Enthusiasts carried it on longer, and the Montanists were among those who did so. They also had a milder kind of fast called a xerophagy in which they rationed themselves very strictly, not eating any kind of food with juice or fat. Fasting, like sexual asceticism, had always been looked upon as a means of obtaining visions. We find this in Hermas too.

But fasting was more than a private devotion, and included more than abstinence from food. In Hermas it was a day of devotion for a whole family or household. There were readings of some sort; food was restricted to bread and water; an offering was made for the poor; and a 'liturgy' of this type was acceptable to the Lord. Since the devotional practices of the church all had a Jewish background, it is worth noting that a day of fasting or humiliation among the Jews was a dramatic liturgical observance. Trumpets were blown, solemn assemblies were held, earnest prayer was offered, sackcloth and ashes were worn. Special fasts were ordered in case of invasion by enemies and such calamities as might endanger the harvest. They were specially associated with prayers for rain, and therefore appropriate at certain seasons of the year. The great compulsory calendrical fast was the Day of Atonement which preceded the Feast of Tabernacles, and marked the autumn New Year. On this fast the pious Jew could obtain forgiveness of all his former sins.

The only traditional seasonal fast among the Christians was the Pascha, when the death of Christ upon the cross was solemnly commemorated. Unfortunately we have very little light on the method by which it was kept, except that it was the traditional season for baptisms, and the Passion narratives from the four Gospels appear to have been used on this day; for the observance of the different days was based on the use of different Gospels, and caused bitter controversy in the Christian community. Which side the Montanists took, we do not know; but there came a time, we do not know how soon, when they parted from the Jewish calendar altogether and chose a fixed day in the Roman calendar, 25 March, on which their fellow-countrymen were mourning the death of their shepherd-god Attis. Some, however, as if to avoid this synchronism, deferred the Pascha till 6 April: this date is related calendrically to 25 March as 6 January is to 25 December.

It does not seem likely that this move had been made so early as the time we are considering. What we learn from Tertullian is that there were two extra weeks of fasting, or rather of xerophagy, during the year. We owe to St Jerome the information that one of these weeks came after Pentecost,[1] the concluding day of the fifty days which follow the Pascha. Since this was a fixed occasion, the other was probably a fixed occasion too; possibly the Day of Atonement, or its pagan equivalent, the Syrian and Greek New Year, which came in the autumn.[2]

Neither the Saturday nor the Sunday in these weeks was kept as a fast, Tertullian says.

While Montanus elaborated the system of fasting and made it much stricter, and formed a compulsory system out of it, it seems likely that he was working from traditions which he found in existence; but the enemies of the movement compared these fasts of his to the similar customs in the rites of Isis or Cybele, which were fundamentally lamentations for the dead; but Tertullian defended them as a training for martyrdom.

THE PROPHETIC ORGANIZATION

The three annual seasons of fasting must have been the principal occasions when the crowds flocked to Pepuza and Tymion. Apollonius says that Montanus gave the name of Jerusalem to these villages, because he wanted people from all quarters to assemble there. He appointed agents for collecting money, he goes on to say; he engineered schemes for receiving gifts under the name of oblations or sacrifices; he supplied salaries to those who preached his word. They all made a very good thing out of it, he insinuates. The business side of the new movement offended the catholic minded; for the tradition had been that all offerings were free-will offerings, and that the clergy were maintained out of the common fund. If you get food and lodging, you should be content with that, St Paul had said. The false prophet or the false teacher never had been content with it; he was a christmonger rather than a Christian, as the *Didache* had said; and yet that mysterious

[1] Represented now by the Whitsun 'Ember Days'.
[2] Represented now by the autumn 'Ember Days' which succeed 14 September (Holy Cross Day).

document rather anticipated what was being done in the New Jerusalem, The prophets, it said, are your high priests, and you must bring them first-fruits of everything you have. The first-fruits given to these prophetic high priests of the *Didache* are in line with the oblations given to the Montanist hierarchy; the assembly of people from all parts at the New Jerusalem, and the observance of three seasonal fasts fit into the picture, for the Jews came up to the old Jerusalem three times a year. It was not far out of line either with the native Phrygian system; the god was the owner of the surrounding territory, and offerings had to be brought to him by all and sundry, and various ascetic taboos had to be observed. It would appear that Pepuza and Tymion had been taken possession of for the new religion. The Christian god had ousted the local deity, and had his own entourage of prophets, priests, and virgins.

The head of the business side of the organization was a certain Theodotus who is described by the Anonymous as the high steward of the so-called prophecy.

It may be felt that the picture which has emerged is too fantastic to be real; but numbers of parallels could be found in the long strange history of the church, especially under missionary or pioneer conditions.[1] What we are watching is the emergence of a new national form of Christianity. The Christian faith in its prophetic form took hold of the mountains and glens of Mysia like a forest fire. It blazed ahead in uncontrollable force. A great man of the native type, a born leader and a fiery fanatic, rose up and took command. He rode in the whirlwind and directed the storm. His voice was heard throughout the Christian world. He preached a harsh inhuman self-discipline which matched the emotionalism of the revival orgies. It was the Phrygian temperament asserting itself in Christian terms. The forms it created were obviously fantastic; its language was too high and exalted; it cultivated a spiritual intoxication; it was to madness near allied; but it had a frightful sincerity mixed with a touch of genius. It brought increase of vision to the church far and wide.

[1] It would be interesting to compare the prophetic movements which occurred among the Maoris in New Zealand, who had prophets and healers, and even their sacred towns like Hiruharama (Jerusalem); or with the American sects of the early nineteenth century.

THE *ACTS OF PAUL*

South of the highway, and south too of the Sultan Dagh Mountains were the east Phrygian cities of Little Antioch, Iconium, Lystra, and Derbe, which Paul and Barnabas had evangelized from Antioch in Syria, in their first missionary journey a hundred years before. The memory of this visit was affectionately cherished, and had given birth to the noble legend of Thecla, which sheds considerable light on the special views about Christianity which were held in this region.

We have noted the historical consciousness developing in the church and expressing itself by the formation of succession lists, the recounting of old traditions, the revisiting of sacred places, the reverence due to the days of the martyrs, and so forth. Another expression of it was the historical novel, such as the *Wanderings of Peter* and the *Ascents of James*, which were being produced in Palestine or Syria, and the *Acts of Paul* in Asia Minor. Fortunately we are not without information about the latter document; for Tertullian remarks in his treatise on baptism,

But what if the writings falsely ascribed to Paul [the text is not perfectly clear at this point] do defend the right of a woman to teach and baptize? Let them know that in Asia the presbyter who composed that scripture, as if with the idea of adding to Paul's glory [Tertullian is being heavily sarcastic here], was condemned; and though he confessed that he had done it out of love for Paul, he was degraded from his office.

(Tertullian, *De Baptismo*, XVII.)

Tertullian was writing about A.D. 200, thirty-five years after the ending of the Parthian war. The book to which he alludes had then gone through the four successive stages of composition in Greek, translation into Latin, circulation in the west, and acceptance there as authentic. It need not have been written so early as the hundred-and-sixties, though some scholars assign it to that period; it surely cannot be a great deal later.

This book was the so-called *Acts of Paul*, and large portions of it still exist in Greek in a form which seems to have been edited by later hands. It was not a church book, and therefore was subject to re-writing. The style and imagination of the presbyter who wrote it were puerile; he was a man of no intellectual ability, though he could tell a tale in a popular manner, which is no mean gift. He was no critic or historian, however, and that is why we are astonished to find a few details which agree with historical conditions in the first century. The narrative follows the road-system of the first century, and the relations of historical characters are accurately given. The inference is that he had an old legend to work on which had connexions with the first century.

Eastern Phrygia, therefore, had its own respectable historical tradition. Paul was its patron apostle, but he was associated with the native-born virgin and martyr Thecla. Whether Thecla actually cut her hair short, and hitched up her dress so as to look like a boy; whether she really taught and baptized—a feature which is no longer preserved in the text; whether the lion in the arena actually lay down and licked her feet; whether there was an actual Thecla at all; all these are questions to which the historian can find no ready answer. She and her lion may come out of native romance or native mythology;[1] but many scholars have believed that she was a historical person; and her legend is certainly ancient.

Tertullian is our witness that in the earlier form of the text Thecla taught and baptized.[2] As it is now, there is no such reference; but she does perform the amazing feat of baptizing herself in public in a tank full of ferocious seals, which seem to be regarded by the presbyter as man-eating animals; from which one would judge that he was not familiar with the sea.

FEMINISM AND ASCETICISM

The cult of Thecla proves the existence of a strain of feminism in the church, which is said to have been characteristic of social conditions in Phrygia, where the mother-goddess was worshipped and women were influential in society. As we think of Thecla teaching and baptizing in the legends of eastern Phrygia, we cannot help thinking of Maximilla and Priscilla prophesying in western Phrygia. We think, too, of their predecessors, Ammia in Philadelphia and the daughters of Philip in Hierapolis; also of Marcellina and Philumene, who came to Rome from Alexandria.

[1] Lions still existed in Asia Minor. The local mother-goddess was attended by lions.
[2] Women baptized in the Marcionite sect, Tertullian said.

Scholars describe the *Acts of Paul* as 'catholic', and doubtless they are not written in the interests of any heretical school; but their emphasis on virginity approaches the border-line. Perhaps the reverend author was an 'encratite' himself like Melito, and gloried in virginity; but the legend lent itself to this purpose. This is what the author makes of the beatitudes, as Paul preaches them at Iconium, and Thecla listens in a condition which is very close to 'ecstasy'.

Blessed are the pure in heart; for they shall see God.
Blessed are they who keep the flesh chaste; for they shall become the temple of God.
Blessed are they who are continent, for unto them shall God speak....
Blessed are they that possess their wives as though they had them not, for they shall inherit God....
Blessed are the bodies of the virgins; for they shall be well-pleasing unto God. *(Acts of Paul, II, 5, 6.)*

When Thecla had recovered from her ecstasy, she broke off her engagement with the socially eligible Thamyris and abandoned everything to follow Paul. This antipathy to marriage is an exaggeration of a well-known Pauline doctrine, and resembles the views of the anti-Pauline heretics who are combated in the Pastoral Epistles. These heretics forbade men to marry or to eat flesh; and in the *Acts of Paul* a vegetarian asceticism also appears; for Thecla finds the apostle hiding in a tomb on the road from Iconium to Daphne, and living on bread and water; some textual authorities add salt.[1] There is a curious field for research in these allusions to sacred foods. Why did the Marcionites allow fish but not flesh? Why did some Montanists lay so much stress on cheese as to be called the 'artotyrites', the bread-and-cheese men? Why does Hippolytus bring olives and cheese[2] into such close association with the bishop's first eucharist.

Our author knew the Pastoral Epistles of St Paul, but only used them as a source-book for names, such as Demas and Onesiphorus. It has even been suggested that he was writing a counterblast to the Pastorals, which are favourable to marriage and allow all kinds of foods. As a source of ideas, he naturally prefers I and II Corinthians; and he

[1] Salt had a semi-sacramental character in Ebionism, which is partially anticipated in the Gospels, and is based on old oriental ideas.
[2] Cheese in Hippolytus is 'coagulated milk', and milk and honey had their place in the tradition. In the vision of Perpetua, cheese represents the sacrament.

composes on his own account a *Third Epistle to the Corinthians*, against Cleobius and Dositheus, who deny the resurrection of the body; so he was no docetist, and agreed with the Pastorals against Hymenaeus and Philetus on this important doctrine. He makes Onesiphorus the father of Thecla; for Thecla, like Onesiphorus, visited Paul in prison.

But Thecla at night took off her bracelets and gave them to the doorkeeper, and when the door was opened for her, she went into the prison, and gave the jailer a mirror of silver, and so went in to Paul, and sat by his feet and heard the wonderful works of God. And Paul feared not at all, but walked in the confidence of God; and her faith also was increased as she kissed his chains. (*Acts of Paul*, II, 18.)

THE CULT OF THE MARTYRS

We recognize in this passage a picture of the kind of thing that was going on among Christians at the time, or more likely the kind of conduct which was idealized in a fanciful way, and held up for imitation. We think of Polycarp kissing the chains of Ignatius. We think of the would-be martyr Peregrinus and the pilgrims from Asia who smuggled dainties into his prison. The value of the book is that it illustrates the ideals and aspirations and wishful thinking of the Christian reading public; perhaps some circle of devout ladies to whom the presbyter read it aloud. It holds up to reverence the figures of the virgin, the ascetic and the martyr.

We noticed in the case of Polycarp that there were two attitudes in the church with regard to persecution. There was the official attitude, which offered some respect to the state, played a defensive game and avoided conflict; and there was the attitude of the enthusiast or fanatic who threw caution to the winds and provoked conflict. It is no accident that Marcianus, in composing the story of the martyrdom of Polycarp for use in an east Phrygian church (Philomelium), drew attention to the apostasy of Quintus the Phrygian, who had offered himself for martyrdom with others, a policy which the church could not 'approve as true to the pattern of the gospel'. Martyrdom, it is suggested, was according to the will of God, not the will of man; and the bishops had the onerous and dangerous duty of maintaining the unity of the church during persecution, providing for the care of the prisoners and their families, dealing discreetly with the lapsed, and reconstructing the church life when the fury of persecution was spent; if, of course, they were still there.

The enthusiast or fanatic cared for none of these things. When Agathonice rushed into the flames, she had her young son by her. 'Have pity upon your child', the spectators cried out. 'He has God to have pity on him', Agathonice replied; but God, in this case at least, meant the bishop. Martyrdom was her glory and her road to heaven. As Montanus had said,

Do not hope to die in bed or in abortion or in languishing fevers; but in martyrdom; that he who suffered for you may be glorified.

(Tertullian, *On Flight in Persecution*, IX.)

It was rather in this style that Roman generals exhorted their troops just before the battle. It reminds us, too, of the spirit of Ignatius.

CHAPTER 12

DIONYSIUS OF CORINTH

ACCESSION OF SOTER, A.D. 166

While the Montanist crisis, with its synods and excommunications, was going on in Asia Minor, Soter succeeded Anicetus as bishop of Rome, his approximate dates being 166–178. This period coincides approximately with the second period in the reign of Marcus Aurelius. Lucius Verus returned home in 166 and celebrated a triumph with Marcus for the victories of his armies in the far east. Avidius Cassius, the Syrian general, who had actually won the victories, was left in Antioch to rule over the eastern part of the empire. A strange interplay of cultural forces was taking place. Syria was being Romanized, but Rome was being Syrianized. Lucilla, the daughter of Marcus, married a Syrian soldier named Pompeianus, who became the prefect, or right-hand man of the emperor, in the west.

Oriental refugees, prisoners of war and slaves must have poured into Rome; soldiers, merchants and officials must have passed from Syria to Rome, and from Rome to the new province of Mesopotamia. The trade in eastern luxuries which was destined to impoverish the Roman currency was increased. The eyes of Rome turned towards the east; the eyes of the east turned towards Rome.

THE MARCOMANNIC WARS, A.D. 167–74

Unfortunately Rome had to cope with new dangers on a second front. In 167 came the news of inroads of barbarians from across the Danube. Various tribes or federations of tribes broke into the empire from Germany and Sarmatia (Russia), to loot and ravage and find lands to settle on. The Marcomanni, the 'march-men' or border people, in-

13. THE PARABIAGO PATERA

14. THE DIATESSARON OF TATIAN

vaded the Balkan province of Moesia (Bulgaria) and penetrated as far as Northern Italy. Rome was alarmed. The two emperors moved without delay to Aquileia, near Fiume, and then to Sirmium, a strong-point near Belgrade, which was destined to become an imperial city of some importance. They won some successes in the year 168, and though Marcus was dubious about the finality of the victory, he was persuaded by Lucius to make peace and return to Aquileia in 169. As the two emperors were seated in their carriage and travelling south-ward, Lucius had a stroke, from which he did not recover.

In 171 the Marcomanni, with the Quadi and other tribes, again poured into the Balkan provinces, and desperate fighting took place on the frontiers. Traces of the fortifications which were built at that time still exist. It was in this war that the famous episode of the 'Thun-dering Legion' occurred, which we will discuss more fully in a later chapter. The army, and the emperor himself, were saved from destruc-tion by a sudden tempest of rain and thunder, which came as an answer to prayer. Some gave credit to the Egyptian Thoth, who was identified with the Roman Mercury; others to the God of the Christians; and still others apparently to the ancestral deities in whom the emperor so firmly believed. The event is recorded in stone upon the huge column which Marcus Aurelius erected in front of the Pantheon.

In 174 Marcus returned to Rome. He was sole emperor now without any colleague, and he had to deal with a malady which was destined to become chronic in future years; it was the burden of never-ending defensive action along the line of the Danube and the Rhine, as new hordes of barbarians appeared at one point or another. Marcus was never free from this anxiety to the day of his death.

CELSUS AND THE *TRUE WORD*

The Christian philosophers had by now made some impact on the educated classes, and their attempt to give an orderly and objective acount of their worship and doctrine had produced some effect in making Christians think out their intellectual position in terms of the ascertained knowledge and logical method of the day. It made one or two notable converts, who become the leaders of this movement in the church; but the reaction of many philosophers was unfavourable, as we have seen already in the case of Crescens. Better men than he, however, remained unimpressed. On Marcus Aurelius, the philosophic Caesar, it made no impression at all. The judicious Galen thought the Christian method of teaching was less than scientific; but he must not be numbered among the adverse critics. The Cynics resented it as an intrusion on their own preserves. Lucian laughed at it gently; more gently, at any rate, than he laughed at most things. It fell to the lot of a certain Celsus to deal with it more effectively, with a heavy logic and a heavy humour, in his *Alethes Logos*, or *True Word;* the protean word *logos* here meaning discourse.

About eighty years after the period of our present chapter, the great Christian scholar Origen was shown a copy of this book, but it was new to him in spite of all his learning. He had heard of two philosophers of the name of Celsus; one of whom was an Epicurean, who he thought might be the author in question, though this is not likely; the other was too early to be considered. He wrote an elaborate answer to the book, in which he quoted each paragraph or sentence as he refuted it. We can separate these quotations from the text of Origen and the *True Discourse* rises before us, mutilated but authentic so far as it goes. We have a picture of Christianity as it was seen by an educated pagan in the middle of the second century. We have made frequent use of it in our history.

Perhaps a clue to its date is to be found in its treatment of Christian heresy. Celsus is fully aware of the importance of the heresy of Marcion and appears to quote from Marcionite literature; in spite of some confusions, however, he successfully distinguishes Marcionism from what he calls 'the great church', meaning the catholic church as a whole. He knew of the existence of Simonians and Helenians, named after Simon Magus and his consort; so this sect was flourishing in his time. He also knew of 'Marcellians', named after Marcellina; and 'Harpocratians', connected with Salome; and others called after Mariamne and Martha.[1] We remember the Marcellina who came to Rome from Egypt when Anicetus was bishop; and the reference to her name makes the hundred and sixties or seventies a reasonable date for the *True Discourse*; the seventies perhaps, more probably than the sixties; we may be taking it rather too early here.

The 'Harpocratians' must be a mistake for the Carpocratians, the

[1] The names occur in the third-century Egyptian gnostic work called *Pistis-Sophia*, which may have some literary connexion with the 'Egyptian Gospel'.

Egyptian sect to which Marcellina belonged. Harpocrates was an Egyptian god.

We are fortunate in having a recent translation of this book, with introduction and notes, by H. Chadwick.

Celsus deals with the church as an illegal and intractable secret society, which was ruled out of consideration on that account. Its existence was incompatible with the autocratic government of the day, under which all vestiges of democracy and self-government were disappearing from public life. He brings into play the heavy artillery of rationalism with which the Epicurean materialist was wont to destroy the Stoic faith in providence, or the Marcionite controversialist make fun of the Hebrew God. He laughs heartily at the notion that God would concern himself with such low creatures as the Christians in their conventicles; rats in a hole or frogs in a pond would be just as important. Yet he can speak in a very interesting way about the intelligence of animals and even of their supernatural knowledge, about which he is distinctly credulous.

He seems to be a Platonist, and speaks of a beneficent deity who is perfect and blessed and remote from this world. Origen smells out an inconsistency here since he believed him to be an Epicurean; but actually the high view of the deity matches with the low view of the world. There was a God for the philosophic mind, but not for the kind of persons who were found in the Christian conventicles, where young people and old women and tradesmen discussed matters which were above their heads, and were deluded by unqualified teachers whose last resort was always to say, 'Do not question; only believe.' It appears that these teachers were often the skilled technicians who were employed in great houses; a most interesting point.

After discussing various points of Christian philosophy he embarks on a defence of polytheism, or of the 'daemons' as he calls the accepted gods and goddesses, maintaining that they were the officers of the one supreme deity. Indeed his invisible world was a monarchy, very like the Roman empire with its emperor and subordinate governors. It was a situation to which the sensible man should submit.

The Christians must make a choice between two alternatives. If they refuse to render due service to the gods and to respect those who are set over this service, let them not come to manhood or marry wives or have children, or indeed take any part in the affairs of life, but let them depart hence with all speed, and leave no posterity behind, that such a race may become extinct from the face of the earth.

(Celsus, *True Word*, in Origen, *Against Celsus*, VIII, 55.)

He admits that there may be an occasion on which a philosopher, as Justin pointed out, must refuse to obey the earthly powers.

We must encounter all kinds of torment, or submit to any kind of death, rather than say or even think anything unworthy of God.... But if anyone commands you to celebrate the sun, or sing a joyful triumphal song in praise of Athene, you will seem to render even higher praise to God by celebrating their praises. (*Ibid.* VIII, 66.)

He points out that if everyone refused to obey the emperor, the result would be that the civilized world would be overrun by the barbarians, and there would be an end of the Christian religion itself. He concludes by urging the Christians to help the emperor with all their might, to labour with him in the maintenance of justice, and to fight in his armies if necessary.

THE JEW IN CELSUS

In addition to his own arguments, Celsus has a number of older documents which he weaves into the *True Discourse*. In his two opening books he introduces a Jew, who attacks Christ and delivers an appeal to members of his own race who have become Christians; it was composed in a dialogue or dramatized form. This *Dialogue with Jesus* was regarded by Origen and subsequent scholars as a literary device invented by Celsus himself; but surely it is a genuine Jewish document of early date which Celsus found in existence and used for his purposes. Its writer shows a better knowledge of certain points than Celsus does in the remainder of the book, as Origen himself pointed out. It suggests the period of 'Barnabas' or the *Preaching of Peter*, rather than that of Justin or Tatian. The author had formed his ideas by studying one Gospel, which was obviously Matthew, and expresses his sense of disturbance at finding that there were more. He accuses the Christians of combining and re-coining their original single Gospel, until it has become two-fold, three-fold, five-fold, or manifold. He may have received his impression of Christianity as early as the hundred-and-twenties.

The tone of the Jew is harsh and blunt, but his criticism is sometimes acute. He takes the usual line, found in the Talmud, that Jesus was a magician who deceived the people and was rightly put to death for his crimes. He is pictured as a stupid and ineffective person; he is unable to plan or design anything; what captain of brigands would suffer his leading men to betray him and desert him as Jesus did? The Jew has no feeling at all for his genius or personal character.

This document is the earliest authority for the Jewish legend that Jesus was the bastard son of a Roman soldier named Panthera, and that he went down into Egypt to learn magic. The story was made up after the Virgin Birth story was current in a Greek form; for the word Panthera is an anagram on the word *parthena*, and *parthena* is an illiterate feminine form of the Greek word *parthenos*, a virgin, which happens (illogically) to be a masculine form.[1] Its origin, therefore, is likely to be Hellenistic, not Palestinian. One would assign the document, provisionally, to a Jewish author in a Greek-speaking Jewish community which had been weakened by conversions to Christianity.

BISHOP SOTER'S EPISTLE

Very little indeed can be said about Bishop Soter of Rome. It seems possible that the controversy with the Asians over the proper observance of the Christian Passover, which had been so amicably arranged under Xystus and Anicetus, caused him some trouble. The statement of Irenaeus that the 'elders previous to Soter', by which title he dignifies the Roman bishops, had maintained peaceful relations on this vexed subject, rather suggests that Soter himself had not done so. Perhaps some storms blew up. The controversy in Asia may have communicated itself to Rome.

Soter had friendly relations with the Corinthians and sent them a generous gift on behalf of the Roman church, accompanied by a letter which has not survived; but Eusebius quotes a paragraph or two from the acknowledgement which was penned by Bishop Dionysius. The Roman letter was read in Corinth at the Sunday service, and Dionysius wrote his reply on the same day, saying that the Corinthians would always be glad to receive admonition from it, as they had done from the earlier Epistle, which had been written to them through Clement; both

---

[1] But Epiphanius quotes obscure Jewish-Christian traditions which make the word *Panthera* a name of Jacob, the father of Joseph of Nazareth.

Epistles being looked upon as Epistles from the church written 'through' its bishop. It is interesting to learn that they were read traditionally in the Sunday service.

The Epistle of Soter appears to have contained some reference to the work of Peter and Paul in Rome; for Dionysius remarks that the excellent admonition which Soter had sent was a link between the 'plantings' of these apostles in the two cities. 'They both of them planted in our Corinth, and they taught us in the same way; and in the same way too in Italy, teaching together and witnessing at the same time.' This is a valuable supplement to the evidence of Paul, who is thought by some to refer to a visit of Peter to Corinth, and to the evidence of Clement which refers to their martyrdoms in Rome. It insists that their teaching was not at variance, as Marcion, for instance, believed. It also suggests that Corinth was as much an apostolic-see city as Rome; and this, no doubt, is exactly the effect that Dionysius intended his words to convey. He must have been quite sure of his ground in writing as he did.

He warmly commends the Roman Christians for their benefactions to other churches especially in times of persecution, and thanks them for help of this kind which has just arrived.

For this has been your custom [he says] from the beginning, to do good to all the brethren in a variety of ways, sending provisions to many churches, city by city; at one time relieving the poverty of the needy, and at another generously supporting the brethren who are in the mines by the provisions which you are in the habit of sending...preserving as Romans the custom of the Romans, which you inherited from your fathers; which your blessed Bishop Soter has not only preserved, but even augmented, by generously supplying the bounty which is being distributed to the saints, and exhorting with blessed words the brethren who come up [to Rome?] even as a loving father comforts his children.

(Dionysius, *Epistle to the Romans*, in Eusebius *E.H.* IV, 23, 10.)

A gratifying picture is here given of the strong, warm-hearted, wealthy, well organized church of the imperial city, interesting itself in the troubles of other churches, receiving their envoys and sending them relief. This letter contains the first reference to Christians who were condemned to hard labour in the mines, a miserable condition of life in which few survived. It rather looks as if the Corinthian church had experienced such a persecution, and had received help.

THE EPISTLES OF DIONYSIUS

The Epistle to the Romans was not by any means the first which Dionysius had composed and sent abroad; for he refers in it to earlier Epistles which he had written at the desire of the brethren; and Eusebius, to whom we owe our information, tells us of six more 'catholic Epistles' which he wrote to churches, and one to a lady named Chrysophora, a most faithful sister, to whom he wrote suitably, communicating to her the profitable food of the word.

Eusebius gives us a catalogue of these letters with a short account of their contents; but we cannot be sure that he gives us the precise words of the author. It would be interesting to know, for instance, whether Dionysius himself used the word 'catholic' in describing his Epistles, and if so, what exactly he meant by it. About this time Themiso the Montanist composed a 'catholic Epistle', we are told, in which he imitated the apostolic style. It suggests, therefore, a letter on the lines of the apostolic Epistles, and intended for the church at large. Such was the character of the Epistle which described the martyrdom of Polycarp; it was addressed primarily to the church at Philomelium, but also to all the 'sojournings' of the catholic church. No doubt the Epistles of Dionysius were of the same character, and their collection and publication supports such a view. If he was prepared to go on reading the Epistle of Soter in his church, he probably expected the other churches to read his Epistles. It was a revival or continuation of the apostolic practice.

The list begins with two Epistles to Greek churches. The Epistle to the Lacedaemonians taught right opinion and suggested peace and unity. The Epistle to the Athenians urged the need of faith and the social virtues in accordance with the gospel. It was for lack of this, he thought, that the Athenians had made such a bad showing in the 'persecution of that time', when their bishop had become a martyr, and great numbers had apostasized; but he bears witness to the splendid way in which his successor Quadratus had reorganized the church by his zeal and energy, and reanimated it by his faith. He referred to Dionysius the Areopagite, who was mentioned in the Acts as a convert of St Paul and was the first to take in hand the episcopate of the Athenian *paroikia*. His own church looked back to Stephanas as its first bishop, as we learn from the Epistle to Corinth in the *Acts of Paul*.

This brief summary is full of interest. There is an apparent reference to the Acts, and there is an interest in local history, which was stimulated no doubt by the visit of Hegesippus to Corinth in the days of his predecessor Primus.

His other epistles were written to churches further afield. Nicomedia, the capital of Bithynia, was a growing city. It was a strong military point, like Sirmium on the Danube; and both would become centres of imperial administration as the frontiers of the empire became more important than its central parts. The neighbour province to Bithynia was Pontus, where Marcion had been born, and Dionysius warned the Nicomedians against the heresy of Marcion, and commended the 'rule of truth', a phrase which suggests a creed-form.

Gortyna in Crete had gone through a persecution, and Dionysius wrote to Philip its bishop, congratulating him on the numerous courageous acts for which his church was famous and warning him against the guile of the heretics. Bishop Philip may not have needed any such warning, for he was the author of a book against Marcion.

Two envoys from the church of Amastris in Pontus, Bacchylides and Euelpistus, had arrived in Corinth and requested a letter. In this Epistle Dionysius expounded the divine scriptures, which meant, of course, the Old Testament, doubtless in opposition to the Pontic heretic, Marcion. He also wrote on the subject of marriage and chastity. He was no rigorist. He recommended that there should be no undue severity in restoring to communion those who had fallen into heresy or immorality. He mentions Palmas their bishop, of whom we shall hear again.

There was another important city in Crete which also had a literary bishop, Pinytus of Cnossos. Dionysius wrote to the Cnossians, urging Pinytus not to lay on the brethren the heavy burden of chastity as a necessity, but to show some sympathy with the weakness of the many. Pinytus wrote back a letter full of compliments to Dionysius, expressed in an extremely elegant style (if we may judge from the sentence which Eusebius quotes) but tinged possibly with a suggestion of sarcasm; for he exhorts him that it is now high time for him to provide some stronger meat and to nourish his people once again with the more perfect literature, lest perchance by continuing permanently on a diet of milk, they might insensibly come to old age without ever having passed out of their spiritual infancy.

THE ATHENIAN CHURCH

We have had a fair amount of information about the history of the Athenian church, but the uncertainty about the chronology makes it impossible to weave it into a connected story. St Paul had founded the church, and his principal convert had been Dionysius the Areopagite, who was regarded now as its first bishop. The apostle had made a speech in the Areopagus, which read like a sketch for an apology or reasoned statement of the faith; it made use of testimonies from Stoic writers. The tradition reappears in the second century. The church in Athens was a learned and literary church. It went on producing apologies. It was its *métier* to explain the faith to the cultured Gentile mind.

There is no evidence to connect Justin Martyr with Athens, except that his *Apology* seems to take its place in the stream of apologies or addresses to the Greeks which are Athenian in origin. First come Quadratus and Aristides of Athens; then Justin and Tatian; then Athenagoras of Athens. There is a community of manner and subject-matter which establishes itself in this tradition and spreads throughout the church. It deals with the worship of the one deity, the philosophy of the Logos, the argument from prophecy, the chronology of the ancient world, the criticism of the pagan myths, and the arguments in favour of the resurrection of the body. They are in the nature of pre-liminary studies prior to the consideration of the Christian gospel itself; Justin is unique in allotting so much space to actual Christian teaching and liturgy. A Christian teacher could embark on any one of these preparatory topics without disclosing the fact that he was a Christian at all. That would be revealed according to the discretion of the teacher or the penetration of the hearer. The procedure is com-mended and illustrated in the books of Clement. It is followed by Theophilus. It was based on Jewish antecedents.

These subjects must all have been taught in Christian academies; and such academies must have been in existence in Athens. They must have accepted the dangerous principle that Greek literature and philo-sophy, which formed the average higher education of the time, were a necessary prerequisite to the serious study of the Christian faith. The character of the Christian professor of this type is well represented by Athenagoras of Athens, whose conversion to the faith cannot be placed much later than the period we are considering. He carries on the work of Justin in a more academic style.

Athenagoras was the nearest to a pure intellectual of all the great Christian teachers of the period whose works have come down to us. He was at home in the academic tradition. He was learned in Greek literature, and was able to support his criticism of the Greek gods and heroes by apt quotations; and these quotations are of value to classical scholars today, though he was sometimes deceived by an imitation. He followed in the wake of Justin, with whose writings he seems to have been familiar; but he is less enthusiastic in his recognition of elements of truth in the Greek philosophers. The true successor of Justin in this respect was Clement of Alexandria, who knew something of Athens, and may have learned his Christianity there from Athenagoras.

THE ATHENIAN SCENE

The *Address to the Greeks* proves that Tatian had personal knowledge of the Athenian scene. He is very sarcastic at the expense of the philosophers, some of whom, he says, received as much as six hundred gold pieces a year from the emperor, and did little more for it than to wear a long beard; and it is a fact that beards were coming into fashion with philosophy. Antoninus Pius and Marcus Aurelius both wore beards; and so did Commodus. It was one of the marks of the philosopher, along with the gown and the staff. It was also the guise in which the Christian teacher appeared. Clement of Alexandria fought a battle for the beard, and Tertullian of Carthage fought one for the gown. These men of devoted and ascetic lives are thought to be precursors of the monastic movement. They entered into competition with the Cynic school of philosophy, which cultivated a rough and ready simplicity and a contempt for polite manners and class distinctions. The Cynics looked on worldly or material conditions as 'indifferent', and professed to be concerned simply with the truth. Socrates and Diogenes were their patron saints; Socrates, who went round examining and cross-questioning the citizens of Athens in his search for wisdom; Diogenes, who scorned mankind and went round Athens in broad daylight with a lantern looking for an honest man.

The other philosophic schools had well endowed colleges, which perpetuated the dogmas and rule of life of their founders. They also attracted wealthy benefactors. They bore historic names. That of Plato was the Lyceum, and that of Aristotle was the Academy. Athenagoras may have been studying in the latter, when Tatian was proclaiming his barbarian philosophy. The tenets of Zeno, the founder of Stoicism, were taught at the Porch, or *Stoa*; those of Epicurus in the Garden. The Cynics roamed the streets, or found their way into the houses of the wealthy. Not all of the exponents of this creed were worthy of Diogenes or Epictetus; there were some who preyed on the rich by using a mixture of flattery and familiarity; and Crescens of Rome must have been a notorious example of this class.

The time-honoured schools of Athens had been newly housed and endowed by the liberality of Hadrian and Herodes Atticus; the old city, considered as a centre of classical and antiquarian culture, was at the height of its glory.

PROTEUS PEREGRINUS

The Christian intellectuals whom we have been considering were men who turned from some kind of philosophy, or philosophical study, to the gospel. We have one case of a man who turned from the gospel to the Cynic philosophy. Among the sights of Athens was the ex-Christian Peregrinus, who had been given the additional name of Proteus, possibly because he had played many parts in his time; for Proteus was the old sea-god who could change his form at will.

Peregrinus had tried his fortunes in Rome, but had been expelled for his harsh criticisms of the emperor. It is good to hear of a philosopher who had not forgotten how to criticize an emperor. Between 160 and 165 he lived in a little hut on the outskirts of Athens, practising self-sufficiency and indifference, and abusing the rich. Tatian and Athenagoras both mention him. Aulus Gellius, a literary critic from Africa, who wrote in Latin, mentions him more than once with approbation. The satirist Lucian of Samosata was also living in Athens, and was a witness of the strange end of a strange life. He saw him throw himself into the flames, and burn to death, before great crowds in the Olympian Games of 165. It was a theatrical end to a fantastic life, designed to demonstrate the Cynic's perfect indifference to death; but may we read into it some deeper psychological motive? Was there some sense of frustration about his failure to become a martyr at Antioch, and of guilt about his apostasy from the Christian faith? Did the man who was noted for his changes of front wish to prove to himself that he was capable of a determined heroic act? Was it an act of reparation to those Grecian gods whom he had denied and vilified when he became a Christian? It seems wrong, with Lucian, to find nothing to admire in this fantastic end of a fantastic life, with its last word of pagan faith, 'Spirits of the fathers, and spirits of the mothers, receive my soul.'

His death was not quite without parallel. A Brahmin from India had immolated himself in the same way before the Emperor Augustus many years before; and the Christian martyr Agathonice rushed headlong into the flames in a similar spirit of self-sacrifice.

So great was his fame that a statue was erected in his honour in his native city of Parium, which had disowned him in his youth. Works of healing took place there, Athenagoras tells us. We note again that there was something in common between the wandering prophet or teacher of the *Didache*, the wandering magician and wonder-worker from the east, and the wandering ascetic or philosopher of the Greek tradition. All of them were conscious of a divine mission to enlighten mankind and release it from sin or error or disease or mental bondage. All were liable to the same temptations, to fraud or exhibitionism. Many imposters were found among them. Some years later, Lucian wrote an account of a pagan imposter of the wonder-working sort, named Alexander of Abunoteichos, whose principal field of activity was in Phrygia. This little sketch was dedicated to the Epicurean Celsus. Alexander carried round with him a serpent with a human head, which gave oracular responses to inquirers at a price. Lucian notes that the Christians refused to be taken in. Pontus was so full of Christians and Epicureans that he had no success there. The Epicureans resembled the Christians in not believing in the gods; they, too, were 'atheists'; they were the only philosophers outlawed in the Christian academies.

CONFEDERATIONS OF CHURCHES

As we contemplate this picture, an interesting pattern emerges. Dionysius writes two letters to Greece, two to the Black Sea Provinces, and two to Crete. He avoids Asia and Phrygia. Now Asia and Phrygia formed a group of interrelated dioceses, without any central organization of course, but held together by the possession of common traditions, the leadership of the greater bishops, and their fraternal relations.

Dionysius was the bishop of the richest and most powerful city in Greece, the capital of Achaea, a centre of maritime trade. Was he planning another federation of churches, neither Roman nor Asian, based on the coastwise trade-routes, in which his church, with its tradition of Peter and Paul, would exercise the hegemony? Such leagues of cities had precedents in Greek history.

What we might call families of dioceses do come to light in his Epistles. The Epistle to Gortyna is addressed to the church sojourning at Gortyna 'with the rest of the *paroikiai* of Crete'; and the Epistle to Amastris is addressed, 'to the church which sojourns at Amastris with those throughout Pontus'. Gortyna and Amastris, therefore, would seem to resemble what were later called metropolitan churches; at least they had facilities for copying manuscripts and distributing ecclesiastical communications. Some twenty years later, we find Bishop Palmas presiding over a synod of the bishops of Pontus, but he is said to have done so on grounds of seniority. This synod did not fall in with the views of the Asian and Phrygian bishops on the question of the date of Easter. They belonged to the same tradition as Rome and Corinth.

The holding of synods of bishops which was now taking place in Phrygia would necessarily call into existence regional families of dioceses. In relation to such synods the older and stronger apostolic sees had positions of commanding influence from the first, a fact which is apparent in the New Testament in the cases of Jerusalem and Antioch and possibly Ephesus, and in the Epistles of Ignatius in the case of Antioch and Rome. We can now see why Bishop Dionysius was anxious to establish the apostolic character of his own see. He must have been a man of importance in his day; the fact that his seven letters were collected, copied, distributed and preserved, proves as much.

ENCRATISM

His Roman letter was one of the last to be written, so that the correspondence which we have been considering may have begun early in the episcopate of Soter, or even before it. There is no sign of any controversy over the date of Easter or the Phrygian prophets; so that the period 160–5 suits it much better than 170–5.

The great enemy is the heresy of Marcion, and next to that an undue emphasis on asceticism or chastity, by which, of course, celibacy is meant. Bishop Pinytus in Crete appears to be insisting upon virginity as the normal condition of a Christian. This rigorous attitude came to be called 'encratism' from the Greek word *encrateia* which may be translated continence or abstinence. This word came next to faith in many old catechisms, but had not this meaning of complete sexual abstinence; it meant renunciation or self-control. A word with a very similar history was *hagneia* or sanctification. Both these words were being pressed into the service of a propaganda in favour of a Christian celibacy.

The docetic heretics, whose phantom christology was the result of a low view of creation, were being absorbed into the Marcionite church. There still remained many ascetic brothers and sisters who looked on marrying and having children as something Satanic. Some repudiated the Hebrew God who gave his blessing to this sort of thing; but a great number accepted the Hebrew revelation as Tatian did; they were orthodox about the creation and the resurrection, and yet extolled the celibate life as the path of perfection. We have come across this combination already in the *Acts of Paul*; and Paul was their patron saint, though they were not slow in appropriating John and Andrew as well. They could remain in the church so long as they did not deny their Creator; the church had possessed its celibates since the days of Clement, or even longer.

Melito was obviously a man of this type, a celibate living continuously in the Spirit, if not a eunuch in the literal sense of the word. Pinytus in Crete was another. Tatian was a third; and just as Marcion drained off the docetics into his rival church organization, so Tatian succeeded in gathering many of the encratites into his peculiar sect or party.

CHAPTER 13

TATIAN AND THE EAST

TATIAN IN ROME

It was during the episcopate of Soter that Tatian departed from the church. He is a figure of commanding influence, of whom we know too little. We have seen him as the pupil of Justin and as a Christian teacher, dividing his time between Athens and Rome. We learn from Irenaeus that he set up a school in Rome after the martyrdom of Justin and drifted into heresy. He was inflated, Irenaeus says, with the pride of being a teacher. He was fascinated by the realms of spiritual being which were revealed in the speculations of Valentine. He had an intense faith in the power and reality of the Spirit which was given to the Christian man. Life in the Spirit was not compatible with life in the flesh or the indulgence of the passions. It must possess and overrule the whole being. At length he parted from the church, Irenaeus says, and established 'his own type of school'; the same expression which he had used to describe the secession of Valentine.

He taught that marriage was the work of the devil and he denied the salvation of Adam, which means in modern speech that he thought that nothing could be done with the common man. It is the mark of all these ultra-spiritual heresies; it is the same in Marcion, in Valentine, in Montanus and in Tatian; the ordinary run of Christians are 'psychics', animal creatures devoid of the divine spark. On the other hand, we must say for Marcion, for Montanus, and for Tatian, that they took the hard way to heaven; they did not find their religion an easy thing; it was a struggle with the powers of darkness.

Such is the account of Tatian's defection which we find in Irenaeus, who is obviously recording a personal impression. We are practically compelled to assume that Irenaeus was in Rome at this time. It is not stated anywhere in so many words that he was a member of the school of Justin, but we may safely assume that he was. We cannot date his arrival in Rome or chronicle his doings. All we know is that he entered very fully into the old Roman tradition which he came to regard as his own. 'It came even unto us', he says more than once.

TATIAN AND THE UNIVERSE

Tatian ended his life teaching among the Syrians on the banks of the Euphrates or Tigris; Irenaeus among the Celts and Germans on the banks of the Rhone. They could not have been more unlike. Tatian had a first-rate mind; he had a touch of genius; but he was excitable and unbalanced and extreme in his views; a dangerous man. Irenaeus was a safe man. He also had a first-rate mind; but fair, well-balanced, methodical, comprehensive, reliable.

Tatian is what used to be called a Byronic figure; the outcast of society, the victim of fate, the sport of the universe. He cultivates a superb indifference, in which he outdoes the Cynic.

I do not wish to be a king; I am not anxious to be rich; I decline military command; I detest fornication; I am not compelled by an insatiable love of gain to go to sea; I do not contend for chaplets; I am free from a mad thirst for fame; I despise death; I am superior to every kind of disease; grief does not consume my soul. Am I a slave, I endure servitude. Am I free, I do not make a vaunt of my good birth. I see that the same sun is for all, and one death for all, whether they live in pleasure or in destitution.

(Tatian, *Against the Greeks*, XI.)

This histrionic attitude appears in his theology. He invents something very like the Miltonic myth. He puts together the fall of the angels out of Enoch, the garden of Eden story out of Genesis, the war of the Titans out of the Greek poets, and the fatalism of Babylonian astrology. Others had experimented in these fields of syncretism, and doubtless he was following in the footsteps of other men.

When a pagan became a Christian, he renounced the old gods, but he did not necessarily cease to believe in them. He walked forward into the new faith, but he remained in the old universe; the universe of all educated men. Justin, for instance, had not changed his God on becoming a Christian, since it was agreed that Moses and Plato believed in the same God; and that is why the Logos theology was so important

15. THE ROMAN ROAD TO ANTIOCH

16. THE THEATRE AT LYONS

for him and Tatian; they needed the divine Word to be the chief actor in the Hebrew revelation and the Christian gospel. In the same way, he had not given up his belief in the pagan gods; he had simply demoted them to the rank of daemons.

Tatian carried into Christianity the oriental faith in astral determinism which he had already identified with Greek mythology. The Greek gods, who were fixed as constellations in the sky, determined the fate of human beings. Their king was the devil himself, whom the Greeks had accepted as their chief deity; they called him Zeus, the father of gods and men. He was the lord of the whole universe. He was 'the spirit that was about matter'. He had been given this authority by God himself, but had rebelled and been cast down. Evil had been infused into God's universe.

Tatian thus had all the advantages of the old Syrian gnosis, without actually being a gnostic. He was formally orthodox, and yet he could regard matter as evil. This was the basis of his encratism; and it even allowed a little scope for astrology.

THE FOUR GOSPELS

Irenaeus, on the other hand, remained loyal to the Asian and Roman tradition, with its background of Hebrew faith and worship, and its legacy of testimony theology, and its historic church order. He fought hard against the tendency to dissolve Christian history into spirituality or merge it in pagan myth. It is interesting that his view of catholic Christianity hardly includes Syria, though some scholars hold that he made use of the works of Theophilus. He does not actually quote the old Roman masters like Clement or Hermas; what he seems to have valued in the Roman church was the solid tradition of the elders and bishops in their successions, like the successions which he had known in Asia; for practical people know that stability and progress depend on people more than on theories or literature. He includes within this double succession the baptismal creeds, the four Gospels and the remaining apostolic books, which he does not hesitate to call scripture.

With regard to the four Gospels, Irenaeus inherited a piece of orthodox gnosis which has come down in the tradition to this day. Heretics had said that it was absurd to have four Gospels; on the contrary, Irenaeus said, it was natural to have four Gospels, one for each of the cardinal points of the heavens; the bull, the lion, the eagle, and the man (Aquarius). Tatian inherited the same four Gospels from the school of Justin and from the Roman church; but he saw nothing sacred in the number four; he decided to harmonize it with the number one.

THE *DIATESSARON*

The greatest literary achievement of Tatian was his gospel-book, which he called the *Diatessaron*, a musical term which means a harmony formed by four notes. The work must have taken years of study, for every verse of the four Gospels was worked into a continuous narrative. He did not know of any other Gospel worthy of consideration.

The selection of four Gospels for church use was a simple matter, if they were merely to be kept in a chest for reference and study, or read in church according to the wish of a preacher; but it would be another matter if a gospel was designed to be read continuously in the service, Sunday by Sunday, in course. Under these circumstances the appearance of a new gospel would cause awkward problems.

It has been suggested that Mark and Matthew were written for continuous reading, Sunday by Sunday, throughout the calendar year;[1] we may not press this theory too hard, but we hope it is fair to say that such an arrangement had been brought into use by the time of Tatian. In the ancient manuscripts the Gospels are divided into numbered lections, and the systems of enumeration in Mark and Matthew agree remarkably closely with one another and with Tatian. The structure of these two Gospels was so similar that this type of chapter-enumeration made it possible to substitute one for another without much difficulty. Now Luke does not fall into the same pattern, and we learn from Irenaeus that the common practice was to use it as a storehouse of additional 'Gospels', such as were not found in Mark or Matthew.

These factors are reflected in the *Diatessaron* of Tatian. Mark-Matthew is the basis of its structure, with a distinct leaning towards Mark. The Lucan text is combined with the Mark-Matthew text in the cases where it supplies the same material; but Lucan material which has no Marcan or Matthaean parallel is placed to the best advantage without disturbing the Mark-Matthew order; sometimes in its obvious position, but often quite arbitrarily.

[1] P. Carrington, *The Primitive Christian Calendar* (Cambridge, 1952).

In the case of John, Tatian had a problem of greater difficulty, since it has a totally different structure. He began by boldly transposing some of the earlier Johannine sections so as to approximate to the Mark-Matthew-Luke order; and when he had done this, he combined all his sources. As if to compensate for this bold action, he adopted the Johannine order for the ministry in Jerusalem and the story of the Passion, fitting the Mark-Matthew-Luke material into it. His work is most ingenious and interesting. The resultant unified Gospel, in fifty-five chapters, could be put into operation in any church on a Sunday-by-Sunday basis, in succession to Mark or Matthew. Its calendrical structure is obvious. Its chapter-enumeration agrees on the whole with the standard chapter-enumeration of Mark.

The work was probably done from the Greek text; for the notion that it was done in Syriac is losing ground. We know now that a Greek text existed, for a small fragment of it has turned up at Dura-Europus on the Euphrates; it formed part of a parchment roll, and was necessarily made before A.D. 250 when that outpost of the Roman empire was wiped out of existence. A translation into Syriac was made at a very early date and became the regular liturgical Gospel of the Syrian churches. It was a long time before the 'Separated Gospels' were able to replace it. There was also a Latin translation which was current in the west, and this exists in more than one form. The *Diatessaron* was made from the so-called Western text, which was also used by Justin, Marcion, Irenaeus, Tertullian, and the Latin versions. The original Greek no longer exists except for the Dura-Europus fragment; what we have is an Arabic translation of the Syriac translation; and this can be supplemented from the various descendants of the Latin translation, which, however, have gone through a number of changes.

TATIAN IN SYRIA, *c.* A.D. 173

Tatian left Rome in the episcopate of Soter. Epiphanius says that he established his school in the 'Midst of the Rivers' in the twelfth year of Antoninus Pius. This would be 150; but Epiphanius means Marcus Aurelius, for, like other writers of his time, he mixes up the Antonine emperors. The year he means would be 173, which is accepted by scholars as reasonably correct. The 'Midst of the Rivers' is Mesopotamia, and the 'school' of Tatian was doubtless a schismatic church.

If that was the year in which he established his schismatic church, he may have left Rome no later than 170 or 171.

It does not look as if he went directly to Mesopotamia. He came from Rome, Epiphanius says, to the parts of the east, and lived there. He preached a modified form of Valentinianism, and a rigorous form of encratism and this preaching of his was influential in Antioch and in Cilicia and in Pisidia. The encratites, who regarded Tatian as their founder, were still numerous in these regions when Epiphanius was writing. Now Pisidia is the local name for the east Phrygian country where Iconium and Derbe and Lystra were situated; and this is the local setting of the encratite *Acts of Paul*. The success of Tatian was in the Pauline country; in Cilicia, the province where he was born; and Pisidia, which cherished his memory as an evangelist and ascetic; and Antioch, where he undoubtedly left his mark.

Avidius Cassius was still in command in Antioch, lord of all Asia Minor, all the east as far as the Euphrates and Tigris, and virtually of Egypt too. Marcus Aurelius had left him there too long. He was a native Syrian, and he was planning to revolt against Marcus, and set himself up as Emperor. Theophilus was the bishop of Antioch, or would soon succeed Eros. We know of two heretical schools in addition to Tatian's, if Tatian's is so reckoned; their leaders were Marcianus and Hermogenes. Marcianus was the docetic who used the *Gospel of Peter*. Hermogenes was a painter who had a gnosis of his own. He believed that prior to creation there was an original uncreated formless matter which was divided between light and darkness. The conflict of these two principles led to an intervention by the supreme God. It looks as if his theology owed something to Basilides. It was very influential in the east and even reached Africa, where Tertullian had to contend with it.

We have no information about the Marcionite or Valentinian schools in Antioch.

THEOPHILUS OF ANTIOCH

Theophilus was an Antiochene scholar who contended with Hermogenes and rose to be bishop of Antioch. He was obviously a Syrian with Syrian sympathies; but that does not mean that he was born in one of the eastern Syrian principalities like Tatian. His reference to the Tigris and the Euphrates as bordering on our latitudes does not warrant this inference. He was much more at home in Greek culture than Tatian, and wrote fluently and attractively in the Greek language. He was not a Christian by birth, but had been drawn to Christianity by the study of the Hebrew scriptures, like Justin and Tatian and Athenagoras. He was acquainted with that whole school of Christian philosophy and theology to which they belonged; but his own approach was a different one.

In his only surviving book, which is called *To Autolycus*, he refers to various historical works which he had composed. He loved poring over the records of times long ago, and learning about gods and wars and chronologies and genealogies and origins; not only in the Hebrew scriptures but also in the Hellenistic annalists of the time of Seleucus and Ptolemy; Berossus, the Babylonian priest who wrote down the chronicles of the old Semitic empires, Menander the Ephesian, who composed a history of the Phoenicians, and Manetho the chronicler of the Pharaohs of Egypt; books which have long disappeared from the earth. Tatian had studied this literature too. The Syrian had a love for chronicles, lists of names, pedigrees, and so forth. Though his style was more graceful, and his spirit less harsh, his mind moved in much the same way as Tatian's in this respect.

It we consider carefully the genuine interest which Theophilus had in this work, which must have made a romantic appeal to his imagination, we cannot help thinking that there was a streak of national or racial pride in it. He was no Roman or Hellene. His treatment of the Greek poets and philosophers is far from respectful; it is not even fair. On the other hand, he has a sympathy for Judaism which is rather unexpected. His praise of Melchizedek as the originator of all priesthood everywhere, and of the Jerusalem Temple where the priests worked their miracles of healing, is not quite the kind of thing that we have found in Christian writers. He seems to stand nearer to the Jewish race, and to the synagogue phase of the church's development, than any of his contemporaries; but not nearer than Clement of Rome perhaps, whose Epistle was undoubtedly known to him. Perhaps he used Jewish sources.

St Jerome says that Theophilus composed a commentary on the Gospel. In one place he says that it was a commentary on Matthew, but in another he says that Theophilus combined the things that were said by the four evangelists into one corpus, thus leaving a monument of his genius. Here is an undeniable link with Tatian. Did Theophilus really make a harmony of the Gospels, or did he comment on the *Diatessaron* itself? Was the *Diatessaron* circulated in Antioch before it reached the Syrian churches on the Euphrates? Did Tatian teach for a time in Antioch before proceeding further? It seems likely.

We know very little about the use of the Gospels in Antioch, except for the unparalleled position of Matthew in Ignatius and the *Didache*. Other Gospels were read and quoted in Ignatius and in Theophilus, but Matthew seems to have been 'The Gospel' still. On the other hand, the sect called the *Docetae* was using the *Gospel according to Peter*, which had been freely composed by a literary man who had the four Gospels spread before him and possibly other material. A 'dia-Tessaron', a one-in-four, might be just what the situation demanded, especially if it was so constructed as to take the place of Matthew in the church service. The *Diatessaron* may have been brought to Antioch, or even composed in Antioch, and used there for a time in succession to Matthew; and this would explain how it spread to the Syrian kingdoms.

This is of course a mere conjecture, designed to fill out the very meagre evidence. Many scholars still think that it was composed in Syriac in the first place, in the land between the two rivers. On the other hand, we have to explain its translation into Latin and distribution in the west. The theory of a Greek original makes it easier to do so; but perhaps the question of priority is not one of great importance in the case of a bilingual scholar.

THE CHURCH IN MESOPOTAMIA

When Tatian arrived home and set up his school in his native country, he found a great change. It had been formed into a Roman protectorate. King Manu of Edessa had taken the Roman side in the recent war, and had been established in his kingdom. According to the legend he was the monarch who put to death Aggai the disciple of Addai, on the grounds that Aggai would not weave him a pagan diadem for his coronation, an Iranian emblem of deity and royalty.

According to the life of Bar Daisan which we have previously quoted, Hystasp was bishop of Edessa; it is an Iranian name, and perhaps he was the one who wove a crown for Manu. Bar Daisan himself, it says, had been born in Edessa on 11 July 154. He was twenty-five years old when he passed by the church which Addai had built, and heard Hystasp explaining the scriptures to the people; it was in the year 179. Bar Daisan was pleased with the discourse and desired to be initiated into the Christian mysteries. Hystasp instructed him and baptized him and ordained him deacon. There is no evidence that Bar Daisan became a pupil of Tatian; but there is an interesting resemblance between the two great Syrian teachers. Both repudiated Marcionism which was propagated in Syria by a man named Prepon; both were attracted by Valentinianism though they did not become Valentinians; both were heretics or near-heretics, out of line with the theologies which prevailed in the Greek-speaking churches of the Roman empire. The special theology of Bar Daisan may have been influenced by Hermogenes of Antioch; it has an Iranian touch.

We lose sight of Tatian after his arrival in Mesopotamia, but his influence on the Syrian churches must have been considerable, since they accepted his *Diatessaron* as their official church Gospel; in a Syriac translation, of course. It remained in use into the fifth century; and the Syrian churches also had a strong encratite flavour.

SYRIANISM

The evidence which we have reviewed in connexion with Syrian Christianity is small in quantity but highly suggestive.

The reading and thinking of Theophilus, so far as it can be assessed from his only surviving book (which he finished writing after 180) shows many curious negative signs. There is, first of all, the massive silence on the credal and sacramental elements in Christianity. He has a Logos theology, or a Logos-and-Sophia theology; and he quotes the Gospels as if they were well-known books; but the name of Jesus is never mentioned, though it may be hidden under certain references to healing, or *iasis*. He confines himself to the prolegomena of Christianity which could safely be spoken of in public in the heathen world; and so, of course, did Tatian in his *Address to the Greeks*; and Athenagoras, too.

Actually he works from the Old Testament, with which he is very familiar. He loves it, and knows it well in its liturgical and catechetical and historical setting. He specializes in the latter and relates it to oriental history generally. He champions the Hebrew culture against the entire Greek culture with all its wise men and philosophers and poets; though indeed he finds a prophetess 'among the Greek and other nations' in the Sibyl and quotes her as an ally, and is grateful for sporadic testimonies from classical Greek authors in favour of a monotheistic faith, imperative morals, divine justice, a resurrection from the dead and eternal retribution in a future life.

Nevertheless his attitude to the Greek culture is uncompromisingly hostile, and his knowledge of it surprisingly superficial. He seems not to have had any personal contact with the exponents of a formal Greek philosophy, for his inaccuracies could not have passed uncorrected in the course of actual encounter. His knowledge is second-hand. He knows his material in literary form, and even so he is not deeply versed in it.

Now Justin and Athenagoras knew Greek philosophy from personal contact, and had a respect for it. Furthermore, they were prepared to affiliate Christianity with it to some extent. Theophilus repudiates it altogether; he never forgets that Christianity is an oriental religion with an oriental background. It was an indigenous religion for him.

Furthermore, his attitude to the Roman empire is not friendly. Clement, Justin and Melito all admire the imperium, and are loyal to it. They are prepared to compliment the emperors on their piety or philosophy. There is no sign of this attitude in Theophilus. He repeats the conventional Jewish teaching about honouring God and the king, which he quotes from Proverbs, not from the Gospels; but that is as far as he goes. He admits that the monarch has a stewardship which he has received from God; but his pattern of Roman monarchy is Tarquin the Proud, whom he paints as a monument of arrogance, a murderer and adulterer, and a patron of every kind of crime.

We are tempted to discover here a racial or political motivation. The Romanized or Hellenized east was proud of its own history and its own cultural inheritance. The wealth and power of Syria was increasing, and would before long dominate the Roman world. The Syrian proconsul, Avidius Cassius, was preparing plans for an independent oriental empire; and the time would come when Syrian emperors and empresses would reign in Rome itself. Was Theophilus the exponent of an oriental Christianity which would know how to co-operate with them when the day came?

Theophilus, in the course of his three volumes *To Autolycus*, strives to wean his reader from an infatuation for the Greek culture and to win him to a Christianity which he presents as the oldest and truest oriental monotheism. The Hebrews are 'our ancestors'; Moses is 'our legislator'; the prophets are 'our scriptures'; and it is by such a pedigree that Christianity, in or near the land where it was born, could appear as the legitimate heir of the oldest oriental culture and the natural form of religious self-expression for the growing Syrian nationalism. He even provides holy places of immemorial antiquity; the high city of Jerusalem; and the garden of Eden bordering on our latitudes; and the mountains of Arabia, where the remains of the ark were to be seen; Arabia no doubt being a copyist's error for Armenia.

Among the varieties of Jewish, Jewish-Syrian, and non-Jewish-Syrian Christianity which ramified east and north from Palestine and Antioch, there was one which actually developed into a form of national self-expression before the end of the century, the Christianity of Edessa. In the time of which we were writing, the king of Edessa was pro-Roman and anti-Christian. His successor Abgar was anti-Roman and pro-Christian. A Christian cult could wed itself to a national sentiment as it had done in parts of Phrygia.

In the series of wars which began in 161 it may be that some Syrian Christians were not on the Roman side.

THE REBELLION IN SYRIA, A.D. 175

In 174 there was a period of peace, following the wars on the Danube; but it was only short-lived. In 175 Marcus was considering the organization of new Roman provinces north of the Danube and east of the Rhine, which would form a protective area against barbarian aggression when news came of a rebellion in Syria. Avidius Cassius, the successful general of the wars of 162–5 had been the ruler of the east for nearly ten years; he was a Syrian by birth, and saw an opportunity of reviving the old Syrian empire of Seleucus and Antiochus. He declared his independence. Marcus was obliged to abandon his plans, and march east with his armies. He took with him his wife the empress Faustina, and his son Commodus, who was now fourteen years old. He had recently been invested with the *toga virilis* which marked his coming of age, and had been given the title of Caesar. It would not be long before he would succeed his father as emperor.

We have now had before our eyes examples of most of the weaknesses which would affect the empire in succeeding centuries; the undue family feeling of the Emperors as they became godlike hereditary autocrats; the perpetual incursions of the barbarians from Germany; the growing wealth and power of the eastern provinces; and the temptation felt by a popular and successful general to assert his independence. To these factors we must add others which are harder to estimate. As the central government increased in power, there was a corresponding loss of independence in the local civic life, where some show of democracy and self-government still existed when St Luke wrote the Acts. The codification of the law tended to identify the source of authority with the will of the prince. Commercial expansion in the eastern countries was accompanied by a serious deterioration of the currency. There was a general decline, historians suggest, in moral vigour, social enterprise, and intellectual originality. The ordinary reader of history, however, cannot help admiring the amazing power and resilience of the empire which succeeded so often in rallying its forces and throwing back its invaders, though each time at fearful cost to itself.

Avidius Cassius was assassinated, and his attempt to found a Syrian empire collapsed with his death. Marcus Aurelius, like Hadrian forty years before, could make a tour of the east. It seems that he made a good impression. He is probably the emperor who is spoken of in the Talmud as visiting Rabbi Judah the Holy, the Jewish patriarch or prince of the sanhedrin, whose court was in Galilee. Judah was the lineal descendant of Hillel and Gamaliel, and presided over the compilation of the Mishnah itself, surviving until about 220. Marcus Aurelius also visited Alexandria, but returned to Antioch for the winter. Early in 176 he passed through Cappadocia where the empress died. He reached Smyrna in the spring and so returned to Rome.

THE *CLEMENTINE RECOGNITIONS*

Some effort must now be made to deal with the Ebionite material which has survived, in a diluted form, in the long philosophic romances which are written in the name of Clement. The difficulty is that they did not appear in their present literary form before the end of the fourth century and the sparse amount of second-century material which they contain is overwhelmed in a flood of religious philosophizing. The supposed narrator is Clement of Rome, who is alleged to have made a visit to Palestine and attached himself to Simon Peter as his attendant and secretary in the Greek tongue. He was influenced to do this by Barnabas, who preached the gospel in Rome shortly after the ascension.

Clement was thought of as a member of the imperial family. His mother Matthidia had disappeared when he was a child, taking with her his twin brothers Faustinus and Faustus. His father Faustinianus had gone in search of his wife and children, and none of them had ever been heard of again. This situation provides a secondary plot for the narrative, and gives it the name by which it is known in one of the two recensions: The *Clementine Recognitions*; for Clement eventually succeeds in finding all his lost relations. The other version is called the *Clementine Homilies*.

The name of Clement connects him with the Flavian emperors and the martyred consul who bore the same name, and his wife Domitilla, whose property at Rome was in use as a Christian cemetery. Antoninus and Marcus Aurelius had both married wives of the name of Faustina, and Hadrian had a female relative named Matthidia, to whom he gave imperial rank. The story of Clement's family is mere machinery which helps to give the heavy narrative a little life; but it also commended Christianity to loyalist circles by connecting it so closely with the imperial family. It may even suggest that Faustina was not unfavourable to the faith.

THE EBIONITE LEGENDS

The next step is to disentangle the older 'Ebionite' legends which were woven into this romantic framework. Epiphanius, in the fourth century, knew of two Ebionite books which seem to answer to this description; one was the *anabathmoi* or *Steps* or *Ascents of James*; the other was the *periodoi* or *Circuits* or *Wanderings of Peter*. There is material corresponding to those titles in the Clementine books, and this material has an Ebionite colour. Origen shows some knowledge of the Petrine material and speaks of *Dialogues with Appion* which are contained in it. We are in touch here with second-century Palestinian tradition.

Among the Jewish-Christian traditions of Hegesippus, who was still living in Rome at this time, there was an account of a scene in the Temple at Passover, when James the brother of Jesus was placed on a pinnacle or high point, and interrogated by representatives of the seven sects into which the Jewish people was divided. The story of James in the *Recognitions* begins in the same way except that he stands at the top of the Temple steps, with the twelve apostles. He has been arguing against the maintenance of the sacrifices, and has announced that the Temple will be devastated unless they are discontinued. He commends Christian baptism as a substitute. After seven days of argument, he has persuaded Caiaphas and the priests to accept baptism, when a mysterious 'enemy' arrives on the scene with a few followers. There is a riot in which much blood is shed. There is a confused flight, in the midst of which 'that enemy' attacks James and throws him headlong from his exalted position, and leaves him there thinking that he is dead; which also resembles the story of Hegesippus. Eusebius makes this story the prelude to his martyrdom but in the *Recognitions* it is a separate incident, and the enemy who does the deed is Saul of Tarsus.

A note in one of the manuscripts explains this identification, but no note is needed; for Caiaphas, who now seems to be on the anti-Christian side again, sends him to Damascus, where it is believed that Peter had taken refuge. Here, then, is the substance of the story of the lost *Ascents of James*.

We now come to the *Wanderings of Peter*, who had been sent by James to Caesarea. There he finds himself in conflict with the sinister figure of Simon Magus, the Samaritan sorcerer and heresiarch. He disputes with Simon, who decamps from Caesarea and makes his way by stages to Rome. Peter follows him from city to city along the Phoenician sea-coast, until he reaches Antioch, where he makes his headquarters. In these encounters it is clear from time to time that the figure of Simon really means Paul. He is the rival of the true apostles who claimed after a brief discipleship, in a single vision which lasted but an hour, to be an apostle and to resist Peter himself. Phrases out of Paul's Epistles are woven into the orations of Peter in which Paul is denounced. But these attacks have more in mind than the historical Paul of the Acts and the Epistles; they have Marcion and possibly Basilides. It is the other side of the Marcionite controversy that comes into view here. Marcion and others like him maintained that Paul alone possessed the truth, and that Peter and the Twelve had not properly understood their Master. Here in the Ebionite propaganda is the Paul that Marcion believed in and the Peter that he objected to, mixing Jewish legalities with the gospel of Christ, and opposing the work of Paul.

It is impossible to doubt that these legends are old second-century material, and reflect the bitter controversy between the churches of the Marcionite and Ebionite types: the ultra-Gentile and the ultra-Jewish.

THE EBIONITE PETER

Peter appears in the New Testament as the champion of a liberal Jewish Christianity, and a friend of the Gentiles. In the *Books of Clement* his liberal Jewish Christianity is of a peculiar type. He denounces the sacrificial rites in the Temple and the holy fire that burned upon the altar; these elements in the Jewish tradition are traced back to the authority of Aaron, who was a representative of the evil power. The two powers which operate against one another in the universe always send their prophets into the world simultaneously: Moses and Aaron, Jesus and John the Baptist, Simon Peter and Simon Magus. The condemnation of John the Baptist is an odd feature of this legend; he is the one born of woman, whereas Jesus is the son of man; he represents the moon and has thirty disciples, whereas Jesus represents the sun and has twelve; he is the master of the heretics; Simon and Dositheus are his pupils.

The true prophet has come into the world many times, appearing first in Adam; Jesus is one of his several incarnations, if incarnation is the right word. He is the new Moses, purifying the old religion of its Aaronic features, and making it a universal religion for all mankind. The sacrifices are replaced by Christian baptism; but a certain amount of the legal ceremonial is retained; how much it would be hard to say. The third- and fourth-century authors who have worked on this material have made Peter into a wandering philosopher of the familiar Hellenistic type, the Pythagorean sage, who has imbibed some wonderful oriental form of illumination, and become a master-mind. He was used as a mouthpiece for all kinds of theological and apologetic propaganda. This process may well have begun in the second century, however; it may be that a refined universalistic form of Ebionism was already being worked out on the Phoenician sea-coast.

It certainly seems to belong to the second-century pattern that James the brother of Jesus has a high position in Jerusalem. He is styled the bishop of bishops, and Peter reports to him from time to time. Peter is the founder of the Gentile church at Caesarea, and endows it with its first bishop, his principal pupil Zacchaeus, to whom he allots twelve presbyters and four deacons. He passes through all the coast-towns, Ptolemais, Tyre, Sidon, Berytus, Tripolis, and Laodicea, making similar arrangements in some of them, and arrives finally at Antioch, where the important citizen Theophilus, or Cornelius, consecrates the great hall of his house as a church, and a chair is placed in it by all the people for the apostle Peter. And these statements may be of value as evidence for the local tradition at the time when the legends took form.

As for Simon Magus, he is not exclusively Paul or Marcion; he is the voice of Gentile error in general, and the assailant of the genuine Christian tradition, with Peter at its head. But now and then he is simply the magician of Samaria, who has become a purely legendary figure; but true facts may linger in the legend, which must also have existed in a pro-Simonian form among those who still accepted him as their cult-leader. Such genuine traditions will be few and far between; they may include, for instance, his connexion with John the Baptist and the name of his companion and rival, Dositheus. The daemonic character of Simon took a firm hold upon the Christian imagination; his legend assumed many forms and enjoyed a long life; its last transformation is said to be the medieval legend of Dr Faustus which was used by Marlowe, Goethe and Gounod.

THE *EPISTLE OF THE APOSTLES*

In recent years another work of the Christian imagination has turned up which may be regarded as an answer to the Ebionite onslaught on Paul, but this time from the catholic point of view, which accepted the traditions of both apostles. It is the *Epistle of the Apostles*, which its editor, Dr Schmidt, assigns to Asia Minor; but we depend on Coptic and Ethiopic translations for the text, and this shows that it was well received in Egypt, even if it did not originate there. There is one leaf of a Latin translation, however, which proves its wide distribution at one time. It is much concerned about the advent of heretical teachers, among whom it mentions Simon and Cleobius.

It has a conventional opening. The author assembles the twelve apostles on a mountain, where they receive instruction from the Lord. He even attempts a list of their names, but with a sad lack of success. He begins with John, Thomas, and Peter, and ends with 'Judas

Zelotes' and Kephas. There may be a copyist's error here, but Clement of Alexandria agrees with him in separating Peter and Kephas and making two men of them, an error which Origen corrects.

It supports the catholic church tradition against docetism. It touches on most of the orthodox points, the Word made flesh, the bodily resurrection, the final judgement, and so forth; but it gives these doctrines in a popular pictorial and apocalyptic form. It is not above a little mythology; for so we must describe the descent of Jesus through the heavens and his appearance to the Virgin Mary as the angel Gabriel. Nor is it above a little legend; like the story of Jesus as a child, learning his alphabet. Nor does it despise a little allegory, even in the case of the Gospels:

We did set pieces of bread before them and they ate and were filled; and there remained over, and we filled twelve baskets full of the fragments asking one another and saying, 'What mean these five loaves?'

They are the symbol of our faith in the Lord of the Christians, even in the Father the Lord Almighty, and in Jesus Christ our redeemer, in the Holy Spirit the comforter, in the holy church, and in the remission of sins.

(*Epistula Apostolorum*, 5, in M. R. James, *Apocryphal N.T.*)

in which we see how the old Trinitarian formula of baptism has given birth to a creed-form in five points; it is a eucharistic creed-form.

One purpose of this book is to substantiate the claim of St Paul to be enrolled with the Twelve as an apostle. It makes the Lord prophesy his arrival and instruct the Twelve to receive him. It quotes an apocryphal scripture to clinch the matter;

Behold out of Syria will I begin to call together a new Jerusalem;
And Sion will I subdue unto me and it shall be taken;
And the place which is childless shall be called the son and daughter of my
     father, and my bride.   (*Ibid.* 33.)

and Paul is described as coming out of the land of Cilicia unto Damascus of Syria.

There is an eschatology of a cloudy and indefinite character. There will be confusions, wars, heresies and scandals in the church. The advent of Christ is to take place during the fifty days between Pascha and Pentecost, when a hundred and fifty years are passed after the Resurrection—if this is the correct text. This works out at A.D. 180, so that the Epistle itself must have been composed prior to that date.

CHAPTER 14

THE PERIOD OF MELITO

The genius of Syrian Christianity expressed itself naturally in myths and legends and psalms and hymns. In literature it affected the pseudonymous; it liked historical romances. It also liked church-orders and chronicles and new editions of sacred texts; but the identity of the author was concealed in these cases too. The work of Tatian and Theophilus is really rather exceptional. Clement of Alexandria says that the great teachers of this generation did not write books.

On the other hand the correspondence of Dionysius of Corinth revealed a network of communication among learned and literary bishops, including two in Crete, Philip and Pinytus; and Eusebius knows of other writers of the period, such as Modestus and Musanus. Asia Minor also had its literary bishops and its learned schools, which profoundly influenced the course of Christian thought; but we have nothing but a few extracts, and a few shadowy synchronisms, and lists of lost books. Yet this country was the source of theological and prophetic movements which stirred the Christian world; it continued to fertilize the thinking of the Roman church to the end of the century, after which its great creative period came to an end.

THE THUNDERING LEGION, A.D. 171

Marcus Aurelius visited Smyrna in Asia Minor, with his son Commodus, on his way back to Rome in the year 176; and this is the only occasion known to us for the presentation in person of the *Apologies* of Claudius Apollinarius and Melito of Sardis. These *Apologies* have not been preserved, but we know something about them. In one of his books Apollinarius referred to the famous episode of the 'thundering legion', which Eusebius assigns to 174 but some modern scholars to

171;[1] and the book in which he did so is likely to have been his *Apology*. His other books, *To the Greeks*, *Concerning Truth*, and *To the Jews*, do not seem to be so likely; nor his Epistle against the Phrygian heresy. This incident had occurred during a campaign on the Danube against the Quadi. The Roman army was suffering from lack of water owing to a drought and were in a bad way, when they saw the enemy approaching. In their desperation they knelt on the ground and offered prayer. No sooner had this been done than a thunderbolt fell from heaven, followed by a torrent of rain which saved the situation. Such is the way in which the story is told by pagan and Christian authors, though details differ, of course.

The providential downpour of rain is illustrated on the Antonine column which was erected in Rome in front of the Pantheon to commemorate the victories of Marcus. It is sculptured with a number of scenes illustrating the war on the Danube. In one of these Jupiter Pluvius, the god of rain, can be seen pouring it down in streams upon the soldiers, who are collecting it in every sort of container. In the pagan account of the miracle, the credit is given to the prayers of the emperor himself, or to an Egyptian magician who was present; but the Christians ascribed it to the prayers of Christian soldiers. Tertullian, writing nearly forty years later, says that Marcus himself gave the Christians the credit, and that he wrote a letter to the senate in consequence, ordering the cessation of persecution; before long, copies of this imaginary letter were in circulation. Marcus did write a report of the matter to the senate, but we may be sure that he gave the credit to Jupiter Pluvius or to some other appropriate pagan deity; and we know that the persecution continued.

Apollinarius is the earliest witness to the story; but Eusebius does not quote him; he merely says that he told the story in a simple and artless manner, and added that, from that time, the legion which had wrought the marvel received from the emperor a title appropriate to the event, being styled the Thundering Legion. Actually however, it had been known for a long time as the '*legio fulminata*' (the legion which was armed with the thunderbolt) and no change at all was made in the name.

It was the Twelfth Legion, and had been stationed before the war at Melitene near Caesarea in Cappadocia, where, no doubt, it had taken in

[1] See Eusebius, *Ecclesiastical History*, Lawlor and Oulton, vol. II, p. 161.

its Christian recruits. Wherever it went, it would be conspicuous because of its shields bearing the figure XII and the emblem of the thunderbolt. Christian legionaries, we may be sure, would not be backward in giving their version of the story, and claiming that their prayers had saved the emperor and his army; and Christian apologists would not be backward in pushing this claim. What is of interest to the modern historian, of course, is the discovery that there were a number of Christians in the army, a fact which implies a certain degree of religious accommodation on both sides. These legionaries could not have evaded the duty of offering religious homage to the emperor and to the standards of the legion; but perhaps there were ways of making things easy for Christians who were prepared to serve as soldiers; and perhaps there is a grain of truth in the story that the emperor stopped the persecution of Christians. He may have been lenient to Christians who would undertake military service. And, after all, the case of Jewish soldiers must have presented exactly the same problems, and have been met in some way.

THE APOLOGY OF MELITO, A.D. 176

The Apology of Melito is generally dated by scholars after Commodus became co-emperor; but the reference to Commodus in the text is not very formal, and the deduction hardly seems necessary. It would have been perfectly natural to include a reference to the young Caesar, if the *Apology* was presented to Marcus Aurelius when he visited Smyrna with his son in 176 on his way home from Syria. No other opportunity for actual presentation seems to suggest itself.

The few sentences which are quoted from it by Eusebius give some idea of the kind of approach which Melito adopted. In accordance with the spirit of the period, he indulges in historical retrospect. He looks back on the last few years. An unheard-of thing has happened. The race of the God-worshippers in Asia is being persecuted and harried as a result of new decrees, a statement which suggests that some new directives of some sort have been issued against the Christians. Shameless informers and coveters of other men's goods are taking advantage of these decrees to attack and plunder innocent people. There was a reference to the looting of Christian homes as early as the Epistle to the Hebrews, and we shall find it described in the Acts of the Gallican Martyrs. Some new decrees, issued by somebody in authority, have encouraged it, but Melito affects to doubt whether the emperor was responsible. The mob has been let loose again. He asks for an impartial investigation, and for the punishment of scandalmongers and informers, the very point which Hadrian had insisted upon. It would seem that there had not been many actual martyrdoms recently.

The Christian philosophy, he remarked, had appeared in history at the same time as the empire itself. It had been the foster-sister of the empire and had brought it good fortune. Nobody had harmed it in any way until malicious persons had brought untrue slanders to the attention of Nero and Domitian, emperors of whom nobody was very proud. Their hostile policy had been corrected by the 'pious father' of Marcus, who had frequently admonished, even in writing, those who had made attacks on the Christians; he reminds Marcus of the rescript of his adoptive grandfather Hadrian, and the edict by which his 'father' Antoninus had restrained the anti-Christian demonstrations in Athens and Larissa and Thessalonica. There is a document in existence which purports to give the text of this edict, but its fictitious character is very obvious, though some scholars are prepared to think that traces of an authentic document may be found in some of its phrases. Our real knowledge of it, however, is entirely confined to what Melito says about it. We have ventured to date it about 150–5.

Melito appeals with confidence to Marcus, as he is even more philosophic and philanthropic than his fathers; but his argument fell on deaf ears. It is possible, however, that Commodus listened.

CHRISTIANITY AND THE EMPIRE

These fragments give a valuable review of the history, which confirms our reconstruction. We see, however, that he is answering new objections. It had been contended, we must suppose, that the calamities suffered by the empire during the reign of the present philosophic and god-loving prince had been due to the impiety of the Christians. A plausible theory. On the contrary, Melito replies, Christianity and the empire had originated and prospered side by side. The good emperors, he pleads, had protected the church; the bad emperors had persecuted it. There is a note struck here which we may also detect in the reference of Apollinarius to the Thundering Legion; perhaps, too, in the Clementine legends which never mention persecution, and affiliate the first bishop of Rome with the imperial family. It is an assurance of loyalty. It is a note of fraternization and conciliation towards the empire if the empire will have it. Far from being a hostile or baneful force, Christianity was a fortunate influence and possibly a predestined ally. Here, too, are hints of future historical developments.

This is very different from the Syrianism which we found in Theophilus of Antioch. If indeed some Syrian Christians had been on the wrong side in the recent rebellion, the riots complained of by Melito could easily be explained, and the hostile attitude of the new imperial edicts accounted for. We could also see the special point of the references by Apollinarius to the prayers of Christian soldiers recruited in the border province.

AVIRCIUS MARCELLUS

High up in the headwaters of the Glaucus River, which was the main tributary of the Meander, was the part of Phrygia known as the Pentapolis or Five Cities. Here, it would seem, Montanism was not so powerful. Among the Five Cities were Otröus and Hieropolis, which is not to be confused with the much larger city of Hierapolis. This country was the home of the 'Anonymous' writer on Montanism; he mentions Zoticus of Otröus as his fellow-presbyter, and dedicates his book to Avircius Marcellus of Hieropolis. The three men were members of an anti-Montanist group which was active early in the hundred-and-nineties; or earlier than the hundred-and-nineties, since Avircius had asked the 'Anonymous' to write a pamphlet on Montanism some time previously.

All three may have been bishops, since it was customary for bishops to allude to one another by the honourable old title of presbyter or elder. We do not know whether this Zoticus was identical with the Zoticus of Cumana who examined Maximilla at Pepuza; it seems rather unlikely; but we know something about Avircius. He had a considerable reputation as a holy man and wonder-worker. About the year 400 somebody wrote a legendary *Life of Abercius*, which is far removed from history, but preserves the information that he was the bishop of Hieropolis, and quotes the epitaph which he caused to be inscribed upon his tombstone.

All doubts about the epitaph were set at rest by the discovery of the tombstone in 1883 by the famous archaeologist Sir William Ramsay.

Avircius composed the epitaph himself, and had the stone erected in his seventy-second year, which was probably no later than 200 or 210, since it was imitated by another citizen of Hieropolis, who dated his in 216.

According to this computation, Avircius was in his thirties or early forties in the year 175 when the Syrian revolt was put down. His epitaph tells of a journey to Mesopotamia, which could have taken place as early as 170–4, when the new province must have been well organized; more likely perhaps during the five or ten years after 176. Time has to be allowed before this eastern journey for a visit to Rome. He tells the story in lame hexameters, which recall the ambiguous oracular style of the Sibylline verses rather than the strong-winged music of Homer. They are full of mysterious symbols and literary allusions in the Phrygian manner, with pagan imagery interwoven with the Christian; or at any rate the Christian treated in pagan style.

I who am a citizen of the elect city, erected this in my lifetime, that I might have in due season a place therein for my body.

My name is Avircius: I am a disciple of the pure shepherd who feeds his flocks upon mountains and plains: he who has great all-seeing eyes. He taught me the faithful scriptures of life. (Cf. Revelation v. 6.)

The shepherd symbolism might have suggested to the pagan passer-by the Phrygian shepherd-god Attis, who, however, could hardly be described as pure. The Christian would think of the Gospels.

To Rome he sent me to see my king and to see my queen, golden-robed and golden-sandalled. I saw a people there who bore a splendid seal.

The king would seem to be the emperor and the queen the empress, though some scholars suggest that the queen means the city. If it means the empress, the journey must have been taken before the year 175 when Faustina left Rome, never to return. There was no one after her, until the last years of the century, who bore the imperial title of Augusta. The church of Rome lies hidden under the reference to the people with the seal.

I also saw the plain of Syria and all the towns, and Nisibis. I crossed over the Euphrates, and everywhere I had companions.

Nisibis lies beyond Edessa, so that Avircius saw something of the new Syriac-speaking Christianity. It was all under Roman rule.

Everywhere I had companions. Paul was my companion, and faith everywhere led me forward; and served food everywhere, the fish from the fountain, immense and pure, which the pure virgin caught, and gave to her friends to eat continually, having good wine, and giving the mixed cup with the bread.

This suggests that he followed the trail of Paul through Phrygia and Cilicia and Antioch and Damascus, finding hospitality everywhere in the mysterious sacramental fellowship of the church.

The modern Christian can easily see the reference to the eucharist in these lines, but he may not notice at first that the pure virgin is the church which dispenses these mysteries. The use of the fish as a symbol for Christ appears here as an established tradition. The famous lines in the *Sibylline Oracles* are not much later; for Christians were already producing these mysterious verses in their own interests, as Celsus says in the *True Word*. The second division of Book VIII begins with an acrostic, the initial letters of the first twenty-seven lines reading as follows: ΙΗΣΟΥΣ ΧΡΙΣΤΟΣ ΘΕΟΥ ΥΙΟΣ ΣΩΤΗΡ—'Jesus Christus God's Son Saviour'; and the initial letters of these five words give the word ΙΧΘΥΣ, which means fish.

The fish symbol was a sacramental emblem, suggested by such passages in the Gospel as the feeding of the five thousand in Mark, which may have been in the mind of Avircius throughout; for Mark mentions the shepherd and the mountain in this connexion, and of course the bread. The poetry on the tomb of Avircius is catacomb art in words. In the catacomb pictures of the eucharist, a fish or fishes often appear with the bread and the cup as a symbol of Christ; and a fish, like a lamb or a dove, could also be used as an image of the soul of the believer. In Theophilus the fishes which are born in the water on the fifth day are symbols of Christian souls reborn in baptism. It may also be used as an image of the convert or believer. Tertullian says of baptism, 'we little fishes, like our big fish, were born in the water.' Such symbolism was something more than a cryptic code-language designed to protect Christian devotion from the scrutiny of the hostile world; it was like the artist's or poet's language of images; it was an imaginative exuberance, arising out of evangelical mass-enthusiasm, and creating an idiom of its own, similar to the speaking with tongues of the apostolic period. The hymns of modern popular usage often show the same characteristics. But to return to Avircius.

These things, I Avircius, standing by, ordered to be inscribed here. I am truly seventy-two years old. He who understandeth these things, let him pray for Avircius, even he who hath knowledge.

But no one is to put another into my tomb, and if he does, he is to pay the Roman treasury two thousand gold pieces, and to my native city of Hieropolis one thousand gold pieces.

Avircius, therefore, was a person of consequence in his native city. His name is Roman or Celtic. He was a Romanized Phrygian grandee, or a Phrygianized member of some Roman family. He was obviously a loyalist in politics. He seems to have been unmarried, in all probability a spiritual and ascetic like Melito; indeed, it is a long time since we heard of any Christian bishop or teacher of whom it is perfectly certain that he was married; not since the apostles in fact, and the married bishops of the Pastorals, and Valens of Philippi, and the prophet Hermas; to which we may add the father of Marcion and the family of bishops in Ephesus to which Polycrates belonged. I doubt if we meet another case before Tertullian and possibly Clement of Alexandria. The evidence is too scrappy, of course, to permit any generalizations on the subject; but it is certainly interesting. The episcopate in Asia could produce its own celibate 'spirituals' to confront the Montanist prophets.

Other Christian intellectuals also expressed themselves in verse. No doubt the Asian, probably Ephesian, elder, who wrote verses against a Valentinian magus of the name of Marcus was flourishing about this time. They may be paraphrased as follows.

> Maker of idols, O Marcus, and warden of wonders,
> Adept in astral learning and magical cunning,
> Ever confirming thereby the teachings of error,
> Showing thy signs to them whom thou makest to wander,
> Worked in the power of the dark apostate spirit,
> Even as Satan thy father in bounty supplies thee,
> By the might of the fallen angel Azazel to do them,
> So making thee the forerunner of atheistical evils.
>
> (Irenaeus, *Ad. Haer.* XVIII, 17.)

Marcus had looked too deeply into the parables and sacraments of Jesus which made use of symbols which had long been known in the mysteries of the ancient world. After all, the cup of wine or the ear of corn reaped were not new with the gospel; what made them new was the new shepherd who took them into association with himself. Marcus brought them back into association with the oldest of the deities in his part of the world, the great mother, whom he magnified into a heavenly spirit, after the manner of Valentinus. When he celebrated his sacrament, he used a cup of water, which turned red as it was changed into the blood of the mother, the 'grace which is above all things'.

The cup was a symbol of prophecy; but it was also a symbol of the bridal rite, when the prophet took one of the sisters to himself and made her a prophetess.

First of all take grace, from me and through me; make thyself ready as a bride awaiting her bridegroom, that I may be what thou art, and thou what I: Consecrate within thy bridal chamber the seed of light; receive from me the bridegroom: give place unto him and let him give place unto thee: behold grace hath come upon thee; open thy mouth and prophesy.

Here is the prophet of the wrong sort, and this may be what the *Didache* calls a cosmic mystery of the church.

To return to Avircius, however; he supplies us with our first perfectly clear example of a request for prayer on behalf of the departed; but these also appear in the catacomb burials.

MELITO AS A THEOLOGIAN

The loss of all the works of Melito is a serious deprivation to the student of church history and theology. He was probably the leading theologian of catholic Christianity between Justin and Irenaeus. He had made the pilgrimage to Jerusalem. He could address an emperor in a worthy and dignified manner. He could deal with an Old Testament story in the imaginative vein of his liturgical tradition. He could preach a sermon in a fervent mystical style which is rather too rich and ornate for our modern western taste; his flowers of speech are suggestive of the east rather than the west. On the other hand he could handle points of doctrine and was in advance of his time in theological terminology, speaking of two 'substances' or *ousiai* in Christ, and contrasting his human 'nature' or *phusis* with his divine nature, almost in the style of later theologians. His works reached Rome, where they were treated with respect, as we learn from definite references in the pages of Tertullian, and in the *Little Labyrinth* which is ascribed to Hippolytus. His influence has been discerned by scholars in the great masterpiece of Tertullian, the famous *Liber Apologeticus*.

A number of his books were preserved in the library at Caesarea where Eusebius worked, and he gives a catalogue of them which is repeated by Jerome. It is a very impressive list, though it does not mention the six volumes of *Extracts* from the prophets, or the *Homily on the Passion* which is the oldest surviving Christian sermon. They are,

Concerning the Pascha [two volumes], Concerning Christian conduct and the prophets, Concerning the church, Concerning the Lord's Day, Concerning the nature of man, Concerning the creation, Concerning the obedience of faith, Concerning the senses, Concerning the soul and body, Concerning Baptism, Concerning truth, Concerning the creation and the birth of Christ, Concerning prophecy, Concerning hospitality, Concerning the devil and the Revelation of John, The key, Concerning the embodied God, and To Antoninus [his apology]. (Eusebius, *E.H.* IV, 26, 2.)

He must have contributed a great deal to the theologians of the next generation.

MILTIADES AND ALCIBIADES

This list of books, together with the other evidence which we have reviewed, proves that there was a vigorous literary and theological life in Asia Minor which was stimulated by controversy of all kinds. The old bishops like Polycarp who had been content to handle the oral tradition had given way to literary bishops who wrote books in the Greek manner. Elders and teachers adopted the style of the philosopher, founded schools and produced books, the great majority of which are lost. Among these cultured writers we must rank Miltiades, whose works are entirely lost, though Tertullian praises him as 'the sophist of the Christian churches' and Hippolytus in the *Little Labyrinth* includes him among the stalwarts who upheld the divinity of Christ. He wrote, as they all did, a treatise *To the Jews* and a treatise *To the Greeks* and an apology *To the Rulers of the World*. It also appears that he wrote a book against the Montanists, *That a Prophet ought not to Speak in Ecstasy*.

The New Prophecy was passing into its second phase. In connexion with the Gallican martyrdoms of 177 or 178, Eusebius remarks that 'just then, for the first time, the disciples of Montanus, of Alcibiades, and of Theodotus, in the region of Phrygia, were winning a wide reputation for prophecy', adding that a controversy arose about these persons to which the brethren in Gaul made their contribution by submitting a pious and orthodox judgement. Time has passed. It is the disciples of the original leaders who are now becoming prominent, and the universal church is being drawn into the controversy. The names of the leaders, however, are not free from difficulty in one particular, and the text of Eusebius may have been corrupted by errors in transmission. He has a reference to Alcibiades (v, 16, 17) where he seems to have meant to write Miltiades; and he once names Miltiades (VI, 16, 3) as if he were a Montanist. Some error seems to have crept into his text which cannot be corrected now. But we are sure of the catholic Miltiades and the Montanist Alcibiades.

THE MONTANIST TRADITION

The form of the New Prophecy which spread to the west in the latter part of the second century does not seem to agree in all respects with the picture which comes to us from Phrygia. It is a more moderate and reasonable movement, albeit very harsh and severe. It knows nothing of the descent of the New Jerusalem at Pepuza, if that was really meant to be taken literally; nor do we find the well organized prophetic ministry, with its high steward and oblations.

A Roman Montanist named Proclus is said to have claimed Philip of Hierapolis and his daughters as the ancestors or predecessors of the movement, but the local theory of the prophetic succession, as reported by the 'Anonymous', goes back no farther than Quadratus and Ammia of Philadelphia. He mentions Agabus, and Judas, and Silas, and the daughters of Philip, with Ammia and Quadratus, as examples of prophecy of the right kind; but he mentions them as part of his own argument and does not connect them with the Phrygian succession. The 'succession' was a purely local one, and was not reinforced by Bible names.

If the talk of Proclus about Philip's daughters (as reported by Gaius) is to be taken seriously, we may be looking at two different successions, one connected with Hierapolis, the home of Philip and Papias; the other with Philadelphia through Ammia and Quadratus; both of them going back to the Revelation of John; the Hierapolis succession looking for the New Jerusalem in Palestine, the Philadelphian in Phrygia.

The views of the movement which are given by the two principal authorities are by no means identical. The Anonymous, who was a local bishop or presbyter with first-hand knowledge, has in mind Ardabau and the first prophesyings of Montanus; he refers a good deal to Maximilla, but never mentions Priscilla or Pepuza, at least not in the extracts given by Eusebius. Apollonius, however, is interested in Priscilla and Pepuza; he also mentions the examination of Maximilla at Pepuza by Zoticus, Eusebius says, but does not quote his actual words. No doubt there were different sects within the movement, and everybody may not have approved of what went on at Pepuza. Even in Rome there were two sorts of Montanism, one headed by Aeschines, which was 'monarchian' in theology, like Montanus himself, the other by Proclus, who seems to have represented the same Asia Minor tradition in theology as Justin and Melito and Irenaeus. The tendency of Montanism to split into groups following personal leaders may be the point in the popular description of them as 'Kata-Phrygians'. *Kata* means 'according to'; and we do find the preposition used rather often, 'according to Aeschines', 'according to Proclus', 'according to Asterius Urbanus', and even 'according to Miltiades'.

The references to Quadratus and Ammia on the one hand, and to the daughters of Philip on the other, may do no more than identify the particular local variety of Montanism which was in question. When Epiphanius wrote his great book on heresies, he listed the Priscillians (or Pepuzans) as a separate sect.

THE EXPANSION OF MONTANISM

The Montanism which reached Rome and Gaul was not of the Pepuzan or Priscillian type, though Priscilla was numbered among the prophets. It was a popular imaginative revival movement with visions and ecstasies. It was welcomed by the martyrs in their prisons. It advocated a rigid discipline which the church generally did not accept. It fasted for longer hours and for more days. It condemned second marriages of any sort. It refused absolution for grave sins, though indeed there grew up a strange idea that the martyr had a privilege in this respect. It is probable that it exercised a powerful influence on the Latin church. Asia Minor had always found a field of expansion in the west; where Asian theology and liturgy had led the way, Phrygian prophecy could follow.

The New Prophecy added to the flood of literature which was deluging the church. The gnostics had their apocryphal Gospels and other additional literature; the Ebionites had their legends; fictitious Acts and Epistles were also being circulated; and the number of genuine Epistles had also been added to. The apostles had been succeeded in this respect by Clement and Ignatius and Polycarp; and these were being succeeded by Soter and Dionysius and Themiso. The *Revelation of Peter* and the *Shepherd* of Hermas were read in the Roman church. The oracles of Montanus and his women were being written down, and these oracles were regarded by the adherents of the New Prophecy as being at least equal in authority to the apostolic writings. The Paraclete had said more things in Montanus than in Christ or the apostles; and not only more, but better and greater; according to the account of Hippolytus as preserved in the Latin *Libellus*. It was a supplementary revelation which made additions to the old apostolic tradition; the authority of the Paraclete through Montanus could not be gainsaid, as Tertullian makes perfectly clear.

The dissemination of this literature forced the church to consider seriously the definition of what is now called the New Testament canon; and it also marked the end of the creative period in the New Prophecy. There are no more revelations on the grand scale. There may have been others who claimed the prophetic gift, but Maximilla would not concede it. 'After me', she said, 'there will be no more prophets, but only the end.' It sounds as if she was the last of the three to be left. She prophesied wars and confusions and persecutions; but actually wars and confusions were drawing to a close for the time being. The Anonymous wrote his book about thirteen years after her death.

Surely this falsehood too is now evident [he writes]; for it is more than thirteen years today since the woman died, and there has been neither a partial nor a universal war in the world; nay rather, by the mercy of God, the Christians have enjoyed continuous peace.

(The Anonymous, *Against Montanism*, in Eusebius, *E.H.* v, 16, 19.)

The only period of thirteen years that could possibly be described in this way is the thirteen and a half years reign of Commodus, from 180 to 192.

THE DEATH OF MAXIMILLA, *c.* 178 A.D.

We may place the death of Maximilla in 178 or 179, and the date when the Anonymous wrote about 192. He claimed that he wrote some forty years after the New Prophecy began, which would make the date of its origin about 152. This is reasonably close to 157, the date that Epiphanius gives.

THE ASIAN SCHOOLS

Montanism was not the only subject which was being discussed by Christians in Asia Minor. There were debates on doctrinal points, in which the first steps were being taken which led to the formulation of the doctrines of the incarnation and the Trinity. Christ is the Son of God, Melito said. He is the Word of the Father, begotten before the light, the creator of all things with the Father, the fashioner of men, the all-in-all; he became incarnate in the virgin's womb; he was born a perfect man that he might save lost mankind and gather together his scattered members. But once he has said this, he does not insist, as a theologian should, on the distinction between the Son and the Father. It is God who comes down to earth to take our flesh from the holy virgin, to be mocked by the Jews, to be fastened on a tree, to be buried in the ground, and to rise from the dead. In an exalted moment he can say, 'God has been slain by an Israelite hand', just as Ignatius could talk about the Passion of his God. In fact this is the kind of talk that went on, we may suppose, when Christians met for the Paschal rites. It would appear that Montanus talked in this way of the Paraclete; for it was God himself who spoke through him.

This old evangelical theology was christened 'monarchianism'. Its watchword was 'One God'. The preachers of this school did not hesitate to assert that God had died on Calvary. In the apocryphal Acts, the great apostles preach in this style. It is the old Jewish monotheism in rather too close union with the Christian gospel.

On the other hand, Melito revels in the doctrine of the two natures. Christ is simultaneously true God and perfect man. Melito is fighting Docetism, but he is also fighting some sort of Ebionism which thought

237

in terms of the man Jesus and a Spirit which descended upon him at his baptism. He asserts that the divinity was hidden in the flesh of Jesus from the beginning; Christ established both his natures during his earthly life; the humanity in the thirty years before the baptism, and the divinity in the three years after; a chronology based on Luke and John.

There was an opposition school of 'monarchianism', however, which defended the Ebionite point of view. This school preached Jesus as a man uniquely endowed with the Holy Spirit; so closely integrated with the Holy Spirit as to have become, to all intents and purposes, God. A christology of this kind was developed at Byzantium, and has come to be called 'adoptionism'. We have some light on the controversies on this subject, which divided the Roman church at the end of the century, but very little on its earlier stages in Asia, where the monarchian schools originated. We are informed, however, by Tertullian and by the author of the *Little Labyrinth*, who was probably Hippolytus, that Melito and Miltiades were the predecessors of Irenaeus in the enterprise of working out a satisfactory theology of the person of Christ. Asia continued to carry onward, in the realms of theology, the creative thinking of Paul, John and Ignatius.

CHAPTER 15

THE MARTYRS OF GAUL

COMMODUS CO-EMPEROR, A.D. 177

Before considering the martyrdoms of Lugdunum and Vienne in 178, we may glance at the imperial background to our story. In 177 Marcus Aurelius elevated his son Commodus, who was now fifteen or sixteen years of age, to the position of co-emperor, with the title of Augustus. It was a disaster. He should have chosen a mature, experienced, and seasoned administrator as his successor. He was only fifty-six, but his philosophy should have taught him that even emperors are mortal. A third Marcomannic war broke out; the two emperors hastened to take command of the troops; and Marcus died of the plague at Sirmium at the age of fifty-nine.

A new plea for the Christians was presented to the two emperors by Athenagoras, a philosopher from Athens. He called his little book a *Presbeia* or 'Embassy', a word which suggests that he went on a journey to present it. The same word, in its verbal form, is used of the 'embassy' of Irenaeus to the bishop of Rome in the following year. As it is unlikely that Athenagoras would pursue the emperors into the Balkans, we may assume that he waited on them in Rome early in 177. It is addressed to the emperors Marcus Aurelius Antoninus and Lucius Aurelius Commodus, conquerors of Armenia and Sarmatia, and best of all, philosophers.

Our first impression of this apology is that it continues faithfully along the lines which had been laid down by Justin. Our second is that it is written in a more moderate, learned and judicious manner. It is non-rhetorical. It aims apparently at giving a clear, dry, unemotional statement of the Christian case.

THE *PRESBEIA* OF ATHENAGORAS, A.D. 177

In his introduction Athenagoras deals briefly with the condemnation
of the Christians by the Roman courts for the mere confession of a
name, when no impartial inquiry has been made into the nature of
Christianity. He feels that if Christians have actually committed crimes
against the law, they should be charged with these crimes, and, if found
guilty, condemned on that account. He refers to a law which is adverse to the Christians, and this falls in with Melito's allusion to 'new
decrees'. The existence of such a law is demonstrated by a reference to
it in the trial of Apollonius five years later. It would appear that no
such law existed in the period of Trajan and Hadrian; and there is no
reference to it under Antoninus. It must have been passed in the prin-
cipate of Marcus. Perhaps the *Presbeia* of Athenagoras is an answer to
it; if so, it is singularly academic for its purpose.

He then enumerates the common scandals which are circulated
against the Christians. They are three in number, atheism, cannibal
banquets and incestuous intercourse. He does not take the latter very
seriously; his short book is mainly occupied with the charge of atheism.

He begins by outlining the Christian doctrine of God. It is a pure
monotheism, towards which the Greek poets and philosophers have
been feeling their way; it was fully revealed, however, in the Hebrew
prophets. Athenagoras expresses the hope that the learned emperors
have had time to read Moses and Isaiah and Jeremiah. His view of the
prophets suggests the theology of Montanism; they were like musical
instruments in the hand of the Lord, and he made use of them to express
his truth. He also agrees with Montanus in his stern disapproval of
second marriages.

His doctrine of God and of the Logos is carefully related to the
speculations of philosophy; it is also very cautious from the point of
view of Christian theology. The one God creates through his Word
and inspires men through his Spirit; but the unity of God must be
preserved even though these distinctions of being are real. He actually
anticipates the classical doctrine of the Trinity. Like Justin he mentions
the army of the angels in close connexion with the Trinity; and like
Justin he goes from this point to the Sermon on the Mount, and the
injunction to love one's enemies. He is far more succinct than Justin,
however; and this dry statement of the content of the faith, with the

17. COMMODUS

vescepline scificatesunt pertiretiam ad
laudecenses alia ad alexandrinos pauli no
mine pincte adhesem marcionis et alia plu
ra quae incatholicam eclesiam recepi non
potest felenim cummelle misceri non con
cruit epistolas ane iude et superscricio
iohannisduas incatholica habentur et sapi
entia ab amicissa lomonis in honore ipsius
scripta apocalapse etiam iohanis et pe
tri tantum recipimus quam quidam ex nos
tris legi inecclesia nolint pastorem uero
nuperrim e temporibus nostris inurbe   *Herma*
roma herma conscripsit sedente cathe   *Pastor*
tra urbis romae aeclesiae pio eps frater
eius et ideo legi eum quide oportet se pu
plicare uero inecclesia populo neque inter
profetas conpletu numero neque inter
apostolos infine temporum potest.
Arsinoi autem seu ualentini uel mitiadis
Nihil intotum recipemus. Qui etiam nouu
psalmorum librum marcioni conscripse
runt una cum basilide assianum cataphry
cum constitutorem

Abraham numerauit seruolus suos uer
naculos et cum trecentis deo ducto
uiris adeptus uictoriam liberauit nepote
pro uatur diuisio nisad fectus quando sic
amabat nepotem, ut pro do necuelli decla
nare periculum qui est numerauit. hoc
est elegit unde et illud nonsolum ad scien
tiam dei reperitur. Sede etiam ad gratiam iustorum

addition of the duty of divine love, makes up his compendious summary of Christianity. His doctrine of daemons is given at a later point, when he is dealing with the deities of Greece and Rome, with whom, of course, they are identified.

He devotes a great deal of space to the polytheistic religion of the empire, which he criticizes, with considerable ability and learning, as absurd and immoral. This counter-attack is more and more the burden of Christian propaganda, both for the philosopher and the martyr, in the lecture room and in the courts of justice. It was, no doubt, the strongest and most effective line of argument. Christianity was persecuted because it attacked the religion of the empire; it was strong and confident because it reposed on a rational faith in one God, who had created the world by his 'reason', and inspired men by his Spirit. As we read the acts of the Gallican martyrs, we shall observe how every one of these points appears in their flesh-and-blood reality.

He deals very briefly with the charges of cannibalism and incest. He asks again for an impartial inquiry, and he assures the emperors of the prayers of the Christians on their behalf.

THE LAWS AGAINST THE CHRISTIANS

There has been a certain amount of study recently on the subject of the persecutions, and it has been argued by some scholars that the last years of Marcus Aurelius, 177–80, were marked by a very severe official persecution which followed years of comparative peace. This theory has some truth in it, but it attempts to prove too much; and it calls for a rearrangement of the evidence which is not very easy to accept. The martyrdom of Polycarp, and the Epistle of Marcianus, in which it is described, are assigned to 177, and made part of the same empire-wide official persecution of Christians to which this theory attributes the Gallican martyrdoms of 177 or 178. The *Apology* of Melito in 176 foreshadows the approaching storm; new decrees have been issued. The *Apology* of Athenagoras in 177 refers to a definite law. In 178 the storm burst both in Smyrna and in Gaul.

Previous to this, the Christians were not seriously disturbed, it is claimed. There was a certain amount of what is called 'police action' from time to time, but that was all. This is a little too facile. The persecution of the early Christian church has been over-dramatized in

liturgy, literature and art; a process which began in the period of persecution itself, and has been consummated in the modern film; on the
other hand, certain scholars and historians, beginning with the great
Gibbon, have taken in hand to prove that the persecutions were
negligible affairs.

It is difficult to make generalizations from sporadic evidence scattered
over a century of history. It is clear that Christians might live for a
number of years without molestation; but it is equally clear that once
they admitted in a law-court that they were Christians, their life was
not safe. On the other hand, if they abandoned their Christianity they
were released. This state of affairs appears in Pliny about 111 and in
Justin Martyr about 150–65. These are examples of 'police action'.

But persecution of another type broke out suddenly from time to
time. There was uproar and disturbance and rioting and looting by
the mob. There was also the ordeal of the arena as we see it in the case
of Ignatius in 115, in whose letters it is perfectly plain that it was no
strange thing. He knows exactly what to expect. And the same picture
is given before his time by Clement, Hermas and Tacitus. Then there
is the horrible orgy which was so graphically described in the case of
Polycarp. We do not fully understand all the factors that contributed
to these horrible demonstrations; an aboriginal festival with a contest to
the death in devotion to some old myth? ancient emotional rituals by
which human scapegoats atoned for communal sin? or simply a savage
delight in blood and death and combat? Clement uses the word
'athlete' of the Christian martyr. Ignatius uses the word 'off-scourings',
by which he means the human scapegoat. So does Paul. All the world's
an arena to him.

Too little thought has been given to the psychology of the persecutors in this grisly question. Tertullian puts his finger on the point
with his usual psychological accuracy. When calamity suddenly falls,
or plague or famine or flood or war, the mob demands a victim, and will
not be refused. Nominally it may be offered to the darker or more
vindictive gods; but actually it is the fear and fury of the superstitious
multitude that demands it. 'Persuade the mob', is what Statius Quadratus, Rome's proconsul, said to Polycarp.

The Roman authorities knew that the mob must be provided with
these sacrifices from time to time, particularly at the prehistoric festivals
of nature, when law was powerless for the time, and wretched slaves

or outcasts dressed as kings or gods were fêted and mocked and murdered. The civic and imperial magistrates provided 'games' at these times, in which men fought with men, or beasts with beasts, or men and beasts together. Victims were provided in the name of the emperor; outlaws, or prisoners of war, or Christians. The proconsul was there to give the thing the emperor's sanction. He was unable sometimes to oppose the demands of the mob. In 129, the proconsul of Asia asked the Emperor Hadrian whether he should yield to 'popular clamour' in the case of Christians; it sounds as if he was referring to the scenes in the amphitheatre. The emperor did not like it.

Trajan had extended a measure of protection to Christians in the case of 'police action'; Hadrian and Antoninus had extended it in the case of 'popular clamour'; but there was no absolute protection. The convicted and self-confessed Christian must die.

Why the 'name' itself should be a capital charge is an enigma. Christians were hated and feared. They were the enemies of gods and men, and of the whole civilization by which men lived their insecure lives. They were foreign and mysterious and secretive and unpatriotic. They would not give a grain of incense to the emperor's image. They were rebels, traitors and atheists. What happened in the years 175–8 was that such protection as had been given by imperial rescripts was relaxed. The great philosopher-emperor may have issued new decrees, in which it may be that the Christians were not actually named.[1] It was decided, however, that they would be firmly dealt with. On the other hand, this view of the matter must not be made too much of; Aurelius was remembered in the Christian tradition as one of the good emperors who did not persecute.

THE GAMES AT LUGDUNUM, 1 AUGUST 178

The kind of tragedy which had occurred in Smyrna in 155 or 156 was repeated at Lugdunum, the modern Lyons, in the south of France, in 177 or 178. It was a great religious and imperial festival, a national one too, of old standing. The festival of the Three Gauls was celebrated annually on August 1 in honour of the divine emperor, whose month it was. It had been established in 12 B.C., but no doubt it was the

---

[1] See R. M. Grant, *The Sword and the Cross* (New York, 1955), p. 87.

continuation of prehistoric rituals. It was a time of licence and violence in which the crowd was king. Nothing could be refused them.

In this case the mob was allowed to indulge in a wild hunt for Christians in the two cities of Lyons and Vienne, which are situated close together on the River Rhône. It was accompanied with every kind of violence, and with the plundering of Christian houses. Those who were discovered were taken before the 'chiliarch', or tribune and examined by him in the presence of the crowd and of the city authorities; if they confessed, they were put in prison to await the arrival of the proconsul. No doubt numbers of non-Christians suffered in these preliminary riots, in which many old scores may have been worked off.

THE EXAMINATIONS; VETTIUS EPAGATHUS

The next stage was the examination before the proconsul, which also took place in public. A young Christian who was present in court, a neophyte apparently, named Vettius Epagathus, unable to bear the unfairness of the proceedings, stood up and made a defence on behalf of the brethren. It was not listened to, of course. He was simply asked if he was a Christian; and when he 'confessed' it, he was 'received into the portion of the martyrs', and nicknamed the 'paraclete of the Christians'.

The word paraclete means in general a champion or defender, and in particular, a legal counsel for the defence. It is the word used in St John's Gospel for the Holy Spirit which would come to the aid of the Christian in his hour of martyrdom (Mark xiii. 11). It is generally translated 'comforter', but more correctly 'advocate'. It was a key-word in the Phrygian prophecy, and this passage sheds light upon its use. A divine power, the Paraclete himself, had entered into Vettius Epagathus, and become in him the advocate of the Christians. For what was taking place was a battle between the powers of heaven and the powers of hell. The grace of God in the martyrs was conducting a counter-offensive (*antistrategei*) against the adversary of mankind; or, as we should say, in our less realistic way, the new religion was defying the old.

One notes, too, a certain system of tactics, and a certain vocabulary, which had been worked out on both sides. No doubt it was expected that the Spirit would move some Christian in court to stand up and make a protest, as Lucius had done in the case of Ptolemaeus. It would not be right for the case to go undefended; the man who was giving his life for his faith must have comfort and help. Equally clearly it was the proconsul's part to make no real answer to the protest, but to put the incriminating question, 'Are you a Christian too?'

The answer '*I am a Christian*' was sufficient in itself to incur the death penalty, but the martyrs were racked and tortured after their confession to get them to deny what they had confessed or to give further information, which was not necessary, except perhaps to incriminate others.

THE TORTURE; SANCTUS THE DEACON

In addition to this, the servants of the Christians were seized and examined by torture, a legitimate process under the Roman law, as the evidence of slaves without torture could not legally be accepted. These slaves soon confessed that their Christian masters and mistresses indulged in cannibal feasts and unholy sexual lusts. This news inflamed the 'Gentiles' even more, and gave them grounds for still further investigations.

Meanwhile the imprisoned martyrs had been separated into two 'churches'; for a number of the captives had denied their faith. It did them very little good, for they were still open to the charges of murder and incest, for which evidence had now been found. They remained in prison, but had no communion with the faithful.

The faithful were then examined by torture. Sanctus, a deacon from Vienne, answered every question with the two Latin words, '*Christianus sum*'. What is your name? they asked; Of what race? Of what city? Are you a slave? Or free? He made the same reply to each: '*Christianus sum*', 'I am a Christian'. This form of defensive tactics was suggested of course by the tactics of the court with its demand for this incriminating reply; what else mattered? Sanctus endured every kind of torture without giving way. They applied red-hot brass to the most sensitive parts of his body, 'and these were indeed burned, but he stood erect and unshaken, firm in his confession, receiving a dew of refreshment and power from the heavenly well of the water of life which proceeds from the side of Christ'. In much the same language Ignatius, the pattern martyr, had prayed that his persecuted Syrian church might be refreshed with the dew of God. This idea of a supernatural coolness and dew was drawn from the Septuagint version of Daniel's story of the three young Jews in the 'burning fiery furnace', a favourite theme in the literature and art of the period.

Sanctus came back to the prison with his whole body 'one entire wound and weal, contorted out of human shape'. After the wounds had stiffened, and blood-poisoning had set in, he went through the whole business again. He came back with his body straightened, and the use of his members restored, as if the second torture had been healing rather than torment.

BLANDINA AND BIBLIAS

About Blandina, they were dubious. She was a slave-girl of poor and weak appearance. Her mistress, who was also among the martyrs, doubted whether she would go through with it; other slaves had made false confessions. She was tortured from morning till evening, till her whole body was torn and opened; it was a wonder that she lived; but her rest and refreshment and 'analgesia' was to repeat the blessed words, '*I am a Christian*' and ,'Among us no evil thing is done.' Blandina, as events will show, was the greatest of them all, and may be regarded as the mother of French Christianity.

They began work then on those who had denied, in order to make them give evidence against those who had confessed. One of these, named Biblias, obviously another slave-girl, recovered herself during her torments by thinking on the eternal torment in hell, and spoke a word of truth, 'How would such as they eat children, when it is not lawful for them to eat even the blood of animals?' And she confessed herself a Christian, and was added to the portion of the martyrs. Inharmonious as it may be with the tenor of the narrative, we pause to note the interesting fact that this church in Gaul, with its Asian contacts, still kept the Jewish food-law which had been laid down in the Jerusalem council of A.D. 49. Evidence comes in from other quarters too that this was still the case.

THE INNER PRISON; POTHINUS THE BISHOP

The martyrs were then moved into a completely dark and unpleasant part of the prison, and underwent such torments as minor officials, especially when angry and full of the devil, are wont to inflict upon their prisoners. The majority of them died of suffocation. Those who had been badly tortured were the ones who endured it best. The new prisoners who had not endured any tortures were the ones who died soonest.

Among the newcomers was the bishop of Lyons, old Pothinus, now more than ninety years of age, who as a child could have heard St John. He had been hunted down and dragged before the tribunal, and had borne a good witness. When the proconsul had asked him who was the God of the Christians, he had replied, 'If thou art worthy, thou shalt know.' He was dragged away; he suffered many blows of fists and feet; they pelted him with missiles of all kinds; 'they all thought that it was a great sin and wickedness to omit any insult, for they all considered that they were avenging their gods'. He was hardly breathing when he was thrown into the prison, and he died in two days. We hear nothing about a bishop in Vienne; he had, perhaps, succeeded in concealing his place of retirement.

And now a great difference became apparent between those who had confessed, and those who had denied. Those who had denied were downcast and mournful; they were despised too by the 'Gentiles' as inglorious and unmanly. The martyrs, on the other hand, were refreshed by the joy of witness and the hope of the promises. Their joy was visible in their faces; they wore their chains like bridal ornaments; and they breathed forth the sweet savour of Christ, so that there were some who thought they had been anointed with actual ointment. In more modern words, they were in a high state of spiritual tension, and had achieved perfect morale.

It is a picture which we have not been privileged to see before, the long slow agonizing process of the 'perfecting' of the martyrs. Many martyrs, at this point, became unduly exalted, and assumed high spiritual authority; but these, we are told, were modest and humble. They would not allow themselves to be called martyrs. They were gentle to those who had denied, and, one by one, the majority of these were received into grace and 'learned how to confess'. 'They defended all and accused none; and as for those who administered the torments, they prayed for them, like Stephen the perfect martyr.' We are thus permitted to see how the accredited martyrs in their prison took on themselves the pastoral ministry of the presbyters, reconciling the lapsed, and restoring them to the 'virgin mother', as they called the true church; and we can see how this might lead, in due course, to a claim on the part of the martyr to presbyteral rank; a claim which Hippolytus himself appears to concede.

THE MONTANIST TOUCH; ALCIBIADES

The brotherhood in the prison, cut off from the world, acted as a church of God, having its own endowment of the Spirit. An interesting example was the case of Alcibiades, an ascetic who had been accustomed to lead a 'dismal life', never eating anything but bread and water. This perpetual fast he tried to keep up in prison; but his brother-martyrs advised him against it. Finally Attalus of Pergamum, after his first contest in the arena, had a revelation to the effect that Alcibiades was not doing well by refusing to use the creatures of God, and was leaving behind him an example which would prove a stumbling-block to others. Alcibiades was persuaded, and took part in the food of all, and gave thanks to God inasmuch as they were not unbishopped (*anepiskeptoi*) by the grace of God, the Holy Spirit being their counsellor; a sentence in which a reference to the sacrament of the eucharist seems to be enfolded.

It is not to be supposed, however, that there was no connexion at all with the outside world; or how could this inside story have been written? Somehow or other, Christian pertinacity and ingenuity found its way in with material and spiritual relief. It also found its way out with messages from the martyrs to the Christian world.

THE EPISTLE OF THE MARTYRS

It was the time, Eusebius says (and we are following Eusebius here, who has preserved the Acts of these martyrs at great length), it was the time when, for the first time, the disciples of Montanus, Alcibiades and Theodotus, in the region of Phrygia, were winning a wide reputation for prophecy. We have seen that the Montanist crisis had reached just this stage; and it may be that the martyr Alcibiades of Gaul is the Montanist Alcibiades of Phrygia; for there was a close connexion between the two countries, and the brethren in Gaul were at this very time making their second contribution to the controversy by issuing a pious and orthodox judgement on the subject, as Eusebius says. With this document, they sent various letters of martyrs who had been perfected among them, letters which they penned while actually in bonds, to the brethren in Asia and Phrygia, and also to Eleutherus who was then bishop of the Romans, sending an embassy (*presbeuontes*) on behalf of the peace of the churches. The man who carried these letters was Irenaeus, and Eusebius gives us the words in which he was recommended by the martyrs in their epistle.

Once more, and always, dear father Eleutherus, we pray that thou mayest be glad in God. This Epistle, we have charged our brother and companion Irenaeus to convey to thee, and we beseech thee to hold him in commendation as one who is zealous for the covenant of Christ; for if we knew that rank ever brought a man righteousness, we would have commended him first and foremost as a presbyter of the church, which office he holds.

(Eusebius, *E.H.* v, 4, 2.)

It would appear from the tone of this passage that the Epistle went out with some slight assumption of authority as a martyrs' communication to the church; yet it is friendly and even affectionate.

This is our first contemporary reference to Irenaeus. The letter which he carried cannot have been unfavourable to Montanism, and it was clearly anticipated that it would have a sympathetic reception in Rome. The phrase 'brother and companion' is taken from the opening verses of the Revelation, where it describes the apostolic and prophetic author who was enduring affliction for the word of God. The phrase 'zealous for the covenant' seems to be borrowed from the Maccabaean literature, which provided the church with model stories of persecution and martyrdom. It is curious that the day devoted to the Maccabaean martyrs in the old Roman calendar was August 1, a commemoration which was afterwards changed to St Peter's chains; the Gallican persecution took place at a pagan festival, the high day of which was August 1.

MATURUS AND SANCTUS

Every one of these men and women was destined to die. They came out of that dark hole into the broad daylight of the amphitheatre, where thousands of men and women and children were waiting to see them. The leaders among them were Sanctus, the deacon from Vienne; Maturus a neophyte, 'newly-illuminated'; and Attalus of Pergamum, whose courage and steadiness had been their support throughout. There was also the marvellous Blandina, who may be said in modern terms to have stolen the show.

Maturus and Sanctus were put through the old series of torments for a third time. Then they passed along a line of men who lashed them with whips as they went by, this being the customary form of introduction into the arena. Then they met the wild beasts, and felt their claws and teeth. Meanwhile the crowd, mad with excitement, was howling out its demands. Then came the iron chair which was made red-hot to receive their bodies. At last their throats were cut.

Blandina had been tied crosswise to an upright stake, as food for the wild beasts, and she inspired the martyrs with her earnest prayer; for they kept up their faith by looking at her, and seemed to see in her the image of the one who had been crucified for them. None of the beasts would touch her, and she was taken down and reserved for another day.

Attalus too was remanded. He was led round the arena with a title carried in front of him in the Latin language: 'This is Attalus the *Christian*'; but the proconsul was informed that he was a Roman citizen, and he decided to refer his case to the emperor. It was during this further delay that the reconciliation of those who had formerly denied took place. There were, therefore, more martyrs than ever, and the cause of Christ was correspondingly glorified.

ATTALUS AND HIS COMPANIONS

When the instructions of Marcus Aurelius arrived, they were to the effect that those who confessed were to be executed, and those who denied were to be released, thus sanctioning the mode of inquiry which Athenagoras had denounced as illogical. Those who were Roman citizens were to be beheaded; the others were to be given to the beasts. In spite of this grim news, the whole augmented body of martyrs stood firm.

While the further examination was going on, there was a physician from Phrygia named Alexander who stood by and encouraged the lapsed Christians who were now making their confession before the proconsul. He had lived in Gaul many years, and everybody knew his love for God and his boldness in the word; for he was not without his share of the apostolic *charisma*. He stood there encouraging the Christians as they made their confessions of faith; indeed, they may well have been his patients and pupils. As he did this, nodding to each one in turn, the crowd began to shout against him, and the proconsul asked him who he might be. '*I am a Christian*', he replied. Once more the solemn procedure of a Roman law court had been interfered with by the advocate of Christ.

On the next day the last martyrdoms took place. Attalus and Alexander went through the whole series of tortures before they were put to death. Alexander neither groaned nor complained, but conversed with God in his heart. Attalus, as he sat in the iron chair, and the air was filled with the stench of burning flesh, made the following observation in the Latin tongue: 'Look,' he said, 'what you are doing now is devouring men; but we neither eat men, nor do any other evil.'

Blandina was brought in with Ponticus, a boy of fifteen years of age, who had been brought every day to watch the punishment of the other Christians. He refused to save himself by sacrificing to idols. The crowd was wild with anger, and they were put through the whole round of tortures, omitting nothing, Blandina encouraging Ponticus until he died. She was then left alone 'like a noble mother' who had encouraged her children and sent them before her as conquerors to the king; and 'after the whips, after the wild beasts, after the iron chair, she was rolled in a net and thrown to a bull; and when she had been tossed by the bull, without having any sensation of what was happening to her, through the hope and understanding of those things in which she believed, and her converse with Christ, she too was killed; and even the Gentiles confessed that never a woman among them had suffered so many and such grievous things'.

The simile of the mother is obviously derived from the story of the mother who gave her seven sons as martyrs in the fourth book of the Maccabees.

THE SIGNIFICANCE OF THEIR WITNESS

So went Pothinus the aged bishop, Sanctus the heroic deacon, Maturus the neophyte, Attalus the strong and outstanding citizen, Vettius Epagathus the young aristocrat, Alexander the beloved physician, Blandina the poor little servant-girl, Ponticus the young and brave, Alcibiades the ascetic, and Biblias who had denied and come back to the faith, 'awaking as it were out of sleep'; and many more. A whole community is created before our eyes as we read this painful record. We see an ancient polytheistic civilization, at a very low level of culture, subject to daemonic recurrences of pure savagery; its Roman piety and Greek philosophy was not strong enough or willing enough to cast out the daemon. It would take men and women with the spirit of martyrdom in them to do that.

Against this background we see a new kind of people, introducing a strange and foreign worship. They are called *Christians*. They live a good life, though they are accused of unmentionable crimes; they have the ordinary social virtues, as we recognize them today; but they have also a frightful courage which their enemies call obstinacy. This courage, they said, was due to a divine Spirit in them which was more than equal to the devilish spirit which animated their persecutors.

Their strange apocalyptic dreams of a better world to come were practical and true in a sense which they could not understand, but only hold on to by faith. They were before their times, as the saying is. They belonged to a new age, and a new world, and a new social order, which had not yet appeared but was to come. It would be established on this earth, as least to some degree, wherever the gospel of Christ infused men's minds; it was already established among them in their Christian fellowship by anticipation. If the dreams which they cherished sometimes seem to us to be too brightly coloured or too simply conceived, we must forgive them for that; the point is that they had a dream at all. Their faith was the faith of children, the wise Clement of Alexandria said. How far the intellectuals and mystics were ahead of them, the reader must judge.

The argument which Athenagoras had presented to Marcus Aurelius was the clearest intellectual summary so far of the ideology which created the tragic scenes in the arena. The monotheism which expressed itself in terms of reason and inculcated the gospel of love was pitting itself against the polytheism which expressed itself in terms of passion, and knew no final argument except force. The best emblem of Christianity in our whole century is the naked figure of the slave-girl Blandina, advancing without fear against the whips, the red-hot irons, and the wild beasts which were the weapons of those pagan gods in whom the philosophic Marcus Aurelius put his trust.

THE LOSS OF THE RELICS

There came then the usual strange contest over the bodies of the martyrs. The 'Gentiles' were in a condition of hysterical triumph. Those who died in the prison had been thrown to the dogs; but the fragments in the arena, the heads and trunks and limbs, charred or shredded as they were, they guarded night and day; 'and among us there was great lamentation because we could not cover the bodies with earth; night was no help to us, nor could money persuade or entreaty move'. For six days this suspense continued, and then the remains were burned by the Gentiles and the ashes swept into the River Rhône, which was in flood at the time; 'and this they did as if they could overcome God and deprive them of the rebirth: as they said themselves, "lest they should attain the hope of the resurrection in which they trust".'

This church, so sadly torn, needed a wise and fatherly bishop, a man with a missionary and pastoral spirit, firm, sympathetic and peaceful. They were fortunate in obtaining Irenaeus. And so the church of France was born; and for many centuries Lyons was the see of its primate.

The idea that Irenaeus himself composed the Acts of the Martyrs is only a modern guess. It may be so. Their memory was long preserved, and further names, with additional details, are to be found in later martyrologies. The day assigned to them in the 'Hierony mian' martyrology, strange to say, is 2 June.

CHAPTER 16

THEOLOGY IN ROME

ELEUTHERUS AND HEGESIPPUS

Eleutherus, who became bishop of Rome about 174, had grown to manhood under the episcopate of Pius, the brother of the prophet Hermas. In his youth he had listened to elders who survived from the period of Clement. He had been deacon, or chief of staff, to Anicetus, who became bishop about 154 or 155. He occupied a position of dignity and influence, therefore, in the Roman ecclesia for a considerable period, for he remained bishop till about 189. It was the memory of this long ministry in the councils of the church, perhaps, which led Tertullian to make the blunder of placing the first preaching of Marcion and Valentinus 'in the episcopate of the blessed Eleutherus'. Little as we know about the man, we must conclude that he exercised a steady and continuous influence on the development of the Roman church during this period of about thirty-five years.

It was only eighty years since the persecution of Domitian and the crisis at Corinth, and the writing of Clement's Epistle. Eleutherus and his elders, and their friends of senior age, must have been well informed about the events of that time. The grandfathers of the present generation had lived in those days, and their graves were known in the cemeteries which were established at that time. Every family would have a tale to tell. They could remember the arrival of the great heresiarchs in the thirties, whose successors were now carrying on their schools. The visit of Polycarp to Rome in the fifties was fresh in their memories. There was no haziness at that time in anybody's mind about the course of events.

Not long after the visit of Polycarp the Jewish-Christian scholar

Hegesippus had arrived, and continued in residence at Rome. He had brought with him similar information about the old mother-church in Jerusalem, as Irenaeus called it. He knew something about James the brother of the Lord, just as the Romans knew something about the apostles Peter and Paul; but he had an advantage over them there; he had a narrative tradition about his holy life, and his arguments with the scribes and Pharisees in the Temple, and about his martyrdom. So far as we know, the Romans had no narrative about the martyrdoms of Peter and Paul. All they knew were the bare facts and the places where they were buried. There were scraps of tradition, but there is no trace of any narrative such as might have been recited when they were remembered before God.

Hegesippus had explored the Roman tradition. He had compiled a succession-list of the bishops. He knew what there was to be known. He was encouraged now to write down what he knew. He did so in the episcopate of Eleutherus, and during its earlier years, since Irenaeus used his writings during its later years. The *Hupomnemata* of Hegesippus may safely be placed between 175 and 180.

THE *NOTE-BOOKS* OF HEGESIPPUS

The word *Hupomnemata* is often translated *annotations*. It is a word which seems to mean a note or minute or record of a transaction or spoken discourse. It is used, for instance, of the summaries of their master's philosophy which were made by the pupils of Valentine. It suggests a rather informal sketch of some great subject or course of teaching. The word 'note-books' might be a sufficient translation. The *Note-books* of Hegesippus were written in the simplest style, Eusebius says, and 'noted down' (or placed on record) the unerring tradition of the apostolic kerugma. There were five volumes of them, and their loss is much to be regretted.

Hegesippus was a pioneer in the application of the argument from history to the Christian controversies. In the hundred-and-forties or -fifties, before he had reached Rome, he had grasped the importance of the general principle that the apostolic tradition as it existed in the great churches was older than the various heretical schools which were dated by using the names of their founders to distinguish them. In order to establish this argument, however, he considered it necessary to verify the origins of these churches; and that was one motive for his travels. He seems to have been the originator of this type of inquiry, but we do not know to what extent he developed the arguments that could be drawn from it. Irenaeus was deeply indebted to him, and so perhaps was Tertullian.

The word *hairesis* is better translated as 'sect' than 'heresy', and this is the primary meaning which Hegesippus read into it. Harnack referred to the great heresiarchs as the first Christian theologians; but they were more than that; they were the founders of sects which were called after their names. Hegesippus became an authority on sects. He knew of sects which had existed in Palestine long before the Roman sects were heard of. Unfortunately they are little more than names to us, and apparently they were little more than names to the Romans. He maintained that they were the ancestors of the Gentile schools which had invaded the Roman church; and of 'all the false Messiahs and false prophets and false apostles who had divided the unity of the church with destructive words'; but nobody in Rome seems to have been interested. There is no sign of such a theory in Irenaeus and Hippolytus.

Hippolytus, in his enormous *Refutation*, gives a much inferior list of Jewish sects, and maintains that the heresies of the Gentile church were all derived from forms of Greek philosophy. Of course they had taken much Greek philosophy and pagan mythology on board; but there was something worth attending to in the theory of Hegesippus, supported as it was by his unique historical knowledge. Eusebius acquaints us with the outline of this theory; Epiphanius realized its value though he did not fully understand it; both were men with Palestinian experience. It would be of great assistance to the modern historian if a copy of the *Note-books* should turn up in some obscure monastery; but even as it is we should not be able to reconstruct our history so well without the aid which we derive from the fragments of it which have come down to us.

THE SCHOOLS OF ROME

Under Pius and Anicetus, the leading Christian school had been that of Justin; but it is hard to say who had succeeded to Justin's position after the defection of Tatian. Tatian had left behind him a pupil named Rhodo, who was an Asian like Justin. He is one of a number of theo-

19. SEPTIMIUS SEVERÚS AND JULIA DOMNA

20. 'ALEXAMENOS ADORES HIS GOD'

logians who are little more than names to us, and their dates cannot be clearly ascertained. We may assign them, however, to the episcopate of Eleutherus, and must do the best we can with them.

A great change had passed over the Christian church during the fourth Christian generation (150–90). Christian teachers of all sorts became proficient in the intellectual methods of the Greek schools. During the reign of Marcus Aurelius, the great medical scientist Galen had resided in Rome, and he was there intermittently throughout his long life, which extended into the third century. He was an exponent of the logical methods of Aristotle. He admired the Christian blend of martyrdom and asceticism; and he refers to the dogmatic statements which were made in the schools of Moses and of Christ, where men heard laws enunciated without adequate logical proofs. His words are worth quoting.

Most men cannot follow a chain of demonstrative reasoning, and therefore need to be taught in parables. So in our time we see those who are called Christians gathering their faith from parables; and yet sometimes they do just the same things as the genuine philosophers; for we can all see with our own eyes that they despise death, and further that they are led by modesty to shrink from carnal lusts; for there are among them men and women who have maintained unbroken chastity throughout their lives. There are even those who, by their self-discipline and self-control, and by their ardent desire for virtue, have advanced so far that they are not in any way inferior to the genuine philosophers.

(Galen, *Commentary on one of the Platonic Dialogues*.[1])

It would appear, too, that Galen saw the limitations of the purely logical and academic schools of philosophy. He regarded some of the men whose minds had been trained in this way as harder to convince of new truth than the disciples of Moses or of Christ. He must have had some contact with Christian intellectuals, therefore, and his mind was large enough to see that they were not to be despised. He even convinced them of new truths.

There is evidence in Roman writings, attributed by modern scholars to Hippolytus, that his influence was not unfelt in the church. The mysterious *Little Labyrinth* tells us that the 'adoptionist' school in Rome, in the third century, was familiar with the works of Aristotle and

[1] From C. Bigg, *The Origins of Christianity* (Oxford, 1909), pp. 245–6.

Euclid and Galen; and we now begin to find Christian discussions that proceed by way of logical and literary analysis. We find an emphasis upon the *monarchia* or sole sovereignty of God, a word which has an Aristotelian sound; and while the sovereignty of God is unquestionably a Jewish doctrine, the more stringent discussions of this period were based on the principle of the one *arche*, the single beginning or first cause of the universe. These arguments told rather heavily against the Logos theology of Justin, and its second centre of personality in the godhead, and his pupil Irenaeus is careful to avoid such incautious terminology. It told even more heavily against the theologies of Marcion and Valentine.

THE MARCIONITE SCHOOLS

Marcion had left several successors, who seem by now to have been obliged to debate the philosophic basis of their faith. Marcion himself had never had a very exact theology, and had spoken freely of two gods, in addition to a formless substance called matter, out of which the universe had been fashioned. The latter was a legacy from the old Babylonian mythology which had survived as a philosophical concept in the Greek schools. The question which the monarchian philosopher now put was how there could be more than one *arche* or first cause in the universe. A number of Marcionite theologians were prepared to answer this question. Potitus and Basilicus affirmed that there were three; Syneros believed in two; Apelles in one. These second-generation Marcionite names are no more than names to us, with the exception of Apelles. Equally indistinct are the names of Lucan or Lucian, the head of the Marcionite school in Rome, and Prepon, the head of the Marcionite school in Assyria, who disputed with Bar Daisan.

APELLES

Apelles was an old war-horse of the Roman school, who became its leading figure in his old age. Like Melito and Proclus, he was held up as a model of the celibate life and the ascetic virtues; but Tertullian says that he had an affair with a girl, which necessitated his leaving Rome for a time; a similar tale was told about Marcion himself, though Tertullian does not seem to have heard of that one. In any case Apelles went off to Alexandria in the days of Marcion himself to spread the Marcionite gospel in Alexandria. In Alexandria he fell under the influence of the Valentinian school, and modified the uncompromising views of his master. He no longer talked about two gods; he demoted the God of the Jews to the rank of a 'fiery angel', an expression which he may have borrowed from Basilides. He returned therefore rather more of an intellectual. He brought back with him a virgin named Philumene ('sweetheart') who saw visions; and he published them under the title of *phaneroseis* or 'manifestations'. He had taken a leaf out of the book of Montanus; for the visions of his virgins had also been committed to paper. Naturally eyebrows were raised and insinuations made among the orthodox; but it is clear that the reputation of Apelles stood high, and perhaps these slurs on his character were unworthy.

What stung the orthodox was the vigour and ability of his attacks upon the Hebrew Bible and the God of the Jews; for the whole strength of the orthodox position depended on this foundation. Marcion had attacked the Hebrew revelation savagely in his book called the *Antitheseis* or *Contradictions*, which seems to have set going a whole stream of books with similar laconic titles. Tatian had pored over the Old Testament and produced his book of *Problems*, about which we know nothing except for his original and perverse explanation of the second verse of Genesis, in which he makes the Creator pray to some higher power for light: 'May there be light', he implores weakly, an interpretation which may have been traditional in the Syrian school. His pupil Rhodo meditated on the task of producing a sequel which he intended to call *Solutions*; but there is no evidence that he ever did so.

Apelles made his contribution to the argument under the ominous Aristotelian name of *Syllogisms* or *Logical Proofs*; and the extracts which have survived show that it was the work of an acute and merciless mind. He attacked the story of Adam and Eve, which was deeply embedded in the current catholic theology. He analysed it and tore it to pieces. The god who appeared in its pages was no god at all. He lacked the power, and the knowledge, and even the will to arrange things better. Did he not *know* that Adam would break his commandments? Did he lack the *power* to prevent him doing so? and so forth. Like his master, he had a matter-of-fact mentality to which poetry and mysticism meant nothing whatever. It is to be feared that his book was very successful. It looks as if Theophilus and Irenaeus were both answering him, though neither mentions his name.

Eusebius says that Apelles made blasphemous attacks upon the Law of Moses, and accomplished 'its refutation and overthrow as he thought'; an interesting phrase; for Irenaeus chose it as the title of the great book in which he made his counter-attack: *The Refutation and Overthrow of the Gnosis which is Falsely so-called*; it is the book which is often quoted as *Against Heresies*, and we have made considerable use of it. The voice of Apelles was not so easily silenced, however; he was still read in the fourth century, and was quoted by Epiphanius in the east and Ambrose in the west. It would appear, therefore, that the book was translated into Latin.

The principal opponent of Apelles and his neo-Marcionite school was Tatian's pupil Rhodo, of whom less is known. He was a young man who had been well trained in the traditions of the church and the allegorical interpretations of the Old Testament histories and prophecies. He tried to drive the old gentleman into a corner with logical proofs; but the old gentleman declined to take up the position. The scene comes out very clearly in the extracts from Rhodo given by Eusebius. Rhodo was certain that he had refuted Apelles in a number of errors; but Apelles evaded him. The question of the unity of God was the most obscure of all problems, he said. It was not really necessary to examine the matter too closely. Let both of them stick to their own form of faith. All those who set their hope upon the crucified would be saved if they were found occupied in good works.

Rhodo pressed him further. Apelles had affirmed his faith in the unity of the first principle; but how could he be sure of this without proof?—without the Hebrew Bible and the testimony arguments, is what Rhodo meant. Apelles admitted that he did not know how to prove it; all he knew was that he was *moved* to believe it; and Rhodo laughed at him for setting up as a teacher without having any proofs to support his teaching. It sounds a little like the voice of Galen; but Apelles might have appealed to Aristotle (and to Basilides) for some support for the idea that there was a faculty in the soul by which God was known, which was higher than the methods of logical analysis.

It strikes us that Rhodo was a bright young man with all the 'solutions', whereas Apelles was a man of character, bearing witness to the greatest thing in the tradition of his master Marcion; the pure evangelical faith which witnesses to itself and is superior to all other modes of knowledge. Marcion and Apelles had no needs of proofs from the

Hebrew prophets or any other quarter. Their gospel was unique, and authenticated itself.

O wealth of riches [said Marcion]—folly, power, ecstasy—seeing that there can be nothing to say about it, or to imagine about it, or to compare it with.
(Marcion, *Antitheseis*, quoted in Epiphanius, *Panarion*, 42.)

THE VALENTINIANS: PTOLEMAEUS

The Marcionites abolished the Hebrew Bible altogether; Marcion found it cruel and immoral; Apelles proved that it was false and inconsistent; but the Valentinians had a more refined and discriminating approach. It was their *métier* to philosophize and allegorize and find spiritual meanings everywhere. Their principal leader now was Ptolemaeus, who systematized the fantasies of the master, and gave to those airy nothings a local habitation and a name. He produced those *Note-books* or *Hupomnemata* which Irenaeus laboriously summarized and refuted and overthrew.

Ptolemaeus touched on the Old Testament problem in his *Epistle to Flora* (or can this name be a manuscript error for Florinus?) which is preserved in the pages of Epiphanius. He approached the matter as a literary critic, with some light from the teaching of Jesus as recorded in the Gospels. It was indicated, he thought, that there were three levels of authority in the old Bible; some of it was given by a God, some by Moses, and some by the elders of the Jews. He then divided the material which came from the God into three classes. First there was pure legislation, free from evil, which the Saviour came to fulfill; this included the Ten Commandments and similar passages. Then there was the secondary material which was mixed with evil, involving ideas of retribution and vengeance, which the Saviour came to remove; but he admits that these precepts possessed a sort of justice, and therefore they came from a God. The third class consisted of the Levitical ritual, and this had a symbolic value. He concludes that the God who gave the Law cannot have been the perfect God; he was the Demiurge, who occupies a middle position between good and evil; intermediate, that is, between the high God and the devil.

The refined polytheism of this Epistle would be repugnant, of course, to Christians of the catholic tradition; but the attempt to classify the different precepts of the Law is very like similar treatments in such authors as 'Barnabas' or Justin or Irenaeus.

HERACLEON

The Valentinian gnosis, which had coloured the thinking of Tatian and Apelles, had at least four exponents in Rome: Ptolemaeus, Secundus, Heracleon and Florinus; and it is interesting to remark that two of them have Latin names, which suggests that this school appealed to the Roman mind. Valentine himself, though he is said to have been a native of Egypt, had a Latin name. We have evidence in Marcionite and Valentinian circles of an interchange of persons and ideas between Egypt and Rome; though any such interchange on the catholic level is entirely a matter of conjecture, unless we are prepared to take into account the reception in Egypt of the Gospel of Mark, and the *Pastor* of Hermas, at an earlier date.

The gnostic schools in Egypt had been the first to take an interest in the Gospels as literature, to write commentaries on them, and to deduce theology from them. The *Exegetica* of Basilides, which was written in the previous generation, was the first Gospel commentary of which any trace remains, unless the *Interpretations* of Papias may be regarded in this light. Neither appears to have been a formal commentary page by page; but such a commentary was now produced by Heracleon. It was on St John's Gospel, which it interpreted in accordance with the Valentinian theology and with the help of a good deal of allegorization. Origen quoted a number of passages from it in his own commentary on John, and these give us some idea of its tone. Heracleon does not shed any light on the Gospel, but there are two interesting historical points about him. He is the first writer to quote the apocryphal *Preaching of Peter* by name, citing the following extract,

We must not worship in Greek fashion, accepting the works of matter, and adoring wood and stone; nor worship the deity in Jewish fashion, since they, who think they are the only ones to know him, do not know him, and worship angels and the month and the moon.

(Heracleon on John, from Origen, *Comm. in Joann.* XIII, 17.)

And he has a passage on martyrdom in which he remarks that there was a kind of confession which did not imply the death of the confessor as a martyr, mentioning Matthew, Philip, Thomas, and Levi as examples. He had a tradition, therefore, that these apostles had died a natural death; it is odd that he distinguishes Matthew from Levi (like Tatian) and that he does not mention John; but very likely he was discussing the case of John, and brought in the other names as illustrations.

FLORINUS

Eusebius in his History mentions at this point the Epistles of Irenaeus to Blastus and Florinus. Florinus was a presbyter of the Roman church when Irenaeus addressed him. He had been a pupil of Polycarp, together with Irenaeus, a generation earlier, when Florinus was in the service of the emperor, and visiting Smyrna.

For I saw you when I was still a boy in Lower Asia, with Polycarp, and you were faring sumptuously at the royal court, and doing your best to win his favour. (Eusebius, *E.H.* v, 20, 5.)

We have assigned this intercourse of Irenaeus and Florinus with Poly-carp to the year 129, which would make Irenaeus about sixty-five at this time. The interest lies in the fact that the subject of the conversation of Polycarp was his intercourse with John and others who had seen the Lord; and we have supplied the rest of the extract in an earlier chapter.[1] It is a most significant fact that a man of this experience should have been converted to Valentinianism, and is a warning to us not to under-estimate the influence of this school. Irenaeus wrote two Epistles to him, both of which are lost, except for the Eusebian extracts; one was called *Concerning the Monarchia*, that fashionable subject; the other *Concerning the Ogdoad*, which was the highest circle of deity in the Valentinian system.

Some scholars place the Epistle of Irenaeus to Florinus at a later date, on the strength of another letter which Irenaeus wrote to Bishop Victor in the hundred-and-nineties; we possess a sentence or two of this letter in a Syriac translation, and it reads as if Florinus were now deposed from his position as presbyter; indeed, he is spoken of as if he were dead; it is his books that are doing harm.

The Epistle we are now considering was addressed at an earlier stage to Florinus himself. 'These dogmas, my dear Florinus, not even the heretics outside the church have had the audacity to utter; these

---

[1] Vol. II, chapter 2.

dogmas, the elders who were before us, those who accompanied with the apostles, never delivered to us.' He has hopes that Florinus will not depart from the church as Tatian had done.

PHRYGIANISM IN ROME

When Irenaeus arrived in Rome during the latter months of 178, he found these schools debating against one another; but it is possible that the rank and file of the church was not greatly interested. He was the bearer of letters from the Gallican martyrs to the brethren in Asia and Phrygia, and also to 'father Eleutherus', the Roman bishop, pleading for a peaceful solution of the conflict over Montanism, which was now spreading throughout the church. The first period of Montanism was over. Montanus and his prophetesses were dead, and there were sinister rumours abroad about the manner of their deaths. It was reported that the insane spirit with which they were inspired, had driven Montanus and Maximilla to hang themselves; Themiso had been lifted up into the air by the spirit that possessed him, and had been dashed to the ground and killed. The Anonymous, who reports these rumours, did not really believe them himself; but the prophets were gone, and their memories were darkened by scandalous stories of this sort.

Their movement went on, however. It entered into a new phase. An inspired literature had accumulated. The oracles of the original group had been written down. Themiso had issued his catholic Epistle. It was natural for the Phrygians to think that these revelations of the Paraclete would be accepted in the churches as other prophetic books had been; the Revelation of John, the *Revelation of Peter*, and the *Pastor* of Hermas; and others perhaps in various places. It would follow, too, that the church would adopt the prophet's legislation on fasting, and marriage, and church discipline, and other points. It does not appear that more revelations were forthcoming, though the prophetic gifts did not cease.

Oriental ideas flooded Rome at different levels. The Lord's people were not all philosophers. There were technicians and merchants and civil servants; there were also great numbers of slaves; and in due course a slave might become a free man and rise to a position of wealth and influence or high position in the church, like Pius and his brother Hermas, who had been the leader of a previous prophetic revival.

Another instance was Callistus, who was a boy or youth at this time, and would in due course become bishop, as Pius had done. Many of the slaves in Rome were of Phrygian origin, and this large community had its own ancient sanctuary on the Palatine Hill, where the Great Mother was worshipped and the death of Attis celebrated every spring with wild frenzy and excitement. It could not be long before the Christian form of Phrygian revivalism was communicated to the Phrygian groups in the city. Perhaps the title 'Phrygian heresy' or 'Phrygian sect' (or Phrygianism as we would say) was given it to discredit it as a slave religion. In any case it arrived sooner or later, and had grown to be a powerful force by the end of the century, when it succeeded in converting the great Tertullian himself. One of its leaders at that time was the venerable Proculus or Proclus, who may have been at the beginning of his career when Irenaeus arrived. He was a healer, ascetic, and theologian of the same school as Melito and Irenaeus himself.

There were features in the old Roman Christianity which were not discordant with a moderate Montanism. Rome had always had her prophets and inspired men; she read Hermas and the apocalypses; she had her virgins and ascetics from the time of Clement; but as we pass on into the third century, we find many ideas which we noted for the first time in Asia and Phrygia. Among these are the birthdays of the martyrs, the added emphasis on virginity, the composition of Acts of Martyrs, the extended series of fasts and calendar days, the holding of synods of bishops, and the closer definition of the canon of the New Testament. Some of these developments may be due to the influence of Montanism or the impact of controversy with Montanism.

It would appear, too, that the intensification of persecution would be favourable to the extension of Phrygianism, which idolized the martyr. In fact it assisted any theologian to gain a hearing if he had spent time in gaol.

PRAXEAS THE MARTYR

Another visitant from Asia Minor was the high-powered 'martyr', Praxeas, with his dramatic monarchian gospel. It was not at all the logical monarchianism of the schools; it was the popular monarchianism of the evangelistic preaching. It taught quite simply that God had come into the world and died for men. Language like this had always been used in the course of Christian evangelism. Creed-forms had grown up which embodied this form of the faith. It is clear, however, that it was not the way in which Hermas had visualized it; or Justin Martyr for that matter.

In the *Acts of Paul* the gospel which Paul preached is summed up in the words: 'Fear one only God and live chastely.' When Thecla was delivered from the wild beasts in Pisidian Antioch, there was a cry of thanksgiving from the women in the theatre; they gave praise to God as with one mouth saying, 'One is the God who hath preserved Thecla.' In the *Acts of Peter* they cry out, 'One is the God of Peter.' 'One God, One Lord' was the watchword of this paradoxical form of the Christian faith; paradoxical because it preached Jesus Christ as the Son of God, and at the same time as the one God himself; faith did not explain how; it looked no further. It was a martyr faith, anticipated in the words of Ignatius: 'Suffer me to imitate the Passion of my God.'

It was well received in Rome. It must have inspired the younger generation; Zephyrinus for instance, who became bishop about 200, and Callistus, who became his deacon. But when did Praxeas come to Rome? and under which bishop? The answer to these questions is uncertain, and depends almost entirely on the evidence of Tertullian.

PRAXEAS AND THE ROMAN BISHOP

We have mentioned the advent of Praxeas at this early point because Tertullian regarded him as the pioneer or forerunner of the high monarchian doctrine which was favoured in Rome when he wrote his book against Praxeas about 205, not long after Zephyrinus became bishop.

He was the first man [Tertullian says] to import from Asia this kind of perversity, a man who was restless in other ways too, and inflated besides with the pride of 'martyrdom', though he had suffered nothing whatever but the boredom of a brief imprisonment. (Tertullian, *Adversus Praxean*, I.)

By the time of Zephyrinus a regular school of the monarchian theology had been established in Rome, and its master Cleomenes had already succeeded its founder Epigonus. A number of years, surely, have to be interposed between this state of affairs and the arrival of the first importer of the doctrine. He must have appeared well before the episcopate of Zephyrinus, either under Eleutherus or Victor.

Hippolytus does not help us much. In the Latin adaptation of his

Syntagma (which he wrote about the same time that Tertullian was writing his book *Against Praxeas*) he says that Praxeas introduced the doctrine which 'Victorinus' was careful to strengthen; but here some copyist has confused the text. Who is Victorinus? Victor or Zephyrinus? Whichever it was, we knew already that these bishops favoured the high monarchian view.

Praxeas was a great success in Rome. His monarchian gospel pleased the multitude. He got the ear of the bishop. He passed on to Africa and taught his gospel there. But he met with some redoubtable opponent and disputed with him.[1] He recanted his errors and after that he disappeared from view. It was later still that Tertullian penned his sarcastic refutation of his theology, with the object of implicating the bishop of Rome, who favoured it.

THE ROMAN BISHOP AND THE NEW PROPHECY

According to Tertullian, Praxeas did two jobs for the devil while he was in Rome; he 'crucified the Father and he drove away the Paraclete'; that is to say he brought in the monarchian gospel that the Almighty Father died on Calvary, and he put to flight the holy dove of the New Prophecy. The bishop of Rome had actually recognized the New Prophecy when Praxeas arrived, and had sent off 'letters of peace'. Praxeas pointed out the unwisdom of what he had done; he referred to the policy of his predecessors who had not been so favourable; he made damaging statements about the prophets; he turned the tide of battle, and the bishop rescinded his action. It is an important moment in Roman church history, and it does not seem possible to place it so late as the episcopate of Zephyrinus; that prelate cannot have been ignorant of the true character of the New Prophecy.

This is what Tertullian says,

After the bishop of Rome had acknowledged the prophecies of Montanus and Prisca and Maximilla, and by this recognition had brought peace to the churches of Asia and Phrygia, Praxeas compelled him to call back the letters of peace which he had already sent, and to recede from his purpose of recognizing the prophetic gifts; he did this by making false statements about the said prophets, and by defending the authority of the bishop's predecessors.

(Tertullian, *Adversus Praxean*, I.)

[1] Was it Tertullian himself? P. C. de Labriolle thinks so.

The influence of the New Prophecy at Rome was at its highest point then, though the facts about it were not perfectly known apparently. The critical attitude of the previous bishops was in danger of being forgotten. Full recognition was being extended to the prophets, their gifts, and their oracles, which probably meant the reception of their scriptures for reading in church. Then there was a change. The great monarchian preacher became the idol of the church. The cause of the New Prophecy was lost. The Paraclete was put to flight.

The arrival of Irenaeus in Rome in 178 has to be placed before this great decision, though not necessarily very long before it. The matter was under discussion when he arrived, and he came as an ambassador for the peace of the churches, first in Rome, but afterwards in Asia and Phrygia. The affectionate tone of the Gallican appeal to Eleutherus suggests that he was regarded by the martyrs as potentially favourable to their cause; and the writings of Irenaeus defend the place of prophecy in the church. It was a normal part of its life. Perhaps the recognition of the New Prophecy was decided upon during this visit, or at any rate seriously considered. Praxeas must have come later with his new theology and his information about the excesses of the Montanist leaders; and then the decision was reversed. The advent of Praxeas could be placed quite late in the eighties, but still under Bishop Eleutherus. Anicetus and Soter would be the predecessors who had condemned the New Prophecy.

If we place the advent of Praxeas in the nineties, during the episcopate of Victor, Eleutherus then becomes one of the predecessors whose policy towards Montanism was unfriendly; so that in either case he ends his episcopate by condemning it.

IRENAEUS AND THE NEW PROPHECY

The sympathy of Irenaeus himself for a moderate prophetism appears in the *Refutation*, which was composed a year or two after his visit to Rome and Asia. He proudly claims that prophetic gifts continued to exist in the church, with other marvellous graces; some cast out daemons in strength and in truth; others had foreknowledge of future things; they saw visions and uttered prophecies; others healed the sick by the laying on of hands; there had even been cases when the dead had been raised and survived among us for many years. Such statements may very truly express the principal features of Phrygianism as it first appeared in the west, but they do not require Phrygianism to explain them. When Phrygianism first appeared in the west it may have looked very like a revival of prophetic and spiritual activities with which the older Christians were quite familiar.

There is nothing to show whether Irenaeus had heard of the Montanist extravagances or excesses; but he has heard of an opposition to the prophetic movement, which was so strong that it rejected the Gospel of John because of the use the New Prophecy made of it.

In their desire to frustrate the gifts of the Spirit which has been poured out according to the pleasure of the Father upon the human race in these last times, they do not accept that aspect [of the Gospel as a whole] which is according to the Gospel of John, in which the Lord promised that he would send the Paraclete; but they reject at one and the same time, both the Gospel and the prophetic Spirit. (Irenaeus, *Ad. Haer.* III, 11, 12.)

The anti-Montanist party or sect, which he alludes to here, seems to be an obscure group in the Roman or Asian church, which objected to the Logos theology of Justin and his friends, as much as they did to the Paraclete theology of Montanus. They have no name. Epiphanius nicknamed them the *alogoi* or irrationals; the people who live without 'logos' or reason. Nothing very much more is known about them except that they found a spokesman in Rome at the opening of the next century in the mysterious Gaius who held a dispute with the Montanist leader Proclus, and backed the Roman tradition against the Asian and Phrygian.

THE MISSION OF IRENAEUS

We have run ahead of our chronology in considering the arrival of Praxeas in Rome. We may assume that the Phrygian movement was assured of fair consideration when Irenaeus arrived there in 178. The probability seems to be that Eleutherus extended full recognition to it, a recognition which he subsequently withdrew.

The mission of Irenaeus was not addressed simply to Rome; it was also addressed to the brethren in Asia and Phrygia. We have no record of what happened when he arrived in Rome; or of the events in the course of his journey in either country; but he wrote a book on his return to Gaul which has the situation in Asia and Rome for its background. In Asia he learned something about Marcus, who was the head of the Valentinian school in those parts and operated a degraded magical gnosis with barbaric and primitive features. He also knew about Theodotion of Ephesus, a convert to Judaism, who had made a new translation of the Old Testament into Greek, for use in the Hellenistic synagogue; a fact which shows how powerful the Greek-speaking Jews still were in Ephesus. This translation was also adopted by the Ebionites, a new name for the Christians of Jewish descent who still observed the Jewish Law; they, too, must have used Greek in their services.

Irenaeus formed the conviction that the time had come to refute all the heresies in a comprehensive work, which would at the same time give a full and trustworthy account of the authentic Christian tradition. He had the Marcionites in view, but he was even more alarmed at the way in which the Valentinians were gaining ground; and he felt that the older and better theologians had failed to deal with them effectively mainly through lack of information about their rules of faith. Considerable research was required. When he reached Lyons again, he took up the duties of bishop; and this position required a great deal of travelling and sheer missionary work among strange tribes who spoke barbarous tongues. He was not deterred from his task, however, for even in the Rhône Valley he found Valentinian practitioners at work. He had his library. He had much the same New Testament that we have today, apart from Hebrews and, possibly, one or two of the lesser Epistles; he had his copies of Clement, Hermas, Polycarp and Ignatius; he had the works of Papias and Justin and Hegesippus; he had the *Notebooks* of Ptolemaeus and other sketches of gnostic mythology; no doubt he had some of the works of Melito and Miltiades and Rhodo and other contemporary scholars who are only names to us. By dint of much hard labour he ground out his five magnificent volumes in the hundred-and-eighties. No sign appears in these volumes that Montanism or Monarchianism can be classed as a heresy. It would appear that when he wrote them Praxeas had not yet appeared at Rome, and the Montanist-Monarchian crisis was still in the future.

CHAPTER 17

ORIENTAL CHRISTIANITY

THE ACCESSION OF COMMODUS, A.D. 180

It was a tragic day for the empire when Marcus Aurelius died of the plague at Sirmium on 17 March 180, just when he had conquered the barbarians and was prepared once again to put into effect his plans to organize protective provinces north of the Danube. He was succeeded by his eighteen-year old son Commodus, who had been educated for the purpose; but higher education had done little good to the son of Faustina. He broke with his father's advisers. He patched up a peace with the Marcomanni and the Quadi. No doubt everybody was tired of war.

He returned to Rome to enjoy life. In physique at least he was more like a god than his predecessors. He affected the style of some sun-god or sun-king from the east. He walked about the camp with gold dust in his hair; he competed successfully with gladiators in the arena; he transfixed ostriches running at full speed, with specially designed arrows. He left the tasks of administration to the praetorian prefects, who were the principal military and legal officials of the empire. He was no persecutor. It is unlikely that he had studied the arguments of the apologists; and it is perfectly possible that he felt that he ought to persecute as a matter of duty; but in practice he did not enforce it. Perhaps he had had more than enough of his father's stern sense of logic and public duty. But these are only surmises; it is a fact that he had, among the three hundred ladies who constituted his harem, a favourite named Marcia, who exercised considerable influence over him. She had a leaning towards Christianity.

We may begin our study of the reign of Commodus with a survey of the east, where the Christian church begins once again to come into view. We will start on our travels from Athens.

THE SCHOOLS OF ATHENS

The glory of Athens, which had been revived under Hadrian, was not destined to endure a great deal longer, and the Christian schools entered into a decline after Athenagoras. We have dated his *Embassy* in the year 177, since it was presented to Marcus Aurelius and Commodus as co-emperors.

The fame of Athenagoras soon faded away, partly because the Athenian schools were themselves eclipsed. Eusebius seems not to have heard of him; but he was mentioned by the elegant Methodius, who wrote in the generation before Eusebius; and two of his works have come down to us, his *Embassy* and a treatise on the Resurrection, if indeed it is his. He can hardly be called original. He runs through the topics which had now become the regular subjects for discussion with the heathen; the injustice of the persecutions, the absurdity of the charges brought against the Christians, the pure monotheism which inspires their worship, the elevated morality which they practise, the doctrine of the Logos, and the doctrine of the daemons. We seem to have here a curriculum of studies which did not vary much from one school to another; but we may note perhaps a growing tendency to retort back upon the Greeks, or upon their gods, the charges of atheism, cannibalism and incest which were still being brought against Christians.

Athenagoras promised to write a treatise on the Resurrection as a supplement to the *Embassy*; for the subject demanded more extended treatment than he could give it there. But it is not certain that the book on the subject which goes under his name is really his. The idea of a bodily resurrection was of Hebrew origin and was not very acceptable to the Greek mind, which took more naturally to the idea of the survival of the soul. The doctrine was discarded in the heretical schools, and those Christians who maintained the apostolic tradition had to fight hard to defend it. The treatise attributed to Athenagoras tries to prove that it was not merely a possibility, but a logical necessity, if one accepted the teleological doctrine of Aristotle. If it is granted that everything in the universe is designed to fulfill some purpose, it can be argued that the purpose of man's creation is not realized in this life, and therefore he must continue his existence, body and soul, in another. The author does not disdain by any means the popular Christian argument from justice; for if a man does not rise again in his body, the rewards or punishments which he earned in the body cannot be appropriately enjoyed or suffered. The book is thought by some to be as late as the third or fourth century, but it follows the *Embassy* in the manuscripts.

If the church in Athens now diminishes in historical importance, it did not do so before it had given to the church universal a child of rare genius in the great Clement, who did something to rescue Christian thought from the pedantic and pedestrian arguments in which it was becoming involved. In the time of Epiphanius Clement was claimed by some as an Alexandrian by birth, and by others as an Athenian. The first claim may be explained as a guess or inference, based on his distinctive appellation; the second is supported by the internal evidence of his books. It is hard to read the charming chapters at the beginning of his *Logos Protreptikos—The Word Persuasive*—without feeling convinced that he had an Athenian background. He loved the songs and myths; he was versed in the philosophers; he had read the poets; he knew something of the Eleusinian mysteries; and he felt the beauty of all these things, even as he condemned their immoralities. He is the last exponent of the old literary tradition with its grace and charm, and its wide and level appreciation of intellectual truth wherever it may be found. He took up Justin's bold defence of the Greek intellectuals just when it seemed to be losing ground. Indeed, he went further than Justin by maintaining that Greek literature provided an excellent introduction to the study of Christianity. He had learned something from Tatian, but he did not approve his harsh and ugly asceticism or his barbarous pride. He developed an attractive and moderate asceticism of his own. He was a civilized man.

He was born of a Roman family. His full name was Titus Flavius Clemens, the same as the Roman consul and cousin of the emperor who was put to death in the nineties for his sympathy with Christianity. He was descended from the imperial family, perhaps, or from some humbler family which was dependent on the imperial house of those days. His outlook is that of the well-to-do educated classes.

THE WANDERINGS OF CLEMENT

We cannot be said to have any proof that he was a pupil of Athenagoras. Our documentary evidence is tantalizingly meagre. Philip of Side, the same fifth-century historian who provided us with a dubious quotation from Papias about the death of St John, comes to our aid with a statement that Athenagoras was the head of the Alexandrian school, that Clement was a pupil of Athenagoras, and Pantaenus a pupil of Clement. Philip is wrong on one point at least. Pantaenus was not a disciple of Clement; he was Clement's revered master. The statement that Athenagoras was head of the Alexandrian school appears to be another blunder; but of course he may be reproducing in a garbled form some true historical statement that he found in a reputable source;[1] for he was the head of the Alexandrian school himself in his own day and he may have had access to good records. It has been pointed out in his favour that there is a reference to camels in Athenagoras, which seems oddly out of place in Athens. It is possible, after all, that Athenagoras did go to Alexandria; but, if so, it is odd that Eusebius had not heard of him. It is certain that Clement went there, and the Athenian tradition went with him.

Clement roamed round the Christian world in the hundred-and-seventies, wandering from school to school and learning from many masters. For the most part they were exponents of the venerable oral tradition, men of the vintage of Hegesippus, younger than Papias or Polycarp but older than Irenaeus or Eleutherus. He tells the story in a careless lyrical style, which has left the exegetes baffled. Perhaps the text is not secure.[2]

Of these, one in Greece, an Ionian; some in Greater Greece [which means southern Italy]; the one from Coele-Syria, the other from Egypt.

He appears to be speaking of three men, an Ionian in Greece, who may be Athenagoras, and two in southern Italy, one from inland Syria, and one from Egypt. None can be identified in any case.

And others in the east, one born in the land of Assyria, and the other, a Hebrew, in Palestine.

The first of these is commonly identified with Tatian.

When I came upon the last—but he was the first in power—having tracked him down concealed in Egypt, I found rest. He was the true Sicilian bee,

---

[1] Or of course some copyist may have garbled him.
[2] Text from *Sources Chrétiennes* (Paris, 1951).

gathering the spoil of flowers from the prophetic and apostolic meadows, engendering in the souls of his hearers a deathless element of knowledge.

So they, preserving the tradition of the blessed apostles, Peter, James, John, and Paul, the son receiving it from the father—though few were like the fathers—came by God's will to us also, to deposit those ancestral and apostolic seeds. (Clem. Al., *Strom.* I, 1.)

What can we get in the way of plain prose out of this rhapsody? The last teacher of all is Pantaenus, who was the head of the Alexandrian school; but the metaphor of the Sicilian bee is probably no more than a stray piece of poetic diction from the poet Theocritus; it does not prove that Pantaenus came from Sicily.

At any rate, Clement began his wanderings in Greece and southern Italy, but went no farther west. He turned to the oriental churches. His first teacher in the east was an Assyrian, and we cannot help thinking of Tatian. The second was a Jewish-Christian in Palestine, where no doubt he came into touch with the tradition of James, whom he mentions next to Peter. It is most illuminating. This is how Hegesippus had travelled from city to city twenty or twenty-five years earlier. Many other Christian teachers and prophets did precisely the same thing; we think of Marcion, Valentine, Justin, Melito, Tatian, Peregrinus, Avircius, Apelles, and Rhodo, as examples. In these oriental lands Clement picked up a tradition which was different from that of Asia or Greece or Rome. In the hundred-and-nineties, he began to write it down 'as a remedy against old age': and he was departing from precedent in doing so.

THE APOSTOLIC TRADITION IN CLEMENT

It is worth collecting his references to his oral tradition, which appears to be independent of Papias or the Papias tradition, so far as we can see. He knows a number of legends about Peter, including his contest with Simon Magus at Rome. He is the earliest witness to this. He knows that Mark composed his Gospel from the teachings of Peter, but adds that Peter commended his work and approved it for reading in the churches. He says, like Irenaeus, that it was written at Rome, a statement which is not made by Papias, at least not in the extracts known to us. He remarks that Peter had a family of children. He has a story about Peter encouraging his wife at their martyrdom. Such pictures of

Peter and his work at Rome were not necessarily received by him from Rome; we may be looking at the Petrine legend as it was transmitted in the east, in Syria or in Alexandria.

He has two traditions about John. One is the story of his appointing bishops in Asia Minor, when he returned from Patmos after the death of the tyrant, and his reclaiming the young Christian who had joined a band of robbers. He says that it was current in more than one locality, and that there were some who named the city where it had happened. The other is that he wrote his Gospel at the entreaty of his friends, a story which the *Muratorian Fragment* gives in greater detail. He has a story about James the brother of John. He says that the man who brought him to trial was converted on hearing him give his witness, and asked to be forgiven. James said, 'Peace be with thee', and kissed him, and they were beheaded together.

He more than once mentions 'James the Just' the brother of the Lord; and since he refers to Jude as a brother of the 'sons of Joseph', he must have looked on them as only half-brothers of the Lord. This is the more likely, as he had heard the tradition of the perpetual virginity of Mary. He says that after the resurrection Jesus imparted knowledge to James the Just and John and Peter, and they imparted it to the rest of the apostles; the rest of the apostles communicated the knowledge to the seventy disciples, among whom he includes Barnabas. The apostles Peter and James and John, though they were so highly honoured by the Lord, did not contend for glory, but made James the Just bishop in Jerusalem. His interest in James the Just suggests that he received these stories from his Jewish-Christian teacher in Palestine.

He includes Paul among the four apostles whose tradition he had received, but he has no special information about him, unless we include his opinion that he was a married man. He had heard a scandalous story about Nicolas of Antioch, the seventh 'deacon' of the Acts of the Apostles, and the way in which he treated his wife; but he refuted it out of his personal knowledge.

We have here a cycle of stories which are different from those which came down by tradition in Asia and the west; but they had descended by similar steps, though these cannot be documented now. A vigorous church life of the catholic type existed in Cappadocia, Syria, Palestine and Egypt, though we do not happen to have its story; but Clement affords us a glimpse of its floating tradition. These were the tales told by the old men in the schools that he frequented. They are on a level with the tales of the first-century rabbis which are preserved in the Mishnah, or with the traditions of Irenaeus.

ALEXANDRIAN CHRISTIANITY

It is not possible to make out the history of the catholic tradition in Alexandria, which formed the foundation for the catechetical school which was presided over by Pantaenus when Clement arrived there in the hundred-and-eighties. Pantaenus had predecessors of the orthodox type, but we only know the name of one, Agrippa Castor, whose learned books refuting Basilides Eusebius had read. Unfortunately they have not survived.

The Alexandrian church inherited a large and liberal apostolic literature, which included Hebrews, I Clement, Hermas, the *Revelation of Peter*, the *Preaching of Peter*, and the *Epistle of Barnabas*. It is thought by many scholars that Barnabas was written in Alexandria; it is an example of learned mystical writing; it is based on the Hebrew scriptures but is anti-Jewish; it is strongly anti-docetic, and holds the catholic faith with regard to the Creation, the Incarnation, and the Resurrection. A more popular treatise was the *Epistle of the Apostles*, which was current in Egypt and quite probably written there. It is based on apostolic tradition, a full New Testament canon, orthodox doctrine, sacrament, and apocalypse. It is written in a simple imaginative prose to catch the popular attention.

The existence of an orthodox and conservative substratum of church life in Alexandria seems to be proved by the opposition which Clement encountered to the liberal studies which were carried on in the catechetical school. There was a solid old-fashioned uninformed body of opinion in the church which objected to his interest in Hellenic culture, and even to his practice of writing books; but, if we may judge by later Egyptian Christianity, it may have had a touch of gnosis and magic as well as apocalyptic.

PANTAENUS

Pantaenus, the Sicilian bee of Clement's encomium, was the first of the three great masters of the catechetical school which was destined to become the glory of the Alexandrian church. By the end of the century it was under the control of the bishop, but its status twenty years earlier is not so clear; all we know is that Pantaenus was its leading teacher, and that Clement studied under him and became his successor.

Eusebius tells us that he had been a Stoic philosopher, and Origen bears witness that he introduced his students to the widest range of Greek literature. Origen could remember him; and Leonides, the father of Origen, had been a Christian of the same broad-minded type. Pantaenus must have expounded the Old and New Testaments, since Clement remarked that he derived his honey from the prophetic and apostolic meadows. He was a teacher of the traditional eastern type and wrote no books. All he left was a school of disciples who celebrated his fame but eclipsed it with their writings. The only quite certain statement of his which is preserved is an observation about Hebrew grammar. Eusebius had heard that at some time he went on a mission to India, and found a group of Christians, who had a copy of St Matthew's Gospel written in Hebrew characters. It had been taken there by the apostle Bartholomew. There is nothing to object to in this story, since there was a regular trade connexion from Egypt to India and Ceylon; but it is said that the name India could be applied to the coast of Arabia.

Perhaps Pantaenus was the 'blessed elder' mentioned by Clement who defended the Pauline authorship of Hebrews; he explained its anonymity by the theory that Christ himself had been the apostle to the Hebrews, and therefore Paul could not have put his own name as an apostle on a communication addressed to them. This proves, at any rate, that Hebrews was included at Alexandria with the Pauline Epistles before the time of Clement, and that the words 'To the Hebrews' appeared as its title. This title must have been supplied when the epistles were collected, just as 'To the Ephesians' was supplied at the head of that epistle. The three facts, or possible facts, about Pantaenus, are connected with the Hebrew language or the Hebrew people; they suggest an interest in Jewish Christianity, which may have been well represented in Egypt. The Gentile churches of Palestine and southern Syria formed a group which was in very close touch with Alexandria.

NARCISSUS OF JERUSALEM

The two principal cities of Palestine were the old political capital Caesarea, which had a more or less continuous history since the days of Pontius Pilate, and the new city of Aelia, which had been built on the site of the old Jerusalem. We have already given the list of Gentile bishops of Aelia subsequent to the Jewish defeat of 135; this list begins with the name of Mark, and ends with the name of Narcissus who became bishop before about 190. According to his own account, he was even then about ninety years old; but even if we deduct ten or even twenty years for a certain amount of exaggeration, we must conclude that he was old enough to have a very good idea of affairs in Palestine previous to the Jewish War of 132–5. The list of bishops would appear to constitute his title-deeds, as he is the last name on it.

Some rather extraordinary tales were current about Narcissus a century later, and Eusebius picked them up when he was a young man working in the libraries of Caesarea and Aelia. They doubtless had some foundation in fact, and they contribute to the picture of the man as it was impressed upon his church. Some time after he had become bishop, it was said, he disappeared from the haunts of men to cultivate 'philosophy', which meant a life of asceticism and meditation. A bishop named Dios was appointed in his place; Dios was succeeded by Germanion, and Germanion by Gordius; then Narcissus reappeared and resumed the episcopate, having won the admiration of all by his retirement and philosophic life. The seclusion of Narcissus, however, had not been brought about solely by a passion for philosophy; there had been certain wretched persons who could not endure his firmness and energy. They devised a plot against him and spread a number of scandals about him, which they supported by imprecating various disasters upon themselves if the charge they made were not true. During the absence of Narcissus in the deserts, these disasters fell upon them exactly in accordance with their words; and not till then did he return.[1] It is possible, therefore, that his retirement was not entirely voluntary; though a voluntary retirement of this kind in view of dissension in the ecclesia was a course commended by Clement of Rome as honourable.

According to another story, there was no oil once in the lamps on the night of the Paschal vigil. He ordered the lamps to be filled with water which he had blessed; the water was changed into oil and burned brightly. Eusebius had actually seen some of this oil, which had been preserved into his time. The legend is of great historical interest. To this day the Greek patriarch in Jerusalem conducts a fire-ceremony on

[1] Were these 'wretched persons' Dios, Germanion, and Gordius? There seem to have been three of them.

the night before Easter, and the festal Epistle contained in the first chapter of II Maccabees strongly suggests that a fire-ceremony of some antiquity was traditional in Jerusalem; it is connected in II Maccabees with a well of 'thick water' which was called 'nephthar'. The Narcissus legend seems to show how seriously the Gentile church in Aelia took its position as the legitimate heir and successor of the old Jewish church or indeed of Judaism itself. The list of bishops preserved in Eusebius, the monument to James which Hegesippus speaks of as standing by the old Temple site, and the chair of James which Eusebius saw for himself, all support this idea. The chair may well have been the chair of Narcissus.

The fire-ceremony should not be looked upon as a pious fraud, since the 'thick water' was thought of, no doubt, as a strange gift of God. The Paschal fire-ceremony of the Jerusalem liturgy is vouched for in the fourth century, and has spread throughout the Christian world.

THEOPHILUS, BISHOP OF ANTIOCH

Our picture of the Antiochene church since the time of Ignatius is not quite so dim as that of Alexandria. We noted the return of Tatian from Rome with his curious theology, the organization of his 'encratite' ascetics, and the dissemination of his *Diatessaron*. The theological writer Theophilus, who was the opponent of the Basilidian Hermogenes, became bishop of Antioch, and went on with his learned researches and literary works. He was still engaged in these labours when Commodus became emperor in 180, since he brings his chronology down to that point; but he cannot have survived very much longer, since he was succeeded by Maximin, who was succeeded in his turn by Serapion about 192.

The books of Theophilus were useful books, a book of 'Histories', a commentary on *Proverbs*, a commentary on the Gospels, or rather on a harmony of the four Gospels (which we have noted is a point of contact with Tatian), his books against Marcion and Hermogenes, and his defence of Christianity which goes under the name of *To Autolycus*. The latter is the only one that survives.

TO AUTOLYCUS, c. A.D. 185

The Autolycus to whom this book is addressed is regarded by some scholars as a fictitious character; but he has some life-like qualities when he appears. Theophilus loses sight of him for long periods; but he is brought in at the beginning of each of the three books. He is just such a character as Theophilus himself. He is prepared to go through long hours of study in the literature of the ancient world. This work must have been done in a library, and that may be where they met. That, at any rate, was a common interest. On the other hand, he was fascinated by Greek art and philosophy, which Theophilus savagely attacks.

A day came when Autolycus discovered who and what Theophilus was, and taunted him with being a Christian. Theophilus maintained that it was a good name to have, since it meant good or serviceable; which was a play on the Greek word *chrestos*, and one of the conventional answers. The argument went further. 'Show me your god', Autolycus had said; and this is the text of the first book, in which Theophilus is at his best. The eternal invisible God cannot be seen by mortal eyes; but he is not the far-off essence of Alexandrian speculation or Iranian mysticism; he is the creator of the universe, and can be discerned in its order and beauty. We are on the same ground that we found ourselves in studying Clement of Rome. Theophilus is one of those who see the glory of God in the order and beauty of the universe and in the processes of nature; he believes that the God whose spirit nourishes all creation and sheds light upon it will be able to raise our flesh, immortal, with the soul. He sees many resurrection processes going on in nature itself.

Autolycus says, 'Show me even one who has been raised from the dead, that I may see and believe'; but Theophilus says that he must learn to rely upon faith. He tells Autolycus of his own conversion, and refers him to the writings of the prophets, which had moved him so profoundly, closing on the certainty of judgement and the destinies of eternal life and eternal fire. It is the Christianized synagogue Hellenism which we found widespread at the beginning of the century, but it is being expounded by a skilled writer with a pleasant Greek style.

The second book contains a detailed commentary on the first chapters of Genesis, and this is the part of Theophilus, which some scholars believe was used by Irenaeus.[1] The argument is not entirely convincing. Both men may have been working from some older book such as the *Six Days' Work* of Rhodo.[2] Rhodo was not a Roman. He was an Asian who spent time in Rome where he studied under Tatian. He had left Rome before he wrote his book and may have journeyed to the east in the trail of his master. Eusebius groups him with Clement of Alexandria and Narcissus of Aelia. In any case these pieces of allegorical interpretation were common property and passed from one book to another.

In his third book he attempts a chronology of the world, the object of which was to establish the antiquity of the Hebrew scriptures, *our* sacred writings as he calls them, in comparison with the Greek philosophers and poets, of whom he has little good to say. The work is done in the Syrian fashion rather than the Hellenic, being full of names and pedigrees and other chronicle material. A beginning of this historical work is to be found in Tatian, and Clement of Alexandria carries it on; and Clement had studied under Syrian and Jewish masters in the east. Julius Africanus, who was now growing up in Aelia as a boy or youth under Narcissus, inherited this tradition, and became the master of it.

Theophilus approaches Christian theology from the point of view of the Hebrew synagogue tradition. His faith in God springs from the contemplation of his activity in nature and in history and in liturgy and in scripture. He has a strong substantial doctrine of revelation and inspiration in nature and in history; but the revelation is primarily in the Law of Moses, and especially in the Creation narratives and the Ten Commandments, of which he gives an interesting traditional text which omits the fourth. He brings in his quotations from the prophets, and even from the Gospels, as confirmations and supplements to the Law. It is one solid unity for him. He thus has a threefold canon of holy writings rather like that of Hegesippus. He quotes from Matthew and John, naming the latter when he does so; he uses the Pauline Epistles including the Pastorals; he also used I Peter, to which we may probably add the pseudo-Petrine writings and I Clement. He wrote something on the Revelation of John, we are told, but he shows no

---

[1] F. Loofs, in *Texte und Untersuchungen*, 1930.
[2] Eusebius had seen two other books of this period on the same subject by authors who are otherwise unknown, Candidus and Apion. Hippolytus also wrote one.

sign of the chiliasm of Papias. The church over which he presided had a catholic faith and order which had developed apart from the western theology. It was still at home in the Judaeo-Christian synagogue tradition and in the Syrian world where it had originated.

JEWISH CHRISTIANITY

Some light is shed on the continuance of a Jewish form of Christianity in the eastern part of the empire by the story of Symmachus. The use of the old Greek Bible, known as the Septuagint, was being abandoned in the Jewish synagogue and in such Ebionite churches as used the Greek language. It was becoming to all intents and purposes a Christian book. The new translation which had been prepared fifty years before by Aquila was a scholar's handbook, and could not be used for liturgical purposes. A more literary and attractive translation had been prepared in Ephesus for use in the synagogue, and some Ebionite churches were using it, Irenaeus says; but there was room for a standard version for the Jewish churches. Such a translation was made about this time by Symmachus, a Jewish Christian of Cappadocia. It does not appear that it was ever widely used, but it had reached Alexandria by the time of Origen. About the year 235 Origen was in the Cappadocian Caesarea, a city of growing importance on the highroad through Asia Minor to the east, where he lodged with a lady named Juliana, who presented him with the original manuscript. Symmachus had also written a book of *Hupomnemata*, or *Note-books*, in which he attacked the Gospel of St Matthew; so that he seems to have belonged to some branch of Jewish Christianity which rejected the doctrine of the virgin birth of Christ. As his church was Greek-speaking or bilingual, it must have used some form of 'Hebrew' Gospel in a Greek translation or some shortened version of Matthew itself.

We have evidence here of a Greek-speaking Jewish Christianity with a scholarly tradition operating in the province of Cappadocia, probably in its capital city of Caesarea. We shall find other evidences of this active Jewish Christianity. The days of Jewish Christianity were numbered; but its story was not finished yet.

Syrian and Jewish forms of Christianity were spreading farther to the east. Mesopotamia was fully open to Roman and Greek travellers, and the hundred-and-eighties are the latest probable dates for the journeys of Avircius Marcellus, the Phrygian bishop, to the country beyond the Euphrates, where, he says, he found companions everywhere. Progress was fast. By about 220 Bar Daisan could speak of Christians in Parthia and Persia as well as Mesopotamia. A legend about the establishment of Christianity in India had come into existence by that time.

THE ROAD TO INDIA

There were three roads to India; by sea from Egypt, by sea from the Gulf of Akaba, which was linked by road with the Roman province of Arabia, and down the Euphrates and Tigris to the Persian Gulf. Communication was slow and difficult and dangerous, but it was established; Buddhist monks had turned up in Egypt in the time of the Ptolemies; Brahmins had visited the court of Augustus; trade missions had come to the court of Antoninus. Towards the end of the second century, the Romans had built permanent trading posts on the Indian coast, and a certain amount of information was disseminated. Romantic pictures of the Brahmins were current; it was understood that they lived naked, abstained from almost all bodily appetites, and had incredible mental powers.

A religious romance about India was written around the personality of the first-century philosopher, Apollonius of Tyana. The story is told by a pupil named Damis; and it describes how he set out with a couple of stenographers, and Damis himself as his adoring friend and biographer, to renew the links between Greece and India which had been lost since the days of Alexander and his successors. The story of the journey down the Euphrates is quite interesting, and so is the arrival in India, where he finds the Brahmins far ahead of the Egyptians or any other exponents of spirituality. They had reached a peak of spiritual power which could afford to look down on mere miracles as vulgar. This story of Damis was a source-book for the official *Life* of Apollonius which was written early in the third century.

LEGEND AND SONG

The interest in India appears in Christian sources too, in the report of the journey of Pantaenus and in the Syrian legends. In the Pantaenus story it is the apostle Bartholomew who is said to have taken the gospel there; in the Syrian legends it is the apostle Judas Thomas. Judas Thomas, or Judas the twin, is an apostle who appears only in Syrian sources; in the Syriac Gospels for instance, and in the legend of Addai. He sends Addai to Edessa, but he does not go to Edessa himself. The Syrian *Acts of Thomas* tell how he went, very unwillingly, to India, and undertook to build a palace for King Gundaphor, who was a historical personage of the first century, as we know from his coins; it tells, too, how that palace was built in heaven and not on earth; for Thomas spent the king's money on the poor and the sick and the distressed. Fortunately for Thomas, the king's brother, who died opportunely at that time, returned to life, and described to the king the beauties of the palace which was awaiting him in heaven. It is not unlike the anecdote of King Monobazes of Adiabene in the Talmud (Baba Bathra), whose son Izates was a circumcised Jew.

We are not at all too early in treating these legends at this point, and it seems necessary to do so in order to bring them into comparison with the story about the mission of Pantaenus to India. Eusebius gives it simply as a tradition; but there is nothing incredible about it, since the way to India was open and India must have participated in the great expansion of oriental Christianity which was going on at this time.

The Syrian legends are better than history in one way. They are evidences of the imaginative fervour of the far-eastern Christianity of this period, which was based on ascetism, gnosis and the mystic's dream. It created fables and songs rather than doctrines and theologies. An interesting legacy from this period, or even earlier, is the *Odes of Solomon*, a collection of spiritual and sacramental psalms which have something of the spirit of Ignatius, and just a touch of something which resembles Valentinianism.

He hath caused me to know himself, without grudging, by his great simplicity: his kindness hath humbled his greatness.

He became like me in order that I might receive him: he was reckoned like myself in order that I might put him on.

And I trembled not when I saw him: because he was gracious to me.

Like my nature he became that I might learn him: and like my form that I might not turn back from him.

The father of knowledge is the word of knowledge; he who created wisdom is greater than his works.   (*Odes of Solomon*, VII.)

285

CHAPTER 18

LATIN CHRISTIANITY

THE RULE OF COMMODUS, A.D. 180–92

Before surveying the progress of the Christian gospel in western Europe, we must take up again the state of the empire and city under the new emperor, whose reign of thirteen years, 180 to 192, was a time of greater ease for the Christian church. Commodus paid no deference to the senate; he magnified his own divine and imperial office; and he ruled the empire through the army. The troops which were stationed in Rome were known as the praetorian guard, and their relation to the emperor was very close. Their prefect was the real ruler of the empire; for he was the supreme military and legal authority under the emperor. A succession of such officers held sway for a few years each, and succumbed to intrigue or violence. Palace revolutions were sometimes directed against the emperor himself, who became more suspicious and unpredictable as time went on.

Marcus Aurelius had left excellent generals in command of his legions on the frontiers; but the day was fast coming when these legions would appoint their generals as emperors and determine the destiny of the empire. Gaul and Britain formed a powerful block in the north-west. The long line of the Danube provided another, and this was more important since it was closer to Rome. The east with its headquarters at Antioch resembled a separate empire. The line was held; risings in Spain and Africa were put down; Britain was held with a firm hand.

We must note the names of three young men who grew up in Rome, or across the water in Africa, during the reign of Commodus. They were Callistus, Hippolytus and Tertullian. Callistus and Hippolytus were ecclesiastics and theologians who fought one another until they eventually set up as rival bishops. Callistus was a slave; Hippolytus was obviously an aristocrat; we shall depend on his writings for the inner history of the Roman church and for light on its liturgical order. Tertullian, the lawyer-theologian of Africa, was the son of an army officer, and a convert to the faith; he wrote copiously on subjects of all sorts, and his books contain many lively and penetrating comments on his times. He is the first great literary figure in western Christianity, and corresponds in age and in importance to Clement of Alexandria in the east. The two writers were very different in character.

THE *EPISTLE TO DIOGNETUS*

For want of a better place we may take here the famous document known as the *Epistle to Diognetus*. It was found in a codex of some 260 pages which contained five treatises, which were all attributed (quite wrongly) to Justin Martyr. It has been lost by fire, but a transcription was made and published. The titles of these treatises (which are, on the whole, likely to be third-century rather than second-century productions) show the kind of subjects in which the Christian schools were interested. They are

> Concerning the Monarchia.
> An Exhortation to the Greeks.
> Concerning the Resurrection.
> To the Greeks.
> To Diognetus.

Fronto and Rusticus, the tutors of Marcus Aurelius, had been strongly opposed to Christianity; but there was another of his academic advisers whose mind may have been more open on the subject; for it has been suggested that he was the person to whom the fifth of these tracts was dedicated. His name was Diognetus. The identification is a modern conjecture but it is not impossible. Some scholars, indeed, regard the Epistle as a third-century production; but it reads more like an early apologetic treatise drawn up under the influence of the *Preaching of Peter* or the *Apology* of Aristides. It has no theological or philosophic argumentation. It is content to eulogize, and possibly to idealize, the pure monotheism and blameless life of the Christian people.

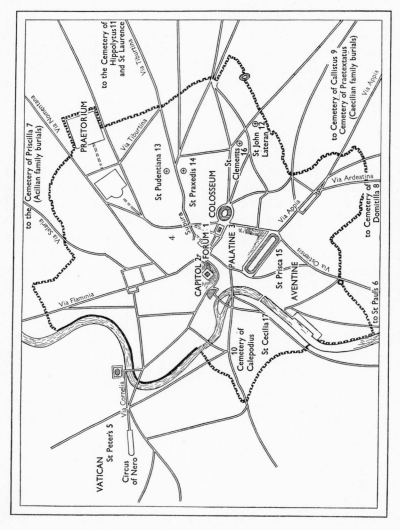

Map 3. Christian sites in Rome.

VATICAN
St Peter's 5

Circus
of Nero

Via Cornelia

Via Flaminia

to the Cemetery of Priscilla 7
(Acilian family burials)

Via Salaria

Via Nomentana

PRAETORIUM

to the Cemetery of
Hippolytus 11
and St Laurence

Via Tiburtina

St Pudentiana 13

St Praxedis 14

Subura

4

FORUM 1

CAPITOL 2

St
Clements
16

COLOSSEUM

St John
Lateran 12

to the Cemetery of Callistus 9
Cemetery of Praetextatus
(Caecilian family burials)

Via Appia

PALATINE 3

Via Appia

Via Ardeatina

to Cemetery of
Domitilla 8

St Prisca 15

AVENTINE

Via Ostiensis

to St Paul's 6

Cemetery of
Calepodius
10

St Cecilia 17

288

(1) The *Forum Romanum* in the centre of the original city lies between

(2) The *Capitoline Hill*, with its temples of Jupiter and Juno, and

(3) The *Palatine Hill*, with its imperial palaces.

(4) Some Jews lived in the neighbourhood called the Subura, but the Jewish quarter was on the opposite side of the river near the Island.

(5) The site of the burial of St Peter is on the right hand of the Via Cornelia as one ascends the Vatican Hill. The martyrdoms of 64 took place in the *Circus of Nero* on the left.

(6) The site of the burial of St Paul is on the *Ostian Way*, and lies south of the city.

(7) In ancient times all burial places were situated outside the city. A first-century Christian cemetery is that of *Priscilla* on the Salarian Way leading north.

(8) Another first-century cemetery is that of *Domitilla* on the Ardeatine Way, leading south.

(9) First-century cemeteries were taken into the *Cemetery of Callistus* on the Appian Way, leading south.

Callistus took charge of this cemetery about 200. It contains the *Crypt of the Popes*, dating from 235.

(10) Callistus, who died in 222, was buried in the *Cemetery of Calepodius* in the district called Transtiberim: across the Tiber. (In Italian: Trastévere.)

(11) Hippolytus, his rival as bishop, died 235, and was buried in the *Ager Veranus* on the Tiburtine Way leading east. St Laurence, who died in 258, was buried nearby.

(12) The Emperor Constantine in 322 gave the bishop of Rome the buildings which became *St John Lateran*. It became the parish church and cathedral of Rome.

(13, 14, 15) According to fourth- or fifth-century legends, the oldest churches in the City were *St Pudentiana* (13), *St Praxedis* (14), and *St Prisca* (15).

(16, 17) *St Clement* (16) and *St Cecilia* (17) are also regarded as old churches.

Note. The expression 'first-century cemeteries' is used to mean a first-century cemetery in continuous use in the family which it is named after, and showing copious signs of Christian use in the second century.

They dwell in their own countries but only as sojourners. They bear their share in all things as citizens, and they endure all hardships as strangers. Every foreign country is a fatherland to them and every fatherland a foreign country. They marry, like other men and beget children; but they do not cast out their offspring. They have everything in common except their wives. They are found in the flesh, but do not live according to the flesh. Their existence is here on earth, but their citizenship is in heaven.

The description of the Christians as sojourners or aliens is not pure rhetoric. It is based firmly on their unhappy and insecure condition in a state which did not recognize their existence; but it passes in the last sentence from the literal to the mystical—having no citizenship here, they claim one in heaven.

The relation between the heavenly and the earthly is precisely the question which will come into prominence from the reign of Commodus onward. Will the church be able to maintain its other-worldly character, or will it compromise with the empire and with society? The themes of this little document reappear in the Latin apologies of Tertullian and Minucius; and so does the notion of the spiritual kingship which does not exercise force; but it is nowhere expressed with such simplicity and skill as we find here. It contains a veiled protest against persecution, and seems to have Marcus Aurelius and his son Commodus in mind.

[He sent us his Son.] Was he sent, do you think, as a man might suppose, to establish an empire or to inspire fear and terror? Not so; but in gentleness and meekness he sent him, as a king might send his son who is also a king. He sent him as God; but he sent him as a man to men. He sent him as a saviour; using persuasion and not force; for force is not an attribute of God. He sent him to invite and not to persecute. He sent him in love and not as a judge; for he will send him in judgement, and then who will endure his presence?

THE AFRICAN MARTYRS, c. A.D. 180

The vision of the spiritual empire appears clearly in the Acts of the Scillitan martyrs; for there were martyrdoms early in the reign of Commodus, only four or five weeks after his accession in 180. They were the work of the African consul Saturninus, who was 'the first to draw the sword against us', Tertullian says.

The first outbreak was at a country town named Madaura, and the first martyr was a native African with the Berber name of Namphamo, or so we judge from the fact that St Augustine calls him the 'archimartyr'. His companions also bore 'barbarous' names, whose forms are uncertain; Lucitas, Mygdon (Miggin), and Samae or Saname. We have no further information about them; but we have an excellent objective record of a trial of Christians in the court-house at Scilli on 17 July 180. The Christians were ordered to swear by the genius of the emperor and to offer sacrifice, to which their leader Speratus made answer in the name of the rest,

I do not recognize the authority of this age; I am a servant of that God whom no man sees or can see with these eyes. I have not committed theft; and if I have bought anything I have paid the tax; for I recognize my own Lord as king of kings and ruler of all nations.

The suggestion of the proconsul that they should abandon their profession of faith was answered by a chorus of protest from the martyrs, whose names now begin to appear.

> *Cittinus.* There is no one for us to fear except the Lord our God who is in heaven.
> *Donata.* Honour to Caesar as Caesar, but fear belongs to God.
> *Vesta.* I am a Christian.
> *Secunda.* I intend to remain what I am.
> *Saturninus.* You persevere in being a *Christian?*
> *Speratus.* I am a Christian.
> *Saturninus.* Would you like time to think it over?
> *Speratus.* In so righteous a matter there is no need to think it over.
> *Saturninus.* What have you got in your box?
> *Speratus.* Books; and Epistles of Paul, who was a righteous man.
> *Saturninus.* Why not take a remission of thirty days and think it over?
> *Speratus.* I am a Christian.

There was nothing now for the proconsul to do but to read the sentence of execution, and the martyrs gave thanks to God. 'Today we are martyrs in heaven', said Nartzalus; 'thanks be to God.' Twelve names in all were read out, and there the records come to an end. 'They were all crowned with martyrdom', the document concludes, 'and they reign with the Father and the Son and the Holy Spirit for ever and ever. Amen.'

The record reminds us of the Acts of the Martyrdom of Justin and his companions in Rome, so that Speratus with his simple answers and his New Testament books may have been a teacher like Justin, witnessing to his faith with his pupils. The dialogue was taken from the records of the court, or written down at once while the memory was still fresh, repeating simply the more significant sayings on each side; but its liturgical close suggests that it was meant to be read aloud at a service. There is no account of the execution such as we find in the Asian and Gallican Acts. It is not a Passion story.

THE YOUNGER CHURCHES

One of the most important points about this document is that it is composed in Latin, and that the martyrs have Latin or barbarous names. There are no Greeks or Asians or Phrygians. We are witnessing the birth of a Latin Christianity.

One of the strange powers of Christianity has been its ability to enter into union with a new language and national culture, and so create a new species or variety of itself. At the very outset of its history in Palestine itself, it appeared in Greek as well as in Aramaic, and this initial bilingualism enabled it to spread along the main trade-routes of the world and establish itself in the main cities. This wonderful faculty for linguistic adaptation seems to be hinted at in the story of the gift of tongues in the Acts of the Apostles with which the record of the world-wide expansion begins. Language was no obstacle to the gospel. It was not a philosophy. Its parables and words of wisdom and apocalyptic dreams and hymns and creeds and sacraments were equally effective in any language; and the figure of the crucified appeals equally to all nations. It had spread through the medium of the apostolic church-order and had won converts of many kinds; not the top of wealth or power or birth as a rule, though there had been distinguished exceptions; not the highest official class in the state, since its duties were too mixed up with pagan ceremony to be regarded as legitimate; nor the greatest of the intellectuals, though there had been Christian thinkers of repute. Nor, so far as we can see, was it a proletarian movement winning its way principally among slaves, though slaves could find their way into the highest orders of the ministry. It is better described as middle-class or bourgeois. It went where the common

Greek of the day took it, among business men, students of literature and philosophy, civil servants perhaps, skilled technicians, and so forth. Celsus makes some interesting remarks about Christian technicians. It ramified at this level, and expanded in a kind of cultured society which was much the same throughout the empire and even beyond it; it was the average enlightened Hellenistic culture of the day.

The case of Rome is an interesting one. The church of Rome wrote and prayed in Greek, so far as we can see; its teachers were almost all foreigners; even its bishops, before Victor, do not appear to have been Romans, though Clement and Pius have Latin names, and possibly also 'Sixtus'. It operated as a part of the international Hellenistic church. But what about the local and popular church life which is not disclosed in the documents—the part of the iceberg, so to speak, which is under the water? It seems quite possible that a Latin Christianity with a vigorous life had been in existence in Rome for a considerable time.

Great progress was being made at this same time in the development of a Syriac-speaking Christianity in the principalities beyond the Euphrates. This development was destined to create a national literature and culture, and a church organization of imposing proportions which would extend as far as Persia, India, and China. Egypt, too, is about to show proof of a vigorous indigenous Christianity.

In Phrygia we have observed the rise of a national form of Christianity which expressed itself in the movement known as the New Prophecy; but here there was a difference. There was no national language or organized culture which was capable of giving permanent expression to this Christian Phrygianism. It was obliged therefore to propagate itself in Greek, and very soon in Latin as well; it had its diaspora in every city of the empire; and it was able to influence the church very widely both east and west.

We must now survey the west. In Gaul we were unable to detect a true national form of Christianity; the martyrs spoke in Latin or in Greek. Attalus and Alexander represented Asia and Phrygia; Sanctus and Blandina had Roman names. The Gallican Epistle was written in Greek and belonged to the literary tradition of Asia Minor. The leading local presbyter was Irenaeus of Asia and Rome. There is no sign of Celtic. When Irenaeus became bishop, he had to speak in Celtic, but he tells us that there were no Christian books in that language; the same observation seems to be true of the Germanies and the Spains, as he calls them. There is no sign of it yet, but Latin was destined very soon to become the language of Christianity in all these regions; and Latin Christianity would become the religion of western Europe. The Acts of the Scillitan martyrs is the first clear glimpse which we get of the earliest stage of this majestic development.

THE PROVINCE OF AFRICA

Just as the name Asia was applied in ancient times to a small district at the western extremity of Asia Minor, so the name Africa was applied simply to the promontory of Tunisia which looks towards Sicily. In the Gulf of Tunis Semitic settlers from the Palestinian coast had established a colony in the ninth century before Christ which they called Kiriat Hadeshat (*Kart Had'shat*), the New Town, a name which has been corrupted into Carthage. Its kings were descended from the royal family of Tyre, which was connected by marriage with the royal family of Israel. The Phoenician settlers intermarried with the native Berbers, and both languages were spoken there. The city flourished and grew strong and became the principal rival of Rome in the western world. There was a long and desperate series of wars, and eventually Rome laid her enemy low and destroyed the old city in 146 B.C. For over a century the site remained desolate and uninhabited; but a colony was settled there by Julius Caesar and had made extraordinary progress. It was within two days' sail of Rome on a fair day, and figs from Carthage had been known to reach Rome in good condition.

Relations between the two cities were now as close and cordial as they had once been hostile and dangerous. Carthage was more Roman than Rome. While Rome was entertaining Greek philosophers and Syrian *littérateurs* at the court of Pius or Marcus, Carthage was producing a respectable Latin literature which inspired a revival of interest in Latin letters in Rome itself. Aemilius Fronto, the anti-Christian tutor of Marcus Aurelius was an African; Aulus Gellius, the Latin grammarian at Athens, was an African; and so was Apuleius, the writer of that delightful novel called the *Golden Ass*, which begins as a comic study of witchcraft in Thessaly and ends with a serious confession of faith in the mysteries of Isis. Soldiers and lawyers and theologians came to Rome from Africa: Tertullian the future theologian, Victor the future bishop of Rome, and Septimus Severus the future emperor, who was of Phoenician descent, and spoke the old 'Punic' language. Severus married Julia Domna the daughter of the high priest of the sun at Emesa in Syria; and this marriage was a forecast of the new cosmopolitan empire which was taking shape.

It is natural to assume that Christianity was introduced into Africa from Rome. This must have happened some time before the persecutions in 180, but not too early in the century, if this is really the first persecution, as Tertullian and Augustine seem to say. The first missionaries must have arrived as early as the hundred-and-sixties. They had to make converts and organize churches, though doubtless the way was prepared for them; they had to spread out into the country towns such as Madaura and Scilli; and they had to provide 'books and Epistles of Paul' in the Latin tongue. Fifteen years does not seem too much to allow for all this. It may have begun in the last years of Justin. The years 165 to 175 are the latest possible period for the first evangelistic work; and there must have been Christian groups even earlier, some of them Greek-speaking.

THE LATIN NEW TESTAMENT

The mention of the books and Epistles of Paul suggests another line of inquiry. What sort of a New Testament was in use in the African church? We can give a good answer to this question, because Tertullian, who began writing about 195, made numbers of quotations in Latin from the African New Testament; and these can be supplemented and checked from the writings of Cyprian a generation later. It was a text of the 'Western' type very like that which was used by Justin or Tatian or Marcion or Irenaeus; it was, in short, the kind of text which was in general use in Rome.

The official Bible of the Roman Catholic Church today is the translation called the Vulgate, which was made by St Jerome at the end of the fourth century from excellent Greek texts; but it is well known that there was an older version or versions which are alluded to by scholars as the Old Latin. Their oldest ancestors must have come into existence in Latin-speaking circles no later than the hundred-and-sixties or -seventies. Judging by the existing remains, there must have been at least three varieties or lines of transmission: the African, which seems to represent the oldest, the Italian or European,[1] and the Marcionite. However this evidence is interpreted, it shows that an immense amount of labour was being expended on the provision of literature for Latin-speaking churches no later than the time of Justin. There were, therefore, Latin churches, Latin schools and Latin liturgical traditions. Nor need we confine this activity to Rome and Carthage. There were churches in the rest of Italy, and in the western provinces where Latin was spoken, such as Gaul, Spain and Britain. Latin was spoken wherever the army was settled, or the Roman law administered: and this included Syria.

It was a large enterprise, which may have gone on piecemeal at different centres. A wide range of books was translated, including Hermas, Clement, Polycarp, Barnabas, and some form of the *Didache*. The works of Irenaeus seem to have been translated quite soon after they were written. It seems reasonable to suppose that the mainspring of this work was a strong Latin-speaking organization in Rome itself. It may be older than we think. Were there no Latin-speaking converts in the days of Hermas? His own Greek style is marked by numerous 'Latinisms'.

THE LATIN TRADITION IN ROME

We have reviewed the evidence about the origins of the church of Rome from time to time, and have remarked that it is not a Latin tradition. Its apostolic inheritance was expressed in the Greek language and in the old Judaeo-Christian liturgical forms. It communicated in Greek with the rest of Christendom. It exercised unbounded hospitality to teachers from other centres of learning. The strongest evidence of a native Roman tradition is to be found in the paradoxical association with the family of the emperor at the close of the first century, and apparently with certain important Roman families with old names. The solidity of this evidence is guaranteed by the existence of old cemeteries like those of Domitilla and Priscilla.

Further evidence of the Roman character of the church is somewhat subjective. Clement, in his Epistle, most decidedly shows a certain pride in the imperial administration and in the discipline of the Roman army, on which he does not hesitate to dilate when addressing a city of lesser rank. But the Roman quality of Clement can be exaggerated;

[1] The Italian type can itself be divided into two.

his doctrine of submission to authority is thoroughly Jewish, and owes more to apostolic catechisms than to the edicts of the praetors. A certain tendency to promote discipline runs through Clement and Hermas, but it can be explained by the needs of the times rather than by the influence of antique Roman piety; and it was balanced by a feeling for forgiveness which was quite un-Roman. Under Pius and Anicetus, the Roman church organized a stout resistance to heresy, and well before the end of the century it was a strongly organized body which exercised a widespread influence in the church universal; a paramount influence many scholars think.

We have come across no evidence whatever of anyone in the Roman church using the Latin tongue; but there is an explanation for this; the nature of our evidence is such that it would not appear. The writings of Clement and Hermas as we have them were intended for distribution in the Greek-speaking world: and all our other evidence comes from foreign visitors. The native Roman, Latin-speaking, tradition would leave no marks on any of it. It may illustrate this point if we make another observation. We have not had a single reference to any Italian church outside Rome; yet there must have been many. Hippolytus tells us that a new bishop was consecrated by other bishops, so that other bishops must have existed in the vicinity. There must have been a Latin-speaking Christianity, not only in Rome, but in Italy generally; but it was not the face which Rome turned to the Christian world.

THE TITLE-CHURCHES

Another avenue of research is the shadowy line of tradition which is associated with the catacombs and the old Roman title-churches, as they are called. One of the points in apostolic Christianity which must have appealed to the Roman mind was its sanctification of the family and its incorporation as a unit into the church. The old Roman feeling about the family (the 'piety' which was so strongly venerated by the Antonine emperors) was supported by a remarkable cult of the dead, which regarded the ancestors as present members of the family circle; indeed, the deification of dead emperors, from one point of view, was an aspect of this family religion. It is not astonishing to find that a pious interest in the dead occurs within the Christian organization.

The oldest churches in Rome, some of which can be proved to have existed in the third century, are what is known as title-churches; they preserve the name of a founder in whose household they originated. Such at any rate is the tradition. The oldest church in Rome according to the fourth-century tradition was that of Pudentiana, on the Viminal Hill, who was said to be the daughter of a Roman senator named Pudens who received St Peter into his house.[1] Another ancient title-church is dedicated to her sister Praxedis. This family was said to have been buried in the cemetery of Priscilla, and there is a church by the title of Prisca on the Aventine Hill. This Prisca, or Priscilla, was said to have been the mother of Pudens. The churches and their names are old; the legends about them are very late.

Another church which has a claim to first-century foundation is that of Clement on the Lateran; another is that of St Cecilia across the Tiber. The archaeological evidence is not decisive in any case. All that can safely be said at present is that they are among the most ancient churches in Rome and bear venerable names, which are probably as old as the churches. It is in their favour that they are *not* named after apostles and martyrs. Future research may discover more reliable evidence about them.

THE CATACOMBS

The cemeteries are situated outside the city, and consist of underground tunnels or galleries along the sides of which are the resting-places of the dead; sometimes opening out into a chapel or chamber which contains the bodies of a family or special group. We have already mentioned the Vatican cemetery on the Via Cornelia, where a shrine was erected about the hundred-and-fifties over the supposed resting place of the body of St Peter. No excavation has yet been carried out at the site of the burial of St Paul on the Via Ostiensis, which was also marked by a monument in the second century. Apart from these there are three important cemeteries of first-century origin which were enormously extended, as time went on, for purposes of Christian burial.

The cemetery of Priscilla on the Via Salaria is associated in legend with the family of Pudens. It is one of the largest and one of the first to

[1] It has been suggested that it was originally the *ecclesia Pudentiana*, the church connected with Pudens.

be used as a common cemetery. Christian inscriptions in Greek and Latin are to be seen there, which date from the middle or latter half of the second century. It included the burial place of the aristocratic Acilian family, among them perhaps the consul Acilius Glabrio who was killed in 91, probably as a Christian. Equally old is the cemetery of Domitilla which is situated on the Via Ardeatina, so called because this property belonged to Domitilla, the Christian niece of the emperor Domitian. The third is a group of cemeteries on the Via Appia, including the cemetery of Praetextatus and the crypt of Lucina; here the noble family of the Caecilii were buried, including the legendary virgin and martyr Caecilia who witnessed under Marcus Aurelius, according to one tradition. This group of cemeteries passed into the ownership of the church before the end of the second century, and is known as the cemetery of Callistus after the archdeacon (later bishop) Callistus, who was placed in charge of it.

The most striking point about these traditional names is the predominance of women; and this is worth a moment's thought. The pre-eminence of women as evangelists or prophets or teachers is obviously a characteristic of the heresies, where Jewish social traditions were relaxed. 'How *forward* their women are!' said Tertullian in his pre-Montanist days. Apostolic writers had insisted that they should be modestly attired, keep silence in the church, and be obedient to their husbands; but this did not mean that they were not given a characteristic position of dignity. There are some interesting points in the Roman Clement on this subject. He suggests at the end of his Epistle that the leaders of the Corinthian schism should make a great act of renunciation and quit the church, and backs this up by referring to examples both in pagan and in biblical history. It is peculiar that he should single out women in this connexion, mentioning particularly Judith and Esther. There were women, therefore, among the leaders of the schismatic group, and he is appealing to them to make the act of sacrifice. This enables us to understand why he emphasizes so strongly the proper position of women in the church, and why he is so careful to mention women among the martyrs who suffered with the noble apostles. They were people of influence in the ecclesia.

Perhaps this explains why he makes so much of the story of Rahab, which he tells at great length; for she is an example of faith *and hospitality*. He tells in some detail how she received the spies sent by Joshua into her house, and hid them from the king's officers. Is she a 'type' of the wealthy believer who gave shelter in her house to the Christian evangelists and made it a centre for the church? Is she one of the wealthy persons praised by Hermas, who gladly receive the servants of God into their houses? She is contrasted with Lot's wife, who represents the dissentient groups.

In any case there must have been properties in Rome belonging to the church and used for church purposes. How could they be legally held? Only, so far as we can see, by their being vested in some individual, by whose name they would come to be known. The theory of house-churches therefore, is bound to remain the one that holds the field, while it awaits confirmation by the archaeologists. That Christians did own properties is a fact vouched for by Irenaeus.

Whence came the house we live in, the clothes we wear, the vessels we use, and all the other gear of our daily life, if not from the possessions which we acquired by avarice when we were Gentiles, or what has come to us from parents or relations of friends who acquired them by unrighteous means? [He has in mind the gospel phrase 'mammon of unrighteousness'.] Not to mention that we who live by faith are still acquiring them. For whoever sells anything without wishing to make a profit from the buyer.

He then adds, what is most significant for our period,

And those of the faithful who are in the royal palace, do they not get the necessities of life from what belongs to Caesar?

(Irenaeus, *Ad. Haer.* IV, 46, 1.)

Not even the early Christians could live so completely off the kingdom of heaven as Diognetus was led to believe. It was reasonable to 'spoil the Egyptians' in moderation, Irenaeus thought. Hermas seems to have thought so too.

THE EVIDENCE OF THE CATACOMBS

Historians are bound to turn to the catacombs for further evidence on Christian life in Rome at this period, for the oldest inscriptions and wall-paintings are said by the experts to date from the latter half of the second century. The inscriptions are few, and consist in this early period of little more than a name and such words as 'In peace', or 'Peace be with thee', or 'Rest in peace', or 'Has refreshment'. The old

Roman tradition was marked by restraint; there were no elaborate Acts of Martyrs yet; or birthdays of the martyrs, so far as we know, except perhaps in family reunions in small groups. A memorial supper of this kind appears in Tertullian and Hippolytus. It is all the more affecting to find that the deepest feelings of the Christian mind should express itself in simple symbolic drawings.

The legends of the famous martyrs of this period only took form in much later times when pilgrims came to Rome from all over western Europe; but these legends are attached to names which may be historical. One such legend is that of Cecilia, and her husband Valerianus, and her brother Tiburtius, whose martyrdom is placed in the time of Marcus Aurelius in one form of the tradition. Another is that of Petronilla, who achieved fame in the middle ages as the daughter of St Peter; but her name seems to be a Latin formation from Petro or Petronius, which was a common name in the Flavian family, so that she may have been a relative of Domitilla. The church which is named after her seems to be an ancient one.

Another ancient cemetery is that of St Felicitas on the Via Salaria. According to the legend she suffered with her seven sons like St Symphorosa; and both stories would seem to be influenced by the story of the martyrdom of the mother with her seven sons in the fourth book of the Maccabees. If there is any truth in the legend, she may have been the leading figure in a mass execution like Blandina at Lyons, or Potamiaena at Alexandria, or Perpetua at Carthage. Could not Felicitas and Symphorosa be Latin and Greek forms of the same name, both of them having the meaning of good luck? The same legend being preserved in two parallel traditions, one Greek and one Latin?

While these legends cannot be admitted into our history, this does not mean that they do not contain authentic names. Meanwhile the catacombs themselves preserve the remains of uncounted actual Christians from our period; and about half the inscriptions are Latin, and half of them Greek. The Roman church was definitely bilingual.

THE DECORATION OF THE CATACOMBS

There is nothing peculiar or mysterious about the catacombs, which are simply underground burial chambers, connected by long galleries, in the walls of which lesser burial places were hollowed out and sealed with tiles. There were Jewish catacombs also, and catacombs have been discovered in other parts of Italy and also in Africa. They were rendered necessary by the doctrine of the resurrection of the body; Jews and Christians could not adopt the Roman custom of burning the dead.

The decorations on the walls were in line with the decorations which are found in the ordinary pagan buildings of the day; but the artists avoided anything suggestive of the pagan gods, or war, or drink, or sex; the cup is found in connexion with the fish or the loaf of bread, not alone. There are no obviously Christian signs; we do not find a cross, for instance, though the common device of the anchor looks like a disguised form of it. The Christian character of these places had to be concealed.

Many of the designs on the walls are the conventional decorations of the day. Amid a trellis-work of lines and ribbons and branches and wreaths, we see flowers and masks and faces, or dolphins sporting in the sea, or butterflies fluttering among the flowers. The little babies with wings are said to represent the souls of the dead; and so are the birds in the air or the fish in the sea or the lambs with their shepherd. The artists keep fairly close to the restrictions which Clement of Alexandria laid down for signet rings: a dove or fish or ship or anchor, or the fisherman at work; all of which admit of a Christian interpretation.

Old Testament scenes, borrowed from the art of the Jewish synagogue, were also in use at this time; among them Noah in the ark, Daniel among the lions, Susanna with the elders, and the 'three children' in the burning fiery furnace. All these paintings symbolize deliverance from death, or endurance of martyrdom. They are the examples which are found embedded in old Hebrew prayers for deliverance, and in the old Roman litanies for the dead or dying. The book of Daniel was the martyr's handbook, and contained the story of Susanna and the song of the 'three children'. Clement of Rome had brought these ideas together in a majestic passage.

What are we to say, my brethren? Was Daniel thrown into the lions' den by men who feared God? Were Ananias and Azarias and Misael shut up in the furnace of fire by men who worshipped according to the majestic and glorious worship of the Most High? God forbid.

Who was it then who did these things? Hateful men and full of all malice were brought to such a degree of rage as to plunge into torment men who served God with a holy and blameless purpose, not knowing that the Most High is a defender and champion of those who in a pure conscience worship his all-virtuous name: To him be glory for ever.   (I Clement, XLV, 5–7.)

This connexion of thought appears again at the end of the century in the commentary of Hippolytus on the Book of Daniel, which is in the same tradition. The references to worship are suggested by the 'Song of the Three Children' in the Septuagint version of Daniel, which passed into Christian liturgy as the 'Benedicite Omnia Opera'.

A few Gospel scenes were also presented in their relation to the Christian sacraments; the baptism of our Lord, the fisherman drawing the fish out of the water, the banquet on fish and loaves of bread, with a cup of wine added to show more clearly what was intended. Other Gospel scenes are rare in this period; but in an old chamber or chapel in the cemetery of Priscilla there is an impressive scene which has the virgin and child on one side and the three magi coming to adore him on the other; but perhaps the Christians of our period would have classed this as an Old Testament subject, since the figures were predicted by Isaiah. In the centre there is a larger figure of a woman, heavily veiled and lifting her hands in prayer; it is a favourite symbol for the soul of the departed. It was probably coming into favour at the end of the second century, and so was the figure of the good shepherd with the lamb carried on his shoulders; the figure is youthful and beardless, and recalls the shepherd-god of the Phrygians, or the angel who instructed Hermas.

We are brought into touch here with the beginning of Christian art, and see it developing in the most natural way out of the Jewish and pagan art-forms which were current at the time. No doubt more ambitious efforts were to be found in the gnostic chapels. We hear of the chapel of Marcellina with its portrait of Christ; and there is the recently discovered vault of the Aureliani which preserves more elaborate efforts in a pagan setting; but the simple, sincere art of the ordinary catacombs speaks to us more directly of the regular central tradition. The study and analysis of these Christian art-forms, as time goes on, may tell us more about primitive Christianity than the documents written by learned theologians; or rather we may be able to use the one to interpret the other. What they do for us is to pick up the story of ordinary church-life in Rome on which we have had no direct light since Clement and Hermas. They are the connecting link between Clement and Hippolytus.

THE MARTYRDOM OF APOLLONIUS, A.D. 183–5

We are fortunate now in having a good account of the trial of a Roman martyr of high rank. Jerome tells us that Apollonius was a senator, and the fact that his trial took place before the senate corroborates this statement. The praetorian prefect presided as the representative of the emperor. Commodus inherited two praetorian prefects in 180, Paternus Tarrutenius and Tigidius Perennis; in 183 Perennis secured the deposition of his rival and controlled the administration for two years, being deposed and put to death in 185. The Greek Acts of the martyr give the name of Perennis as the prefect who conducted the trial; but the Armenian version has transformed this into Terentius, which is thought by some scholars to be a corruption of the name Tarrutenius. In any case we have a very close date for this important trial. The acts are written in the Roman manner, which simply reports the dialogue at the trial, though there seems to be some literary elaboration in this instance. There is no account of the execution.

Apollonius was asked why he had refused to sacrifice to the gods, and gave the traditional reply, '*I am a Christian*'. He had come quickly to the point, and Perennis remonstrated with him and advised him to consider his case and take thought for his life. Such remonstrances seem by now to have become a regular part of the procedure.

On the following day Apollonius announced his determination to abide by his religious convictions and was reminded by Perennis of a decree of the senate which imposed the death penalty on those who would not sacrifice. This seems to be the law to which Athenagoras referred in the last year of Marcus Aurelius. In reply he delivered a discourse in the manner of the apologists on the follies of idolatry, referring, like Justin, to the example of Socrates.

'You have given us enough of your excellent philosophy', said Perennis, 'but the senate has forbidden Christianity.'

Apollonius continued his apology, however, debating the question

21. THE NORTH AFRICAN MARTYRS: AN INSCRIPTION, A RELIQUARY,
AND A CEDARWOOD COFFIN

22. ROMAN TOWNS IN NORTH AFRICA

with Perennis and with a brother-senator who belonged to the Cynic school. He went on to speak of the Logos, and his appearance on earth in the person of Jesus Christ. He quoted the famous passage from the *Republic* of Plato, which said that if a truly righteous man appeared on earth, he would be scourged, bound, have his eyes put out, and at last be crucified. He touched on the prophets, and concluded with a reference to the resurrection and the judgement of God. He belonged, therefore, to the theological school of Justin.

Perennis was reluctant to sentence him, but had no other course of action. 'I wish I could release you,' he said, 'but I am forbidden by the decree of the Emperor Commodus.'

The law could not be evaded once it had been invoked, and Apollonius was beheaded; but the informer who had brought the accusation against him was sentenced to have his legs broken; an action which would effectually discourage other would-be informers. We may hazard the guess that he was a slave in the household of the martyr.

THE CHRISTIAN AND THE ROMAN OFFICIAL

It is clear from this narrative that Perennis was reluctant to put into force the laws against Christians, at least when they affected men of high social or official standing; and the evidence is increasing which shows that there were many of them among the noble families and in the imperial service. He was the chief administrative authority in the empire, and his example would be widely followed. The law was not changed; indeed, it would seem that it had been strengthened; but its actual operation depended upon the action or non-action of the local official in each instance. Tertullian, in a book addressed to the persecutor Scapula, gives instances of local governors who did manage to evade the law. Arrius Antoninus, a relation of the emperor, who was proconsul in Asia in 184–5, arrived at a village where all the inhabitants came out and offered themselves for martyrdom. Such an action was in the nature of a challenge, since no government was likely to wipe out a whole community. He executed some, and drove the rest away. 'Cowards!' he said; 'If you hate life so much, have you no halters or precipices?'

Cincius Severus, at Thysdrus in Africa, suggested safe answers to the accused. Vespronius Candidus and Pudens dismissed certain cases.

It looks as if the tide were turning in favour of the Christians for the moment. The policy of persecution must have been abhorrent to many decent people who were fully informed of the facts of the case; some of them would have friends and relations whom they knew to be Christians; and the policy had not proved effective. As Tertullian said in his *Apology*, 'The blood of Christians is like seed; the faster you mow us down, the thicker we spring up'; an aphorism which is usually quoted in the form 'The blood of the martyrs is the seed of the church.'

CHAPTER 19

THE REFUTATION OF GNOSIS

THE *REFUTATION* OF IRENAEUS, *c.* A.D. 185

The great book of Irenaeus, in five volumes, was written in the hundred-and-eighties, while Eleutherus was bishop of Rome. In the preface to the first volume he asks to be pardoned for his poor Greek; for how can anyone expect elegant Greek from a man who spends his time among the Celts and has to talk to them in their barbarous speech? And in any case it is not an accomplishment that he has ever mastered. The person for whom he is writing obviously did not live among the Celts. He was an important personage who had teaching responsibilities in the church and had asked him, some considerable time before, for a book on the subject of the heresies. Unfortunately his name and rank are not known.

Irenaeus proposes to deal principally with the Valentinian gnostics, since he has a number of pamphlets which give their secret doctrines, and so is in a good position to tackle the subject. The weakness and ineffectiveness of older and better men was due to the fact that they had not been well informed on the heretical 'rules of faith'.

The title of his book was the *Refutation and overturning of the Gnosis which is falsely so called.* The knowledge or 'Gnosis falsely so called' is a phrase from I Timothy, which Hegesippus may have used before him;[1] and the words 'refutation and overturning' may have been borrowed from the Marcionite Apelles, who had undertaken to refute and overturn the revelation of God given by Moses, Eusebius says.

Large portions of the original Greek of Irenaeus are preserved, and

---

[1] See Eusebius, *E.H.* III, 32, 8.

20-2

there is a complete translation into Latin, which seems to have been made not long after the book was written. It is 'barbarous' in character, but fortunately it is very literal. We have to depend upon it for the greater part of the text, and in consequence the book is generally referred to by its Latin title, *Adversus Haereses*, or 'Against the Heresies', which is abbreviated to *Ad. Haer.*, or even *A.H.*; but for general purposes the Greek word *Elenchos*, or even its English equivalent *Refutation*, is coming into fashion.

Later on, he wrote a shorter and simpler volume which he called the *Demonstration of the Apostolic Preaching*, which may similarly be shortened to the *Epideixis* or *Demonstration*. It is a positive outline of Christian teaching, which is interesting for its almost entire dependence on the Old Testament, which was still in the mind of Irenaeus the real Bible of the church. It was discovered not long ago in an Armenian translation; and some fragments of an Armenian translation of the *Refutation* also exist. His writings, therefore, were very widely known.

We shall make no attempt to summarize the *Refutation*, or do justice to its controversial or theological abilities. We shall simply use it to throw light on the development of the Christian religion, as Irenaeus saw it.

THE RULE OF FAITH

Irenaeus opens his first volume of the *Refutation* with a long transcript or summary of the Valentinian system, as it was expounded in the lecture-notes of Ptolemaeus, who was teaching in Rome at this time. It suggests strongly that this was the situation to which the book was primarily addressed, and that the person to whom he dedicated it was a leading Christian in Rome, possibly Bishop Eleutherus himself. The *Demonstration* was dedicated to a certain Marcianus, who may be the Smyrnaean author who wrote up the story of the martyrdom of Polycarp.

Irenaeus goes on to criticize the gnostic allegorization of the Gospels, and to recommend the best defence against their propaganda, which is to hold fast to the rule or 'canon' of truth which the believer had received at his baptism; for this is the faith, he says, which the church dispersed throughout the world had received from the apostles or from the disciples of apostles. It was a faith in

One God the Father Almighty who made heaven and earth and the sea and all that is in them;

And one Christ Jesus, the Son of God, who was made flesh for our salvation;

And the Holy Spirit, who announced by the prophets the dispensations and the advents, and the birth from a virgin, and the Passion, and the resurrection from the dead, and the taking up of the flesh of the beloved Christ Jesus our Lord into the heavens, and his coming from the heavens in the glory of the Father. (Irenaeus, *Ad. Haer.* I, 2.)

He adds to this an eschatological passage which accentuates the supreme exaltation of the Christ, and includes the general resurrection and the righteous judgement.

Here is our first clear view of the baptismal creed in which the faith of the believer was confessed. It embodies in an act of devotion the gospel which had been received by the whole church; 'which is dispersed throughout the world, and yet dwells together as it were in one house; preaching and teaching and transmitting everything in harmony, whether it be in the Germanies or the Spains, or among the Celts, or in the east, or in Egypt or Libya, or in the central parts of the earth', by which he means Asia Minor, Greece, and Rome.

This creed is a formula; no doubt not a fixed formula, but a formula nevertheless; beginning with Hebrew monotheism and ending with apocalyptic music; gathering into unity the powerful phrases in which the gospel had come down from the mouths of the apostles; containing all the passwords of the common Christianity; not complete yet; not perfectly formed; but saying what was needed; what God's people had always believed; in the old language to which they were accustomed; stirring the heart, not merely summarizing doctrines.

It is not a doctrinal diagrammatic statement about the deity or the incarnation or the atonement; it is not an abstract system of definitions, such as we shall find attempted at the end of the century; it is the answer of the Christian believer to God at his supreme moment of personal dedication; and its power and significance is derived from the existential situation in which it was uttered; the entrance into a new life with God which may prove to be the road to martyrdom. It is pre-theological.

MARCUS THE MAGUS

Irenaeus naturally goes on to draw a contrast between this unity in faith and the large amount of variety and difference which existed among the heretical schools and cults. In the course of this he gives a portrait of the head of the Valentinian school in Ephesus, a man named Marcus, a practitioner of the lower type, who excelled in magic and ritual and numerology. He had transformed the Christian parables and sacraments into a sexual mystery-cult, in which he was the chief performer. A deacon in Asia had received this charlatan into his house, and his wife had fallen a victim to his arts. The woman eventually made her profession of penitence and returned to her husband and to the church; so here at any rate there was no doctrine that sin committed after baptism could not be forgiven.

Irenaeus adds that this form of gnosticism had invaded the Rhône valley, where he was now bishop, and this helps to explain his special interest in Marcus. It is also an illustration of the fact that gnosticism operated at different levels. An examination of the mystical theology of Valentine as expounded by Ptolemaeus fails to give the whole picture; gnosticism lacked the moral discipline of the church, and sorcerers like Marcus could make a living out of it.

Irenaeus gives several examples of his numerological and astrological extravagances, and then goes on to gnostic misinterpretations of the scriptures. He mentions too, the inexpressible multitude of apocryphal and bastard scriptures which the gnostics forged; and he gives a story from one of them.

When the Lord was a little child, and was learning his letters, the master said to him, as the custom was, 'Say Alpha', and he said Alpha. But when the master ordered him to say Beta, the Lord answered, 'You tell me first what Alpha means, and then I will tell you what Beta means.'

(Irenaeus, *Ad. Haer.* I, 13, 1.)

The story is also found in the 'Epistle of the Apostles', which is a second-century writing, and in the so-called *Gospel of Thomas*; but here we have it in Ephesus about A.D. 180, which attaches it to a definite time and place. We shall return to this question of apocryphal Gospels in a later chapter.

The apocryphal Gospels and the fantastic rituals are an efflorescence of the Christian imagination when it was liberated from the controls of the apostolic tradition; and they are of great importance to the historian. Strange as they may seem to be, they are attached to the Christian roots at some point and shed light on Christian life at certain levels.

THE *SYNTAGMA* OF JUSTIN

In the making of an ancient book there was no law of copyright or feeling against plagiarism to hamper an author; if a thing had been well written by a previous writer, there was no need to do the work over again. Whole chapters or sequences of chapters were taken over with very slight changes. The limits and origins of these sources can often be detected by modern critical methods.

In the fifteenth chapter of his first volume, we are conscious that Irenaeus is entering upon such a source. It is the *Syntagma of Heresies* which Justin had written in the hundred-and-forties. Irenaeus gives a series of short sketches of the eminent heresiarchs of that time: Simon, Menander, Saturninus (for so Justin spelt the name), Basilides, Carpocrates, Cerinthus, the Ebionites, the Nicolaitans, Cerdo, and Marcion. The same portrait gallery is found, with some changes, in the writings of Hippolytus, the pupil of Irenaeus; and it seems clear that he too was using the *Syntagma* of Justin, which does not survive independently. Both men edited it for their purpose, Irenaeus seems to have omitted the section on Valentine, about whom he has already said so much. He seems to have added the sections on the Ebionites and the Nicolaitans.

The word 'Ebionite' appears here for the first time, and it is the name of a recognizable group or party; but there was no recognizable heresy of Ebionism, it would appear, when Justin wrote. There were simply Jewish Christians of various sorts and degrees. The Ebionite sect described by Irenaeus has no traces of Jewish gnosis; it kept the Law of Moses, practised circumcision, rejected the Virgin Birth, used the Gospel of Matthew, rejected Paul as an apostate, and adored Jerusalem as the house of God. As for the Nicolaitans, it is usually thought that Irenaeus or some informant invented them by combining the Nicolaitans of the Revelation with the Nicolas of Antioch who is mentioned in the Acts; but Clement of Alexandria knew something about this sect.

It would seem that the Ebionites and the Nicolaitans were more active in Asia than in Rome; and the Cerinthians too. Irenaeus has Asia in mind as well as Rome.

It was necessary for Irenaeus to add an appendix to the *Syntagma* of Justin to bring it up to date. It dealt with the encratites, or ascetics, who were on the border-line of heresy, and with Tatian who is described by Jerome as their grim patriarch. Irenaeus regards them as an offshoot of the oriental schools, and affiliates them with Saturninus of Antioch and Marcion of Pontus. He says that the Egyptian sects, which followed Basilides and Carpocrates, tended to develop in the opposite direction, and thought nothing of promiscuous sexual intercourse, a multiplicity of marriages, and participation in the banquets of the gods. His remarks are based on his own observation, but they may be rather sweeping; and his personal feeling against Tatian is not concealed. Irenaeus will not concede him even the virtue of originality. He borrowed all his opinions from others except for his dogma that Adam could not be saved; that one he invented for himself. (Now Irenaeus had an affectionate interest in Adam.)

He follows this discussion with a number of obscure Ophite myths, which should be treated under the heading of Christian imaginative writing, or possibly Christian polytheism.

THE TRADITION OF THE ELDERS

We may excuse ourselves from the task of ploughing through his second volume, in which he refutes the gnostic mythology on logical and metaphysical grounds; but we may take from it a typical example of the 'tradition of the elders', which he knew in his youth and used now as a supplementary authority which explained and elucidated the apostolic gospel. We have already given one or two of these, which he took apparently from the pages of Papias, though he claimed personal access to the tradition through his contact with Polycarp.

There was a controversy of long standing on the length of the Lord's ministry, from his baptism to his Passion, which is of interest also to modern scholars. There was a view which was based apparently on Mark (or Matthew) that the ministry of Jesus lasted for exactly twelve months; but Irenaeus was able to meet this theory with evidence and inferences from the Gospels of Luke and John;[1] and these arguments in their turn could be supported by the living voice of the apostolic 'elders'.

And all the elders bear witness, those who accompanied [*convenerunt*] with John the disciple of the Lord in Asia, saying that this was the tradition of

[1] This chronology based on Luke and John was also known to Melito: see chapter 14.

John; for he continued with them up to the times of Trajan; and some of them had seen, not only John, but other apostles too, and had heard the same things from them, and bear witness to this report.

(Irenaeus, *Ad. Haer.* II, 33, 3.)

Here is a tradition from the Asia Minor school which Irenaeus was in a position to transmit out of his personal knowledge. The word 'elder' had been used by Papias of the apostles themselves; it is now used by Irenaeus of the venerable men who had heard the apostles and instructed him; it has the general meaning, in either case, of the senior men, now beyond recall, who were the bearers of the tradition in their day. He uses the word of Ignatius of Antioch, and of the Roman bishops prior to Soter. It is the same conception of succession that we find in the Rabbinic schools; it is an inheritance from the Jewish period of Christianity.

THE GOSPELS IN THE CHURCH

In his third volume Irenaeus takes up again the question of the apostolic gospel, which he regards as the creative and unifying impulse in the church. He insists that it was originally an oral 'kerugma' or preachment; and that is what in essence it continues to be. It was taken to the bounds of the earth by the apostles, each of whom had perfect knowledge of it and possessed it in its entirety. He is refuting here the criticisms of the gnostics, who held that the original apostles did not fully understand it; he is also preparing the way for the phenomenon of diversity in its presentation.

Matthew, he thinks, was the first to reduce the oral gospel to writing.

Now Matthew produced among the Hebrews, in their own language, a written form of the gospel, while Peter and Paul were proclaiming the gospel in Rome, and laying the foundation of the church. After their departure [by which he means their martyrdom] Mark, the disciple and interpreter of Peter, handed down to us himself in written form what had been preached by him [Peter]; and Luke the follower of Paul set down in a book the gospel which was preached by him. Then John the disciple of the Lord, who reclined upon his breast, himself produced the Gospel while living in Ephesus of Asia.

(Irenaeus, *Ad. Haer.* III, 1, 1.)

Irenaeus impresses us throughout his book by his strong feeling for history. He harbours no legendary or miraculous or picturesque additions to the apostolic tradition; the Christian world was full of it, and he rejects it all. The Gospel was written down in four forms in accordance with its fields of expansion: they represent the schools of Matthew, Peter, Paul and John.

This is another formula, a Roman formula. It has a date concealed in it which has a Roman sound. The Romans counted their years from the foundation of the city, *ab urbe condita*; in this document the fixed point is the founding of the Roman church. That was the time when Matthew was writing his Gospel in the Hebrew language. The statement, as a statement, is unobjectionable; we know that Irenaeus, in some way or another, identifies this Hebrew Gospel with the canonical Matthew, and doubtless that was very generally done now; but the formula does not say this. It says that Matthew gave out his Gospel in the language of the Hebrews.

It was after the martyrdoms that Mark delivered the preaching of Peter in a written form 'to us'; that is to say to the Romans. We are in a part of the *Refutation* where the words 'to us' are constantly appearing with this meaning. It is a Roman document, a Roman source perhaps, though Irenaeus obviously shares its sentiments. He grounds his treatment of the Gospels in the year of the foundation of the Roman church;[1] he enumerates the succession of Roman bishops from that date as a means of measuring historical time; he leads up to a statement about the Roman church which glorifies it as old and famous and apostolic.

The Gospel formula has two more interesting points about it. One is that while it contains two statements which are also found in Papias, it is not dependent upon him; Papias was not interested in the places where the Gospels originated, or their relative dates. The other is that it is plain and realistic and has no legendary colouring; it does not profess to know where Luke wrote his Gospel, though others did. It reads like prologue-material. Marcion or someone in his church had been equipping the Pauline Epistles with brief introductory notes saying where and why they were written; they were widely copied in the catholic church, and appear in medieval manuscripts. 'Anti-Marcionite' prologues were composed for the four Gospels, which we made use of in our first volume. The Marcionite church would only require one Gospel prologue of course, since it had only one Gospel;

---

[1] For the 'foundation' of the Roman church, see the note at the end of this chapter.

the 'anti-Marcionite' prologue to Luke looks like an answer to such a single prologue; and this Roman formula which is used by Irenaeus looks like a single prologue or preface which might serve for a unified fourfold Gospel. A more extended collection of prologue material is found in the Muratorian Catalogue.

THE ROMAN TRADITION

The four Gospels had been criticized by the heretics, who claimed that they were not accurate, or had no authority, or disagreed with one another; but Irenaeus does not regard them as the primary authority. The primary authority was the living voice, and we may perhaps have an echo of Papias here. The living voice, or gospel message, or oral tradition, was entrusted by the apostles to a flesh-and-blood corporation which Irenaeus calls the succession of the elders in the churches; and he associates with these 'elders' the bishops who were appointed in the churches by the apostles, and the successions which are derived from them.

It was quite possible, he says, to enumerate the various lists of bishops to whom the apostles had entrusted their own positions as teachers or masters; but this would take too long; so he contents himself with taking the ancient and glorious church of Rome, so well known to all, 'having been founded and constituted by the two apostles, Peter and Paul, and holding firm the tradition which it had received from the apostles, and the faith which was proclaimed to mankind and had come down through the successions of bishops as far as ourselves'; and here again is the inclusive 'we', which intimates that Irenaeus is writing as a Roman for Romans at this point.

And to this church, on account of its more powerful leadership,[1] it is necessary for every church to gather [*convenire*]; that is to say the faithful from all quarters; because the tradition from the apostles is preserved there by those who come from all quarters. (Irenaeus, *Ad. Haer.* III, 3, 1.)

We have already made use of this important passage which unfortunately is only extant in the Latin translation. There has been a good deal of discussion about its precise meaning. The word *convenire* which I have translated as 'gather', is sometimes translated 'agree'; but the

---

[1] 'Potentiorem principalitatem': see note at end of chapter.

expression *convenire ad* ought to mean motion to. The word was used in our previous extract about the elders to translate the original Greek word *sumballein*, which means to accompany; and in a quotation which I give later it translates *sunelthein*, which means to come together; and these instances seem to show what the usage of the translator was. In any case the international character, the powerful leadership and the central position of the Roman church are fully vouched for.

There were two great historical causes which gave the Roman church its position of 'more powerful leadership'. One was the tradition of the two apostles, who had preached in Rome and founded the church by their witness to death. The other was that all roads lead there. There was no other international centre with schools and local communities representative of so many races. Jewish, Syrian, Egyptian and Asian teachers 'convened' there, each representing the apostolic tradition in one form or another. The faith was preserved there by the representative men who came from all quarters. Traditions and interpretations could be checked; error could be refuted and overthrown; the true character of the universal faith could be clarified.

A third point must be added—the solidity, conservatism, hospitality and generosity of the Roman church itself. We may also add its record of fidelity to the faith. Clement still had the oral teaching of the apostles ringing in his ears, Irenaeus says; or is it Hegesippus quoted by Irenaeus? Ignatius had declared that the Roman church was filtered free from any foreign stain. It was invaded by heresy under Hyginus, but it recovered under Pius. It had the Roman virtue of stability, and was in communication with what was called the whole world; but there is no evidence whatever of any centralized organization. The nature of inter-church action through regional councils and correspondence will become apparent when we come to the records of the Paschal controversy.

THE EPISCOPAL SUCCESSIONS

We are now in a part of the book where Irenaeus is deriving his material from Hegesippus, and it is perfectly possible that what he had to say about the Gospels and the Roman church was based on Hegesippus, too, though there is nothing in it which would not have been common knowledge. The Gospels could not have been distributed with less information than that.

Hegesippus had made his list of Roman bishops in the episcopate of Anicetus, and continued it down to the episcopate of Eleutherus, under whom Irenaeus was writing. It was through this order and this succession, he says, that the tradition of the apostles and the preaching of the truth came even unto us. Once again the words 'we' and 'us' emphasize his personal participation in the Roman tradition; but he is careful to insist that it was not unique.

The other great apostolic see-cities had their episcopal successions too, a statement which he supports by referring to the tradition of Asia, which was his first love. He gives a good account of Polycarp, who had been 'made a disciple' by apostles, and had associated with many who had seen the Christ. He had been established by the apostles as a bishop for Asia in the church at Smyrna; and there Irenaeus had seen him personally, in his early manhood;[1] for he survived for a long time, and was a man of great age, and witnessed gloriously as a martyr. He mentions Polycarp's visit to Rome to confer with Anicetus, and his refusal to recognize the heretic Marcion. He gives Polycarp's anecdote about John and Cerinthus, and mentions his Epistle to the Philippians. He also refers to the church at Ephesus, which had been founded by Paul, and where John had survived into the times of Trajan, some eighty years before the date of writing: that is to say, the boundary of living memory.

THE FOUR-GOSPEL CANON

Irenaeus then gives further information from Hegesippus which deals with the arrival in Rome of the great heresiarchs, and after some argument on this point returns to the topic of the written Gospels. There were heretics who made capital of the fact that their beginnings were all so different. These heretics were content with one Gospel only: the Ebionites with Matthew; the Marcionites with their abbreviated Luke; the Cerinthians with Mark; while the Valentinians favoured John above the rest.

This argument about the different 'faces' or 'beginnings' of the four Gospels appears in other sources. A book in the form of a roll was necessarily known by its beginning, since one would unroll a little of it

---

[1] He had listened to Polycarp *with Florinus* as a boy (*eti pais ōn*). He is thinking now of a later period when he was a young man.

to identify it, if it had no *frons* or label attached to it. Irenaeus had an old piece of orthodox gnosis which glorified this diversity; it was based on the accepted apocalyptic mysticism. The whole work of God in creation and revelation was fourfold, or was so described in the mystical tradition; there were four winds, four points of the compass, four seasons of the year, four principal constellations in the skies. He who sat on the throne of the heavens sent out his spirits north and south and east and west; the Lamb of God in the Revelation, who is also the Word, unsealed the scroll of mystery, and four riders on four horses rode out into the world. (Revelation vi. 1–8; see also Mark xiii. 27, Matt. xxiv. 31.)

It is impossible to unravel all this astral symbolism here; but it is possible to make two points about it. One is that the expansion of the gospel is universal; it speeds out in all directions. The other is that it is diversified; it assumes different forms; and that is what is symbolized by the number four. The four living beings which uphold the throne of God in Ezekiel and John have different faces; the bull, the lion, the eagle, and the man, corresponding to the four constellations which mark out the cardinal points of the heavens. These are the 'faces' which he assigns to the four Gospels; the lion for John representing the princely and glorious birth, the bull for Luke representing the priestly and sacrificial character; the man for Matthew representing his birth as a man; the eagle for Mark representing the descent of the Spirit and the gift of prophecy.

This ancient mythological wisdom is not without its more profound meaning. It is easy to see that the creative power never repeats itself identically. It expresses itself diversely and requires all the diversities in order to express the truth. The church would have been poorer with only one form of the gospel tradition. It had to have four; and four was enough.

The four apocalyptic animals have continued to be used in the church tradition as emblems of the evangelists, though the lion has been allotted to Mark and the eagle to John. We have here another example of the poetic or artistic efflorescence of the gospel which found its way into the devotional life of the church. It would appear that this imaginative art-form is more characteristic of primitive Christianity than the definitions of the philosopher. The poet and the artist may be able to interpret something in the work of the prophets and evangelists which the theologian does not always see: the theologian comes later and works out the implications of the tradition. Irenaeus attempts this task himself with the help of his predecessors. He distinguishes and defines.

THE NEW TESTAMENT

From the Gospels he passes to the Acts, in which the most authoritative parts for him are the speeches of the apostles and the decrees of their council at Jerusalem, the old mother-city of Christendom. The apostles are his authority, rather than the book. He also uses the Revelation, the Epistles of Paul, I Peter and two Epistles of John. He includes an interesting dissertation on Luke, in which he says that everybody made use of selected extracts from his Gospel, some of which he enumerates; thus suggesting that he was not always read through in course, as we have presumed to suggest that Matthew and Mark were. He points out how absurd it is for the heretics to use these Lucan 'Gospels', as he calls them, and at the same time to reject the book of Acts by the same author; or to set a high value on Paul and reject the narrative which was written by his trusted companion.

Irenaeus, therefore, had a New Testament very like ours; and he sometimes alludes to a Gospel or an Epistle as 'scripture'; but it is not right to attach too precise a definition to this word in the second century. The word *graphe*, or 'writing', is obviously used for holy books in a religious tradition, but more cannot be said. Among the Jews it was the third and last class of inspired books that were given the title of the 'writings', *kethubhim*, a name which was used to distinguish them from the Law and the prophets. Irenaeus also applies it to Hermas, which he quotes once, but no precise deduction as to inspiration or canonicity can be drawn from this, except that he regards it as a holy book. He takes them all as he finds them in the church tradition; they are all holy writings. At one moment he treats them as a sacred text; at another he can discuss their origin or authorship in an objective way. Nevertheless, he had a collection of apostolic or near-apostolic books, whose authority stood apart from the rest; and the glimpse we thus get of the development of a New Testament is very important.

The striking point about this embryo New Testament is its conservative and critical character. He makes no use of the numerous 'apocryphal' books, the apocalypses, visions, oracles, manifestations, and Sibylline verses which abounded in his time; still less the apocryphal Acts or Gospels. He does not even use the *Revelation of Peter*, which was read in the Roman church; he does not use II Peter or Hebrews. It is doubtful whether he uses James. There are no traces of III John, but the lack of a quotation from so small an Epistle does not prove that he did not know it. He mentions the Epistle of Clement, and more than one of Polycarp. He quotes once each from Hermas and Ignatius, but without naming the author. He supplements these writings with the testimony of his Asian elders, specially mentioning Papias.

He must have had a very full apostolic and sub-apostolic library, to which must be added Justin and Hegesippus among his senior contemporaries.

THE OLD TESTAMENT

The real Bible of Irenaeus was the Old Testament. When he comes to write his *Demonstration* which is a manual of the Christian faith, he uses the Old Testament throughout to prove his points.

The principal theological emphasis of Irenaeus is the historical solidarity of Judaism and Christianity. The God who created the world and revealed himself to the Jews was also the God of the Christians. His revelation was continuous; Jesus Christ was his Son; the apostles proclaimed no other God. The scriptures of the Jews are the scriptures of the Christians.

But when he takes up the Old Testament he is obliged to refer to the new interpretations and the new translations, just as preachers and writers have to do today. He mentions the new translation by Theodotion of Ephesus and the earlier one by Aquila of Pontus, both of whom, he says, were converts to Judaism. These translations were also used by those Ebionites who asserted that Jesus was the son of Joseph; they translated the famous text from Isaiah as, 'The maiden shall be with child and bring forth a son'; not, as in the Septuagint, 'The virgin shall be with child and bring forth a son.'

Irenaeus points out the antiquity of the Septuagint translation, which was made by the Jews themselves long before the coming of the Lord. It is plain that he knows no Hebrew himself. He tells the story of the translation of the Hebrew scriptures by the seventy 'elders' in the days of Ptolemy II, and is the first to add the miraculous feature that they each made a separate translation, and, when they came together

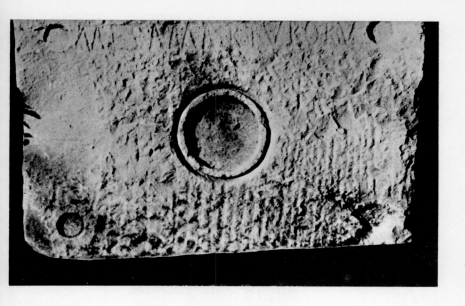

23. CHRISTIAN SYMBOLISM IN NORTH AFRICA

24. CATACOMB PAINTING

(*convenientibus ipsis*), it was found that they had all translated the Hebrew by the same phrases and words from the beginning to the end; so God was glorified, and it was established beyond doubt that this translation was inspired. Here is a tale accepted by Irenaeus which does not stand up to critical investigation. The legend had been amplified since Justin wrote it down. The Septuagint is an inspired translation, it asserts; the new ones cannot compete with it.

Irenaeus goes on to point out that the apostles, Peter and John and Matthew, all used this translation, made by the 'elders'. He establishes a succession, that is, from the prophets who wrote the Hebrew books, through the elders who translated them, down to the apostles who used them in proclaiming the gospel. This biblical succession was a fact of history, though in a rather different way from this. The Septuagint had been the Bible of the Hellenistic synagogue, and had never lost that position when the Hellenistic synagogue was transformed into the Hellenistic church; it was one of the continuous liturgical factors. Its position was not unchallenged, however, even among Gentile Christians. The new 'adoptionist' schools in Rome which had some affinity with Ebionism, interested themselves in the textual criticism of the Hebrew scriptures, and it would not be long before Origen devoted himself to the same task in Palestine.

We must not look for such an attitude in Irenaeus. He was no more interested in textual criticism than in philosophic speculation; he was interested in the historical revelation which had come down to him through the Hebrew prophets within the Christian church; the incarnation of the Son of God; the apostolic preaching; and the succession of elders in the church. Not that he approved of all elders without distinction. He condemns the minute studies and legal elaborations of the Jewish elders of the Pharisee tradition, and he reprobates those elders of the church who separated themselves from the episcopal succession, and held assemblies by themselves; they were heretics or schismatics or hypocrites; they were playing with strange fire like Nadab and Abihu. He was thinking perhaps of his quondam friend Florinus and other suspected members of the Roman presbytery.

THE LAW OF MOSES

Irenaeus has an interesting analysis of the Law of Moses, which should be compared with the analysis of it which was made by the contemporary gnostic, Ptolemaeus. There were two classes of precepts, Irenaeus says. First there were the precepts of nature, or common morality, by which men were justified before ever the Law of Moses was given. They are summarized in the Ten Commandments, and similar passages, which the Lord came to 'fulfil'. These had a certain quality of servitude or slavery about them which had to be removed so that men could follow God without fetters. They had to be transformed by Jesus into a law of liberty, a possible echo of the Epistle of James. Irenaeus, with his feeling for history, could sense the idea of progress in a historic revelation. It was necessary to begin with secondary things, he says, before attaining to the primary. Men were called through types and symbols to the reality; through temporal things to the eternal; through the fleshly to the spiritual; through the earthly to the heavenly. So there was law and discipline and prophecy of better things in the future for Israel in that period.

The second class of precepts was given them because of the 'hardness of their hearts', and even the new covenant was not free from legislation of this kind; the apostle Paul had made concessions to his flock because of the 'weakness of their flesh'; a statement which bears some resemblance to the views of Montanus. But what Irenaeus really has in mind at this point is the ceremonial law, which was given to the Jews as a second best when they failed to accept the higher revelation at Mount Sinai. It was a necessary discipline for them and was not without its symbolic significance, since it was a gift from God; but its binding character had been cancelled by the new covenant of liberty; and those laws which were natural and free and common to all mankind had been increased and broadened.

This criticism of the Old Testament is based on principles which had been expounded in the Pauline Epistles, and Hebrews, and Barnabas, and Justin. Its attempt to distinguish a universal and spiritual morality which was harmonious with the inborn moral feeling of the human heart was the work of a mind which could distinguish between different levels of insight in a religious tradition. It presents Jesus as a teacher of ethics who worked within an imperfect but progressive revelation, expanding it into full perfection. Irenaeus is perfectly familiar with the idea of organic growth in history. It is his strong point.

Furthermore, he can make a penetrating analysis of holy books and develop the general principles which underly them.

THE GOSPEL OF INCORRUPTIBILITY

Enough has been said to show that it is very difficult to assess Irenaeus as a theologian, since more than one emphasis is to be discerned in his thinking. It is best to look upon him as an expositor; the expositor of an ancient traditional religious culture. He accepts it as he finds it. He never invents what he writes. He is an interpreter.

We dare not enter deeply into the question of his theology or theologies. It would seem that he did not have the theological approach. At any rate he did not have a system of philosophy or doctrine through which he could unify his various points of view. What he had was a certain vision and appreciation of the prophetic and evangelical and catholic tradition as a whole. It may be rather audacious to attempt a sketch of it, but we will try.

It was determined by history. He was not interested in what God did before creation. He did not begin in eternity with an infinite being and a co-essential thought-process or logos-power. He began with a spiritual deity who had involved himself in matter and materialism; his joy was to create, and to continue creating, and to reveal himself in his creation. The nature of his creation was to be organic and responsive and progressive and free; but these words are inadequate; in the language of Irenaeus himself, its nature was to be fertile and to 'fructify'. It is the theology of the Marcan seed parables. God's creation and revelation is perpetually growing, increasing, enlarging, maturing, and coming to perfection. God was revealed to man within this process, and so the process of revelation was organic and progressive too. It came to a precocious maturity at one point in cosmic history, when man, the darling son of the universe, and the image of his Creator, first came into existence. He was perfectly made, but immature. He was a child;[1] God's child; and he was lost. He gave way to the powers of evil, and passed under the dominion of death and corruption. The rather

---

[1] The Ebionites held that Adam was a perfect man, being made in the image of God and animated with his Spirit.

dramatic, rather materializing, perhaps-too-flesh-and-blood imagination of Irenaeus comes out here. It is not death-and-*sin* he thinks of, like St Paul in Romans, but death-and-*corruption*, though that is a Pauline word too. Man is not so much under judgement and needing to be atoned for by blood; he is lost and dying and under the dominion of the evil power, and needing to be saved and set free and restored to life.

The word 'corruption' must not be understood simply as bodily decay; it is the process of ruin or deterioration which goes on in the whole man, body, soul and spirit. It is the inheritance of mortality in which death is the decisive point so far as our present bodily life is concerned.

There is something Greek, perhaps, in the thought of a salvation from mortality; something Greek, too, in his conception of the remedy, and in the 'mythological' turn of his thinking at this point. Man must be deified. Divine power and spirit must be infused into him to overcome the powers of dissolution, to which his mortal nature is subject; a transfusion of life and spirit by which he will become God as he was originally destined to do. The divine Son of God, the eternal true Man from heaven, enters the world with new life and power, and takes that ruined and corrupted nature into union with himself. He comes in the heart of the sacred preordained area of redemption, and brings everything that man needs; he takes up the curse; he endures the death; he overcomes it; he rises again in glory; he offers all mankind the victory. He infuses new life; incorruption; immortality.

The creative energies of God never pause; they constantly bring forth more fruit. The Son of God moves onward as his gospel is proclaimed to the world in the church; he bestows his spirit; he bestows incorruption; through the gospel preaching, through the teaching, through the waters of baptism, and in the universal sacrifice of the eucharist. He restores, he renews, he mends human personalities, he liberates men from death and decay; he endows them with immortality; they become once again God's darling sons.

God becomes man that man may become God.

THE END OF THE MYTH

Such, in a paraphrase, is the picture one gets of the vision of Irenaeus. How far it is a logical systematic theology one is not prepared to say. Certainly it coheres.

At any rate it represents the preaching of a theologically minded, deeply learned, highly imaginative pastor of souls. It is how he talked, how he lectured, how he preached, how he dealt with scripture and how he answered questions. And now at one point it verges on theology, and now at another it verges on myth, or, as we would say, poetry. And while, at one moment, we have the poetic genius of the Asian mind with its love of sensuous imagery, at another we have the practical Roman mentality with its feeling for order and history and succession. Quite steady, however, is the vision of the whole creation as the ever-growing medium of God's creative power, and man, as his darling child, ever growing nearer to his likeness as he is infused with divine grace; and if the thinking of Irenaeus seems to the pure theologian or the Lutheran evangelical to be too sensuous, and insufficiently aware of the reality of guilt, or the terror of God's judgement upon sinful man, let it be remembered that it was formulated in opposition to the glossy and unsubstantial mirage of the gnostic other-world, and the notion of an automatic salvation for superior minds through knowledge. The salvation which he proclaims is the salvation of Adam, the common man.

His preoccupation with this world and its destiny leads him to close on the vision of the redeemed earth; and now the Asian mysticism with its dreams of an earthly paradise takes complete control. He accepts all the promises of the prophets with a child-like literalism which is in complete contrast to his profound analysis of the symbolism of soteriology. A new earth, restored and redeemed, rises before his eyes. The chiliasm of Phrygian prophets and elders, to whom he had listened in his younger days, takes possession of his imagination. He quotes the sayings of the men of that generation. Matter and substance will not pass away, but the fashion of the world will be changed. Jerusalem on earth will be rebuilt according to the image of the Jerusalem in heaven. Men will forget how to die. The earth will bear fruit out of its own fertility, and by means of the dew of heaven. The wolf and the lamb will feed together, and the lion will eat straw like the ox; and if the straw in those days can feed a lion, what manner of wheat will it produce for men?

Irenaeus loves this world. He will not have it destroyed by fire; he will have it infused with more creative life. He has no interest in an other-worldly Elysium; this world is good enough for him. What can be better for man, than God's own creation, when it has reached perfection?

APPENDIX

Text of the 'Anti-Marcionite' Gospel Prologues

1. *To Mark*: extant only in Latin.

Mark comes next, who is called stumpy-fingered,[1] because he had fingers which were too short in proportion to the rest of his bodily development. He was the interpreter of Peter. After Peter's own 'departure' he wrote this Gospel in the regions of Italy.

2. *To Luke*: extant in Greek as well as in Latin.

There is Luke, a Syrian of Antioch, a physician by profession, who had been a follower of the apostles, and afterwards followed Paul until his martyrdom, serving the Lord without distraction; he was unmarried and had no children, and fell asleep at the age of eighty-four in Boeotia, full of the Holy Spirit.

There were already Gospels in existence, the one according to Matthew written in Judaea, and the one according to Mark in Italy; but he, being moved by the Holy Spirit, composed this whole Gospel[2] in the regions about Achaea, making plain in the introduction this very point, that there had been others written before him, and that it was necessary to set forth the accurate narrative of the dispensation for the benefit of the faithful from among the Gentiles, so that they would not be disturbed by Jewish mythologizings, or be deceived by heretical and vain fantasies, and so depart from the truth. Of necessity, therefore, we have received, at the beginning, the birth of John, who is the beginning of the gospel, having been the forerunner of the Lord, and a participant in the perfecting of the gospel and in the management of the baptism, and in the fellowship of the Spirit; of which dispensation the prophet Malachi makes mention, being one of the Twelve.

And then after that Luke wrote the Acts of the Apostles; and after that John the apostle, being one of the Twelve, wrote the Revelation in the island of Patmos; and after that the Gospel.

3. *To John*: extant only in Latin.

The Gospel of John was manifested and given to the churches by John, while still living in the body, as a certain person, Papias by name, a man of Hierapolis, a dear disciple of John, has related in the *Exoterica*, that is to say in the last five books; for he wrote down the Gospel correctly, as John dictated it. But Marcion the heretic, when he had been rebuked by him, because his opinions were contrary, was rejected by John;[3] for he had brought writings or letters to him from the brethren who were in Pontus.

Notes. (1) The nickname 'stumpy-fingered' for Mark is used by Hippolytus also in an anti-Marcionite context. (2) Luke's Gospel is the *whole* Gospel, not the shortened version used by Marcion. (3) Perhaps in the original Greek Marcion was rebuked by Papias, and rejected on the authority of the writings or teachings of John: *abjectus est ab Johanne.*

The Lucan prologue was obviously composed in connexion with an incipient canon which included as a minimum the four Gospels with the Acts and the Revelation.

A NOTE ON THE FOUNDATION OF THE ROMAN CHURCH

We have ventured to suggest that the 'foundation' of the Roman church by the apostles Peter and Paul in Irenaeus is a date which may be compared with the foundation of the city by Romulus and Remus. Since writing this, we have noted the importance of the fact adduced by O. Cullman in his recent book *Peter: Disciple, Apostle, Martyr* (tr. by F. V. Filson, Philadelphia, 1953) that the date assigned to the foundation of the city was 29 June, which was also adopted for the commemoration of the martyrdoms of Peter and Paul.

We point out in chapter 26 that the latter date first appears in the Liberian Calendar opposite the year 258 where it is allotted to the 'deposition' of Peter and Paul, the word 'depositio' being used in this document for the burial of a bishop. It is clear if we connect these three points, that the founding of the Roman church was associated with the martyrdoms of the two apostles; and this of course is the point from which the episcopal years are calculated. Perhaps the word 'depositio' (laying down) originated as a figure of speech derived from the laying of foundation stones. Such an idea could then be connected with the imagery of tower-building in the Visions of Hermas, in which apostles, teachers, bishops, and deacons form the foundation stones of the church.

However this may be, the glory of the ancient Roman church is certainly associated in the mind of Irenaeus with its foundation by the two apostles. He also allots it a 'more powerful leadership' *(potentiorem principalitatem)* or 'very powerful leadership' as it may be translated. There is no agreement unhappily about the meaning of the latter word; but it can be argued that the word 'principalitas', being connected with 'princeps' (the first man of a number) contains the idea of primacy or presidency; and this is connected by some scholars with the statement of Ignatius that the Roman church presides in the region of the Romans: see vol. 1, chap. 24. It is true that the word 'princeps' was a title of the Emperor, but only in virtue of his position as the first man on the senatorial roll. But the word certainly does suggest someone who has a position as first in relation to others of the same standing.

It is remarkable indeed that nobody refers to the promise made to Peter in Matthew xvi. 18. Indeed, the apostolic pre-eminence of Rome at this time was founded on her possession of both the great apostles, who were coupled together in connexion with her by Clement and Ignatius and Dionysius; and also by Gaius in his reference to the two monuments. It was the fusion of their two traditions which took place in the latter half of the first century, and its alliance with the tradition of John which took place early in the second century, that gave Rome its unique position. It had also accepted from Syria at about the same time the Gospel of Matthew, and had awarded it the premier place among the four; it had accepted it as representing the Jewish Gospel of Matthew which it looked upon as contemporary with the preaching of Peter and Paul at Rome. Matthew must, to some extent, have displaced their own Gospel of Mark.

We see here an example of what Irenaeus meant by his statement that the faith was preserved in Rome by those who flocked there from all parts. It is all very different from the Syrian picture of Peter transmitting his authority to Clement as first bishop, a view which may, for all we know, single out for attention one important factor in the multiple tradition of the 'ancient and glorious church'.

CHAPTER 20

CREED, CANON AND LITURGY

OLD CREED FORMS

We saw in the *Refutation* of Irenaeus that the candidate for baptism received a creed which became his rule of faith. It is not considered likely that the words of this creed were rigidly fixed or everywhere the same; but Irenaeus implies that the agreement in the catholic church was great enough to be counted on. The text given by Irenaeus owes something, no doubt, to his own special theological interests, but its substance and form were traditional. It consisted of two parts; a 'trinitarian' part which expressed faith in the Father, the Son, and the Holy Spirit; and a 'christological' part which included the content of the gospel message.

Creed forms of many kinds had existed from the first. The oldest of all was the Jewish *Shema*: 'Hear, O Israel, the Lord is thy God, the Lord is one.' This 'unitarian' form, as we may call it for convenience, persisted in the Christian church in the watchword 'One God', but gave birth quite early to the form 'One God, One Lord', which has been called a 'binitarian' form. We recognize it in such apostolic salutations as 'Grace be with you from God the Father and our Lord Jesus Christ'. But these forms were not associated with baptism. The baptismal forms seem to have been either trinitarian or christological; and finally they were both.

St Paul summarizes the act of faith which was made at baptism in the words 'Jesus Christ is Lord', accompanied by the conviction in the heart that God raised him from the dead; that is to say it was a vocal assent to the gospel message given with faith. Other forms were 'Jesus is Lord' or 'Jesus is the Son of God'; their meaning being dictated of course by the content of the gospel message to which assent was being given. In some instances the act of faith continued to be an assent to the gospel message; in others the content of the gospel message was incorporated into the act of faith; and we can see the steps by which this was managed as early as the Epistles of Ignatius and the *Apology* of Aristides; but we cannot assert that these declarations were used at baptism.

There are also trinitarian forms in the writings of Paul, the finest of which is the formula of blessing at the end of II Corinthians; but it does not look as if these were used at baptism. The use of the trinitarian formula in baptism was established in a rather different way. There was a form of words which was used by the baptizer, which involved an 'invocation of the name', though of course the act of faith made by the candidate might be described by this term. Christians were alluded to as those who called upon the name, or more probably those who called the name upon themselves, or occasionally those who had had the name called upon them. Such invocations were also used in the case of exorcism, and exorcism was closely related to baptism. In fact it became the general custom to exorcize every candidate for baptism during his preparation period; and Justin tells us how devils were exorcized in the name of Jesus Christ who was crucified under Pontius Pilate, which sounds like a credal phrase.

In the Acts of the Apostles we read of baptism into the name of the Lord Jesus; but in Matthew and the *Didache* we have baptism into the name of the Father and of the Son and of the Holy Spirit, where it is connected with the command to baptize the Gentiles. This trinitarian form or outline became the general one, and we found it in Justin in an expanded form. The developed baptismal creeds included all these elements.

THE BAPTISMAL CREEDS

In order to transform the baptismal creed given by Irenaeus into the creed form which everyone knows today, all that was necessary was to take the christological part of it, with its emphasis on 'born, suffered, died, rose again', and insert it into the middle section of the trinitarian part. This simple rearrangement was effected very soon; in fact it may have been done already. We find it in the *Apostolic Tradition* of his pupil Hippolytus, written some thirty or forty years later, but embodying in a fixed written form the customs and traditions of his youth.

There was a dialogue in which the convert gave assent to the credal material, which was put to him in the form of a question. The baptizer stood by the candidate in the water, and asked him three questions, to each of which he answered 'I believe', and each time the baptizer laid his hand upon his head and immersed him. These questions were:

Dost thou believe in God the Father Almighty? *I believe.*

Dost thou believe in Christ Jesus the Son of God, who was born of the Holy Spirit from the Virgin Mary, and crucified under Pontius Pilate, and dead and buried, and rose again on the third day living from the dead, and ascended into heaven, and sat on the right hand of the Father, and will come to judge the living and the dead? *I believe.*

Dost thou believe in the Holy Spirit and the holy church and the resurrection of the flesh? *I believe.*

This is the earliest known form of the old Roman Creed. It is interesting that it does not begin with the words 'one God the Father Almighty', as it does in Irenaeus and Tertullian, a difference for which learned scholars have supplied more than one explanation; the presence of the word 'one', which appears in the oriental creed, guards against Marcionism and kindred heresies; its absence might be accounted for by a reaction against 'monarchianism'. This creed had an interesting history after this period, and appears not very much changed as the baptismal creed of the west, commonly called the Apostles' Creed.

The 'interrogatory' form of the creed used at baptism may be older than the declaratory form, in which the candidate says the creed for himself; but an early 'declaratory' form is found in the Western Text of the Acts, which puts into the mouth of the Ethiopian eunuch a simple christological declaration, 'I believe that Jesus Christ is the Son of God'.

THE BAPTISMAL RITE

It would be unwise to attempt to form a theory of the development of the baptismal rite by arranging the *Didache* and Justin and Hippolytus in an ascending scale. The *Didache* and Justin give only partial impressions, and we should have to take into account other literature such as the *Epistle of Barnabas* and the heretical rituals, as well as the apostolic and sub-apostolic literature. There was a variety of elements in the baptismal ritual from the beginning which were consolidated in the second century, and our different authorities deal with it from different points of view. We would also have to take into account the Jewish rituals which preceded the Christian sacraments. Recent study has proved that the pattern of Jewish liturgical usage reappears in the Christian sacraments, and must have been a controlling factor from the first.

It would not be right to assume that every phrase in Hippolytus came down to him from the period of Eleutherus, but most of the customs which he regulates must have been old even then. He tells us that the sacrament of baptism was preceded by a period of preparation which included prayer, fasting and exorcism; as a rule it lasted three years. The catechumens were excluded from the prayers of the brethren, but had their own prayers in the house of their teacher; they even had a substitute for the eucharist, since they were permitted to attend the 'agape' or love-feast. Devotional and disciplinary exercises increased as the day approached. We are told about the Thursday preparation; the Friday and Saturday fasts; the final exorcism, the insufflation, and the long Saturday vigil with its readings from the scriptures and special instructions. This pattern was doubtless very old, and is still embedded in the rites for Holy Saturday in the Roman Missal.

At cock-crow on the Sunday, Easter Sunday normally, prayer was made over the water. The candidates put off their clothes. The bishop blessed two vessels of oil, one for exorcism and one for thanksgiving. Each candidate then renounced Satan and all his servants and all his works, after which he was anointed by a presbyter with the oil of exorcism. Then came the three immersions with the threefold creed form which we have already described. After this he was anointed with the oil of thanksgiving, and resumed his clothes. Such anointings, from head to foot, were the normal accompaniment of the bath in those days, but were given a special significance as part of the sacrament.

The candidate was then brought to the bishop for the laying on of hands with prayer, and this was followed by a third anointing, by the bishop, and on the head only. This was the major anointing which was the outward sign of the gift of the Holy Spirit. The candidate was then admitted to the prayers of the brethren and to the kiss of peace. At the eucharist which followed there was a cup of water and a cup of milk and honey, as well as the cup of wine.

These rites are already very complicated, but on the whole the

332

procedure must be old; very old indeed; the anointing seems to be alluded to in Barnabas and Theophilus and was part of the Marcionite and Valentinian rituals also. As the evidence comes in during the third century from Syria, it becomes clear that there was a family resemblance between the various rites of christendom. It is the order that is different. In Syria the major anointing preceded the baptism; what happened afterwards was that the candidate was taught the 'Our Father' and received the laying on of the hand; but this prayer may have been delivered at this point in Rome too. The two tracts of Tertullian *On Baptism* and *On Prayer* suggest something of the kind; for his exposition of the Lord's Prayer is clearly a traditional one associated with the liturgy; and the first act of the newly baptized, on being received into the church, is to spread out his hands and call upon the heavenly Father.

THE CANON OF THE NEW TESTAMENT

Just as there was no fixed text of the creed and no fixed service for baptism, but only a generally accepted pattern, so there was no official list of the 'New Testament' books as we call them; nor is there anything to suggest that such a 'canon' was imposed upon the churches by some ecclesiastical authority, though doubtless the subject was dealt with at the regional councils and in the inter-episcopal correspondence. The Montanist crisis had made this question an urgent one, and it was in Asia Minor that the expression 'New Testament' or rather 'New Covenant'[1] first appears in this connexion. The 'Anonymous' writer on Montanism excuses his delay in writing his book on the grounds that he did not wish to seem to add to the books of the New Covenant of the gospel. It is clear that there was a movement now to define or restrict the list of books which might be read in the services and treated as having sacred authority. Irenaeus worked from a restricted canon of this sort, which he alluded to as scripture.

It is an impressive fact of history that the church as a whole received four Gospels, which were different in form and came from different ecclesiastical centres, and set them in a position of unassailable authority. It is unfortunate, however, that decisive evidence does not come in from Syria on this point, though of course the four Gospels were known

[1] The Greek word '*diatheke*' means covenant or testament.

and used there. The church in Edessa had received them in the harmonized form which Tatian had bestowed upon them, and it is conceivable that Antioch went through a similar stage. It is possible that Antioch came along more slowly than the other centres in the definition of the canon. At the end of the century a bishop of Antioch took time to study the question of the introduction of a new Gospel at Rhossos, a fact which suggests that it was still possible to use supplementary gospel material.

The writing of Epistles to be read in churches had gone on continuously; indeed, it has never ceased. Bishops still issue pastoral letters, and councils send out encyclicals. What was necessary towards the end of the second century was to distinguish from the rest those that might be grouped with the Gospels, though in a subordinate rank. Such a distinction had been made by the time that Irenaeus wrote, and further light is shed on the subject by the Muratorian Catalogue, which is generally dated in the period which we are discussing, since it refers to the episcopate of Pius as recent. These two authorities are both western, and some scholars think that the church of Rome was in advance of the others in defining the limits of this literature. It is quite likely, however, that similar action was taken in Asia, where the pressure from Montanism was very heavy. It has been suggested, too, that the place given to the Pauline Epistles in the Marcionite church may have suggested the idea of placing the Acts and Epistles next to the Gospels in the catholic church; and the pressure of Marcionism existed everywhere.

ACTS, EPISTLES, AND APOCALYPSES

The promulgation by Marcion of an unsatisfactory edition of the Pauline Epistles must have emphasized the necessity of establishing a true one. We know of three such collections which circulated in the second half of the century. The first was the collection used by Irenaeus which contained all the Epistles, including the Pastorals, but not Hebrews; it may have included the short version of Romans without the last two chapters, from which Irenaeus never quotes; and this version seems to have stood in some Old-Latin Bibles. The second was the Roman list or lists, as given in the Muratorian, which was the same as that of Irenaeus; we are able to see, however, that the Pastorals and

Philemon were regarded as a distinct group from the rest. The third was that used in Alexandria, which contained Hebrews as a Pauline Epistle. We have an actual copy of this Alexandrian collection in the Chester Beatty papyrus (P46) now in the University of Michigan, which is thought to have been made about A.D. 200. It contains Hebrews after Romans, but it seems that it did not contain the Pastorals. What remains of the codex is eighty-six leaves out of an original one hundred and four; and it is said that there would not have been room for the Pastorals in the missing leaves. They may have been included in a separate book, as they were at Rome. Codex Vaticanus (B), which may be regarded as Egyptian, was copied from an older manuscript, now lost, in which Hebrews stood between Galatians and Ephesians, as is proved by the chapter enumeration; the Pastorals were not included in this system of enumeration. The evidence shows that the history of the canon at Rome and Alexandria was different. Similar evidence from other centres is not available.

It is an interesting confirmation of the special position of the Pastorals that they are never set for Sunday reading in the Latin Mass. Hebrews is set on one Sunday only. The subordinate position of the Epistles to the Gospels is very strongly marked in the ritual.

With regard to the other apostolic Epistles, the study is a complex one. The First Epistle of St John is vouched for in the Roman and Alexandrian evidence; the Second has left clear traces; the Third appears very indistinctly. We could say that the position of I Peter was unquestioned, but for the fact that it is not found in the Muratorian, a strange omission for a Roman document; but the bad state of the manuscript does not justify us in taking this omission very seriously. The Muratorian mentions Jude, and so does Clement of Alexandria. With regard to the rest, it is best to say that the collection and classification of the catholic Epistles was proceeding, but that the evidence is imperfect; only I Peter and I John can be thought of as securely established on the same level as the Pauline Epistles. This is not to say that James and II Peter were not known.

The Acts seems to have taken its place quite naturally along with the four Gospels; it was originally circulated no doubt along with Luke, as its sequel. It is mentioned after the four Gospels in the Muratorian, though a reference to I John intervenes; and in the Chester Beatty papyrus (P45) the four Gospels and Acts made a single large codex.

This codex was made in Alexandria about thirty years later than the Pauline codex (P46), the experts think. The sixth-century Codex Bezae (D) at Cambridge is also limited to four Gospels and the Acts, but the volume is not in its original form. Enough evidence remains to show that the Epistles of St John once intervened, a point in which it calls to mind the Muratorian.

The prophetic books are a difficult study. The Revelation was popular enough in Asia Minor where it was written, and it was highly esteemed by Justin and Irenaeus. It is included in the Muratorian, but had difficulties in attaining canonical rank in the east, where it was widely rejected in the fourth century. It is quoted by Clement of Alexandria, however, and is said to have been used by Theophilus of Antioch. The *Revelation of Peter* is also included in the Muratorian, though it was spoken against by some. The *Pastor* of Hermas is quoted by Irenaeus as scripture, but rejected for public reading in the Muratorian; Clement thought highly of it. The fact is that we have reached the penumbra of the New Testament Canon. The process of canonization, if we may so call it, definitely included the Acts, the Pauline Epistles, I John and I Peter (with due respect to the Muratorian). The position of the rest cannot be determined, and varied from church to church.

THE SACRED MINISTRY

The outline of the liturgy which is given in the *Apostolic Tradition* of Hippolytus begins with the sacred ministry. The bishop is to be chosen by all the people, a very important piece of information. He is ordained by the other bishops, who lay their hands upon his head, the presbyters standing by; there is a period of silence, the people praying in their hearts; then one of the bishops, chosen for the purpose, lays his hands upon the new bishop's head, and utters the consecration prayer.

The laying on of hands was an ancient Hebrew ceremony in which grace or authority was handed on to a son or successor. The classical instance is the appointment of Joshua by Moses; and we find it in Acts and Pastorals on the one hand and rabbinic sources on the other.

Hippolytus derives the opening clauses of his consecratory prayer from the Pauline Epistles. He then traces the descent of the ministry from Abraham, through princes and priests, in a manner which recalls the Epistle of Clement, who was the exponent of the Roman liturgical

25. CATACOMB PAINTINGS

26. CATACOMB PAINTINGS

order nearly a century before. He refers to the Temple at Jerusalem, and prays for the same princely Spirit which Jesus Christ had given to the apostles, who had established churches in every place to be a sanctuary for the glory and praise of God's Name; that is to say the world-wide federation of worshipping churches which was the appointed substitute for the old Jerusalem. He prays that the Spirit of the high priesthood may be given to the bishop now being ordained, that he may propitiate the countenance of God, and offer the gifts of the holy church, and remit sins according to the commandment, and loosen every bond according to the authority given to the Apostles.

The author of the *Didache* also looked upon the Christian diaspora as the new form of the old Jerusalem dispensation; and his queer ministry of prophets, bishops and deacons, was regarded as the new form of the old priestly succession. Clement had compared the ministry of the apostles and bishops and deacons to the ministry of the sacred orders in Israel; but while the prayer of Hippolytus shows every sign of continuity with the thought of Clement, it also shows signs of development. In Hebrews and Clement, the high priest was Jesus Christ himself. In Clement the ministry of bishops was priestly in character, but it was closely related to the ministry of presbyters; in fact some scholars regard his bishops and presbyters as identical persons. In Hippolytus the distinction has been clarified along the lines of the oriental episcopal system, for which our earliest authority is Ignatius; the bishop has the priesthood and is assisted in his liturgical work by deacons; the presbyters form a sacred council of government like the Jewish sanhedrin.

The origin of the Jewish sanhedrin was traced back to the presbyterate which was instituted by Moses at the foot of Mount Sinai; and the prayer of Hippolytus for the ordination of a presbyter begins with this holy precedent. This clear distinction between the presbyters and their bishop is in line with the usage of the words in the oldest Christian documents, since they have different connotations, or refer to different functions, even if they are applied to the same person; but the sole liturgical position of the bishop in Hippolytus, and the powers which are bestowed upon him, seem to have been accentuated, and the non-liturgical position of the presbyters rather unduly insisted upon. He insists that, so far as the Spirit was concerned, the presbyters received but did not confer; but it is clear from his own text that they did have some share in the ministration of the Spirit, however subordinate it might be.

It might almost seem that they may have been, in some degree, the legatees of the old plural episcopate of apostolic times, which we noticed, so far as our surviving documents inform us, does not seem to have had the power to ordain, which is presumably what Hippolytus means. It is a sign, however, of their solidarity with the bishop, and his with them, that they join with him in the laying on of hands in the eucharistic offering and in the ordination of a new presbyter; but not of a new deacon, since deacons were the bishop's officers. The bishops and deacons were thus quite independent of the council of presbyters from the point of view of order.

It might be argued that Hippolytus is resisting the idea that the presbyters should have some large or predominant share in the choice and appointment of the new bishop, as the legend asserts they did in Alexandria. He insists on popular choice and episcopal consecration, the presbyters standing by; whereas Clement had insisted on appointment by eminent men and popular acclamation. But is it likely that presbyteral nomination was entirely lacking in Rome in the time of Hippolytus? or popular acclamation in Alexandria? We cannot assume that a clear-cut constitutional procedure was laid down in either place which had to be followed *au pied de la lettre*. Nor need we assume that the old bishop had always been removed by death; he may have had a voice in the choice of his successor, as was regarded as normal in the story of Addai and actually occurred in the case of Narcissus. Hippolytus does not seem to envisage this possibility at all.

So soon as the new bishop had been ordained, he received the kiss of peace from all present, and proceeded to offer the holy eucharist. The deacons brought up the oblations of the people, which included, or might include, oil and cheese and olives as well as bread and wine. He laid his hand on these oblations with the presbyters, who thus asserted their solidarity with him; and this laying of the hand upon the oblation seems to be illustrated in the catacomb pictures.

He then offers the bishop's prayer, a form for which is given, though Hippolytus points out that the bishop is not tied to any fixed form, but may pray according to his ability. The *Didache* allows the same liberty to the prophets. This consecration prayer contains a clause in which the bishop gives thanks for being made worthy, or deemed worthy, to

338

stand in God's presence and minister to him; which is specially suitable to the day of his consecration. The same form is to be used, with appropriate changes, for the oil. Lesser benedictions are supplied for the cheese and olives.

THE BAPTISMAL EUCHARIST

There are two other accounts of the eucharist, or two other types of eucharist, in Hippolytus, which must be taken into consideration. The first of these is the baptismal eucharist. After the candidate has been confirmed and anointed by the bishop, with the sign of the cross in all probability, and given the kiss, and welcomed with the salutation, 'The Lord be with you', he was admitted to the 'prayers of the brethren', which were followed by the kiss of peace from all; the men kissing the men and the women kissing the women, Hippolytus explains.

The oblation was then brought up by the deacons to the bishop. It consisted of the bread, with three cups, one of water, one of milk and honey, and one of wine and water. The bishop then uttered a prayer of thanksgiving, by which the bread became the pattern or 'antitype' of the flesh of Christ, and the cup of wine and water became the antitype or 'likeness' of the blood which was shed for all who would believe in him. The Latin translation, which we are following, explains that the words 'antitype' and 'likeness' were the actual words of the Greek text. They are frequently found in later eucharistic prayers, and seem to be introduced here as if they were parts of the bishop's prayer in the baptismal eucharist; but as no text is given we cannot be sure of this, and may suppose, if we wish, that the prayer assigned for the bishop's consecration was a sufficiently useful model for all occasions.

The direction for the benediction over the milk and honey has a reference to the fathers, that is to say the Israelites of the Exodus period, and their introduction into the Holy Land; a mystical connexion of thought which goes back into the New Testament period, and was well established before the *Epistle of Barnabas*; for baptism was closely associated with the Passover night. The benediction over the cup of water regards it as effecting a baptism of the inner man.

The bishop is then directed to explain all these things, after which he breaks the bread, and distributes the fragments saying, 'The bread of heaven in Christ Jesus.' The breaking of the bread is definitely a preparatory act before communion, rather than a distinct ritual act. The words of administration are an echo of the story of the manna and its application to the eucharist, which we find in St John. The communicants say 'Amen' as they receive it.

The presbyters, with the help of the deacons if necessary, administered the cups. The one who administered the water said, 'In God the Father Almighty'; the one who administered the milk and honey said, 'And in the Lord Jesus Christ'; and the one who administered the wine and water said, 'And in the Holy Spirit and in the holy church'; thus echoing the trinitarian formula of the baptism. We are reminded of the five-point credal formula in the *Epistle of the Apostles*, which was connected with the five loaves which were broken and blessed by the Lord for the five thousand.

The communicant says 'Amen' to the words of administration, and tastes three times of each cup.

OTHER EUCHARISTS AND THANKSGIVINGS

The third kind of eucharist mentioned by Hippolytus is the regular eucharist on the first day of the week, when the bishop communicated all the people from the broken bread with his own hand if this was possible, the cups being managed by the presbyters and deacons. This third type is omitted in the Latin translation, but has adequate support from the other authorities. There is no description of this Sunday service, which must have been a very protracted one.

We have here one of the points of resemblance between the literary arrangement adopted by the *Didache*, Justin and Hippolytus; first comes the baptism and baptismal eucharist; then the reference to Sunday and the Sunday eucharist. Hippolytus was not the first to write out an order of prayer and sacrament; it was an established literary pattern; what appears to be original with him is that he composed it from the bishop's point of view; it was what liturgiologists call a pontifical.

The text of the bishop's eucharistic prayer in Hippolytus is free from the old Jewish associations with the fruits of the earth, which are strongly represented in the *Didache* and Justin and Irenaeus; but the ordination and baptismal eucharists both retain traces of them in the offerings of oil, cheese, olives, milk, and honey; and the offering of the fruits of the earth continued in the Roman rite for a long time and has never become quite extinct. Hippolytus preserves some of these old Jewish rites as separate features, the offering of first-fruits for instance, and the benedictions over various gifts of nature. We also find the 'agape' or love-feast, in which some rich person gives a supper in the evening for less privileged brothers and sisters. There was prayer and the reading of scriptures; the bread was broken and blessed by the bishop, who was to be present if possible; otherwise by a presbyter or deacon. Each guest said the 'eucharist' or thanksgiving for himself over his own cup.

Catechumens might be present at the agape, but they received a bread of exorcism, not a bread of blessing, and the bread of blessing in the agape was distinguished in its turn from the bread of thanksgiving of the eucharist. According to the Books of Clement, the reason why the catechumens could not eat with the baptized Christians, was that the catechumens were subject to possession by evil spirits which took advantage of meals to enter into them. Some idea of this sort might explain why the catechumens had to eat 'exorcized bread'; indeed, the unbaptized adherents must have had to live their lives with the aid of continual exorcisms.

The bishop was also the normal officiant at the offering of the first-fruits, at which he uttered a benediction into which he inserted the name of the giver. The first-fruits were doubtless offerings made according to Jewish precedent and devoted to the maintenance of the church and clergy as in the *Didache*.

An important distinction now appears in the terminology. The noun *eucharistia*, which means thanksgiving or thank-offering, and the verb *eucharistein*, are beginning to be restricted to the sacramental action. In the New Testament this word is interchangeable with the noun *eulogia* and the verb *eulogein*, which simply means to bless. They are both used of the doxologies which were offered over the gifts of nature or on other appropriate occasions. In Hippolytus, however, the bread of the sacrament is referred to as *eucharistia* and the bread of the love-feast is only *eulogia*.

The distinction is not consistently observed, however. At the love-feast the private Christian or catechumen says his own *eucharistia* over the cup, following the old Jewish precedent; the blessing of the first-fruits is also called a *eucharistia*.

THE BISHOP'S PRAYER

These trains of thought prefigure the way in which a eucharistic terminology will develop. The consecration of bread and wine, in accordance with the command of the Lord which was given within the Paschal commemoration, was continued in a liturgy of Jewish origin, which had been a sabbath liturgy in the case of the Jews, but had become a Lord's Day liturgy in the case of the Christians. If we set aside the important matter of lections from holy books, and psalms, and common prayers, the first movement in such a liturgy is bound to be the worship of Almighty God as the creator, and a thanksgiving for all the good things of this earth; 'over everything which we offer', as Aristides and Justin had said. The synagogue tradition provided appropriate prayers and benedictions.

In the Hebrew liturgy there was a second great reason for thanksgiving, and this was the historical one; the choice of the holy people by Almighty God through Abraham; their deliverance from Egypt; the giving of the Law on Mount Sinai; and their establishment in the Holy Land. Hippolytus does not give a form of prayer for the Sunday service, but these Hebrew ideas are fully represented in his prayers of ordination; and they explain how he can speak of the Israelites in the desert as 'our fathers' in his benediction over the milk and honey. He was but carrying on the rich and complex tradition of the apostles and of the elders who succeeded them. The catholic tradition knew no other mode of worship; but the Hebrew historical *eucharistia* was continued and completed by a thanksgiving for the coming of Jesus Christ into the world, his voluntary death and Passion, his resurrection on the third day, and the incorporation of the Gentile believers into a new holy people through faith in him. Here is the basis of the Christian liturgical tradition as we find it everywhere. It appears, for instance, in widely different forms, in Clement, in Barnabas, and in Theophilus; Rome, Alexandria, and Antioch.

No doubt there were long prayers of this type offered at the second-century *eucharistia*; indeed Justin says that the bishop's prayer was one of no ordinary length; but there was another type. The Mishnah gives us many examples of quite short doxologies or benedictions for all sorts of occasions. The following grace before meals is an example.

Blessed art thou, O Lord, king of the world, who bringest forth bread from the earth.

We may compare it with various benedictions from apostolic and near-apostolic sources.

> Our Father who art in heaven, blessed be thy Name....
> Blessed be the God and Father of our Lord Jesus Christ who....
> We thank thee, O God, through thy beloved Child, who....
> Glory be to thee....

Sometimes the reason for the doxology is lengthened or extended; sometimes it turns into a prayer; and sometimes it concludes with a second doxology; and this would appear to be the forerunner of the Christian 'collect'. An extended prayer of this sort is found as early as Acts iv. 24. This is the kind of thanksgiving-prayer which the *Didache* supplies for the baptismal eucharist, one over the cup, one over the broken bread, one for the unity of the church, and one after 'being filled', all rather in confusion. The prayer in the *Martyrdom of Polycarp* is an example with better connexion.

The bishop's prayer in Hippolytus is not as different as might be supposed. It begins as follows,

We give thanks to thee, O God, through thy beloved Child Jesus Christ who....

But what follows is the whole apostolic kerugma, arranged in a series of short clauses. The new bishop appears to be solemnly voicing his faith in the true apostolic gospel; each clause, however, might have formed the core of a short doxology of the *Didache* type:

1. Whom thou didst send to us in the last times as saviour and redeemer and angel of thy will:
2. Who is thy inseparable Word:
   Through whom thou madest all things and it was well-pleasing to thee:
3. [Whom] thou didst send from heaven into the Virgin's womb...[and so forth].

These clauses lead up to the narrative of the institution of the eucharist at the Last Supper. This recitation is perfectly natural, and we are accustomed to it; but it is not included in the prayers of the *Didache*, and it is given apart from the description of the rite in Justin. It may be that the relation of the narrative of institution to the connected eucharistic prayer was not an easy problem to solve. Traces of uncertainty are found even at a later date than this.

It is followed by an act of remembrance and offering:

1. Remembering, therefore, his death and resurrection, we offer to thee bread and a cup (giving thanks unto thee because thou hast made us worthy to stand in thy presence and minister to thee),
2. And we pray thee to send thy Holy Spirit into the oblation of the holy church,
3. Gathering into one,
4. Grant to all who partake of holy things [or, Grant to all the holy people who partake],
5. For fulfilment of the Holy Spirit and for strengthening of faith in the truth...[*ending with a doxology*].

It looks here as if fragments or phrases of the old liturgical tradition have been strung together in a logical order, but they produce a confused text, at least in the Latin translation on which we depend. Perhaps they are first lines, or key-words, of well-known devotions. The sequence of the main verbs suggests the practical logical Roman mind finding formulas to explain exactly what was being done or said, very different from the older Hebraeo-Christian idiom which gloried in the language of oriental ritual and apocalypse. The framework of thought seems to be, 'We remember...we offer...we give thanks...we pray'. The clause in brackets in the first paragraph looks like a special thanksgiving on the occasion of the ordination.[1] The following prayers, which do not flow on very grammatically, visualize and present before God the oblation of the whole church, not merely of the local ecclesia. The 'gathering into one' is an echo from the prayer for unity which is given at much the same position in the *Didache*; it refers there to the unity of the whole catholic church. 'Holy Spirit: holy church' is a credal expression, the intention of which is to look beyond the local ecclesia to the far horizon.

Such would be our way of studying this important prayer. The ancient material in it is more important than the form which has been imposed upon it; but the form must be very much earlier than the time

---

[1] But compare the liturgical formulas in Rev. i. 5–6 and v. 9–10.

of Hippolytus. No doubt Eleutherus prayed very much in these terms; or at any rate Victor. The outline of the prayer, it may be added, bears a curious resemblance to the outline of the baptismal creed. In both cases a christological kerugma has been given a place within a trinitarian formula. The christological part of the Roman creed has been found separate from the trinitarian framework; similarly the narrative of the Lord's Supper has been found distinct from the eucharistic prayer. In both cases the latter has been inserted into the former. The likeness to the structure of the baptismal creed is accentuated by the addition of Holy Spirit to holy church in the petition which follows the act of oblation.[1] It is a neat, logical, satisfactory arrangement of old material; the exuberance of the old Hebraeo-Christian benedictions has been curbed; theological continuity has been supplied.

THE EUCHARISTIC DOCTRINE

The petition of the bishop's prayer in Hippolytus is to the effect that God will send down his Holy Spirit upon the oblation of the holy church. We may ask whether this descent is supposed to effect any change in the nature of the elements of bread and wine; for none is asked for in the prayer. The object of the petition is for 'fulfilment of the Holy Spirit and strengthening of the faith in truth'. Even if we interpret the prayer as asking for the descent of the Spirit upon the bread and wine there present, it is still true that there is no expressed idea that the invocation of the Spirit is intended to effect a change in their nature. If it was so, it would be a novel idea. According to Justin and Irenaeus the predecessors of Hippolytus, both of whom he venerated and followed, there was a change indeed; but it was not connected by those fathers with the descent of the Holy Spirit. The food is called eucharist, Justin says, and it is not received as ordinary bread or ordinary drink; for, just as Jesus Christ was made flesh by the Word of God, so this food which has been 'eucharisted' by 'a Word of prayer which is from him', is now the flesh and blood of that Jesus who was made flesh by a Word of God. The language is far indeed from being precise; but it establishes the fact that in the year 150 it was the common teaching that the elements were to be received as the flesh and blood of Christ,

---

[1] And in the concluding doxology; and in the administration of the cups at the baptismal communion.

after they had been blessed by the word of the prayer, or better, perhaps, the 'prayer of the word, that is from him'.

This phraseology recalls the passage in I Timothy which says that all food is to be taken with thanksgiving, or *eucharistia*, since it is made holy by a 'word' of God and intercession. In Justin, however, the phraseology has been coloured by his special theology of the Logos, and there appears to be a comparison between the consecration of the elements and the incarnation of the Logos. The words of Irenaeus are much less definite, but attempt to say the same thing: 'Bread from the earth, when it receives the invocation of God, is no longer ordinary bread, but eucharist, being composed of two things, heavenly and earthly.' The author of the *Didache* probably had the same idea in mind when he called it 'spiritual food'; for the word spiritual means charged with Spirit or energized by Spirit. And so did Hippolytus when he spoke of the 'antitype' or 'likeness', words which imply more than similarity or imitation.

Much discussion has taken place about the meaning of the 'prayer of the word that is from him' in Justin, and the 'invocation of God' in Irenaeus, without arriving at any certainty. Some have suggested that it might be an invocation of the Logos, as in the later Egyptian rite; others have suggested an invocation of the Spirit, as in the later Syrian rite. Another possibility is the invocation of the name. In all the old Jewish doxologies the mind was directed upward to God, not downward to the food; the name of God was solemnly blessed, and so powerful was the invocation of the name, in faith, that the food itself was made holy; 'it is made holy by a word of God and prayer'. This upward motion of the mind is strongly emphasized in the eucharistic prayer of Hippolytus in its opening salutations and biddings.[1]

> The Lord be with you:
> And with thy spirit.
> Lift up your mind:
> We have, unto the Lord.
> Let us give thanks unto our Lord God:
> It is worthy and righteous.

He proceeds along the lines of the old Jewish doxologies, 'We give thee thanks, O God, through thy beloved child Jesus Christ who . . .'; he

[1] See also Colossians iii. 2, which opens a eucharistic passage, cf. iii. 15–17.

adds many clauses and finally comes to rest on the same note: 'That we may praise and glorify thee through thy beloved Child Jesus Christ, through whom, to thee, be glory and honour; to the Father and the Son with the Holy Spirit in thy holy church, now and unto the ages of ages. Amen.'

Need we look much closer or with much more precision for the word of prayer or the invocation of God?

APPENDIX

Text of the Muratorian Fragment

It will be convenient to give a translation, so far as possible, of the Muratorian Fragment, since this document, mangled as it is, sheds a good deal of light on the formation of the New Testament at this stage. The original Greek text is usually assigned to the episcopate of Eleutherus or Victor; some scholars assign its composition to Hippolytus. It is closely related to the controversies with which Irenaeus dealt in his *Refutation*.

Captions have been added to the text for convenience in reference.

The beginning is lost. It had said (presumably) that Matthew wrote in his own name; that Mark began his Gospel from the preaching of the Baptist, and that he obtained his information from Peter, at whose preachings (?) he was present and wrote accordingly. (It has been suggested that it alluded to I Peter at this point.)

1. THE FOUR GOSPELS

[The text begins]. . .at which [in the plural] he was present and so put [them]. The third book of the Gospel: according to Luke. Luke, that physician, after the ascension of Christ, when Paul took him with him as one eager for the Law[1] wrote in his own name[2] from his point of view; yet neither had he seen the Lord in the flesh; and he too, so far as he could follow [?] began to speak from the nativity of John.

Of the fourth of the Gospels: John, one of the disciples, when his fellow-disciples and bishops were urging him, said, Fast with me today three days, and whatever may be revealed to any one, let us tell it to one another. The same night it was revealed to Andrew, one of the apostles, that all should certify [or call to mind] and John should write everything down.

2. NOTE ON THE FOUR GOSPELS

And so, even if different beginnings[3] are taught in the several books of the Gospels, it makes no difference to the faith of believers, since they are declared in all by the one princely Spirit: concerning the Passion, concerning the resurrection, concerning his intercourse with his disciples, and concerning his double advent, the first in the humility of rejection which is past, the second in the glory of royal power which is to be.

3. EPISTLES OF JOHN

What wonder is it therefore if John brings forward so firmly, one by one, in his Epistles, saying in reference to himself: What we saw with our eyes, and heard with our ears, and our hands have handled, these things we have written for you? and thus claims that he is not only one who saw and heard, but also the writer of the marvellous acts of the Lord, in order.

4. THE ACTS OF THE APOSTLES

Now the Acts of all the Apostles were written by Luke in one volume to the most excellent Theophilus. It contains the different events which occurred in his presence, as he makes perfectly clear by omitting the passion of Peter, and also the journey of Paul, when he set out from the city for Spain.

5. THREE EPISTLES OF PAUL

Now the Epistles of Paul themselves make plain to those who desire to understand it, from what place or for what reason they were sent: first of all to the Corinthians condemning the schism of heresy; then secondly to the Galatians on circumcision; to the Romans however on the order of the Scriptures, but intimating that their origin was Christ, he wrote at length on points which it was necessary to discuss with us one by one.

6. SEVEN EPISTLES OF PAUL

Since the blessed apostle Paul himself, following the order of his predecessor John, writes only to seven churches by name, in the following order: first to the Corinthians, second to the Ephesians, third to the Philippians, fourth to the Colossians, fifth to the Galatians, sixth to the Thessalonians, seventh to the Romans; and even if he does write a second time, by way of rebuke, to the Corinthians and the Thessalonians, it is still made known that there is one church dispersed throughout the whole round world; and John too, though he writes in the apocalypse to seven churches, nevertheless speaks to all.

7. PERSONAL EPISTLES OF PAUL

And there is one to Philemon, and one to Titus, and two to Timothy, on account of affection and love; they are sanctified however in the esteem of the universal [catholic] church, in the regulation of the ecclesiastical discipline.

8. PAULINE FORGERIES

Now there is one current to the Laodiceans, and another to the Alexandrians, which have been forged in the name of Paul for Marcion's heresy; and many others which cannot be received in the universal [catholic] church; for gall with honey may not be mingled.

9. OTHER EPISTLES

The Epistle of Jude indeed and two of the above-written John are received in the universal [catholic]. . . .

10. MISCELLANEOUS[4]

And the Wisdom written by the friends of Solomon in his honour. . . .

11. APOCALYPSES

The apocalypses of John and Peter we also receive, and no others, which latter some of ours do not wish to be read in church.

But the Shepherd was quite recently[5] composed by Hermas in our own times when Bishop Pius his brother was sitting in the chair of the church of the city of Rome, and so it certainly ought to be read, but not publicly in church to the people, neither among the prophets, since their number is complete, nor among the apostles at the end of the seasons.

12. HERETICAL BOOKS

Now of Valentinus of Arsinoe [?] or of Metiades, we receive nothing whatever.[6] Those also who composed a new book of psalms for Marcion, together with Basilides: Assianus founder of the Catafrygians. . . .

Notes. (1) 'Eager for the Law': according to Irenaeus Luke emphasizes the priestly and sacrificial aspect. (2) 'His own name' proves that the gospel circulated as his, though his name is not mentioned in it: the text may mean that he wrote under his own name but represented Paul's point of view. (3) Irenaeus mentions this argument about the beginnings of the Gospels. (4) The text has been broken after 'Other Epistles' since something appears to have dropped out; but there is no break in the manuscript. (5) 'Quite recently': perhaps in answer to the theory, known to Origen, that he was the Hermas of Romans xvi. 14. (6) 'Arsinoi seu Valentini' looks as if Arsinous was a name given to Valentinus; there was a place called Arsinoe in Egypt. Metiades and Assianus are unknown names; the translator or copyist has hopelessly confused them.

349

The Pauline Epistles. Either the carelessness of the copyist has robbed us of the conclusion of the first attempt to list the Epistles of Paul; or perhaps there was an old roll or codex containing three Epistles with titles: *Concerning the Schism of Heresy, Concerning Circumcision,* and *Concerning the Order of the Scriptures.* If so, there was a second roll containing the seven (nine) Epistles to churches, and a third containing the personal Epistles.

There are traces of an enumeration in the first list: 'primum' is placed before Corinthians, 'deincepsb' before Galatians, but no numeral before Romans. The capital B at the end of DEINCEPSB may represent the Greek beta which was also the numeral 2, as Westcott pointed out. If this is correct, we have traces of a system of enumeration here which has partially disappeared.

The Non-Pauline Epistles. Section 9, 'Other Epistles', is linked with 6, 7, and 8. Sections 7, 8, and 9, all close on a reference to the universal or catholic church. Such repetitions are frequent causes of blunders by copyists. In Section 9, 'Other Epistles', the word church is missing, and this meagre list of non-Pauline epistles is thus brought into immediate contact with the Wisdom of Solomon in Section 10 which also seems to have lost some words.

The text is in a terrible state as may be seen from such forms as DEIN-CEPSBCALLATIS (then secondly Galatians) or TENSAOLENECINSIS (Thessalonians); and Sections 9 and 10 seem to have suffered from omissions.

Symbolic Numbers. The use of symbolic numbers is reminiscent of Irenaeus. The author of the catalogue may have begun by explaining why there were four Gospels with different beginnings. He considers seven to be the right number of Epistles, signifying that they were addressed to the whole church; the collection of Ignatius contained six, with an extra one for Polycarp; the collection of Dionysius contained seven, with an extra one for Chryso-phora. In consequence we would expect to find seven non-Pauline epistles; and eventually the number of catholic epistles was seven. The number of the prophets was well known to be twelve; twelve prophets and twelve disciples are mentioned in the Anti-marcionite gospel prologue.

General. When it speaks of the scriptures it means the Old Testament. The 'order' of the Old Testament may mean its authority in the church.

Does the 'end of the seasons' mean the end of the calendar year?

CHAPTER 21

EXTRA-CANONICAL LITERATURE

THE NEW LITERATURE

We have moved on a matter of forty or fifty years since the early half of the reign of Hadrian, at which point we attempted a consideration of the anonymous and pseudonymous literature which appeared on the fringe of the New Testament. Many apocryphal books have appeared during these four or five decades, and it is not possible to assign exact dates to them; some of the books which we shall consider may not have received their final form until the third century; but it is more convenient to take them together. It is a fictitious literature for the most part, and its touch with history is slight. The *Acts of Paul*, for instance, of which we have given some account already, is simply a historical romance. It was written to amuse and instruct and entertain, and to point a moral or two at the same time. The older non-canonical books like the *Revelation of Peter* were written for church use.

THE NEW GOSPELS

It is not possible, however, to draw a line of demarcation between these two types of literature. The Hebrew Gospel seems to have been a serious piece of Gospel-making designed for liturgical use in Jewish churches, and the Marcionite Gospel was designed to meet the needs of an anti-Jewish gnosis. The new Egerton papyrus is such a small fragment that we cannot tell what it was: a number of selections for the use of a preacher perhaps. These Gospels retell the old narratives with differences of detail. In the Hebrew Gospel, the man with the withered hand says, 'I was a mason earning my bread by my hands; I pray thee, Jesus, to restore me to health lest I beg my bread in shame'.

In the British Museum Gospel, the leper says, 'Rabbi Jesus, by travelling with lepers, and staying with them in the inn, I became a leper myself; if therefore thou wilt, I am made clean'. This is the kind of dramatization which a preacher introduces almost instinctively as he goes along. They are 'homiletic variations', not fictional writing.

The *Egyptian Gospel* may also have been made for actual use. It was quoted by the Alexandrian docetic, Julius Cassianus and seems to have been a gnostic expansion of the Gospel in the form of a dialogue between Jesus and the women, with some of the disciples. Celsus mentions a sect of 'Harpocratians' who followed Salome, and others who followed Martha and Mariamne. Hippolytus mentions a group of Ophites who received traditions from Mariamne, who had received them from James the Just. *Pistis Sophia*, a third-century compilation contains conversations between Jesus and these three women. We only possess a single group of sayings from the Egyptian Gospel, and these are quoted by Clement of Alexandria. When Jesus had finished speaking on some apocalyptic subject, Salome asked, 'How long will men continue to die?' and the Lord made answer, 'So long as women bear children', a cryptic answer which conceals within it the docetic abhorrence of sex; for he also says 'I came to destroy the works of the female'. It must have been a secret tradition that was being delivered, for Salome goes on to say, 'When will these things become known?' 'When you have trampled on the garment of shame', Jesus answers, 'and the two become one, and the male with the female, neither male nor female.'

The last saying is also found in II Clement, though it is given a different and more respectable interpretation. It may have been one of the extra-canonical sayings of Jesus which were going the rounds.

It is more blessed to give than to receive.   Acts xx. 35.
Wherein I find you, there will I judge you.   *Justin and others.*
Be ye approved bankers [or money changers: or good business-men?].
                                        Clement of Alexandria and others.
He that is near me is near fire: he that is far from me is far from the kingdom.
                    (Origen; and compare Ignatius, *Smyrnaeans*, IV, 2.)

Such sayings were collected into anthologies, and examples of these anthologies have cropped up among the Egyptian papyri.

The only other Gospel which can be safely assigned to so early a

28. THE SYNAGOGUE, DURA EUROPOS

period, and to actual church, use is the *Gospel of Peter* which is a literary rewriting of the four-Gospel story for a docetic sect; it was in use at Antioch, and probably at Alexandria too. The 'Ebionite Gospel', quoted by Epiphanius, seems to be a later composition. None of these Gospels was widely received, or considered for inclusion with the four.

APOCRYPHAL EPISTLES

We have dealt in some detail with the various types of Epistles which succeeded the apostolic period, and carried on the apostolic tradition. There was the fringe of the New Testament group to consider, like Hebrews and James, neither of which was strictly apostolic; there were the Epistles of apostolic men like Clement and Ignatius and Polycarp; there were the nameless writings which acquired apostolic associations, like Barnabas and II Clement; there were actual pseudepigraphs like II Peter.

The Muratorian Catalogue mentions two epistles 'forged for the Marcionite heresy', which it calls Laodiceans and Alexandrians. The Marcionite Epistle to the Laodiceans was simply our Epistle to the Ephesians under another name; but at a later date an orthodox Epistle to the Laodiceans was made up by combining passages from the genuine Epistles. Such an Epistle seems to be demanded by the reference in Colossians iv. 16. About the Epistle to the Alexandrians we know nothing at all. There is a third Epistle to the Corinthians in the *Acts of Paul*. It is painfully orthodox. Stephanas and the elders write to Paul and tell him that Simon and Cleobius have come to Corinth and are overthrowing the faith of many by saying that they must not use the Old Testament, that the 'Almighty' is not God, that there will be no resurrection of the flesh, that man was not made by God, that Christ was not born of Mary, and that the world was not made by God, but by the angels; a pretty summary of the position of Simon, Satornil and Marcion. Paul's reply covers all these points, but especially the resurrection of the flesh.

The much longer *Epistle of the Apostles* was put together to correct much the same erroneous opinions, in opposition to Simon and Cerinthus, who were chosen as typical opponents of leading apostles. It expressed the received theology in a semi-apocalyptic form. It has a good knowledge of most of the New Testament.

THE *ACTS OF JOHN*

The Muratorian does not name any apocryphal Acts, but seems to have them in mind when it alludes to the canonical Acts as the Acts of *all* the Apostles, thus ruling out the Acts of one particular apostle; and also when it defends the Acts for omitting certain points which are supplied in the *Acts of Peter*.

We have given some account of the *Acts of Paul*. In its original form it was one of the oldest of the apocryphal Acts, and the text we have has passed through numerous revisions. The story of Thecla, the Corinthian correspondence, and the martyrdom of Paul, circulated as separate documents. There is only one manuscript of the book as a whole, and it is in such bad condition as to be little more than a mass of fragments. It is a Coptic translation. It glorifies martyrdom, asceticism and virginity; but it cannot be called unorthodox. No doubt it has been corrected. It is full of miracles, hairbreadth escapes and marvellous conversions. It was written by a presbyter in Asia and was condemned there at a synod.

Some scholars place the original form of the *Acts of John* earlier than the *Acts of Paul*. Photius of Constantinople, at the end of the ninth century, found a corpus of five books of apocryphal Acts, which had been put together by the Manichaeans; they were the Acts of John, Paul, Peter, Andrew and Thomas; and they were all ascribed to an author named Leucius Charinus. It is thought that Leucius may be the author of the *Acts of John*, which is the first-named, and so they are sometimes called the Leucian Acts. But nothing is known about Leucius except for a statement in Epiphanius that he was a disciple of John.

A good deal of the *Acts of John* has survived, and it is apparent that it is a Valentinian production. The apostle appears as a mystic and wonder-worker. The book is written in a verbose high-flown style, and does not seem to add anything of historical value to the church tradition about John, which it fully accepts; John of Ephesus is the disciple who reposed on the bosom of the Lord at the Last Supper; he dies peacefully at a great old age in Ephesus. It has been suggested that some of the stories about John in the church tradition may have been taken from this book, but none of them are to be found in the portions of the book which survive. There is a Roman tradition, mentioned by Tertullian, that John was immersed in a cauldron of boiling oil, from which he emerged without hurt; but it is not found in what remains of the *Acts of John*; and it is not known to any Greek writer, so that it is quite unlikely that it ever stood there. It was known to Hippolytus, and so was the tale of the lion who licked the feet of St Paul, but this fails to appear in the *Acts of Paul*, which tells how a lion licked the feet of Thecla. It will be seen that the traces of the apocryphal Acts in church writers of this period are very slight, or even non-existent.

It is probable that the better-known anecdotes about the apostles were very widely told, and need not be traced to one source or another. A certain number would be in the common stock. We can see the beginning of this in Papias.

In the Leucian Acts, John has a supernatural power over death and the devil. One episode tells of a lady named Drusiana, who gave up marital relations with her husband Andronicus for the sake of godliness and persuaded him to agree with her on the subject. Much to her mortification, she was courted by a wealthy Ephesian named Callimachus, and was so grieved by his attentions that she died. Callimachus, who was devoid of gnosis, was still enslaved to his passion, and decided to visit her dead body. Fortunatus, the steward of Andronicus, admitted him to the tomb; but a serpent appeared from some quarter and slew him. As for Callimachus, it wound itself round his legs, brought him to the ground and sat on him.

On the next morning, which was the third day after the death, John and Andronicus and the brethren came to the tomb at dawn to break bread.[1] A beautiful youth with fiery eyes appeared to them, smiling, and told John that he was to raise to life those who were dead. After a number of speeches and prayers, the two corpses were raised to life. The eucharist was then celebrated in the tomb, but when they came out they found Fortunatus lying on the ground, dead and black. This tale illustrates the gnostic division of mankind into three species; Andronicus and Drusiana are the spirituals or true gnostics; Callimachus is the psychic, capable of salvation; Fortunatus is the *choic* or material. He has no possibility of salvation. He is a compound of death, earthly matter and fire. John looks at his dead body, and says, 'Thou hast thy child, O devil'.

---

[1] It is suggested by some that this represents a common Christian practice. This third day celebration in the *Acts of John* is based on the Easter morning narrative.

THE *ACTS OF PETER*

We have already referred to the Palestinian *Ascents of James*, and the *Wanderings of Peter*, which were worked into a tale about Clement and incorporated into the later Books of Clement called the *Recognitions* and the *Homilies*. The first of these recorded the arguments of James the Just in the temple with Caiaphas and the priests and the attack upon him by an enemy, who was intended to represent Paul; the second recorded the contest between Peter and Simon Magus in southern Syria, and at some stage or another the figure of Simon Magus was so handled as to represent Paul. In these Ebionite documents the figure of James gives added weight to the witness of Peter and the Twelve, just as Paul does in the catholic tradition. James is almost, if not quite, the superior of Peter.

There is no trace of these theological tendencies in the *Acts of Peter*, which is almost a catholic book. It is usually assigned to about 200–220 and is thought to have been written in Syria. It brings Peter to Rome to continue his controversy with Simon Magus, a conclusion which is foreshadowed in the Ebionite legends. It shows no first-hand knowledge of Rome whatever. It says nothing at all about Clement or his family.

Like all the Acts, it is encratite or ascetic in character, but it is not far removed from orthodoxy, except for some gnostic devotions and a gnostic exposition of the mystery of the cross which is allowed to take possession of the story of Peter's martyrdom. This material closely resembles certain passages in the *Acts of John*, from which it may be borrowed; but it is liturgical in character and was probably circulating independently.

When Peter reached Rome, he found that Paul had departed on his voyage to Spain; and this excludes the idea of antagonism between Peter and Paul. Simon Magus was living in the house of a rich senator named Marcellus, who had been a convert of Paul and the patron of the church; but he was now under the influence of Simon. Peter knocked at the door of the house and asked Simon to come out; but Simon would not come; in fact he told the porter to say that he was not at home. So Peter sent in the dog to deliver his message, and the dog went in and stood up on his hind legs and delivered it; in fact he said more than Peter told him to say. There were several contests of wit and eloquence between Peter and Simon, and more miracles were performed. Before long Peter reclaimed Marcellus to the true faith.

There is a certain rough humour about this book. There is a rather peculiar miracle in which Peter animates a dried herring; and such stories may perhaps be poking fun at the miracles attributed to Simon in the Simonian tradition. The account of Simon's death may also have been intended to raise a laugh. He decided at last to give his supreme display of the magic art; he would fly up into the air over the city of Rome; and so he did, but Peter put up a prayer and Simon crashed, breaking his leg in three places. He retired into the country and died. Now this is not the form of the legend which was known in Rome. According to Hippolytus, he had himself buried in the earth, and promised that after three days he would rise again, which, however, he failed to do; 'for he was not the Christ'.

The account of Peter's martyrdom, which may have been a separate document, contains the celebrated 'Quo vadis?' story. Peter was persuaded to leave the city by night during the persecution of Nero; but as he was going out of the city, he met the Lord who was coming into it. 'Where are you going, Lord?' said Peter. 'I am going to Rome to be crucified,' said the Lord. So Peter came to himself, and returned to Rome rejoicing and glorifying God. The legend of his crucifixion head downward then follows.

THE LEGENDS ABOUT PETER

The story of the passion of Peter is extremely weak, but the 'Quo Vadis?' story has become famous. It is the only episode in the *Acts of Peter* which stands up and looks solid. The rest is two-dimensional; highly-coloured but flat. This author could not have invented such a story; or was he successful, just for once? It is an audacious story which reveals Peter as very nearly failing his Lord and Master again; and of course it might be taken as a rebuke to those bishops who retired into the background in persecution. It is quite possible that it was picked up out of the living tradition. We have drawn the conclusion that the Roman church did not possess a passion-story about Peter similar to the Jerusalem passion-story about James; for surely it would have been preserved; but no doubt they did possess little pieces of anecdote and tradition, such as persist in the wake of all great historic events, and attach themselves to great personages. Where did Clement of Alexandria get his story about Peter encouraging his wife when they were facing martyrdom? He spoke her name, and said, 'Remember the Lord.'

The substance of the *Acts of Peter* is fairy-tale, but what about the framework of 'history' within which it moves? Paul's journey to Spain? Peter's journey to Rome? and his crucifixion head downwards? It looks as if these points were firmly fixed in the consciousness of the church. And whence came the idea of a contest between Simon Peter and Simon Magus in Rome, which does not appear before Clement of Alexandria? The readers of the tale would look for the points which were familiar to them, and the writer would use these points to provide a semblance of historical outline for his inventions. He would not conflict with such ideas as were very generally accepted.

On the other hand, he does not trespass on New Testament territory; and the same is true of *John*, though not of *Paul*, which is related in part to Paul's Galatian adventures. *Peter* and *John* answered the question which had now arisen, What happened after the sudden close of the canonical Acts? The Acts itself was obviously well established in the church before they were written.

CHRISTIAN FICTION

What was the value of this literature? It had the value that fictions, fairy-tales and folk-lore have in every time and place. They give expression to a faculty for day-dreaming that cannot be eradicated from the heart of man; and if they are well-written he sees something of himself and his friends reflected in the events and characters. A number of equally fanciful novels and films, dealing with the life of Jesus and his apostles, have appeared in the last few years in America and been very popular.

It is probable too that the type of Christian for whom they were written may have thought it wrong to read the Greek or Latin literature of the day, which was full of pagan mythology and sexual adventure; instead of this they provided a Christian mythology, enlivened with ascetic adventure and stories of heroic martyrdoms. It is possible that pagan myths or folk-tales have been taken into them. They should be compared with the occasional short stories of eminent rabbis which enliven the pages of the rabbinic writers, and on the other hand with the biographies of Hellenistic sages, who were also ascetics and wonder-workers.

From the point of view of the historian, they allow us to penetrate into a level of Christian life and culture which would not otherwise be accessible to us. Those who read these stories were romantics. The characters are quite unreal; their fancy names and fine speeches are hopelessly 'literary'; they are such things as dreams are made on; but they do show us what the Christian imagination achieved when it was liberated from the limitations of actual history and real life. They show us the popular conception of a great apostle like Peter or Paul, and the gnostic conception of a great apostle like John; their idea, that is, of what the apostles *ought* to have been like; great orators and wonder-workers and confounders of all opponents. They give us the picture of the apostolic tradition as it was visualized and magnified in the Christian imagination. They expressed it in a readable form, no doubt, for the pagan inquirer.

A long account is given, for instance, of a Friday service at the house of Marcellus, which was purified for the occasion by the sprinkling of water and the invocation of the name of Jesus, a ceremony which reminds us of the dedication of the tower in Hermas. The widows and old people assemble, and each one of them is given a gold coin. Narcissus the presbyter is present.[1] The Gospel of the transfiguration is read from the scroll of the Gospel, and Peter gives an exposition of it; a rather gnostical exposition, for it was a favourite gnostic passage. It had to do with the opening of the eyes for mystical vision. When the ninth hour arrived, the point at which the day's fast normally terminated (at about three in the afternoon, that is), they rose up to make prayer; and Peter prayed that their eyes might be opened to see Jesus Christ. And they did see Jesus Christ. The whole hall shone with light. Some saw an old man, some a young man, some a boy gently touching their eyes. They saw him in different forms. Fasting and prayer were rewarded by vision.

The favourite form in which Christ appears in these Acts is as a young man with a bright torch or with shining eyes, and the favourite time for his appearance is at a baptism. It is the Hellenistic idea of an angel or spirit or divine being.

[1] A Narcissus is mentioned in Romans xvi. 11.

GNOSTIC RITUALS

These Acts contain liturgical forms which may be older in origin than the Acts themselves. The *Acts of Peter* are orthodox on the whole, and even make use of the Hebrew scriptures at one point; but there is an infusion of gnostic liturgy and mysticism; and there are traces of the view that the twelve apostles did not fully understand the Lord. The *Acts of John* gives this material in a fuller and clearer form, and we find a great advance upon the primitive or degraded forms which Irenaeus discovered in the Valentinian schools in Ephesus. It is of real importance to the scholar; for, erratic as it well may be, it is still a form of Christian worship, and must have some relations at some points to the liturgical development as a whole. The difficulty of the gnostic was that all authentic Christian prayers were originally Jewish prayers, glorifying and blessing the creator of heaven and earth, and he was obliged to produce prayers which were free from this association with the demiurge. He had to compose new books of Psalms. He fell back on the mysticism of the Gospels, and especially of the fourth Gospel, and also no doubt on pre-Christian and non-Christian Hellenic forms.

The baptisms, the acts of prayer, and the eucharists, are of particular interest. Baptisms were taken in the name of the Trinity, and anointing with oil followed. Prayers were built up round the invocation of the name, or the offering of glory and thanksgiving for the name, meaning of course the name of Jesus, not the name of the Creator. In the eucharist, bread and water were used, or bread alone.

What praise or what offering or what thanksgiving shall we name, *as we break the bread*, save thee, O Lord Jesu? We glorify thy name which was given through the Father.... We glorify thy entering of the door; we glorify thy resurrection shown to us by thee; we glorify thy way; we glorify thee the seed, word, grace, faith, salt [and so forth at great length].

(*Acts of John*, 109, in M. R. James, *The Apocryphal New Testament*, p. 268.)

When the prayer was finished, the bread was broken, and given to the brethren with prayer, and sometimes with the laying on of hands. As a rule, there was no cup, or else a cup of water.

There is an important liturgical text in the *Acts of John*, which is set for the evening of the Last Supper and the day of the Crucifixion; it was therefore a paschal ritual. It is preceded by references to earlier events in the gospel story which also had a cultic significance, the call of the first disciples, the transfiguration, and the meals of Jesus with his disciples, which are turning points in the structure of Mark's Gospel. It is made clear that the Lord did not actually eat and drink, since he had no real human body. Nor did he really suffer. He was the Word of God, but not the Word made flesh.

On the night before the Passion, the disciples form a ring round Jesus and join in a mystic dance as they sing a hymn to the Father. Jesus sings, and they respond with an Amen.

I would be saved and I would save: *Amen.*
I would be loosed and I would loose: *Amen.*
I would be wounded and I would wound: *Amen.*
I would be born and I would bear: *Amen.*
I would eat and I would be eaten: *Amen.*

and so forth indefinitely.

A lamp am I to thee that beholdest me: *Amen.*
A mirror am I to thee that perceivest me: *Amen.*
A door am I to thee that knockest at me: *Amen.*
A way am I to thee the wayfarer: *Amen.*
Behold thyself in me who speak, and, seeing what I do, keep silence about
  my mysteries.   (*Acts of John*, 94–5.)

There is a great deal more of it, and it is related to the heavenly ogdoad and zodiac.[1] To some modern minds it is poetry of a high order; to others it is merely idle chatter of a transcendental kind. Perhaps some poetic insights lie hidden under its mechanical iterations.

During the Crucifixion, John retreats to a cave on Mount Olivet, and the Lord stands by him and exposes for his benefit the unreality of the scene that is taking place on Calvary. He shows him the real cross, a cross of light, which was called word or mind or Jesus or Christus or door or bread or seed or resurrection, and so forth.

I suffered yet I did not suffer,
Pierced and yet I was not smitten,
Hanged and yet I was not hanged,
Blood flowed from me and it flowed not [and so forth].

[1] The Valentinian year began in the spring, that is to say at Passover, which was also the commemoration of the creation in Philo and some of the Jewish authorities. The disciples represent the twelve months of the zodiac circle; Jesus was betrayed in the twelfth month by the twelfth disciple.

He was taken up, John says, and yet not one of the multitudes beheld him; 'and when I went down, I laughed at them all, for the Lord had contrived everything in symbols, and by a dispensation towards men, for their conversion and salvation'.

In this way John is given the inward gnostic understanding which the Valentinians believed that they had received through his Gospel. The life of Jesus was an allegory, revealing and yet concealing the heavenly mysteries.

SPECIAL-PURPOSE GOSPELS

The older apocryphal Gospels were succeeded by a number of lesser Gospels which were written to shed light on special points and illustrate special views. One class is that of the Passion Gospels. Possibly the *Gospel of Peter* was such a Gospel. The existing *Acts of Pilate* or *Gospel of Nicodemus* is a late compilation, but seems to have had second-century forerunners, as we have indicated. Its theme is the descent of Christ into Hades and the liberation of the souls of the righteous dead. To this extent, therefore, such a Gospel would be supplementary to the canonical Gospels.

The same is true of the infancy Gospels. There is a late Gospel, called the *Gospel of Thomas*, which contains stories of the childhood of Jesus, including the one about his learning his letters which we have found in the *Epistle of the Apostles* and in the Valentinian school at Ephesus; so this Gospel too looks as if it was descended from a second-century ancestor. We have confirmation of this supposition in Hippolytus and Origen, who both speak of a *Gospel of Thomas* which was used by a branch of the Ophites. No doubt it contained some of the other miracles which are found in the extant texts. The child Jesus makes little birds out of clay, which fly away when he claps his hands. Joseph finds that a piece of wood which he is using is too short, and Jesus pulls it out to the correct dimensions. He strikes his school companions dead with a casual word, when they offend him. These stories may come out of pagan myth or folk-lore; they would offset the adoptionist statements that he did no miracles before his baptism by John.

Another field of speculation which is not illuminated as brightly as was desired was the history of the Virgin. There is a late Gospel called the *Book of James*, the so-called *Protevangelium*, which gives a long account of her birth and childhood, and names her parents as Joachim and Anna. The name Joachim seems to be derived from the last Davidic king[1] in the royal genealogies, and the name of Anna from the mother of Samuel or the Anna of St Luke's second chapter. This book shows a quite remarkable indifference to the realities of Jewish religious and social life; its origin is Gentile. In the text as we have it an angel announces to Anna that she will become the mother of a child, and the birth takes place without the intervention of Joachim. Mary is born and brought up in the Temple, where her virginity is carefully guarded until Joseph, who is a widower with children, takes her as his virgin-spouse. Her virginity is maintained, and is certified by a midwife after the birth of Jesus. This legend about Mary's continued virginity was in existence in the second century; it is found in the *Ascension of Isaiah*. Origen knew of a *Book of James* which says that the 'brethren' of Jesus were the sons of Joseph by a former wife. Clement knew of the story about the midwife.

The growth of legend round the person of the Virgin during the second century is an obscure point. In catholic theology she was the second Eve, whose obedience offset the disobedience of the first Eve and so made the salvation of man possible. She was also the mysterious Virgin foretold by Isaiah; and so she appears in a second-century painting in the catacomb of Priscilla.

The doctrine of her continued virginity appears in writings of Egyptian origin. It was developed in a peculiar manner by Valentine, who does not allow that Jesus took anything at all from the Virgin in being born of her. This was very different from the catholic belief about Mary, which emphasizes the true human nature of her child; the doctrine of the continued virginity as expressed in these legends undoubtedly diminished it. The second-century evidence does not take us any further. The legend existed and may have been orthodox in intention. Perhaps its principal purpose was to offset the stories put about by the Jews that Jesus was illegitimate, and of course the adoptionist theories which made him a 'mere man' on whom the divinity descended at his baptism.

[1] Identified by Hippolytus in his lectures on Daniel with Joachim the husband of Susannah.

OTHER GOSPELS

All these Gospels are a little shadowy; no doubt they made their appearance in the second century, but we do not know them in their second-century forms. Still more shadowy is the Ophite *Gospel of Judas* mentioned by Irenaeus, or the *Gospel of Matthias* or *Traditions of Matthias* mentioned by Clement and Origen; sources from which Basilides is said to have helped himself. Many scholars assign the *Epistle of Barnabas* to Alexandria, and the *Homilies of Clement* identify Barnabas with Matthias, and assign the preaching of Barnabas to Alexandria; the *Recognitions* place it in Rome.

Our list would not be complete without a reference to the 'Ebionite Gospel', of which we know nothing at all except for the quotations which are culled from it by Epiphanius. It must not be confused with the much earlier Hebrew Gospel, which was orthodox by comparison. The quotations from the Ebionite Gospel are of a heretical colour which harmonizes with the Clementine legends. It commended an ascetic diet of herbs, and made Jesus say that he came to destroy the sacrifices, the very announcement which James the Just is said to have made in the Temple in the Books of Clement. It refers to Jesus himself as a 'man named Jesus', so that its theology would seem to be prophetic or adoptionist.

EXTRA-CANONICAL SAYINGS OF JESUS

Clement of Alexandria quotes a saying or two from the *Traditions of Matthias*:

Wonder at the things that are before thee, making this the first step in further gnosis.
Fight with the flesh and abuse it...making the soul grow by faith and gnosis.

The former resembles a saying found in the famous Oxyrhynchus papyrus; the latter resembles a saying attributed to the Nicolas of Antioch who is mentioned in the Acts of the Apostles. As we have seen they were handed down in the 'apostolic' schools and passed, no doubt, from mouth to mouth. Some were collected into anthologies; others even found their way into manuscripts of the canonical Gospels. We may give examples of both.

The two fragments of papyrus which were found at Oxyrhynchus are too mutilated to give a complete text, but some twelve or thirteen sayings can be recovered in whole or in part. One of them has a little introduction which claims that the words were spoken to Thomas. In the following extracts the words in brackets are supplied by conjecture.

Let not him that seeketh cease [seeking till he] find, and when he find [let him wonder, and] having wondered, he shall reign, and [having reigned] he shall rest.

If ye fast not from the world, ye shall not find the kingdom of God, and if ye keep not the sabbath for the whole week, ye shall not see the Father.

Wheresoever there are [two, they are not without] God, and where there is one alone, I say I am with him: lift up the stone and there shalt thou find me: cleave the wood and there am I.

The best example of a floating tradition which found its way into one or another of the texts of the canonical Gospels is the story of the woman taken in adultery, which is found in the Latin Vulgate and the English Authorized Version as John viii. 1–11. Another interesting anti-rigorist story has been inserted into Luke in the Cambridge Codex Bezae (D), immediately after Luke vi. 4. The story must be ancient since it deals with a purely Jewish problem.

On the same day he saw a man working on the sabbath, and said unto him, O man, if thou knowest what thou doest, blessed art thou: but if thou knowest not what thou doest, thou art accursed and a breaker of the Law.

OPHITE MYTHS

Another kind of sacred literature which should not be overlooked is the myth. Some of the old 'testimony' material, like the saga of Moses and Joshua, was on its way to become myth (see Barnabas, XII); and the stories of creation and of the Garden of Eden, in the first chapters of Genesis, invited this treatment and had long ago received it. There was an old apocryphal book called the *Book of Adam*, which is thought to have been Jewish, but may have been Christian. Catacomb pictures of Adam and Eve and the serpent are assigned to the third century.

The supreme example, however, is the Ophite myth of Sophia and the serpent, which was transformed into a connected story with a dramatic appeal. It reached its highest form of literary expression in the Valentinian school in which the sorrows of Sophia were presented as a passion play.

> For at times she wept and sorrowed, as they say, because she was left alone in the darkness and the void; sometimes, when she thought upon the light that had left her, she was confused and laughed; sometimes again she feared; and at other times was perplexed and amazed. And indeed there was a remarkable tragedy there now, and an imaginative creation, as each of them, some in one way and some in another, pompously announced from what emotion it was, or from what element, that material subsistence took its origin; and these things, it seems to me somehow, they have no desire to teach openly, but only to those who can afford a heavy price, worthy of these mysteries. (Irenaeus, *Ad. Haer.* I, 1, 7–8.)

The sorrows of the mother were the principal feature of the inner mysteries; they represented in an allegorical form the desperate case of the human soul, in its conflict with sin and evil and ignorance and death. Its main features are illustrated in later gnostic documents, like the third-century Coptic *Pistis Sophia* (which draws upon the Psalms of David and the *Odes of Solomon*), and an apocryphal Gospel (probably the *Egyptian Gospel*), to help it out devotionally.

Numerous written forms of the myth and ritual are referred to by Celsus, Irenaeus, Hippolytus and Origen. Those mentioned by Celsus were closely related to the mystery-religion type of ritual. He possessed a diagram or map of the seven heavens, on which a ladder of seven metals was indicated, which symbolized the ascent of the soul to the realm of real existence; strange animal figures guarded the various portals. There was something similar in Mithraism. Origen had a different version of this diagram. Irenaeus had a connected story of the primal man and his offspring, and their love for the primal woman. He follows it with fragments of alternative myths which are not so literary, and are much harder to follow. Those given by Hippolytus are more advanced and sophisticated and radically pagan. The infinitesimal point, or small seed, develops into the tree of life, which is the universe itself, and God, and primal man; in one colossal system of Phrygian origin, the pagan cults, and especially those of the Egyptian Osiris, are taken into consideration, every male image and every temple is a representation of the gnostic primal man or divine fertility-principle.

Hippolytus gives an account of a writer named Justinus, who combined the story of the twelve labours of Heracles with a system of Ophite myth. His books were to be committed to the initiates under an oath of secrecy such as Elkhasai had demanded from his followers; but Hippolytus had managed to obtain a copy of his *Book of Baruch*, who was the third angel of the Father and creator, whose name was Elohim. Elohim was an emanation from the high God, and the world came into existence as a result of his love for Edem, or pleasure; he representing the spirit, and she the soul. Her third angel was Naas, the serpent who seduced Eve. In Elkhasai, too, there was some special significance about the third of a series, and in Ebionism the male principle is strong, and the female weak. Elohim sent Baruch to inspire the Jewish prophets, but all of them succumbed to the evil influence of Naas. Then he selected Heracles, who went valiantly through his twelve labours, but was enticed and overcome by the half-virgin half-serpent Omphale, who was also called Babel or Venus. Lastly he found Jesus, who was the son of Joseph and Mary, at the age of twelve, minding the sheep—a Davidic touch; and Jesus remained faithful to the inspiration of Baruch, who appears to be the Holy Spirit. Out of jealousy, Naas caused him to be crucified; but he left the 'body of Edem' hanging on the tree, and ascended to the Father, saying to Edem, 'Woman, behold thy son', meaning thereby his natural and earthly man.

This narrative does not look like a system of religious faith. It looks more like a mythical romance of the Greek type, mixed in equal proportions with Ebionite gnosis, to form agreeable reading and illustrate certain religious ideas. The gnostic Justinus is not otherwise known, and is very likely a literary fiction. Justin Martyr had pointed the way to possibilities of this kind by making use of a Socratic myth, which he took from Xenophon, in which Heracles comes to a place where the road divides and has to choose between two female figures, one of whom represents Virtue and the other Vice. Even Tatian had a good word to say for Heracles; he was a popular god in eastern Syria and represented the sun driving in his chariot round the circle of the heavens; Commodus identified himself with Heracles. It is possible, therefore, that since Justin Martyr had originated the idea of allegorizing Heracles in the interests of Christian preaching, our author boldly took the name of Justin as a suitable one for the quite imaginary narrator of his mixture of mythological material. The oaths of secrecy may have been another literary touch, designed to give artistic verisimilitude and awaken interest.

PAGAN AND CHRISTIAN MYTH

Justin Martyr had been troubled by the obvious resemblances between the pagan myths like those of Heracles, Orpheus, and Bellerophon, and the central facts of the Christian gospel. Now myths were not, in their origin, connected stories or fables, such as the Greek poets had made of them. They were the fragmentary imaginative conceptions which accompanied the ancient rituals, and often personified the forces of nature or the history of the tribe. They expressed in poetic form the conflict with evil and the mysteries of life and death. We may take as an example the myth of Perseus, which is known to all of us in its Christianized form of St George and the dragon. The Christian populace did not need to have a biography of St George with historical references; the imaginative concept of the hero on his horse slaying the dragon, was sufficient; but it could have, in addition, the picture of the virgin tied to the tree and in danger from the dragon, she being a king's daughter, of course.

These primitive mythical ideas are quite limited in number, though they were capable of an indefinite number of artistic affiliations and spiritual applications. They revolve round the topics of life and death or good and evil; the hero born to be king, the maiden giving birth to the hero, the hero riding on his horse, the hero slaying the dragon, the hero wedded to the maiden. They symbolize the fundamental realities with regard to man's life in a dark and mysterious universe.

Such figures are as ancient as civilization itself and as widespread. We find them in the Bible from the first chapters of Genesis onward; they appear in the apocalypses either in heaven or in the imagined future. Pagan poets placed them in the skies as constellations, where the gnostics found them and used them for their fantasies. The author of the Revelation adapted them for his own purposes; the hero born of the virgin, the hero slaying the dragon, the hero riding his horse in the heavens, the hero coming to his wedding day. The docetic myth recalls them in the Spirit who descends from heaven to do battle with Death and Hell and to set their prisoners free. Even Paul in his Epistle to the Romans is using this kind of language at times.

Primitive Christianity loved the language of myth, falling now and then into the snare of literalism, but handling it on the whole with a creative freedom. No council ever decreed dogmas about Adam and Eve or the tree of life or the serpent or the mysticism of the cross or what was called in the Middle Ages the harrowing of hell. John, Barnabas, Justin and Irenaeus knew the old tradition well. Its central paradox in its Christian form was the picture of the hero who conquers the dragon by dying on the cross.

The reader should be warned that the word dragon or *drakon* is simply a Greek word for a snake or serpent; but the serpent is apt to appear in strange forms. But fantastic dragons are of ancient origin, being found in Babylonian art and mythology and passing into the Jewish and Christian apocalypses. In John's apocalypse a monster with seven heads rises out of the sea. In the catacomb art a dragon-like monster rises out of the sea to swallow Jonah. The home of the primeval dragon was in the sea; he is the Leviathan of Psalm lxxiv. 14 and civ. 26, and probably of Job too.

The language of myth passed very easily into Christian art and poetry, and continued to be used in the popular tradition to express fundamental religious ideas, especially the idea of a conflict between man and his sinful self, or between innocence and malevolence, or between life and death; that is to say the fundamental existential situation of Christians face to face with the pagan world and the facts of life.

HYMNOLOGY

The *Little Labyrinth*, which is thought to be the work of Hippolytus, speaks of psalms and songs which had been written by faithful brethren from the beginning, celebrating Christ as the Word of God, and speaking of him as God; and Pliny, a century earlier, had mentioned the songs which were sung at dawn to Christ as God. There are only a few traces of them and little record of the music of the churches, though Celsus remarks that it was the custom of the Christians to use instrumental music in order to excite the emotions. The Muratorian Catalogue mentions a Marcionite Psalm-book; and certainly Marcion would have to find some substitute for the Hebrew psalmody which was one of the legacies of Judaism to the church.

Clement of Alexandria, who weaves verses from pagan Greek

poetry into his Christian prose, denominates Christ himself as the new song, and appends two hymns to his *Paidagogos*, or *Leader of Youth*. The first of them begins as follows.

1. Bridle of untamed colts,
   Wing of unwandering birds,
   Sure helm of babes,
   Shepherd of lambs.

2. Assemble thy simple children,
   To praise holily,
   To hymn guilelessly with innocent mouths
   Christ the guide of children.

3. O King of saints,
   All-subduing Word of the most high Father,
   Ruler of Wisdom, support of sorrow,
   Rejoicing unto the ages.

4. Jesu, Saviour of mankind,
   Shepherd, Husbandman, Helm, Bridle
   Heavenly wing of the holy flock.
   Fisher of men who are saved.

It need hardly be said that it would be a mistake to think of this as a children's hymn; he is thinking of those simple believers who make good martyrs, even if they are not cut out for philosophers. The birds, the lambs, the babes, are to be found in the catacomb art as symbols of the souls of the faithful; and so are the shepherd and the fisherman as symbols of Christ; and the ship as the ark of Christ's church. For the wing, the reader might consult Basilides, or one of his followers in Hippolytus, *Refutation* VII, 10: see page 67 of this volume. The untamed colt is that on which Christ rode into Jerusalem, and symbolizes the Gentiles who lived apart from the Law.

Hippolytus knew a collection of Ophite hymns, from which he quotes the following. It visualizes the descent of the Saviour through the heavenly spheres to save mankind.

Then said Jesus, Father:
The pursuit of evil upon the earth
   makes men to wander from the Spirit.
He seeks to escape the bitter chaos:
   but knows not how to flee.
Wherefore send me, O Father!

> With the seal will I descend,
> All the aeons journey through,
> All the mysteries disclose,
> Forms of gods will I impart:
> Secrets of the Holy Way—
>   which men call gnosis—
> Will I impart.

Another collection of hymns which may be assigned to the second century is the so-called *Odes of Solomon*, not to be confused with the older Pharisee *Psalms of Solomon*. They exist only in Syriac, but it is considered probable that they were written in Greek, and in the second century, possibly quite early in the second century. There is a Johannine touch about them; they recall the ardent poetry of Ignatius of Antioch; they are spiritual, mystical and sacramental; they express themselves in oriental images, without the flesh-and-blood feeling of the popular Judaeo-Christian apocalyptic; they are perceptibly nearer to Valentinus than to Papias or Justin. Perhaps they come from the Syrian border-land where the Christian tradition had not been fixed yet on western lines. Here is a very simple one, which we may call 'The Fountain'.

> Fill ye waters for yourselves,
>   from the living fountain of the Lord;
>   for it is opened unto you.
> And come all ye thirsty,
>   and take the draught,
>   and rest by the fountain of the Lord.
> For fair it is, and pure,
>   and giveth rest to the soul.
> Much more pleasant are its waters than honey:
>   and the honeycomb of bees is not to be compared with it.
> For it flows forth from the lips of the Lord:
>   and from the heart of the Lord is its name.
> And it came infinitely and indivisibly:
>   and until it was given in the midst they did not know it.
> Blessed are they who have drunk therefrom:
>   and have found rest thereby. Alleluia.
>
> (*Odes of Solomon*, xxx.)

THE NEW CHRISTIAN LITERATURE

There was no lack, therefore, of imaginative writing in orthodox, encratite, semi-orthodox, semi-gnostic and gnostic circles; historical romances about apostles, fanciful imitations of the Gospel narrative, anthologies of sayings attributed to Jesus, imitation Epistles, prophetic oracles, mythical tales, poetry, psalmody and song; but what impresses us is that it never entered into competition with the apostolic writings which were being organized into a New Testament. The popular idea that the New Testament books were selected by ecclesiastical authorities from a larger mass of possible literature is the reverse of the truth. It was always a rather small and select tradition. The New Testament of the Muratorian Catalogue is not so large as ours, unless we include the *Revelation of Peter* and the *Pastor* of Hermas, both of which were being questioned; neither is the New Testament of Irenaeus, or Origen, or even Eusebius, unless we add Hermas in the case of Irenaeus, and Hermas and 'Barnabas' in the case of Origen.

Dr Montague James, whose *Apocryphal New Testament* is the most convenient collection of this extra-testamental literature,[1] has a very fair statement on this point. 'We may fairly say that the only books which had a real chance of being included in the canon of the New Testament were the Epistles of Clement and Barnabas, the *Revelation of Peter*, and the *Shepherd* of Hermas; for I do not think we need to reckon in the *Didache* or the *Acts of Paul*.' And we might add that there came a time when the church might have lost the Revelation of John if the east had had its way, and the Epistle to the Hebrews if the west had had its way; and that the canon of seven 'catholic' Epistles does not appear before the time of Origen, James and II Peter being disputed even then. This is the penumbra of doubt and debate within which the main structure of the New Testament stands as a catholic institution fully accepted by the end of the second century.

This does not mean that all the apocryphal books were banned by churchmen. Far from it. The non-heretical literature was read, and enjoyed, but not in church. In later, less critical times, the apocryphal Acts, and the infancy Gospels, were accepted at their face value as history; though not as scripture. The stories of the apostles, and of the Holy

---

[1] Unfortunately it lacks the *Recognitions* and *Homilies of Clement*; but there are translations of these in the Ante-Nicene Library.

Family, were still further elaborated. *Acts of Thomas* and *Andrew* were composed in the third century. The myths and symbols inherited from the wisdom of the ancient world passed into Christian art and poetry. In one shape or form, most of the extra-canonical imaginative inheritance of the Middle Ages was present in germ at least at the end of the second century; we might almost say the poetry and art of Christian Europe. It is an authentic creation of the primitive Christian genius for poetic expression, which, after all, is the natural form of intellectual expression for Christian enthusiasm.

Note. Since writing the above it has been announced that the MS. of a second-century *Gospel of Thomas* has been discovered in Cairo and will be published. It appears to be identified with the Thomas gospel mentioned on p. 365, not that on p. 362.

CHAPTER 22

THE PASCHAL CONTROVERSY

THE ACCESSION OF VICTOR, *c.* A.D. 189

The accession of Victor as bishop of Rome took place about 188–90. He had a Latin name, and the later Roman tradition, preserved in the *Liber Pontificalis*, says that he was an African by birth and that his father's name was Felix. Jerome spoke of books which he had written in the Latin tongue. It looks as if a native Latin element asserted itself when he became bishop.

There were two young men at the time of his accession who were destined to become leaders in the controversies of the next generation and thorns in the sides of future bishops of Rome. One was Tertullian, whom we have already introduced, a brilliant young lawyer whose conversion, whether in Rome or Carthage, is generally assigned to the neighbourhood of the year 190; the other was Hippolytus, who was probably ordained a presbyter by Victor, but possibly by Eleutherus. We have made use already of his attempt to reduce to written form his conception of the old Roman church order as it existed in Victor's time or even earlier. He was a great scholar and a rugged traditionalist of the school of Justin and Irenaeus. He and Tertullian were both rigorists with regard to morals and church discipline, but seem to have been satisfied with the way in which the Roman church was conducted in the time of Victor. Both of them viewed with displeasure the rise to power of the humble-born Callistus, who favoured the new 'monarchian' theology of Praxeas who had come and gone in the later years of Eleutherus, or the first year or two of Victor.

THE EPISODE OF CALLISTUS

By mere chance we are able to read in the pages of Hippolytus a detailed and ill-natured story of an episode which occurred early in the episcopate of Victor and before the assassination of Commodus on 31 December 192. The first scene, in fact, may belong to the episcopate of Eleutherus. There was a wealthy official of the imperial court, named Carpophorus, who happened to be a Christian, and had a Christian slave named Callistus, a young man of great energy and ability, with a gift for managing affairs and influencing people. Callistus and Hippolytus were of the same age; and as Hippolytus died as a martyr in 235, they are not likely to have been any older than twenty-five to thirty in the year 190.

Carpophorus entrusted his promising young slave with sums of money and he acted as a financial agent, making loans or accepting deposits. The time came when he found himself insolvent, and there were clients who wanted their money back. Carpophorus, too, wanted an accounting. Callistus attempted to escape by sea, and when he found he was pursued, he plunged into the water with the intention of drowning himself, Hippolytus says. He was rescued, however, and sent to a slave-prison. After that we see him vainly endeavouring to rectify the finances of his 'bank'. Finally he made an appearance in a Jewish synagogue on the sabbath day, with the object of collecting sums of money which were due to him from Jewish creditors, *he* said, but with the hope of making a martyr of himself, Hippolytus says; there was a commotion, and he was arrested and sent to the mines in Sardinia, not as a Christian, Hippolytus is careful to explain, but as a criminal. In the Sardinian mines, the convicts did not live very long. Hippolytus himself ended his days there as a martyr, and perhaps he thought more kindly of Callistus then.

Now Victor had influence with Marcia, who was the mistress of the emperor's harem, and on the whole appears to have used her great personal influence for good. She was virtually empress. She was a devout woman, Hippolytus says, and anxious to perform some good work. There were a number of Christians now in the imperial service; Carpophorus himself was one, and Hyacinthus, who was a eunuch attached to the palace and also a Christian presbyter, was another. Marcia's influence with the Emperor Commodus was strong enough to secure the release of all those who had been condemned as Christians, and Hyacinthus was despatched to Sardinia with a written order to that effect. The name of Callistus was not on the list which Victor had supplied, but he begged on his knees to be taken back to Rome, and his request was granted. His health had suffered, and on his return he was sent by Victor to a town on the sea-coast named Antium, and a small monthly allowance was made to him on grounds of compassion; not as a confessor, Hippolytus insists, thereby implying that there were some who did regard him as a confessor. No doubt all the captives who returned to the church after their terrible ordeal were greeted with affection and pride.

This man, who was despised by Hippolytus as a slave, an adventurer and a criminal, became his hated rival in the Roman church; the patron of the opposition school of theology; and finally his rival as bishop. The theological divisions which were the ostensible and very real cause of this grave schism obviously had their social and political and personal antecedents. There were, as there always are, some non-theological factors involved.

THE CASE OF BLASTUS

When Victor became bishop c. 188–9 he inherited some theological problems from his predecessor. The affair of Praxeas, and the condemnation of the Montanists has already been discussed. We assigned it to the last years of Eleutherus, but the first years of Victor are not impossible. We also assigned to the episcopate of Eleutherus the affair of Florinus, the Roman presbyter who embraced the doctrines of Valentine. Irenaeus wrote a letter to Victor about certain books of his which were still being read by the faithful; but the days of Valentinianism in Rome were over; martyrdom and monarchianism were winning the day.

The affair of Blastus may conveniently be taken here. It was an article of his creed that the Passover must be kept on the fourteenth of the Jewish month Nisan; he was a 'Quartodeciman', a 'fourteenthite'. Irenaeus wrote him an Epistle to which he gave the ominous title *Concerning Schism*. The book no longer exists, but the title suggests that Blastus had taken too strong a line in organizing his liturgical protest against the traditional practice of the Roman church;

Hippolytus, in the *Libellus*, says that he was introducing Judaism secretly. It seems that he was the chief of a die-hard group, probably in the Asian community, which observed the Jewish Passover rite and expected everyone else to do the same; it would appear that the common Asian custom was to keep the fourteenth as the anniversary of the death of Christ, neglecting its connexion with the Passover.

The Roman bishop had suffered a good deal from the vagaries of the Asian minority in his see-city, and made up his mind to bring about a measure of uniformity. The trouble may not have been entirely calendrical. The Asian group had contributed in its time to the stability of the Roman church, but it was also capable of giving trouble. Many of the teachers whose peculiar views had disturbed the church of Rome had come from Asia; we think of the Logos theology of Justin, the New Prophecy of Montanus, the monarchianism of Praxeas, and doubtless the 'Judaism' of Blastus. It would seem that Victor had decided that the time had come to end the privileged position which had been granted to the Asians by Xystus seventy years before and confirmed by Anicetus after his conference with Polycarp. He knew that this would involve him in conflict with Ephesus, and he realized that it would be necessary for him to get the support of powerful churches overseas. No doubt he did so. He had the support of Irenaeus on the Paschal question, and possibly of other Asians too. He held a synod at Rome and wrote letters to the leading bishops overseas requesting them to hold synods, too, and consider the matter.

The consideration of the same question by the whole catholic church through concerted regional synods is a landmark in Christian history as important as the Council of Nicaea itself. We have not seen the church acting simultaneously before, and it is interesting to see how it does it. The 'more powerful leadership' of the Roman church, of which Irenaeus had spoken, is very evident, for it is Victor who initiates action; but the work of consideration remains regional. The details cannot be fully ascertained but the story as a whole is perfectly clear. A time came when Victor found that he had enough support to justify action. At some point, he wrote a letter to Polycrates, the bishop of Ephesus, requesting him to call a synod of bishops to consider the matter, and it would appear that he included in the letter some reference to what might happen if the Asians did not comply with his requests. This, at any rate, is where the controversy begins to come clearly into view;

but matters must have proceeded a long way before such a point was reached. We do not possess a copy of the letter which he wrote to Polycrates, but very fortunately Eusebius has preserved some extracts from the reply which Polycrates made to it; and these are very revealing. They give us our last good picture from Asia Minor.

THE EPISTLE OF THE ASIAN SYNOD

Polycrates called a synod of the Asian bishops, who unanimously supported him in defending their ancestral customs. They authorized him to write a firm letter, which he did. He is not to be moved by threats, he says. He may be a small man (can Victor have said that?) but the support which he has received shows that he has not worn his grey hairs in vain. He has lived sixty-five years in the Lord, and seven of his family have been bishops; he is the eighth. He has conferred with bishops from all over the world. Greater men than he have said that we should obey God rather than men; it is a form of citation which recalls a favourite phrase of Irenaeus, 'A better man than we are has said'; it would appear to be an Asian idiom; these two men, Irenaeus and Polycrates, were much of an age, and had the same ecclesiastical background.

It is a spirited reply, and the information which it gives is of great historical value. The sixty-five years of Polycrates 'in the Lord' had begun about A.D. 125 or 130. He was at least twenty-five when Polycarp died. In his highly episcopal family he had mixed with men who remembered John and those other disciples. Victor, in his Epistle, seems to have alluded to the Roman founders, St Peter and St Paul, in support of the Roman custom; for Polycrates states that 'great lights' had fallen asleep in Asia *too*. He commences his list of them with St Philip and St John, taking them in the order of their deaths.

Among these are Philip, one of the twelve apostles, who fell asleep in Hierapolis; and his two aged virgin daughters; and another daughter who lived in the Holy Spirit, and now rests at Ephesus.

And there is John too, who reclined upon the breast of the Lord; he became a priest, wearing the *petalon*, and was both witness [*martus*] and teacher; he sleeps in Ephesus.

And there is Polycarp in Smyrna, both bishop and 'witness', and Thraseas both bishop and 'witness', from Eumeneia, who fell asleep in Smyrna.

And what need to mention Sagaris, bishop and 'witness', who sleeps in Laodicea.

And Papirius too, the blessed, and Melito the eunuch who ever lived his life in the Holy Spirit, and lies in Sardis awaiting the visitation [*episkope*] from heaven. (Polycrates, *Epistle to Victor*, in Eusebius, *E.H.* v, 24, 2–6.)

This catalogue or litany of glorious and well-remembered names is a part of the appeal to apostolic and catholic history which was being stirred up everywhere by the controversy. These are the witnesses on which the churches of Hierapolis and Ephesus and Smyrna and Laodicea and Sardis depended to establish their case. These are the real and spiritual signatures to the conciliar letter. Others must find more glorious names if they can.

We cannot help noting the same stress on martyrdom and asceticism, along with episcopacy and apostolic origin, which we have noted in the records of the Montanist controversy. Polycrates belongs to the Asian tradition, and writes in strong figures of speech. The word *martus*, or witness, means no more than confessor if so required. The word 'eunuch' probably means no more than an ascetic and celibate, and the description of St John is expressed in figures of speech drawn from the Jerusalem Temple, the *petalon* being the golden plate which the high priest wore on his forehead. James the Just is described by Hegesippus in a very similar way; 'he alone went into the sanctuary', and so forth. The concept of the apostolic founder as a mystical and priestly personage was no foible of Polycrates. We remember the ordination prayer of Hippolytus in which the apostles are regarded as having established sanctuaries everywhere after the pattern of the Jerusalem Temple; Irenaeus and Clement treat the apostolate as a form of the priesthood; and Paul describes his apostolate to the Gentiles in priestly terms (Romans xv. 16).

THE EPISTLE OF THE GALLICAN SYNOD

The answer of Victor to Polycrates was a sentence of excommunication. We must give the actual words of Eusebius based on his study of the original documents.

Victor, the president of the church of the Romans, without any trepidation, attempted to cut off the *paroikiai* of all Asia, together with the adjoining churches, from the common unity, as heretics, and actually certifies it [or denounces them] by means of documents, proclaiming that all the brethren in those parts were entirely cut off from communion.

But this was not by any means pleasing to all the bishops; indeed they replied urging him strongly to think upon those things which belong to peace and to neighbourly unity and to love; and the actual words of these bishops are extant, in which they assail Victor with great severity; among whom was Irenaeus, who wrote a letter in the name of the Gallican brethren over whom he presided, in which he laid it down that the mystery of the Lord's resurrection should be celebrated only on the Lord's day, and also bestows a great deal of advice on Victor, in a suitable manner, to the effect that he should not cut off whole churches of God on account of their preserving the tradition of an ancient custom.   (Eusebius, *E.H.* v, 24, 9–11.)

In the days of Eleutherus, Irenaeus had glorified the stability and orthodoxy of the Roman church; he had said that it was necessary for all other churches to convene there (or agree with it, as some scholars translate the word); and it had been established that a majority of churches did agree with it on the point under debate. Nevertheless, it now fell to his duty to voice the general disagreement with the bishop of Rome in his policy towards the minority group. It was made clear that the church as a whole would not support any attempt to force the liturgical custom of the majority upon apostolic churches which had inherited a different one.

Eusebius preserves parts of the conciliar Epistle issued by Irenaeus, and we have made considerable use of it in reconstructing our history. He traces back the differences of custom to the most ancient period of church history; he points to the policy of toleration which had existed in Rome for seventy years; he supports the Roman Easter, but he asks for a recognition of divergences. His role is that of an ambassador for peace, as it had been in the Montanist affair rather more than ten years earlier.

The question which naturally arises is whether this inter-episcopal and inter-synodical procedure had been employed before. Eusebius says that Victor attempted to cut off the Asian churches from the common unity *as if they were heretics*; so that it looks very much as if the heretical schools had been cut off from the common unity by concerted action of this kind, and it becomes likely that the world-wide agreement of the catholic church on such points of common interest had been effected and registered during the previous generation by the exchange of episcopal and conciliar letters, and also that the church of Rome, with its old tradition and its international character, had exercised considerable influence, and even taken the lead.

The visits to Rome of overseas bishops, like Polycarp and Avircius, are thought by some scholars to be related to the leadership of the Roman church in action of this kind. The letter of the Gallican Christians addressed to Rome and Asia in 178 seems to be in line with this supposition; and Irenaeus, who acted as a mediator in that dispute, was acting as a mediator in this one, Eusebius says. The interlocking conciliar system must have been operating in the church fairly widely before its appearance in our records on a large scale in connexion with the Paschal question.

THE CHRISTIAN YEAR

We are thus able to complete our survey of the second-century church order by a consideration of the conciliar system and the festal calendar.

The ancient world understood, better than the modern, how much the lives of men are influenced and even governed by the recurrence of nights and days and seasons and years, which are conditioned in their turn by the revolutions and variations of suns and moons. The first moon of spring was a disturbing and exciting moon. The Jews called it Nisan, and held their Pascha or Passover when it was full. On the fourteenth day of that moon, they fasted all day, they killed their lamb in the Temple (so long as it was standing), and then, when the sun set and the full moon rose, they ate it in their houses and thought upon the deliverance from Egypt, when the angel of death passed over them and smote the Egyptians; they drank the cup of blessing; they partook of the spotless lamb; they ate of the unleavened bread.

It was at this spring festival that Jesus had been crucified, and when it came round, the tides of faith and feeling rose to their highest point. The scroll of the Gospel was brought out and the narrative of the Passion read. The day was kept as a solemn fast; it was the day when the bridegroom was taken from them, and the Lord had said that they would fast in that day. The new converts were baptized; the faith of the veteran Christians was renewed.

The argument about the day among the Christians was an intricate one, and it is probable that we do not altogether follow it. The Asian Christians had a custom which dated from the time of John, and very likely from the time of Paul, which consecrated the actual day of the Jewish Passover. The divergence in Asia seems to have arisen from a divergence in the Gospel records. According to Matthew the Lord had kept the Passover before his death, and therefore Christians should do the same; according to John he had not; he had died on the Passover day, and Christians should observe it simply as the anniversary of his death. He was the true Paschal Lamb.

The Romans looked at it in a different way. They were more concerned with the days of the week. Everybody agreed that the Lord had been crucified on a Friday, and risen again on a Sunday. The important day was the Sunday which came immediately after the Passover. The Passover might come on any day of the week; but the Romans always observed the following Sunday with a fast on the preceding days; there was some divergence in detail, Irenaeus says, but in Hippolytus the fast was on the Friday and the Saturday; Good Friday and Holy Saturday (as we call them now) and these were the days which were devoted to the baptismal rite.

It is a curious fact that the Sunday after the Passover was a festal day in its own right in the old Jewish calendar, according to the Sadducee computation;[1] it was the Omer or First-fruits which the Pharisees kept on Nisan sixteen. It looks very much as if the Asian custom had been fixed originally in accordance with the Pharisee computation, and the Roman in accordance with the Sadducee.

This festival of the Omer was the first of the fifty days which led up to Pentecost, and the church observed these days. They were suitable for baptisms, Tertullian says, though Easter Eve was the best of all days for that. No fast should be kept during this period, and there should be no bending of the knee. According to the *Epistle of the Apostles* it was the time when Christians should look for the return of their Lord.

There is some evidence that attempts were being made to work out a

---

[1] And this made Pentecost a Sunday too. This computation is connected by some scholars with the ancient agricultural calendar of Canaan which was based on periods of fifty days. See J. Morgenstern in *Vetus Testamentum*, vol. v, no. 1 (Leyden, 1955).

fixed system of festivals based on the Roman calendar. The Basilidians of Alexandria had their festival of the birthday of the Christ on 6 or 10 January, thus consecrating the pagan New Year. They studied such matters in Alexandria and made close calculations, but, like other learned men, they did not always agree. There were some who preferred the Syrian New Year or birth of the sun on 18 November, as we learn from Clement of Alexandria and Epiphanius. Hippolytus in Rome spent much time on research of this sort and worked out the dates of the Annunciation and the Passion for 25 March; it followed that the Nativity occurred on 25 December, which coincided with the old Roman New Year festival of the Saturnalia. Somewhat similar calculations were being made by the obscure sect called the *Alogi*. The Phrygians, at some time or another, fixed their Paschal day for 25 March, which was the high day of their god Attis, who also had a sanctuary in Rome. At the time of the great Paschal controversy these calculations may not have been much more than speculations; but they eventually captured for Christian use the old pagan rituals of the great turning-points of the sun's year.

SOME EASTERN SYNODS: CAESAREA

Eusebius, who studied in the library at Caesarea before he became the bishop of that city, found a quantity of correspondence which had been preserved there ever since the days of the Paschal controversy, and he was therefore in a position to say a good deal about the various councils and conciliar Epistles. We have mentioned the Epistles issued by Victor, Polycrates and Irenaeus, on behalf of Rome, Asia and Gaul respectively. Eusebius had also seen the Epistle which was issued by a synod in Pontus, which was presided over by Palmas of Amastris as the senior bishop; he was the same Palmas who had been addressed by Dionysius of Corinth about thirty years before. Bachyllus was bishop of Corinth now, and had issued a letter on his own account; Eusebius does not mention a synod there. A Palestinian synod was held at Caesarea, and was presided over by Theophilus of Caesarea and Narcissus of Jerusalem, a rather peculiar arrangement, one would think; Cassius, bishop of Tyre, and Clarus, bishop of Ptolemais, were among those who attended it. The Epistle which was sent out by this council was preserved in the Caesarean archives. It treated at length of the 'tradition concerning the Pascha which had come down to them out of the succession of the apostles', and concluded by saying,

Take care that copies of our Epistle be sent to every *paroikia*, that we may not be responsible in the case of those who readily delude their own souls. (Eusebius, *E.H.* v, 25.)

—from which we infer that there were churches in Palestine and southern Syria which kept the Christian Pascha on the Jewish day. The Jewish Christians would certainly do so.

There is an additional note of great interest,

We inform you that they observe the same day as we do in Alexandria; for letters have been sent from us to them and from them to us, so that we may keep the holy day harmoniously and together. (*Ibid.*)

ALEXANDRIA: BISHOP DEMETRIUS

This letter seems to prove the existence of a regional church organization for the Gentile churches in Palestine and Southern Syria, whose presiding bishop might be either the bishop of Caesarea, or the bishop of Aelia; more likely the former, since that was the custom which established itself in later times. This network of churches depended on Alexandria for guidance in regard to the calendar. This is not surprising, since Alexandria was a centre of astronomical study; and we doubtless have here the beginning of a custom by which the bishop of Alexandria issued 'Festal Epistles' on the Feast of the Epiphany (which was already being kept in that city) informing the church at large when the Pascha would fall. Alexandria supported Rome on the question of the Paschal tradition, and no doubt Victor had assured himself of this before attacking the Asians. Clement, who was by now the head of the Alexandrian School, in succession to Pantaenus, wrote a treatise *Concerning the Pascha*, of which a few scraps are preserved in the *Paschal Chronicle*; but it is not at all clear that he took the same line as his bishop. He may have favoured the Quartodeciman side.

Alexandria, like Rome, had a strong man as bishop, and his date of accession was about 190. He must have been a young man, since he administered his *paroikia* for over forty years. According to Jerome, he was a rustic of no great intellectual ability, and, if this is true, it makes it all the more remarkable that the school which he controlled had such a liberal policy. He was the bishop, according to the tenth-century annalist Eutychius, who appointed other bishops, for the first time, in the land of Egypt. There were three of these, he says, which would have been a sufficient number to consecrate a new bishop. The effect of the change would be to lift the responsibility for an episcopal appointment out of the control of the presbyters and lodge it in an episcopal college. However, Jerome says that the appointment of the bishop of Alexandria from among the presbyters and by the presbyters continued into the time of Heraclas, the successor of Demetrius; Eutychius makes it continue down to the time of the Council of Nicaea.

SYRIA: BISHOP SERAPION

Eusebius also has a record of a council in the far-Syrian kingdom of Osrhoene, presumably in the capital city of Edessa, which agreed with all these councils in supporting the Roman position. This city came under strict Roman control in the year 195, and the council probably represented the views of the western influx of population and the pro-Roman element in the population. There is evidence of serious divisions along these lines in Edessa at this time; for the tradition speaks of a new bishop named Palut, who was consecrated by Serapion of Antioch, who is quite erroneously said to have been consecrated by Zephyrinus of Rome.

Theophilus, the scholar and author, had been succeeded by Maximinus, and Maximinus by Serapion about 191 or 192. There is no evidence at all about the views of Serapion on the Paschal question; the controversies in which we find him engaged are with Montanists and Docetae. In the first of these he preserves for us interesting evidence about Phrygian synods of an earlier date; in the second he preserves interesting evidence about an apocryphal Gospel.

The omission of any reference to Antioch by Eusebius in connexion with the Paschal controversy strongly suggests that it did not agree with Rome in spite of the line taken in Osrhoene. It may be that the east in general sympathized with the Asians and supported the Quartodeciman position. Later evidence confirms this conclusion. Athanasius says that in his time, Cilicia, Mesopotamia and Syria were Quartodeciman; and Chrysostom, who was an Antiochene himself, says that Antioch was formerly Quartodeciman. These statements explain the silence of Eusebius, and prove that the Asians had wide-spread support. We are reminded of the general attitude of Theophilus; Syria is not entirely at one with the Greco-Roman world. On the other hand, Jerusalem is in line with Rome through its affiliation with Alexandria; and this is a new alignment, though it is not unlike the understanding between Palestine and Rome which is suggested in the Books of Clement.

CONTROVERSY IN PHRYGIA

There is no news about the Paschal controversy from Phrygia, but the controversy over the New Prophecy was blazing fiercely. In the last years or year of Commodus, that is to say about 190 or 191, there were great arguments in Ancyra, the modern Ankara, one of the chief cities of northern Galatia, a country which had been settled by invading Gauls as much as four centuries before, giving their name to the whole region where they settled, and later to the Roman Province into which it was incorporated.

Two visitors from the Phrygian Pentapolis were invited to be present. One of them was something of an expert on the history of the New Prophecy; but unfortunately his name is not recorded; he is referred to as 'the Anonymous'. His companion was Zoticus of Otröus, who, perhaps, is to be distinguished from Zoticus of Cumana, who had confronted Maximilla in the earlier days of the movement. The discourses and arguments of the Anonymous were so effective that the local presbyters requested him to leave them a written memorandum of what he had said. He had been asked to write a treatise on the subject a long time before by his neighbour, the venerable Avircius Marcellus of Hierapolis, but had hesitated to do so because he did not want to incur the accusation of seeking to add a new document to the 'New Testament' of the gospel; but, on reaching home, he addressed himself to the task. He dedicated his book to Avircius and sent off a copy to Ancyra.

His sensitiveness on the subject of the New Testament indicates that the limits of the New Testament were a subject of hot discussion between the churchmen and the prophets. He is the first writer to use this name for the list of apostolic books which were read in church.

About the same time, 'the fortieth year after Montanus began his pretended prophesying', Apollonius wrote on the same subject. He was much concerned about a certain Alexander, an ex-bandit and ex-martyr, who was flourishing with his prophetess somewhere in Asia or Phrygia and indulging in high living at the expense of the widow and orphan.

Tell me [asks Apollonius], does a prophet dye his hair? Does a prophet paint his eyelids? Does a prophet love adornment? Does a prophet play at gaming-tables and dice? Does a prophet lend out money on usury? Let them agree as to whether these things are permitted or not, and I for my part will prove that they took place among them.

(Apollonius in Eusebius, *E.H.* v, 18, 11.)

It looks as if Apollonius was an Ephesian. He refers inquirers about Alexander to the official records of Asia, and mentions the name of the proconsul under whom Alexander was condemned for the crime of robbery at Ephesus, prior to his imprisonment as a martyr. This statement reminds us of the story of Callistus at Rome, and there may be two sides to it in both cases. It was a strong recommendation, apparently, for any new teacher or prophet, to have spent time in gaol; we have Praxeas and Noetus and Theodotus, all from Asia. Apollonius uses the Revelation of John, and mentions a story about the apostle John raising a dead man in Ephesus, which is a point of contact with the *Acts of John*. He dates the encounter with Maximilla by the martyrdom of Thraseas, which is said by Polycrates to have taken place in Smyrna. He may have been the successor of Polycrates as bishop of Ephesus; a fifth-century writer, Predestinatus, gives him this title.

The Anonymous mentions a persecution at Apamea on the Meander, in which Gaius and Alexander, a catholic Alexander it would seem, bore their witness; and he says that on this occasion the martyrs from the church severed themselves from the communion of the martyrs from the Phrygian heresy. He says that frightful tales were being circulated among the orthodox about the deaths of Montanus and Maximilla and Theodotus, but he doubts their truth. He is the more judicious writer of the two, and probably the better informed.

THE EVIDENCE OF THE *SYNODICON*

At the end of the ninth century a catalogue of historic synods was drawn up by some unknown writer who made use of ancient sources. This book is called the *Synodicon* or *Libellus Synodicus*. Its earliest entries concern the synods which dealt with the Montanist and Paschal controversies. Our first impression might be that these particulars were derived from the pages of Eusebius himself, with the aid of a rather free use of the imagination; but the *Synodicon* is a serious compilation and is entitled to as much respect as the fifth-century Philip of Side, or the eighth-century Georgios Hamartolos, or the tenth-century Eutychius. Any one of them may be following some ancient authority of real merit. Furthermore, it appeared that the details which it gave about the Montanist synods of an earlier date were worthy of consideration.

Similar details are supplied for the councils held about the Paschal question; there were thirteen bishops at the council in Gaul presided over by Irenaeus, fourteen in Rome under Victor, fourteen in Jerusalem under Narcissus, twelve in Caesarea under Theophilus, fourteen in Pontus under Palmas (whose name appears as Plasmas) and eighteen in Osrhoene, the name of the president not being given. It will be seen that this is the list of Eusebius, except that it slips in a synod at Jerusalem under Narcissus in addition to a synod at Caesarea under Theophilus, whereas Eusebius speaks of a synod at Caesarea only, presided over by both bishops. The *Synodicon* adds a council of eighteen bishops in Mesopotamia, which looks like a duplication of that at Osrhoene, and a synod at Corinth under Bacchyllus, without giving the number of bishops.

Eusebius has no synod in Mesopotamia or Corinth, though he says that Bacchyllus of Corinth wrote a letter on his own account. Nevertheless, the list in the *Synodicon* looks like his, with added particulars. Is there any reason to suppose that these particulars were invented? Is there any purpose that would be served in the ninth century by inventing them? Now Eusebius had before him the original documentary records of the Montanist and Quartodeciman synods to which he refers, with conciliar Epistles and lists of bishops attending. He gives a few very short extracts from these, and in one instance he mentions actual signatures, two of which he copies. These documents existed in his time, and there is no reason why they should not have been preserved, or possibly some more complete catalogue of them. It is quite within the bounds of possibility, therefore, that the compiler of the *Synodicon* could have had access to these Caesarean documents or some précis of them; his numbers could have been derived from such a source. The larger number of bishops present at Hierapolis under Claudius Apolinarius is quite consistent with the impression which we receive of church organization in Phrygia; bishops appear to have been numerous there. The other numbers are rather uniform perhaps; but they rather suggest that twelve was regarded as a quorum or minimum number of bishops for a regional council, just as it was thought of as the appropriate number of presbyters to be associated with a bishop in the local *paroikia*, according to the Palestinian and Alexandrian traditions. On the other hand, Narcissus of Jerusalem is given fourteen bishops at his council, and Theophilus of Caesarea twelve at his; and this agrees exactly with the number of Gentile predecessors of Narcissus in the Jerusalem episcopal list, and the numbers of presbyters allotted to Zacchaeus of Caesarea in the Clementine books. If these are fictions, they interlock in a truly remarkable manner.

When we turn to the other early councils on other theological questions, which are listed in the *Synodicon*, we find weakness and confusion; and no numbers are given. We are entitled to infer that he drew his particulars of the Montanist and Paschal synods from a distinct source of better quality, and did not invent details where his source did not supply them.

There is a chance, therefore, that he is right about his additional synod in Aelia, and that Eusebius is wrong in combining it with Caesarea. Did Eusebius, in working from notes which he had made, lose track of an Aelian council under Narcissus, and come to regard the list of signatures to it as an episcopal succession? The double presidency which he affirms for the Caesarean council might have corresponded to conditions in his own day, when Caesarea claimed metropolitical rights over Aelia, and yet Aelia had a certain dignity and independence as the successor of Jerusalem. Caesarea was his own see, and the picture which he gives would be in line with its claims. Or alternatively did Narcissus, when signing the conciliar letter, enumerate his predecessors as co-witnesses with him to the 'tradition concerning the Pascha which had come down to them out of the succession of the apostles'? In just that style Polycrates had appealed to the tradition of Philip and John; and Victor, apparently, to that of Peter and Paul. Narcissus could appeal in the same way to the tradition of James the Just. This would explain how Eusebius found himself in possession of this episcopal list, and at the same time it would explain the numbers given in the *Synodicon*.

CONCILIAR ACTION

The picture which has emerged from this study is the objective opera-tive counterpart of the generalized statements about the doctrinal unity of the church which were given by Irenaeus in the *Refutation*. The addition which it makes to it is the interlocking regional councils of bishops, which seem to have come earlier in the more numerous and ancient churches of the east than in the more missionary west, where Rome was the only great apostolic see, Corinth and Athens coming a poor second and third. Its position there could not be rivalled, and its grandeur would increase. How far it had won or lost in prestige in the Paschal controversy is a matter for debate. It was on the winning side over the actual point of the controversy, but it was not supported in its effort to excommunicate the Asian churches, which were not without friends. The geographical distribution is almost exactly the same as it was in the days of Dionysius of Corinth, thirty years earlier; then it was Italy, Greece, Pontus, Bithynia and Crete; now it is Italy, Greece, Pontus, Bithynia, Palestine and Alexandria, with a friendly voice from distant Osrhoene. The other group extends along the old Pauline trail from Ephesus to Antioch; it is made up of Asia, Phrygia, Cilicia, Syria and Mesopotamia. The cultural and political duality of the Empire seems to be represented here in ecclesiastical terms.

The church councils were a remarkable development. The men who attended them had been elected or appointed with the consent of the communities which they served. They were the first representative bodies of a democratic character in history. They proceeded by means of free debate and the discussion of differences. They had no central executive which could impose their decisions on dissentient churches. They could only proceed by registering general agreements.

The bishops were often strong men with considerable powers; for the democratic tone of the church life was not incompatible with vigorous leadership. They stepped into their place in the succession, and appeared at the council table as spokesmen of their several tradi-tions. It was not the merits of the various ways of celebrating the Pascha that were under discussion; the object was to discover what the apostolic custom had been, on the assumption that the apostles had bequeathed a single tradition to the church. The outcome of the inquiry was that, in this case, they had bequeathed a double tradition, and in consequence the heirs of the secondary tradition were not to be disturbed.

A hundred years before this time, the various churches had depended for their external unity on their relations with the apostle or apostolic man on whom they depended for guidance and direction; a generation later we find them related to one another through the episcopate, which had inherited the functions of guidance and direction from the apostolic founders, and was also integrated constitutionally with the local ecclesia and its presbytery. By now the bishop was in a stronger position constitutionally than he had been in the days of Ignatius and Onesimus and Polycarp; and this increased strength was based on the fact that he was an elected, ordained, responsible officer, constitutionally related to his people and to the church at large; his authority being limited, however, by the form of 'apostolic' tradition to which he belonged, and for which he spoke. Ignatius had seen these possibilities in the episcopate as it existed in his time, and had commended the holding of synods on a wide geographical basis.

Along with the development of regional councils went the growing influence and importance of those bishops who were the logical men, for geographical or historical reasons, to preside over them. Irenaeus in Gaul, Victor in Rome, Bacchyllus perhaps in Corinth, Polycrates in Asia, Apollinarius during an earlier conflict in Hierapolis, Serapion in Antioch, Theophilus in Caesarea, and Demetrius in Alexandria, were becoming what were later to be called metropolitans; bishops of mother-churches. Palmas of Pontus may be an exception; it is said that he presided because he was the senior. The wider authority or influence of the greater bishops was no new thing. It may, indeed, be a primitive feature and represent the area of the original apostolic mission. It was certainly anticipated by Ignatius, who called himself bishop of Syria, and seems to regard the church of Rome as possessing a similar position of regional leadership in the west.

CHAPTER 23

TERTULLIAN AND CLEMENT

The Afro-Syrian Dynasty, A.D. 193–235, *p.* 392. The Accession of Severus, A.D. 193, *p.* 394. Tertullian's *Apology*, c. A.D. 197, *p.* 396. Early writings of Tertullian, *p.* 399. Minucius Felix, *p.* 400. The Parthian wars, A.D. 197–202, *p.* 401. Bar Daisan (Bardesanes), *p.* 401. Syrian Christianity, *p.* 402. Serapion of Antioch, *p.* 403. Clement of Alexandria, *p.* 404. Clement and the tradition, *p.* 406. Clement and the New Testament, *p.* 407. The Alexandrian texts, *p.* 408. The *Word of Invitation, Logos Protreptikos*, *p.* 409. The *Paidagogos* and the *Stromata*, *p.* 410. The pupils of Clement, *p.* 412.

THE AFRO-SYRIAN DYNASTY, A.D. 193–235

(Synopsis of Christian Chronology)

A.D.

185   Birth of Origen. Pantaenus is head of the Alexandrian School; Clement is his pupil; Narcissus is bishop of Aelia, Irenaeus of Lyons, Eleutherus of Rome, Polycrates of Ephesus.

189   *Victor, bishop of Rome*; episode of Callistus before 193.

190   *Demetrius, bishop of Alexandria, and Serapion of Antioch, c.* 191.
      Period of the Paschal controversy; Letters of Irenaeus and Polycrates.

192   Council at Ancyra on Montanism; the 'Anonymous' treatise on Montanism addressed to Avircius.

193   *Septimius Severus emperor, Julia Domna*   Writings of Clement, 190–202.
      empress.

194   Severus in the East.   Monarchian Schools in Rome.

195   Submission of Abgar IX (Africanus, Bar Daisan, in Edessa).

196   Fall of Byzantium.

197   Severus returns to Rome.   Tertullian, *Apology*, etc.

198   Severus returns to the East.

199   *Zephyrinus, bishop of Rome, Callistus his deacon; schism of Natalius.*

200   Edicts of Severus against Jews and Chris-   Apollonius writes against Montanism.
      tians.

201   Severus in Egypt.   Tertullian, *Prescription* and other books.

202   *Persecution in Alexandria* (pupils of Origen): *Clement leaves Alexandria.*

203   *Persecution in Africa* (Perpetua).   *Origen head of Alexandrian school.*

204   Gaius and Proclus on Montanism?

205   Hippolytus, *Syntagma, Against Gaius*, etc.

206   Origen studying under Ammonius.

207   Tertullian accepts Montanism by 207.

208   Severus goes to Britain.   Tertullian, *Against Marcion*, etc.

209   Tertullian, *Against Praxeas?*

210   *Persecution continuing.* Alexander in prison in Cappadocia, Clement at work in Cappadocia.

211   *Caracalla emperor, Julia Domna queen-mother. Asclepiades, bishop of Antioch. Clement in Antioch.*

212   *Persecution in Africa* under Scapula.   Origen visits Rome, 210–12.

213   *Alexander, bishop of Aelia*, Narcissus still   Sabellius in Rome?
      living.

A.D.

214		Origen visits Arabia.
215	Birth of Mani, Iranian religious founder.	Origen at Caesarea.
216	Edessene Monarchy suppressed, Abgar IX captive, Caracalla in Edessa.	
217	*Callistus and Hippolytus, bishops in Rome,* Caracalla assasinated, Macrinus emperor.	
218	*Elagabalus emperor, Julia Maesa queen-mother.*	
219		Hippolytus, *Apostolic Tradition.*
220	*Murder of Elagabalus and his mother.*	*Chronographies* of Africanus.
	Severus Alexander emperor.	
221	Africanus visits Rome.	Last works of Tertullian, *On Modesty,* etc.
222	*Alexander Severus emperor, Julia Mamaea queen-mother. Urban and Hippolytus, bishops of Rome.*	
223		Statue of Hippolytus.
224		Paschal computations of Hippolytus.
225		Origen on St John, and *De Principiis.*
226	Coronation of Ardashir I of Iran as king of kings.	
227		Hippolytus, *Refutation of Heresies.*
228		
229		
230	*Pontian and Hippolytus, bishops in Rome, schism of Artemon.*	
	Persians invade Mesopotamia.	Hippolytus writes against Artemon.
231	Origen travels in Greece and settles in Caesarea, is ordained: condemned by Demetrius.	
232	Alexander and Mamaea in Antioch.	Origen's visit to Mamaea.
	Roman failure in Mesopotamia.	Origen resumes literary work.
233		
234		Hippolytus, *Chronicle.*
235	*Murder of Alexander and Julia Mamaea.*	Origen in the Cappadocian Caesarea, 235–7.
	Maximin emperor; Persecution, Pontian	
	and Hippolytus die as martyrs in Sardinia.	

Notes. The first entries on this chart, A.D. 186–92, are all approximate, and form an introduction to the reigns of Septimius Severus and his successors. The lives of two men bridge the whole period: Demetrius, bishop of Alexandria, and Hippolytus who became (in his own estimation at least) bishop of Rome.

Clement of Alexandria seems to have died about 216, and Tertullian about 222; Callistus was martyred in the latter year.

The entries on the left-hand side are solid dates. The entries on the right-hand side are approximations, unless a figure is actually given. Sometimes they draw attention to some general tendency or activity which was going on.

The bishops of the Adoptionist schism in Rome, Natalius and Artemon, are placed opposite the names of the bishops whom they opposed. Actually all we know is that Natalius was Adoptionist bishop in the time of Zephyrinus, and Artemon late in the episcopate of Hippolytus; he was still bishop over thirty years later: he is not actually called a bishop.

The name of Geta is omitted; he was co-emperor with his brother Caracalla in 211, and murdered by him in 212. Caracalla, Elagabalus and Alexander Severus all perished by assassination.

The indications are that the Paschal controversy should be assigned to the last years of the emperor Commodus and the first years of Severus, that is to say about 188–95 inclusive. No doubt it raged for a long time, and we have even ventured to suggest that the synod in Osrhoene was held as late as 195. It has the historical value of bringing on to the stage many of the leading figures in the catholic church. It forms another divide in church history, comparable to that which occurred about the year 100. The old order, in the persons of Irenaeus and Polycrates and Narcissus, joins hands for a moment with the new order in men like Demetrius and Serapion and Victor.

A new order appears with even greater dramatic effect in the political world. The age of the Antonines comes suddenly to an end with the death of Commodus, the son of Marcus Aurelius. The reign of the Hellenic philosopher, with his appeal to reason and his sense of the freedom of the spirit, is a thing of the past; the importance of free and responsible institutions has almost disappeared; the oriental spirit has captured the Greco-Roman civilization.

THE ACCESSION OF SEVERUS, A.D. 193

The influence of Marcia must have waned rather fast, for one day, as she was looking through the emperor's papers, she saw her own name on a list of persons who were to be summarily executed. Commodus had become a suspicious and tyrannical man and his violence and bad government had made him intolerable. It was not hard to find people who were ready and willing to assist her in ending his life, which they did on the last day of the year 192. He was thirty-one years old, and had reigned thirteen years. He was suffocated in his bath by his trainer in athletics. So ended the dynasty of the Antonines. A distinguished general named Helvidius Pertinax was made emperor. He tried to introduce discipline into the garrison troops at Rome, and to restore constitutional powers to the Senate; but he was too late. A serious deterioration had taken place in public life, and the golden days, such as they were, had gone. The army was now the master, and the praetorian guards took action. They murdered him on 28 March, and put up the empire for auction to the highest bidder. It was bought by a certain Didius Julianus. The century of peaceful succession was over.

The praetorian guard formed the garrison of Rome and were the emperor's personal guards; but they could not speak for the whole army. The reign of Commodus had been a peaceful one, largely because he had good generals in the field, a fact which speaks well for his father. Three of these were proclaimed emperor by their legions. The nearest legions were those in the Balkans, whose commander-in-chief was Lucius Septimius Severus, an African of Carthaginian descent who spoke the Punic language better than he spoke Latin. He marched on Rome, and was received by the senate, who had anticipated his arrival by executing Julianus on 2 June. He regarded himself as the successor of Pertinax. He was a great soldier, a man of iron will, with extra-ordinary energy and ambition. He began by recognizing his western rival, Clodius Albinus, who commanded the legions in Gaul and Britain, granting him the lesser title of Caesar, and reserving for himself alone the higher title of Augustus. He then marched eastward to attack Pescennius Niger, who had been proclaimed emperor in Antioch and had the riches and military might of Syria at his command. The Balkan general had to fight a major war. There were two years of desperate fighting before he made himself master of the east; for he had to carry the war across the Euphrates, where the Syrian kingdoms had sup-ported Niger. He subdued Abgar IX, the king of Edessa who favoured the Christian church, and its native theologian and astrologer Bar Daisan. He enrolled the Edessene archers in his army and used them with great effect in his subsequent wars.

On his way to the east, he had left in his rear the strong city of Byzantium, where there was a Christian church and a local theologian, Theodotus the Adoptionist, known as the tanner or leather-worker. It was taken by one of his generals in 196, and it is recorded by Tertullian that when it surrendered the defeated general, Caecilius Capella, is said to have cried out, 'Christians, rejoice!' Exactly how much cause the Christians had to rejoice over the triumph of Severus is a matter for debate. Byzantium suffered severely; for Severus showed no mercy on those who opposed him.

In 197 he defeated his western rival and nominal ally, Albinus, at Trevoux near Lyons, where Irenaeus may still have been bishop; Lyons suffered severely too, and many of its citizens were massacred. Severus now held the whole empire in his ruthless grasp. There were great festivities when he re-entered Rome, and the Senate trembled. There were executions and severities. There were Christians apparently who were not sufficiently prominent in the ceremonies of welcome; doubtless there were many in the palace itself of whose loyalty he did not feel very confident; and they felt his resentment. This occasion seemed to have moved Tertullian to write his *Apology*, in which he alludes to recent actions against Christians in the emperor's domestic circle. In his later writings, however, he speaks with some favour of the emperor, and says that he had protected eminent Christians in time of persecution.[1] In particular he mentions the Montanist theologian, Proculus Torpacion, a venerable person of holy and ascetic life, who had healed the emperor of some sickness by means of oil; he sought him out, Tertullian says, and kept him near him till the end of his life. He adds that the sons of Severus were brought up on Christian milk, which is more likely to mean the catechism than a wet-nurse, as some have interpreted it. They were also provided with the best that pagan culture could afford in the personal tuition of the philosopher Philostratus, the author of the *Life of Apollonius Tyana*, the Pythagorean sage of Domitian's reign who was now proposed as a pagan substitute for Christ.

TERTULLIAN'S *APOLOGY*, c. A.D. 197

The *Apology* of Tertullian is generally assigned to the year 197, in which Severus defeated Albinus in Gaul, and returned to Rome to settle the empire. It points to a recrudescence of anti-Christian feeling. It is clear that their loyalty was suspect. It was impossible for Christians to join in the ovations offered to the emperor on state occasions. No laurel garlands graced their door-posts; no lamps flamed and smoked before their portals. The populace grew excited and old scandals were brought out again. Scurrilous pamphlets were handed about. Tertullian mentions a cartoon with a figure in a philosopher's gown, and a book in his hand, and the head of an ass. Archaeology has unearthed a similar sketch which was scratched on the wall of the emperor's palace; it was a crucified figure with the head of an ass, and another figure kneeling in front of it; underneath it is the legend, 'Alexamenos adores his God'.

Scenes of violence occurred. Christians were dragged before the magistrates, and ordered off to torture and execution.

The '*Apologeticum*' gives a picture of the Christian religion in its rise to power and the Roman empire approaching its decline. The second century had seen a vast growth in population and apparent

---

[1] Perhaps there was a political division in the church. The bishop Victor was associated with Marcia (who was put to death by Severus) and therefore with the regime of Commodus. Was the new bishop, Zephyrinus, more acceptable to Severus?

prosperity. New cities had sprung up; vacant territory had been settled; and everywhere Christians abounded. Even beyond the confines of the empire, in lands where Roman arms had never penetrated, the Christian faith was establishing itself. The empire was alarmed; the church was exultant; the faith was still misunderstood. With telling sarcasm, he ridicules the legal proceedings by which the Christians were done to death in order to pacify a howling mob or gratify a sadistic governor. He reduces to absurdity the old scandals about a ritual of cannibalism and incest. He follows Melito in reviewing the relations between the empire and the church, but his history is open to criticism. The thesis that the bad emperors persecuted and the good did not could no longer be seriously maintained.

He works his way through the regular course of subjects: monotheistic faith, Jewish prophecy, and the crucifixion of Jesus in the reign of Tiberius. The array of gods and goddesses are declared to be daemons. The emperor is accepted as God's viceroy, but not as a god; and the loyalty of Christians is strongly asserted. None of them supported Niger or Albinus, he claims.[1] Their worship is outlined in general terms; but there is no mention at all of baptism or eucharist or bishop. In his thirty-ninth chapter, however, he gives a picture of the Christian assembly in non-technical terms and without reference to the mysteries. Prayers were offered for the emperor and those in authority, for the peace of the world and for the delay of the Day of Judgement. The sacred writings were read aloud; exhortations, admonitions and disciplinary action followed; but no graver sentence was ever passed than that of excommunication from the common prayer. (In the Jewish synagogue, it should be remembered, the luckless offender against the Law of Moses received in public the penalty of the thirty-nine lashes; no such discipline had yet invaded the Christian church.) Approved elders presided on these occasions, and were not to be influenced by bribes. The common fund was kept up by voluntary monthly contributions, which were devoted to the burial of the poor, the support of orphans and aged people and the relief of prisoners. All were brethren, and even the pagans were known to say, 'See how they love one another.' 'One in mind and soul, we do not hesitate to

---

[1] He seems to be answering an accusation here, but does he protest too much? Doubtless few actual Christians had borne arms against Severus in lands known to Tertullian. Abgar had certainly been an enemy.

share our worldly goods; all things are in common among us except our wives.'

He goes on to describe the 'agape' or love-feast, the name of which was the ground of scandalous accusations. Before reclining, he says, we taste first of prayer to God; we eat and drink in moderation; we talk like men who know their Lord is listening. After the supper we wash our hands; lights are brought in (it is the evening hour by now); individuals stand up and sing hymns to God, either from the scriptures or of their own composing. When all is done the meeting closes with prayer. This is the setting of the little rituals which we find in Hippolytus. It is a charming picture; but of course we must not think that the agape was always so orderly and blameless as he suggests; we know from Clement of Alexandria that it could be otherwise; and no doubt the pagans had heard a few tales of rowdiness or unseemly behaviour. Hippolytus finds it necessary to specify that men kiss men, and women kiss women.

After this chapter Tertullian proceeds to answer a number of criticisms, which were circulated, no doubt, in a written document. The Christians are blamed for every public disaster. If the Tiber floods its banks, or the Nile fails to do so, the cry goes up to throw the Christians to the lion. They are called an idle non-cooperating breed of men. They are never seen at the public festivities. They vainly attempt to rival the philosophers, whose doctrine and ethics they have stolen. They create general amusement by announcing that God will judge the world and send some to Gehenna, which is a subterranean fire, and others to Paradise, which is a place of heavenly bliss. The poets and philosophers have said exactly the same thing, but they are only described as arrogant speculations, or even insanity, when the Christians say them.

Well, the Christians, as they die, are more than conquerors.

Go on, go on, good good judges. You will gain glory with the populace if you sacrifice us at their demand. Kill us, torture us, condemn us, grind us to pieces.... The more you mow us down, the thicker we rise up. The blood of the martyrs is a kind of seed.   (*Apology*, 50.)

The intemperance of Tertullian is kept well under control in the rolling rhetoric, sudden paradoxes and fiery argumentations of this great appeal. The author only seems to reach the same heights again in his

Testimony of the Soul, in which he puts the human soul in the witness-box, and makes it confess itself Christian by nature and origin. '*O anima naturaliter Christiana*', he cries out; 'O soul of Christian birth and nature.'

EARLY WRITINGS OF TERTULLIAN

Tertullian must still have been a young man. He is not yet tainted with the harsh Montanist spirit which dried up his streams of generosity and turned his romantic admiration of popular Christianity into a waspish irritation at the weakness and worldliness with which it was often infected. His output of literature was prodigious. In his early period he turned out a stream of text-books and pamphlets which made available, in an exciting and idiomatic Latin, the traditional material of the older Greek schools. His book *Against the Jews* (for surely it is his) is the first systematic outline of the testimony material from the Hebrew prophets; it is thought that it preserves some of the work of Aristo of Pella. His books *On Prayer* and *On Baptism* were intended for catechumens and contain valuable information about the liturgy which enables us to supplement the church order of Hippolytus. His simple exposition of the Lord's Prayer may be based on older liturgical practice. His controversial genius displayed itself in his book *Against the Valentinians*, in which he makes use of Irenaeus. The *Prescription of Heretics* dresses up the old arguments from priority and apostolic origin and catholic consent in a novel and arresting style. He has high praise for the church of Rome, which he afterwards came to think very hardly of. He pillories Greek philosophy as the source of heresy. 'What has Athens to do with Jerusalem? What concord is there between the Academy and the Church? what between heretics and Christians?'

His happy ending to his book on baptism may serve to conclude this brief notice of some of his earlier books. He is speaking to his class of catechumens, who are now very near to their baptism.

Therefore ye blessed, for whom the grace of God is even now waiting, when you shall ascend from the sacred fountain of your new birth and spread forth your hands for the first time in the house of your mother, together with your brothers, ask from your Father and from your Lord special treasures of grace and distributions of *charismata*—and when you are asking, be mindful also of Tertullian the sinner.

MINUCIUS FELIX

The *Octavius* of Minucius Felix was written in a very different tone from the *Apology* of Tertullian, though it traverses many of the same subjects. They are discussed by a couple of friends, Caecilius and Octavius, at the sea-side resort of Ostia near Rome. The dialogue consists for the most part of two long speeches, Caecilius presenting the case against Christianity and Octavius speaking in its favour. There is a narrative introduction which provides a charming social and domestic background. We are conscious of the waves coming in on the beach throughout the long summer's day. The children are throwing pebbles into the sea. Their elders are discussing philosophy. None of the mysteries of the faith are touched upon. The talk circles round the familiar topics of monotheism, philosophy, Judaism, judgement, resurrection, persecution, and so forth. Caecilius had read the works of Fronto, with their low view of Christianity and their stupid belief in the crimes with which Christians were charged. The object of the dialogue seems to be to answer his book in an atmosphere of serene unclouded familiar conversation, though a deep-felt sincerity appears on both sides.

This book is commonly dated about A.D. 200, though some scholars place it as much as fifty years later; but the reference to Fronto supports the earlier date. The works of Tertullian and Minucius mark the appearance of the Christian faith in Latin literature, and, more than that, a revival of Latin literature itself; for they are among the best specimens of it in their time. Minucius is aware that Cicero had written dialogues in which noble Romans, who had drunk from the cup of Greek literature, debated in a measured prose which did not lose in strength by being graceful and exact. Those golden days of classical Latin were now past; but the *Octavius* is regarded as one of the fine examples of what is called 'silver Latin'. The genius of Tertullian was of another character; it was not so closely tied to classical precedents, and moulded the Latin idiom according to its needs in new and surprising forms of verbal expression which rank him as a great creative artist.

THE PARTHIAN WARS, A.D. 197–202

Severus is described by Tertullian as the most immovable or conservative of princes. He set himself to hew down the immense jungle of Roman law and precedent and to enforce firm and efficient government. In constructing the great *Corpus Juris* he had the assistance of distinguished jurists such as Plautian, Papinian and Ulpian, and possibly of Tertullian himself, since a lawyer of that name is mentioned in its pages. The will of the prince became more than ever the mainspring of the system; the senate became a cipher. This great code of law was the machinery by which he circumscribed the old liberties; the army was his instrument of power. His ambition was boundless; his character was cruel and unforgiving.

In 198 the Parthians overran Mesopotamia and he returned to the east, where he fought a brilliantly successful war. In 199 he captured Seleucia and Ctesiphon, the royal cities of the Parthian monarch, but did not occupy them permanently; he was content to enlarge and strengthen the Roman province of Mesopotamia, fortifying the city of Nisibis, east of Edessa, which became the centre of the Roman administration. He remained in the east during 200 and 201, and there are obscure references to a rising among the Jews and Samaritans. We are ignorant of what happened in Palestine, but it led him to put out some decrees forbidding conversions to Judaism and Christianity. Perhaps he found the Jews and Christians were not perfectly loyal? The circumcision of non-Jews had long been forbidden by law, but the prohibition of the baptism of new Christians was a novelty. It does not seem to have been very widely enforced.

BAR DAISAN (BARDESANES)

During these wars Abgar IX, the patron of Syrian Christianity, retained his throne in Edessa; and it was at this time that Julius Africanus of Aelia, who was a young cavalry officer under Severus, went hunting with Bar Daisan and admired his skill in archery.

Information comes in from various quarters about Bar Daisan. He was educated with Abgar (Epiphanius); he was a skilled archer (Africanus); he was a missionary in Armenia (Moses of Chorene); he stood firm in some sort of persecution under Caracalla (Epiphanius); he conversed with a delegation of Indians who came to the imperial court (Porphyry); he argued with the Marcionite leader Prepon (Hippolytus); he wrote a hundred and fifty hymns; he wrote a book called 'Books of the Laws of Countries'. He dabbled in astrology.

The treatise on the laws of countries is also known as the *Dialogue on Fate*. It is still in existence, but proves not to have been written by Bar Daisan. It is the work of a disciple named Philip, but he is the principal speaker in it. He appears as a learned and scholarly person who knows how to reason like a Greek philosopher without passion or personal feeling. He refutes the native pagan astrologer Awida and convinces him that there is room in the universe for free will. One ruling principle is nature, by which he means the orderly predictable element which Victorian philosophers called law; the second is fate, by which he means the unpredictable or accidental element which we might call chance. Man cannot change either law or chance, but there remains a considerable area of existence in which he can exercise his free will, which is the third ruling principle. He thus decides his own character and to some extent his destiny. Bar Daisan had strange ideas about the heavenly powers, and the creation of the world, and the composition of man; but he seems to have been the exponent of a remarkable Christian philosophy, though it was not precisely that of the catholic church.

He must also be regarded as the founder of Syrian literature, a literature which grew and prospered in succeeding centuries. He was a poet and wrote several songs, which have not come down to us, unless we accept as his the mystical *Hymn of the Soul* in the *Acts of Thomas*. It appears to be derived from the story of Joseph and the coat of many colours, which it has transformed into a transcendental myth. The bondage in Egypt represents the bondage of the human soul in this world; it forgets its heavenly origin until its father, the king of kings, sends down the heavenly robe, which is the Christus; he is the twin or other self of the soul, which puts him on and is united with him, so returning to its true home above the skies.

SYRIAN CHRISTIANITY

The *Acts of Thomas* are the most attractive of the apocryphal Acts. They tell the story of Judas Thomas (Judas the Twin), who was the twin brother of the Christ, and was sent by him, against his own will, to preach the gospel in India, where he converted King Gundaphor. The approximate date of the *Acts of Thomas* is thought to be about 220, and no doubt it gives us our best idea of the older Syrian Christianity, to which Addai, Hystasp, Tatian, Abgar and Bar Daisan, all contributed. Bar Daisan died in 222 at the age of sixty-eight, the chronicle says. It would appear that his ideas did not die with him; for his school of Syrian Christianity was a potent force in the far east. No doubt Syrian Christianity sobered down under the influence of Palût and his successors, but it retained for a long time its strongly 'encratite' character mixed with a gnostical mysticism. Among its treasures was the *Diatessaron* of Tatian, which was not dislodged from its place in the liturgy until the fifth century; and also the *Odes of Solomon* with their lyrical spirituality. The whole Syrian church was tinged with these ideas. The Syrian father Aphraates (Afrahat), who wrote in the fourth century, shows the marks of it; he uses the *Diatessaron*, and he advises those who are thinking of marriage not to come to baptism.

SERAPION OF ANTIOCH

Serapion of Antioch, whose accession date was about 191, remained bishop for twenty years. He was a writer of *Hupomnemata* or 'Notebooks', like Hegesippus and Symmachus, including one called *An Exercise concerning Words*, which sounds as if it must have been grammatical or lexical; but even Eusebius had not seen them. He knew of an Epistle, however, which was addressed to a certain Domnus, who had lapsed from the faith in a time of persecution and had taken refuge in Judaism; and another, which was addressed to Pontius and Caricus, 'ecclesiastical men', on the subject of the New Prophecy. His principal problems, therefore, seem to have been Montanism and Judaism. He also had to adjudicate on the *Gospel of Peter*.

Serapion had visited the church at Rhosus, about thirty miles away from Antioch, and found it divided by an argument. As the only point at issue seemed to be the question whether the *Gospel of Peter* should be read or not, and as he judged them all to be sound in the faith, he allowed it to be read. Later on, however, he was informed that the champions of the disputed Gospel were adherents of heresy. This led him to make inquiries, and he found that it had been composed in the sect of the Docetae, apparently in a previous generation; for he says that he conferred with 'their successors', and received information from them, thanks to which he was able to compose an analysis of the Gospel, indicating what parts of it were in accordance with the true teaching of the Saviour and what parts were added.

Two interesting points emerge. One is that the bishop of Antioch was in a position of regional or metropolitical importance, which seemed to be the case under Ignatius eighty years before. The other is that it was still possible to have a new Gospel read in church, or at least to assent to it for the sake of peace. Indeed, if the *Diatessaron* could be read at Edessa, why not the *Gospel of Peter* at Rhosus? But it is possible that steps were being taken even now to introduce the four 'separated' Gospels in the Syrian language at Edessa; unsuccessful steps, so far as the liturgy was concerned.

It should be noted that Serapion had never heard of the *Gospel of Peter* before. On the other hand he had a standard Gospel text with which he could compare it; and he rejected it because it made certain additions. Did he compare it with all four Gospels, a difficult feat in those days? Or did he compare it with the *Diatessaron*, which was a handy compendium of the four? And did he regard the *Gospel of Peter*, when it was first shown him, as a new harmony rather like the *Diatessaron*? And was his own *Diatessaron*, if he had one, the *Diatessaron* of Tatian or of Theophilus? These are only some of the questions which are raised by this interesting episode.

Serapion sent his analysis to the church at Rhosus, and told him they could expect another visit from him in the near future.

His correspondence on Montanism has been dealt with in an earlier chapter, since it gives information about the period of Apolinarius.

CLEMENT OF ALEXANDRIA

The year 190 marks the end of the fourth Christian generation, and very soon there will be no venerable bishops or teachers like Irenaeus and Polycrates, who had received the tradition from men who could remember the apostles. The fifth generation (190-230) produced brilliant scholars, however, who were nourished in the church tradition, studied the Christian literature, and branched out unhesitatingly into new fields of creative work. These men represented the old teaching order which had existed in the church since apostolic days, but it had assimilated itself now to the pattern of the Greek philosopher or *littérateur*, taking in too a certain amount of asceticism. They travelled a good deal from church to church, and wore the gown or pallium which was the habit of the philosopher as a man dedicated to the search for truth. They seem originally to have been a lay order, working primarily with the hearers and catechumens, but there was a tendency now to draw them into the presbyterate. Clement was a presbyter, and possibly Tertullian too; but there were some who might be described as free-lances, and it is thought that these were the precursors of monasticism. It is noticeable that we hear little more about prophets who may have been absorbed into the same movement.

Clement of Alexandria was the most illustrious of these teachers. It is probable that he was the head of the Alexandrian School early in the hundred-and-nineties; but Pantaenus, his tutor and predecessor, may have lived into this decade. Among his scholars were Alexander, who became a bishop, first in Cappadocia and then in Aelia; Origen,[1] who established a famous school at Caesarea; and possibly Heraclas, who became bishop of Alexandria. This network of churches, which was infused with the spirit of Pantaenus and Clement, became by far the most important influence in Christianity. It was an intellectual movement of a very rare kind, spiritual, conservative and liberal. Clement had entered very fully into the Alexandrian tradition of Philo, the gnostics and Pantaenus himself, not to mention hosts of non-Jewish and non-Christian authors. He is proud of the word 'gnostic' which he tried to rescue from the heretics. The true gnostic, he thought, was the Christian who understood his faith and practised it intelligently.

There was a battle in Alexandria between the champions of simple faith and the exponents of the new theology. Alexandrian Christianity was not all gnostic by any means. There was a strong substratum of plain traditional faith and practice and apocalyptic, which was accepted by the rank and file without much intellectual scrutiny; and Clement had to prove against hard opposition the usefulness and value of the current academic training in Greek language and logic and critical thinking. He even had to defend the practice of writing books, for his predecessor Pantaenus had written none; nor had the other apostolic teachers whose memory he revered.

[1] This has been questioned. At any rate he belonged to the same circle, and seems to have been able to remember Pantaenus.

CLEMENT AND THE TRADITION

It is rather ironical that Clement, who idolized the old oral teachers of the church tradition, should also be the defender of book-writing and an author of numerous volumes. He says that he is writing down the teachings of the ancients as a remedy against forgetfulness, in anticipation of his old age; but this is one of his pleasantries, half serious, half comic. Clement writes because he must; and, as he does so, he illuminates every aspect of Christian life. He is far from being a systematic writer, though he tries to be systematic. He plans out a series of volumes, one growing out of another, which he never completes. His thought is too fertile. It grows and expands too richly as he proceeds with it. A modern theologian says that his powers were not great enough for the task; but it may be that they were too great. He made use of intellectual formulas and approaches and generalizations, but he was unable to prune down the vast forest of the Christian tradition as he saw it into compliance with his intellectual formulations.

He was a connecting link. The old tradition flows very fully into his work and everywhere appears, though it may be in strange company and in a new guise. We find the Jewish prophecies, the Logos theology, the apostolic literature, and so forth; but it has undergone a change. He has civilized it. A certain barbarous quality which Tatian highly approved of, has disappeared. It is brought into line with the whole range of Greek thought and literature and learned research; for truth is truth, wherever it is found, and it is everywhere the work of the Word of God. Its meaning and message is developed in the form of general principles which can be related to the general principles of the great Hellenic thinkers as expressed in poetry and philosophy; he even makes some use of the mystery religions.

In doing this work on the scripture, Clement frequently resorted to allegorization, and often on highly artificial lines, which were inspired by the example of Philo. Clement enjoyed doing this, but it is quite wrong to give the impression that his work was vitiated by it. He had a remarkable understanding of the scriptures, including the New Testament as well as the Old, and his use of it shows great penetration and insight. It may be that this is the point at which he owes most to his master Pantaenus, who, he said, gathered his honey from the apostolic meadows; indeed the mystical exposition of the New Testament may have been a learned tradition of old standing in Alexandria, dating from the days of the great gnostic founders. But however this may be, the work of Clement inaugurates the intelligent study of the New Testament in the Christian church. He does not merely use it to prove theological points from, or to build up theology with, though he is an adept in both; he loves it for its own sake as an expression of heavenly wisdom in beautiful forms.

CLEMENT AND THE NEW TESTAMENT

The picture of the New Testament which we obtain from Clement is different from that which has appeared in Rome. The range of literature is wider; the process of restriction or canonization has not gone so far; the distinction between the core of the canon whose position is sacred and unassailable, and the periphery or penumbra of more debatable literature, is even less easy to make out. Moreover, the picture itself is not quite identical.

The four Gospels, of course, stand by themselves, and have no rival; but he gives them in the order Matthew, Luke, Mark, and John, placing first those which are provided with genealogies, and giving notes on the origin of each. His book of Pauline Epistles contained Hebrews, which he thought had been written by Paul in Hebrew and translated into Greek by Luke; in Rome Hebrews was not regarded as Pauline or as canonical. He made use of Acts and of the Revelation of John. He wrote a commentary, or at any rate comments, on all the catholic Epistles, Eusebius says; but all we have of this is a Latin translation of some of his notes on I Peter, Jude, and I and II John. He quotes, without any great sense of difference so far as we can see, from I Clement, 'the apostle Clement'; and the *Epistle of Barnabas*', 'the apostle Barnabas'; and the *Pastor* of Hermas; and the *Preaching of Peter*, and the *Revelation of Peter*. His quotation from the *Didache*, as 'scripture', is less certain since he might have derived it from one of the catechetical sources used by the *Didache*.

If Clement had been asked to divide this literature into canonical and non-canonical, he might have been very much perplexed. He was no critic. He had received a good deal of apostolic and near-apostolic literature without necessarily canonizing it all, even when he calls it scripture. He had a love of good literature wherever he found it, and he valued it in proportion to the truth and beauty which he saw in it. On the other hand, we have used his uncritical acceptance of these additional books as a sign of their early date; he could hardly have used them as he did if they were of recent composition.

THE ALEXANDRIAN TEXTS

There are some 'Western' readings in Clement's quotations from the Gospels, but on the whole he uses a different type of text from that which was current in Rome. It would appear that three types of text were current by this time in Alexandria, and modern critics distinguish them as follows, though it is now known that the nomenclature is misleading.

(1) The so-called 'Neutral' or 'Alexandrian' type, which is represented by the great fourth-century codices Vaticanus (B) and Sinaiticus (Aleph or S), and used by the Alexandrian fathers like Athanasius and Cyril.

(2) The so-called 'Caesarean' type which is represented by the Chester Beatty papyri and the ninth-century Koridethi manuscript (Theta), and used by Origen in his later works, his earlier works being based on the 'Neutral'.

(3) The so-called 'Western' type which is represented by the Old Latin translation and the Codex Bezae (D), and was used by Marcion, Irenaeus, Tatian and Tertullian.

The type of text current in eastern Syria was related to the 'Western' text, judging from the old Syriac 'separated' Gospels. Perhaps it should be regarded as a fourth class.

The text used by Clement was not a 'Western' text; it seems to have resembled the 'Neutral' rather than the 'Caesarean'; Origen began by using the 'Neutral', but changed to the 'Caesarean' before he left Alexandria. The nomenclature is now admitted to be misleading, and sheds little light on the local origins of the various types of texts. The 'Caesarean' text might just as easily be 'Athenian', since Origen started using it after his return from Athens.

The Neutral text is a conservative text made from early manuscripts, but showing signs of scholarly revision and correction; the Caesarean text is like it in being non-Western, but has its own history and ancestry. The Western text was the popular widespread text of the second century, as is proved by the use made of it by the writers of the period, and the Latin and Syriac translators; unfortunately we have no early manuscript of this type. There is an interesting contrast between the early manuscripts of the Caesarean and Neutral types; the Chester Beatty gospels with their long lines of script running right across the page and their complete lack of marginal apparatus, look very different from the formal script of the parchment pages of B and Aleph, with their narrow columns and their chapter enumerations. The two types of text may be associated with different methods of book-production, one possibly for private reading and study, the other for use in church.

THE *WORD OF INVITATION, LOGOS PROTREPTIKOS*

It is utterly impossible to summarize the voluminous writings and diversified theological ideas of Clement; still less to reproduce the wise, poetic, playful, deeply sincere style which colours every page. Even the titles of his great books defy translation.

His first book, the *Logos Protreptikos to the Greeks*, I have seen translated into English as the 'Hortatory Discourse'; but the Logos means the divine Word of God as well as a discourse or treatise, and the verb *protrepein* has the suggestion of stimulation and persuasion. The 'Word Persuasive' is a fairly literal rendering. It is written in a graceful literary style which is full of allusions to Greek poetry, mythology and ritual, drawn from a wide acquaintance with the best authors; and this is blended with the poetry and wisdom of the Hebrew prophets and sages. The Word of God, Jesus Christ, is the new song, sung by David and the prophetic choir, excelling that of Orpheus and the Muses, even as Mount Zion excels Mount Helicon, and the mysteries of Jesus excel those of Eleusis. Clement is full of the newness of the gospel, just as Marcion was. He presents the faith as a youth-movement in an ageing world, and perhaps the school of Clement was a youth-movement, which attracted the young intellectuals though it was not approved by everyone in Alexandria.

It says much for the statesmanship of Demetrius, who was not an old man himself, that he patronized a theology of this kind in the cate-chetical school, over which, apparently, he had complete authority; or was he quite happy about it all the time?

A bolder paraphrase of the title of this book, which unveils the barbarism and superstition of the established Greek religions, would be the 'Invitation to Music', since Clement makes his divine Word and Saviour invite his erring children to the true music and harmony of God as it has been realized on earth in the church.

THE *PAIDAGOGOS* AND THE *STROMATA*

His second book is the *Paidagogos* which is surely not very well represented in English by the word 'Instructor'? The Greek 'pedagogue' was not an instructor, in any case, but a leader of children; in Clement's language the divine Word now assumes the character of the *Youth-leader*. The youth which he leads and inspires and trains are the ordinary baptized Christians, who have a pleasing child-like quality about them and respond to his words of encouragement and admonition, which are given through the prophets and the apostles and mediated by the wisdom of Clement. Clement covers all the problems of social life, sleeping and waking, talking and feasting, marrying and giving in marriage; always with great wisdom and moderation. He appears, if we may say so, as a man of the world, at home in all classes of society. He gives us a vivid picture of the whole social life of the time, which he knows very well. The wise Christian is a married man; he mixes with society, but always governs himself by the use of reason; his asceticism consists in a sweet reasonableness and self-discipline. He is a man of prayer. He is the educated gentleman of the day, Christianized; not the savage ascetic, or the wild untamed prophet, or the enemy of social life. Clement invariably respects the order of the church from which he draws his counsels and general principles, but he does not look to episcopal or prophetic authority as the way by which the church will be saved; he looks to an intelligent understanding of the Christian faith.

His third book, which is far longer, is a collection of miscellaneous studies, which he calls the *Stromateis* or *Stromata*, a word which means 'blankets'. No one has ventured to translate this literally. There was a vogue for such names, though they were usually prettier and more poetical. Africanus, for instance, called one of his books the *Cestoi*, or 'embroidered girdles'. The books in question were collections of studies on various topics, written in a more or less popular and attractive style. Clement seems to have meant by his a travelling-kit or equipment for the journey of life; I have carried on the train of thought, therefore, and paraphrased it as *Equipment for the Road*.

It contains an immense variety of material which defies classification; the account of his teachers, for instance, and their apostolic oral tradition; a long series of notes on the Greek philosophers; an outline of world-history in the style of Tatian and Theophilus. He brings the latter down to the death of Commodus in 192, showing that when he was writing he was already in the mid hundred-and-nineties. So far as it has a theme, it is the character of the true Christian gnostic, as contrasted with the false gnostic of the heretical schools. He deals in great detail, for instance, with the whole question of sex, controverting the errors of those who insisted on complete celibacy for all, and also those who advocated indulgence in the sexual act as a holy rite. He controverts, too, those who took too literally the command to renounce all property; Christians do not have to give all their goods away. Neither do they have to rush on martyrdom; God intends us to preserve our lives if we honourably can. It looks rather as if he was a married man himself, with a modest competence; an educated member of the higher bourgeoisie, or even the aristocratic classes.

What then is his picture of the true gnostic? He finds it hard to define it clearly. The true gnostic is an intelligent Christian, who has come to the knowledge of the divine Word of God through study and sacrament and prayer; his mind is in true harmony with the mind of God; he controls the passions by means of the reason.

He thus achieves the objective of the Platonic sage or Stoic philosopher. It must be granted that the picture falls short of the Pauline evangel of sin and grace and salvation through faith; but he tells us himself that there are mysteries with which he does not deal. He has managed to hold himself in some degree to his self-imposed intellectual task, and has worked it out on the lines of his special formulation of it. He has shown the world of his day the picture of a reasonable civilized Christianity.

There was a fourth book which was called the *Hupotuposeis*, which may be translated 'Images' or 'Patterns' ('Blue-prints'?), but it has not survived, except for a few fragments. The ninth-century Photius had read it, and was shocked by its unorthodoxy.

THE PUPILS OF CLEMENT

No one knew better than Clement that the work of a great teacher was personal. The true teacher is paternal. He gives his pupils living seed from within his own mind which lives fruitfully in their minds. They are his sons; though books, too, may be described as the children of their authors. It emphasized very happily the personal quality in the old oral tradition, and indeed in education generally.

The pupils of Clement multiplied and expanded his creative teaching. There was Alexander in Cappadocia and Aelia. There was Origen in Alexandria and Caesarea. Horigenes Adamantius was destined to become one of the half-dozen greatest figures in the glorious list of Christian intellectuals. He was a Christian by birth. He was born in 185 or 186. His father Leonides was fully aware that his son was a child of great intellectual genius, and of a pure and ardent spirit. He took pains to see that he was well grounded in Greek literature, and that he had contact with the circle of Clement and Pantaenus.

CHAPTER 24

THE REIGN OF SEVERUS

NOETUS OF SMYRNA, MODALISM

The interest in a 'monarchian' theology had appeared in Rome in the
episcopate of Eleutherus. Theologians of all sorts were trying out their
systems in the light of the doctrine of the one 'arche' or beginning, or
first cause, or sovereign ruler of the universe. Before long various
monarchian theologies began to arrive from Asia Minor. Praxeas, the
keen opponent of Phrygianism, brought in a paradoxical form of it,
using the watchword 'One God', which meant one indivisible deity.
In its most provocative form, it led to the statement that the one
indivisible God had become man in Jesus of Nazareth. It could even be
said that the Father had been crucified, or at any rate that he had suffered;
he had died and risen again, and, as Hippolytus sarcastically added,
ascended into heaven and sat down at his own right hand. This evangelical form of the doctrine was nicknamed 'patripassionism'; but the
more careful theologians taught it in a form which has been christened
'modalism'; the one God had revealed himself at different times in
different modes; sometimes as Father, sometimes as Son, and sometimes as Holy Spirit; but always it was the one God.

There was a certain Noetus who taught this theology in Smyrna;
but after a while he was called upon to give an account of himself before
the local presbyters and was accused of identifying the Father with the
Son, and saying that he had been born and had suffered and had died.
According to Hippolytus he answered his critics by saying, 'What
harm am I doing in glorifying Christ?' According to Epiphanius he

413

said, 'What harm am I doing in glorifying one God?' He was condemned by the presbyters, but he was so carried away by his self-confidence as to 'establish a school'. He was the Moses of this school, and his brother was the Aaron; doubtless the bishop; and it looks as if this succession was recognized by the Roman church. At any rate Rome failed to condemn it. This schism in the ancient church of Smyrna may be one example of widespread dissensions in Asia and the east.

It does not appear that Noetus ever visited Rome. His theology was introduced there by a pupil of his named Epigonus and carried on into the episcopate of Zephyrinus by a certain Cleomenes. It received the approval of the Roman church. It taught a high evangelical theology with a respectable ancestry; and the fact that it was welcomed at Rome suggests no less; but Hippolytus bitterly opposed Cleomenes and obviously thought that he should have been condemned at Rome, as Noetus had been at Smyrna. There were the makings of a schism here such as existed in Smyrna, but Hippolytus and his friends accepted the situation as it was, so long as Zephyrinus was bishop.

THE SCHOOL OF HIPPOLYTUS

The old Logos theology possessed a formula which saved it from the paradox of patripassionism. It was not the eternal Father, they said, who had been incarnate in Jesus; it was the divine Word or Reason, which was generated in the mind of the Father; at first residing only in himself but then active in creation; coming forth from the Father like the stream from the fountain or the ray of light from the sun; mysteriously the same and yet mysteriously different. This school of theology tended to make the Logos a little too different.

The theology of the secondary centre of personality in the godhead had not been satisfactorily expressed and was open to criticism. It was taught in Rome by Hippolytus, who was the successor of Justin and Irenaeus. He inherited the theology of the Son of God as Word or Angel, and expounded it angrily and exactly and dogmatically. We have come to a new point of development in our history; it is the clash and rivalry of the dogmatic schools within the catholic tradition; for Hippolytus used the word 'catholic' in its derived sense of the non-heretical non-schismatic body which holds the true tradition of faith and order. Down to and including Irenaeus, it had meant little more than universal or world-wide, 'dispersed throughout the earth'; now it carried the additional significance of holding to, and maintaining, the doctrines and church order of the apostolic tradition as accepted by the universal federation of churches which recognized one another.

The war with the gnostic sects had been won, and still more the even older war with the Ebionites. No one could bring in another god who was superior to the creator; no one could proclaim another Christ whose humanity was unreal; everyone accepted the Old Testament scriptures, and the four Gospels, and the Acts, and the other apostolic books; and there was a solid tradition of theology and liturgy which had authority in the churches. For Hippolytus this was the tradition of Justin and Irenaeus on the one hand and Eleutherus and Victor on the other. He was a learned and industrious man with a powerful but not original mind. He maintained the old tradition as he understood it. He put all the heresies in their place. He classified them and traced them back to remote and improbable origins. He refuted them one by one, from the first pagan philosophers and mystics, who were the original fountains of error, down to the new schools which had obtained control in the Roman church, the last and latest heresies of his own rivals, headed by Praxeas and Noetus and Cleomenes and Sabellius and worst of all, Callistus. He pursued them with untiring pertinacity; it was a vendetta, not a theological inquiry.

THEODOTUS OF BYZANTIUM, ADOPTIONISM

There was another monarchian school, however, which established itself in Rome during the episcopate of Victor, and also claimed a respectable ancestry. Its leader was Theodotus of Byzantium, known as Theodotus the leather-worker (tanner or shoemaker). The fortifications of Byzantium were destroyed by order of the Emperor Severus in 196, and he may have been a refugee from this calamity, if indeed he had not anticipated it. He taught that Jesus was a 'mere man', or so Hippolytus reported him, who was the recipient of a divine *dunamis* or power, which came down upon him at his baptism, after which he was able to work miracles. It was rather nearer to the election and anointing of Ebionism than to the spirit-christology of Cerinthus. The spirit which Jesus received was not a distinct person as Cerinthus taught; it was the spirit of the one indivisible deity; it was the power of the Most Highest which overshadowed Mary and was with the human Jesus from his conception and birth. Room could be found in this way of thought for the Ebionite idea of the advance of Jesus in holiness and righteousness, and he could be thought of as being progressively adopted into ever-closer connexion with the deity, and so acquiring the value or status of God, or even becoming God in some sense of the word. It was a serious attempt to form a Christian theology out of traditional materials, preserving the monarchian idea of the indivisibility of God, and dispensing with the idea of the incarnate deity. It is known as 'dynamic' or 'adoptionist' monarchianism. Jesus was a man who became God rather than a God who became man.

The 'adoptionist' way of thought spread widely in the east, which was no doubt its original home; its most illustrious exponent being Paul of Samosata, who was bishop of Antioch in the two-hundred-and-fifties.

Theodotus of Byzantium came to Rome in the episcopate of Victor and founded a school there. There were some who professed to recognize in his teachings an old tradition of the Roman church itself; for the successors of Theodotus, some thirty years later, claimed that the older generation in Rome, and even the apostles themselves, had received and taught these doctrines, which had been preserved into the times of Victor. It was in the episcopate of Zephyrinus, they asserted, that the truth of the kerugma had been 're-minted', a weighty statement, in reply to which Hippolytus (in the *Little Labyrinth*) was able to point out that Victor himself had excommunicated Theodotus.

Yet we would infer that he must have found supporters in Rome in Victor's time who thought that his teaching was in line with an old Roman tradition of some sort; and we think inevitably of the un-formed christology of Hermas, and the humanistic christology which is referred to in the pages of Justin. It had seemed legitimate in earlier times to think of Christ as a combination of human 'flesh' and divine 'spirit'; but the Roman church under Victor would not accept a rationalized theology along these lines, which located the personality of the Christ exclusively in the human being, and not at all in the indwelling 'spirit'.

At the end of the episcopate of Victor, therefore, the theology of incarnation had won a resounding victory over the theology of

adoption; and when Zephyrinus succeeded him, a 'monarchian' theology of this type became the official theology of the Roman church.
We cannot resist the impression that the election of Zephyrinus came
as a blow to some of the old-fashioned Roman Christians, some of
whom may have venerated the memory of Justin, and others Hermas.

THE ACCESSION OF ZEPHYRINUS, *c.* A.D. 199

Zephyrinus succeeded Victor about 199, when Severus was occupied in
his eastern war. He continued as bishop for about eighteen years. He
was not fitted by nature to adjudicate upon rival theologies; Hippolytus
caricatures him as a weak man and a poor administrator; he even
suggests that he took bribes; but we must discount these statements.
He appointed as his adviser and right-hand man the ex-slave and so-
called confessor Callistus, whom he recalled from his retirement at
Antium and appointed as his 'deacon', putting him in charge of the
cemetery, which is the first we hear of this venture.

Ever since the times of Clement in the first century there had been a
group of Christian cemeteries on the Appian Way, including the crypt
of Lucina and the cemetery of Praetextatus, in connexion with which
was the private burying-place of the Caecilian family. They had by now
become the property of the church; and the fact that the church could
own property shows that it had been recognized as a corporation,
perhaps under some legal fiction; it was making rapid progress on the
economic, social and political levels. It is possible that Zephyrinus had
been interested in the cemeteries himself before he became bishop.
There is a medieval document which states that he was buried 'in his
own cemetery close by the cemetery on the Appian Way'; an interesting statement, since the tradition says that previous bishops had been
buried near the body of St Peter. It is unfortunate that none of these
early episcopal burials have been confirmed by archaeology or by older
literary evidence; they are still nothing but late tradition. The transformation of the cemeteries on the Appian Way into a church cemetery
is a matter of history, however. They are now known as the Cemetery
of Callistus, after the energetic deacon of Zephyrinus who succeeded
him as bishop.

The interest in cemeteries and memorials at this time must be connected with that strong sense of history and continuity which was

the strength of the whole church; the reverence for the apostolic founders, the growing cult of the martyrs, and the old Roman reverence for the dead. It would also appear to be connected with the importance of certain families, the growth of financial organization, and the promotion of political relations. Hippolytus, who was a likely person to succeed Zephyrinus, regarded the rise to power of Callistus with dismay. The two men are likely to have been still in their thirties; probably no more than forty.

THE ADOPTIONIST SCHISM: NATALIUS

The position of Zephyrinus as bishop was not uncontested. The adherents of the adoptionists had been defeated, but they did not accept this position, since they held themselves to be the true representatives of the old Roman tradition, and had some financial backing. They found a confessor named Natalius (a native Roman if we may judge by his name), whom they established as bishop, paying him a monthly salary of 1500 denarii, which is represented by Hippolytus as a new and shocking idea. Among his backers was a new Theodotus, who was called the banker (or money-changer) to distinguish him from his predecessor, Theodotus the leather-worker; no doubt he was the financial strength of the party. The new Theodotus carried on the theology of the old Theodotus, adding a strange piece of speculation about Melchizedek, the mystical priest-king of Salem in Abraham's time, whom he looked upon as superior to the Christ, his critics said. Another supporter was a certain Asclepiades, sometimes spelt as Asclepiodotus, perhaps by confusion with Theodotus.

Natalius was not happy in his position as bishop. One night he had a dream in which holy angels came and scourged him severely, a story not without parallel in the records of abnormal psychology. Jerome had a similar experience, and so did Laurentius, the second archbishop of Canterbury. Natalius arose in the morning, ran to Zephyrinus and showed him his shoulders covered with the marks of the beating. He confessed his sin and begged forgiveness, embracing the knees of the bishop, the presbyters and even the laity who were present. His plea was granted, and he was restored to communion. Heaven itself had approved the episcopal standing of Zephyrinus. The story is told in the *Little Labyrinth*.

It must have been a severe blow to the adoptionists to lose their bishop in this ignominious fashion, but they continued their separate existence. A new bishop must have been found; for the proclamation of the 'kerugma of the truth' as they understood it, continued. They occupied themselves with literary criticism. They compared and emended the manuscripts of the sacred scriptures, by which the Old Testament would seem to be meant. They invoked the names of Euclid, Aristotle, Theophrastus and Galen, and emulated their techniques. Their church or school was still in existence between 230 and 270, and its leader at that time, in all probability its bishop, was a certain Artemas or Artemon; the true bishop of Rome in his own estimation.

The picture which we have been able to give of the fortunes of the Roman church at this point is available through the accidental preservation of the controversial writings of Hippolytus, whose evidence can be supplemented from those of Tertullian. There is no reason to suppose that these controversies and disputed elections were exceptional; it is not improbable that they were common features of the democratic way of life of the church of this period, not only at Rome but elsewhere. On the other hand, the great mass of Christian people may not have been very deeply concerned with the disputations of the scholars; and the rivalries of the parties may not have been due solely to theological differences. The enmity between Hippolytus and Callistus was coloured by strong personal feeling, and the two men represented different types and different social classes. Probably, if we knew more about these church divisions, we would find that there were social, racial and personal interests involved.

EXOMOLOGESIS

The story of Natalius gives us a picture of the procedure known as *exomologesis*, or public confession, by which open and notorious sinners who had been expelled from the communion of the church were reconciled after due penitence had been shown. Tertullian gives an account of this important element in the church order in his book *Concerning Penitence*, which he wrote while he was still a catholic himself. The penitent appeared in sackcloth and ashes; he bewailed his sins; he entreated the faithful for their intercessions, as Natalius had done. The sentence of restoration was pronounced by the bishop, though it would seem that the presbyters had a voice in the decision; it was one of their most important functions.

Little is known about the development of the system of penitential discipline in the church. There was a tradition which dated from the earliest times that there was no forgiveness for post-baptismal sin of a grave character; but this idea was not universally accepted. Dionysius of Corinth, for instance, had urged Palmas of Amastris to welcome back those who returned from any kind of 'falling away', whether it was misconduct or heretical error. Tertullian, at this period of his life, allowed for one repentance or restoration after baptism, and this concession to human frailty had been sanctioned since the episcopate of Pius, or earlier, by the spiritual authority of the Roman prophet Hermas, whose revelation of God's will was still widely accepted. The ministry of repentance was, in some way or another, carried on, and the doctrine of no repentance after baptism was mitigated in practice, though it may have been maintained in principle.

At a later date Tertullian brought forward another view of the matter, which also had a tradition of some sort behind it. He thought that idolatry, murder, and adultery, the three major sins of the old Jewish moral theology, could not be forgiven by the church, and Hippolytus has a similar tradition. Idolatry meant relapse into paganism, and especially the denial of Christ in times of persecution, which was known technically as 'apostasy'; but Hermas had envisaged the possibility of the reconciliation of some classes of apostates. The Gallican martyrs had actually taken it upon themselves to restore their lapsed brethren to communion in the prison. The third century would present the church with the problem of great numbers of apostates seeking restoration, and also of martyrs assuming the right to restore them. As for adultery, it was well known that Hermas was lenient towards adulterers and at a later date Tertullian strongly attacks him for his leniency. Indeed, the writings of Hermas may have been under fire from more than one quarter. They were on the way out.

Two points should be borne in mind in considering this topic. One is that in spite of the authoritative statements about ancient customs, it is very unlikely that any clear-cut or consistent procedure did exist in the churches. The other is that an increasing number of Christians were deferring their baptisms so that they did not come under this discipline at all. The Christians in the army, in the civil services and in high social positions may have been in many cases catechumens. The number of catechumens who appear as martyrs may be partially explained in this way; their martyrdom was their baptism. It accounted for all sins.

PERSECUTIONS UNDER SEVERUS;
APOCALYPTIC FERMENT

The edicts which Severus issued in Palestine forbidding the baptism of converts may also have served to keep Christians in the catechumen class; but it is not clear to what extent this edict was enforced. In 201 he arrived in Egypt, and his arrival coincided with an outbreak of persecution in Alexandria, perhaps as part of the demonstrations of loyalty to the emperor. So sudden and severe was this wave of persecution, which went on under two successive prefects, that a leading Christian named Judas was moved to write a book in which he sought to prove that the day of judgement was at hand.

There are other signs of unrest and apocalyptic ferment among the Christians at this time. There came to Hippolytus in Rome two strange stories from the east. One came from Syria; it was the case of a bishop who was so carried away by his studies in the scriptures as to lead out a great crowd of brethren, with women and children, into the desert to meet Christ. The proconsul naturally thought that they were 'robbers', and was prepared to arrest them and put them to death; but fortunately his wife was a believer and persuaded him to settle the matter quietly and so avoid a mass persecution.

The other case was that of a bishop in Pontus, a man of humility and piety, but unfortunately he trusted in visions which he received. He set up as a prophet and announced the day of judgement in a year's time. His hearers gave themselves up to prayer and lamentation; they fasted even on the sabbath and the Lord's Day; they left their farms uncultivated and sold their livestock. When the year ended and the judgement had not come, the bishop was covered with shame, the scriptures were discredited, and the brethren so gravely upset that their virgins married and their men returned to their farms. Those who had sold their farms were reduced to beggary.

HIPPOLYTUS ON DANIEL

These stories may be exaggerated of course, but they must be borne in mind in estimating the character of Christianity at this time. We see here a fanatical element, which was allied in some ways with Montanism and in others with Encratism; it cannot have had any sympathy with the civilization of the day. Even Hippolytus, writing in Rome itself, gives a sombre and satiric picture of its history, not at all like the friendly approaches of Melito and Tertullian. He comments gravely on the uncertainty of the favour of princes. He seems to have in mind some recent instances of the mutability of imperial favour.

We get a good picture of him now, lecturing to the faithful, and working on the scriptures, and relating them to current events. These stories are taken from his commentary on Daniel, which is assigned to this period. He was a great commentator, though this is the only commentary of his which has come down to us entire. He uses, of course, the Septuagint Daniel, with the story of Susanna and the Song of the Three Children in the burning fiery furnace, which Clement had also referred to. He talks a great deal about martyrdom, and urges his hearers to prepare for it. His book could be illustrated from the catacomb pictures of the time.

He was also concerned to defend the church against an extravagant apocalypticism. He believed that the only sound approach to this subject was through the canonical scriptures. With some degree of diffidence and protest, he proceeds to give his own interpretation. His picture of the last days is calamitous in the extreme, especially for the saints; Antichrist will reign in Jerusalem; the earth will be reduced to misery and confusion; there will be no millennial kingdom on this earth; but these evils will culminate in the appearance of Christ and the final judgement. His fiery pictures of the end owe something to the eschatology of II Peter; he is the first Christian writer who quite certainly makes use of this book, though its use may be considered possible in Justin and Theophilus.

He pursues the same subject in his book *Concerning Christ and Antichrist*. Fortunately none of these things will happen for five hundred years.

THE ALEXANDRIAN MARTYRS, A.D. 201–4

The catechetical school in Alexandria was closed, and Clement left the city. His action was not criticized so far as we know, and we find him ten years later standing by his friend and pupil Alexander during a persecution in some city of Cappadocia where Alexander was bishop.

Leonides, the father of Origen, died as a martyr; but not in consequence of the emperor's decree, since he was already a baptized Christian. Origen himself, who was now sixteen years old, would have died with him, had not his mother, who was a woman of resource, hidden his clothes. His father's property was confiscated, and he had to support his mother and his younger brothers by giving classes in the Greek language and literature. He also carried on a class for the instruction of catechumens in the faith. The numbers became so great, and the calls upon his time so pressing, that he gave up his classes in Greek literature and devoted himself entirely to this work. In order to finance it he sold his library, and invested the proceeds in a small annuity. He also found a wealthy patroness in whose house he lived. She had another Christian teacher under her roof, a gnostic from Antioch, whose name was Paul, a skilful and popular lecturer; but Origen refused to associate with him, and this early brush with heresy may have served to strengthen him in his adherence to the church tradition. This Christian school or college in the house of a wealthy lady is not without precedent. Had not Paul and Silas taken up their abode in Lydia's house at Philippi? Had not Hermas spoken of wealthy Christians who received the servants of God into their houses.

The name of this broad-minded lady is not known.

Origen stood by his pupils in their trials and during their executions. It seemed to the Christian mind an act of God that he was not touched himself, though the mob howled for his blood at times. He saw his pupils pass from baptism to martyrdom. Among the martyrs were five men, Plutarch, Serenus, Heraclides (a catechumen), Hero, and a second Serenus; there were three women, Herais, Potamiaena, and her mother Marcella. Potamiaena was the heroic figure of this persecution, like Blandina at Lyons, and she had her seven companions as in the story of the Maccabaean mother. Eusebius says that her praises were sung long afterwards in songs and hymns. The soldier who had charge of her, whose name was Basilides, did his best to protect her from the insults of the mob and she promised him a reward before she died. Three days later she appeared to him in a dream by night and placed a crown on his head, and he too became a Christian and a martyr. The figure of the soldier who is deeply impressed, or even converted, is a feature of the Acts of martyrdom; doubtless there were many soldiers who were half-persuaded of the truth of Christianity or even admitted as catechumens.

These martyrs may have suffered under the edict of Severus, since they were mostly new converts. They were what Clement called children in the faith; the first Christian youth-movement that we clearly see, under a youthful leader.

THE CATECHETICAL SCHOOL

It says much for the vision and courage of Bishop Demetrius that he recognized the work that Origen was doing, and appointed him at the age of eighteen to be the successor of Clement as head of the catechetical school; or did he think that it would be easier to control the school under so young a man? Was that indeed how he acquired control of the school? In any case Origen must have possessed the confidence of the bishop and the presbyters at this time. Perhaps he ranked as a confessor.

Origen was acutely aware of his lack of qualifications for the position, and he undertook strenuous intellectual and spiritual disciplines to fit himself for it. He attended the lectures of Ammonius Saccas, the leading philosopher of the day, then at the beginning of his distinguished career. He had begun his life as a porter carrying bags, and had acquired the name of Saccas in consequence; for the word 'sack' is the same in many languages. Origen had been led to him by an older friend and pupil, Heraclas, a brother of the martyred Plutarch. Among his later pupils were Plotinus the great systematic philosopher of the third century, and Longinus the great literary critic. Origen was their equal in intellectual power, and their senior in years. The neo-platonist philosophy which this school developed required rigid preparation in mathematical and logical subjects—the very qualifications in which Justin had been lacking. It also encouraged the ascetic and holy life. Clement had emphasized all these points, but Origen carried matters farther than Clement would have approved.

Origen, at this age, did nothing by halves. Ascetism was the fashion of the time, and he treated himself hardly, wearing only one garment, sleeping on the floor, and discarding the use of shoes; all in accordance with Gospel precepts, taken rather literally. He ate sparingly and drank no wine. Unfortunately he took too literally a statement in St Matthew that there were some who had made themselves eunuchs for the sake of the kingdom of heaven. Some fifty years before, Justin says, a young Christian in Alexandria had decided to do this, but had failed to get the requisite permission from the prefect which was required by the law. With or without permission, Origen did it; but the Christian conscience generally did not approve, as he was to discover. In due course he took a different view of it himself, and learned to interpret scripture less literally. At present, however, Bishop Demetrius was indulgent to this brilliant young catechist. He had the glamour of martyrdom about him; he was a mystic and ascetic and completely absorbed in his vocation; but we never find him seeing visions or hearing voices. He was too much of an intellectual for that.

THE AFRICAN MARTYRS, A.D. 203

It was otherwise with the African martyrs. In the case of these young people, as some of them were at any rate, there was more of the prophet than the scholar. It was on 7 March and in the year 203. Once again a young woman was the leader of the martyrs; her name was Vibia Perpetua; she was twenty-two years of age, and came of one of the leading families of Carthage. Her father was not a Christian, and was deeply distressed by her determination to die as a martyr for the faith which she had so recently espoused. This family grief was her severest trial. She wrote the earlier part of the story herself in the prison; the following chapters being written by the presbyter Saturus, who had doubtless been her instructor in the faith and had surrendered himself with his pupils; the account of the actual martyrdoms was added by another hand.

She was the mother of a small infant, and her slave and fellow-martyr Felicitas gave birth to a child in the prison. There were three men: Revocatus who seems to have been the husband of Felicitas, Saturninus and Secundulus; they were all catechumens. The name of another catechumen, Rusticus, occurs in the last chapters. The deacons, Tertius and Pomponius, visited them in prison from time to time, and were successful in inducing the guards to let them walk in the fresh air once a day.

It was felt right under such circumstances to ask the Lord for a vision, and as Perpetua had been permitted to converse with the Lord, it was agreed that she should ask him what the issue was to be. She was given a dream in which she saw a golden ladder going up to heaven, with a dragon couching under it, and swords and lances and sharp weapons bristling from it. Saturus went up first, and called to her to follow him. She followed him, naming the name of the Lord Jesus, and setting her foot on the dragon's head. She found herself in a vast garden, where there was a white-haired man in the dress of a shepherd, milking his flocks. 'Thou art welcome, my daughter', he said to her, and gave her a piece of the cheese that he was making. She received it with folded hands, and as she ate it all who stood by said 'Amen'. 'And at the sound of their voices I awoke, still tasting a sweetness which I cannot describe.' So she knew that the outcome would be martyrdom and that Saturus would be the first to go.

After their trial, she had two dreams about her little brother Dinocrates, who had died at the age of seven, presumably without baptism. In the first she saw him in a place of darkness and distress, but in the second she saw him delivered and happy in answer to her prayers. In her next dream she fought with an Egyptian gladiator and won her fight. After this the presbyter Saturus records a dream of his, in which he took part in company with martyrs of an earlier persecution in the worship of heaven. He was given a message of his bishop Optatus, who was not on good terms with the presbyter Aspasius. Optatus is the first African bishop whose name we know. He was given the title 'papa' which means grandfather. This word appears in English as 'pope'. It is first found in Carthage and Alexandria.

Secundulus died in prison. Felicitas, without much trouble, gave birth to a little daughter, who was committed to one of the 'sisters' to bring up. The narrative of the martyrdom tells how the men were made to fight with wild animals, a leopard, a bear and a wild boar; but the boar attacked the huntsman who had charge of it, and he died later on from wounds received. Revocatus apparently was killed by the leopard but Saturus escaped alive. He had been savagely bitten, and so much blood flowed from the wound that the crowd shouted out, 'Washed and saved! Washed and saved!' in imitation of the language of the

Gospel. A soldier named Pudens asked for a ring from his finger, and Saturus gave it to him saying, 'Remember my faith.' He was then condemned to an encounter with the bear; but the bear refused to come out of its den.

Perpetua and Felicitas were stripped naked, enveloped in nets, and gored by a wild cow; like Blandina at Lyons, Perpetua was in a trance and felt nothing, as she declared to a young catechumen, Rusticus, who came to her assistance.

It was then decided to finish off the martyrs with the sword, and they all kissed one another, and prepared for death. Saturus was killed first. They received the sword-thrust without moving or making a sound, except for Perpetua herself, who gave a loud cry as she was pierced through the breast, but then guided the hand of the young swordsman to her throat; 'and possibly', the narrator adds, 'such a woman could not have been slain unless she had willed it herself, since she was feared by the impure spirit'.

The epitaph of these martyrs has been discovered in recent years, so that we know that their relics were not lost.

MARTYRS AND CONFESSORS

Such, then, was the quality of the new generation of champions of the faith. If it seems to the critical modern mind that they had become a little too concrete in their views about demons and gehenna and paradise, perhaps it can be forgiven them. They may have taken their dreams and visions rather literally, though it looks as if they well understood the nature of poetry and symbol; yet these dreams were strong enough to carry them through, for they expressed in the simplest possible form the faith in God the Father and the Lord Jesus Christ which gave them their victory over fear and death and every other evil power which barred their road to glory. They have something of Hermas, something of the *Revelation of Peter*, something of the Phrygian prophets, something of the art-forms and mottoes of the catacombs. It is a Christian folk-lore. It is the new Gentile dress for the old Christian gospel; but it is none the less the old Christian gospel for that. It is a mistake to look on the visionary Perpetua as a 'Montanist'; she is an example of simple evangelical piety, stimulated into vision by the prophetic movement; or, if it is Montanism, then it is a liberal-minded unreflective Montanism of the second degree, set free from the harshness of Ardabau or the fancies of Pepuza.

During the third century the Roman church adopted the custom of keeping the birthdays of some of the greater martyrs. A martyrology, or calendar of martyrs, came into existence, in which the oldest commemoration was that of St Perpetua and her companions. This movement seems to have been a feature of the growth and development of the native Latin tradition, which may of course have received help and stimulation from the sister-church of Carthage at this time. It is not that Rome had been backward heretofore in honouring the martyrs, but her way had been a simple stone slab with little more than a name upon it; or not even a name. Now the pictorial decorations, the Christian inscriptions, and the keeping of birthdays, begin to appear. Tertullian speaks of memorial banquets and other rites. The status of the martyr continued to be exalted, and, with it, the status of the confessor. Hippolytus admits that a genuine confessor has the rank of a presbyter. We have seen that they undertake to reconcile penitents.

THE DEFECTION OF TERTULLIAN, A.D. 205–7

The Montanist movement was still active on both sides of the Mediterranean, and Tertullian himself was drawn into it. In the year 207 he was writing the first volume of his ponderous work *Against Marcion*, and he makes it plain that he was already a Montanist. He announced his withdrawal from the company of the 'psychics', as he calls the catholic church, in his book *Against Praxeas*, which would therefore seem to be a work of the same period. It must have been the result of serious tension. It appears from the Acts of Perpetua that the catholic bishop, Optatus, was at odds with one of his teachers named Aspasius, and was unable to control his church. Jerome says that Tertullian's defection was due to the jealousy of the Roman presbyters, and we have seen that there was division and party-feeling there too. The two principal points of controversy were the same in both churches, Phrygianism and monarchianism.

Praxeas, who was the forerunner of the higher monarchianism, had left little impression in Rome, since he had founded no school there. He had gone over to Africa with the glory of his 'martyrdom' and the favour of the Roman bishop of that day, Eleutherus or Victor. He had taught his doctrine and clashed with a redoubtable opponent, whose name Tertullian does not give; he admitted his error and signed a recantation which remained on record in the church. After that he disappeared from view. But the seeds of his heresy remained. The church at Carthage must have espoused his theology in a modified form, just as the Roman church had done. When Tertullian parted from the catholic church, he expressed his theological views in his book *Against Praxeas*; but it was meant to be, by implication, an attack on Zephyrinus and Callistus and Cleomenes, who were spreading the new theology in the Roman church.

It seemed to the rather practical Latin mind that the theology of Praxeas and Cleomenes represented the old faith in one God and one Lord Jesus Christ. The word *monarchia* was on everybody's lips. 'The simple,' said Tertullian, 'not to say the foolish and the senseless, who are always in the majority among the faithful, are crying out, "We hold to the *monarchia*"; they are terrified of the *oeconomia*.' The first Greek word was certainly easier to understand than the second, for which no adequate Latin or English equivalent has ever been found. It means literally the management of a house, and hence any arrangement or system or plan or disposition; it is sometimes translated, but most inadequately, by the words dispensation or disposition. Tertullian used it of the real and eternal personal distinctions within the deity: the inner relations of Father and Son and Spirit. Naturally it was a little beyond the simple, who had no comprehension of purely theological problems.

It becomes clear that the administrations of Optatus in Carthage and Zephyrinus in Rome were firmly based on popular support. Monarchianism was in and Montanism was out.

PROCLUS THE MONTANIST

Montanism meant for Tertullian a special outpouring of the Spirit, which expressed itself in dreams, visions and oracles; an outpouring of the Spirit which was cultivated within a very small circle. It meant a sour disapproval of the ordinary Christians, whose cause he had championed in his *Apology*. He had discovered that they were prone to the temptations of the world and the flesh; for the number of worldly Christians was every day increasing, and the standards, in his opinion, were becoming much too elastic. These standards had been stiffened

up, he thought, by new legislation which had been given by the Paraclete through Montanus. There was to be no more repentance for the
idolater, the murderer or the adulterer. Second marriages were anathema,
and any marriage was to be deplored; though Tertullian himself was a
married man, and wrote a treatise *To his Wife* in which he urged her
not to marry again should anything happen to him. Fasts were to be
longer, more frequent and more severe. Life was to become a system
of training for martyrdom.

There were two sects of Montanists in Rome, one 'according to
Aeschines' and the other 'according to Proclus'. Aeschines followed
the fashionable Monarchian theology, which was in line with the
utterances of Montanus himself. Proclus, or Proculus, was a theologian
of the school of Melito and Irenaeus. He was the master of Tertullian in
theology, who speaks of him with affection as 'Proculus noster', our
own Proculus, adding the information that he was medical adviser to
the emperor. He was an old man now, and famous for his life of
celibate sanctity.

During the episcopate of Zephyrinus he engaged in a debate with a
certain Gaius or Caius, which was reduced to written form by the
latter and came into the hand of Dionysius of Alexandria and Eusebius.
Eusebius quotes from it more than once. In the course of this debate
Proclus referred to the 'four' daughters[1] of Philip, who had been
prophetesses and were buried at Hierapolis, where their tomb was to be
seen. He was conscious of the Phrygian origin of the New Prophecy,
but was not very well informed about it, since he confuses Philip of
Hierapolis with Philip the deacon and evangelist who is mentioned in
the Acts.[2] It would seem therefore that he was not a Phrygian himself,
or at any rate had never been in Hierapolis; but he sheltered himself and
his teaching under the prestige of the Asian tradition.

Gaius had a prompt and effective answer to the claim of Proclus.

I myself can point out the trophies of the apostles; for if it is your pleasure to
proceed to the Vatican or to the Ostian Way, you will find the trophies of
those who founded this church.

(Gaius, *Dialogue with Proclus*, in Eusebius, *E.H.* II, 25, 5.)

[1] The better-informed Polycrates speaks of three, and says that one was buried
at Ephesus.

[2] Many scholars prefer his evidence to that of Papias (as understood by Eusebius)
and Irenaeus and Polycrates, and therefore identify this Philip with the 'deacon' of
Acts who had four daughters who prophesied.

This reference shows, quite apart from the archaeological confirmation, that the tombs of St Peter and St Paul were shown in Rome at the present traditional sites, and must have stood there long before the time of Gaius. He calls them 'trophies' or monuments of victory, but he would appear to mean actual tombs, since he was using them to outshine the prestige which Hierapolis derived from the Philippian tombs.

GAIUS OF ROME

Eusebius had no idea who Gaius was, and describes him vaguely as a churchman. The ninth-century Photius, who had also read the *Dialogue*, says that he was a Roman presbyter; but if so he is a further example of the theological discord which could exist in that venerable presbytery.

Hippolytus wrote a book against him called *Chapters against Gaius*; or at any rate that is the name that it went under in the Syriac translation. No such book exists, and no such title is found in the list of books which is engraved upon the statue of Hippolytus; but perhaps it is identical with the book called *The Defence of the Gospel and Revelation of John*, which is included there; for Gaius rejected both Johannine books. A few quotations from this lost work of Hippolytus survive in the twelfth-century Syriac writer Dionysius bar Salibi, and one of them says:

Hippolytus of Rome said: A man named Gaius appeared who said that the gospel was not John's, nor the Revelation, but that they were the work of Cerinthus.

(Dionysius bar Salibi, from R. M. Grant, *Second-Century Christianity*.)

and another:

The heretic Gaius charged John with disagreeing with his fellow-evangelists, since he says that after the baptism Jesus went into Galilee and wrought the miracle of the wine at Cana.   (*Ibid.*)

It is not likely that these views about the Gospel appeared in the *Dialogue with Proclus*, since Eusebius does not seem to have noticed them; but he does quote a sentence which refers in a guarded manner to the Revelation.

And Cerinthus too, by means of revelations which were ostensibly written by a great apostle, brings in some marvellous things which were shown him, as he asserts, by angels; saying that after the resurrection the kingdom of Christ will be established upon the earth, and the flesh will dwell in Jerusalem, serving once more the pleasures and desires...and that there will be a period of a thousand years to be spent in nuptial festivities.

(Gaius, *Dialogue*, in Eusebius, *E.H.* III, 28, 2.)

Here is the Phrygian millennialism of Papias, in a rather gross form, based on the Revelation, which is attributed to Cerinthus. Neither Irenaeus nor Hippolytus attributes any apocalyptic opinions to Cerinthus; and it is possible that Gaius is not a very good authority. It would appear that he was an enemy of the whole Asian tradition, not merely of Montanism. Eusebius would approve his rejection of chiliasm, and even of the Revelation of John, which he did not accept himself.

THE 'ALOGI' IN EPIPHANIUS

It would seem that the party which Gaius represented is referred to by Irenaeus in his statement (quoted in an earlier chapter) that there were some who rejected the Gospel of John because of their opposition to the New Prophecy. The same point of view was developed in a document which fell into the hands of Epiphanius. Unfortunately it had no name or title, and so he invented a name for the sect which had produced it; he called them the 'Alogi', the people devoid of Logos or Reason.

This document analysed the points on which the Gospel of John gave a different chronological order from the other three, and in this connexion it discussed a number of calendrical questions on which the Alogi had peculiar and interesting views. It used sarcastic language about the imagery of the Revelation, and made the extraordinary statement that when it was written there was no church at Thyatira.[1]

It has been suggested that Epiphanius found this sect described in the short *Syntagma* of Heresies, which Hippolytus wrote at this time. We only know this book through the use made of it in the Latin *Libellus*, and the copy of it which the author of the *Libellus* used had lost a few pages at the end, and therefore did not include the last one or two heresies with which Hippolytus dealt. It is an ingenious suggestion, but the document which Epiphanius had before him was a pamphlet written by the sect itself, or by a leading member of it; it was longer

[1] This statement is fully discussed by P. C. de Labriolle in *La Crise Montaniste*.

432

and more detailed than the short notices in the *Libellus* could have been; and if the sect had been included in the *Syntagma*, it would have been given a name.

Both Gaius and the Alogi remain something of a mystery.

SABELLIUS OF LIBYA

At some point in the episcopate of Zephyrinus a new teacher appeared in the dominant monarchian school; his name was Sabellius, and he is said to have come from Libya, a country lying west of Egypt. He was a man of real ability, and seems to have been the first of the trained theologians who candidly recognize intellectual difficulties and attempt to solve them by working out an acceptable terminology. He began by defining the nature of the deity, and asserted that there could be only one eternal being or essence, using the Aristotelian word *ousia*, which is derived from the verb to be and means existence or sometimes substance. He suggested, however, that the one being or existence might have more than one mode of revealing itself in creation and revelation; and in order to express more clearly these modes or aspects of revelation, he chose the word *prosopon*, which means literally a mask or face, or even the character assumed by an actor. There was but one eternal reality or ground of being; but there were three modes of manifestation or revelation. It rather seemed to follow that, while the unity was absolute and eternal, the three aspects or persons might be transitory manifestations; but possibly he guarded himself against this conclusion.

Tertullian, who was no philosopher at all, but a theologian of considerable originality and penetration, was working out a somewhat similar terminology in Latin. There was one *substantia*, he said, a word which could be used as a rough equivalent for *ousia*; and there were three *personae*, a word which had the same meaning as *prosopon*. But words taken from different languages rarely coincide in their meanings and common usage. Tertullian was a lawyer, and his two words had legal connotations. In law the word *substantia* was a word for the property owned by an individual or corporation; *persona* was used for the individual or trustee who could legally hold the property. The terminology, therefore, was rather in the nature of an analogy, as all abstract terminology fundamentally is. The eternal reality and distinction of the three 'persons' could not be questioned in his case; they formed a *trinitas* or threefold unity, a word which is found for the first time in his writings. It corresponds to the Greek word *trias*, which was used by Theophilus and Hippolytus.

We have not attempted to do justice to the subtlety of thought of Sabellius, which is very imperfectly known. He invented the historic term *homo-ousios*—of the same essence—which encountered strong criticism, being condemned in certain Syrian councils; but it was finally adopted at the Council of Nicaea, and put into the creed. The Son of God, it says, is 'of-one-essence', or 'of-the-same-substance' as the Father. On the other hand, the word *prosopon* was rejected, though the corresponding Latin word *persona* continued in use in the west, and passed into Latin theology. Sabellius himself was classified as a heretic; his trinitarianism was regarded as too shadowy and unreal; and yet the Roman church was able, from these beginnings, to build an acceptable theology.

CALLISTUS AND HIPPOLYTUS

Hippolytus, who stoutly maintained the old Logos theology, had no sympathy with the modalism of Cleomenes of the refined trinitarianism of Sabellius. He did not hesitate to attack the administration of Zephyrinus, which condoned such errors; but Zephyrinus had the majority on his side and managed to maintain an equilibrium between the competing parties in the church. He was no philosopher, however, and contented himself with making pronouncements from time to time which seemed to settle the matter for the time being, though they were hardly compatible with one another. 'I know there is one God, Jesus Christ,' he is reported to have said on one occasion, 'and I know no other who was begotten and capable of suffering.' 'The Father did not die,' he explained on another, 'it was the Son'; leaving matters where they were before.

Hippolytus 'withstood him face to face', he says, using language from St Paul's account of how he withstood St Peter face to face (Galatians ii. 11); an interesting comparison. Callistus, he says, played a double or triple part, which is the inevitable criticism of the non-partisan churchman. Callistus was concerned with the task of keeping the peace in the church, or assisting Zephyrinus to do so. He would appear to yield, at one time to Hippolytus, and at another to Sabellius; Sabellius would be half-persuaded, now by Callistus and now by

Hippolytus. It strikes one that Callistus was playing off his two theologians against one another, and encouraging Sabellius as a counterbalance to Hippolytus. Sabellius, perhaps, was making a sincere effort to meet all the difficulties. But the decisive factor in the situation, after all, was the personal antagonism between Hippolytus and Callistus. Hippolytus despised Zephyrinus and hated Callistus; yet he remained a presbyter in good standing in the Roman church. It was hardly possible for them to condemn the old Logos theology; and it was quite impossible for Hippolytus to leave them and go in with the Adoptionists. And so matters continued to the end of the long episcopate of Zephyrinus.

A NOTE ON THE MONARCHIAN TERMINOLOGY

There is another line of research into the terminology of the monarchian schools. The monarchian faith in 'One God' may be traced back to Jewish origins in the 'Shema' (see p. 329, etc.), 'Yahweh is one'. The Greek word *ousia* may have been regarded as an equivalent of the name Yahweh which is explained in the LXX translation of Exodus iii. 14 as meaning '*ho ōn*', 'he who is'. 'One Yahweh' is thus one self-existent being or one *ousia*.

The word *prosopon* may have been regarded as an equivalent of the Hebrew *panim*, which means a face and was used of the presence or manifestation of Yahweh locally. In rabbinic Hebrew it was used to mean a person.

The word *dunamis* or 'power' seems to represent the Hebrew *hayil* or *hēl*, as in Hel-Khasai (Elchasai), 'the hidden power', or in the *Gospel of Peter* (see p. 11). It was commonly used in gnosis and in the Christian schools of a spiritual energy issuing from the divine unity; see *Dialogue with Trypho*, LXI and CXXVIII, and Tatian's *Address to the Greeks*, v. It had its Hebrew antecedents; the unity of the Hebrew deity was dynamic and multiform.

The word which Tatian uses for the unity is not *ousia* however; it is *hupostasis* or fundamental reality, literally what stands under; the Latin word *substantia*, used by Tertullian, has the same derivation.

CHAPTER 25

THE CHURCH AT PEACE

THE AFRO-SYRIAN DYNASTY

(Pedigree of the Emperors and Empresses)

(1) SEPTIMIUS SEVERUS an African, emperor 193; died at York 211.
married to
JULIA DOMNA of Emesa in Syria, who was the sister of JULIA MAESA

(2) CARACALLA and GETA	Sohaemias and Mamaea (JULIA MAMAEA)	
co-emperors 211		
Geta murdered 212	(3) ELAGABALUS	(4) ALEXANDER SEVERUS
Caracalla assassinated 217	emperor 218	emperor 222
(Macrinus emperor 217)	assassinated 222	assassinated 235

Notes. (1) Publius Septimius Severus on accession took the additional name of Pertinax, whose death he had avenged. (2) 'Caracalla' is a nickname: his official name was Marcus Aurelius Antoninus, after the great second-century emperor. (3) 'Elagabalus' is a nickname from 'El gabal', the name of the fetish stone from Emesa. His name had been Bassianus, but he took the name of Marcus Aurelius Antoninus. (4) The original name of Alexander Severus was Alexianus; he took the name of Marcus Aurelius Severus Alexander.

ACCESSION OF CARACALLA, A.D. 211

In the year 208 there was a revolt in Britain and Severus, with his usual energy, took the field himself in this far frontier of empire, achieving certain dubious successes in the highlands of Caledonia. He firmly stabilized the Roman dominion as far as the Wall of Hadrian, and confirmed the city of York as the headquarters of the military administration. There he died on 4 February 211. It is probable that he was attended by the Montanist physician or healer, Proclus, since Tertullian says that he kept him in 'his palatium' or governmental headquarters, until the day of his death. As Severus lay dying, he asked to see the urn that was to contain his ashes; he took it up in his hands and said, 'Thou shalt contain one whom the world itself could not contain.' Feared, hated and respected, he had restored the whole empire from the River Tigris to the Grampian Mountains. He left his empire to his two sons, Caracalla and Geta, whose hatred for one another was of a pathological intensity and reflected their father's vein of cruelty and vindictiveness. Caracalla, whose official name was Marcus Aurelius Antoninus—for everyone now revered the memory of the philosopher-emperor—murdered Geta in 212, and ordered his name to be erased from every public monument in the empire.

Their mother, the powerful and imperious Julia Domna, was distressed at this act of violence but continued to exercise her influence upon public affairs, virtually sharing with her son in the government of the world. He, too, had come under the influence of the mysterious Proclus, though his character shows no sign of the Christian graces. Yet the church had peace now for nearly forty years, except for the sudden persecutions under Maximin in 235.

The period from 211 to 235 is the subject of the present chapter.

ALEXANDER AND CLEMENT

Persecution had become more intense again during the last years of Severus, and was not extinguished until the accession of Caracalla and Geta. In 210 or 211, there was a governor in Africa, named Scapula, to whom Tertullian wrote an address, out of which we have already taken a good deal of information. He tried to intimidate Scapula by rehearsing stories of persecutors who had suffered for their sins. Saturninus, who had been the first to unsheath the sword against African Christians, had lost his eyesight. Claudius Lucius Herminianus, who was governor of Cappadocia, persecuted the Christians because his wife had embraced the Christian faith; and God afflicted him with a sore disease. He vainly hoped that other Christian wives might not hear of his affliction.

Alexander, the old friend and pupil of Clement of Alexandria, had become a bishop now somewhere in Cappadocia (probably at the 'New' Caesarea), and Clement was his adviser and doubtless the head of his school. Alexander was thrown into prison, and was still in bonds when he heard of the death of Serapion of Antioch and the

437

appointment of his successor, Asclepiades. He was liberated shortly after (on the accession of Caracalla perhaps), and lost no time in sending an Epistle to Antioch by the hand of Clement, who had been working in his diocese during his imprisonment. Eusebius quotes a paragraph from it:

Alexander, a servant and prisoner of Jesus Christ, to the blessed church of the Antiochenes, greeting in the Lord: The Lord made my bonds light and easy, when I heard in my prison, that, by divine providence, Asclepiades, whose worthy faith makes him most suitable, had been entrusted with the episcopate of your holy church of the Antiochenes.

(Alexander, *Epistle to the Antiochenes*, in Eusebius, *E.H.* VI, 11, 5.)

The new bishop, therefore, unlike his adoptionist namesake in Rome, was able to pass the Alexandrian standards of orthodoxy, which were based on the new understanding of the Logos doctrine.

Alexander concludes,

I am sending you this letter, my dear brethren, through Clement the blessed presbyter, a virtuous and approved man, of whom also you have heard, and with whom you will be well acquainted; when he was with us here, by the providence and direction of God, he strengthened and increased the church of the Lord. (*Ibid.* 6.)

Any information about the Antiochene church is of value, since it is so scarce. The work of Clement in Cappadocia and Antioch must have been of great importance, and spread the influence of the Alexandrian school. During this period, no doubt, he completed some of the books which we have mentioned already. He also wrote one for Alexander, which he called *The Ecclesiastical Canon*, or *Against the Judaizers*. We do not possess a copy of it, but its title serves to confirm what we have gathered from other sources, that Jewish Christianity, or a too-Jewish form of Gentile Christianity, was still a strong enough force north of Antioch, and doubtless in its neighbourhood, to cause the bishops of those parts some concern; Apamea and Beroea, both in the neighbourhood of Antioch, were Jewish Christian centres.

We hear no more of Clement except for a brief reference in a letter written by Alexander to Origen, perhaps about 216, from which one infers that he was then dead.

For we know as fathers those blessed ones who have gone before us, with whom we too shall be ere long; Pantaenus the truly blessed who was my master; and the holy Clement who became my master and profited me; and others like them; through whom I came to know thee, who art in all respects the best, my master and my brother.

(Alexander, *Epistle to Origen*, in Eusebius, *E.H.* VI, 14, 9.)

ALEXANDER AND NARCISSUS

About this time (211–15), Bishop Alexander, in obedience to a vision which he saw in the night, made a journey from Cappadocia to Aelia, to pray and to visit the holy places. The Christians of Aelia, the old Jerusalem, gave him a cordial welcome; for they had received a revelation to the effect that someone was coming to them whom they were to welcome as their bishop; and so, with the common consent of the neighbouring bishops, they compelled him to remain as such. This story, which Eusebius accepts without demur, points to three features which may have been expected to occur at an episcopal election: the sign from heaven, the consent of the people, and the approval of the neighbouring bishops. It may even point to a fourth feature, the reluctance of the bishop-elect. Narcissus, it is to be noted, was still living.

Those who see in Alexander the first 'co-adjutor' may be guilty of an unconscious modernization. According to the Syrian legend, Addai, the first bishop of Edessa, had consecrated one of his pupils named Aggai as his successor, and Aggai would have consecrated another of them as his successor, but for his martyrdom. This legend points to the existence, in the east at least, of a belief that a bishop would naturally and normally consecrate his successor. On the other hand, the case of Alexander is our first indubitable instance of the 'translation' of a bishop from one see to another.

The illustration is all the more in order since there was a connexion at this time between Aelia and Edessa; for Julius Africanus, the friend of Bar Daisan, who had campaigned in Syria with Severus and was a friend of Abgar himself, was now living in Palestine, not far from Aelia. He was the chief magistrate of the town of Emmaus, which was situated in southern Judaea, and called itself by the Greek name of Nicopolis; it was not the Emmaus of the Gospel. Africanus assisted Alexander to establish his library in Aelia, and there Eusebius worked some seventy or eighty years later, and found the documents from which he took much of this information. Africanus was working at this time on his *Chronographies*, a universal history of the oriental kind, full of genealogies and lists of kings. He had a very complete knowledge of the literature on the subject and a keenly critical mind, which he was prepared to apply to biblical subjects.

Narcissus continued to take part in the liturgy at Aelia, as we learn from an Epistle written by Alexander to the people of Antinoe in Egypt. Eusebius makes the following quotation from it.

Narcissus salutes you, who held the position of bishop before me here, and is still associated with me in the prayers; he is a hundred and sixteen years old, and urges you, even as I do myself, to be of one mind.

(Alexander, *Epistle to the Antinoites*, in Eusebius, *E.H.* VI, 11, 3.)

The last link with the apostolic past is broken with the disappearance from history of Narcissus; for, even if we discount his estimate of his age, we must conclude that he remembered the time when old men of the same generation as Papias and Polycarp were still handing down their memories of old disciples or near relations of the Lord.

The correspondence of Alexander reveals the linkage between the oriental church in Cappadocia, Syria, Palestine and Egypt, and proves that the ascendancy of Alexandrian theology was established prior to the amazing career of Origen. This may have tended to check a too-Jewish or too-adoptionist theology which may have been influential in Syria.

THE RISE OF ORIGEN

Origen was already rising to fame. It must have been about 210–12, when he was about twenty-five years of age, that he visited Rome, 'desiring to see the most ancient church of the Romans'. He listened with approval, Jerome says, to a sermon from Hippolytus, who was therefore in good standing as a presbyter. The contact thus established between these two men, both of whom adhered to the Logos theology, must have provided an important link between east and west, though nothing could have been more unlike the free intellectualism of Origen than the crusted dogmatic and literal-minded exegesis of the Roman scholar. Yet his literary works found their way to the east, and were read there long after it was forgotten who exactly he was.

On his return to Alexandria Origen began his studies in Hebrew. He found a Jewish scholar who was willing to give him instruction and assist him in his Old Testament studies. It does not seem that he ever progressed very far in the language, but it is significant that he grasped the importance of the study of source-books in the original language, and the effort must have brought him rich rewards.

A year or so later, perhaps in 213 or 214, he visited Arabia. The change in the imperial policy may be judged by the fact that the military governor of Arabia sent an escort to fetch him. The capital city of the Roman province of Arabia was named Bostra, and it had a bishop, Beryllus, whose theological views seem to have approximated to those of the adoptionists at Rome; Origen convinced him of their unsoundness, but this may have occurred during a later visit. He did not stay long in Arabia, but soon returned to Alexandria. In 215 he visited Palestine, where he received a warm welcome from the friends of Clement. There had been no small warfare in Alexandria, Eusebius says, and this is probably a reference to the massacre of the Alexandrians which Caracalla perpetrated during his visit in that year. There may have been anti-christian demonstrations too, and it may have been thought wise for Origen to withdraw, as Clement had done thirteen or fourteen years previously.

It may be asked how the catechetical school was managed during these frequent absences of Origen. The work was carried on by his old pupil and colleague Heraclas, to whom he had handed over the main duties of administration.

Origen took up his residence at Caesarea, and lectured on the scriptures in the church, on the invitation of the bishop Theoctistus, who is not to be confused with his predecessor Theophilus, or his successor Theotecnus. Now Origen was a lay teacher, and his own bishop Demetrius held that laymen ought not to preach in the presence of bishops. He protested in vain. The bishops of Aelia and Caesarea could not understand how he could have made a statement which was manifestly so untrue. They quoted a number of Phrygian precedents to support their case. Demetrius was not mollified, and sent some of his deacons to Caesarea to bring Origen back. He returned to Alexandria, perhaps in 219, and resumed his academic duties; but his relations with his bishop were obviously not what they should be.

During this period, Origen must have begun his acquaintance with Africanus, and Africanus must have paid his visit to Alexandria to see Heraclas.

THE ACCESSION OF ELAGABALUS, A.D. 218

A completely new picture of the church and empire now emerges, which we must pause to consider. It was marked by the military despotism of religious emperors, the importance of the eastern empire, the decline of Rome as the emperors ceased to frequent it, the ascendancy of the neo-platonic philosophy, and the dissemination of a broadminded monotheism based on Syrian and Persian ideas. All religions would be welcomed into what might almost be called a state-church. A place was vacant among the gods for Jesus of Nazareth, if he would accept it. The sun in heaven was the symbol of the new monotheism, which was devised so as to include every form of polytheism. The emperor was its priest and embodiment.

Julia Domna, the widow of Septimius Severus, was the daughter of the high priest of El Gabal at Emesa in Syria. Emesa was a sun sanctuary; and the *gabal* or stone was a fetish representing the sun-god. She was a remarkable woman, quite capable of governing the empire, her biographer remarks. She was well versed in Greek literature and philosophy. She studied these things in her palace at Rome, and thought the new paganism needed something to offset the Christian gospel. She asked her literary adviser Philostratus to prepare a life of the Pythagorean sage Apollonius of Tyana out of the existing second-century memoirs and a few apocryphal Epistles. He did it rather in the style of the apocryphal Acts. The *Life of Apollonius* is better literature than the apocryphal Acts, and has secured greater fame; but it is doubtful whether it exercised much influence on the religious situation. Nevertheless it is interesting to see paganism beginning to answer the challenge of Christ.

Apollonius heals the sick, casts out devils, and raises a young girl from the dead. He appears before the judgement-seat of Domitian, and saves himself by vanishing into thin air. On the afternoon of the same day, he appears to two disciples in a cave; one of them doubts, but Apollonius stretches out his hand and says, 'Touch me.' In general, however, he is the exponent of the highest type of Greek intellectualism which was able to come to terms with the highest intellectualism and mysticism of the east. This was to be found in India, it was believed. It is the same formula that we find in the Books of Clement, in which Peter is the exponent, in terms of Greek intellectualism, of a refined

Hebrew monotheism which had been mediated through Jesus as the 'True Prophet'. Their history seems to be very much the same as that of the *Life of Apollonius*. They were put together early in the third century, out of stories which had already appeared in the second. In their third-century form, they may have been designed to win the approval of the empress.

When Caracalla was assassinated in 217, Julia Domna starved herself to death; but her commanding position was inherited by her equally potent sister Julia Maesa, who had two grandchildren who she freely stated were descendants of Septimius Severus. She persuaded the eastern legions that this was the case, and succeeded in placing on the throne the elder of the two, Bassianus, who had become the high priest of the sun-god at Emesa at the age of fourteen; he was sixteen when he became emperor. His mother took him to Rome, and they brought the sun-god from Emesa with them and installed it in a temple at Rome. There they proceeded to gather the sacred emblems of the various higher deities of the empire and group them round it. Apparently there was a place in this union of religions for the Jews, the Samaritans and the Christians. A great honour was reserved for Tanit, the old Carthaginian queen of heaven from Africa; she was brought over to Rome with great pomp and ceremony and formally married to the black stone from Emesa.

Bassianus was surnamed Elagabalus (or Heliogabalus), as the earthly representative of the sun-god of Emesa, El Gabal. It was his greatest joy to take the leading part in the rites and ceremonies of the various foreign deities, which were celebrated with the utmost splendour, barbarous dances and sexual climaxes.

THE ROMAN SCHISM, A.D. 217

The brief episcopate of Callistus was practically concurrent with the reign of Elagabalus. It lasted about five years. Zephyrinus died in 216 or 217, and when the episcopal elections were over there was the usual schism. Callistus and Hippolytus both claimed to be bishops. A certain amount of mystery still surrounds this unfortunate period, and the nature of the schism is not perfectly clear; but it is not possible to place the episcopate of Hippolytus anywhere else than in Rome.

Callistus began his short episcopate by excommunicating the

unfortunate Sabellius, who was very much disappointed, since he thought he had received encouragement from Callistus; or so Hippolytus states. It looks rather as if Callistus had used him while it was convenient to do so and had discarded him when he reached his objective. On the other hand, Callistus may really have come to see that there was something unsatisfactory about his theology. He may have receded a little from the 'modalism' of the dominant monarchian school; he may have seen some value in the teaching of the 'adoptionist' school. Or, of course, he may have been hoping for adoptionist support. At any rate, according to Hippolytus, he proposed a theology which started out in the one camp and had the appearance of ending up in the other; but it is hardly likely that the scornful report of it given by Hippolytus is to be trusted. After all, he ranks Callistus as a heretic, and has to prove that he is one.

Callistus condemned Hippolytus in one trenchant utterance: 'You are ditheists', he said, worshippers of two gods; and the stricture was not devoid of justice, for the theology of Hippolytus did suggest that the Angel or Logos was a second god, or a secondary manifestation of the one deity, though he worked hard to get rid of this unfortunate impression. Hippolytus had found sufficient support among the local bishops, presbyters and substantial laity to set himself up as a bishop; the bishop of Rome in his own estimation, for he obstinately refers to the 'school' of Callistus. He admits that the majority sided with Callistus, but he was not impressed by that. The claim to legitimacy on the part of a bishop was much strengthened by the recognition of outside bishops; and it is probable that many bishops recognized him; in particular the oriental bishops must have regarded him with respect, since his books were received and preserved in the east. He certainly thought that he had a mission to instruct the Christians of all nations.

The Roman church counts Callistus as the legitimate bishop; indeed it knows only of Callistus. Hippolytus was revered as a presbyter and martyr, and his true story was completely forgotten. Except for the *Chronicle*, his books, which were written in Greek, have left no trace in the Roman tradition. How are we to explain the fact that there was a grave schism in the Roman church, which left no memory behind it? It is likely that the old Greek-speaking tradition of the Roman church which Hippolytus represented, was fast disappearing, and that the native Roman and Latin-speaking elements rallied to the cause of Callistus.

CALLISTUS

The attempt of Callistus to reconcile the conflicting monarchian theologies did not exhaust his efforts to restore peace to the Roman church. He relaxed what many regarded as the ancient discipline of the church and undertook to forgive sins committed after baptism. It had been freely stated, even in the time of Hermas, that such sins could not be forgiven; but we have ventured to doubt whether this perfectionist principle was ever translated into what might be called canon law. Yet we are dealing now with a view which seems to be regarded as well established, that the baptized Christian who relapsed into idolatry, or committed murder, or was guilty of adultery, could not be received back into communion. God could forgive him, but the church could not; he must be left to the judgement of heaven. What Callistus did was to announce publicly that he would extend the ministry of reconciliation to include adultery.

Tertullian gives a sarcastic account of this announcement in his book *Concerning Modesty*. The supreme pontiff, he remarks with heavy humour, the bishop of bishops, has spoken; he has issued an edict; he has undertaken to remit the sin of adultery. There is no doubt that he means Callistus, though he does not name him. Tertullian, by now, was harsh, censorious and grumpy. Hippolytus was grim and conscious of his rectitude. Sinners cast out by Hippolytus were being received into communion by Callistus. He was allowing high-born ladies to marry men of the slave-class, from which, of course, he had risen himself. Men who had been twice or three times married were allowed to become presbyters; and presbyters who were not yet married were allowed to marry after ordination. He even sanctioned re-baptism, Hippolytus says, referring possibly to the case of persons who had been baptized by heretics.

It is plain that something which was regarded as an ancient discipline was being broken down, and the new policy offended the Montanist rigour of Tertullian as deeply as it offended the legalism of Hippolytus. Some scholars have suggested that a 'primitive' standard of spiritual and moral perfection was being abandoned, and a general lowering of standards was taking place. It would certainly appear that the picture of the church as a race of other-worldly 'spiritual' enthusiasts was becoming rather unreal. It was penetrating the world and being penetrated by the world. Some Christians were government officials, some enjoyed wealth and social prestige, and many adapted themselves to the social standards of the day. What was the right policy for the church under the new circumstances? Before we condemn men like Clement of Alexandria who sketched out a way of life for the gnostic Christian, which took some account of social conditions, or men like Callistus of Rome who made it easier for the lapsed Christian to start again, we ought to remember two facts. One is that the problem had always existed and had never been solved; the first Epistle to the Corinthians and the first Epistle to Timothy show that it was quite possible for unworthy Christians to exist in a church which was supposed to be governed by apostolic standards. The other is that a moral and spiritual perfectionism had given way during the second century to a harsh puritanism and a rigid legalism; the champions of what were supposed to be the primitive standards had lost the primitive spirit.

Callistus decided, as Clement and Hermas had done before him to exercise a ministry of mercy and reconciliation towards erring Christians, even if it did involve him in some logical perplexities. We could build up a very pleasant picture of Callistus out of the sarcasms of his two enemies, which provide the only evidence we have. He made allowances for the weakness of human nature. He knew how to lead and handle the church. He had risen from the ranks, and knew what hardship and temptations were like. He had some claims to be considered a confessor. He was kind and compassionate. He had read the Gospels, and thought that it was his duty to restore the lost sheep to the flock. His eucharistic chalice was engraved with the figure of the Good Shepherd.

Tertullian observed that he was in danger of restoring the lost goat rather than the lost sheep; but he probably did not mind that unkind cut; catacomb pictures of the period show the Good Shepherd bringing back the lost goat. And it is possible that this idea was wise and Christian. In any case it triumphed.

ALCIBIADES OF APAMEA

It was in the reign of Elagabalus, and in the episcopate of Callistus, that Alcibiades of Apamea brought to Rome the teachings of the Jewish-Christian prophet Elkhasai. The Apamea from which he came must have been the Syrian Apamea on the Orontes River, not far from Emesa, the holy city which had supplied Rome with its dynasty of empresses and emperors. Where one could go, the other could follow. Elkhasai, it will be remembered, had appeared in Transjordania in the third year of Trajan, and had announced a second baptism which washed away all sins; not merely sexual irregularities of the grossest description, but apostasy as well. In fact the prophet had said that it was lawful to deny in time of persecution, provided one did not deny 'from the heart'. Hermas, too, though he regarded the restoration of an apostate as virtually an impossibility, thought that it might be done provided he had not denied 'from the heart'.

Callistus had not made provision for the repentant idolater, so far as we know, though it would not be long before the church did so; but there is a certain significance in the fact that Hippolytus compares Alcibiades with Callistus. Both exercised a ministry of repentance for fallen Christians; and both did it on the strength of a declaration or edict; in one case it was the scroll which Elkhasai had received from heaven, in the other it was an episcopal pronouncement. There is a possibility that Callistus still relied upon the authority of the scroll which had been received from heaven by Hermas, which had ranked as scripture at one time in the Roman church and had not entirely lost its authority; but he seems to have laid greater stress upon the authority of the episcopal office to forgive sins, to 'loosen every bond', as Hippolytus expressed it in his ordination prayer. He made use of many Gospel texts, as we can tell quite clearly from Tertullian's replies to his arguments; and one of them seems to have been the authority which had been given to St Peter to loosen and to bind.

We have here a very interesting but obscure subject. The high authority of Peter in the evangelical tradition appears to be an oriental doctrine, but after all it had been communicated to the whole catholic church in the Gospel according to St Matthew. The Ebionites in Syria had made much of the figure of Peter, and believed that Clement had been appointed by him as the first bishop of Rome. This idea had reached Rome by the end of the second century, and was known to Tertullian.[1] It was but a step to the theory that any special authority which was given to Peter was transmitted to subsequent Roman

[1] When Tertullian sarcastically describes Callistus as the 'bishop of bishops', he may be quoting from the Clementine legends, in which James is given this title.

bishops; or, more probably, to the episcopate as a whole, for Antioch claimed Peter too, and before very long were showing his chair, since they could not show his tomb. Both theories appear in theological debate in the mid third-century.

THE LAST PERIOD OF TERTULLIAN

Tertullian maintained, in answer to whatever claim it was that Callistus had put forward, that the authority given to Peter had stopped with him. He admitted that the authority to forgive sins had been committed to the church; but not to the 'psychics' as he now called the catholic church, and not to a 'quantity of bishops'. Such forgiveness was to be exercised by a 'spiritual man', if it was exercised at all; but it was not to be exercised at all since Montanus had forbidden it.

As for the *Pastor* of Hermas, its long life as a piece of Christian scripture was coming to an end. Tertullian attacks it as being quite alone in favouring adultery, and adds that it had been rejected now by various councils. Its position cannot have been strong; but it looks as if Callistus, or some one on his side of the argument, had referred to it. As for Tertullian, we hear no more of him. His numerous books seem to have been written within about twenty-five years, that is to say from 197 to 222. He was completely isolated from the church now, in his peculiar sect, which came to be called the Tertullianists. He was a bitter enemy of the catholic church, and yet the catholic church treasured his writings and studied them, and they helped to form the mind of Latin Christianity.

Despite his inhuman rigorism, and his increasing lack of sympathy with the ordinary Christian of his day, he was a man of deep Christian character, moral fervour, and acute intelligence. He could write a splendid oratorical prose which arrests the attention even today. He saw that an intense faith ought to express itself in an uncompromising moral life, which meant to him a strongly anti-social life; but it looks as if moral compromise actually was the danger of the church in his time. He has continued to command the respect and admiration of Christians in all ages.

ACCESSION OF SEVERUS ALEXANDER, A.D. 222

In the year 221, Julius Africanus paid a visit to Rome on municipal business. He is an interesting example of the so-called worldly Christian; for he had been a cavalry officer under Severus in the Syrian wars, and was now the chief magistrate of the town of Nicopolis in Judaea. He did not find these duties incompatible with his Christianity, apparently. He had finished his great book called the *Chronographies* in the third year of Elagabalus, that is to say 220–1, and he arrived in Rome in time to see the end of his brief but lurid career. After five years of sumptuous fertility rituals and religious carnivals, the people of Rome tired of their Syrian boy-emperor and his ambitious mother. They rose against them and threw them both into the Tiber—which may have been an ancient ritual too, for all we know. His cousin Alexianus, who took the name of Alexander Severus, succeeded him in 222, and was a complete contrast. He was a student, an ascetic and an idealist. Whereas Elagabalus had gathered the sacred images and fetish stones of the various nations far and wide, Alexander sent them home and built himself a chapel in which he placed the images of Orpheus, Abraham, Apollonius and Christ. His mother Julia Mamaea, who kept up the tradition of her dynasty by presiding in the senate and giving orders on the field of battle, was a patroness of the Christian intellectuals. She permitted Hippolytus to dedicate his treatise *On the Resurrection* to her, and at a later date she sent for Origen to confer with her when she was at Antioch. The days of peace had certainly come with the ascendancy of Syria.

It is likely enough that Alexander already knew Africanus. At any rate he requested him to arrange his library for him in the Pantheon, the famous round temple with its enormous granite columns and its concrete dome which Agrippa had built for all the gods, before the time of Christ, and Hadrian and Severus had restored. It is natural to suppose that Africanus met Hippolytus, and that the two chroniclers exchanged notes, and discussed difficult points in the emperor's library. On his return to Judaea, Africanus helped to organize the episcopal library at Aelia. As we consider these contacts between east and west, it is not hard to understand how the works of Hippolytus and the older Roman writers were transmitted to the east and became available to students like Eusebius and Epiphanius. There must have been many similar contacts.

THE MARTYRDOM OF CALLISTUS, c. A.D. 222

Africanus may also have been in Rome at the time of the martyrdom of Callistus. Across the Tiber today, in the 'Trastevere', the visitor may see the church of St Cecilia and the cemetery of Calepodius. It was in this neighbourhood, not far from the Jewish quarter, that Callistus was killed in a riot. He was buried in the cemetery of Calepodius, not in the church cemetery on the Appian Way which he had managed himself when he was the deacon of Zephyrinus. His successor was named Urban, and in his episcopate, or more probably in the episcopate of the next bishop Pontian, a beautiful crypt was laid out for the burial of the bishops of Rome; Urban is there, and so is Pontian, but not Callistus, after whom the cemetery is now named. The reason for the exclusion of Callistus from the 'Crypt of the Popes' is probably a very simple one. The good people of the Trastevere held on to him; he was a bishop and a martyr, and why should they let him go?

The suggestion which comes into one's mind, that the residence and headquarters of Callistus were situated in this district, is supported by two considerations. One is that the cemetery of Callistus on the Appian Way contained the burial lots of the Cecilian family, whose church was near the cemetery of Calepodius.[1] The other is that there was undoubtedly a church-building at this time in the Trastevere, for a guild of cooks or tavern-keepers tried to take it away from the Christians by a legal action, and the new emperor awarded it to the Christians on the grounds that it was better for the property to be used for the worship of God, whatever name he might be called by. The right of Christians to hold property was thus officially recognized, and it looks as if their religion was now perfectly lawful in every respect.

When Urban succeeded Callistus as bishop, Hippolytus abated none of his pretensions, so far as we can see.[2] It can hardly have been later than 222 that his adherents had his statue made, seated in his chair, and wearing the philosopher's gown or cloak. It stands today in the Vatican Museum, and it is much to be deplored that its head is missing, and even more to be deplored, perhaps, that it has been restored. The

---

[1] Was the church of St Cecilia originally simply the church of the Cecilian family?

[2] Some degree of recognition was extended to Hippolytus by the Roman church after his martyrdom. Is it possible that some reconciliation or partial recognition took place after the death of Callistus?

list of his books, to which we have referred from time to time, is engraved upon it, and so are his tables for calculating Easter by the moon, which were intended to set the church free from dependence upon the Jewish calculators. The full moons for 217–23, about the period of the episcopate of Callistus, are correctly given; but after that date they begin to go wrong, so that 222–3 seem to be the latest years that we can assign to the statue. It was found in the cemetery of Hippolytus, on the Via Tiburtina, which runs eastward from the city; and, as it was erected in the lifetime of the saint, it suggests that this was his residence and headquarters.

THE PHILOSOPHY OF ORIGEN

It was under the rule of this emperor that the mind of Origen began to turn towards authorship. The fruit of his studies with Heraclas, under Ammonius Saccas, begins to appear. He writes his great book which is called *Concerning First Principles*, or *De Principiis*, from the Latin translation, which unfortunately is all that survives, except for a few extracts from the original Greek. He also began his *Commentary on John*. Neither can be called orthodox. The commentary made use of the work of the Valentinian writer Heracleon; and the *De Principiis* is based on the neo-platonic philosophy of the day, which Ammonius was adapting to the requirements of the new paganism. Ammonius resembled Pantaenus in the fact that he wrote nothing. He is known through his pupils: Origen and Heraclas in his early period; Plotinus and Longinus later. Christian and pagan could both drink from his fountain; but it cannot be accepted that he was ever a Christian, as Porphyry, a pupil of Plotinus, states. He seems to be confusing him with a Christian Ammonius, who also lived at Alexandria, probably during his later period; this Ammonius was known for his synoptic studies of the Gospels and did work of lasting importance which Eusebius carried further.

Philosophy had been used so far by Christian teachers in an unsystematic way to illuminate this or that doctrine of the faith, and express it in terms which would be more generally comprehensible to educated men; or to support difficult doctrines with weighty arguments; and even so the procedure was felt by many to be very dangerous. Hippolytus traces the origin of every heresy to some form of philosophy, and Tertullian quite agreed that its influence was evil. In

Alexandria, however, it had been maintained from the time of Pantaenus at least that philosophical and literary studies were essential prerequisites for theology. This view had been objected to, but Clement had done much to disperse the opposition. Even he, however, had not attempted to produce a thought-out philosophy of the Christian religion. Basilides and Valentinus were the true precursors of Origen in this respect; but he owed little to them; he leans on nobody.

Origen loyally accepted the common Christian tradition as the essential material with which he was to do his work, and in this connexion he gives a list of articles of faith which were beyond dispute. It is an enlargement of the usual creed-forms. He also accepted the Old Testament and the New Testament scriptures, of which he gives a list. With regard to the latter, he uses our New Testament exactly as it stands today, though he admits that there are some who have their doubts about II Peter and II and III John. He thinks that Hebrews was written by a disciple of St Paul. Possibly we should add Hermas and Barnabas to this New Testament canon; and, if we do, it agrees exactly with the contents of the Vatican Codex B. Indeed, that manuscript, which was made in Egypt in the fourth century, represents very exactly the text that Origen used in this early period; it must have been copied from such a manuscript of this period.

Nobody ever studied the Bible more diligently, or loved it more devotedly, than Origen; but his method of allegorical interpretation, which he inherited from Philo and Clement, enabled him to derive from the text any philosophical conclusion which he required, though he did not disturb the literal meaning or the moral or spiritual significance. He studied them very carefully, but he also filled his commentaries with indefensible deductions of an allegorical character which were additional to the literal, moral and spiritual interpretations.

DE PRINCIPIIS

It is not possible to give an adequate account of the great system of thought which he created; for this would be a long study in itself. It begins with the concept of eternal being. It was conceded now in philosophic circles that it was not possible to think of an all-wise, all-good, eternal mind, without an element of plurality within its unity; it had to be a trinity. A bare monarchianism had been surpassed already by the philosophers. The multi-personal or poly-dynamic deity of the old Hebrew revelation found his counterpart now in the highest realms of philosophic speculation. The Logos theology, in its Clementine form, took its place as an essential element in the philosophy of monotheism; it was the divine reason, eternally expressing the mind of the high God to himself and in relation to the cosmos. An element of inferiority or 'subordination' still clung to the Logos in Origen's thinking; for though he is co-eternal with the Father, he is still the derivative God with which the cosmos must be content.

It will do little justice to the thought of Origen to give a thumbnail portrait of his 'system' as Justin and Irenaeus did for Satornil and his fellows; but it must be attempted. The creator, in his boundless love, made all souls free and equal at the beginning of time. Some fell from virtue and obedience before the creation of the material universe, and they were condemned to be clothed in bodies, that they might work out their redemption, some as angels, some as daemons, and some as men. This cosmos is their purgatory, in which they make progress towards perfection. All will be saved, some in this life through faith and works; some in the next after passing through purifying fires; for aeonian fire must naturally mean spiritual fire for Origen.

What then of the Saviour of mankind? The Logos united himself with a pure soul which had not sinned; he was born of the virgin, and passed through suffering, death and resurrection. His function was to deliver man from the devil, to reveal the truth and to give him grace through faith and knowledge. Origen lacks the acute sense of spiritual crisis which we find in the Pauline language about salvation from sin; but is he unorthodox? The framework of his thinking is decidedly gnostic, but does he contradict the faith of the gospel at any point? Does he take on board profound heretical errors? Subsequent generations argued the question with fury, and eventually he was condemned. Epiphanius, who admires him very much, includes him with regret among the heretics. In the middle ages it was a point of debate in the schools whether he could be saved.

There is no sign that his views occasioned any comment in Alexandria. Demetrius, who was quick to notice uncanonical irregularities, did not concern himself too much perhaps with what the intellectuals talked about in the schools. Like Callistus, he seems to have been primarily an administrator.

AMBROSE

There was another reason perhaps for Origen's immunity from interference. He had a powerful patron in the wealthy high-born influential Ambrose, who stood by him to the end of his life. It has even been suggested that he accompanied him to Rome, where he would have seen the enormous literary output of Hippolytus, who, incidentally, must have had powerful support himself from substantial laymen. Ambrose seems to have belonged to the governing class. He had been a gnostic, but had been reclaimed by Origen. He took him into his household, and provided him with a corps of stenographers who took down his lectures in shorthand. These notes were then transcribed in longhand by others, and the transcripts were handed over to expert women who copied them on papyrus rolls. Research and discussion went on far into the night. The day's labour began again early in the morning and continued until three or four in the afternoon; for in those days the hours of daylight were precious. Three or four was the usual hour for the main meal of the day; but meals were constantly sacrificed to business. The pace at which he lived, and the number of books he wrote, is terrifying to think of. Six thousand volumes was one estimate.

Ambrose took his part in the intellectual work, and urged Origen on to undertake greater labours. Origen calls him his taskmaster, and rather blames him for certain errors that crept into his books owing to the speed with which they were produced. Actually Origen had little notion of literary grace or style, and this method of composition would not contribute to it. He was financially independent of Demetrius, however. He was in the position of the free-lance teacher of the second century; and what Christian scholar has ever had such independence and such facilities for publication?

THE *APOSTOLIC TRADITION* OF HIPPOLYTUS

Hippolytus was a dry-as-dust scholar, who lived in the world of books and doctrines. He conducted theological wars on paper, and sometimes in public debate. It is hard to think that the church over which he presided was a true democratic flesh-and-blood ecclesia with full pastoral responsibilities; it is easier to think of it as a learned academy based on an ecclesiastically organized community, but chiefly occupied in learned research, controversy, propaganda and the dissemination of theological literature. His knowledge of philosophy, mythology, astronomy and magic was encyclopaedic. He delved into ancient history, wrote biblical commentaries and laid down the law on eschatology. His surviving works, with some help from Tertullian, have enabled us to make a partial reconstruction of some events and trends in the Roman church.

During his last years, 230–5, Hippolytus worked on his *Chronicle*, which contained among other things a list of Roman bishops with their episcopal years. This list was incorporated into the 'Liberian' or 'Philocalian' Calendar, which was compiled in Rome about 354, for this document states that it made use of an older document, the last entry of which was dated in the thirteenth year of Alexander Severus, that is to say 234. It was undoubtedly the *Chronicle*.

These books are all full of historical information, though they make hard reading, but he produced a more human work in his less ambitious *Apostolic Tradition*, and in recent years it has attracted a great deal of attention from liturgical scholars. Its text has been fairly successfully reconstructed from various sources. Its date is uncertain, but a recent editor, the much lamented Gregory Dix, assigns it with good reason to a date not long before the death of Zephyrinus in 217. The first volume, which does not survive, dealt with *charismata* or gifts of grace. The second volume is a pontifical, or outline of liturgical procedure from the point of view of the officiating bishop. It is a priceless picture of the liturgy and holy order of the Roman ecclesia as it existed in the time of Eleutherus and Victor, defined and expressed in clear outline by the exact and dogmatic mind of the man who claimed to represent the old Roman order as it had come down from apostolic times. It stands to reason that he would not and could not seriously alter this tradition; indeed, he does not charge Zephyrinus and Callistus with doing so; they observed the customs and the traditions, he says. Yet of course he could not commit it to paper without endowing it with considerable precision of form, and settling points which might be variable or doubtful; but if we make allowances for this tendency, and for the impress of his own opinions here and there, we are bound to regard the customs to which he bears witness as the tradition which was established and operated in his younger days; and we have seen that the prayers which

he commits to writing and the customs to which he refers can sometimes be explained as originating in the Hellenistic synagogue-order of
the earliest times. We can recognize their background in the liturgical
passages of older Christian writings.

The book has two features which are necessary in a liturgy, purity
of outline and gravity of style. It never sins by exuberance or excess. It
is a notable work with which to close our survey of the first two
Christian centuries; for it is obvious that the whole life of the church in
all its departments was supported and carried forward by the corporate
worship of Almighty God, through faith in his Son Jesus Christ, in the
spiritual fellowship of the apostolic church, in accordance with the old
Judaeo-Christian tradition. It was in this living succession that the
Gospels and Epistles were publicly read and expounded, and the evangelical concepts of God the Father and the Lord Jesus Christ were
formed in the mind. They were not obtained from the reading of books
nor in the lecture-halls of the theologians.

It also closes the story of the old Hellenistic Roman church, which
had become, for a time, the forum of international Christianity. As the
emperors shifted their courts into Syria, or Asia Minor, or the Balkans,
the swarm of philosophers and purveyors of religion went with them.
Christian theology gravitated in the same direction. By the time we
come to the two-hundred-and-fifties, a Latin-speaking church has
evolved out of the conflicts of the earlier part of the century. As the
Greek language passed out of use, it was cut off from its past, and also
from the eastern churches, by the barrier of language. Hippolytus and
his works were forgotten in his own city.

The prophet who was without honour in his own country was
singularly influential abroad, however. His books were received far
and wide throughout the east. In particular the *Apostolic Tradition*
became the basis of numerous later church orders, especially in Egypt.
His eucharistic prayer survives almost entire in the liturgy of the
Ethiopian church, and its influence may be traced far and wide. The
original text only exists in a Latin translation, and even that only exists
in part.

HIPPOLYTUS THE MARTYR, A.D. 235

In the year 230, which closes our historical period of two hundred years from the Crucifixion, Pontian succeeded Urban in the succession of Zephyrinus and Callistus; and from the time of Pontian Latin names predominate in the Roman episcopal succession. There were still three bishops in Rome, if not more; for Artemas, or Artemon, must be regarded as the bishop of the Adoptionist succession.

In 235 Alexander and his mother Mamaea were assassinated in the course of a war on the Danube. They were succeeded by a general of marked ability, who was a native of the Balkans. His name was Maximin. There is no clear evidence that he was a persecutor, but local persecutions broke out in his reign. Both bishops of Rome, Pontian and Hippolytus, were sent to Sardinia, where they died as martyrs. After the years of confusion, their bodies were brought back to the city. Pontian was buried in the famous 'Crypt of the Popes' in the 'Cemetery of Callistus'. He was probably the first to be buried there, for the body of Urban seems to have been brought in at a later date. This chamber was probably set aside for episcopal burials when the troubles had subsided. Hippolytus was buried in the 'cemetery of Hippolytus' in the Ager Veranus, where his headless statue was discovered. Neither he nor Callistus lies with the other Roman bishops. It may be that both rest in their places of residence and administration.

Pontian was honoured as the legitimate bishop; but Hippolytus was honoured as a teacher and martyr. His schism was forgotten and very soon nobody knew who he was. Catalogues of martyrs and bishops were now kept in official form; the birthdays of the former and the 'depositions' or burials of the latter were entered in a calendar. Liberius, who was bishop of Rome in 354, commissioned the scholar Philocalus to prepare a new 'catalogue' based on the old material, including in it the *Chronicle* of Hippolytus himself, which had survived in Rome to that year, though its authorship was no longer known. The *Liberian Catalogue* says:

At that time Pontian the bishop and Hippolytus the presbyter were exiled and deported to the unhealthy island of Sardinia in the consulship of Severus and Quintian [i.e. 235 A.D.].

and that is all they seem to have known about it at that time.

THE CHRISTIAN LITERATURE AVAILABLE IN LATIN

A partial list of the Christian literature which was available in Latin at the opening of the third century can be attempted, and is offered here to supply background material for the study of the development of the Roman church as it emerges from its predominantly Greek-speaking phase.

(1) The New Testament with the apocalypses of Esdras and Baruch: translated from Greek.

(2) Clement, Hermas, Polycarp, Barnabas, the *Two Ways*, and the *Refutation* of Irenaeus: translated from Greek.

(3) Literature written in Latin begins (according to Jerome) with Victor; then follow Minucius Felix and Tertullian.

(4) The early *Syntagma* against heresies of Hippolytus was translated into Latin (or re-edited in Latin) and at a later date ascribed to Tertullian. His *Apostolic Tradition* was also translated, but Gregory Dix propounded the rather unlikely theory that it was done at a later date from a Syriac version. The *Chronicle* was also translated. But none of these were known as his.

We may also add the catalogue of New Testament books which is preserved in the *Muratorian Fragment* in a Latin translation. Some scholars attribute this to Hippolytus.

(5) The *Acts* of the African martyrs which provide the oldest names in the Roman calendar of martyrs.

Note. There was also of course the Marcionite version of the New Testament and possibly other Marcionite literature, since the *Syllogisms* of Apelles seems to have been translated into Latin at some time.

I can find no trace of other heretical literature in Latin, but the polemic of Tertullian against the Valentinians and others suggests that they were making headway in Latin. It is hard to suppose that the popular Montanist and Monarchian schools had no literature in this language. Some of the apocryphal Acts and similar literature also became available.

CHAPTER 26

THE THIRD CHRISTIAN CENTURY

CHRONOLOGICAL TABLE

A.D.

230 Ardashir of Persia invades Mesopotamia.
Emperor Alexander and his mother Mamaea in Antioch.

232 Origen settles in Caesarea of Palestine.
Heraclas succeeds Origen in the Alexandrian school.

233 Assassination of Alexander and Mamaea; *Maximin* emperor.
Persecution; Pontian and Hippolytus martyrs in Sardinia.
Origen in Caesarea of Cappadocia with Firmilian.

237–8 Persians overrun Mesopotamia.

238 Maximin overthrown by *Gordianus* family.

241 Shapur I succeeds his father Ardashir, who died at Antioch.

242 Coronation of Shapur; Mani proclaims his new religion.

243 Persians driven out of Mesopotamia.

244 Gordianus III assassinated; *Philip the Arabian* becomes emperor.
Philip makes peace with Persia.

247 Dionysius becomes bishop of Alexandria.

248 Thousandth anniversary of Rome.

249–50 Gothic attacks on Moesia.

249 Philip assassinated; *Decius* becomes emperor.
Persecution; martyrdoms of Babylas, Fabian, Alexander; Origen
imprisoned.

251 Death of Decius in battle. *Gallus* emperor. Cessation of persecution.
Cornelius, bishop of Rome: correspondence with Cyprian; schism of
Novatian.

252 Goths invade Greece and Asia Minor.

A.D.

253   *Valerian and Gallienus* emperors. Death of Origen at Tyre.
Invasion of Armenia by Shapur of Persia.

254   Stephen, bishop of Rome; controversy with Cyprian of Carthage.

255   Persian invasions continue; barbarian pressure from north.

256   Second Gothic raid; Valerian at Antioch.

257   *Persecution* of Valerian.

258   Martyrdoms of Cyprian in Africa and Xystus and Laurence in Rome.

259   Dionysius, bishop of Rome.

260   Defeat and capture of Valerian by Shapur.
Edict of Toleration for Christians by Gallienus; sole emperor.

262   Success of Odenatus of Palmyra against Persians.
Odenatus virtual sovereign in the east.

263 (approximate)   Bishops at Antioch condemn Paul of Samosata.
Continued invasions of Goths and other barbarians.

267   Murder of Odenatus; his widow Zenobia succeeds him.

268 (approximate)   Second council at Antioch condemns Paul and appoints Domnus.
Death of Gallienus; *Claudius* emperor.

270   *Aurelian* emperor; builder of the walls of Rome.

272   Aurelian defeats Zenobia. Death of Shapur, succeeded by Hormizd I.
Ejection of Paul of Samosata; Domnus succeeds him.

273   Final defeat of Zenobia. Vahram I succeeds Hormizd.

274   Triumph of Aurelian in Rome; restoration of empire.

275   Murder of Aurelian.
Approximate date for crucifixion of Mani.

276–283   War with Persia; Tacitus, Florian, Probus, Carus, Carinus and Numerian are emperors in quick succession. Diocletian succeeds in 284 defeating Carinus in 285.

ORIGEN LEAVES ALEXANDRIA, A.D. 231

We have now reached the terminal point of our history, which is the year 230, having completed the fifth generation of forty years each since the Crucifixion, two hundred years in all. It has not been treated in as great detail as the preceding four, but an attempt has been made to indicate the connexions and inter-relations of persons and events. The present chapter will cover a hundred years of history, necessarily omitting many important new developments, but continuing some of the principal topics, and so forming an epilogue without which our narrative would not be complete or self-explanatory.

The year 231 was marked by the emergence of the Persian power, a sign of ill omen for the Roman empire. Artaxerxes (Ardashir I) of Persia was successful in wresting the province of Mesopotamia from the Roman garrisons. The Emperor Alexander and his mother Mamaea spent the winter in Antioch in preparation for an eastern campaign which was far from successful.

Origen was now the rising intellectual luminary of the Christian church, and indeed of the philosophical and religious world. He was much in demand outside of Alexandria. He travelled and lectured constantly; and in this year he paid a second visit to Caesarea, where he was again asked to lecture in the church. He was still a layman, but he was now forty-five years of age, and his episcopal friends ordained him presbyter. It was a provocative act, and the news was not well received in Alexandria, where Demetrius had now been bishop for forty years and the presbytery was a highly privileged and exclusive corporation. He was the last remaining figure of importance from the days of the Paschal controversy, when Irenaeus and Victor and Polycrates and Narcissus were maintaining the traditions which they had received from disciples of the apostles. He was a strong man, and not to be trifled with.

Origen went on to Greece and spent some time in Athens. On his way back to Caesarea he stayed at Nicomedea in Pontus, which was one of the new centres of imperial and military administration and a city of growing importance. He went on to Ephesus and Antioch. It is quite possible that he never returned to Alexandria at all; for the patience of Demetrius was exhausted. It was not a question of Origen's philosophy, it seems, that was charged against him; it was his uncanonical ordination and the old question of his mutilation. At a later date, canons of the church strictly forbade the ordination of a eunuch, though this had happened in Rome, it would appear, in the case of the eunuch Hyacinthus who had attended Marcia;[1] they also directed that a man could only be ordained presbyter by his own bishop. These rules or customs may already have been observed in Egypt, but in any case Demetrius was prepared to take action. He called a council of

---

[1] Bishop Melito of Sardis is so described but the word may not have been intended to be taken literally.

presbyters, and Origen was dismissed from his position as head of the catechetical school; he was 'ordered to remove', says Photius, who had read the correspondence. Demetrius followed this by calling a council of bishops, who deposed him from the presbyterate. Whatever may have been the case in earlier days, there was nothing defective about the episcopal order in Alexandria now. Demetrius communicated this decision to the other bishops of the catholic church, and all concurred in it, Jerome says, except the bishops of Palestine, Arabia, Phoenicia and Achaea. Rome and Antioch, therefore, must have decided against Origen, if Jerome is accurate; but in the case of Rome, this would mean Pontian rather than Hippolytus; for Rome was still divided.

Heraclas became the head of the catechetical school in Alexandria, but its glory had departed. The great Alexandrian tradition was now removed to Caesarea, where Origen worked in harmony with Theoctistus and Alexander and Africanus. Ambrose followed him, and re-established the library and the scriptorium. Origen revelled in his new-found freedom. He referred to the providence of God, which had delivered him from the Egyptian bondage; and it was at this time most likely (231–3) that he was summoned to Antioch to meet the empress, Julia Mamaea.

In 233 Demetrius died. He was now a very old man, and the diocese of Alexandria owed much to his resolute administration. He was succeeded by Heraclas; and Dionysius, another pupil of Origen, became head of the catechetical school. Dionysius succeeded Heraclas as bishop in 247. The theological tradition of Pantaenus, Clement and Origen continued without a break; but it was not apparently in perfect harmony with the Origenists in Palestine.

ORIGEN AT CAESAREA

In the year 235 the young Emperor Alexander and his mother Mamaea were assassinated in the course of a campaign on the Danube, where barbarian invaders had crossed the river, and swarmed into the Balkan provinces. The new emperor, Maximin, was a native of the Balkans who had risen from the ranks, the first of a number of emperors of this sort. There seems to be no good reason for enrolling him among the persecutors; but persecutions did break out in his reign. The Christians were no longer favoured. It was in this year that Pontian and Hippolytus of Rome were condemned to the mines in Sardinia and died there as martyrs. There may have been persecution in Palestine too, but not apparently in Cappadocia, where Origen was visiting Firmilian, the bishop of the Cappadocian Caesarea, which was now one of the most important military centres of the empire and a rival of Antioch itself. Firmilian had visited Origen in the Palestinian Caesarea and had invited him to his diocese to work there, much as Clement had worked for Alexander. The Cappadocian Caesarea became the centre of a leading church which maintained the theology of Origen in the following century when his memory was reviled. It formed a base for the evangelization of Armenia.

Origen seems to have remained there as long as two years. He resided with a lady named Juliana, who presented him with the autograph copy of the translation of the Old Testament made by the Jewish-Christian Symmachus, and also a copy of his book against St Matthew's Gospel. Clement, too, had had to deal with Judaizers in Cappadocia. Jewish Christianity was weakening now, but it was not dead; for it flourished in the Syrian cities of Beroea and Apamea. In Samosata, a young man named Paul was growing to manhood; he became a student of theology, and combined an adoptionist theology of a semi-Ebionite kind with a measure of Origenian philosophy.

Origen returned to Caesarea in Palestine about 237. His literary labours continued, and so did his travels. He visited Jerusalem, Jericho, the Jordan Valley, Galilee and Sidon, to investigate the footsteps of Jesus and his disciples and the prophets. Allusions to these investigations occur in his Gospel-commentaries. He paid at least one more visit to Bostra in Arabia, and it may have been at this time that he conferred with the bishop, Beryllus, and convinced him of the error of his (apparently) adoptionist theology. His sphere of influence is clearly indicated. He never returned to Alexandria, where his old colleague Heraclas, the 'blessed pope' as Dionysius called him, seems not to have been sympathetic. He wrote to Fabian, the new bishop of Rome; for the war of Epistles was always going on. It is unfortunate that the letters of Origen are lost; but it would seem that he was defending his views against criticism. Rome was not sympathetic with the Logos theology.

About this time he was engaged in an enormous labour, the determination of the true text of the Old Testament; and many years were spent on the making of the *Hexapla*, a six-column codex. The first column contained the text in Hebrew; the second contained the Hebrew text transliterated into Greek letters; the remaining four were devoted to the Greek translations of Aquila, Symmachus, the Septuagint and Theodotion. In appearance it must have resembled the Vatican manuscript of the Bible, Codex B, which has three columns to the page; and it is interesting to know that magnificent and expensive books of this type were being produced in Christian workshops at this time; the original volumes from which Vaticanus (B) was copied may quite possibly have been in existence at this time.

A similar book was made in Alexandria at this time by the 'blessed Ammonius'. It was a harmony of the four Gospels made in a more modern way than that of Tatian. There were four columns to the page; the Gospel of Matthew was placed in the first column, divided into numbered sections or paragraphs; opposite each section of Matthew he placed the corresponding section from the other Gospels, each in its appropriate column. This book must have resembled the Sinaitic manuscript (Aleph), which is written in four columns and has a set of section-numbers based on those of Ammonius.

These scientific studies indicate the thorough methods of the Alexandrian school. The *Hexapla* also had a critical apparatus, which consisted of a number of asterisks, obeli etc., which drew attention to agreements and disagreements. In the long run, the influence on the textual tradition was not good, for the importance of these marks was forgotten, and subsequent copyists based their work on a confusion of the evidence. It is doubtful, in consequence, whether we possess a pure copy of the Septuagint. The best text is thought to be that contained in Codex B, which may be closely related to the *Hexapla* text. The *Hexapla* itself was seen by Eusebius and Jerome, but does not survive any longer. It was presumably a parchment book.

Origen was aware that there was a New Testament textual problem, though it was not so complicated or serious as the problem of the Old Testament. The earlier work of Origen is based on the so-called Neutral text which is represented by Aleph and B; but shortly before he left Alexandria he began to use the so-called Caesarean text, represented by the Chester Beatty papyrus and the manuscript Theta (Θ). He used this increasingly in later life during his residence at Caesarea; and that is why it has been called Caesarean.

29. ROMAN REMAINS IN BRITAIN

30. (i) PALMYRA

30. (ii) THE ARCH OF CONSTANTINE

During this period he enrolled among his pupils two brothers of noble birth who came to him from Pontus; their names were Theodore and Athenodore. The former took the name of Gregory, and was known in after generations as Thaumaturgus, the wonder-worker. He became the apostle of Armenia, which soon became a Christian state, and at a later time boasted a distinguished theological school which inclined to the theology of Nestorius. When Gregory left Caesarea, he delivered a valedictory, or *Farewell Address*, which has been preserved and gives an attractive picture of Origen as a teacher. The power of Origen over his pupils was due even more to his personality than to his intellectual genius. His literary style has little art or beauty about it, but he had the gift of awakening interest and inspiring love and devotion. He was selfless and sincere, and wore his halo of learning, asceticism and sanctity with modesty and restraint. His deeply emotional nature was kept under control by prayer and intellectual discipline. He was completely absorbed in his vocation, and always at the service of others. His pupils were led to express themselves freely in discussion, but soon found their ideas analysed by a master of the Socratic dialectic. Then he would lead them on with irresistible charm to new light and new truth, through the pathways of divine philosophy.

PHILIP THE ARABIAN, A.D. 244

Maximin, who was something of a dictator, was overthrown as early as 238 by the Gordianus family of Africa, with the co-operation of the senate, which now makes its last bid for power. The Persians were driven out of Mesopotamia, but Gordian III was murdered in 244, and the Syrian legions put in as emperor a competent soldier named Philip the Arabian. Philip was the last emperor to represent the east and to carry on the Syrian policy. He was believed by many to be a Christian, and there is a story of his appearing at the Easter rites and being repelled by the bishop until he had joined the ranks of the penitents, on account of certain sins; in the fourth century Antioch claimed to be the scene of this event. The story is not accepted by modern historians, but it serves to mark the fact that Christians were in favour again.

Origen was now sixty years old, and was persuaded to allow his sermons to be taken down by stenographers. Many of these reports are included among his *Homilies*. He was working hard on his commentaries, which included the twenty-five 'tomes' on Matthew, some of which still survive. In spite of his fantastic allegorism, Origen was a great biblical scholar, often displaying keen critical insight. He fully accepted the literal, moral and spiritual implications of the text, and it was his constant labours on the scriptures that kept him within the current of legitimate Christian thinking. It was in this period that Ambrose came upon the *True Word*, in which Celsus, the philosopher of the Antonine period, had so strongly attacked the Christians of his day. He insisted that Origen should compose a rejoinder; and the result was his long laborious learned book *Against Celsus*, which is now such a valuable source-book for the story of second-century Christianity.

In 248 the city of Rome celebrated its one thousandth anniversary, which was a sign that the old Roman and Latin spirit was asserting itself, though its actual power and importance was diminishing. It had ceased, or was ceasing, to govern the empire. The government was administered from the army headquarters, and that would usually be on the boundaries rather than in the centre. Nor was the city of Rome the political centre. The strength of the empire was definitely in the east, a feature which was reflected in the ecclesiastical situation. In the east, too, was its greatest military danger, the strong and aggressive Persian empire; but hordes of 'barbarians' were constantly pressing down from the north, the Franks in Gaul, the Alamanni in northern Italy, and the Goths in the Balkans.

THE PERSECUTION OF DECIUS, A.D. 249–51

In 249 Philip the Arabian was assassinated in Moesia while fighting against the Goths, and Decius became Emperor. In view of the dangerous situation, he endeavoured to bring back the empire to the old religious and patriotic traditions which had been the source of Rome's greatness, as he believed, during its thousand years of history. He determined to make everyone conform to the state religion. All the inhabitants of the empire had been given the Roman citizenship by Caracalla, and they were now called upon to appear personally and sacrifice to the gods, and obtain a *libellus* or certificate that they had done so. He was advised and assisted in this programme of compulsory return to religion by his 'censor', Valerian, who had been engaged in purging the membership of the senate. Persecution of Christians had already broken out in Egypt under the prefect Sabinus, accounts of which are given by Eusebius from the interesting letters of the bishop, Dionysius. Fabian of Rome, Babylas of Antioch and Alexander of Jerusalem suffered martyrdom; Cyprian of Carthage and Dionysius of Alexandria were persuaded to retire into the country. Origen was imprisoned and subjected to torture.

Dionysius, a pupil of Origen, had become bishop in 247. He was a distinguished theologian and wrote on many subjects. Some of his Epistles are extant, including a correspondence with Dionysius, bishop of Rome, in which he defended his views against the criticism of his namesake. The Alexandrian Dionysius, who had ventured to attack the Sabellian theology which was current in Libya, was a little tinctured with Origenism, and his conception of the Logos was far from satisfactory; the Roman Dionysius was the exponent of a fortified and reasonably orthodox Sabellianism, a kind of theology which the easterns did not, as yet, either understand or like. They were more in line with Hippolytus, it would seem, than with the legitimate Roman succession.

Egypt was troubled with teachers who took the apocalyptic expectations rather literally, and expressed them in rather wild forms. There was a bishop named Nepos, who had written a book *Against the Allegorizers*; and it was in connexion with this dispute that Dionysius wrote his critical analysis of the grammar and style of the Gospel and Revelation of John, assigning them to two different authors, a conclusion which he supported by saying that there were two tombs of John which were shown to visitors at Ephesus. The Gospel, he thought, was written by the apostle, and the Revelation, which he treated with great respect, by some other man of the same name. He did not know the work of Papias apparently, but he may have read the work of Gaius.

The empire was now entering a phase of great weakness, not to say disaster. The grave emotional tension expressed itself in the form of savage persecution on the pagan side, and savage apocalyptic on the Christian side. The Christian poet, Commodian, who seems to have written his Latin verses at this time, promised the world that it would suffer the ravages of two 'anti-christs', one of them coming from the north across the Danube, the other from the east across the Euphrates. The political animus, which is often not far away in apocalyptic writing, is painfully apparent here. The wiser bishops, who were scholars and men of the world, tried to keep their more fanatical followers in check. At the moment, however, the Persians had been driven back and Mesopotamia reoccupied; but the Goths were crossing the Danube again in force, and in 251 the Emperor Decius was killed in battle in Moesia, after a short reign of three years. His successor, Gallus, was forced to make a bargain with the barbarians and allowed them to settle south of the Danube; an important date in European history.

Origen was released from his imprisonment, but did not live much longer; he died in 253. Cyprian and Dionysius returned to their dioceses. There was a short cessation of religious conflict.

THE CONFLICT WITH THE CONFESSORS

Great numbers of Christians had failed to stand firm in the persecutions. They had sacrificed to the gods or purchased immunity from a corrupt (or Christian?) official. It was no longer possible to refuse restoration to this great multitude. On the other hand the surviving confessors, who had endured imprisonment, were exalted to great spiritual heights and assumed the authority to restore to communion those who had lapsed. A curious bond was thus formed between two very different classes. Cyprian had a situation of this kind to cope with in Africa; but he felt that he could not grant indiscriminate restoration to all who had lapsed, nor could he allow the confessors to decide the matter. His own position was weak, since he had retired from the persecution, and the extreme party regarded him as an apostate himself. A number of older presbyters, who had objected to his election in the first place, made common cause with the confessors and set up a rival bishop; their leader was a presbyter named Novatus. Cyprian endeavoured to restore some sort of order by calling regional councils of bishops. But there was a weakness in that too; the extremists thought that any bishop who had failed to come up to the highest standards of the martyr's code had ceased to be a bishop.

There had been more than a year in Rome with no bishop at all, but Cornelius was elected in 251. He did not satisfy everybody and, needless to say, there was a rival bishop. He was the theologian Novatian, the leader of a party of confessors who refused to assent to the restoration of any who had lapsed or shown weakness in persecution. They were known as the *cathari* or puritans. Strange to say, they made common cause with the dissident party of Novatus in Africa, though their church policy was by no means the same. It would seem that Novatian found similar groups who would communicate with him in most parts of the world; a new schism came into existence which was highly orthodox, highly spiritual and highly moral; it had no room in it for forgiveness and restoration.

Cornelius of Rome wrote an interesting letter to Fabius of Antioch, in which he gives a short biography of Novatian, and remarks that he had in his own organization in Rome, 46 presbyters, 7 deacons, 7 sub-deacons, 52 exorcists, lectors and door-keepers, and over 1500 widows and orphans to support. This count supports the Roman tradition that his predecessor, Fabian, had divided the city into seven regions for purposes of administration, an arrangement which persisted into the middle ages; it is likely that each region was administered from one of the old city churches. It was a considerable organization, and we do not wonder that the Emperor Decius said that he would rather see a rival emperor in Rome than another Christian bishop. All the corre-spondence which passed between Rome and Africa was in Latin; and on the Roman side it was sometimes in very poor Latin. Cyprian and Novatian wrote their theological books in Latin, and in very good Latin. Novatian was a good theologian, rather in the tradition of Hip-polytus; but his grim denial of forgiveness to penitent Christians went far beyond the legalistic position of Hippolytus.

VALERIAN AND GALLIENUS, A.D. 253

Gallus revived the persecution after a while, and Cornelius was sent into exile, where he died; his successor Lucius suffered a similar fate. But Gallus soon perished, and was succeeded in 253 by Valerian (the censor of Decius) and his son Gallienus. In 254 Stephen became bishop of Rome. His controversy with Cyprian over the rebaptism of heretics disturbed the never too peaceful relations between the two churches, and raised the question of the powers of the bishops in their churches and the position of the Roman church in relation to the other churches. Cyprian's letters and treatises are very important theological documents. His views on the rebaptism of heretics, though they had been widely held in the church, were eventually abandoned and heretical baptism was accepted as valid. His views on the equality of bishops were not incompatible with the recognition of some precedence or pre-eminence for the Roman see as an apostolic foundation; but it is not possible to go into these questions here.

In 255 the Goths invaded Illyricum and Macedonia, the Scythians were in Asia Minor, and the Alamanni in Italy. Shapur (or Sapor as the Romans called him), the Persian monarch, had taken Armenia and was threatening Antioch. Matters were worse than ever, and Valerian resorted once again to the persecution of Christians, but in a quite new form. He had grasped the importance for the church, of the episcopal order, and in 257 he issued a decree which required all the Christian clergy to sacrifice to the gods. He also forbade Christian assemblies. Other decrees followed. Dionysius of Alexandria went into retirement again, but Cyprian stood his trial, suffering martyrdom on 14 September 258, as Xystus II had done in Rome on 6 August, and his deacon Laurence a few days later. Laurence was buried near the cemetery of Hippolytus, and the church of San Lorenzo marks the place. He soon eclipsed Hippolytus and all the other Roman martyrs and became the most famous of them all. This year, according to the *Liberian Catalogue*, marked the 'deposition' of the bodies of St Peter and St Paul 'at the catacombs' and 'on the Ostian Way' respectively.[1] The meaning of the entry is not known, but the word 'deposition' in this document is used for the burial of a bishop. The day of this 'deposition', 29 June, has been chosen as their annual festival in the west. St Laurence is commemorated on 10 August, and these two days became the most important fixed points in the Roman calendar between Pentecost and Advent. The shape of Latin Christianity was beginning to appear.

Gallienus, meanwhile, had been winning victories over the Alamanni who had invaded Italy; but his father Valerian, who had checked the Goths in the Balkans, was defeated by the Persian king Shapur in 260 and taken prisoner. This calamity caused great dismay, though Gallienus does not seem to have been seriously perturbed; it was worse than the defeat and death of Decius in 251. It may even have suggested that the persecutors of Christians came to no good end, an idea which had

---

[1] The strange word *catacumbae* is said to have been given first to what is now the catacomb of St Sebastian, which is built over a declivity or 'hollow'; *ad catacumbas* may mean 'at the hollows'. The tradition is that the body of the apostle reposed there for a time. The date 29 June was that of the foundation of the city of Rome by Romulus and Remus; see note to vol. II, chap. 19.

been mooted by Tertullian and would be developed by Lactantius. Shapur's armies advanced into Syria, Cilicia and Cappadocia; but the generals of Valerian were not inactive, and Shapur had left in his rear the strong city of Palmyra. Odenatus, the king of Palmyra, attacked him vigorously and he was forced to retire into Mesopotamia in the following year. Odenatus now saw his way to set up what was virtually an independent Syrian empire, and Gallienus was forced to recognize him. It suited him to do so.

THE REIGN OF GALLIENUS, A.D. 260–70

In 260 Gallienus issued an edict of toleration for the Christians and restored to them the use of their churches, a very important act of imperial recognition. What more could they require? They were undisturbed by persecution for over forty years.

In 262 an incursion of Goths from southern Russia came down by sea through the Bosphorus, ravaged Asia Minor, and burned the great temple of Artemis in Ephesus. Gallienus failed to check this raid, which encouraged the Goths to repeat it. He was obliged to recognize Odenatus as an independent sovereign and the virtual ruler of the eastern empire. Meanwhile he cultivated the intellectual life, after the manner of his Syrian predecessors, and patronized the distinguished philosopher Plotinus, who was now lecturing at Rome. One of his pupils was Porphyry, who had once met Origen at Tyre, and was becoming the leading intellectual opponent of the Christians; for the cessation of persecution was succeeded by intellectual warfare. Porphyry wrote his books against Christianity towards the end of the century, and was answered by Methodius and Eusebius. Plotinus himself never mentions Christianity. These must surely be the last Hellenic schools of any kind in Rome, where Latin was now the dominant language.

A Christian intellectual of very strange proportions now appears in the east; Paul of Samosata, bishop of Antioch, an ambitious and powerful prelate. He was the author of a brilliant theology which managed to blend the Logos theology of Origen in a weakened form with some kind of adoptionism; the Logos dwelt in Jesus 'as a quality', Paul said. Paul was condemned by two councils during the two-hundred-and-sixties, but without effect. The first of these, perhaps about 263, was dominated by the old Origenists; Firmilian of Cappadocia was there;

and so were Gregory and Athenodore; Dionysius of Alexandria excused himself on the grounds of age. They condemned Paul, but there was no more that they could do. He remained in possession of the church property and continued to administer the diocese. Time passed.

The empire was at its lowest ebb. Gallienus had to deal with a rival emperor in Gaul who had some victories over the Franks to his credit. In 267 the Goths made further spectacular raids by sea and by land. They ravaged Illyricum and Thessalonia, and looted Athens. The old civilized countries took long to recover from these raids, and perhaps it may be said that they never did. The eastern empire was virtually independent. Odenatus was assassinated in the same year, but he was succeeded by his widow Zenobia, a Syrian queen of great charm, marked executive ability and no little learning. Longinus, the disciple of Ammonius Saccas, was her philosopher. Paul, the heretical bishop of Antioch, was her minister of finance. This was the last phase of the Syrian Hellenism, which had first appeared under the patronage of Julia Domna; but the 'Syrian culture', having absorbed a measure of Hellenism, was still vigorous and had a further part to play in later history.

A second council of bishops was held, about 268, which deposed Paul from his office, and appointed Domnus, who was the son of his predecessor, to be bishop in his place; but no progress was made in ejecting Zenobia's favourite from the church property and the episcopal dignity. He continued in his grand state, and choirs of ladies sang his praises as he entered his church; or so his enemies asserted. It is rather curious that the *Didascalia*, a church order which emanated from Antioch about this time, is our first evidence, apart from the Montanist and other sects, for a female order of ministers in the church, though Pliny mentioned something of the sort; they were known as deaconesses. It is not incredible that Paul may have been saluted with honorific chants, when he came into church, since existing liturgies make a similar provision. But neither the personality nor the theology of Paul can be clearly discerned, since they are delineated by his enemies. It would appear that he could play the politician, the business-man, the stump-orator and the *bon viveur* as successfully as he could play the philosopher or theologian.

It may be suggested that there were a number of non-theological factors in this notorious case. Paul's appointment, in the first place, may have been due to a party in the church with native Syrian or Palmyrene sympathies, or even to political pressure. Quite a different party, with Roman or anti-Palmyrene sympathies may from the first have favoured a successor from the old episcopal family. Paul was not a native Antiochene.

ACCESSION OF AURELIAN, A.D. 270

And now the resolute Aurelian became emperor. He made a bargain with the Goths, abandoning the provinces north of the Danube, which were now hard to defend. He built a defensive wall round the city of Rome, which stands to this day as a monument of his enterprise and a proof of the alarm which was felt at the time. He succeeded in conquering the Alamanni, however, who had once again invaded Italy. One of his generals recovered Egypt, which had been taken by Zenobia; and in 272 he marched into Syria and defeated the warlike queen in a battle near Antioch. In 273 he defeated her again near Emesa, and destroyed Palmyra itself. Rival emperors in Spain and Gaul were suppressed by his generals. He had restored the empire, and celebrated a triumph at Rome in 274.

Now when he was in Antioch in 272, the bishops submitted to his consideration the case of Paul and Domnus. They wanted Paul evicted and Domnus installed. The emperor made a decision of great importance. The property was to be awarded to whichever party the bishop of Rome agreed with. The bishops were exultant; 'Let him communicate with Artemas', they said; an interesting link with the past, for Artemas must be the same adoptionist leader who was mentioned by Hippolytus forty years before in the *Little Labyrinth*, if that is his work. A sixth generation had now passed. It is forty years since the migration of Origen to Caesarea, and nearly forty since the death of Hippolytus.

Paul was deposed. Longinus was executed. Zenobia was taken to Rome, to appear in the triumph of Aurelian, after which she was permitted to reside comfortably in Italy. The period of Syrian ascendancy in government, theology and philosophy had passed its peak, though its influence was by no means at an end. On the other hand Persian ideas were making themselves felt.

It was between 272 and 277 that Mani was crucified. He was born about 215 in the village of Mardiu, south of the old Babylon. His family belonged to the sect of Mugthasila, or 'baptizers'. His religious background would appear to owe much to the Transjordanian syncretism. He created a new religion, a semi-christian gnosis which was intended to supplement and supersede all existing religions. It was based on the old Iranian ideas and inculcated an extravagant antipathy to everything of a material character, far exceeding the encratite or gnostic asceticisms. Marriage and property were both forbidden to the perfect, and vegetarianism was hardly less sinful than the eating of flesh or the drinking of wine. He proclaimed his new religion in the year of the coronation of King Shapur in 242, and preached it for thirty years. He is said to have gone as far afield as India and China. He aroused the hostility of the Magian priests in his own country and was crucified under a new king, Vahram I, the grandson of his patron Shapur.[1] His followers were known as Manichaeans and carried on his teachings far into the middle ages. The word 'Manichaean' has come to be used in a general way for all who regard this life as inherently evil.

PAMPHILUS AND EUSEBIUS

Eusebius was a child when the deposition of Paul took place. Nothing is known about his parentage and childhood, but at some point in the last quarter of the century, he attached himself to Pamphilus, who was the guardian of Origen's library at Caesarea. Pamphilus himself was a wealthy man of south Syrian origin. He devoted all his property to the poor and lived a life of self-denial. After studying at Alexandria he settled at Caesarea, where he was ordained presbyter and organized an extensive library into which the library of Origen was incorporated. It is not certain that he had been a pupil of Origen himself; but he was devoted to his memory and spent his days in arranging his manuscripts, making new copies of them and studying them intensively. Thus the spell of Origen's personality lingered on.

Eusebius was the devoted pupil of Pamphilus, and in consequence a devotee of Origen. He studied his books and papers, and also the second-century literature which told the stories of martyrdom and church-controversy in which his soul delighted. He visited Aelia, too, and saw the library of Alexander, with its archives and chronicles,

---

[1] Compare the story of Aggai at Edessa in chapter 13.

which took him back to the days of Narcissus, who was still being talked about. He was shown the chair of James the Just and the miraculous oil of Narcissus. Fortunately he possessed great industry and a remarkable respect for ancient documents. He became the greatest chronicler of them all. He read very widely in the ancient literature which was available to him. He had access to the old Jewish Hellenistic literature, which preceded the Christian era. But for him, we would know little about all this.

The day was evil for the empire, but there was no persecution now for the church. It was rich and prosperous, with imposing buildings, dignified services and worldly prelates. Eusebius describes this state of affairs in his stilted conventional manner, and yet imparts to his denunciation a prophetic sincerity. He never acquired a graceful or readable style; he was apt to be impressed by the drama of pomp and circumstance; and yet he was always sincere. He was sincere, above all, in his reverence for the martyrs.

CHRONOLOGICAL TABLE
THE SUCCESSORS OF DIOCLETIAN

A.D.

284 Diocletian becomes Emperor.

302–3 Persecution of Diocletian, egged on by his 'Caesar' Galerius.

305 Resignation of Diocletian and his western colleague Maximian.
Galerius succeeds Diocletian at Nicomedia; *Constantius* recognized as Augustus (co-emperor) at York.
Maximin Daia as Caesar in the east; *Maxentius*, son of Maximian, as Caesar in the west.
Eusebius begins his History.

306 Death of Constantius; *Constantine* recognized as Augustus in York.
Maxentius as Augustus in Rome: *Maximin Daia* as Augustus in Antioch.
Galerius carries on the persecution in the east.

307 Imprisonment of Pamphilus, the tutor of Eusebius.

308 Galerius makes *Licinius* Augustus at Sirmium in the Balkans.

309–10 Martyrdoms of Pamphilus and Lucian.

311 Galerius issues edict of toleration on his death-bed.
Maximin Daia succeeds him as emperor in Nicomedia.
Eusebius completes first draft of his History.
Resumption of severe persecution by Maximin and Maxentius.
Alliance between Constantine and Licinius.

A.D.

312 Battle of the Milvian Bridge; *Constantine defeats Maxentius* and becomes Augustus in Rome; conference with Licinius at Milan; edict of
toleration in west (so-called Edict of Milan).

313 *Licinius defeats Maximin* in east; the Edict of Nicomedia, in the names
of both emperors, proclaims toleration of all religions and restoration
of Christian churches.

  Eusebius, Bishop of Caesarea.

  There are now two emperors; Licinius in Nicomedia is the senior:
  Constantine in Rome is the junior.

  Eusebius completes a revision of his History.

320–1 Licinius begins to persecute.

324 Battle of Chrysopolis; Constantine defeats Licinius; declares himself
a Christian: gives privileges to the church; begins work on the new
city of 'Constantinople'.

  Eusebius completes final draft of his History.

325 Council of Nicaea.

330 Dedication of Constantinople.

335 Division of the empire among the family of Constantine.

337 Death of Constantine, 22 May.

339 Death of Eusebius.

Note. The dates assigned to the stages in the composition of the *Ecclesiastical History* of Eusebius are those advocated in Lawlor and Oulton's edition.

DIOCLETIAN, A.D. 284

Aurelian celebrated his triumph in 274, but his glory was short-lived.
He is said to have issued a decree against the Christians, but he was
murdered in Thrace in the following year as he was marching eastward
to resist a new invasion by the Persian king, who had actually reached
the Bosphorus; few emperors in this wretched period of history died
in peace. A chaotic ten years followed his death. A series of generals
followed one another as emperors in rapid succession; they clashed
with one another, or were assassinated after a brief period of power.
They were not unsuccessful, however, in their efforts. Carus, who
was the last of them, drove back the Persians and recovered Armenia
and Mesopotamia. He was succeeded by Diocletian, an old officer of
Aurelian, who assumed the purple in 284. These emperors were the
creation of the Danubian legions, and Diocletian and his successors
were natives of the Balkans.

It fell to the lot of Diocletian to reorganize the whole empire on new lines. Its duality was frankly recognized, and the city of Rome was quietly ignored; emperors were needed on the frontiers where the work of defence was carried on. Diocletian knew that the strength of the empire was in the east, and chose Nicomedia in Pontus for his capital

Map 4. The empire under Diocletian, showing centres of imperial administration (in capital letters) and other cities of importance in Christian history. (Constantinople was built on the site of Byzantium.)

city; but he appointed a second emperor, subsidiary to himself, whose capital city would be at Milan in northern Italy. Each would have the venerable title of Augustus, and be given an assistant with the lesser title of Caesar, who was allotted his own territory to administer and defend. After twenty years, the Augusti were to resign, and the Caesars would automatically move up into their places, thus ending the old dynastic tradition and the ambitions of popular generals. Each was to be surrounded by religious pomp and circumstance like the Persian monarch, who was an earthly replica of the sun-god and was adorned with the holy diadem or halo. He was to be approached with reverence and awe. This unhellenic and unroman glorification did at least protect their lives.

The Christians were tolerated; indeed, it is said that the wife of Diocletian was a Christian; but not long before his retirement became due he was prevailed upon by his Caesar, Galerius, to launch an attack upon the church, which began in 302. It came as a judgement on the church for its laxity, Eusebius thought. It was a long drawn out, vindictive and competently-organized affair, wherever the local Augustus or Caesar was in favour of it. The churches were looted and sometimes destroyed; the sacred books were burned, a loss which the historian still regrets; and the worship of the gods was enforced with savage penalties. Eusebius catalogued the martyrs of Palestine and told their stories. It is the climax to which his *Church History* moves.

CONSTANTINE THE GREAT, A.D. 305

When Diocletian and his western colleague Maximian retired from their supreme positions in 305, the plans for an automatic succession very soon broke down, and a complicated story of rivalry, intrigue and inter-imperial war was the sequel. Galerius, who succeeded Diocletian in the east was a persecutor; Constantius, who succeeded Maximian in the west, was not. The capital city of Constantius was at York in Britain. He was a veteran officer of the Danubian armies, and his wife Helena was a Christian. The edicts of persecution were not put into effect in his territories. It is true that the tradition preserved by St Bede places the martyrdom of St Alban, the first known martyr of Britain, in this persecution; but it has been suggested that it really took place fifty years earlier under Decius. There were at least three dioceses in Britain at this time, including York and London, and possibly Lincoln; for bishops from these dioceses attended the Council of Arles in 314.

Constantius died in 306 and Maxentius, his Caesar, the son of old Maximian, should have succeeded him as Augustus; but the legions in York would have none of that; they proclaimed his son Constantine as Augustus, presumably in the *praetorium*, the remains of which are to be seen underneath York Minster. Galerius was obliged to recognize both men as Augusti, one in Britain and one in Italy. To balance matters, he elevated his own Caesar, Maximin Daia, whose capital was in Antioch, to the rank of Augustus, and appointed another general named Licinius, who was in command of the Balkans, to the same rank. He died in 311. In the intense rivalry which followed, Constantine came to an understanding with Licinius, but Maximin Daia, now at Nicomedia, was, of course, the senior man, the real Roman emperor.

We have now come to the end of the second period of forty years since 230, completing the seventh generation since the Crucifixion.

In 312, the year after the death of Galerius, Constantine marched on Rome with his legions, to do battle with his rival Augustus, Maxentius, who was a persecutor, and also his brother-in-law. As he crossed the Alps, he saw in the sky a strange sign compounded of a circle and a cross; and in a dream by night he saw it again, and heard a voice which said

TOYTω NIKA or EN TOYTω NIKA

'Conquer by this'.

It would do for Christ and his cross, or for Mithras and the unconquerable sun. He adopted the sign, which came to be called the 'labarum', for the standard of his legions, and won the battle of the Milvian Bridge on October 27, Maxentius being drowned in the river. He met Licinius at Milan, where they settled on a policy of toleration for all religions, and doubtless issued some sort of edict to that effect; but Licinius still had to defeat Maximin Daia before the pair were in control of the empire. He did this in 313, and then issued a decree from Nicomedia, in the name of both emperors, granting toleration to all religions, restoring their property to the Christians, and authorizing grants for the rebuilding of churches. Neither of them came out entirely on the Christian side.

Everywhere church life began again. It is a tangled story, and the stages in the rise to power of the Christian church cannot be clearly made out. Among the Christian writers of the time whose books shed light on the history were Lactantius and Eusebius. Lactantius wrote in Latin; he had been professor of literature in his pagan days, and had received a professional literary training; his grim book *Concerning the Deaths of the Persecutors* attempts to establish the thesis that persecutors come to a bad end. Eusebius had already made considerable progress with his *Ecclesiastical History*; for he hails with joy and thanksgiving the policy of toleration which was promised in the east by Licinius; but once he had defeated his persecuting opponent Maximin Daia, Licinius relapsed into a policy of persecution, and it was not until he was defeated by Constantine at Chrysopolis in 323–4 that real toleration came. So Eusebius had to re-edit his *History*, and compose an additional volume.

Constantine was now the master of the whole empire, as Aurelian and Diocletian had been in their prime. He was able to declare himself a Christian, though indeed he was not baptized, to extend his favour to the church, to declare Sunday, 'the venerable day of the sun', to be a holiday, and to confer on Christian bishops an official status. In 325 he presided over the famous council of three hundred and eighteen bishops (a symbolic, not an actual number: see Genesis xiv. 14) which was held at Nicaea, not far from Nicomedia; with Hosius, the bishop of Cordova in Spain, as his principal adviser, and Eustathius, bishop of Antioch, as the principal spokesman for the east. In 326 he visited Rome for the last time, and it was on this occasion that he put to death his wife Fausta and his son Crispus, the full truth about which is quite unknown. He gave her residence which was known as the Lateran Palace to the bishop of Rome, Sylvester; it was dedicated to St John, and became the cathedral and parish church of the city, a dignity which it still holds. It is not far from the church of St Clement.

But he was making new plans altogether, which would provide a Christian Rome as the capital city of a Christian empire. He founded it in 330 not far from Diocletian's capital of Nicomedia, on the site of Byzantium, the military strength of which he had learned from hard experience in his war against Licinius. It has come to be known by his own name as the city of Constantine, or 'Constantinople'; but the orientals still call it Rome. Its official name today is Istanbul. In 335 he divided the empire between his three sons and two nephews, thus reinstating the dynastic principle, and the partition of the imperial power. At Easter in 337 he dedicated the church of the Holy Apostles at Constantinople; he was baptized on his death-bed a few days later, and passed away on the Feast of Pentecost, being 22 May.

31. THE CODEX SINAITICUS

32. THE GOOD SHEPHERD

EUSEBIUS OF CAESAREA

Eusebius died two years later. He is remembered as the state bishop and fervent admirer of Constantine, whose biography he wrote in much too flattering terms. His admiration was perfectly genuine, however, for, with all his defects of character, Constantine had greatness and sincerity and a simple belief in Christianity as a source of power and a possible bond of union for the empire; indeed, the only possible bond of union. Eusebius hailed him as the heaven-sent deliverer of the church from the long terror of persecution begun by Galerius and Diocletian and carried on by Maximin Daia and Licinius. The Council of Nicaea was beyond all belief. It was the first attempt ever made at a representative world-conference; and it was Christian. Among the great scholars, and worldly prelates, and political adventurers, were grand old stalwarts, ascetics and martyrs, wearing their scars and deformities, and wondering whether this was the kingdom of heaven on earth.

The true Eusebius, however, was not the court bishop. The true Eusebius was the young student who had worked with Pamphilus in the library of Origen. Pamphilus was thrown into prison in 307, and Eusebius attended him there. They collaborated on the first five volumes of the *Apology for Origen*, which was an answer to the many attacks which had been made on his character and theology. They made use of his letters for this purpose and published a selection of a hundred of them. It is very unfortunate that neither the *Apology* nor the letters have come down to us. Pamphilus was kept in prison for two years, and then suffered as a martyr. Eusebius, who proudly called himself 'the son of Pamphilus', had to produce the sixth volume of the *Apology* alone.

He seems to have begun work on the *Ecclesiastical History* as early as 305; and in the preliminary stages, he could avail himself of the help and advice of Pamphilus, whose martyrdom occurred in 309. The first eight volumes seem to have been completed in 311, the year when Galerius died. In 313 he became bishop of Caesarea. A ninth book was added, the text was revised, and the history completed in 314; a tenth book was added later, and it appeared in its final form in 324.

It does not stand alone, for his other works combine with it to create a complete historical survey, such as the oriental mind loves. The parallel work called the *Chronicle* arranged the historical events in order, year by year; and this preliminary labour enabled him to write his

History in its setting of imperial reigns and episcopal successions. His *Prophetic Selections* (or 'Eclogues') were a new version of the old Book of Testimonies, showing how Hebrew prophecy foretold and illuminated the gospel revelation. This kind of work was still very popular; Lactantius devoted part of his *Divine Institutions* to it. The *Preparation of the Gospel* of Eusebius, and the *Demonstration of the Gospel* were massive works of learning which give an enormous amount of information about the pre-Christian Hellenistic thought and literature.

This was by no means all. He perfected the work of the 'blessed Ammonius', who had promoted the synoptic study of the Gospels by arranging them side by side in a four-column codex, using the order of Matthew as the base, and numbering the sections to correspond. Eusebius worked out an ingenious system of figures which could be entered in the margin of an ordinary copy of the four Gospels and enable the reader to refer rapidly to the corresponding section in any other Gospel. They are found in the margin of Aleph (Codex Sinaiticus), a manuscript which was made not long after the death of Eusebius, or even perhaps before his death. The 'Ammonian sections' and the 'Eusebian canons' were universally adopted and are to be found in Bibles of all kinds right down to recent times.

THE NEW TESTAMENT CANON

It is still fairly widely believed that the Council of Nicaea made a decision on the question of the New Testament canon. Actually no General Council has ever considered the matter. The oecumenical church came to a unanimous agreement on the subject slowly and by general consent. The canon of the New Testament was the last of the great catholic institutions to unify and mature. Eusebius has some valuable things to say about it.

His own attitude was critical and conservative. He divided the possible literature into four classes. First came the ancient books, of whose apostolic and canonical quality there has never been any doubt. These were

The Four Gospels.	The Pauline Epistles, including Hebrews.
The Acts.	I Peter and I John.

He admits that many would add the Revelation to this basic New Testament; the Roman church would omit Hebrews.

The second class consisted of books which were widely used and familiar to the majority, but nevertheless were disputed in some quarters; such were James, Jude, II Peter, and II and III John, the five lesser catholic Epistles. The third class consists of the pseudonymous writings: the *Acts of Paul*, the *Shepherd* of Hermas, the *Revelation of Peter*, the *Epistle of Barnabas*, the *Teachings of the Apostles*, and the Revelation of John, unless indeed this is placed in the first class; and some would include the Hebrew Gospel in the third class. The fourth class consists of the heretical apocrypha, such Gospels as Peter and Thomas and Matthias, and such Acts as Andrew and John, which no reputable Christian writer had even mentioned. He did not regard his third class, therefore, as heretical; what he thought was that they were not written by the apostolic persons whose names they bore. For Hermas was regarded as an apostolic name by Origen, who identifies him with the Hermas mentioned by St Paul in Romans.

This classification of the literature shows a very strong critical and historical sense. It also shows that the fully canonical New Testament had not quite arrived. The basic New Testament, with or without Revelation (or Hebrews) was canonically secure; the books of the second class were widely read, but their reception was not unanimous; the books of the third class were also widely read, but not open to inclusion since they were not apostolic; the books of the fourth class were not open to consideration at all. It appears that his classification of Revelation and Hebrews is not perfectly logical; nevertheless it reflects his view of the situation with great accuracy.

Further progress was being made in Alexandria, as we learn from a list put out a little later by the great bishop Athanasius. It consists of

The Four Gospels.	The Pauline Epistles, including
The Acts.	Hebrews.
The seven Catholic Epistles.	The Revelation.

This is identical with our present New Testament; but Athanasius adds to it a secondary group of books, which were sanctioned by the fathers for reading; they were especially useful for converts who desired to be instructed in the word of piety. They were the Wisdom of Solomon, the Wisdom of Sirach (Ecclesiasticus), Esther, Judith, Tobiah, the so-called *Teaching of the Apostles*, and the *Shepherd*. He agrees with Melito in excluding Esther from the Old Testament.

THE SECOND CHRISTIAN CENTURY

The different churches continued to differ from one another on the question of the literature of the third class. Codex Sinaiticus (Aleph) contains Barnabas and Hermas in addition to the canonical New Testament; Codex Alexandrinus (A) adds I and II Clement, and the Psalms of Solomon. It was long before the Syriac New Testament contained all the catholic Epistles, though James was adopted fairly early. It is interesting that the Sunday Epistles for the Roman Mass are never taken from the Pastorals and only once from Hebrews. They were first appointed in a period when these books were still on a different level.

The agreement of all Christians on the subject of the New Testament canon is a remarkable example of the growth of a catholic institution and the power of a diffused authority to reach agreement. Nevertheless it was thought necessary to provide machinery by which the diffused authority could make itself heard on some points; and it was a momentous departure from precedent when this was done under imperial patronage.

THE COUNCIL OF NICAEA, A.D. 325

The Council of Nicaea was called by the emperor to deal with the Arian controversy, to settle certain other vexatious questions, and to foster the unity of the church and empire.

Between the years 260 and 300 a Christian school of some importance had grown up at Antioch, the principal teachers in which were Dorotheus and Lucian. Lucian had been the head of the Antiochene school under Paul of Samosata, and died as a martyr in 308. He did valuable work on the text of the Old Testament, and probably also of the New. It is even possible that he created, or rather took the first steps in the direction of creating, the 'Antiochian Text' of the New Testament, which is a judicious blend of the older texts, expressed in an improved literary style, or what was intended to be an improved literary style. Such a text was accepted at the end of the century in Antioch and Constantinople. It gradually became the official text of the Greek church, passing of course through further stages of revision. The mass of Greek manuscripts belong to this family, the oldest of this type being Alexandrinus (A) at the British Museum. The great vernacular Bibles of the Reformation, including the English Authorized Version, were made from manuscripts of this type.

The church of Antioch is said to have paid particular attention to literary and historical studies, a point which became apparent as early as the time of Bishop Theophilus. Through all its phases, from Ignatius onward, it was always anti-docetic; it aimed to preserve at all costs the humanity of the Christ; and there were times, apparently, when it may have drifted in the Ebionite or adoptionist direction. In this kind of theology the divine power which is recognized as existing in Christ is rather sharply distinguished from the man Jesus; in the time of Zenobia, Paul had attempted to combine a christology of this sort with a Logos theology; the Logos dwelt in the man Jesus 'as a quality'. Lucian seems to have originated the thought that the disjunction might be placed at a higher stage. The Logos might be less closely identified with the eternal deity; he might be a created being. The Logos theology, from Justin to Dionysius, had always tended to suggest that the Word had not existed absolutely from all eternity.

He was an angel or a spirit, though such words were not used, or at any rate not in serious theological debate; he was an emanation like the Persian primal man; he was the Son of God, and might be worshipped as God; but he was not God; not God identically. It had a certain resemblance to older modes of thought; for nobody had analysed at the beginning of Christian history the exact philosophical implications of such terms as Holy Spirit or Son of God.

The new philosophy of the Logos was taken up by Arius, a presbyter of Alexandria, and provided the principal bone of contention at the Council of Nicaea in 325. Alexander, the bishop of Alexandria, had excommunicated Arius; but his cause had been championed by certain bishops of the Antiochene school, such as Eusebius of Nicomedia. Eusebius the historian, who was now bishop of Caesarea, seems to have been reluctant to join the opposition. He was no philosopher, and occupied a conservative or moderating position. It was the first round in the great theological rivalry between the school of Alexandria and the school of Antioch. Arius argued with great intellectual dexterity in favour of the new theology; Athanasius, the deacon of Alexander, argued against him, explaining his bishop's point of view. Eusebius of Caesarea produced the old baptismal creed of his own church as a traditional formula on which all might agree. It was adopted, but was supplemented with stronger words which he only accepted with great reluctance.

One of these words had been coined by Sabellius in Rome, and appears to have been criticized, and possibly even condemned, at the councils at Antioch which condemned Paul of Samosata. It was the word *homo-ousios* or 'consubstantial', which had seemed at one time to stress unduly the identity of the Father and the Son, but now seemed the very word which was required in order to resist too great a degree of disjunction. It was suggested by Constantine himself, on the advice of Hosius of Cordova, a western and Latin-speaking prelate. It was adopted, and the famous Nicene Creed came into existence.

We believe in one God, the Father Almighty, Maker of all things visible and invisible; and in one Lord Jesus Christ, the Son of God, begotten of the Father, only-begotten, that is to say from the essence (ousia) of the Father; God from God, Light from Light, true God from true God, begotten not made, of-the-same-essence (*homo-ousios*) as the Father; by whom all things were made, both in heaven and in earth; who, for us men and for our salvation, came down, and was incarnate; was made man; suffered and rose again the third day; ascended into heaven; and is coming to judge the living and the dead; and in the Holy Spirit.

And those who say that once he was not, and before his generation he was not, and that he came into being out of nothing, or those who claim that the Son of God is of other substance or essence, or created, or alterable, or mutable; the catholic church anathematizes.

This creed was not, of course, a baptismal or liturgical creed; it was a 'conciliar' creed, which dealt strictly with the points which were being debated by the council. It was amended and enlarged at later Councils, and received its final form at the fourth General Council, which was held at Chalcedon in 451; and the form which it then received has been accepted throughout Christendom as the 'Nicene Creed'. It was not, on the other hand, a theological exposition, but an attempt, with some help from the theologians, to define the faith which had been proclaimed in the churches from apostolic times, and for which seven generations of martyrs had given their lives.

Other questions came up, and among them the old Paschal controversy, which was settled, of course, in accordance with the custom of the majority; Easter was to be the first Sunday after the full moon which came next after the spring equinox. And there it is to this day.

EUSEBIUS AS A HISTORIAN

As a theologian, Eusebius has been accused of an undue sympathy with Arius, whereas he seems to have been an old-fashioned churchman who eyed the precise terminology of the new creed with displeasure. As a historian, he has been accused of undue credulity; but in view of the standards of the age he must be regarded as reasonably critical. He accepted the apocryphal correspondence between Jesus and Abgar of Edessa, and recorded without criticism some of the legends of the Holy Land, though not the discovery of the sacred sites in Jerusalem by Helena, the emperor's mother. He rashly identified the ascetic Jews of a treatise by Philo, *On the Therapeutai*, with the early Christians, and he made one or two errors in identification or chronology, which are not hard to detect, since his work on the whole is so reliable. But he rejected the great mass of apocryphal literature, even when it exalted his own see-city of Caesarea. He expressed some doubt about the lesser catholic Epistles, or admitted that doubt existed. He rejected the Revelation of John, in common with the eastern church generally.

His mind moved along well-defined lines. His detestation of heresy was balanced by his glorification of martyrdom. His admiration for Constantine was excessive but sincere. His style is wretched. But he is faithful. He never invents. There are no imaginary narratives or speeches. He uses sources which he generally identifies, and in so doing he is the forerunner of the modern historian; nobody before him seems to have done it. His methods of quotation are not always as exact as we might wish. Sometimes his extracts seem to have been reproduced in part only or to be imperfect in some way; and in these cases, he may have relied on notes that he made, or trusted in some assistant who had not quite grasped his instructions. Nevertheless, we are able to a very considerable extent to make use, through him, of original documents which no longer exist; and, as we can check the accuracy of his quotations in those instances where the originals do exist, we are able to get a good idea of his standards of fidelity, which must be regarded as high.

It is evident that, without Eusebius, we would not be able to construct a history of early Christianity at all.

THE CHRISTIAN WORLD

He saw everything, of course, from his Palestinian point of view, though he travelled widely in the eastern empire, which was now the centre of the imperial administration and the area of maximum culture in the 'world'. He visited Alexandria. He became bishop of Caesarea in 313. He preached at the dedication of the new church at Tyre in 315, where the tomb of Origen was pointed out in succeeding centuries. He attended Constantine at Nicomedia and Nicaea. He was present at the dedication of the church of the Resurrection at Jerusalem in 335. He knew nothing to speak of about Rome, except what he learned through old documents which were preserved in the libraries at Caesarea and Jerusalem; and these closed with the writings of Hippolytus, of whose Roman character he was ignorant.

Rome had declined in importance so far as the east was concerned. It no longer had very much to do with the government of the empire. The means of communication were less reliable. The barrier of language was hard to penetrate. From the Greek point of view Rome was relapsing into barbarism. Not many delegates came to Nicaea from the west; but Hosius of Cordova was there to advise the emperor, who was a westerner himself and did not know much Greek.

The Sixth Canon of the Council deals with metropolitical rights, and reads as follows,

The old custom in use in Egypt and Libya and the Pentapolis should continue to exist, that is to say the bishop of Alexandria should have jurisdiction over all these places, since there is a similar relation in the case of the bishop of Rome. In the same way in the case of Antioch, and in the other civil provinces, the ancient customs are to be preserved in the churches. And this is perfectly plain, that if any one becomes a bishop without the consent of the metropolitan, the great synod decides that he ought not to be a bishop.

The ancient traditions are to be respected and continued; but Alexandria, Rome and Antioch are now the big three. Ephesus has lost its pre-eminence; perhaps it never recovered from the destruction done to it by the Goths. It is included, no doubt, as a metropolitical centre, among the 'other provinces', but it will never regain its glory. Many changes have taken place in church and state during a century of witness and conflict; but none is more important than the disappearance of the old apostolic high-road through Ephesus to Rome, and the appearance of the new catholic pattern in which Rome, Alexandria and Antioch are the leading patriarchal sees.

Among these apostolic foundations, Rome possessed a primacy of honour, which was formally recognized at the later oecumenical councils, Constantinople rising by slow degrees to a similar pre-eminence in the east.

ROMAN EMPERORS FROM AUGUSTUS TO CONSTANTINE

B.C.		A.D.	
27	Augustus	235	Maximin
A.D.		237	Gordian I, Gordian II
14	Tiberius		Maximus Pupienus
37	Caligula		Balbinus
41	Claudius	238	Gordian III
54	Nero	244	Philip the Arabian
68	Galba, Otho	249	Decius
	Vitellius	251	Hostilian, Gallus
	Vespasian	252	Volusian
79	Titus	253	Aemilian, Valerian
81	Domitian		Gallienus
96	Nerva	268	Claudius II
98	Trajan	270	Aurelian
117	Hadrian	275	Tacitus
138	Antoninus Pius	276	Florian, Probus
161	Marcus Aurelius	282	Carus
180	Commodus	284	Carinus, Numerian
193	Pertinax	284–305	Diocletian
	Didius Julianus	286–305	Maximian (and 307–308)
	Niger	305–306	Constantius
	Septimius Severus	305–311	Galerius
211	Geta	306–307	Severus
	Caracalla	306–312	Maxentius
217	Macrinus	306–337	Constantine
	Diadumenianus	307–324	Licinius
218	Elagabalus	308–313	Maximin Daia
222	Alexander Severus		

SELECT BIBLIOGRAPHY

Supplementary to the Bibliography for Volume I, which should be consulted.

A. GENERAL INTRODUCTION

See Bibliography to Volume I.

B. CHURCH HISTORIES ETC.: ADDITIONAL TITLES

Bethune-Baker, F. J. *An Introduction to the Early History of Christian Doctrine*, 5th edn. (Cambridge, 1933).

Duchesne, L. *Christian Worship*, trans. M. L. McClure (London, 1947).

Hefele, K. J. *History of the Councils*, English trans. (Edinburgh, 1871).

Lietzmann, H. *The Founding of the Church Universal*, trans. B. L. Woolf (London and New York, 1938).

Mason, A. J. *The Historic Martyrs of the Primitive Church* (London, 1905).

Srawley, J. H. *The Early History of the Liturgy*, 2nd edn. (Cambridge, 1947).

C. ENCYCLOPAEDIAS, ETC.

See Bibliography to Volume I.

D. LITERATURE OF THE PERIOD: SOURCES AND INTRODUCTION: ADDITIONAL TITLES

Series and collections

Patrologia Graeca et Latina, J. P. Migne; *Latina* (Paris, 1844 ff.); *Graeca* (1857 ff.).

Griechische christliche Schriftsteller (the Berlin corpus) (Leipzig, 1897 ff.).

Corpus Scriptorum Latinorum (the Vienna corpus) (1866, ff.).

Loeb Classical Library (with translations) (London and New York, various dates).

Texte und Untersuchungen, ed. E. von Gebhardt, A. Harnack and others (Berlin, 1882 ff.).

Texts and Studies, ed. J. A. Robinson, etc. (Cambridge, first series, 1891–1952).

Sources Chrétiennes, ed. H. de Lubac et J. Daniélou (Paris, 1941 ff.).

The Ante-Nicene Christian Library (translations only), ed. A. Robertson and J. Donaldson (Edinburgh, 1867 ff.); American edition, ed. A. C. Coxe, 1896 ff. (reprinted Grand Rapids, Michigan, 1952).

Translations of Early Christian Writers (S.P.C.K. series), ed. W. J. Sparrow-Simpson and W. K. Lowther Clarke (London, 1916 ff.).

The Library of Christian Classics (translations), London, S.C.M., and Philadelphia: especially *Early Christian Fathers*, ed. C. C. Richardson, 1953, and *Alexandrian Christianity*, ed. J. E. L. Oulton and H. Chadwick, 1954.

Reliquiae Sacrae (texts of surviving fragments of lost Christian literature with notes in Latin), M. Routh (Oxford, 1846).

Second-century Christianity (translations of surviving fragments with introductions), R. M. Grant (London, 1946).

Selections from Early Christian Writers (text and translation), H. M. Gwatkin (London, 1914).

Documents Illustrative of the History of the Church (translations), B. J. Kidd, 3 vols. (London, S.P.C.K., 1920–41).

Irenaeus against Heresies (text and notes), W. W. Harvey (Cambridge, 1857).

Justin Martyr, *The Apologies* (text and notes), A. W. F. Blunt (Cambridge, 1911).

Justin Martyr, *The Dialogue with Trypho* (introduction, translation, notes), A. L. Williams (London, 1930).

The Apology of Aristides, etc., ed. and trans. by J. R. Harris in Cambridge Texts and Studies, 1891.

Tertullian, *Opera* (Latin text), F. Oehler (Leipzig, 1851 ff.).

Origenes, *Contra Celsum* (introduction, translation, notes), H. Chadwick (Cambridge, 1954).

Acta Apostolorum Apocrypha (text): vol. 1. ed. R. A. Lipsius (Leipzig, 1891); vols. 2 and 3 ed. M. Bonnet (1898 and 1903).

The Earliest Life of Christ (translation of the Arabic text of the Diatessaron), H. J. Hill (Edinburgh, 1910).

The Odes and Psalms of Solomon, J. R. Harris (Cambridge, 1909).

The *Apostolic Tradition* of Hippolytus, ed. and trans. B. S. Easton (Cambridge, 1934).

The *Treatise on the Apostolic Tradition* of St Hippolytus of Rome (translation with introduction, text and notes), G. Dix (London, 1937).

Liturgies Eastern and Western (texts), F. E. Brightman (Oxford, 1896 ff.).

Didascalia Apostolorum (translation), R. H. Connolly (Oxford, 1929).

The *Homilies and Recognitions* of Clement (text), B. Rehm in the Berlin Corpus (1953 ff.), or P. Lagarde (Leipzig, 1865).

E. SECOND-CENTURY CHRISTIANITY: SPECIAL STUDIES

See Bibliography to Volume I.

Church and Gnosis, F. C. Burkitt (Cambridge, 1932).

Gnostiques et gnosticisme, E. de Faye (Paris, 1913).

Early Christian Creeds, J. N. D. Kelly (London, 1950).

Apostolic Succession in the Second Century, A. Ehrhardt (London, 1953).

Jewish Antecedents of the Christian Sacraments, F. Gavin (London, 1933).

Marcion, das Evangelium vom fremden Gott, A Harnack, in *Texte und Untersuchungen*, 2nd edn. (Leipzig, 1924).

Marcion and his Influence, E. C. Blackman (London, 1948).

Marcion and the New Testament, J. Knox (Chicago, 1942).

La crise montaniste, P. C. de Labriolle (Paris, 1913).

Montanismen og de Phrygiske Kulter, V. Schepelern (Copenhagen, 1920); German translation (Tübingen, 1929).

Early Eastern Christianity, F. C. Burkitt (London, 1904).

Irenaeus of Lugdunum, F. R. M. Hitchcock (Cambridge, 1914).

The Biblical Theology of St Irenaeus, J. Lawson (London, 1948).

Clement of Alexandria, R. B. Tollinton, 2 vols. (London, 1914).

The Christian Platonists of Alexandria, C. Bigg, 2nd edn. (Oxford, 1913).

Cambridge Handbooks of Liturgical Study, ed. H. B. Swete and J. H. Srawley (Cambridge, 1910ff.).

The Shape of the Liturgy, G. Dix, 2nd edn. (London, 1952).

The Sword and the Cross, R. M. Grant (Chicago, 1955).

Messe und Herrenmahl, H. Lietzmann (Bonn, 1926).

The Catacombs of Rome, J. P. Kirsch (Rome, 1946).

Rassegne sulle Catacombe, G. Bovini (Rome, 1952).

Roma sotteranea, W. R. Brownlow and J. S. Northcote (based on the work of de Rossi) (London, 1869–79).

Esplorazioni sotto la confessione di San Pietro in Vaticano, B. M. A. Ghetti and others (Vatican City, 1951).

Le problème littéraire et historique du roman Clémentin, O. Cullmann (Paris, 1930).

Dura-Europos and its Art, M. I. Rostovtzeff (Oxford, 1938).

Excavations at Dura-Europos (Yale and Oxford, 1929ff.).

The Christian Church at Dura-Europos, C. Hopkins and P. V. C. Baur (Yale, 1934).

Bardesanes, A. Hilgenfeld (Leipzig, 1864).

Conversion, A. D. Nock (Oxford, 1933).

Les Moralistes sous l'empire romain, C. Marthe (Paris, 1866).

Roman Stoicism, E. V. Arnold (Cambridge, 1918).

Cyprian and his Times, R. W. Benson (London, 1895).

INDEX TO VOLUMES I AND II